URBAN
LAND
ECONOMICS

URBAN LAND ECONOMICS

MICHAEL GOLDBERG
Faculty of Commerce
University of British Columbia

PETER CHINLOY
Department of Economics
University of British Columbia

JOHN WILEY & SONS

New York   Chichester   Brisbane   Toronto   Singapore

This book is dedicated to
Richard U. Ratcliff

Library of Congress Cataloging in Publication Data:

Goldberg, Michael A. (Michael Arthur), 1941–
Urban land economics.

   Includes index.
   1. Land use, Urban—United States.   I. Chinloy, Peter,
1950–   . II. Title.
HD205.G64 1984   333.77'0973   83–23486
ISBN 0–471–09286–X

Printed in the United States of America

10 9 8 7 6 5 4 3 2 1

PREFACE

The present text originates from our need in the faculty of Commerce and Business Administration at the University of British Columbia to provide materials for students in our courses in urban land economics. Since Canadian urban institutions are considerably different from those in the United States, American classroom materials are inappropriate. The educational level of existing books was also a problem. The course for which this text has been designed is an introductory course in the subject, but students who take the course typically have two years of economics behind them, up through the intermediate micro and macro level. Accordingly, we could assume literacy in economics, though not in urban land economics.

Existing books came from two different sources, undergraduate urban economics courses and undergraduate courses in real estate. The former tended to focus on economic analysis to the exclusion of urban institutions; the latter tended to be too descriptive and institutional. In short, we were seeking a synthetic creature that employed economic concepts and economic analysis but which also set these analyses in the context of the appropriate institutions, be they national, regional, or local.

The resulting effort is best viewed as an applied institutional urban economics text. It draws on economic concepts and applies them within an institutional framework. The conceptual and institutional ideas that are developed here are thought to be sufficiently general and applicable that they can be utilized in a Canadian or American setting. Thus, the book is also comparative in nature, demonstrating the generality and utility of the approach in various national and regional and urban contexts.

Given the genesis of the present volume in our need to provide appropriate material for our course, with its real-world application, we see it as being of potential use in analogous courses in which applied urban economic thinking is being introduced for the first time. Urban economics courses in schools or departments of city and regional planning would be other obvious places where the present book might be of use. Courses in real estate and urban economics of an applied nature would also be potential users. Finally, courses in urban economic geography also might fruitfully employ the book. In each case, the

v

book is intended to develop concepts of urban economics, of urban land markets, and of the institutional environment within which these markets must function.

To achieve these objectives, the book is organized into three parts. Part 1 introduces the reader to urbanization processes, cities, and the broadly based discipline of urban land economics. Part 2 develops the necessary economic and institutional constructs to equip the reader to analyze contemporary urban issues. In Part 3 a range of such issues is addressed, including housing and land, changing urban economic patterns, and issues related to urban public finance and government organization.

Isaac Newton noted that each generation's scholars can see so much farther than their predecessors because the more recent scholars stand on the shoulders of the intellectual giants of previous eras. We agree heartily, and if our students can improve their vision and understanding and decision making relating to urban land markets it is because we have been able to stand on the shoulders of earlier giants. The most important of these leaders from earlier generations is Richard U. Ratcliff. His pioneering work, *Urban Land Economics* (McGraw-Hill Book Company, 1949), is still the best in the field despite being well into its fourth decade. The insights provided by Dick Ratcliff in that book, complemented by insights from his more recent writings, are as fresh and stimulating today as they were nearly two score years ago. Dick was directly responsible for the scale and quality of the present Urban Land Economics Program at the University of British Columbia. The present volume is traceable to numerous conversations and endless enjoyable luncheons with Dick. His intellectual imprint is apparent in the Urban Land Economics Program today and pervades this book as well.

Just months before he died, he typed the foreword that opens this book. His prefatory chapter is a model of clarity and thoughtfulness and sets out in extraordinarily economical fashion the crux of urban land economics. Our debts to Richard U. Ratcliff, for his participation in the present project and for allowing us to stand on his shoulders, are truly without limit. It is to his achievements and memory that we have dedicated our effort here.

Other acknowledgments are deserved and due. To our students over the past two years, our thanks and gratitude for their forbearance. Their patience and critical comments, while of little assistance to themselves, have helped us in revising and shaping the book so that future generations might have an easier time grappling with the material.

Similarly, our colleagues, particularly Jonathan Mark, who used the draft version of this text several times, have provided both critical comments and support. George Gau, Stan Hamilton, and Dennis Capozza have provided valuable assistance at various stages in the writing and revision of the manuscript.

Financial support has been provided by the Real Estate Council of British Columbia, which, through its ongoing funding of our research activities in urban land economics, enabled us to develop much of the comparative statistics that fill the volume. Support has also been provided by the Social Sciences and Humanities Research Council of Canada, both in research funding and leave fellowship, during which part of the book was written. The Faculty of Commerce and Business Administration also provided secretarial and clerical support that made the task feasible. Specifically, the entire staff of the Faculty's Word Processing Centre performed the herculean task of typing, retyping, and revising. They tolerated unreadable handwritten revisions and laborious and seemingly endless tables ("Goldberg's awful tables," as they came to be known). Merrill De Vuyst and Joan Ewer helped get initial drafts typed and onto the word processing system. Mabel Yee had the most difficult task of last-minute revisions, and endured tedious hours of glaring into and glowering at the CRT display, as well as having to ride herd on the various bits and pieces of manuscript, tables, and figures that are all embodied in a writing project of this scale. To all of our helpers in the Faculty, our heartfelt thanks.

The traditional disclaimer that must accompany acknowledgments needs to be made by us as well. Despite the best efforts of all involved, and despite the consultation and guidance given by friends, errors remain. We apologize in advance to our readers for these errors and for the confusion that might result from such mistakes. We accept our responsibility for these errors and hope that we may have the opportunity in the future to rectify them.

Michael Goldberg
Peter Chinloy

FOREWORD

The aim of this book is to bring the reader to a comprehension of the economics of urban land and to an understanding of the economically rooted problems of cities, and to the development of remedies. But its first obligation is to lay down a basic structure as a frame of reference for the diverse material to come, a framework that will provide the perspective required for a balanced and realistic consideration of the broad content of this field of study.

The basic frame of reference to be presented in this introduction will be constructed of three types of material: (1) the essential characteristics of land as a natural resource and as a universal economic good; (2) the evolutionary and functional nature of human settlement as a prime land use from which is derived special qualities of productivity; and (3) certain unique features of urban land economics as an organized discipline. As an essay on the general nature of urban land, this introduction will anticipate many of the subject areas to be developed fully in the main body of this volume. (Because of its separate authorship, the introduction will possibly deviate occasionally from later generalizations, but such departures are useful in illustrating the relative immaturity of urban land economics and in challenging the new generation of scholars to search for definitive answers.)

LAND AND NATURE

"Under all, the land," proclaims the motto of a prominent real estate trade association. The implications of this statement are vast and profound. Land provides space and support for all living entities, and the fruits of the soil are the basis of the sustenance of all forms of life. Inextricably associated with the land surface and equally essential to life are the atmosphere and the beneficent rays of the sun. In addition, the supersurface of land is the meeting place of meteorological and astronomical forces and factors that create the various climates at each location on the earth's surface.

Land as two-dimensional space is the entire surface of the earth, but two-dimensional space is a physical, geometric concept of no economic significance. As a productive resource or economic good, land is three-dimensional, elemental space that may be wet or dry, ocean, lake, river, or solid ground. To accommodate plants and animal life including humans, their activities and artifacts, three-dimensional space is essential. The concept of a vertical dimension for land embodies a recognition that associated with the horizontal space of a parcel of land is subsurface space that encloses the subsoil responsible for fertility and gives room for plant roots, minerals, and energy sources. The supersurface is the realm of the atmosphere and the climate, and provides space for building bulk, for multifarious biological and botanical activities, and airspace for everything that flies, from gnats to 747s.

Land has been characterized traditionally as "the gift of nature"; it is the natural attributes of land that impart productivity and utility. The differentiation among various parcels of land is the result of different combinations of natural components inseparably associated. Indeed, land is truly the product of nature, a composite of natural attributes through nature giving of itself. Because land is the essential site of all natural processes, it is difficult to distinguish an identify for land as separate from nature. In the large, land is nature and nature is land.

It may be observed that the essentiality of land and its fruits for our survival may well explain the persistence down through history of the primacy of land as our most valued possession. There is an intriguing hypothesis that humans, along with many other living creatures, respond to a basic and innate instinct to possess and protect territory essential to their welfare. Indeed, some modern aspects of our behavior toward land could be interpreted as a residual instinctive compulsion to hold land, the heritage of a primitive necessity.

Land as a Joint Product

We have defined land as a composite of natural attributes, but land by any definition does not become a productive economic good without some human input. Even the consumption of natural products such as wild berries requires effort in harvesting. Modern farming involves large capital investments in draining and fencing, in machinery and buildings as well as substantial labor in planting, cultivating, and harvesting. Land in urban areas, except for some recreational uses, requires human input and improvements such as clearing and grading, supplying potable water and waste-disposal facilities, and building access roads. To shelter urban activities and provide living quarters, various structures must be erected. Thus, land as the space attribute of nature has no economic value without human capital and labor applied to the space and its natural components. In this sense, land with productive potential is a joint product of nature and humankind. Thus, the traditional conception of land as a gift of nature overlooks the fact that land is nonproductive without essential human contribution.

Fixity in Space

It is well recognized that land as space is fixed at a specific latitude and longitude. But the other physical components of land—the natural materials and the more or less permanently attached man-made improvements—are not all immobile or immutable. Topsoil can blow away, rivers can dry up, houses can be moved, and over time drain tile may deteriorate, smog can pollute the atmosphere, and forests can burn or be lumbered off. These changes and many others can drastically modify land's productivity and its economic value.

From the fact that space is fixed it follows that any given unit of space must be used or exploited where it is found: It cannot be moved into a more favorable market. Furthermore, it follows that each parcel of land is vulnerable to conditions within its special environment, be they favorable or adverse, static or in flux. It is this quality of land which gives rise to the concept of location, an aspect of land about which much will be said in this volume. At this point, we will only introduce the subject with a brief definition and some of the more important implications.

Site location is the complex of special space relationships with other points on the landscape that are linked with a site in some meaningful way. This concept is merely the popular and common-sense notion of location. For example, the locational qualities of a home include exposure to a set of natural features such as a fine view or a strong prevailing wind, and a combination of spatial relationships and travel convenience to various human activities and diverse facilities such as the homes of friends and relatives, schools, churches, shopping centers, and places of work. The special set of significant exposures and conveniences which affect site productivity will vary with each type of land use and with each site devoted to a given type of use.

The locational qualities of a site fixed in space are rarely stable, for there is constant change in the features of the landscape with which it is linked. Each change is likely to affect the productivity of the site in some degree. For example, a home becomes less desirable if the lovely sea view from the living room is contaminated by the appearance of off-shore oil drilling rigs. A potential supermarket site rises in value as the surrounding area develops with subdivisions and new homes.

Environmental change may be sufficiently drastic to bring about a change in the nature of the utilization of the site. For example, farm land on the periphery of a growing city will be subdivided into home sites when population pressures make it more valuable for subdividing than for farming. Thus, land is said to possess economic mobility and, with many exceptions, tends to move into its most productive use as determined by its environment.

One of the more interesting derivatives of this discussion is the observation that locational factors, external to the site, can generate change in productivity and use while the land remains physically unaltered.

Fixity in Supply

It is not debatable that the total area of land on the surface of the earth is fixed and nonexpansible, provided, of course, that we define land broadly as the entire surface of the earth, wet or dry. The statement would be untrue under the popular definition of land as solid ground, as demonstrated by the dramatic achievement of the Dutch in expanding their country by converting the sea into productive land area. But there is a widespread and carelessly accepted assumption that there is an absolute limit to the land area available to us. This generalization is translated by the naive and by the real estate salesman into an assurance that land will always increase in value as growing demand presses against the fixed supply. But, in matter of fact, land is not a homogeneous element traded in a common market; it is highly differentiated in physical and locational characteristics.

Parcels of land may shift from one use to another because of economic forces or political controls. We have earlier alluded to the conversion of farm land to urban uses under economic pressures; modifications of public controls such as zoning can substantially increase or decrease the land area available for commercial or industrial purposes; a new bridge may open up heretofore inaccessible land for development and effectively increase the supply in the market; and so we must conclude that the physical truth that the surface area of the earth is fixed in extent has no practical economic significance, and the naive conclusion that land always rises in value must be labeled as a misleading and dangerous guide in land investment.

Uniqueness

As no two persons are exacely alike, so no two parcels of land are identical. Each parcel has an orientation different from any other parcel, and may have physical differences in subsoil conditions, drainage, and other features. Our concern here is with the economic significance of this quality of uniqueness. Land law recognizes this characteristic of land, and in certain situations specific performance of a contract relating to land is required because of the impossibility of discovering an identical parcel that might be substituted and the injustice of a money award in lieu of a unique land site. In the marketplace, the uniqueness of land parcels requires that each parcel be judged individually. Differences find expression in the variety of bids and offers. Although exact substitutability cannot obtain, economic equivalence is effected through trade-offs of qualities and in the pricing of the product. For example, in a subdivision of nearly identical lots located in a cold climate, buyers may be willing to pay the same price for a lot facing south but with no view and a lot facing north but with a protected view of the distant mountains; or a lot with a few trees may command a premium over an identical and contiguous parcel with no ground cover. It may be said that the land market operates in a manner quite like any other market that deals in nonstandardized goods. Uniqueness of land sites, then, is an accepted fact but not a characteristic that distorts economic behavior in a pattern which is singular to the land market.

Exploitation by Humans

Since the beginning of time, the creatures of the earth, for self-serving purposes, have exploited, within their powers to do so, such natural resources as were accessible and appropriate to their needs. Each species, regardless of the burden on the rest of nature, has conducted this exploitation in a continuing and single-minded quest for survival, for benign conditions of life, and for the assured perpetuation of its kind. Within recorded history, among the denizens of our planet, *Homo sapiens* have made by far the most dramatic progress in improving living conditions. Our resourcefulness and industry have raised the quality of our life from bare existence to a highly sophisticated level. But this advance has been achieved at the expense of nature.

Early humans were sustained by natural foods procured by hunting and by harvesting wild fruits and vegetables. Later, having depleted the supply of wild foods, they learned by necessity to cultivate the land and domesticate wild animals. The raw materials out of which they fashioned increasingly complex artifacts were drawn from natural sources, some of which proved to be exhaustible. But neither the domestication of the food supply nor the development of synthetic materials has emancipated humans from dependence on nature as the ultimate source of food and energy.

Over the centuries, our increasing control over those aspects of nature that could be exploited for our benefit and our ingenuity in evolving a productive technology have nourished a progressively increasing growth in the human population. The needs and demands of this expanding population have pressed on the supply of natural resources to the point of threatening the exhaustion of some critical elements; it has led to a decimation of many wild species and has disturbed the ecological balance in parts of the world; and it has contaminated nature in many places and reduced both material productivity and aesthetic benefits.

There are those who are disturbed by alarmist predictions of an exhaustion of the world's resources and a contamination of the environment so extensive that it leads to the disappearance of humanoids from the face of the earth. But these timid souls can find encouragement in the great versatility of land in productive uses, its economic mobility, and in the demonstrated ingenuity of our species in devising offsets, social and technical, to potentially destructive developments. It may be observed in passing that testimony to the near-identity of land

and nature lies in the fact that most of the social devices aimed at limiting the destructive exploitation of nature take the form of public controls over the use of land.

THE URBAN ENVIRONMENT

The anthropology of cities reveals that human settlements developed as an integral aspect of technological, social, and economic evolution. Early humans discovered that cooperative group action was more productive for the individual than was independent effort in such essential activities as, for example, hunting large animals. At that time, considerations of defense enforced other practical considerations favoring a close-knit congregation of dwelling places. Settlements grew up in proximity to natural resources such as a water hole or where raw materials could be most easily extracted. In later times, with the development of production processes involving specialization and the division of labor, the most efficient arrangement required that the living and working places of the producers be geographically concentrated. The expansion of trade and exchange encouraged the appearance of trading communities that were points of assembly for goods, the loci of trading activities, and the homes of the traders. The need for cross-country transport of raw materials and finished products spawned towns and cities at the junctions of trade routes, where goods were loaded or shifted from one mode of transport to another, such as from canoe to pack animal, or from ship to rail.

This brief and partial account of the functional origins of human settlement serves to suggest certain generalities about cities. First, broadly speaking, most settlements are bifunctional, the locus of both human production and consumption. They are centers of consumption in which people live, use and consume the products of nature's bounty and human effort, and enjoy various services and the benefits and satisfactions of social contacts. In the same urban place, involving the same people for the most part, there are productive economic activities of various kinds by which most of the residents earn their living. The proliferating functions of an advancing society have created an ever-increasing complexity of interaction and interdependence within urban areas. This pattern of interrelationships is organic in the sense that modifications in any one of the components of the system will effect some responsive modifications in one or more of the other components or related processes. For example, the recent demographic shift in Santa Cruz, California, to a greater number and higher proportion of young adults will result in a change in local consumption patterns which, in turn, will affect retailers and places of entertainment. There will be changes in the composition of the labor force which may benefit some lines of business and damage others and which will modify the attractiveness of the area for new industries. This example illustrates the point that the analysis of any one urban component abstracted from the rest of the community may result in a distorted conclusion that ignores significant side effects.

The anthropology of urbanism offers a valuable guide to the analyst and the decisionmaker dealing with urban phenomena. The history of human settlements demonstrates the functional character of cities and establishes their evolutionary adaptation to the changing needs and preferences of society, changes which follow advances in technology or modifications in such factors as social values and political organization.

Now, it is fundamental that the decisionmaker deal with future probabilities. His or her decision, be it in connection with a specific transaction or the adoption of a policy, depends on his prediction of the probable outcome of the decision. Even the analyst examining the past is in search of generalizations that may be useful in forecasting the future. It is clear that analysis for decision making regarding urban land requires forecasting changes in factors affecting future productivity, land values and land use, and evaluating the composite effect of these factor changes. In effect, the analyst seeks to describe and measure the coming phase of the city's continuing mutation in patterns of land values and land utilization. It is of note that the factors of greatest weight are exogenous to the site or area under analysis. Locational factors are probably the most significant in urban areas. A second category of productivity factors is composed of the ever-changing social, economic, political, and technological environment that affects all manner of economic activities. A third class of factors involves physical changes in the land itself from the operation of natural forces or through man-made modifications and improvements. Incidentally, the question of whether there is a difference in urban and agricultural land economics is answered by the fact that all of the productivity factors in the three categories just summarized are active agents in determining the productivity of both classes of land.

THE NATURE OF LAND ECONOMICS

It may be presumed that the readers of this volume are familiar with the field of economics and, in general, with the subject areas it encompasses. They should understand the nature of at least the more familiar economic institutions and processes, and should have been exposed to the various economic theories, laws, and principles which the casual scholar is inclined to accept without serious question. Economics is generally classified as a social science. Without questioning the accuracy of this term, we do perceive a danger in the encouragement of the misconception that the "science" of economics is a systematic and orderly body of internally consistent information and principles that is as immutable as are the laws of nature.

Our view of economics, including land economics, emphasizes its behavioristic aspect. Economics is the study of human behavior in situations where economic considerations prevail. Economic laws or principles are nothing more than genralizations, based on past economic behavior, that permit predictions of probable future behavior within useful limits of reliability. But human behavior is not constant. This fact is observable and widely accepted as a general truth; but there is somewhat less agreement that changing social behavior is explained in part by the fact that, contrary to the tenets of classical economic theory, human nature is not innate and unchanging. The famous psychologist Thorndike has said: "Much, perhaps nine-tenths of what commonly passes as distinctly human nature is . . . not in man originally but is put there by institutions, or grows there by the interaction of the world of natural forces and the capacity to learn." Institutional economics, which is our brand of land economics, accepts this explanation of changing social behavior and discards as unrealistic the classical assumption of hedonism as the universal and unchanging motivating force.

Institutional economics not only views social change which modifies economic behavior as, in part, the result of change in human nature, but also recognizes that changes in individual attitudes are usually associated with corresponding changes in group patterns of thinking and action. Consistent with this view is the application of the Darwinian concept of evolution in the physical world to evolution in the social world, defined here as a continuous adaptation to constantly shifting social patterns and evolving technology.

Central to institutional economics is the recognition that social, political, and economic institutions are powerful determinants of economic behavior. These institutions appear, change, and sometimes disappear in a social form of Darwinian evolution. Thorstein Veblen, an early prophet of institutionalism, summarized the tenets of this school of economics somewhat as follows: Human activity is to be viewed as an evolutionary process; institutions are decisive factors in shaping human behavior; social science must deal with real human beings, not rationalized human nature—with facts, not a normalized picture of them.

Institutional economics does not purport to replace or discredit orthodox neoclassical economics as an analytical device. However, it does offer a different approach and emphasis, one that is particularly well adapted to the problems of land. The following summary of the salient features of institutional economics is adapted from the writings of Professor Edwin Witte, a well-known institutionalist and labor economist:

1. It is not a complete, self-contained, and connected body of thought, but a method approaching particular economics problems.

2. It is problem-oriented economics.

3. Its concerns are more than solely economic motives and thus include whatever leads humankind to act in economic matters.

4. It is interdisciplinary in recognition of the broad range of interacting social and technical factors that affect economic affairs.

5. It recognizes that institutions that are active or that are restraints in our economy are man-made and changeable. In problem solving, it is the present form of the institution and its evolutionary origins which are the materials of analysis.

6. The method is heavily inductive, based on a direct observation of all the facts.

7. It comprehends the associational propensities of our society that lead to group patterns of thinking and action.

Whether or not the authors of this volume will be comfortable with the institutional label, the treatment of urban land economics in this volume conforms to my perception of institutional economics; and, by intent or not, it is the economics of Darwinian change. As genuine, problem-oriented institutionalism, the book is launched with a preview of urban problems. The reader will find that most of these problems are land-related, and as he proceeds through the text, he will discover that all of the criteria of the institutionalist approach are fully met.

But in what sense is this the economics of Darwinian change? Certainly, classical economics does not ignore change, but there are differences in the concept of change and the view of what changes. Basically, the classicist views change as discontinuous, the product of disturbing elements outside the system and calling for adjustment to reestablish equilibrium or a state of quiescence. But to the institutionalist, change is an ineluctable part of the economic process. Technology is in constant flux, institutions are forever changing, and humans continue to strive to adapt to the unending mutations in their physical and social environment. This view of change is useful to the analyst who searches for generalizations out of past economic behavior in order to interpret change or to discover remedies to problems which arise through change. Future change becomes more predictable, the by-products of change are more foreseeable, and the outcomes of remedial steps are more reliably forecast.

We earlier suggested that the *raison d'être* of economic analysis is to solve problems and make decisions and that the constructive economist is necessarily a forecaster. He must predict the probabilities of various possible future outcomes under alternative solutions and courses of action. Thus, economic analysis must start with a study of the prospective physical and institutional changes that may affect his predictions. The institutionalist is not one to seek solutions or sound decisions under the classical assumption that economic behavior is constrained by a fixed body of timeless and "place-less" principles; the economics of the institutionalist is human behavior in an environment of ceaseless and pervasive change. There is no present; there is only the past and the future.

Richard U. Ratcliff

CONTENTS

1

INTRODUCTION AND SETTING

URBAN PROBLEMS:AN INTRODUCTION

Paraphrasing Winston Churchill, it would appear that cities are the worst form of human settlement, except for all the others. The past three centuries have seen a dramatic rise in urban population and urban economies. The experience during the past three decades has been particularly dramatic, with rapid urbanization spreading to the previously unurbanized developing countries.[1]

Along with such an enormous increase in population inexorably comes an enormous increase in urban problems. These problems are highly interrelated, difficult to define, and difficult to treat effectively. Along with additional residents come additional jobs, factories, schools, streets, public facilities and services, housing, offices, and, thus, the potential for even more people or jobs. These in turn breed a host of problems which North American urban residents know only too well. A short list would include traffic congestion, air pollution, slums, crime, and the loss of open space and recreational activities.

The number of volumes dedicated to documenting and commenting on contemporary urban ills is large.[2] Popular newspaper and magazine articles also abound. Scholarly research into urban dilemmas has grown dramatically to meet these growing needs.[3] In both Canada and the United States federal government studies on the state of urban areas have been numerous and ongoing.[4] In sum, there does not appear to be a shortage of problems or of studies and suggested solutions. However, to set the stage for later discussion, a review of some of the most pressing problems facing North American urban dwellers is in order. Such a review will provide us with a convenient point of departure for when we move on to apply the tools developed in this book to analyze contemporary urban problems and their posited solutions.

Urban Environmental Quality.   As more people and jobs fill urban areas, the waste products from human activities build up to levels where they become noxious and potentially hazardous to human well-being. Attention has focused on the pollution of air and water, though there is increasing concern about noise and the removal of solid wastes from homes and worksites.[5]

Transportation, Transit and Traffic.[6]   Given the spatial growth and specialization that occurs in urban areas, it becomes necessary to carry out specialized human activities in separate locations. The need arises, therefore, to overcome this spatial separation of specialized human activities which gives rise to urban transportation systems. The urban transportation system is extremely complex and includes people who walk to work and to shopping; those who use bicycles to get around; automobiles, which predominate in North America for these purposes and require extensive road networks, as well as parking facilities, for their use; and, finally, public transit systems, which include all forms of buses, trolleys, subways and other rail systems, and ferries.

Road systems have become overcrowded, necessitating extensive freeway construction as well as requiring additional parking facilities. After years of declining revenues and patronage, public transit systems are seeing a resurgence but are beset by numerous financial difficulties, old and poorly maintained equipment, and outdated operating procedures. With fuel shortages and rising fuel prices, public transit represents a potential key to energy and urban policy, but it will need major restructuring to fulfill its posited potential. Furthermore, as will be seen in Part 2, transportation issues cannot easily be separated from land use and the spatial distribution of activities in urban areas. Moreover, transportation places heavy demands on the urban environment, with automobiles, trucks, and buses being major sources of air pollution.

Housing and Social Conditions.[7] The literature on housing in urban areas is vast and growing rapidly. Much of it has been devoted to social issues and to questions of poverty and housing for low-income families. Increasingly, researchers have begun to look at housing affordability for all North Americans and not just for the poor. The issue is complex, highly political, and highly personalized and emotional. While North Americans on average have the highest-quality housing stock in the world, there are also significant portions of the North American population who cannot afford conveniently located housing of reasonable quality. Housing, in turn, is a major land user (perhaps as much as one-third of developed land being in residential uses) and, as a result, is a major shaper of urban form and a primary object of urban transportation, education, recreation, and other publicly provided services. Housing has been historically a major focus of social policy, since low-quality slum housing is seen as a major contributor to urban social problems such as disease, crime, and instability in general. Growing commuting distances and costs and rising housing and land values in accessible neighborhoods and suburbs have added the middle classes to the housing problem.

General Metropolitan and Central City Decline. Urban areas in the older Eastern and Midwestern portions of the United States and Canada have been experiencing declining central city populations. More recently, older metropolitan areas have declined as a whole (i.e., both central areas and suburbs alike). At the same time that people, on average, have been moving out of central cities across North America, these areas have had to support large capital investments in streets, schools, public buildings, and social services while their property tax base has been declining or stagnant. Industrial jobs have been deserting central cities for less congested suburban or nonmetropolitan locations, leaving the older cities in poor financial and physical shape. This widely publicized phenomenon has helped create the popular image of urban crises across North America, an image not entirely founded in fact.[8] The physical and financial decline, combined with high crime rates, decreasing environmental quality, and growing concentrations of urban poverty in central areas, has blackened the already tarnished image of these cities.

This very brief review of some of the numerous current urban problems that we face highlights the complexity and interrelatedness of these difficulties (e.g., it is not possible to separate transportation and sprawl, nor is it possible to separate housing and poverty issues). However, despite this apparently bleak outlook for cities, the past century has not been without its significant urban achievements.

URBAN ACHIEVEMENTS

Despite the bleak picture presented above, urbanization continues worldwide, and with some new wrinkles in many highly developed countries.[9] Instead of continually asking where have cities failed or cataloging *ad nauseum* urban ills, a brief inventory of urban achievements should provide a more balanced foundation for our discussions in later chapters.

Urban North America continues to be the focus for the vast majority of economic activities and for housing North America's population.[10] Moreover, the quality of the North American housing stock has increased consistently over the post-World War II period. Urban centers continue to provide the bulk of cultural and recreational activities despite the growing popularity of outdoor recreational activities such as downhill and cross-country skiing, hiking, fishing, and camping, all of which have their basis in an urban life-style that provides high levels of output and leisure time.

Cities and towns have continued to provide North Americans with generally safe, enjoyable, and economically viable places in which to live and work. Along the way, difficulties have arisen and many of the advantages of urban living have been neutralized or, in some cases, reversed as a result of growing congestion, pollution, poverty, and urban fragmentation. The question that must be asked is, "Is there something in the very structure and function of cities that creates these difficulties or do the roots of the problems lie outside the framework of cities and closer to more profound societal and cultural issues?" In view of the large number of enormously successful and livable cities around the world (e.g., Amsterdam, Copenhagen, London, Paris, Toronto, and Vancouver), it would appear that the typical urban problems are not necessary concommitants of urban living.[11] The trick is to understand cities and urban areas to the extent that difficulties can be overcome without destroying, in the process, the cities' underlying vitality and livability.

URBAN LAND ECONOMICS: ITS POTENTIAL ROLE

Having at least raised a number of pressing issues, we can start dealing with them analytically. An understanding of urban land values and use lies close to the heart of the matter, since all activities must occupy space. Analyzing the pricing and production of urban space leads necessarily to an appreciation of the myriad factors that affect, and are in turn affected by, the process of allocating urban land and built form.

As we will see below, the demand for urban land and buildings is a "derived demand," derived from the uses to which the land and buildings can be put. The production and allocation of urban space (i.e., land and buildings) are the results of a series of complex and interwoven decision processes by consumers and producers. By studying the factors that affect these decisions, it is possible to assemble a clear picture of the dynamics of urban growth and change, and to develop significantly the means for intervening effectively in the urban development process.

This, then, is the task that lies ahead: how to allocate scarce urban land and building resources among alternative competing uses. In seeking to find a solution, we shall study demand and supply forces and the socio-political-legal institutions within which the urban development process takes place. Once equipped with the tools to answer the allocation question, we shall apply these tools to important current problems facing urban areas in North America. Such an application will serve to reinforce the usefulness of these tools and concepts as well as to ensure that we have a firm grasp of the essentials. Like pudding, the proof of analytical skills lies in their consumption or use.

Footnotes

1. Considerably more will be said about urbanization in the next chapter. However, for present purposes, some recent data should serve to make the point.

World's Rural and Urban Population: 1950–1977

Population	1950	1960	Projected 1970(A)[a]	1970(B)[b]	1975[c,d]	1977[e]
World (000's)	2,501,894	3,012,659	3,604,518	3,628,000	3,968,000	4,336,000
Urban	706,383	993,718	1,713,378	1,399,000	1,560,309	1,777,760
Rural	1,795,511	2,018,941	2,233,140	2,229,000	2,407,555	2,558,240
World (%)	100.0	100.0	100.0	100.0	100.0	100.0
Urban	28.2	33.0	38.0	38.0	39.32	41.0
Rural	71.8	67.0	62.0	61.4	60.68	59.0

[a]Projection A for 1970 was obtained by summing the projection for individual countries. It is conservative because, although the urban population was projected on the basis of the 1950–60 trend, it was modified in each case to allow for a slight decrease in the rate of change due to the fact that 1960 starting levels were higher than 1950 starting levels. (For the methods used in Projection A, see Kingsley Davis, *World Urbanization*, Volume I, Chapter 1.)

[b]Projection B for 1970 was made by dealing with the world as a whole. The world's total population and its urban population were both projected on the assumption that their 1960–70 growth rate was the same as their 1950–60 rate. The rural population for 1970 was then obtained by subtracting the urban from the total population.

ᶜTake note that 1975 and 1977 data is taken from a different source. Kingsley Davis' definition for urban is 100,000 people. However the U.N.'s definition of urban is 20,000 people.
ᵈUnited Nations, Dept of Economic and Social Affairs Population Studies No. 62, *World Population Trends and Policies, 1977 Monitoring Report, Volume 1: Population Trends* New York, United Nations, 1979, p. 111.
ᵉUnited Nations, *World Statistics in Brief* (New York: United Nations), 1981.

Source: Kingsley Davis, *World Urbanization 1950–1970, Volume II: Analysis of Trends, Relationships, and Development,* Population Monograph Series, No. 9 (Berkeley, Calif.: Institute of International Studies, University of California), 1972, p. 11.

Thus, between 1950 and 1970 the world's urban population almost doubled, while the percentage of the world's population living in urban areas of 100,000 or more people rose from roughly 28 percent to roughly 38 percent.

2. A random sampling of volumes on the urban "crisis" in its several guises would include: Editors of *Fortune, The Exploding Metropolis* (New York: Doubleday), 1958; Edmund K. Faltermayer, *Redoing America* (New York: Harper and Row), 1968; Jeffrey K. Hadden, Louis Masotti, and Calvin J. Larson, *Metropolis in Crisis* (Itasca, Ill.: F. E. Peacock Publishers), 1976; Irwin Isenberg, ed., *The City in Crisis* (New York: The H. W. Wilson Company), 1968; Jane Jacobs, *The Death and Life of Great American Cities* (New York: Random House), 1961; Jeanne Lowe, *Cities in a Race with Time* (New York: Random House), 1967; Albert Mayer, *The Urgent Future* (New York: McGraw-Hill Book Company), 1967; Robert C. Weaver, *Dilemmas of Urban America* (New York: Atheneum), 1969; and James Q. Wilson, ed., *The Metropolitan Enigma* (Cambridge, Massachusetts: Harvard University Press), 1968.

3. Numerous anthologies have appeared recently that bring together scholarly works in related fields and illustrate the range of academic activity in recent years. Another brief sampling would include: Charles Tilly, ed., *An Urban World* (Boston Mass: Little, Brown and Company), 1974; Sam Bass Warner, ed., *Planning for a Nation of Cities* (Cambridge, Mass.: M.I.T. Press), 1966; Kingsley Davis, ed., *Cities: Their Origin, Growth and Human Impact* (San Francisco: W. H. Freeman and Company), 1975; and Henry J. Schmandt and Warner Bloomberg, Jr. eds., *The Quality of Urban Life* (Beverly Hills, Cal.: Sage Publications), 1969. For a Canadian perspective, see N. H. Lithwick and Gilley Paquet, eds., *Urban Studies: A Canadian Perspective* (Toronto: Methuen), 1967; and Lloyd Axworthy and James Gillies, eds., *The Canadian City* (Toronto: McLelland and Stewart), 1975.

4. At the national level, the importance of the "urban crisis" is illustrated by the existence of high-level federal agencies. In the United States, the U.S. Department of Housing and Urban Development carries out an enormous range of research into housing and urban development issues as well as administering funding for billions of dollars of grants each year for U.S. cities. In Canada, the responsibility of the federal government for cities is not clear-cut, and as a result there is no strict equivalent of HUD in Canada. The closest approximation is Canada Mortagage and Housing Corporation (CMHC), which is a Crown Corporation charged with administering the National Housing Act in Canada, which does get CMHC involved peripherally with urban policy; but under the Canadian constitution (the British North America Act of 1867 and the Canada Act of 1982) such involvement must be done in close cooperation with the provinces and municipalities concerned. More will be said in later chapters on urban

policy making in the United States and Canada. The foregoing merely points out that urban areas and problems are viewed as being major national issues and deserving of national attention.

5. The physical and biological quality of the urban environment has attracted increasing efforts from researchers. The following collections bear witness to this activity: A. V. Kneese and B. T. Bower, eds., *Environmental Quality Analysis* (Baltimore: The Johns Hopkins Press), 1972; B. J. L. Berry and F. Horton, eds., *Urban Environmental Management* (Englewood Cliffs, N.J.: Prentice-Hall), 1974; A. V. Kneese and C. L. Schultze, eds., *Pollution, Prices and Public Policy* (Washington, D. C.: The Brookings Institution), 1975; and Peter House, *The Urban Environmental System* (Beverly Hills, Ca.: Sage Publications), 1973.

6. Transportation in and about cities has similarly received a great deal of attention. Some useful summaries and overviews include: John R. Meyer, John F. Kain, and Martin Wohl, *The Urban Transportation Problem* (Cambridge, Mass.: Harvard University Press), 1965; Anthony J. Catanese, *New Perspectives on Urban Transportation Research* (Lexington, Mass: D. C. Heath), 1972; James O. Wheeler, *The Urban Circulation Noose* (North Scituate, Mass: The Duxbury Press), 1974; and John R. Wheeler and José A. Gómez-Ibáñez, *Autos, Transit and Cities* (Cambridge, Mass.: Harvard University Press), 1981.

7. Housing in general, and housing the poor specifically, is such an enormous area of study that it is pointless to go into at this juncture. It is treated below in Chapter 12.

8. See, for example, Michael A. Goldberg, "Canadian and U.S. House Prices," in Michael Walker and Lawrence B. Smith, eds., *Public Property: The Habitat Debate Continued* (Vancouver, B.C.: The Fraser Institute), 1976, pp. 207–254. See also Michael A. Goldberg and John Mercer, *Canadian and U.S. Cities* (Vancouver, B.C.: The University of British Columbia Press), forthcoming.

9. The new wrinkle in urbanization is the migration to nonmetropolitan urban areas from metropolitan urban areas. This has been demonstrated for the United States and other Western countries. See, for example, B. J. L. Berry, ed., *Urbanization and Counterurbanization* (Beverly Hills, Cal.: Sage Publications), 1976.

10. For example, in Canada in 1981 urban housing represented roughly 78.5 percent of the total housing (i.e., 6,567,775 units out of a total of 8,365,465 in Canada as a whole) and housed an equal proportion of the Canadian population. Similar patterns emerge when looking at U.S. housing and population in urban areas in 1980, where there were 60,550,611 urban housing units out of a total of 80,439,837 housing units, or 75.3 percent.

11. Irving Kristol has observed that there is a strong antiurban bias at work among North Americans and among the planning professionals in particular, thus tending to dim urban accomplishments and heighten urban failures. (See Michael A. Goldberg and Michael Y. Seelig, "Canadian Cities: The Right Deed for the Wrong Reasons," *Planning* (May 1975): 8–14.

1

URBANIZATION, URBAN AREAS, AND URBAN LAND MARKETS

URBANIZATION: THE PROCESS

Some Definitions and Examples

As John Palen observes in *The Urban World*, "urbanization is . . . the process by which rural areas become transformed into urban areas."[1] This transformation entails changes in size and also implies significant changes in function and organization. For example, as Vancouver, British Columbia, grew from a small lumber-milling community in the 1880s into its present status as a commercial and service center for western Canada, it not only increased markedly in size but also added functions that it had not previously performed. It became a port to ship lumber, and later wheat and grain, from the prairies. It also added financial and brokerage functions to service the lumber and shipping industries. These functional changes in turn necessitated changes in the spatial organization of the city. First, it had to encompass more land to hold and house these functions and the added residents. Second, the uses to which the land was put became increasingly specialized, mirroring the growing specialization and complexity of the growing Vancouver economy. This same process can be seen to have occurred in all areas that grew from small, single-purpose towns or villages into multifaceted and complex urban realms. So much for urbanization.

One additional definition is needed before proceeding, and a rather central definition and concept it is. What, after all, is meant by "urban," in the urbanization process?

In general, cities and urban areas are rather dense collections of human activities, including houses, jobs, recreation, and transportation and public services to knit together these human activities and provide essential services to residences and worksites (e.g., sewers, water, and utilities).

Once we leave this rather intuitive notion of cities, the issue can become increasingly less coherent as we strive to gain a more precise definition of "urban." In his introductory essay to his book, *An Urban World,* Charles Tilly observes the following about defining a city.

Cities are special kinds of communities in which the coordination and control of widely dispersed activities takes place. Exactly which communities we single out as cities depends on which theoretical approach to community structure we adopt; right now we have four or five distinct ways of theorizing about cities, and no single one of them is clearly superior to the rest.[2]

If we move to a quantitative definition, we will see that the issue does not disappear but again gets more complicated. For instance, Tilly used 100,000 people as his measure of "urban" in his work,[3] as did Kingsley Davis in his study of worldwide urbanization.[4] However, the World Bank relied on the U.N. definition of 20,000 inhabitants in its work.[5] Finally, and more to the point, the U.S. government uses a cut-off of 50,000 people in the core city of an urban region before it designates such a region as a Standard Metropolitan Statistical Area (SMSA); and the Canadian government uses a population of 100,000 in defining a Census Metropolitan Area (CMA), where these people live in one continuously built-up labor market. This, in turn, begs the question of how one defines the boundaries of such areas.[6]

Instead of clarifying things, the issue has become significantly muddied: for instance, how many people to include? How to define the boundaries of the urban region? In the remainder of this book we will rely on two approaches. The first, and more general, is our intuitive notion that cities are rather dense collections of people and of human activities (i.e., cities are very much what the word conjures up in most of our minds—people, factories, buildings for offices, shopping, and living). Over and above this intuitive notion, we will rely on a variety of statistical definitions, depending on the specific data set under discussion. Thus, in the present chapter, when talking about worldwide urbanization, we will be drawing on Kingsley Davis' data and largely relying on his definition (i.e., 100,000 people or more in a built-up area). When later we look at data for U.S. metropolitan areas, we will rely on the SMSA definition noted above. Similarly, when examining Canadian urban areas, we will make use of the CMA definition. However, transcending any of these specific definitions is the intuitive notion of an urban area discussed here, that is, what each one of us thinks of at the mention of the word "city".[7]

An example is in order. Prince George, British Columbia, with a 1976 population well in excess of 100,000 people, is not considered a

CMA because it lacks any contiguous built-up area as required under the CMA definition. Functionally, spatially, visually, and intuitively, Prince George is a city. So much for rigorous formal definitions. At the other end of the spectrum, the remote town of Occidental, California, is classed as urban because the county in which it is situated (Marin County) is part of the San Francisco–Oakland SMSA.

Urbanization Prior to 1800[8]

Prior to 1800 the vast majority of the world's population lived in rural settings, and the rate at which the population was urbanizing was relatively slow and remarkably constant over the preceding several centuries. Kingsley Davis estimates that during the 16th, 17th, and 18th centuries the average rate of growth for the cities in his sample was less than 0.6 percent per year, compared with population growth estimates for the whole of Europe of just over 0.4 percent per year in the period 1650–1800.[9] Hardly a population explosion by any definition. However, with the advent of the industrial revolution the urbanization process accelerated markedly, first in Europe, then in North America, and most recently in the less-developed countries.

Urbanization: 1800–1950

As is clear from Table 1–1, beginning about 1800 there was a dramatic increase in the rate of urbanization as evidenced by the proportion of the world's population living in cities of 5000 or more inhabitants.

Geographer Emrys Jones gives another interesting measure of the degree of urbanization as typified by the number of cities with more than 1,000,000 residents. In the year 1800 there was not a single city with as many as a million people, though London, with 950,000, came close. By 1850 the populations of both London and Paris exceeded one million inhabitants. In 1900 a total of 11 cities could claim a million or more residents, and by 1955 that total had risen to 69 cities.[10]

As would be expected, Britain urbanized first, with other Western European nations lagging somewhat behind, as can be seen in Table 1–3.

Table 1–1 Number and Percentage of World Population Living in Towns Over 5000 Population

Year	Number	Percentage
1800	27.4 million	3.0%
1850	74.9 million	6.4%
1900	218.7 million	13.6%
1950	716.7 million	29.8%

Source: Emrys Jones, *Towns and Cities* (London: Oxford University Press, 1966), p. 32.

Table 1–2   Percentage of People in England and Wales Living in Centers of 10,000 Population or more

Year	Percentage
1800	21.3%
1850	39.5%
1890	61.7%
1901	77.0%
1951	81.0%

Source: Emrys Jones, *Towns and Cities,* p. 30.

Table 1–3   Percentage of Population Living in Centers of 5,000 or more in Selected European Countries

Country	Year				
	1900	*1910*	*1920*	*1930*	*1950*
France	44.0	44.2	46.4	51.2	52.9
Germany	56.1	61.7	64.6	69.8	71.0
Sweden	21.5	24.8	29.5	38.4	56.3
Spain	32.2	34.8	38.4	42.6	60.5
Bulgaria	9.8	19.1	19.9	21.4	24.6

Source: Emrys Jones, *Towns and Cities,* p. 30.

Despite this rapid urbanization in the developed nations of Europe and North America, by 1950 less than 30 percent of the world's people lived in settlements of 5000 or more people. This picture changed rapidly after World War II with the advent of a more widespread industrialization and with the dissemination of modern medical aids.

Urbanization 1950–Present

To put the historical picture in better perspective let us look at Table 1–4, which presents the percentage of the world's population living in urban areas of various sizes at different times. We see that the proportion roughly doubled every 50 years from 1880 through 1950. Since 1950, the rate has increased slightly but the proportion of people living in urban areas has risen quite dramatically, particularly for places with more than 20,000 inhabitants. Two additional tables (1–5 and 1–6) will serve to illustrate this point by setting out the number of cities of different sizes over the 1950–1970 period as well as the number of people living in these different-size cities. By any of these measures, it is clear that there has been a striking increase in the number of large cities and in the number of people living in these larger cities around the world.

Armed with these worldwide trends, we can now look at the urbanization of North America. We will be particularly interested in

Table 1–4 Indices of Urbanization and their Rates of Change, World as a Whole, 1800–1970

	Percentage of World's Population			
Year(s)	In All Urban Places	In Places 20,000+	In Cities 100,000+	Combined Index
1800	3.0	2.4	1.7	2.4
1850	6.4	4.3	2.3	4.3
1900	13.6	9.2	5.5	9.4
1950	28.2[a]	22.7	16.2	22.4
1970	38.6	32.2	23.8	31.5
	Percent Change Per Decade			
1800–1850	16.4	12.4	6.3	12.9
1850–1900	16.3	16.4	19.1	16.8
1900–1950	15.7	19.7	24.1	18.8
1950–1970	16.9	19.3	21.1	19.1

[a]This figure differs slightly from the earlier figure of Jones (Table 1–1) due to slight differences in the definition of urban place.

Source: Kingsley Davis, *World Urbanization 1950–1970, Volume II: Analysis of Trends, Relationships, and Development,* Population Monograph Series, No. 9 (Berkeley, Calif.: Institute of International Studies, University of California, (1972), p. 51.

Table 1–5 Distribution of the World's Population According To Size of Place: Log-Equal Scale

Size–Category Urban Places	Population (000's)			Percentage of World Total		
	1950	1960	1970	1950	1960	1970
12,800,000+	—	14,114	16,077	—	0.5	0.4
6,400,000	22,724	48,613	120,631	0.9	1.6	3.3
3,000,000	50,339	65,970	75,000	2.0	2.2	2.1
1,600,000	61,972	89,144	133,781	2.5	3.0	3.7
800,000	65,524	102,023	144,583	2.6	3.4	4.0
400,000	71,974	89,773	125,737	2.9	3.0	3.5
200,000	67,885	93,075	130,999	2.7	3.1	3.6
100,000	65,600	89,516	116,945	2.6	3.0	3.2
50,000	67,666	91,578	130,409	2.7	3.0	3.6
25,000	67,327	90,905	128,745	2.7	3.0	3.5
12,500	64,284	87,537	116,208	2.6	2.9	3.2
6,250	60,899	82,066	100,863	2.4	2.7	2.8
<6,250	40,189	49,404	58,911	1.6	1.6	1.6
Rural	1,795,511	2,018,941	2,229,000	71.8	67.0	61.4
World Total	2,501,894	3,012,659	3,628,000	100.0	100.0	100.0

Source: Kingsley Davis, *World Urbanization 1950–1970,* Volume II, p. 39.

Table 1–6 World's Urban Places Classified By Size: Conventional Scale

Size–Catetory Urban Places	Number of Places			Percentage of Urban Places		
	1950	1960	1970	1950	1960	1970
16,000,000+	—	—	1	—	—	—
8,000,000	2	3	9	—	—	—
4,000,000	9	13	17	—	—	—
2,000,000	15	27	43	0.1	0.1	0.1
1,000,000	53	71	104	0.2	0.2	0.3
500,000	108	138	179	0.4	0.4	0.5
250,000	189	268	384	0.8	0.8	1.0
125,000	381	551	731	1.6	1.7	1.8
100,000	205	229	309	0.8	0.7	0.8
50,000	957	1,295	1,844	3.9	4.1	4.6
25,000	1,904	2,571	3,641	7.8	8.1	9.2
20,000	1,150	1,566	2,079	4.7	5.0	5.2
10,000	4,450	6,035	7,783	18.3	19.1	19.6
5,000	7,286	9,598	11,751	30.0	30.4	29.5
<5,000	7,564	9,222	10,896	31.2	29.2	27.4
All Urban Places	24,273	31,587	39,771	100.0	100.0	100.0

Source: Kingsley Davis, *World Urbanization 1950–1970*, Volume II, p. 38.

looking at the timing of urbanization in the United States and Canada and in seeing how cities of different sizes fared over time.

The Urbanization of Canada and the United States

Canada and the United States, despite their youth, experienced urbanization at roughly the same time as other developed countries did during the 19th century. Table 1–7 presents data on the percentage of the U.S. and Canadian population that could be classed as urban—from 1790 onward for the United States, and from 1851 onward for Canada.

From these data we can see that both countries urbanized at roughly similar rates and over roughly the same period of time. Moreover, we can see that they are as urbanized as all but the most urban of European nations (e.g. Britain and Germany).

Another interesting measure of urban growth is the growth in the number of cities of different sizes. Accordingly, Tables 1–8 (for the United States) and 1–9 (for Canada) set out the numbers of different-size cities over time.

While the data presented in these tables are not strictly comparable because of the differences in the number of urban places in Canada and the United States necessitating fewer size classes for the Canadian data, the picture that emerges is a consistent one. Larger urban places were experiencing rapid growth both in terms of their number and in terms of the number of people residing in them.

Again, the picture is clear. Up through 1980–1981 larger communities were capturing the bulk of the Canadian and U.S. popula-

Table 1–7 Percentages of Population in Urban Areas:
U.S. and Canada

U.S.[a]		Canada[b]	
Year	Percentage	Year	Percentage
1790	5.1		
1800	6.1		
1810	7.3		
1820	7.2		
1830	8.8		
1840	10.8		
1850	15.3	1851	13.1
1860	19.8	1861	15.8
1870	25.7	1871	18.3
1890	35.1	1891	29.8
1900	39.7	1901	34.9
1910	45.7	1911	41.8
1920	51.2	1921	47.4
1930	56.2	1931	52.5
1940	56.5	1941	55.7
1950 (old def.)	59.0	1951	62.4
1950 (new def.)	64.0		
1960	69.9	1961	70.2
1970	73.5	1971	76.6
1980	73.7	1981	76.7

Sources: [a]U.S. Census, 1790–1980, and includes all places with more than
2500 inhabitants and, after 1950, all places with more than 2500 inhabitants as well as all places in metropolitan areas with a core city of more
than 50,000 people.
[b]D. M. Ray, *Canadian Urban Trends,* Volume I (Ottawa: Department of
Supply and Services), 1976, p. 18. The Canadian data refer to all places
with more than 1000 inhabitants. In addition, the data from 1951 onward include Newfoundland, which was excluded from earlier periods
as it was an independent British Crown Colony prior to 1949.
[c]1981 *Census of Canada.*

tion. However, the most recent experience since has pointed out some
dramatic changes in the urban system in the United States, while during the same period the Canadian urban system remained virtually
unchanged.

After 1970 a dramatic change occurred in the patterns of urbanization in the United States:[11] Smaller, nonmetropolitan communities
that were previously in a long-term decline suddenly began to grow.
This growth occurred at the expense of the existing metropolitan areas
as population growth in the United States as a whole slowed markedly
after 1970.

The data presented show the virtually complete reversal of earlier
trends wherein completely rural counties that were not at all adjacent
to SMSAs lost population durign the decade 1960–1970, yet during
the four-year period 1970–1974 this 0.4 percent annual loss was transformed into a 1.4 percent annual increase.

Table 1–8 Number of Places in Urban and Rural Territory in the United States, 1900–1980

Class and Population Size	1980	1970	1960 Including Alaska & Hawaii	1960 Conterminous United States	1950 1950 urban definition	1950 1940 urban definition	1940	1930²	1920	1910	1900	1890
Urban territory	8,820	7,062	6,041	6,015	4,741	4,023	3,464	3,165	2,722	2,262	1,737	1,348
Places of:												
1,000,000 or more	6	5	5	5	5	5	5	3	3	3	3	
500,000–999,999	16	20	16	16	13	13	9	8	9	5	3	1
250,000–499,999	34	30	30	29	23	23	23	24	13	11	9	7
100,000–249,999	117	100	81	81	65	66	55	56	43	31	23	17
50,000–99,999	290	240	201	201	126	128	107	98	76	59	40	30
25,000–49,999	675	520	432	429	252	271	213	185	143	119	82	66
10,000–24,999	1,765	1,385	1,134	1,130	778	814	665	606	465	369	280	230
5,000–9,999	2,181	1,839	1,394	1,388	1,176	1,133	965	851	715	605	465	340
2,500–4,999	2,675	2,295	2,152	2,140	1,846	1,570	1,422	1,332	1,255	1,060	832	654
Under 2,500	1,061	627	596	596	457							
Rural territory	13,459	13,706	13,749	13,693	13,807	13,235	13,288	13,433	12,855	11,830	8,931	6,490
Places of:												
1,000–2,499	4,430	4,191	4,151	4,113	4,158	3,408	3,205	3,087	3,030	2,717	2,128	1,603
Under 1,000	9,029	9,515	9,598	9,580	9,649	9,827	10,083	10,346	9,825	9,113	6,803	4,887

Sources: U.S. Bureau of the Census, *Historical Statistics of the United States, Colonial Time to 1970* (Washington, D.C.: Government Printing Office), p. 11. U.S. Bureau of the Census, *1980 Census of Population, Volume 1, Characteristics of the Population,* Chapter A, "Number of Inhabitants," ASI 2531–1, 1982.

Table 1–9 Number of Places in Urban Canada by Size of Place, 1901–1971

Number of Urban Complexes	1901	1921	1941	1951	1961	1971
100,000 and over	2	7	8	15	18	23
30,000–99,999	8	11	19	20	25	34
5,000–30,000	43	70	85	102	147	162
Under–5,000	53	88	112	137	190	219

Source: N. H. Lithwick, Urban Canada: Problems and Prospects, (Ottawa, Ontario: Central Mortgage and Housing Corporation), 1970 p. 33; and Statistics Canada, 1971 Census of Population.

The Canadian situation is not nearly so dramatic. The data do not lead to the conclusion that there is a mass movement back to rural places. While it is generally true that during the 1971–1976 period there was a slowdown in growth among the largest metropolitan areas in Canada (notably Montreal, Toronto, and Vancouver), it was also true that the second tier of urban areas had some cities which exhibited very buoyant growth (e.g., Edmonton and Calgary). As a result, the Canadian status is not as clear-cut as that which appears to be evolving in the United States and some other highly developed countries, where major metropolitan centers are losing population to smaller urban areas, many of which are not located in metropolitan regions of any kind.[12]

An Attempt at Some Usable Generalizations

Given the apparently conflicting trends of late and the significant differences that appear to be cropping up between the urbanization process in developed countries and that in developing countries, some generalizations would help considerably at this juncture. Fortunately, a number of useful generalizations can be made but do no violence to the several sets of data presented above, and create some order out of the plethora of trends and countertrends. If we break up the urbanization process into three quite different stages, we can then look more closely at the dynamics of the process at each stage.

Agrarian Urbanization   There was relatively little urbanization prior to the onset of the industrial revolution late in the 18th century. In turn, it is deceptively easy to link urbanization and industrialization directly. However, most writers on the subject stress that urbanization and industrialization and the industrial revolution itself were closely tied to major advances in agricultural technology that led to dramatic increases in agricultural productivity. This enabled fewer people to produce as much, if not more, food from the same or even smaller parcels of land as had been possible previously. Such innovations as the English enclosure movement, the deep plowing of fields, rotation of crops, and the planting of certain crops, like oats and beans, that renewed the soil's natural productivity all contributed to the increased output per acre and per worker.

Table 1–10 Number of People Living in Urban Places in the U.S. by Size of Place, 1900–1980

Class and Population Size	1980	1978	1960		1950		1940	1930	1920	1910	1900
			Including Alaska and Hawaii	Conterminous United States	1950 Urban Definition	1940 Urban Definition					
Urban territory	164,851	149,325	125,269	124,699	96,468	88,927	74,424	68,955	54,158	41,999	30,160
Places of:											
1,000,000 or more	17,530	18,769	17,484	17,484	17,404	17,404	15,911	15,065	10,146	8,501	6,429
500,000–999,999	11,326	12,967	11,111	11,111	9,187	9,187	6,457	5,764	6,224	3,011	1,645
250,000–499,999	12,253	10,442	10,766	10,472	8,242	8,242	7,828	7,956	4,541	3,950	2,861
100,000–249,999	16,756	14,286	11,652	11,652	9,479	9,614	7,793	7,541	6,519	4,840	3,272
50,000–99,999	19,758	16,724	13,836	13,836	8,931	9,073	7,344	6,491	5,265	4,179	2,709
25,000–49,999	23,347	17,848	14,951	14,855	8,808	9,496	7,417	6,426	5,075	4,023	2,801
10,000–24,999	27,681	21,415	17,568	17,513	11,867	12,467	9,967	9,097	7,035	5,549	4,338
5,000–9,999	15,250	12,924	9,780	9,730	8,139	7,879	6,682	5,897	4,868	4,217	3,204
2,500–4,999	9,296	8,038	7,580	7,542	6,490	5,565	5,026	4,718	4,386	3,728	2,899
Under 2,500	1,378	727	690	690	578						
Other urban territory	12,544	15,186	9,851	9,806	7,344						
Rural territory	59,495	53,887	54,054	53,765	54,230	61,770	57,246	53,820	51,553	49,973	45,835
Places of:											
1,000–2,499	7,038	6,656	6,497	6,440	6,473	5,383	5,027	4,821	4,712	4,234	3,298
Under 1,000	3,863	3,852	3,894	3,888	4,031	4,129	4,316	4,363	4,255	3,930	3,003
Other rural territory	47,597	43,379	43,664	43,437	43,725	52,258	47,903	47,637	42,586	41,809	39,533

Sources: U.S. Bureau of the Census, *Historical Statistics of the United States*, p. 11. U.S. Bureau of the Census, *1980 Census of Population, Volume 1, Characteristics of the Population*, Chapter A, "Number of Inhabitants", ASI 2531–1, 1982.

Table 1–11 Population of Urban Centers by Size Group, Canada, 1901–81 (number in thousands and percentage)

Size Group	1901	1911	1921	1931	1941	1951	1961	1971	1976	1981
100,000 and over	476	1081	1659	2328	2645	5222	8401	10426	11685	12593
	(25.5)	(35.9)	(41.8)	(45.1)	(45.2)	(59.2)	(64.0)	(62.4)	(67.2)	(68.3)
30,000–99,999	343	489	496	697	928	1231	1647	1931	1824	1997
	(18.4)	(16.3)	(12.5)	(13.5)	(15.9)	(14.0)	(11.8)	(11.8)	(10.5)	(10.8)
5,000–29,999	503	783	1058	1305	1370	1198	1641	2593	2372	2354
	(26.9)	(26.0)	(26.6)	(25.3)	(23.4)	(13.6)	(12.7)	(15.8)	(13.7)	(12.7)
1,000–4,999	545	655	765	831	910	1167	1595	1641	1485	1491
	(29.2)	(21.8)	(19.1)	(16.1)	(15.5)	(13.2)	(11.5)	(10.0)	(8.6)	(8.1)
Total Urban	1867	3008	3977	5161	5854	8818	13972	16411	17367	18435
	(100.0)	(100.0)	(100.0)	(100.0)	(100.0)	(100.0)	(100.0)	(100.0)	(100.0)	(100.0)

Source: Gertler and Crowley, *Changing Canadian Cities: The Next 25 Years* (Toronto: McClelland and Stewart), 1977 p. 49. 1976 Figures: 1976 Census of Canada, *Population: Geographic Distribution,* Catalogue 92-807 (Ottawa: Statistics Canada), 1978, Table No. 7. 2 1981 Census of Canada, *Population: Age, Sex, and Marital Status,* Catalogue 92-901 (Ottawa, Statistics Canada), 1982, Table No. 6.

Table 1–12   Components of Population Change for Groups of Metropolitan and Nonmetropolitan Counties, 1960–1970 and 1970–1974

Population Category	1974 Population (000's)	Annual Population Growth Rate 1960–1970	1970–1974	Annual Natural Increase Rate 1960–1970	1970–1974	Annual Net Migration Rate 1960–1970	1970–1974
United States	211,390	1.3	0.9	1.1	0.7	0.2	0.2
Inside SMSA (metropolitan)	154,934	1.6	0.8	1.2	0.7	0.5	0.1
Outside SMSA (nonmetropolitan)	56,457	0.4	1.3	0.9	0.6	−0.6	0.7
In counties from which:							
≥20% commute to SMSA	4,372	0.9	2.0	0.8	0.5	0.1	1.5
10–19% commute to SMSA	9,912	0.7	1.4	0.8	0.5	−0.1	0.8
<3–9% commute to SMSA	14,263	0.5	1.3	0.9	0.6	−0.4	0.7
>3% commute to SMSA	27,909	0.2	1.1	0.9	0.6	−0.8	0.5
Entirely rural counties not adjacent to an SMSA	4,618	−0.4	1.4	0.8	0.4	−1.2	1.0

Sources: Richard L. Forstall, Population Division, U.S. Bureau of the Census, unpublished statistics; and Calvin L. Beale, "A Further Look at Nonmetropolitan Population Growth Since 1970," review draft, August 1976; Peter A. Morrison, "The Current Demographic Context of National Growth and Development," reprinted in Bourne and Simmons, eds., *Systems of Cities: Readings on Structure Growth and Policy* (New York: Oxford University Press), 1978, p. 477.

It was thus possible for many fewer people to feed a nation's population. Rural populations could therefore be released for work in urban areas and, more importantly, farming communities could now support much larger urban populations than before. The revolution in agriculture created simultaneously a supply of labor for factories as well as an adequate supply of food for urban residents, both of which were necessary conditions for any sort of urban industrial development.

Accordingly, this first stage of the urbanization process was typified (and made possible) by agricultural innovations and rising agricultural productivity. The supply of labor thus created was then attracted to cities and towns by the existence of factories, which could be fed by the higher agricultural output.[13] From this point onward urbanization and industrialization interacted with further agricultural innovations to move people from the countryside into the cities and towns, where the growing manufacturing activities located.

Such a conception of urbanization was relevant for the now developed countries in the early years of their industrialization, and applied to Canada and the United States throughout much of the 19th and early 20th centuries. This first stage of urbanization also applies to the presently developing countries, who with their enormous stocks of rural inhabitants are the primary force behind the current rates of urbanization for the world's population.

Industrial-based Metropolitan Urbanization This second stage of urbanization encompasses the growth of metropolitan centers in the United States and Canada, particularly in the period between World War II and 1970. This urbanization was typified much less by movements from farming and agriculturally based communities than by movements from smaller urban areas (many of which are in rural parts of North America) to larger ones. Between 1920 and 1970 in the United States, and from 1941 to 1971 in Canada, metropolitan areas grew as a result of growing concentrations of people and economic activities that began to cluster around the larger cities. This concentration was aided by fairly rapid post-war population growth (the so-called "babyboom") as well as by rapid rates of immigration into both countries, particularly from southern Europe. The result was the great concentration of North America's population in metropolitan areas that accounted for more than half of the inhabitants of both the United States (in 1970) and Canada (in 1971). This essentially urban–urban migration pattern was the result of the virtual emptying out of farming areas during the previous phase of urbanization as well as the growing economies of scale that appeared to exist in carrying out production of goods and (more recently) services in metropolitan areas of considerable size.[14] As Brian Berry points out, it was also a function of some deep-seated underlying assumptions about the availability of resources, energy, population growth, and general optimism.[15] However, many of these assumptions are no longer valid, and rising dissatisfaction with the diseconomies of metropolitan growth, such as various forms of pollution, crime, crowding, as well as rising affluence are generally leading people to look for alternatives.

Post-industrial Nonmetropolitan Counterurbanization[16] With growing signs of declining livability for the largest metropolitan areas, smaller areas began to grow. At first these were largely contiguous with SMSAs, but in the 1970–1974 period nonmetropolitan urban areas of fewer than 50,000 began to grow rapidly, reversing the trend for most of the present century. The reversal is most pronounced in the United States but has been observed in most Western European countries.[17] In Britain, post-war attempts to contain the sprawl of Greater London are being replaced now by attempts to stimulate growth in that city, which has lost large numbers of residents during the past two decades.[18] Similar concerns are being voiced in North America's major metropolitan regions.[19]

Changing values and growing disaffection with large cities created a potential for this radical shift, not unlike the growth of industry early in the industrial revolution. However, without the necessary technological changes in agricultural production, the urbanization-industrialization process would have been little more than an unsatisfied set of potential demands. Similarly, in the present case, changing values would have meant little were it not for the technological changes that have allowed, and in some instances promoted, further decentralization. The growth of service industries, with their minimal locational restrictions, has freed a major portion of the U.S. labor force to live where it likes and still conduct business efficiently. Similarly, high-technology production and research are largely independent of location and are much more "footloose" than are the metropolitan-based industries which typified our economy of the 1950s and 1960s. These technological changes are thus analogous to the agricultural innovations of the 18th and 19th centuries in that they made possible the nonmetropolitanization of the United States during the 1970s. How enduring these trends will be and how well they will apply to Canada (a nation whose people are generally satisfied and enthusiastic about their urban environments) remains to be seen.[20] It implies a rather exciting period ahead for city-watchers and, more importantly, for North America's policymakers.

URBANIZED AREA: THE PRODUCT

Before leaving the question of urbanization and the growth of cities, we will look back in greater detail at the variety of forces that have created our present urban areas and, in so doing, learn something for the future. If nothing else, we can begin to appreciate the diversity and ever-changing nature of the city-building forces that are inextricably linked to the urbanization process and to the more general technological and social and economic changes that occur simultaneously in North American society.

As the process of urbanization progressed, cities grew and became increasingly specialized and complex. This specialization and growth were additional factors in the ongoing urbanization of the world's population. The city is thus both the cause and the effect—it being exceedingly difficult to isolate cause and effect here, with some scholars attributing the urbanization process to the increasing lure of cities, while others claim that cities grew as a result of factors beyond their control such as agricultural advances. We are not interested here in this causal argument but rather with exploring some of the forces that worked to create and build cities and to arrange functions spatially within city boundaries.

City-building Forces and Functions

In their pioneering text on urban land economics, Herbert Dorau and Albert Hinman set out five quite general reasons for human settlement in cities. These rather general propositions provide a convenient framework for examining the changing specifics of city-building forces.[21]

1. *Human instinct—fear*: Initially, fear of animals and of the mysterious forces of their natural habitat forced peoples to band together. Later, fear of other bands was another factor.

2. *Human instinct—gregariousness*: As Dorau and Hinman note, human beings like company; thus, clustering of human beings in settlements met their need for companionship.

3. *Defense*: According to Dorau and Hinman, these first two instincts were unconscious, whereas banding together to protect one's clan or group for defense purposes and building towns to effectuate this defense are the first conscious motives for city building.

4. *Religion*: The creation of places of worship and religious ceremony also created the need for human settlements.

5. *Standard of living*: This last and, in many ways, most general of the five reasons for living in cities is also the most dynamic, reflecting changes in production consumption and technology.

Returning to the earliest known cities, we can see these forces at work. Since the first two factors noted are unconscious and since they are to a significant extent covered by the last three factors, we can safely ignore them and focus on defense, religion, and standard of living as constant city-building forces with ever-changing physical forms. Accordingly, let us see how early cities permitted ancient civilizations to defend themselves against natural and human enemies. We can then move on to see how they served their religious and economic functions as well.

Prior to the industrial revolution, the technology of warfare was relatively primitive and required assaulting forces to be in reasonable proximity to the military objective. Accordingly, for defensive purposes, ancient and even medieval cities sought to isolate themselves from their surroundings by locating on hilltops or islands. Excavations of early cities in the Middle East and aerial photographs of extant medieval cities in Europe clearly reveal the early defense motive in locating preindustrial cities.

The importance of religion in early city building has been stressed by most writers on the history and archaeology of cities.[22] Dominating medieval skylines and central areas are the famous Gothic and Renaissance cathedrals. Earlier cities such as Jerusalem, Athens, and Rome were all religious centers, and religious structures played central roles in their form and development. Similarly, Mesoamerican cities of the Aztecs and Mayans focused on massive pyramids and temples. Similar ceremonial structures occupied positions of importance in the earliest cities of Mesopotamia and the Nile Valley.

Turning finally to the economic functions of the preindustrial city, we can begin to see the close relationship that exists between the economic system and the city. For example, cities of the ancient world were founded on the emerging agricultural surplus of their hinterlands. Accordingly, these early cities grew to service these agricultural hinterlands and served as marketplaces for their products, and later as more extensive commercial and trading centers. Given the primitive transportation technology of the preindustrial period prior to the 19th century, such commercially based cities sat astride major trading routes, watercourses, or at the intersections of these commercial avenues. And with the advent of ocean travel and trade, port cities came into being.

Medieval and Renaissance cities were the culmination of these trading and manufacturing activities and featured a broad range of financial, brokerage, legal, and other commercial services. As time passed and technologies changed, cities reflected this evolution as they themselves evolved from simple trade centers, with their bazaars and marketplaces, to urban complexes housing more sophisticated commercial activities, as was the case in the Italian city-states.

City-building after the Industrial Revolution

As Gideon Sjoberg notes, "It was the industrial revolution that brought about truly far-reaching changes in city life."[23] With the coming of mechanical power and machines, agricultural productivity could rise even more dramatically than previously, and factories would require enormous supplies of labor, raw materials, and energy. Implications for the location and form of cities were vast.

Given the technological advances in warfare, defensive considerations became less and less important towards the beginning of the 19th century. North America provided some interesting exceptions to that generalization since a number of cities west of the Mississippi River basin had their origins as forts: St. Joseph's, Missouri; Omaha, Nebraska; Sacramento, California; Calgary, Alberta; and Victoria, British Columbia, to mention but a few.

Similarly, religious functions became less important in the forming and shaping of cities, again with the exception of North America. The Spanish missions in California, for example, founded virtually all of that state's major cities. These missions were also important in Texas, New Mexico, and Arizona. In New England, the importance of organized religion in early town life can still be seen in the traditional white church steeples dotting the New England countryside. In large North American cities, neighborhood churches and large cathedrals also played important parts in shaping urban and neighborhood growth and in serving as foci for the immigrants who began flowing into North America in the middle of the 19th century.

While defense and religion began to wane as city-building forces in the wake of the industrial revolution, economic forces came to the fore. Accordingly, the great shaper and builder of cities in the last two centuries has been what Dorau and Hinman called "standard of living," or economic factors. The emergence of the factory system brought with it the need for materials, labor, and capital on a scale never previously imagined. Accordingly, where earlier cities evolved along commerical lines, trade routes, and defensive locations, industrial cities needed to take advantage of resources—human, natural, and financial. Some cities, such as Duluth, Thunder Bay, and Pittsburgh, grew up near natural resource deposits. Others took advantage of renewal natural resources such as timber (Seattle, Vancouver, B.C.; Coos Bay, Oregon), fishing (Halifax, N.S.; Prince Rupert, B. C., and St. John's, Newfoundland), and agriculture (Saskatoon, Kansas City, and St. Louis). Virtually all North American cities needed access to the rest of the continent and to the outside world.

In the early phases of the industrial revolution, river, canal, or deep-water access were necessary. Later, with the development of railroads, waterborne access could be supplemented with, or its absence overcome by, railroads. The development of the prairie and plains regions of the United States and Canada was particularly dependent on the railroad because of the enormous territory to be settled where there was no watercourse or harbor. Railroad communities still dot the North American continent, from Moose Jaw, Saskatchewan, and Medicine Hat, Alberta, to Chicago, Illinois, and Abilene, Texas.

Changing technology brought roads and motor vehicles, which gave access to cities and regions that had been previously served only by rail or not at all, and these urban fringe communities were brought directly into the urban realm via the automobile and truck.

Technological changes in energy also had significant impacts on city building. Waterpower was supplanted by steam, and the need for coal was in turn replaced by natural gas, petroleum, and electricity. Factories once dependent on waterpower were thus freed to move to areas endowed with other sources of energy. New England's water-driven mills could be replaced with Pittsburgh's coal-fired heavy industry and the hydroelectric power of the Tennessee Valley Authority in the Southeast.

It is not difficult to think of cities that were founded on the basis of defensive, religious, or economic-technological functions. However, cities being complex and highly specialized entities, it is artificial and unreasonable to try to trace the evolution and development of any single city to a single source. Thus, while Calgary may have originated because of its strategic location on two prairie rivers, its development was also related to the early defenses erected there and, later, still, to the oil resources in the province of Alberta. The construction of the Canadian Pacific Railroad gave Calgary a strong push in the 1880s, just as its new airport will do in the 1980s. This point can be repeated using any large North American city. The city of the present is the cumulative result of the various forces acting on it during its history. The city-building forces we have isolated in this section do not act exclusively, but rather act in concert and in varying combinations over time as technological, political, social, and economic forces in society ebb and flow. To understand the growth and development of any specific city or region requires a proper understanding of all of these forces as well as an appreciation of the social, political, cultural, economic, and technological milieu within which these forces must find expression and interact.

City Building in the "Post-Industrial Era"

If there is one trend that can be discussd in all of this, it is that cities are less and less dependent on any single factor for their current and future growth.[24] Cities like Brasilia grow up in the middle of the Amazon jungle as a result of government policy and the availability of sophisticated technologies to move people, goods, and resources to and from the city. Cities are becoming increasingly "footloose" and independent of the constraining city-building forces of the industrial and preindustrial periods of the past 5500 years. Today cities process information as much as they process materials. As a result, they are free to locate wherever information is available or can be made available. In view of the continuing rapid changes in information processing and transmission, it is clear that economic activities that provide the impetus for urban growth are more and more free to locate where they choose. The almost explosive development of the Sun Belt states and the more recent growth of nonmetropolitan areas are both consistent with the greater freedom of choice that economic activities possess today. Increasingly, people (and therefore jobs) are seeking high-amenity locations, since they are no longer inhibited by the constraints that faced earlier industrial-based growth.[25] Hence, the post-industrial era, typified by service-based economic activity and information as opposed to materials processing, has the potential to stimulate quite different city-building forces than those noted previously.

Thus far, we have been addressing questions related to the external forces that drive city growth. However, associated with each of these external forces are internal forces that shape the form of the city and arrange its various land uses into a remarkably orderly pattern. It is to these internal structural forces that we now briefly turn.

The Internal Forces of City Growth and Structure

Along with increased urbanization and industrialization came increased specialization of economic tasks. Technology and technological change were both the cause and effect of this process of growing specialization. As Childe observed, one of the inevitable outcomes of the industrial system was a corresponding class system.[26] The growing mobility of the world's population and the movement from villages to cities and from the Old World to the new further fragmented urban populations according to race, tribe, or ethnic group.

This specialization and fragmentation of work and resident groups, as we will see, has had significant impacts on the internal growth and structure of cities.

The great specialization and complexity of the modern city has presented urban researchers with significant analytical and definitional problems. In turn, they have chosen to subdivide the city into a growing number of subfields, each representing a recognized area for study. Thus, the very specialization and complexity that has given rise to the city is mirrored in the way we study its internal structure and dynamics. Any such division of so complex and interrelated an entity as the modern city is bound to be fraught with oversimplifications and, in many cases, errors where things have been improperly categorized or where interactions among categories have eluded the specialized analysts' tools and framework.

This book, being concerned with urban land economics, will focus quite naturally on economic forces affecting urban land use and value. However, at this introductory stage it is important to note that we could (and different urban specialists do) study the internal structure of the city from any of the following points of view (and from many others as well). Given the complexity of that picture, it will be necessary to break the city as a subject into manageable compartments for study. The principal compartments that we have developed include the following views of urban structure (the specialities are noted in parentheses).

Social structure (sociologists and social psychologists and, increasingly, social planners and social workers)

Political structure (political science)

Governmental and administrative structure (political science, public and business administration, planning)

Economic structure (economics and, increasingly, geography and planning)

Spatial structure (geography and, increasingly, economics)

Land use structure (sociologists, geographers, economists, and planners)

Each provides us with important insights. However, no one discipline or viewpoint is adequate to deal with the true complexity of the issues. Thus, the student of urban land economics is reminded at the outset that the principles set out in this volume are helpful in beginning to understand the growth and development of cities, but they are at best a partial (though important) approach.

Without going into great detail on any one of the above structural categories, we can make some useful generalizations that apply to all. For example, each of these views (and the disciplines associated with them) has to deal with the growing specialization of internal structures in the city. City government, land uses, social groups, economic activities, and political power all reflect the great specialization which was largely the result of (and cause for) urbanization. In addition to specialization, each has to deal with the growing scale of activities which typifies the city. Social, economic, land use, and political problems appear and reappear on a scale of greater size and complexity as urban areas. Finally, each structural view has to take increasing cognizance of the multitude of other factors that influence the city's structure, as we have found that narrow and specialized views have led to ineffective solutions to urban problems and policy making.

The internal structures of present cities therefore do mirror the diversity and complexity of the forces of urbanization that gave rise to our cities in the first place. A significant portion of the study of urban land economics is devoted to the study of the internal arrangement of urban areas, and the present discussion has served merely to introduce the topic, its potential complexity, and to alert readers that our emphasis will be on the economic and land use views of urban structure.

URBAN PROBLEMS: THE INEVITABLE SIDE EFFECT

It is a truism that the problems that are associated with the concentration of large numbers of people in relatively dense settings (i.e., cities) are different from problems facing people residing in less dense, rural environments based on agricultural economies. A complete cataloging of urban ills is not possible in this section, nor is it possible, for that matter, in any single volume. The problems facing cities in developing countries are significantly different from those facing the cities of developed nations. Moreover, the problems facing cities in the United States are quite different from those faced by Canada's cities. The purpose here is to raise a number of representative urban issues to which we can return later, when we are equipped with suitable tools to analyze these problems. At this early stage we can illustrate the types of uses to which urban land economics can be put, as well as provide a bridge between the macrospatial worldwide phenomenon of urbanization and the microspatial difficulties faced by neighborhoods, shopping districts, and office areas of North America's cities.

In developing countries, urban problems are not easily separable from the other problems these countries face, namely, of providing adequate physical and social services for their people. Housing usually tops the list of problems as the rapidly growing urban populations, swelled by immigrants from rural agrarian areas, quickly overwhelm the ability of governments to provide shelter. Related to housing and crowding is the provision of adequate sewage, water, and utilities for the growing number of people inhabiting Third World cities. The automobile poses further problems and creates congestion, noise, and air pollution. In the face of rapid growth (approaching 6–8 percent a year in some Latin American cities), there is a pressing need for government policy relating to land use and urban growth, but many potentially useful policies are thwarted at the outset by speculation and private interests.

In the United States and Canada, urban problems take different forms. Provision of low-cost housing for lower-income urban residents has been, and will continue to be, a growing problem. While North American cities are well served in terms of both hard (e.g., engineering and public works) and soft (e.g. social, educational, and cultural) services, problems have arisen with respect to paying for these high-quality services.

As urban growth continues, many people who moved from dense central areas to more spacious suburban areas resent the growing trend toward higher density and have attempted to contain further growth to maintain their life-style. Guiding urban growth while providing adequate housing and job opportunities for all is one of the major problems that policymakers face in North America and one on which we will focus considerable attention later. Many of the previously used devices to control and order urban growth (such as zoning and other land use controls) have not always had their desired effect, and have at times caused additional problems of their own.

The rapid growth of outlying suburban and exurban areas has caused problems not only for these outlying areas trying to maintain a certain quasi-rural life-style, but for the central areas as well. Claims of rampant speculation speeding the exodus of central city residents and of fragmenting peripheral growth (i.e., suburban sprawl, leap-frogging, etc.) are frequently heard and need to be explored at some length, as these activities are concentrated in the urban land markets that are the focus of this book.

Central area decay is another problem of particular importance in the United States and closely related to peripheral growth. Associated with the loss of central-city middle-income families is the growing concentration of poverty and racial minorities in the centers of many U.S. urban regions. In those cities to which white middle-income households are returning, a new era dawns for their older neighborhoods; but only larger problems loom for the soon-to-be-displaced urban poor. Once again, an understanding of the workings of the urban land market can greatly enhance our ability to analyze these problems and formulate innovative policies that are consistent with both the workings of urban markets and with broader societal goals.

By studying how markets work, we will be able also to study why they do not work (so-called market imperfections). Racial discrimination is a most important example of these imperfections. However, zoning, land use controls, restrictive covenants, and other local government restrictions also act as imperfections impeding the smooth functioning of market processes in seeking social objectives. Once again, by understanding how these imperfections work their way through the marketplace for urban land and buildings, we are in a position to see where such restrictions and policies often run into difficulties and thus fail to achieve their social ends.

Another problem facing both Canadian and U.S. urban dwellers is the rising cost of housing, not just of the urban poor but for all residents. The affordability of housing and the quality of urban living are closely related. However, continued attempts to raise the quality of the physical environment through restrictions on development eventually affect affordability, raising housing costs and thereby diminishing some of the gains in the quality of life.

It has been said that economics is the science of trade-offs. If that is so, then urban land economics can be seen as the science of urban trade-offs and choices. Accordingly, in what follows we shall be attempting to provide readers with the technical and substantive knowledge needed to analyze the complex urban issues facing us and our urbanized societies today. Additionally, and perhaps of greater utility, based upon such analyses, we hope to be able to arm the student of urban land economics with the necessary tools to suggest and analyze policy alternatives that are likely to be consistent with the workings of urban land markets and with society's social, political, and institutional goals and realities.

Footnotes

1. J. John Palen, *The Urban World* (New York: McGraw Hill, Inc.), 1975, p. 6.

2. Charles Tilly, "Introduction," in Charles Tilly, ed., *An Urban World* (Boston: Little, Brown and Co.), 1974, pp. 2–3.

3. *Ibid.*, p. 39.

4. Kingsley Davis, *World Urbanization 1950–1970, Volume I: Basic Data for Cities, Countries, and Regions* (Berkeley, Cal.: Institute of International Studies, University of California), 1969; and Kingsley Davis, *World Urbanization 1950–1970, Volume II: Analysis of Trends, Relationships, and Development* (Berkeley, Cal.: Institute of International Studies, University of California), 1972.

5. World Bank, *Urbanization: Sector Working Paper* (Washington, D. C.: World Bank), 1972.

6. Peter G. Goheen, "Metropolitan Area Definition: A Re-evaluation of Concept and Statistical Practice," in Larry S. Bourne, ed., *Internal Structure of the City* (New York: Oxford University Press), 1971, pp. 47–58.

7. In the remainder of this chapter we will be using the words "city," "urban area," "metropolitan area," "urban region," and "metropolitan region" interchangeably for variety as well as to reinforce the intuitive notions we all have about the characteristics of "urban" as opposed to "rural" or "nonurban."

8. The cutoff date of 1800 is somewhat arbitrary, and any date within 50 years of ths would work adequately. A number of historical studies exist which gather data in 50-year periods, and thus 1800 seemed a reasonable point of division.

9. Kingsley Davis, "The Urbanization of the Human Population," in Charles Tilly, ed., *An Urban World* (Boston: Little, Brown and Co.), 1974, pp. 160–177.

10. Emrys Jones, *Towns and Cities* (London, England: Oxford University Press), 1966, p. 32. It should be noted that these data refer to central cities and not to metropolitan areas as a whole.

11. This change has been documented in a number of places. See, for example, Brian J. L. Berry, ed., *Urbanization and Counter-Urbanization* (Beverly Hills, Cal.: Sage Publications), 1976; Peter A. Morrison, "The Current Demographic Context of National Growth and Development," in Larry S. Bourne and James W. Simmons, eds., *Systems of Cities* (New York: Oxford University Press), 1978, pp. 473–479; Niles M. Hansen, *The Future of Nonmetropolitan America: Studies in the Reversal of Rural and Small Town Population Decline* (Lexington, Mass: D. C. Heath), 1973; and Leland S. Burns, "The Metropolitan Population of the United States: Historical and Emerging Trends" (Los Angeles, Cal.: UCLA School of Architecture), mimeographed, 1980.

12. See Berry, *Urbanization and Counter-Urbanization, op cit.* Also see L. Tweeter and G. L. Brinkman, *Micropolitan Development* (Ames, Iowa: The Iowa State University Press), 1976.

13. See Palen, *op. cit.,* especially pp. 12–14.

14. See H. Craig Davis, "Post-War Migration Patterns in Canada" (Vancouver, B.C.: School of Community and Regional Planning, University of British Columbia), mimeographed, 1973. The belief in the continuation of this process was sufficiently widespread to lend additional weight to the idea of creating a series of new towns in Britain to help take development pressure away from the Greater London and Greater Manchester areas. See Emrys Jones, *op. cit.* pp. 64–69.

15. See Brian J. L. Berry, "The Counterurbanization Process: How General?" in Niles M. Hansen, ed., *Human Settlement Systems: International Perspectives on Structure, Change and Public Policy* (Cambridge Mass.: Ballinger Publishing Co.), 1978, pp. 25–49.

16. *Ibid.*; and Hansen, *The Future of Nonmetropolitan America . . ., op. cit.*

17. Berry, "The Counterurbanization Process? . . .", *op. cit.*

18. For example, Peter Hall in his revised edition of *World Cities* (New York: McGraw-Hill), 1977, estimates that London lost roughly 10,000 office jobs per year from 1963 to 1975, and moreover, that since 1961 London has experienced significant net outmigration (p. 44).

19. For example, the British Columbia cities of Vancouver and Victoria, both leaders in the early 1970s in the area of growth and land-use controls, recently created economic development offices to stimulate lagging economic growth. These offices have had the enthusiastic support of their city councils and mayors and have received good press coverage relative to their small sizes.

20. A recently released study, sponsored by the now defunct Ministry of State for Urban Affairs in Ottawa, showed that in general Canadians are quite pleased with their urban environments and there is little dissatisfaction with urban living overall. See Canada Mortgage and Housing Corporation, *Public Priorities in Urban Canada: A Survey of Community Concerns* (Ottawa, Ontario: Canada Mortgage and Housing Corporation), 1979.

21. Herbert B. Dorau and Albert G. Hinman, *Urban Land Economics* (New York: The MacMillan Co.), 1928, pp. 13–14.

22. In his widely quoted paper on urbanization, V. Gordon Childe sets out ten elements that characterize cities as opposed to earlier forms of human settlement. One of these characteristics was the need for large monumental public buildings, a need which was most often filled by the erection of a central temple. See V. Gordon Childe, "The Urban Revolution," *Town Planning Review* 21(1:1950):4–7.

23. Gideon Sjoberg, "The Origin and Evolution of Cities," in Kingsley Davis, ed., *Cities: Their Origin, Growth and Human Impact* (San Francisco, Cal.: W. H. Freeman and Co.), 1973, pp. 18–27.

24. See Edgar M. Hoover, *The Location of Economic Activity* (New York: McGraw-Hill Book Co.), 1948, for an excellent discussion of the changing locational needs of economic activity and their growing locational freedom.

25. This argument is taken to what initially appeared an extreme position by Michael A. Goldberg and Douglas Webster in their paper on the growth potential of the high-amenity Maritime region of Eastern Canada. See their paper, "The Atlantic Provinces: Canada's Next Amenity Region," *CONTACT: A Journal of Urban and Regional Affairs,* Fall 1979.

26. Childe, *op. cit.*

2

THE TOOLS OF URBAN LAND ECONOMICS

SOME PROBLEMS IN NEED OF ANALYSIS
AND TREATMENT

Earlier, some of the consequences of urbanization were discussed, including a variety of problem areas. The stereotype of these problems is the image of the old decaying central city of the Northeastern and Midwestern United States, surrounded by sprawling suburbs, complex highway networks, and closely tied to racial discrimination and urban poverty. Associated with this dismal picture is the gloomy fiscal condition of cities, exacerbated by the flight of middle-income families and jobs to the suburbs or to the Sun Belt states. This caricature of the "urban crisis" is just that, an exaggeration of the facts. Even in financially troubled New York City there are significant growth activities, such as office industries. Moreover, among the decaying structures there are pockets exhibiting significant rejuvenation and vitality. The problems cannot be, and should not be, abstracted and simplified. They occur within the context of an extremely complex and interrelated system—the city.

In addition to the rather spectacular difficulties typified by say, New York or Detroit, there are a host of less spectacular but perhaps more widespread problems facing not only North American cities but, more importantly, North American urban citizens. Paramount among these is the rising cost of housing, complemented by the rising cost of urban travel. The traditional trade-off between housing costs and travel costs still exists but confronts consumers with rising costs on both sides of the trade-off. Simultaneously, in the face of growing budgetary problems and the desire to provide residents with at least a constant-quality urban environment, local governments have created a range of urban development controls and guidelines to minimize further encroachment on the quality of urban life. In many instances, these very attempts to improve the livability of urban areas have exacerbated elements of the problem by restricting the supply of residential opportunities and raising the cost of available housing.

If we are to avoid continually exacerbating this state of affairs in our attempts to improve it, we must begin to properly analyze problems and develop solutions based on a sound understanding of how the urban land market works in all its complexity and variants. As a result, there is a clear need for a set of tools that will enable us to analyze urban problems and proposed solutions in significant depth so that past unexpected difficulties can be overcome and more appropriate and effective solutions put forward and implemented.

AN INTRODUCTION AND OVERVIEW OF THE TOOLS

Urban land markets function within the context of the urban economy at large. Thus, before we can begin to analyze the specifics of urban land markets, it is necessary to understand the larger economic environment within which the urban land market operates. This is the domain of urban macroeconomics (i.e., the urban economic system). In Chapter 3 we develop a framework within which to study the urban economy and its principal elements. We will develop, as well, a framework for accounting for urban economic activity so that we can measure the state of the urban economy at different points in time. We will also be building on this accounting framework to formulate a set of techniques for analyzing and forecasting these economic activities. Such analyses and forecasts provide a basic building block in any microanalysis of urban problems and are a logical place at which to begin to assemble our urban analysis tool kit.

Having set the macroeconomic stage, we explore the microeconomic world of demand and supply and, of course, their interaction in the marketplace. Chapter 4 sets out the various concepts that underly the study of the demand for urban land. The important role of location will be stressed here, as will be the role of the general urban economic climate.

We consider the supply of urban land and real property in Chapter 5. Of particular importance here are those characteristics that tend to make urban land and real property somewhat unique as economic goods. Accordingly, the discussion will center on the supply from the standing stock of land and structures (i.e., improvements), as well as on the supply of newly developed land and structures.

An essential element in the supply of urban land and improvements is the capital needed to create and maintain this supply. The importance of financing derives from the great costs incurred in subdividing and servicing land, and then in actually constructing buildings on this serviced land. The financing is of two types: private financing to developers, home purchasers, and other consumers of urban real property; and public finance to service and maintain the serviced land and improvements. In Chapter 6 we look into questions and techniques of financing the private sector, with particular emphasis on mortgage markets and analytical financial tools. In Chapter 7 the focus shifts to financing the urban public sector, including the sources and uses of public funds and the major problems facing local governments as they strive to finance the services demanded by residents.

Demand and supply forces do not operate in a vacuum. Rather, they operate within a very complex sociopolitical and legal framework. Because of the unique economic characteristics of urban land and real property, a separate body of legal and political institutions has grown up to define legal interests in land and to govern the way these interests can be transacted. As a result, it is essential that we have some feeling of the institutional setting within which urban land and real property markets bring supply and demand together. This is the function of Chapter 8, where the political nature of the urban development process will be explored, along with the legal institutions that distinguish land and real property from other economic goods.

Having developed suitable analytical tools in these introductory chapters, it is now possible to bring these tools together to tell us something about the price of urban land and real property and about the dynamics of demand and supply and their interaction. This is achieved in Chapters 9 and 10. Chapter 9 introduces us to the various participants in the market and to the functioning of the market under normal conditions; in Chapter 10 we develop a more realistic view of market function by looking at some of the ways in which urban land and real property markets function abnormally, as well as the ways in which the market in reality is broken down into a number of interacting but separable component submarkets.

THE APPROACH

By developing the tools in this manner (e.g., from macro to micro) we will be providing a consistent framework with a reasonably clear-cut logical structure for analyzing a great diversity of problems and solutions. By setting out the tools separately in Chapters 3 through 8 we hope to minimize confusion and complexity. Having mastered these concepts, we bring them together in Chapters 9 and 10 to deal with the complexity of markets in a real-world setting.

Having presented these tools in order, and then having synthesized them under the rubric of urban land and real property markets, we are now equipped to look at a range of current difficulties being faced by urban residents in North America. Accordingly, the final part of the book provides an opportunity to look both at pressing problems in some detail and to provide a framework for applying these tools so that the reader can have the tools reinforced and simultaneously see the utility of having mastered the tools in the first place.

2

INTRODUCTORY OVERVIEW TO URBAN LAND ECONOMICS

WHAT IS URBAN LAND ECONOMICS?

In coming to grips with a similar definitional problem, two pioneers in the field of land economics observed, "The starting point of Land Economics is the relation of population to land. Land Economics deals with the utilization of land by man, but more specifically with the relations of man to man arising out of the relations of man to natural resources."[1] Somewhat earlier, these same pioneers defined *land economics* as "that division of economics, theoretical and applied, which is concerned with the land as an economic concept and with the economic relationships which grow out of land as property."[2]

Urban land economics, by focusing on land within and adjacent to urban areas, is a more narrowly construed field. Important resource issues dealt with in land economics, such as mineral rights and subsurface rights, riparian rights (water), and renewable land-based resources such as forests and agricultural fields, are not of direct interest to the urban land economist, though many of the economic and institutional concepts that we will be developing are general enough to treat these broader issues.

Since we are interested in the economics of urban land, we should spend a moment discussing the economic entity of interest: urban land and, more particularly, those characteristics of urban land that are sufficiently unique or otherwise special to warrant a separate field of analysis, related to, but distinct from, the more general fields of economics and urban economics. A number of differentiating characteristics are set out below.

Some Differentiating Characteristics of Urban Land

Three sets of differentiating characteristics are typically mentioned in the literature of urban land economics.

Physical Characteristics[3] Physical characteristics include such attributes as the slope, altitude, shape, soils, and dimensions of a given site. The following four most abstract physical characteristics differentiate urban land from other economic entities.

Space The dimensional characteristics of a site are probably its most important physical characteristics. With the coming of condominium (strata-title) ownership of three-dimensionally defined parcels of property, the earlier dimensionality expressed by the Fishers takes on new meaning.[4] Thus, the quantity of space occupied by a site, is of critical importance in understanding the economic utility of a parcel of urban land.

Indestructibility Physical space can neither be created nor destroyed. It exists independent of any structure built to make it usable to our society. This indestructibility (and for built forms, their analogous great durability) means that urban land possesses long-run characteristics that are significantly different from those of other economic goods and services. It also implies that the stock of physical space is absolutely fixed, though structures of shorter duration influence the effective supply of real property available at any point in time.

Immobility Space on the earth's surface cannot be moved in any way. It is permanently fixed with respect to the physical location it occupies.

Uniqueness In a narrow sense, every parcel of real property is unique. There is only one of each location on the face of the earth. Moreover, each parcel is characterized by its slope, aspect, altitude, soils, mineralization, neighboring parcels and their characteristics, dimensions, shape, climate, and so on. This uniqueness implies that the supply of sites can be differentiated, requiring in such instances a different sort of analysis from the traditional perfectly competitive situation which assumes homogeneous undifferentiated goods and services. Despite this uniqueness, there are close substitutes for many of the parcels of land within urban areas, allowing us to use assumptions about competitiveness, but these assumptions must be used with great caution and forethought to assess their appropriateness in each instance. These four physical characteristics set land apart from most economic quantities and require special treatment.

Locational Characteristics   There is an old saying in the real estate industry that the three most important characteristics of urban real estate are, in order, location, location, and location. This is something of a simplification, although not as much as one might expect. The point is that location does differentiate urban land economics from the main body of economics. Location is ignored in the main body of economics; it has been called "aspatial" as a result; economic activity is assumed to take place somewhere, but its precise location, and the extent and type of land it requires, escapes traditional analysis.[5] However, location is of central importance in urban land economics and urban economics, and locational aspects of urban land will occupy much of our attention, as they are intimately related to the uses to which parcels of urban land can be put, and to their economic and social value. When we speak here about locational characteristics, we are speaking about much more than the coordinates of the parcel. We mean as well the whole web of economic, social, and spatial interactions that affect economic activity at the particular location in question.

Legal Characteristics   That the physical and locational characteristics of the urban land resource set it apart as an economic good should be clear. In recognition of the uniqueness of the urban land resource, a separate set of legal institutions has developed over the centuries to deal with legal issues concerning the use, disposition, and ownership of urban land and the improvements affixed to it.[6]

In a fundamental sense, the economic good that we have been calling urban land is really no more than the bundle of legal rights that accompany the urban land. These property rights reflect social institutions and attitudes. The institution of real property differs from one jurisdiction to the next, and the precise nature of the property rights must be ascertained before one is in a position to probe more deeply into any economic issues relating to specific parcels or groups of parcels of urban land. As with locational questions, the importance of the legal characteristics of urban real property require that we spend considerable time studying them later. Of note at this stage is the fact that these legal characteristics represent another important differentiating feature of urban land.

These three differentiating characteristics of urban land justify our study. Because of the special circumstances relating to urban land, a special body of knowledge, based on broad principles of economics, needs to be developed. This development must build heavily on other areas of knowledge than economics alone, because of the special institutional, locational, and physical qualities that urban land and improvements possess.

Returning to the opening problem of this chapter (e.g., a proper definition of urban land economics), we can begin to see why the field was so broadly defined: It combines elements of urban economics, of more general economics at both the macro and micro levels, of real property law, and urban political and social institutions.

In essence, we are trying to develop an applied brand of urban economics, one that is rooted in the institutions that affect our special economic good: urban land and improvements. Given this firm grounding in the empirical and institutional realities of the urban land resource, it is clear that urban land economics is also a highly policy-oriented field, one directed at both an understanding of the workings of urban land markets, as well as toward the improvement in the functioning of these markets to help meet broader social and political goals.

Richard U. Ratcliff summed all this up rather well in the preface to his incomparable *Urban Land Economics*.

Urban land economics deals with the process and patterns of land utilization where man and his artifacts are assembled in communities. The subject matter is embraced within the framework of general land economics, which covers the utilization of the entire earth's surface and "the natural forces and productive powers above or below that space over which the owner has property rights." In turn, land economics is but a branch of general economics; economics is a study of the wealth-getting and wealthspending activities of man and is therefore a study of human behavior. When such behavior is consistent and predictable, hypotheses and principles are derived which are the foundations of the science of economics.[7]

THE PURPOSE OF THE BOOK

Given the need for a specialized field in urban land economics, and given the existence of such classics as Ratcliff's book and the growing selection of texts in both real estate and urban economics, why does there exist a need for yet another volume on the subject? A number of shortcomings surround existing offerings, necessitating an alternative. For example, Ratcliff[8] is both somewhat out of date (1949) and certainly out of print, as are other classics such as Dorau and Hinman[9] and even Fisher and Fisher.[10] Newer and readily available texts in real estate tend to be rather descriptive and vocationally oriented,[11] while the urban economics texts are either too theoretical or else lack important institutional elements concerning urban land *per se*.[12] Finally, all extant books deal with the urban situation in the United States to the exclusion of the Canadian city. This is a critical failing, since Canadian cities differ rather markedly from their American counterparts.[13] More importantly, principles and constructs based on the U.S. experience are not likely to be very useful outside the United States, nor are they likely to be necessarily of long-term utility even for U.S. urban settings. We felt very much the need therefore to develop a more generally useful set of analytical tools.

More specifically, there are three goals that we want to achieve with this book.

1. *To provide analytical and institutionally based economic tools enabling students to analyze a range of complex urban problems in a variety of national, regional, and local settings.* The analyses quite obviously will be rooted in economics, but because of the strong institutional and empirical bent of the book, they will be sensitive to the social, political, and environmental forces that impinge on urban land and property markets.

2. *To span the artificial and destructive dichotomy that has been built up between theory and practice.* The good theorist has a very sound grasp of the specifics of the environment within which the theory is derived. Similarly, great practitioners have, embedded in their unconscious, quite sophisticated and complex theories of the urban system that enable them to gain unique and important insights into the intricacies of investing in or making policy for urban areas. Thus, we strive to develop sound concepts based on empirical and institutional realities that are practical but nonetheless quite general and "theoretical."

3. *To overcome the cultural biases of either the United States or Canada with regard to cities and city-based problems, institutions, and issues.* By spanning these cultural specifics we hope to develop more general constructs than would be possible from being grounded in one national setting. As a result, while being aimed primarily at North America, we expect that the resulting concepts and analyses will be sufficiently general to allow the use of the book in countries outside of North America, with the reader filling in local examples to illustrate general principles.

Footnotes

1. Richard T. Ely and George S. Wehrwein, *Land Economics* (New York: The MacMillan Co.), 1940, p. *v*.

2. Richard T. Ely et al., *Characteristics and Classification of Land*, Volume I of the *Outlines of Land Economics* (Ann Arbor, Michigan: Edwards Brothers), 1922, p. 4, quoted by Herbert B. Dorau and Albert G. Hinman, *Urban Land Economics* (New York: The MacMillan Co.), 1928.

3. This discussion drew heavily from Richard U. Ratcliff, *Real Estate Analysis* (New York: McGraw-Hill Book Co.), 1961, Chapter 3, "The Physical Foundations of Real Estate Value."

4. Ernest M. Fisher and Robert M. Fisher, *Urban Real Estate* (New York: Henry Holt and Co.), 1954.

5. William Alonso used this term in a similar context in his *Location and Land Use* (Cambridge, Mass.: Harvard University Press), 1964.

6. Ratcliff, *op. cit.*, Chapter 5, "The Legal Dimensions of Real Estate Value," makes this point and illustrates it in a number of important ways.

7. Richard U. Ratcliff, *Urban Land Economics* (New York: McGraw-Hill Book Co.), 1949, p. *v*.

8. Ratcliff (1949) and (1961), *op. cit.*

9. Dorau and Hinman, *op. cit.*

10. Fisher and Fisher, *op. cit.*

11. We have in mind here such updated standard texts as: G. F. Bloom, A. Weimer, and J. D. Fisher, *Real Estate*, 9th edition (New York: John Wiley and Sons), 1982; H. C. Smith, C. J. Tschappat and R. Racster, *Real Estate and Urban Development*, 3rd edition (Homewood, Ill.: R. D. Irwin), 1981; and C. F. Floyd, *Real Estate Principles* (New York: Random House), 1981.

12. At the theoretical end of the urban economics spectrum is: E. S. Mills, *Studies in the Structure of the Urban Economy* (Baltimore: Johns Hopkins University Press), 1972; and on a more intuitive and conceptual level, Alan R. Winger, *Urban Economics: An Introduction* (Columbus, Ohio: Charles E. Merrill), 1977; and James Heilbrun, *Urban Economics and Public Policy*, 2nd edition, (New York: St. Martin's Press), 1981. At the more applied end would be A. F. Schreiber, P. K. Gatons, and R. B. Clemmer, *Economics of Urban Problems* (Boston: Houghton Mifflin and Co.), 1976, and Harold Hochman, *The Urban Economy* (New York: W. W. Norton and Co.), 1976. In addition, there have been numerous anthologies, such as R. Grieson, ed., *Urban Economics: Readings and Analysis* (Boston: Little, Brown and Co.), 1973. These volumes of readings also fail to bring out the institutional aspects of urban development and fail to focus their attention on urban land and real property in particular.

13. See, for example, John Mercer, "On Continentalims, Distinctiveness and Comparative Urban Georgraphy: The Canadian and American City," *Canadian Geographer*, 23 (1979): 119–139.

3

URBAN
MACROECONOMICS

INTRODUCTION: ACCOUNTING FOR URBAN ECONOMIC ACTIVITY

Urban macroeconomics focuses on the totality of economic activity within an appropriate, defined urban region. The numerous economic enterprises that flourish at different locations within the urban region are aggregated to provide a series of measures of the economic status of the entire urban area, and not just for specific neighborhoods or cities or industries within its boundaries.

In order to develop such an economic status report for the urban area, it is necessary to devise a consistent and logical framework for aggregating the data. This introductory section presents such an urban economic accounting framework and discusses its relationship to the determinants of urban economic activities. We will also look at some of the difficulties such an urban economic accounting system faces, and some of the caveats.

A Mechanism for Studying Urban Income Determination

Before proceeding to develop a system of urban economic acccounts, we need to develop a simple conceptual framework to depict how economic activity proceeds in urban areas. This conceptual framework will allow us to structure our accounts so that they capture key determinants as set out in that framework.

Urban economies cannot easily be viewed in isolation from their national and regional contexts. National and regional economic health or sickness have significant implications for the urban economies that function within these larger boundaries. The boom in the city of Calgary during the late 1970s was certainly closely tied to the feverish activity surrounding the energy sector in the province of Alberta. Simi-

larly, the sluggishness of the Montreal economy during the same period was traceable to the generally slow pace of the Quebec economy.
High levels of economic activity in the U.S. Northwest at the close of
the 1970s were associated with high levels of urban economic activity in
the cities of Seattle and Portland.

However, the situation is not unidirectional. Urban economies can
also provide significant impetus to regional and national economic activity. Rapid growth in Dallas and Houston contributed greatly to the
general economic climate in the state of Texas during the past decade.
Cities are highly interdependent economic systems, closely tied to each
other through intricate trade and communication networks, and to the
regions and nations of which they are important component parts.[1]

Figure 3–1 below serves as a convenient schematic summary of
these networks. We are assuming only two regions with one principal
city in each, but the underlying is quite obviously applicable to any
number of cities and regions.

Turning to the mechanism of income generation in the urban
economy, we can visualize that process in terms of the traditional
circular-flow diagram, shown in Figure 3–2. Here, the economic system is conceived of initially as a sort of closed plumbing system. The
system is in equilibrium when the upper-loop flow equals the lower-
loop flow. These two loops represent a form of double-entry
bookkeeping.

The upper loop represents dollar flows, clockwise, from households (consumers) to businesses (producers). Expenditures are categorized under five headings as follows: C for consumption expenditures
by households (e.g., for haircuts, vegetables, etc.); I for expenditures
by businesses on investment in plant and equipment (e.g., new machin-

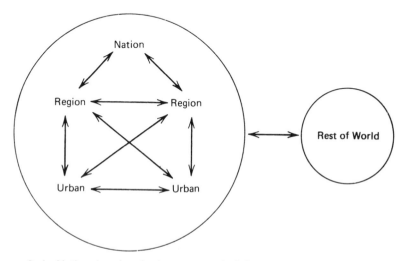

Figure 3–1. National-regional-urban economic linkages.

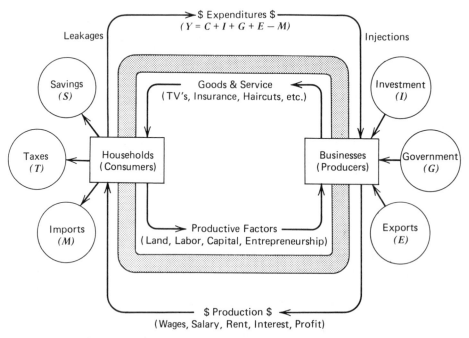

Figure 3–2. Circular-flow diagram of expenditure and production.

ery for automobile plants, a new headquarters for a bank, etc.); G for government spending on goods and services (e.g., stationery, new tax forms, consultants, etc.); E for export spending by people living outside the city or region on goods and services produced inside the city or region (e.g., dresses made in Montreal and bought by women in Toronto, etc.); and finally M for imports, goods and services consumed by local households, businesses, and governments but produced outside the local area (e.g., Palm Springs holidays for, say, Toronto residents, etc., if the diagram represents the Toronto area).

Leakages are drains of resources from the system, and include taxes, imports, and savings. Increased taxes reduce disposable income. Increased savings reduce expenditures on consumption, the "paradox of thrift." Taxes (T) represent government revenues. These can also slow down the local economic system. The final leakage we consider is imports (M). These are particularly important in urban and regional economies because so much of local consumption must come from goods and services produced outside the urban area. We refer to this reliance on imports by urban economies in terms of "openness." Urban economies are open because they are so heavily dependent on trade with the rest of the world, be it with other regions of the same country or other countries.

Investment (I) tends to drive the local economy through increasing spending by nonhousehold units in the private sector. Governments can also inject money directly into the local economy through direct expenditure (*G*). Aerospace and defense spending are often used in the United States for this purpose. Relocating government activity and providing incentive grants have been typical Canadian ways of increasing expenditure in specific and local economies. Exports (*E*) represent an extremely important expenditure in an area because of the openness of the urban economy. The present framework places exports and imports in their broader perspective so that they can be viewed against other components of urban area income determination as per Figure 3–2.

Consider the box labeled "Businesses (Producers)" in Figure 3–2. We require an examination of the structure of the production process and how producers interact to provide the final goods and services represented by the upper-loop total expenditure flow. Figure 3–3 provides this more detailed disaggregated view of the urban economy.

While it takes a very different form from that of our circular-flow diagram (Figure 3–2), Figure 3–3 is related to the circular-flow view of the urban economy. The box on the right-hand side of the figure is a disaggregation of the upper loop of the circular-flow diagram. However, in this instance these expenditures on final demands (e.g., Consumption, Investment, Government, and Export) are also broken down by the industries that produced the goods that comprise final demands.

Corresponding to the lower loop of the circular-flow diagram is the lower box in the present figure. In the circular-flow diagram's

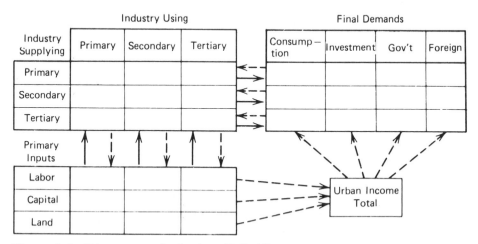

Figure 3–3. Urban economic structure. Dotted lines represent dollar flows, while solid lines represent flows of real goods and services. [*Source:* Adapted from N. H. Lithwick, *Urban Canada: Problems and Prospects,* p. 70 and N. H. Lithwick and G. Paquet, *Urban Studies: A Canadian Perspective* (Toronto: Methuen), 1968, p. 26.]

lower loop, we measured the amount of production from the payments to the several factors of production. This is exactly what is represented by the lower box labeled "Primary Inputs." As in the case of final demands, these primary inputs (and the factor payments that paid for them) are disaggregated by the several industries, thus presenting a detailed picture of how these primary factors of production are employed by industry.

The framework in Figure 3–3 also depicts how inputs ("Labor," "Land," and "Capital") are transformed into outputs ("Consumption," "Investment," "Gov't" and "Foreign"). It achieves this by showing how the outputs of each industry are distributed among these industries to produce the final demand outputs. In a simple example with three industries ("Primary," "Secondary," and "Tertiary" corresponding roughly to resources, including agriculture and extraction, manufacturing, and services), this so-called matrix of interindustry flows depicts how each local industry disposes of its output to the other industries, and also how its output is distributed within the final demand matrix on the right. By reading down each column of the interindustry-flow matrix, the sources of inputs are obtained: first from other industries in the matrix; second from the Primary Inputs matrix, which shows how land, labor, and capital are used by each industry. By reading down each column we get a recipe for the production of output by the industry represented in that column. By reading across the row, we get a picture of the sales of each industry. Since this is a double-entry bookkeeping system, sales (output) must equal purchases (inputs).

This interindustry, or input-output, view of the structure of the urban economy provides all the information of the circular-flow diagram. In addition, it shows in detail how the various economic sectors relate to each other, to their demands for basic inputs, and, finally, to their distribution of output to final consumers. The input-output concept is a generalization of the circular-flow concept, but one capable of significantly greater detail. That it is equivalent to our earlier circular-flow conception should be clear from a final look at Figure 3–3. Income derived from selling primary inputs (land, labor and capital) flows into the several Final Demand sectors. This flows back into the interindustry matrix to pay for the Final Demand outputs. The payments for Final Demand outputs of goods and services combine with similar payments from intermediate industrial users (e.g., those within the interindustry matrix) and enable the producing sector to pay for their primary inputs. The dotted arrows represent money flows, while the solid arrows represent the offsetting real flows of goods and productive services.

Consider an example from Charles Leven of Washington University in St. Louis, Missouri. Leven developed a set of accounts, along the lines of the framework discussed above, for the Sioux City, Iowa, urban region for 1958.[2] They are reproduced below (Table 3–1) to give operational content to the previous discussion. The first tabular listing of Income and Product Accounts corresponds closely to the circular-flow notion introduced initially, where the left-hand columns represent value added at each stage of production and correspond to the lower-loop measure of economic activity. The right-hand columns correspond to upper-loop expenditure measures.

These accounts are disaggregated in Table 3–1 so that a detailed view of the economic struture of the Sioux City region can be obtained. For those interested in the national accounts analogy of these regional accounts, national income accounting is discussed in various introductory economics textbooks.[3]

Table 3–1 Income and Product Accounts, Sioux City Area, 1958 ($000)

Income and Product Accounts			
Value added in the production of goods for export	123,413	Sales of goods to the rest of the world	734,437
		Purchase of goods by consumers	151,646
Value added in the production of goods for investment	6,535	Purchase of investment goods	21,690
		Less: Imports of intermediate goods for production of goods for export	611,024
Value added in the production of goods for consumption	72,852	Less: Imports of final and intermediate goods for investment	15,155
		Less: Imports of final and intermediate goods for consumption	78,794
Charges Against Gross Area Product	202,800	Gross Area Product	202,800

Consumption Account			
Value added in the production of goods for consumption	72,852	Purchase of goods by consumers	151,646
		Less: Imports of final and intermediate goods for consumption	78,794
Charges Against Consumption Product	72,852	Consumption Product	72,852

Investment Account			
Value added in the production of goods for investment	6,535	Purchase of investment goods	21,690
		Less: Imports of final and intermediate goods for investment	15,155
Charges Against Investment Product	6,535	Investment Product	6,535

Rest-of-the-World Account			
Value added in the production of goods for export	123,413	Net investment in the private sector of the rest of the world	13,723
Excess of out-commuter wages over in-commuter wages	(−11,160)		
Net receipts of interests, rent, and dividends from abroad	475		

Table 3–1   (*Continued*)

Rest-of-the-World Account			
Excess of gifts received over gifts given abroad	(−428)		
Excess of profits of outside branches of local firms over profits of local branches of outside firms	(−4,628)		
Less: Imports of final and intermediate goods for consumption	78,794		
Less: Imports of final and intermediate goods for investment	15,155		
Net Current Payments Due To The Area On Private Account	13,723	Net Investment In The Private Sector Of The Rest Of The World	13,723
Excess of direct and indirect nonlocal tax and nontax payments over transfer payments from nonlocal govts.	37,559	Net contribution to non-local government	37,559
Net Current Payments Due To The Area	51,282	Net Investment In The Rest Of The World	51,282
Saving and Investment Account			
Purchases of investment goods	21,690	Undistributed profits of local corporations	3,416
		Personal saving	8,891
		Capital consumption allowances and statistical discrepancy	59,947
		Less: Net investment in the rest of the world	51,282
Gross Investment	21,690	Gross Saving	21,690

Source: Charles L. Leven, "Regional Income and Product Accounts: Construction and Application," in Hochwald, ed., *Design of Regional Accounts* (Baltimore: The Johns Hopkins University Press, 1961), pp. 191–193.

Some Caveats on Urban Income Accounting

The foregoing summary of urban economic accounting overlooks many assumptions and problems. Many will become apparent when we use these accounting concepts to analyze and forecast economic activity in urban regions. Others will remain hidden from view and need to be ferreted out prior to using any system of urban income accounts.

First, all of the problems inherent in national income accounting systems apply in the context of urban and regional accounts. Definitional problems abound, as do problems of measurement. Examples include constructing value added by imputing the value of nonmarket production, such as housewives' time, and the treatment of consumer durable services, such as automobiles. Second, urban regions being much more "open" with respect to imports and exports than corresponding national economic systems require careful accounting for imports and exports, since they constitute such large portions of the total economic activity. Unfortunately, there is a paucity of data on imports and exports for subnational entities, since there is no requirement of any government to keep such detailed accounts. There are no customs duties among various regions of the same country and thus no reliable records of the magnitude and structure of imports and exports. For example, it is exceedingly difficult to record the export of financial services to the rest of the United States, or even to the rest of the U.S. Northeast, by the financial institutions located in the city of New York. However, these services represent a key export for the region. It would be equally difficult to ascertain the exports of automobiles from the Detroit area or to estimate its import of automobile parts. Data problems are thus severe when dealing with urban economic relations and one must be always cognizant of the difficulties associated with estimating these relationships.

Finally, when applying income accounting frameworks to urban areas, one must be vitally concerned with spillover effects where people may be employed within the urban region but live outside it. Vice versa, urban residents may gain their livings from workplaces immediately adjacent to, but lying outside of, the urban region in question. The spatial relationships that exist among work, residence, and disposition of outputs (and inputs) must be considered explicitly at the urban level of analysis. There is no similar requirement when dealing at the national level.

Some other caveats on national income accounting should be borne in mind. First, government expenditure (G), by potentially affecting interest rates, may crowd out private investment (I). Investment is not exogenous, and there may be some feedback from government spending. Second, savings (S) do not necessarily represent a leakage, for they may form part of the supply of funds for investment and capital accumulation.

Summing Up

Above we have borrowed concepts from national income accounting and models of income determination to develop analogous concepts for measuring the level and structure of economic activity within urban regions. These concepts are beginning steps in any analysis of the microeconomics of urban land markets. A proper understanding of the urban macroeconomic environment is a vital starting point, since it provides the necessary overview for understanding how the aggregate of economic activity is allocated among various microeconomic markets, most importantly, in our case, the market for urban land. Suitably armed with an understanding of the macroeconomic environment, we can proceed to analyze the micro market behaviors against their appropriate macro setting.

MODELS OR CONCEPTS OF URBAN ECONOMIES

In this section we shall explore a number of the more commonly used and more useful models of urban economies. We will be developing the material from the most elementary, and most widely used, concepts such as urban economic base analysis and shift-share analysis, and progressively elaborating our analytical framework to include input-output analysis as well as econometric and hybrid models. We will be illustrating specific concepts through examples in which the concept has been successfully applied. This linking of the concept with practice and actual data from real-world cities should help crystallize the concept while simultaneously illustrating its utility.

Urban Economic Base Analysis and Economic Base Multipliers

This is the most elementary and also the most widespread technique of urban macroeconomic analysis. The technique proceeds from a simple, yet intuitively appealing proposition, namely, urban economic activity is dependent upon the level of exports by the urban economy to the outside world. The model has also been called the export-base model. Essentially this model ascribes both the level and growth of the urban economy to the level and growth of exports in an urban area.[4]

Returning to our definitional equation of urban economic activity we have:

$$Y = C + I + G + E - M \tag{3.1}$$

where, as before:

Y = urban aggregate income or product

C = urban area consumption

I = urban area investment

G = urban area spending by government

E = exports from the urban area

M = imports into the urban area

The economic base model simplifies this framework and views urban product or income as being a function of the export sector alone:

$$Y = f(E) \tag{3.2}$$

The whole problem of determining urban income or product thus reduces to determining the level of exports and the relationship between exports and total economic action in the urban region (i.e., the export base multiplier).[5]

To clarify this idea, consider the following schematic representation from H. C. Davis.[6] Figure 3–4 depicts the relationship between

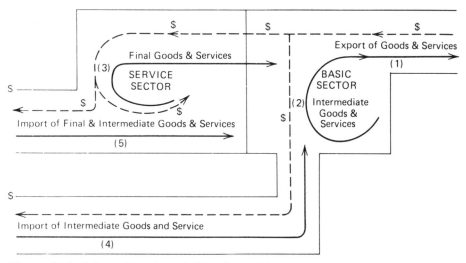

Figure 3–4. Schematic representation of export base
multiplier process. (*Source:* H. C. Davis, *Regional
Economic Base Analysis,* School of Community and
Regional Planning, University of British Columbia, p. 2.)

export activity, import activity and local service activity. Five distinct
flows are identified in the figure: Flow 1 represents the outflow of
goods and services produced by the export sector. It sets in motion
flow 2, the so-called "technological" multiplier process that creates demands for additional inputs of intermediate goods and services to enable the export sector to produce flow 1. This flow gives rise to two additional flows: Flow 3 is the local income multiplier induced by the
need for locally produced intermediate goods and services; flow 4 is
the analogous flow to pay for externally produced goods and services
needed to produce exports. Finally, flow 5 represents the flow of funds
to pay for imports needed to satisfy local consumers and service
producers.

It should be noted that the entire process depends on flow 1.
There is a feedback from locally produced services to local incomes
and therefore back to locally produced services. The existence of this
flow is predicated on that of the export flow, and is called an export-
dependent model of local economic activity.

To put the concept to work requires the determination of a number of simple ratios between export activity and total economic activity,
and between export activity and total population. The typical export
base exercise would proceed using the following ratios to determine
total economic and population activity.

1. The base-service ratio or the ratio of export base activity to local service activity.
    For illustrative purposes, let us assume that $B:S = 1:3$.

2. The base-total employment ratio follows directly from the $B:S$ ratio set out above. In the present instance the ratio would be $B:TE = 1:4$. For each employee in a basic exporting industry, there are a total of four employees in the local economy (three service employees plus the basic employee).

3. The third required ratio is that between total employment and total population. If we assume that half of the population is employed, which is reasonably close to actual figures in North America, then $TE:TP = 1:2$.

4. The final ratio, of total population to basic employment, is $B:TP = 1:8$. For each basic employee, four jobs are needed to sustain him or her, and this requires a total of eight people to provide the four employed people.

The preceding ratios were arrived at by assumption to illustrate the use of the economic base below. The ratios are roughly realistic for the typical North American city. Given these ratios, we can now apply them to a hypothetical urban area to yield a conceptually and operationally simple method for forecasting urban economic and population activity.

Applying the approach is straightforward under two conditions. The first is that the underlying assumptions embodied in the concept of the economic base are reasonable and appropriate in the particular situation to which the concept is being applied. The second is that base ratios can be readily identified.

Turning to the assumptions first, the following are all implied by the use of the concept.[7]

1. Exports are the primary, if not exclusive, driving force in the urban economy. Changes in the levels of C, I, G, and M are not seen as having any role in determining the level of aggregate urban economic activity.

2. All export sectors have homogeneous effects on the regional economy. Exports of automobiles, raw copper, or banking services have the same impact on total population and total employment.

3. The base-service ratio (or basic-nonbasic ratio) is invariant over time and type of export activity. Import ratios are also constant: There is no import substitution as a result.

Table 3–2 Example of Using Base Ratios

Present Urban Employment and Population	Ratio to Base (B) Taken as Unity	Immediate Impact of increase in basic employment (B) of 1,000	Long-run Impact of 1,000 increase in (B)
$B = 2,000$	1	3,000	3,000
$S = 6,000$	3	6,000	9,000
$TE = 8,000$	4	9,000	12,000
$TP = 16,000$	8	18,000	24,000

4. Linkages with other regions are assumed negligible or nonexistent. Exports to another region cannot feedback to the region in question to further influence the level of export activity in the subject region.

5. There are unemployed capital, human and physical resources in the subject region. Otherwise, increases in export activities are faced with the possibility of limiting constraints. The present model assumes that increases in export levels are met by proportional increases in output by the service and import sectors.

6. The economic base is identifiable and separable from the rest of the urban economy.

These assumptions will almost never be strictly met, with the possible exception of the simplest single-resource-based communities of the Canadian and American West. The degree of charity required differs for each of the assumptions. For example, it is not unreasonable to assume the relative stability of the several ratios over moderate periods of time, such as five years. To assume their stability over spans of a decade or more, particularly where the local economy is one that is growing and maturing, is a heroic assumption. Table 3–3 sets out estimates of the base-total employment ratio for selected U.S. cities in 1960.[8] Notice the very significant variation that follows from the size of the urban region, and thus from its economic complexity. The concept of a simple economic base becomes questionable for large, mature and diverse urban economies.

From Table 3–3, as cities get larger the base ratio changes, throwing the assumption of constancy into question. In times of considerable government involvement, it is unreasonable to assume that exports alone can serve as fuel for local economic well-being. Some sizable economies such as those of Washington, D.C., and Ottawa, Ontario, run on government in a direct sense.

Table 3–3 Estimated Base-Total Employment Ratios for Selected U.S. Cities, 1960

City	Population	Base-Total Employment Ratio
New York, N.Y.	10,700,000	1:3.3
Los Angeles, Cal.	6,700,000	1:3.1
Chicago, Ill.	6,200,000	1:3.0
Philadelphia, Pa.	4,300,000	1:2.9
Detroit, Mich.	3,800,000	1:2.8
Washington, D.C.	2,000,000	1:2.6
Dallas, Texas	1,100,000	1:2.4
Richmond, Va.	400,000	1:2.1
Erie, Pa.	250,000	1:2.0

Source: E. L. Cillman, U. I. Dacey and H. Brodsky, *The Economic Base of American Cities,* revised and enlarged edition (Seattle: The University of Washington Press), 1971.

The existence of multibranch firms also undermines the viability of the assumption of export primacy. External inflows of investment capital can have considerable impacts on local economies. Construction of the Alaska pipeline led to significant economic activity in that state.

Construction of pulp mills, development of mines, and the building of office buildings all are forms of investment and all have significant impacts on local economies. None are strictly export activities.

One final blow to export primacy, and closely related to the data in Table 3–3, is import substitution. As areas grow, local markets also become larger until they can support local products. When this occurs, locally produced goods and services are substituted for imported products. Local consumption of locally produced goods increases while imports decline. From (3.1) an increase in C and a decline in M can both lead to increases in urban economic activity independent of exports entirely. The export base concept is most likely to be useful in simple and smaller economies.

There is difficulty in identifying the economic base of larger and more complex urban economic systems. The base for a resort community such as Vail, Colorado, is relatively easily identified. The economic base of Denver, Colorado, is considerably more complex, since many export activities benefit local residents while many of the traditional support services are exported. Apart from viewing basic and export activity as synonymous, there is also the problem of assuming rigid substitution possibilities between exported and nonexported goods.

Measuring the Basic and Nonbasic Sectors

There are four ways to measure the economic base of an urban region.[9] The first, most reliable, and most expensive is the direct measurement from surveys of firms and institutions. The remaining three techniques are indirect approximations and suffer from a number of weaknesses. The objective of the measurement is to identify those economic sectors, or portions of economic sectors, that produce goods and services for consumption outside the urban region, that is basic export activities. Those activities that do not fall into the basic category are therefore nonbasic and local.

Direct Measurement of the Base This requires that a survey be undertaken of the firms and institutions in the urban region to ascertain the proportion of their output sold outside the urban area. Most commonly, a written questionnaire is developed for this purpose. Such questionnaires, when combined with personal interviews and local expertise, provide the most complete view of the structure of the urban economy. A side advantage of this survey approach is that it also provides insights into the linkages among economic units within the region, thus creating a reliable picture of the multipliers that are likely to be at work within the local economy.[10]

An alternative direct method of measuring export activity, and one that is less reliable, derives from a study of waybills of all goods shipped out of the region. The difficulties here are usually enormous. An equivalent method of measuring the outflow of goods (services are difficult to catch in the waybill approach) is to measure the inflow of money paid for the exported goods and services. Here, again, the empirical problems are considerable, with hard-to-trace cash transactions leading the difficulties along with internal corporate bookkeeping transfers, for multiplant and multiregional firms.

Indirect Approaches to Measuring the Economic Base Three approaches have been used here with varying degrees of success. All are considerably cheaper and quicker than direct estimating procedures. All have their drawbacks.

The Assumption Approach This is the simplest; it is also the most difficult to use successfully. The assumption approach proceeds by classifying activities into local and basic by assumption only, with no empirical foundaton necessary. For example, one might assume that all agricultural and manufacturing activity is export-oriented, and that all financial, health, and business services are locally consumed. If such assumptions derive from first-hand knowledge of the urban area, and if the urban area is relatively simple in its economic structure, then the assumption approach need not be unreasonable. It is not particularly useful when one is making assumptions based on experience in other urban regions whose underlying structural and historical characteristics might differ considerably from the subject region.

The Location Quotient Approach This technique seeks to overcome the *ad hoc* nature of the assumption approach by substituting some empirical knowledge for pure intuition. The location quotient approach proceeds by seeking to solve for N_k in the following simple equation,

$$\frac{N_k}{\text{total local employment}} = \frac{\text{national employment in industry } k}{\text{total national employment}}$$

where N_k is local employment in a given industry.

The nation is assumed to be roughly self-sufficient and, if the region were self-sufficient in industry k as well, the proportion of people employed in industry k regionally would match the proportion in industry k nationally. (Solving the above equation for N_k yields an estimate of the number of people employed in industry k locally.) Any observed excesses are attributed to exports.

This approach is weak on several counts. It assumes that the technology is the same regionally as nationally (i.e., production methods and labor productivity are identical regionally and nationally), and that the economy is comprised of regions all using the same technology, with constant returns. It also assumes that the national economy is closed (i.e., self-sufficient), which may not have been unreasonable for the United States economy in the 1950s and 1960s but is not a particularly valid assumption about the U.S. economy in the 1980s, nor was it ever a viable assumption concerning the Canadian economy.

The location quotient technique is generally regarded as being a poor approach to estimating the proportion of export-based activity in a local economy. Table 3–4, based on mid-1950s data, when the United States possessed a more or less self-sufficient economy, highlights the inadequacy of the technique.

The Minimum Requirements Technique   In an attempt to overcome some of the inaccuracies of the location quotient approach, geographers Edward Ullman and Michael Dacey of the University of Washington developed the minimum requirements approach.[11] This is conceptually related to the location quotient idea but is operationally different. The principal notion is that one can determine the export-bound output from a region by comparing a region, industry by industry, with other urban regions of the same size and general structure. By identifying the community with the minimum percentage of employment in each industry, it is argued, one can find the so-called minimum requirements needed to satisfy local demands. Once all of these minimum proportions or requirements have been identified, one can proceed to find export employment, since export employment would be the excess employment over and above the minimum requirements employment identified in the first step.

Table 3–4   Comparison of Export Percentages Based on Survey Results and Location Quotients, 1955–56

	(S = percentage based on survey results;										
	LQ = percentage based on location quotients)										
Manufacturing	**Decatur**		**Ft. Wayne**		**Waterloo**		**Flint**		**Madison**		**Indianapolis**
	S	LQ	S	LQ	S	LQ	S	LQ	S	LQ	S	LQ
Food	87	71	67	26	91	83			92	71	63	24
Chemicals	98	44									100	50
Printing											51	24
Primary metals	97	20	99	20							99	0
Fabricated metals							98	44			98	11
Non-elec. machinery	97	74	91	40	99	87			96	0	98	38
Electrical machinery			99	87			100	81	99	0	100	67
Transportation equip.	100	45	100	68			100	93			100	68

Note: Data are shown only for industries that are relatively important in the particular metropolitan area.

Source: Charles M. Tiebout, *The Community Economic Base Study*, (New York: The Committee for Economic Development), 1962.

The most frequent criticism of the minimum requirements approach is that, given the usual sample size of 50–100 comparison urban areas, there are bound to be some outliers with observed minimum requirements below their own actual minimum requirements. The example of commercial baking or food processing for resource-based communities is relevant where recorded minima might be 0 percent, an understatement of the minimum baking requirement needed to satisfy the local population. The technique also fails to take into account regional variations in prices or production techniques, both of which would lead to sources of error. Further, no rationale is presented as to why minimum requirements exist for the local but not the export sector. Further, this approach, as well as the others, fails to account for substitution possibilities between local and export employment.

Closing Comments on The Economic Base Approach The purpose of the technique is to provide a basis for understanding and forecasting the state of the urban economy. To achieve this objective, the economic base approach seeks to identify export employment and to establish the relationship between export and local employment. The output from such a study would be a table, such as Table 3–5, that summarizes succinctly the various exporting activities and their local components. That table, a model for economic base work, was the result of a detailed direct survey of firms in the Los Angeles–Long Beach SMSA for 1960.[12]

Shift-Share Analysis

The economic base approach is conceptually straightforward and relatively simple to apply. One of its major drawbacks is its inability to assess changes in economic structure, since a key economic base assumption is the constancy of the relative share of basic activities in their relationship to nonbasic local activities. There are techniques available, such as input-output and econometric models, that allow a more detailed structural view, and they will be discussed shortly. A simpler approach that provides insights into regional economic structure is considered first, namely, shift-share analysis.

The shift-share approach views economic growth in a region as being related to three factors: growth of the national economy for all industries taken together (the national component); growth of each industry at the national level compared with the growth of the overall national economy (the industrial mix component); and, finally, growth of each industry within the subject region compared with the growth of the same industry nationally (the regional share or competitive component).

Table 3–5 Allocation of Employment Created by Sales by Industry Groups
Los Angeles–Long Beach, California, SMSA, 1960

Industry From	Sector To	Employment (in thousand)			Distribution of Employment	
		Total	Export	Local	Export	Local
Durable Manufacturers		579.7	381.5	198.2	65.6%	34.4%
Primary metals		26.2	9.5	16.7	36.1	63.9
Fabricated metals		65.2	27.9	37.3	42.6	57.4
Nonelectrical machinery		31.0	45.9	15.1	75.0	25.0
Electrical machinery		113.0	82.4	30.6	72.9	27.1
Transportation equipment		200.7	143.5	57.2	71.7	28.3
Instruments and Ordnance		41.4	34.6	6.8	86.3	16.4
Stone, clay, and glass		22.0	15.4	6.6	70.0	30.0
Lumber products		8.4	32.5	5.9	29.7	70.3
Furniture products		26.0	11.9	14.1	45.7	54.3
Miscellaneous manufacturers		15.8	7.9	7.9	50.1	49.0
Nondurable Manufacturers		233.4	104.6	128.8	44.8	55.2
Apparel		48.2	34.7	13.5	72.0	28.0
Textile–leather		9.5	4.7	4.8	49.5	50.5
Paper		13.7	9.4	4.3	68.8	31.2
Printing		38.4	9.3	29.1	24.1	75.9
Chemicals		23.3	12.9	10.4	55.4	44.6
Petroleum		18.8	6.8	12.0	36.2	63.8
Rubber		23.7	13.6	10.1	57.4	42.6
Food and beverages		57.8	13.2	44.6	22.9	77.1
Total Manufacturing		813.1	486.1	327.0	59.7	40.3
Agriculture, forestry, fisheries, and mining		47.3	5.3	42.0	11.2	88.2
Contract construction		163.9	.5	163.4	.3	99.7
Transportation, communication, and public utilities		147.6	52.4	95.2	35.5	64.5
Wholesale trade		161.7	24.2	137.5	15.0	85.0
Retail trade		429.9	40.2	389.7	9.4	90.6
Finance, insurance, and real estate		131.5	22.1	109.4	16.8	83.2
Services		476.2	63.2	413.0	13.3	86.7
Government		277.8	21.2	256.6	7.6	92.4
Total All Industries		2,649.0	715.2	1,933.8	27.0	73.0

Note: The percentages after the decimal point were included to avoid gross errors in rounding.

Source: Hansen, Robson, and Tiebout, *Markets for California Products,* California Development
Agency (Sacramento, Cal.), 1961, reproduced in Charles M. Tiebout, *The Community Economic Base
Study,* p. 33.

The essential ingredients of the shift-share approach are the following symbols and their definitions.[13]

$E_{i,t}$ = regional total in ith industry, period t

$E_{i,t+1}$ = regional total in ith industry, period $t + 1$

$US_{i,t}$ = national total in ith industry, period t

$US_{i,t+1}$ = national total in ith industry, period $t + 1$

$$N_{i,t} = E_{i,t}\,[US_{i,t+1}/US_{i,t}] - 1 \tag{3.3}$$

Given these ingredients, we can now combine them into the three shift-share components noted previously.

US_t = national total, all industries, period t

US_{t+1} = national total, all industries, period $t + 1$

$N_{i,t}$ = national growth component, ith industries, period t, $t + 1$

$I_{i,t}$ = industry growth component, ith industry, period t, $t + 1$

$R_{i,t}$ = regional growth component, ith industries, period t, $t + 1$

$$I_{i,t} = E_{i,t}[[US_{i,t+1}/US_{i,t}] - [US_{t+1}, US_t]] \qquad (3.4)$$

And finally,

$$R_{i,t} = E_{i,t}[[E_{i,t+1}/E_{i,t}] - [US_{i,t+1} - US_{i,t}]] \qquad (3.5)$$

Let us look at these several equations in order. First, the national growth component (3.3) is being defined as equal to the growth rate of all industries in all regions between periods t and $t + 1$. This national growth rate is then multiplied by the base employment in year t in industry i in subject region j, to provide an estimate of what year $t + 1$ employment would be in region j and industry i if this industry in this region grew at the same rate as did all industries in all regions of the nation.

The second component, industrial mix (3.4), states that growth in the ith industry in the jth region between periods t and $t + 1$ is a function of the differential rate at which i grew nationally compared with national growth for all industries. Thus, the industrial mix (sometimes also called the differential shift component) compares growth in the ith industry at the national level (the left-hand term in brackets) with previously defined growth at the national level for all industries (the right-hand term inside the brackets). The industrial mix component is essentially saying that industry i in region j is growing (or declining) because this industry i is growing (or declining) nationally.

The final component in the shift-share scheme is the regional share, also called the competitive component. It is defined in (3.5), and it "explains" or attributes growth in industry i in region j to the fact that this region appears to have certain competitive advantages in housing this industry when compared with the nation. It does this by comparing the growth rate of the ith industry in region j with the growth of the ith industry nationally. The regional share component is the most important, and the most unpredictable and unstable, of the components. It is the most important because it provides information about the relative competitiveness of the given industry in the subject region, and some insights into underlying locational factors; it is the least stable because such locational advantages are often short-lived, being highly dependent on technological and human behavioral factors.

To try to crystallize the idea, an example is worth looking at in some detail. The following is taken from Bruce Lindsay and Susan Martin and looks at the changes in employment that have occurred in three southern New Hampshire counties during the 1940–1970 period.[14] These counties were sufficiently close to the Greater Boston area, immediately to the south, to experience significant spin-offs from that region as it began to grow in the 1950s as a public and private service center and as a center for high-technology manufacturing. This becomes clear from looking at Table 3–6.

The first column indicates how many people would be employed in each industry if industry employment grew (or declined) at the same rate as did total employment nationally during the relevant period (in this case, the decades 1940–50, 1950–60, and 1960–70). The second column indicates how much each industry would grow (decline) if it grew (declined) at the same rate that the industry grew (declined) nationally once overall national growth was subtracted. This element, industrial mix, tells us whether the industry in question was a rapidly growing industry relative to all industries or whether it was sluggish. This is indicated by the sign (positive for more rapid growth than national averages; negative for less rapid growth than national averages). Finally, the third column tells us how our particular industry fared over the period compared with the performance of the same industry nationally. This regional share component tells us whether the area was better suited for that industry during the period (if the sign is positive) or worse suited (if the sign is negative) than was the nation as a whole—that is, it measures whether the region has a comparative locational advantage for the industry.

Turning to the actual results of the shift-share analysis for southern New Hampshire, we can see the following: During the period 1940–1950 the area grew less rapidly than did the nation as a whole. This is evidenced by the fact that the total employment change in the region over the period was 18,401, compared with the 23,727 employees the region would have added had it been growing at the national rate. The overwhelming reason for this slower growth was the poor comparative advantage of the region over this period, as shown by the −11,101 job-loss figure attributed to the regional share component. The positive industrial mix component of 5775 demonstrates that the area did not have an adverse mix of slowly growing industries (which would have been the case had the industrial mix component been negative), but rather that the region grew slowly over the decade because it did not possess needed locational advantages.

This picture of a sluggish economy is reversed dramatically with the advent of the 1950s and 1960s. The region is growing more rapidly than the nation as a whole. This growth can be attributed to a favorable mix of growing industries (the 4130 industrial mix component in the 1950s bears witness to this) as well as to a strong competitive advantage vis-à-vis the nation as a whole in attracting new jobs (the 5959 employ-

Table 3–6 Shift-Share: Results for Employment In Southern New
Hampshire, 1940–1970

Sector	National Growth	Industrial Mix	Regional Share	Total Change
1940–1950				
Agriculture	1,765	−2,900	575	−560
Mining	40	−38	−36	−34
Construction	1,110	−1,686	−821	1,975
Manufacturing	10,422	4,343	−6,805	7,960
Transportation	1,087	644	−117	1,614
Wholesale/retail	3,527	1,759	−1,211	4,075
Finance	557	81	320	958
Services	4,160	−1,489	−1,108	1,563
Government	659	1,758	−1,110	1,307
Not reported	400	−69	−788	−457
Total	23,727	5,775	−11,101	18,401
1950–1960				
Agriculture	1,112	−3,368	−549	−2,805
Mining	21	−54	27	−6
Construction	1,124	−250	330	1,204
Manufacturing	8,626	2,283	3,918	6,991
Transportation	1,043	−889	350	504
Wholesale/retail	3,171	−648	423	2,946
Finance	558	776	1,633	2,967
Services	3,144	3,426	289	6,859
Government	693	853	4,957	6,503
Not reported	191	2,001	2,417	4,609
Total	19,683	4,130	5,959	29,772
1960–1970				
Agriculture	716	−1,879	596	−567
Mining	24	−30	94	88
Construction	1,608	−583	3,221	4,246
Manufacturing	11,843	−6,448	2,470	7,865
Transportation	1,357	−590	1,577	2,344
Wholesale/retail	4,436	1,007	6,915	12,358
Finance	1,316	965	−1,221	1,060
Services	5,259	5,028	2,837	13,124
Government	2,250	205	−2,380	75
Not reported	1,237	3,430	835	5,502
Total	30,046	1,105	14,944	46,095

Source: Bruce E. Lindsay and Susan E. Martin, "Employment Changes Via Shift Share: The
Southern New Hampshire Experience," *The New England Journal of Business and Economics,*
5(1:1978): 110, p. 4.

ment figure for the regional component supports this claim over the
1950–60 period). Similar but more buoyant growth patterns continued
into the 1960–70 decade, with locational strengths becoming even
more evident.

Shift-share allows us to identify sources of growth concerning the
three components, and also to examine specific sectors and their contributions to the economic growth or decline of the area. In the southern New Hampshire case, much of the acceleration in growth was due

to the existence of strong and rapidly growing construction, manufacturing, wholesale/retail, and service sectors during the 1960s. All of these sectors exhibited large positive regional share figures. The wholesale/retail sector grew by 6915 jobs during the 1960–70 era as a result of favorable competitive conditions in the region (i.e., the regional share component). This component accounted for more than half of the 12,358 added to the area's economy during the 1960s.

The analysis can be extended by a more detailed breakdown of the various industrial sectors into their own principal elements. The great utility of the shift-share technique is that it is so amenable to disaggregation and is easily applied. Data are usually readily available to allow the analyst to perform shift-share calculations such as those in Table 3–6. By performing increasingly detailed shift-share analyses we can develop a more disaggregated picture of the urban area economy, pinpointing major sources of strength and weakness.

In summing up the discussion of the shift-share approach, one benefit is its simplicity in use and interpretation. It allows successively finer levels of disaggregation and pinpoints quite specific sectoral weaknesses and strengths. It can be applied to analyze employment change and changes in retail trade, population, and other principal magnitudes or urban growth and decline. It makes no really limiting assumptions and is practical in urban regions of all sizes.

It does have one major drawback, and that is its inability to "explain" in any behavioral way why particular industries might be growing at the national level (i.e., the industrial mix element). Nor can it provide any insights into the nature of the locational advantages or disadvantages of a particular region during the period of analysis.[15] In this sense it is a descriptive rather than an analytical and explanatory technique. Another drawback is its neglect of prices in computing the employment growth rate. The prices of outputs in the sectors, and the wages of labor in each sector and region clearly affect employment but are ignored here. Further, there is the substitutability between capital and labor by industry, which also affects employment opportunities.

On the plus side, shift-share analysis can focus the attention of the urban analyst on those sectors and those locational questions that are of primary importance to the health of the urban area under study. It is a relatively cheap, easy-to-use, and easily understood technique that has the potential of providing significant savings in time and cost by helping the analyst to concentrate on those industries and those locational questions that are of major importance. However, the limitations mentioned should be regarded as caveats.

Input-Output Analysis

Before proceeding to an example of input-output analysis, let us review its underlying ideas and then look at a hypothetical example to illustrate these ideas. Again, we rely on some of the materials developed by Craig Davis, who has created some very clear numerical examples of how input-output works and how it can be easily interpreted.[16]

Input-output analysis was developed by Wassily Leontief in the 1940s. The technique is designed to capture the complex set of interrelationships that exist within developed urban, regional, and national economies. The purpose is to allow analysts and policymakers to trace the effects on all economic sectors of changes that occur in any one or more of these sectors. Since our economy in North America is large and diverse and highly interconnected, it is important to establish not only the direct effects that derive from increasing production levels in any given sector, but also indirect effects that changes in a given industry induce on other sectors.[17] Input-output is ideally suited to this purpose. Indeed, its first major test came during World War II, when U.S. policymakers were becoming increasingly concerned about the impacts of switching from a wartime economy to a peacetime economy.

Since its inception and first applications, the technique has spread rapidly around the world. Virtually every state and province has some form of input-output model already estimated. Many have done several in different years. Virtually every nation has at least one input-output table, with most developed nations updating and reestimating input-output tables every five years or less. In recognition of his contribution and of the utility and importance of the input-output model, Wassily Leontief was awarded the Nobel Prize in Economics in 1973.

One of the most dramatic and active areas of input-output development is in urban and regional economics. Because of the vulnerability of urban and regional economies to external (exogenous) changes in demand for locally produced outputs, local economies have been in particular need of a reasonably reliable indicator of economic impacts arising from changing final demands (that is C, I, G, and E from national income accounts).

We earlier broached the subject of input-output analysis in our discussion of urban economic structure. The approach gets its name because it is a double-entry system of urban, regional, or national income accounting, disaggregated by industry. Input-output tables are built up by directly recording all transactions within firms within given industries. Sales appear as outputs; purchases, as inputs. By building up a table of transactions between industries (so-called interindustry transactions) and final demands, a complete picture of the sales-purchase (i.e., input-output) interrelationships among the various firms and industries can be developed quantitatively.

Three input-output tables need to be developed to adequately discuss the approach. These appear below as Tables 3–7, 3–8, and 3–9. The economy is usually divided into industrial sectors according to the Standard Industrial Classification Code (SIC). The definition of individual sectors is relatively less important than the condition that all the sectors taken together must completely account for all economic activity in the region. In the following illustration we use a three-industry classification, as shown in Table 3–7. For illustrative purposes we have chosen agriculture, manufacturing, and services as the three sectors (primary, secondary, and tertiary activities, respectively). Final demands include consumption by households, investment, government, and exports.

Since each sector buys from and sells to other sectors within the economy for further processing, each is listed both at the left of the table, as a seller, and at the top of the table, as a purchaser. The 3 × 3 matrix formed by these sectors is referred to as the "processing" matrix.

The Final Sales categories represent all sales that are made not for further processing by business establishments within the region, but for final consumption by households, government, investment, and exports. If a farmer sells milk to a restaurant, the transaction is from Agriculture to Services; if the farmer sells milk to a household, the transaction is from Agriculture to Final Sales (households). Thus, each sector's sales are recorded as satisfying either Intermediate (processing) or Final Sales. Total Output (total sales) of each sector is the sum of Intermediate and Final Sales. Reading along any of the first

Table 3–7 Hypothetical Transactions Table ($1000)

Sellers \ Purchasers	Intermediate Sales			Final Sales				Total Output
	Agriculture	Manufacturing	Services	Households	Investment	Government	Exports	
Intermediate Purchases								
Agriculture	10	5	5	10	5	10	25	70
Manufacturing	20	30	25	5	10	5	10	105
Services	5	10	10	35	5	10	5	80
Final Purchases								
Imports	5	20	5					
Value added	30	40	35					
Total Outlay	70	105	80					

Source: H. C. Davis, *An Interindustry Study of the Metropolitan Vancouver Economy* (Vancouver BC: Faculty of Commerce and Business Administration, Urban Land Economics Division (University of B.C.) 1974.

three rows in Table 3–7, we can see how each sector distributed its output over the period. Manufacturing, for example, sold $20,000 of its $105,000 total output to Agriculture, $30,000 to Manufacturing, $25,000 to Services, and the remaining $25,000 to the Final Sales categories.

Reading down any of the first three columns indicates how the particular sector purchased inputs. For example, Manufacturing purchased $5000 from Agriculture, $30,000 from Manufacturing, $10,000 from Services, $20,000 from Imports (goods and services produced from outside the region), and $40,000 from the Value Added sector (roughly wages and salaries, rents, interest, depreciation, dividends, and profit). Total Outlay (total purchases) must equal Total Output (total sales) as profits are considered to be remuneration to management and thus serve as the balancing item. That is, total sales revenue (Intermediate plus Final Sales) is equal to total cost plus profit (Intermediate plus Final Purchases). The dollar flows are customarily those that have been recorded over a period of one year.

Table of Direct Interindustry Requirements This second table, sometimes called the Table of Direct Coefficients, is formed by dividing the entries in each column of the processing matrix by their respective column totals (Total Outlay). For our illustrative input-output (I-0) model, the table is as follows.

Table 3–8 Table of Direct Interindustry Requirements Per Dollar of Total Outlay

	Agriculture	*Manufacturing*	*Services*
Agriculture	.14	.05	.06
Manufacturing	.29	.30	.31
Services	.07	.10	.12

Source: H. C. Davis, *An Interindustry Study of the Metropolitan Vancouver Economy,* p. 4.

The table reveals that for the average dollar spent by, say, agriculture during the period, 14 cents were spent on agricultural inputs, 29 cents on inputs from manufacturing, and 7 cents on services. Under the assumption that these coefficients remain fixed, we can estimate the effects on the regional economy resulting from a change in one or more of the Final Sales categories. To illustrate, let us assume that the export demand for the output of our regional manufacturing sector increases by $10,000. The manufacturing sector will increase its output by $10,000 to meet this rise in final demand and, to do so, will have to make the following purchases:

Manufacturing: $10,000
Agriculture: 10,000 × .05 = $500

Manufacturing: $10,000 \times .30 = 3,000$

Services: $10,000 \times .10 = 1,000$

However, in order to produce this supporting output, each sector will require the following inputs:

Ag.: $500	Man.: $3,000	Serv.: $1,000	Total
Ag. $500 \times .14 = \$ 70$	$3000 \times .05 = \$150$	$1000 \times .06 = \$ 60$	$ 280
Man. $500 \times .29 = 145$	$3000 \times .30 = 900$	$1000 \times .31 = 310$	1,355
Serv. $500 \times .07 = 35$	$3000 \times .10 = 300$	$1000 \times .12 = 120$	455

These requirements will set off a third round of spending as follows.

Ag.: $280	Man.: $1,355	Serv.: $455	Total
Ag. $280 \times .14 = \$39.20$	$1355 \times .05 = \$ 67.75$	$455 \times .06 = \$ 27.30$	$134.25
Man. $280 \times .29 = 81.20$	$1355 \times .30 = 406.50$	$455 \times .31 = 141.50$	629.20
Serv. $280 \times .07 = 19.60$	$1355 \times .10 = 135.50$	$455 \times .12 = 56.40$	209.70

These rounds of spending will continue, with each round becoming increasingly weaker in its effects. The total increase in sales for each sector resulting from the initial stimulus to the manufacturing sector of $10,000 in export demand can be computed by summing the increases in sectoral sales in each round.

While such series of calculations are helpful in understanding the effects that reverberate throughout the regional economy from the initial stimulus, fortunately they are not necessary to determine the ultimate effects. The final changes in total sales (Total Output) of each sector can be read directly from the third table of the I-O model, the Table of Direct Plus Indirect Requirements (Table 3–9).

Table of Direct Plus Indirect Requirements   This third table is mathematically derived from the second table, as is explained in the appendix to this chapter, and is generally constructed with the aid of a computer.

The table tells us that if there is a $1 increase in the final demand for agriculture, the total output of agriculture will, after all the interdependent transactions have worked themselves out, increase by $1.21. Manufacturing and services in this case will rise $0.57 and

Table 3–9   Table of Direct Plus Indirect Requirements Per Dollar of Delivery to Final Demands

	Agriculture	*Manufacturing*	*Service*
Agriculture	1.21	0.57	0.16
Manufacturing	0.10	1.55	0.19
Services	0.12	0.60	1.22

Source: H. C. Davis, *An Interindustry Study of the Metropolitan Vancouver Economy.* p. 6.

$0.16, respectively. We can read from the table the effects of a $10,000 increase in exports of manufacturing. Total sales of agriculture will rise $1,000 ($10,000 × 0.10); manufacturing sales will increase $15,500 ($10,000 × 1.55); and the output of the services sector will expand by $1900 ($10,000 × 0.19). The Table of Direct Plus Indirect Requirements reveals the economic impact on the regional economy, sector by sector, of an increase in the final demand for the production of any one of the regional economic sectors.

To conclude our discussion of input-output for the present time, we will review an actual study completed in 1974 for the Vancouver, British Columbia, region by Davis.[18] The study is a good model for our purposes because it was modest in scope, dealing with 18 industries, and yet very useful, being the basis for several other economic studies in the Vancouver region during the past decade.

Instead of reproducing all three tables here (i.e., the Interindustry Table, the Table of Direct Requirements, and the Table of Direct Plus Indirect Requirements), we will skip directly to the Table of Direct Plus Indirect Requirements, which is the endpoint of input-output analysis. That table is reproduced here as Table 3–10. Applying our understanding from the previous discussion to the present table, we can learn the following about the Vancouver economy in 1971 as evidenced by Table 3–10. For each additional dollar of output to final demand in agriculture, forestry, fishing, and mining, a total increase of $1.01 results in this sector (i.e., there is an additional $0.01 induced by the initial $1.00 increase). This same dollar stimulates another $0.03 of construction and $0.02 of utilities output. The total direct and indirect requirements to produce an additional $1.00 of output in the agriculture, forestry, fishing, and mining sector is $1.20 (the sum across the entire row, which thus includes all of the direct and induced effects on all the economic sectors of the Vancouver region). We can see that the higher is the figure in any column, the more closely tied to the region's economy is that sector. For example, if we look at the pulp and paper industry, its direct and indirect requirement resulting from an additional dollar of sales to final demand is $1.13 (as compared with the $1.01 figure for agriculture and fishing). We can conclude from this that the pulp and paper industry has more significant feedbacks to itself within the Vancouver region than does the agriculture and fishing sector. By looking at the right-hand column of Table 3–10 we can see the total impact in direct and indirect requirements from additional sales to final demand in each of the 18 sectors. The non-metallic products sector had a total multiplier of $1.46 (the highest in the region), while the chemicals and petroleum sector had a multiplier of $1.09. We can conclude from this that the former industry was very closely linked to other activities in the region, while the latter industry had few linkages to industries in the Vancouver region in 1971.

Two other tables that can be easily developed from the basic

Table 3–10   Table of Direct Plus Indirect Requirements, Metropolitan Vancouver, 1971 (dollars)

	Agriculture, Forestry, Fishing & Mining	Construction	Food & Beverages	Wood Industries	Paper & Allied Products	Chemicals & Petroleum	Non-Metallic Products
	1	2	3	4	5	6	7
1. Agriculture, Forestry, Fishing & Mining	1.01267	0.03014	0.01334	0.00498	0.00234	0.01688	0.00284
2. Construction	0.00079	1.00178	0.00004	0.03283	0.00105	0.00286	0.03890
3. Food and beverages	0.03081	0.00234	1.04939	0.00097	0.05272	0.00599	0.03049
4. Wood industries	0.00001	0.00087	0.00003	1.06429	0.00099	0.00744	0.00042
5. Paper and allied products	0.00001	0.00209	0.00007	0.00370	1.12850	0.01860	0.00014
6. Chemicals and petroleum	0.00000	0.00173	0.00000	0.00012	0.00272	1.01579	0.00052
7. Nonmetallic products	0.00723	0.01111	0.00058	0.00368	0.01569	0.04427	1.10754
8. Metal fabricating	0.00005	0.00180	0.00001	0.01076	0.00596	0.00717	0.00020
9. Printing and publishing	0.00001	0.00454	0.00005	0.00066	0.13312	0.01733	0.00022
10. Manufacturing, nec	0.00001	0.00099	0.00001	0.00691	0.00351	0.00379	0.00083
11. Trade and transport	0.00024	0.00881	0.00041	0.00073	0.00598	0.00954	0.00049
12. Communication	0.00001	0.00822	0.00001	0.00073	0.00276	0.00965	0.00133
13. Utilities	0.00001	0.00538	0.00000	0.00030	0.00030	0.01529	0.00185
14. Finance, insurance, and real estate	0.00000	0.00258	0.00009	0.00011	0.00205	0.00093	0.00012
15. Health and welfare	0.00002	0.00536	0.00057	0.00088	0.00090	0.00781	0.00026
16. Education	0.00011	0.00224	0.00315	0.00017	0.00697	0.00223	0.00315
17. Business services	0.00000	0.00042	0.00001	0.00004	0.00410	0.00097	0.00003
18. Other services	0.00080	0.00316	0.00403	0.00267	0.00257	0.00095	0.00060

Source: H. C. Davis, *An Intermediary Study of the Metropolitan Vancouver Economy* p. 41.

input-output table are given below as Tables 3–11 and 3–12. These tables are derived using a slight variant of the basic Interindustry Transactions Table (e.g., Table 3–7). The variant moves the household sector out of Final Demand and Value Added and puts it into the interindustry processing matrix directly. This procedure allows us to capture the effects of changes in sales (output) on regional incomes and consumption, and allows us to derive multipliers that are much closer to Keynesian income and consumption multipliers.

Table 3–11 presents the 18 multipliers for total sales within the region that result from a $1.00 initial increase in sales in each sector. Thus, a multiplier of 1.97 in the non-metallic products sector indicates that for each additional initial increase of $1.00 in sales by this sector, a total of $1.97 will be stimulated in intermediate and final demand sales. In contrast, an additional initial increase of $1.00 in sales by the chemicals and petroleum sector results in a mere $1.18 total increase in sales. This implies that chemical and petroleum products have few

Table 3–10 (*Continued*)

Metal Fabricating	Printing & Publishing	Manufacturing, nec	Trade & Transport	Communications	Utilities	Finance, Insurance & Real Estate	Health & Welfare	Education	Business Services	Other Services	Multipliers (Row Sum)
8	9	10	11	12	13	14	15	16	17	18	
0.00484	0.00697	0.02588	0.02432	0.00818	0.02103	0.01450	0.00029	0.00206	0.00913	0.00069	1.20115
0.02595	0.00182	0.01288	0.02286	0.00544	0.00565	0.02353	0.00000	0.00045	0.01587	0.00115	1.19396
0.05205	0.00289	0.00756	0.02978	0.00380	0.01863	0.01069	0.00003	0.00180	0.00640	0.00121	1.30761
0.00705	0.00087	0.00100	0.01300	0.00522	0.01050	0.00946	0.00000	0.00013	0.01100	0.00554	1.13787
0.00382	0.00282	0.00489	0.02592	0.00498	0.01981	0.02434	0.00000	0.00219	0.01711	0.01130	1.27031
0.00259	0.00147	0.00479	0.00402	0.00145	0.03640	0.00402	0.00008	0.00159	0.00769	0.00010	1.08515
0.03903	0.00384	0.05957	0.06844	0.00696	0.03432	0.04066	0.00000	0.00012	0.02135	0.00041	1.46493
1.08654	0.00147	0.07732	0.01654	0.00634	0.03332	0.01055	0.00002	0.00002	0.00862	0.00103	1.26781
0.00551	1.05114	0.00288	0.02173	0.01401	0.00917	0.01865	0.00000	0.00028	0.02985	0.00983	1.31906
0.03944	0.00309	1.01770	0.02260	0.00520	0.00594	0.00781	0.00000	0.00001	0.01586	0.00047	1.3429
0.00219	0.01550	0.00315	1.02521	0.01531	0.01056	0.02212	0.00000	0.00003	0.01851	0.00144	1.14031
0.02075	0.00987	0.00421	0.00758	1.00439	0.00444	0.02220	0.00000	0.00011	0.02539	0.00148	0.12322
0.00864	0.00095	0.00686	0.00796	0.00769	1.02857	0.01032	0.00000	0.00002	0.01909	0.00008	1.11339
0.00048	0.01532	0.00081	0.01561	0.01331	0.00302	1.05337	0.00004	0.00003	0.01011	0.00095	1.11890
0.00290	0.00559	0.00525	0.02222	0.00369	0.00928	0.00376	1.00000	0.00218	0.00648	0.00314	1.08037
0.00109	0.02026	0.00852	0.00815	0.00988	0.01762	0.00638	0.00000	1.00607	0.02864	0.00031	1.12501
0.00066	0.02422	0.00044	0.00278	0.01175	0.00537	0.01772	0.00000	0.00011	1.03403	0.00199	1.10471
0.00114	0.00152	0.00278	0.00269	0.01438	0.00970	0.01294	0.00000	0.00001	0.00643	1.01604	1.08250

interindustry linkages with the other sectors of the Vancouver economy, while the non-metallic products sector is much more closely interrelated with the region's other industries.

Finally, by a slight manipulation of Table 3–11 we generate Table 3–12, which sets out employment multipliers that result from each additional $1 million in sales to final demand by the 18 sectors of this study. For example, for each additional $1 million in sales to final demand by the trade and transport sector, an additional 161 jobs are created in the Vancouver region. In contrast, each additional $1 million in sales to final demand by the paper and allied products sector creates only 61 jobs. Thus, Table 3–12 captures not only the sales-generating capacity but, more importantly, the job-creation capacity of each industry. Those industries with high employment multipliers are those that, in general, use less capital and more labor and are linked to other labor-intensive sectors. Those sectors with low employment multipliers are typified by high capital intensity, as a perusal of Table 3–12 will quickly indicate.

Table 3–11 Metropolitan Vancouver Sales Multipliers, 1971

Sector	Sales Multiplier
1. Agriculture, forestry, fishing, and mining	1.61
2. Construction	1.68
3. Food and beverages	1.63
4. Wood industries	1.49
5. Paper and allied products	1.64
6. Chemicals and petroleum	1.18
7. Non-metallic products	1.97
8. Metal fabricating	1.63
9. Printing and publishing	1.67
10. Manufacturing not elsewhere classified	1.50
11. Trade and transport	1.69
12. Communications	1.64
13. Utilities	1.54
14. Finance, insurance, and real estate	1.69
15. Health and welfare	1.64
16. Education	1.68
17. Business services	1.67
18. Other services	1.61

Source: H. C. Davis, *An Interindustry Study of the Metropolitan Vancouver Economy,* p. 26.

Table 3–12 Metropolitan Vancouver Sales Multipliers, 1971

Sector	Employment Multiplier
1. Agriculture, forestry, fishing, and mining	155.21
2. Construction	90.05
3. Food and beverages	61.80
4. Wood industries	70.70
5. Paper and allied products	60.69
6. Chemicals and petroleum	15.03
7. Non-metallic products	91.12
8. Metal frabricating	69.39
9. Printing and publishing	76.81
10. Manufacturing not elsewhere classified	74.32
11. Trade and transport	160.70
12. Communications	89.19
13. Utilities	53.30
14. Finance, insurance, and real estate	85.99
15. Health and welfare	138.38
16. Education	136.25
17. Business services	93.39
18. Other services	145.04

Source: H. C. Davis, *An Interindustry Study of the Metropolitan Vancouver Economy,* p. 27.

Input-output analysis rests on three principal assumptions and some related minor assumptions. First, the model assumes that the relationships between the various industrial sectors remain constant over time (i.e., the Table of Direct Requirements does not change). This assumption is made despite the realization that there are changes in relative prices (some input prices change more than others, such as those for energy), changes in technological production methods employing new and different inputs as well as different combinations of old inputs, and changes in the firms in the region as some die off, shrink or grow, and new firms enter the region's economy.

Second, the model assumes that there are no resource constraints. Final demands can increase without limit, and production can increase to satisfy these growing final demands. This assumes significant excess supplies of labor, capital, and physical inputs, again a questionable assumption in light of past capital, energy and resource shortages.

Third, the input-output model assumes that there are no economies of scale and externalities. Doubling final demand will lead to a doubling of all inputs and outputs. This constant linear proportional relationship between inputs and outputs and final demands is also suspect, given the scale economies and diseconomies that exist in most industries. Finally, when we derived our employment multipliers above, we made one additional assumption—namely, that the relationship between sales and employment is constant.

As was the case with the economic base model, to use input-output intelligently requires an understanding of its underlying assumptions, many of which are tenuous over the long run, particularly in rapidly growing areas and industries. When we are armed with such cautionary knowledge, the model can, however, be most useful to us.

Econometric Models

Input-output is basically a double-entry bookkeeping system for the urban economy. It is based on fundamental accounting identities where the value of expenditures on inputs and outputs must be equal for the accounting system as a whole to be consistent and usable. The input-output framework is a powerful, if costly, tool of urban analysis, one that is grounded in some rather elementary, and therefore intuitively straightforward, accounting principles.

When moving on to discuss econometric models, the picture changes. Like input-output, these are rather costly and complex tools. However, where input-output is founded on basic accounting identities, econometric models derive their roots from economic theory and from statistical methodology. It is not possible to even broach many of the technical methodological issues associated with urban and regional econometric modeling. Our purpose here is to present the basic concepts and ideas of econometric modeling. Discussion will focus on the strategy and structure of econometric model building.

The approach will be analogous to that followed above. We will start by looking at the structure and strategy of econometric models in an intuitive way. En route, we will develop some simple illustrative models. The discussion will conclude with a look at an actual model estimated for a North American city, Philadelphia, using this estimated model as a vehicle for testing our understanding of the concepts and implications of econometric model building. We will leave to the next section of this chapter the task of employing the model in a forecasting situation.

In their overview article on "Econometric Model-Building at Regional Level," Klein and Glickman observe that the construction of econometric models generally includes the following four steps.[19]

1. model specification, with identification

2. data preparation

3. parameter estimation

4. simulation and other applications

The modeling proceeds, according to Klein and Glickman, as follows.

In such systems, the past is used as a guide to present and future, by fitting the theoretical equations (1) to data collected (2). The end result is parameter estimation in (3). Finally, applications follow in the complete and integrated system.[20]

This is an example of a large literature in regional econometric models.[21]

Model Specification The model specification stage requires relationships in the urban economy given our intuitive and theoretical knowledge about urban macroeconomics. We return to a simplified version of our original urban income definition, where there are no imports and exports.[22] We make this simplification so as to be able to illustrate the model specification process with minimum complexity while maintaining realism. The income definition is

$$Y = C + I + G \tag{3.7}$$

where:

Y = aggregate income for the urban area

C = aggregate consumption in the urban area

I = aggregate investment in the urban area

G = aggregate government expenditure in the urban area

To model the urban economy, we need additional equations that provide us with estimates of aggregate consumption, investment, and government spending. Assuming that government spending is a policy variable and therefore not amenable to modeling via an equation, we are left with the task of specifying equations about the factors that likely "explain" the levels of investment and consumption and which therefore can allow us to model the levels of investment and consumption in a logical and usable fashion.

First, consumption in the urban area is likely to be determined by such factors as the level of income, the level of prices of consumption goods and services, and population levels in the urban area. For simplicity, we will look only at the first two factors, income and consumer prices. We thus construct the following equation to explain consumption levels in the urban area.

$$C = aY + bCPI + c \tag{3.8}$$

where:

C = aggregate consumption in the urban area

Y = aggregate income in the urban area

CPI = the consumer price index in the urban area

a, b, c = parameters to be estimated with actual data

An analogous argument applies to investment in the urban area. Intuitively, investment should be a function of income levels, profits, interest rates, inventories, and the age or productivity of existing capital. We can again state this, taking only the first two "explanatory variables" for simplicity.

$$I = dY + eP + f \tag{3.9}$$

where:

I = investment in the urban area by private interests

P = business profits after taxes

d, e, f = parameters to be estimated

Substituting (3.9) and (3.8) in (3.7), we obtain

and
$$Y = aY + bCPI + c + dY + eP + f + G$$

$$Y = \frac{(c + f)}{(1 - a - d)} + \frac{(b)}{(1 - a - d)} CPI + \frac{(e)}{(1 - a - d)} P + \frac{(G)}{(1 - a - d)}$$

where $1/(1 - a - d)$ is the multiplier on government spending (G).

Despite the simplicity of such a model, it is a usable, estimable conceptualization of an urban economy. As Beach observes, this model has been estimated for the entire U.S., as distinct from an urban region, using data for 1930–1948.[23] In its estimated form, the model appears as

$$C = 0.535Y + 0.214CPI - 3.06 \qquad (3.8a)$$

$$I = 0.221Y + 0.339P - 11.20 \qquad (3.9a)$$

$$Y = C + I + G$$

As measured, the model dealt with annual flows in billions of dollars, for C, I, G, Y, and P. The CPI is an index and is not stated in dollar terms. The multiplier is then $1/(1 - 0.534 - 0.221) = 1/0.244$, or approximately 4. A stimulus of \$1 in G yields another \$4 in output in this case.

What does the estimated model tell us? First, it says that our intuition was right. Second, it tells in quantitative terms how the variables are related to each other. The model tells us that the dollar value of consumption is determined by income and the consumer price index. Moreover, consumption can be estimated indirectly (in billions of dollars) by taking observed GNP and multiplying it by 0.535 and adding to it 0.214 times the observed CPI. Finally, if we subtract the constant term 3.06 (billions of dollars in this case), we will obtain an estimate of consumption spending without having to observe it directly.

While the foregoing model was stated in urban terms but actually measured in national terms, the principles of model construction and estimation are the same whether we are working at the national, regional (state or provincial), or metropolitan level. The simple model above served as a convenient vehicle to broach the discussion of econometric modeling.

Given this intuitive introduction to the subject, we can turn to discuss briefly one of the better known and documented urban econometric models, that done by Norman Glickman of the University of Pennsylvania for the Philadelphia metropolitan region.[24] The Philadelphia model is considerably more complex than our simple model, which had only three equations, just as the Vancouver input-output model with 18 industries was considerably more complex than the simple three-industry table we used for introducing the model.

The Philadelphia model is comprised of 26 equations and was estimated over the period 1949–1966 for the Philadelphia Standard Metropolitan Statistical Area (SMSA). The strategy for developing the model followed closely the steps discussed earlier, though with some interesting side issues that arise from working at the metropolitan level as opposed to the national level. The biggest issue derives from the "openness" of metropolitan economies that we mentioned at the outset of this chapter, namely, metropolitan economies are much more dependent on imports and exports than are nations generally.

When modeling the metropolitan economy, one must include a significant number of variables to represent these outside forces. Such variables, whose values are determined outside of a particular modeling framework, are called exogenous variables, and their values are fed into the model as data. The variables whose values we are attempting to model (such as consumption in our earlier three-equation model) are called endogenous. As a general rule, urban and regional econometric models take as exogenous a range of national economic magnitudes such as GNP, interest rates, national unemployment, and national price levels. Most urban and regional econometric models proceed in what has been called a "topdown" fashion, whereby they take exogenously determined national economic conditions from a national econometric model (or, from historical data when estimating the models initially) and then translate these national trends and conditions to the urban scale. This is exactly the procedure followed by Glickman in constructing the Philadelphia model set out below.

The metropolitan economy is broken into three sectors:

Sector 1 = manufacturing (SIC 19-39).

Sector 2 = wholesale and retail trade and selected services (SIC 50-59, 70-79).

Sector 3 = all other sectors.

Next, the general intuitive structure was developed. For instance, in equations 2 and 3, output in wholesale and retail trade and selected services (sector 2) and in all other sectors (sector 3) were assumed to be a function of levels of personal income in the Philadelphia metropolitan region, though not necessarily the same function. On measuring the relationship in equations 2 and 3, the functions differed, with services and trade being less dependent on local personal income (with a coefficient of 0.124) than was sector 3 (with a coefficient of 0.466). Table 3–13 sets out the 26 equations in full, including measures of goodness of fit (i.e., the reliability of the equation as estimated). The numbers in parentheses below each coefficient are the values for Student's t-distribution, a measure of the reliability of each coefficient. As the R^2 figures approach unity, the equation approaches 100 percent in its ability to represent completely and fully the variables that determine the behavior of the dependent variables on the left-hand side of each equation. As the t-values get larger, the reliability of the coefficient increases. Generally, t-values greater than 2.0 can be taken as indicating quite reliable estimates of the true underlying value of each coefficient.

As with economic base, shift-share, and input-output, we need to conclude this stage of our discussion with some words of warning about assumptions. First, if econometric models are to be useful for forecasting and analyzing the impacts of proposed policies, then it is essential to have confidence in the appropriateness of the model. We can obtain statistical measures of reliability such as the t-value and the adjusted R^2 (adjusted for the number of observations and degrees of freedom) noted above. Other statistical measures are also available to provide confidence in the statistical reliability of the model. However,

Table 3–13 The Structural Equations of the Philadelphia Econometric Model

Dependent Variable	*Regression Estimate*	R^2
(1) Output in sector 1	$Q1 = -132.370 + 10.988 \, USGNP \, (30.918)$	0.984
(2) Output in sector 2	$Q2 = 202.890 + 0.124 \, PY \, (32.358)$	0.985
(3) Output in sector 3	$Q3 = -29.870 + 0.466 \, PY \, (6.704)$	0.727
(4) Gross regional product	$GRP = Q1 + Q^2 + Q^3$	—
(5) Investment in sector 1	$I1 = -322.912 - 0.123 \, (K1) \, (2.842) + 0.224 \, Q1 \, (3.857) + 0.958 \, (I1) \, (3.982)$	0.818
(6) Capital stock in sector 1	$K1 = K1_{-1} + (I1 - D)$	—
(7) Employment in sector 1	$E1 = 381.809 + 0.058 \, Q1 \, (3.993) - 128.183 \, TIME \, (4.788)$	0.645
(8) Employment in sector 2	$E2 = 185.384 + 0.122 \, Q2 \, (11.751)$	0.891
(9) Employment in sector 3	$E3 = 528.469 + 0.024 \, GRP \, (10.247)$	0.862
(10) Total employment	$TEMP = E1 + iE2 + E3$	—
(11) Average	$MAW1 = -524.468 - 6.263 \, UNNO \, (4.990) + 1.302 \, MAW^a \, (41.017)$	0.991
(12) Average annual money wage in sector 2	$MAW2 = 15.552 - 5.645 \, UNNO \, (3.743) + 1.086 \, MAW2^b \, (23.118)$	0.970
(13) Average annual money wage in sector 3	$MAW3 = 345.919 + 0.732 \, MAW3^a \, (7.865)$	0.792
(14) Consumer price index	$P = -0.050 + 0.077 \, GRP \, (7.604) + 0.00059 \, TEMP \, (6.688)$	0.958
(15) Average annual real wage in sector 1	$RAW1 = MAW1/P$	—
(16) Average annual real wage in sector 2	$RAW2 = MAW2/P$	—
(17) Average annual real wage in sector 3	$RAW3 = MAW3/P$	—
(18) Non-wage income	$NWY = -1085.563 + 0.385 \, GRP \, (6.915)$	0.733
(19) Personal income	$PY = (RAW1) \, (E1) + (RAW2) \, (E2) = (RAW3) \, (E3) + iNWY$	—
(20) Labor force	$LF = 1055.133 + 0.404 \, TEMP \, (3.270) + 79.381 \, TIME \, (4.724)$	0.937
(21) Population annual money wage in sector 2	$POP = 2265.356 + 0.758 \, LF \, (2.041) + 568.620 \, TIME \, (5.894)$	0.970
(22) No. of employed	$UNNO = LF - TEMP$	—
(23) Unemployment rate	$UNR = UNNO/LF$	—
(24) Consumption	$C = 2683.267 + 0.217 \, PY \, (11.203)$	0.887
(25) Local government revenues	$GREV = 43.470; +0.377 \, TAXR \, (2.020) + 0.036 \, PY \, (1.856)$	
(26) Local government expenditures	$GEXP = -52.584 + 1.097 \, GREV \, (12.669)$	0.941

Definitions of Variables

$Q1$ = Output in sector 1
$USGNP$ = United States Gross National Product (1958 dollars)
$Q2$ = Output in sector 2 (millions of 1958 dollars)
PY = Personal income (millions of 1958 dollars)
$Q3$ = Output in sector 3 (millions of 1958 dollars)
GRP = Gross Regional Product (millions of 1958 dollars)
$I1$ = Investment in sector 1 (millions of 1958 dollars)
$K1$ = Capital stock in sector 1 (millions of 1958 dollars)
$(K1)$ = Capital stock in sector 1 lagged one period (millions of 1958 dollars)
$(I1)$ = Investment in sector 1 lagged one period (millions of 1958 dollars)

D = Depreciation (millions of 1958 dollars)
$E1$ = Number of employees in sector 1 (thousands of employees)
$TIME$ = Time (1949 = 0, 1950 = 1, . . . , 1966 = 18
$E2$ = Number of employees in sector 2 (thousands of employees)
$E3$ = Number of employees in sector 3 (thousands of employees)
$TEMP$ = Total employment
$MAW1$ = Average annual money wage in sector 1 (current dollars)
$MAW1^a$ = Average annual money wage in sector 1 in U.S. (current dollars)
$MAW2$ = Average annual money wage in sector 2 (current dollars)
$MAW2^a$ = Average annual money wage in sector 2 in U.S. (current dollars)
$MAW3$ = Average annual money wage in sector 3 (current dollars)
$MAW3^a$ = Average annual money wage in sector 3 in U.S. (current dollars)
$UNNO$ = Number of employed in SMSA (thousands of employees)
UNR = Unemployment rate (%)
P = Consumer Price Index (1958 = 100)
TWB = Total money wage bill (millions of current dollars)
$RAW1$ = Real average annual wage in sector 1 (current dollars)
$RAW2$ = Real average annual wage in sector 2 (current dollars)
$RAW3$ = Real average annual wage in sector 3 (current dollars)
NWY = Non-wage income (millions of 1958 dollars)
LF = Labor force (thousands)
POP = Population (thousands)
C = Consumption (millions of 1958 dollars)
$GREV$ = Total local government revenue (millions of 1958 dollars)
$TAXR$ = Local tax rate (%)
$GEXP$ = Local government expenditures (millions of 1958 dollars)

above and beyond such statistical measures, we must be reasonably sure that the coefficients as measured are stable and not likely to change either in the future or as a result of policies. Such an assumption is analogous to the assumptions of constant base-service ratios and constant technical coefficients in the interindustry input-output model. The stability issue is an important one and deserves careful exploration when using, or contemplating the use of, any econometric model.

One last issue about econometric models relates to the possibility that, despite good statistical and theoretical reasons to believe in their validity, they may be incorrect. The famed paradox of thrift is a good example of the trouble that can result from employing the wrong model. Keynes noted that the household model of thrift is inappropriate and counterproductive at the national level. The household model tells us that if we want to have more cash available to spend next year, then we should save more this year (i.e., spend less). Keynes noted that if everyone pursued such a policy, the aggregate demand for goods would decline, resulting in lay-offs, unemployment, and fewer cash resources for the average household. When applied to the entire economic system, thriftiness for the household can lead to dissaving and lower incomes.

When developing or using a sophisticated econometric model, regardless of its theoretical and statistical properties, the intelligent user must consider the possibility that there are other models that might explain the observed phenomenon or system better. We cannot rely too heavily on any of our tools of analysis. Whether a chef needs a knife or a meat grinder depends on the task at hand. The same circumstances surround the selection and use of our economic tools. Such care begins with knowledge of the tool and of their actual and potential limitations.

Other Models of Urban Economies

Economic base, shift-share, input-output, and econometric models are tools for studying the urban economy in the aggregate. They have stood the test of numerous applications to local planning and forecasting problems. There are other techniques, or combinations of the preceding techniques, that have been developed recently as means for overcoming some of the assumptions and weaknesses noted above. We review these briefly below.

Simulation Models   Simulation models are different from econometric and input-output models, which are also widely used to simulate the effects of a range of policies and investments.[25] Simulation models here apply to those comprehensive models of urban growth which draw on a range of mathematical techniques and statistical methods. The models here are all computer-based. One virtue of their structure is that they are easily flowcharted, a necessary first step in the computer programming process. Accordingly, we can look briefly at flowcharts for two quite different types of simulation models (see Figures 3–5 and 3–6). The first is typical of a large class of urban simulation models designed not only to forecast aggregates such as employment, housing, and population, but intended to enable investigators to disaggregate forecasts to subareas (see Figure 3–5). The more ambitious of these efforts have dealt with close to 30 industrial sectors, more than a dozen age-sex cohorts (groups), and nearly 1000 subareas. The cost in constructing and using such enormous models is great, running into the millions of dollars for the most ambitious efforts.

The second type of model does not disaggregate urban economic totals to small areas. Instead, attention is focused on the interactions among sectors (see Figure 3–6). These models are considerably simpler than the spatially disaggregated models, though their internal dynamics can be complex.

The model begins with an economic forecast for total economic activity in the region, usually in terms of employment by major industrial sectors (see Figure 3–5). Any of the preceding techniques for forecasting employment will do, although economic base variants have been the most popular. Population is also forecasted in a separate routine which usually interacts with the employment forecasting structure to develop estimates of migration.

Given the population and employment forecasts from these first

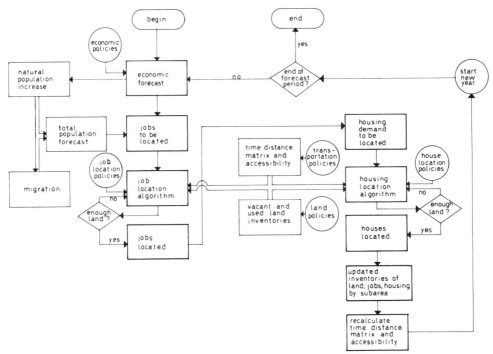

Figure 3-5. Schematic flow chart of spatially disaggregated land use simulation model. [*Source:* Michael A. Goldberg, "Simulating Cities: Process, Product and Prognosis," *Journal of the American Institute of Planners,* Volume 43, No. 2, p. 152.]

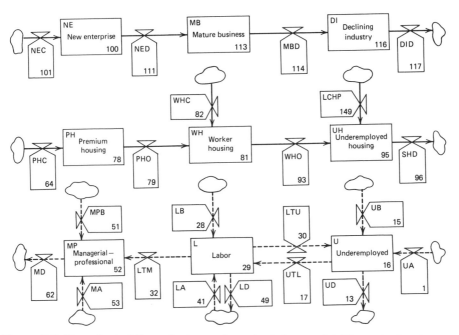

Figure 3-6. Flow chart of Forrester-type urban simulation model. The major levels (rectangles) and rates (valve symbols) for the Forrester model of an urban area. [*Source:* From Jay Forrester, *Urban Dynamics* (Cambridge, Mass.: M.I.T. Press), 1969, p. 16.]

two submodels, the simulation models then move on to simulate the spatial location of jobs and housing needed to accommodate the forecast population and employment.

In this allocation phase of the model's operation there is typically some close linkage with a transportation submodel that is used to provide estimates of accessibility, travel time, and cost to the allocation model. Once the forecast of houses and jobs are spatially distributed, they are fed back into the transportation submodel to estimate the growing congestion as more people are located in houses or jobs around the urban region.

The final phase of each iteration (i.e., each loop through the model) is to test if there is sufficient land to hold the newly located houses and jobs. If not, excesses have to be allocated to subareas with available land supplies. Once all activities have been successfully allocated to subareas, all data files are updated to reflect the new housing and job locations and the model returns to the next iteration and another employment and population forecast, until the terminal year of the simulation is reached.

Such urban spatial simulation models were generally developed as part of the large transportation and land-use planning studies, principally in the United States, though a number of operational models have also been developed in Canada and Britain. These models, because of their spatial focus, resulted in forecasts of land use, housing population, and employment for subareas in the urban area, usually roughly approximating neighborhoods.

These spatially oriented computer simulation models are tools of enormous question-asking power. The power is achieved at some considerable expense. First, these models are costly. They are also very time-consuming, as it takes years to construct the larger ones. Finally, they are fraught with theoretical, technical, and empirical weaknesses. They have often been described as "black boxes." For example, all the rigidities of the economic base approach obtain in large scale in models of this type. Their complexity does not easily allow users to appreciate all of the assumptions. *Caveat emptor* could have been written especially for potential buyers of these large-scale computer-based simulation models.

The second class of simulation models are attributed to Jay Forrester, who had previously developed elaborate models of large industrial firms and who then turned his attention to modeling urban systems. Club of Rome simulation studies done by Dennis Meadows and his associates, originally published as *The Limits to Growth* were global extentions of the urban dynamics framework.[26] Subsequent refinements were made to the *Limits to Growth* model and much attention was focused on these efforts.

Forrester-type models received much attention when first published and led to often vigorous debates in both the popular and academic presses. Forrester enjoyed a great deal of notoriety for a time in the late 1960s and early 1970s, and because of the attraction of his models to policymakers, they deserve some mention here in our survey of urban macroanalytical tools.[27]

The key to understanding Forrester-type models lies in the concept of a feedback loop (see Figure 3–6). Forrester saw dynamic processes as the result of some flow (such as water or electricity) controlled by a valve, which determines the rate of flow. As the flow continues, it adds to previous period flows, to establish a level (such as the level in a reservoir resulting from the flow of a river). As the level changes (say, in our reservoir again), there is a simple feedback between the level and the valve controlling the flow. As the level increases, the valve is closed (a negative feedback), slowing the rate of flow and therefore stabilizing the level. There is no spatial dimension. The disaggregation of economic activity is not done by industrial sector, but rather by whether the firms in the urban economy are new, mature, or declining.

The so-called Urban Dynamics Model looks at three aspects of the urban system: firms, housing, and employment/population. The business and housing components have much in common. In both cases there is a progression from new to old to underutilized. The dynamic of the model relates to the rates of flow of new housing and new enterprises and their subsequent movement through the system. Due to their complexity, the linkages among the various rates and levels are not shown.

While the popularity of the Forrester-type urban simulation models have declined somewhat, work still continues on their development, refinement, and testing. The initial model constructed by Forrester was soundly criticized by urban professionals on the basis that it lacked firm empirical foundations and that many of the assumptions and linkages built into the model were naive or unrealistic.

To Forrester's credit, all of the assumptions embodied in the model are carefully set out. They are available to the interested reader, though hardly accessible in the normal sense, given the complexity of the model. This is easier said in theory than accomplished in fact, again a function of the complexity of the model and its linkages among rates, flows, and levels in almost all of its submodels.

In summarizing the utility of the Forrester-type models, it is important to distinguish between the particular models that Forrester built and the technique itself. The Forrester model (as distinct from Forrester-type models and the general approach) was filled with questionable assumptions, lacked a credible empirical base, and had questionable linkages among its numerous elements. If these models are to result in major contributions to our knowledge of cities, considerably more work must be done in bringing these assumptions and linkages into conformity with empirical realities.

Time Series and Hybrid Models   Because of the shortcomings of the first four techniques, attention has shifted to means for overcoming weaknesses by building alternative types of models. Our review of these techniques will be brief, as they are largely in their infancy, but they should be mentioned as they do point the way toward the future. This is particularly true of time series models, which have been proposed as alternative statistical specifications for econometric models.

Where econometric models rely heavily for their structure on economic theory, and for their utility on the stability of the estimated relationships, time series models require neither.[28] Instead, time series analysis seeks to minimize forecast error. Time series analysis is unconcerned with causality (e.g., the underlying theoretical relationships among the variables) and with the analytical and structural qualities of the time series model. It is a purely empirical tool and merely seeks to describe the properties of a given system over the past and into the future without attempting to explain or otherwise analyze these properties and their observed dynamic behavior. There is a rapidly growing body of literature relating to time series analysis, and interest is shifting rapidly to the application of these techniques to urban and regional forecasting problems.

Finally, let us turn to some of the hybrid combinations. Two such combinations stand out as holding particular promise for forecasting at the metropolitan level and are depicted schematically in Figure 3–7. The first combines econometric (perhaps later time series) models with input-output models to construct consistent forecasts of the economy, because all of the interactions and requirements among an area's industrial sectors are accounted for.

Input-output analysis is a static technique. It assumes that its technical coefficients are constant over time and over price and resource changes. It also lacks any means for forecasting future levels of final demand. The scheme above seems to overcome these shortcomings by linking an input-output structure with an econometric model that forecasts final demands, which are then allocated across all economic sectors via the input-output model. The result is a forecast of employment and incomes that is consistent with respect to the needs of all sectors and their interindustry linkages and technical requirements.[29] As time series models gain in popularity and use, we can easily envision hybrids based on time series and input-output models.

One other hybrid combination is worth noting, combining shift-share and econometric techniques to provide a forecasting model that draws on the simplicity of shift-share and the explanatory power of econometric techniques.[30] One of the significant drawbacks of shift-share as a forecasting technique is the volatility of the regional share or competitive component. Accordingly, it seems worthwhile to develop econometric (or time series) models that deal with the behavior of the regional share component. Such models could draw heavily on the ex-

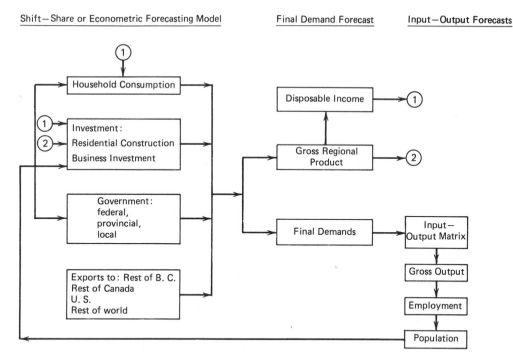

Shift—Share or Econometric Forecasting Model   Final Demand Forecast   Input—Output Forecasts

Figure 3–7. Integration of input-output models with shift share of econometric forecasting models.

tensive literature on location analysis to begin to explain why people or firms prefer or avoid a given region. This behavioral model of the regional component could then be combined with the national and industrial mix components in a straightforward manner to provide a relatively inexpensive yet usable and understandable forecasting device.

FORECASTING URBAN ECONOMIES

In the preceding section we presented, discussed, and illustrated a number of techniques of urban macroeconomic analysis. Part and parcel of such an improved understanding is a heightened ability to gaze into the future, since the future is in many instances (especially during relatively stable times) a direct continuation of the past.

Economic Base Forecasts

An interesting economic base forecast, because of the complexity of the study area, was provided by the Economic Base and Population Study as part of the Eastern Massachusetts Regional Planning Project in the late 1960s.[31] Eastern Massachusetts is a complex and advanced economic region, centered on Boston but including several other historically important manufacturing areas such as Brockton (shoes) and

Lowell (textiles). In 1963 (the base year for the study) there were roughly 1.3 million workers in the region and 3.5 million inhabitants.

Using location quotients, the study proceeded by classifying each three-digit industry as being either export or local-population serving. Any industry with a location quotient greater than 1.55 (apparently arbitrarily chosen) was defined as an export (national market) industry. Otherwise, it was defined as a local market industry. Having defined the economic base in this manner, the study then set out to forecast output in each three-digit industry by linking it with its national counterpart over time. Employment estimates were then dervied by using productivity forecasts to convert output into employment (i.e., by dividing output by labor productivity—output per worker—one can estimate employment in a direct way). The results of these several calculations appear in Table 3–14 below.

Table 3–14 Eastern Massachusetts Economic Base Study—Forecasts National Market Gross Product by Manufacturing and Nonmanufacturing

	1963	*1970*	*1980*	*1990*	*2000*
	(Millions of 1960 Dollars)				
National Market	3238.8	4016.0	5789.7	7802.6	10396.8
Manufacturing	2403.2	2934.1	4130.2	5495.1	7232.9
Nonmanufacturing	835.6	1081.9	1659.5	2307.5	3163.9
	(Percent Distribution)				
National Market	100.0	100.0	100.0	100.0	100.0
Manufacturing	74.2	73.1	71.3	70.4	69.6
Nonmanufacturing	25.8	26.9	28.7	29.6	30.4
National Market as Percent					
of GRP	33.1	33.3	34.0	33.5	32.7

Local Market Gross Product
by Manufacturing and Non-Manufacturing

	1963	*1970*	*1980*	*1990*	*2000*
	(Millions of 1960 Dollars)				
Local Market GP	6548.2	8050.9	11260.0	15460.4	21439.8
Manufacturing	999.3	1221.0	1564.8	1987.4	2624.5
Nonmanufacturing	5548.9	6829.9	9695.2	13473.0	18815.3
	(Percent Distribution)				
Local Market GP	100.0	100.0	100.0	100.0	100.0
Manufacturing	15.3	15.2	13.9	12.9	12.2
Nonmanufacturing	84.8	84.8	86.1	87.1	87.8
Local Market as					
Percent of GRP	66.9	66.7	66.00	66.5	67.3

Source: Metropolitan Area Planning Council, *Economic Base and Population Study for Eastern Massachusetts* (Boston: Metropolitan Area Planning Council, 1967).

Table 3–15 Eastern Massachusetts Economic Base Study—Employment Forecasts Export and Local Market Employment by Manufacturing and Nonmanufacturing

	1963	*1970*	*1980*	*1990*	*2000*
All Export	433.3	470.6	561.6	628.4	706.3
Manufacturing	284.7	292.8	324.5	342.7	365.3
Nonmanufacturing	148.5	177.8	237.8	285.7	341.0
All Local	851.3	914.7	1056.5	1172.6	1309.4
Manufacturing	109.3	115.0	125.3	135.9	155.6
Nonmanufacturing	742.0	799.7	931.2	1036.7	1153.8

*Source:*Metropolitan Area Planning Council, *Economic Base and Population Study for Eastern Massachusetts.*

This study applied the economic base concept to a large and complex urban economy, which was made possible by removing some of the limiting assumptions of the traditional economic base exercise.[32] For example, no constant relationship was assumed between basic and nonbasic activities. Rather, both were forecast using a consistent forecasting framework. This avoided a major shortcoming of most base studies, while introducing its own weakness such as the forecasting mechanism itself, which was rather *ad hoc* and relied on constant relationships between industries in the region and their national counterparts. The reliance on location quotients to define the economic base, and the further reliance on location quotients of 1.55 or more, subjected the study to unknown errors, since the reliability of the location quotient approach varies from region to region and no backup or confirming method was employed in this study. For all of its pitfalls, the Eastern Massachusetts Economic Base Study demonstrates the utility of the economic base notion, even in quite complex urban economies. Moreover, the various assumptions are clearly stated and subject to *ex post* scrutiny.

Shift-Share Forecasts

Using shift-share techniques to forecast urban and regional growth has been one of the more contentious and active areas of urban macroanalysis during the past decade. Claims and refutations of these same claims have gotten much attention in the academic literature.[33] Some portion of the argument has derived from differences in notation, data bases, and forecasting horizon. Even taking these into account, there is still an underlying question about the stability of the regional share (competitive) element and thus a question about our ability to use shift-share to forecast.[34] The regional component basically reflects the competitiveness of the region, vis-à-vis other regions in the nation, to produce goods in a given industry. Such a competitive position can be changed dramatically over time as a result of technological changes, availability or depletion of resources locally and in other regions, and changing institutional factors such as local taxes, incentives, and relative prices. All of the foregoing raises questions about the stability of the competitive component and the use of shift-share in forecasting.

Given this intuitive understanding of the problem of forecasting using shift-share techniques, we can turn to explore a shift-share forecast done several years ago for the Ocean County, New Jersey, urban region by Rae Zimmerman.[35] To keep our notation straight, let us review quickly the shift-share model presented above. The essential ingredients of the shift-share approach are the following symbols and their definition.

Zimmerman sets out the shift-share forecasting framework as follows. Most shift-share forecasts proceed from an equation similar to (3.10) where i is industry; j, region; k, the benchmark economy; t, time; and E, employment, value added or some other indicator of regional activity.

$$E_{ij(t + 1)} = \left(\frac{E_{ijt}}{E_{ikt}}\right) E_{ik(t + 1)} + \left[\frac{E_{ij(t + 1)}}{E_{ik(t + 1)}} - \frac{E_{ijt}}{E_{ikt}}\right] E_{ik(t + 1)} \qquad (3.10)$$

The first term in (3.10) represents the share of the benchmark economy (the nation, in most studies) for the urban area in time t for industry i. The second term is the shift term and depicts how this share is changing over time (here between time periods t and $t + 1$). It shows how well the region is competing against other regions over the period. In this formulation the national and industrial elements are ignored for forecasting purposes, which is not unreasonable given the primacy of the regional share (competitive) component.

On inspecting equation (3.10), it becomes immediately apparent that some changes must be made if it is to be useful for forecasting since our objective is to forecast the value of $E_{ij}(t + 1)$, though this term appears on both sides of the equation. Zimmerman proposes the following alternative.

$$E_{ij(t + 1)} = \left(\frac{E_{ijt}}{E_{ikt}}\right) E_{ik(t + 1)} + \left[\left(\frac{E_{ij(t + 1)}}{E_{ik(t + 1)}}\right)^* - \frac{E_{ijt}}{E_{ikt}}\right] E_{ik(t + 1)} \qquad (3.11)$$

where all of the variables are defined as above.

The important element in equation (3.11) is the starred (*) element representing the forecast value of the shift of economic activity i into the region j from the benchmark economy. Zimmerman used a particular type of projection of this term, though any sound projection device will work in the context of the equation as specified. The forecasts yielded by this procedure appear in Table 3–16.

A question that one always asks about a forecast is how good it is. Using a technique developed by Henri Theil, Zimmerman compares

Table 3–16 Employment Projections Using the Modified Shift-Share Technique for Ocean County, New Jersey

		Employment in Ocean County		
		1964	1972	1980 (projected)
SIC	Industry			
	Total	19,700	35,100	68,900
	Agriculture Services, Forestry, Fisheries	200	300	—
07	Agriculture services and hunting	100	200	—
09	Fisheries	100	100	0
	Mining	200	100	200
	Contract Construction	2,600	3,500	6,100
15	General building	900	1,000	1,600
16	Heavy construction	200	400	1,300
17	Special trade	1,500	2,100	3,500
	Manufacturing	3,300	4,700	8,400
20	Food and kindred products	400	200	100
22	Textile mill products	—	—	—
23	Apparel and other textiles	600	600	800
24	Lumber and wood products	100	300	400
25	Furniture and fixtures	—	500	900
26	Paper and allied products	0	0	0
27	Printing and publishing	200	400	700
28	Chemicals and allied products	1,200	1,400	1,500
29	Petroleum and coal products	0	0	0
30	Rubber and plastic produce	100	300	500
31	Leather and leather products	0	0	0
32	Stone, clay, and glass products	200	300	500
33	Primary metals industries	0	0	0
34	Fabricated metal products	0	100	300
35	Machinery, except electrical	0	200	500
36	Electrical equipment and supplies	300	300	500
37	Transportation equipment	300	200	100
39	Miscellaneous Manufacturing	0	0	0
	Transportation and Other Public Utilities	1,200	2,100	2,900
42	Trucking and warehousing	200	200	100
44	Water transportation	100	200	400
48	Communication	—	900	900
49	Electric, gas, and sanitary services	500	700	1,100
	Wholesale Trade	800	1,100	1,300
	Retail Trade	5,900	11,800	18,100
52	Building materials and farm equipment	400	600	900
53	General merchandise	900	1,900	2,800
54	Food stores	1,300	2,600	4,200
55	Automotive dealers and service stations	900	1,600	2,200
56	Apparel and accessory stores	300	500	100
57	Furniture and home furnishings	200	500	900
58	Eating and drinking places	1,200	2,900	4,900
59	Miscellaneous retail stores	700	1,200	1,500
	Finance, Insurance, and Real Estate	1,300	3,200	4,600
60,61	Banking and credit	500	1,100	1,500
63,64	Insurance	100	400	1,100
65,66	Real estate	600	1,600	2,200

Table 3–16 (*Continued*))

| SIC | Industry | Employment in Ocean County | | |
		1964	1972	1980 (projected)
Services		4,200	7,900	13,000
70	Hotels and other lodging places	1,000	700	2,000
72	Personal services	400	500	1,000
73	Miscellaneous business services	100	400	1,000
75	Auto repair, services, and garages	100	200	400
76	Miscellaneous repair services	100	200	300
78	Motion pictures	200	300	1,600
79	Amusement and recreation services	—	—	—
80	Medical and other health services	1,300	3,400	4,200
81	Legal services	200	400	500
82	Educational services	300	500	1,200
86	Nonprofit membership organizations	200	800	2,100
89	Miscellaneous services	200	500	900
Unclassified Establishments		100	400	—

Source: Rae Zimmerman, "A Variant of the Shift and Share Projection Formulation," *Journal of Regional Science* 15(1:1975): 29–38, p. 32.

these results with those resulting from other formulations of the shift-share and shows that these results are superior. In absolute terms, compared with national economic forecasts, for example, the modified shift-share approach compares favorably. Thus, despite the much-discussed shortcomings of the shift-share approach as a forecasting tool, the present modified shift-share approach appears to overcome many of these weaknesses and provide a reasonably simple and economical urban forecasting device.

Input-Output Forecasts

The input-output model by itself cannot be used for forecasting purposes. It needs forecasts of changing patterns of final demands. However, given such estimates of final demand changes, the input-output framework is an extremely powerful technique for gaining valuable insights into changes in the urban economy resulting from changes in final demands.

Input-output has had broad application in the policy field, where policymakers and policy analysts use the input-output model to assess the impact on the subject economy of contemplated changes in government policies (i.e., final demands). The following impacts were developed using the Philadelphia input-output study as a base.[36]

The impacts of both direct and indirect U.S. government Vietnam war expenditures were estimated for the Philadelphia region by first estimating the level of these expenditures by the U.S. government and then by using the input-output multipliers to calculate the direct and indirect impacts. Moreover, the input-ouput model was used to see what impacts would have been obtained in the Philadelphia region had the estimated $284 million that went to the Vietnam war effort in the region been redirected toward other government programs. Assuming that the money would be reallocated along the following lines (direct impacts), the input-output model multipliers provided estimates of the total impact these redirected expenditures would have had on the region's economy.

Elementary and secondary education	$170,400,000
Institutions of higher education	56,800,000
Low-income housing construction	56,800,000

That net cost was estimated to be on the order of $40 million in 1968.

A second application of input-output models of significant interest was that surrounding changes in final demands from a private firm, not from the public sector. In the late 1960s the Boeing Company of Seattle, Washington, found itself with a large excess of employees resulting from the termination of its supersonic-airplane program, and from a general slackening in demand for airframes. Boeing is a key employer in the Seattle region and an estimate of the impacts of Boeing's cutback was of vital importance to state and local policymakers. Researchers at the University of Washington had started their second input-output table for the state of Washington only two years before the massive Boeing layoffs, which began in late 1968 but were felt in earnest beginning in 1969.[37] Table 3–17, from the *University of Washington Business Review,* sets out in step-by-step fashion how the input-output table was used by Philip Bourque and his associates.

These two foregoing examples show how input-output analysis can be used to evaluate the impacts of sizable public and private decisions on urban and regional economies. Input-output analysis has served as a highly useful and quite powerful tool of economic impact analysis, primarily, and general purpose forecasting, secondarily. We must, however, keep in mind the previously discussed caveats that surround the use of the input-output technique.

Econometric Forecasts

Whereas input-output models are restricted in their forecasting ability by the need to have a set of final demand forecasts, there is no similar restriction on econometric models. One of their *raison d'être* is precisely that of forecasting. Table 3–18 presents just such a forecast done using Glickman's model for the Philadelphia metropolitan region.[38]

These forecasts to 1980 are based on two different sets of national growth assumptions.[39] The Philadelphia econometric model is a so-called "topdown" model, which relies on national variables and forecasts to drive it. The first growth assumption is that the national economy will grow at an annual rate of 2.9 percent over the 1966–1980

Table 3–17 Economic Impact Paradigm

Problem: Impact Analysis: Appraise impact of aerospace employm ent changes on income and employment in Washington State.

Given information:

(a) Employment in Washington State aerospace averaged 91,000 in 1969.

(b) Aerospace employment is projected to decline and stabilize at a rate of 32,000 by end of 1971.

(c) Shipments per employee ratio are estimated at $25,000.

Translation for I/O Model:

(a) Implied value of aerospace production will decline by (91,000 − 32,000 × 25,000 = $1475 million.

(b) Virtually all aerospace production in Washington is exported. Making some allowance for interindustry shipments in Washington, assume exports decline by $1400 million.

1. Income impact of decreased exports (change in GSP).

  (a) Direct income loss in aerospace (value created per dollar of production is $.429): $.429 × $1400 million-$600 million

  (b) Total income loss (direct, indirect, and household-supporting); multiplier times export change, or $0.82 × $1400 million = $1148 million

  (c) Total income loss, if state and local government expenditure adjusts: adjusted multiplier times export change, or $.99 × $1400 million = $1380

  (d) Total income loss if investment spending adjusts: not calculated

2. Employment impact of decreased aerospace exports: Based on estimated GSP of $17.0 billion in 1969 and employed labor force of 1310 thousand, GSP per emplo yed is $12,980.

Decline (in thousands):

  (a) Direct employment decline in aerospace (given datum) = 59

  (b) Total employment loss (direct, indirect, and household-supporting): $1148 million + 12,980 = 88

  (c) Total employment loss if state and local employment adjusts = 106

  (d) Total employment loss if investment spending also adjusts = not calculate d

---

Source: Philip J. Bourque, "An Input-Output Analysis of Economic Change in Washington State," *University of Washington Business Review* (1971): 5–22, Table 4, p. 1 9.

forecast period. Second, a more buoyant set of assumptions uses the Wharton econometric model of the national economy, which provided a more optimistic forecast for the nation than a 2.9 percent annual growth over the period.

In addition to their use as forecasting models, econometric models have been useful in assessing impacts of government policies on economic systems, just as we saw input-output used in the preceding section. Table 3–19 presents such an impact analysis, once again using the Philadelphia econometric model. The objective of the exercise is not, as before, to provide a forecast for the urban area of its output or employment, but rather to provide insights as to how these levels of economic activity are likely to differ under two different sets of government policies.

The policies compared in Table 3–19 are the imposition of restrictive fiscal and monetary policies during 1970. These are compared with the less restrictive policies in force at the time. It can be seen from the table that the more restrictive policies did take their toll on the

Table 3–18 Forecasts for 1980 from a 1966 Base Year

Variables	2.9 Percent Annual Growth Rate of GNP		1980 Wharton–EFU Forecast	
	Level	Percent Change 1966–1980	Level	Percent Change 1966–1980
Q1	10,756	47.4	11,934	63.6
Q2	2,669	41.0	3,273	72.9
Q3	9,293	69.1	10,938	99.1
GRP	22,718	54.7	26,146	78.1
E1	599	4.2	670	16.5
E2	510	19.7	582	36.6
E3	1,080	20.0	1,155	28.3
TEMP	2,189	15.1	2,407	26.5
PY	21,516	60.8	24,912	86.2
NWY	7,669	68.4	8,786	92.9
TWB	13,848	59.9	16,127	82.7

Note: Dollar values (*Q1, Q2, Q3, GRP, PY, NWY,* and *TWB*) are in millions of 1958 dollars; employment (*E1, E2, E3,* and *TEMP*) is in thousands of em ployees.

Source: Norman J. Glickman, *An Econometric Forecasting Model for t he Philadelphia Region,* Regional Science Research Institute, May, 1970, p . 44.

Table 3–19 The Effect on the Philadelphia Region of Restrictive Monetary and Fiscal Policy, 1970

Variables	1970 Level: Restrictive Policies	1970 Level: Present Policies	Column 1 Column 2
Q1	7991	8106	−115
Q2	2227	2270	−43
Q3	7255	7406	−151
GRP	17473	17782	−309
E1	566	572	−6
E2	456	462	−6
E3	953	961	−8
TEMP	1975	1995	−20
PY	16340	16678	−338
NWY	5648	5776	−128
TWB	10692	10902	−210

Note: Dollar values (*Q1, Q2, Q3, GRP, PY, NWY,* and *TWB*) are in millions of 1958 dollars; employment (*E1, E2, E3,* and *TEMP*) is in thousands of employees.

Source: N. J. Glickman, *An Economic Forecasting Model for the Philadelphia Region* (Philadelphia, Pa.: Regional Science Re- search In stitute), Discussion Paper Series, no. 39, 1970, p. 41.

Philadelphia economy. For example, total employment is estimated as being down by 20,000 people; gross regional product is forecast to de- cline by $309 million; and personal income in the area is seen as declining by $338 million. These were significant impacts for an urban area, even one of Philadelphia's size, to absorb over a short period of time, and forecasting them provides policymakers with the opportunity to take offsetting actions to cushion their impact.

As before, with our other forecasting techniques, we must put the econometric forecasts and impacts in the context of the assumptions that are built into the technique. Most important among these is the assumed stability of the model's estimated coefficients and parameters, not just over time but over the range of policy changes for which the model was used. Methodological issues also need to be checked before being satisfied that the econometric model is methodologically sound and its assumptions are sufficiently viable.[40]

Other Urban Economic Forecasting Tools

There are a number of other forecasting techniques that deserve some attention. Paramount among these is simple trend extrapolation wherein past trends, with or without some modification, are extrapolated into the future. This is what econometric models do, though they perform this extrapolation using highly disaggregated data and sophisticated statistical techniques. Exactly the same statement would apply to the time series models discussed earlier; they are a very sophisticated and elaborate technique for extrapolating past trends. Virtually all forecasting techniques are rooted in moving past trends forward through time with some form of adjustment mechanism to account for changing environmental factors (here environment is used in its broadest sense to include business, social, and political as well as physical environments).

Simple trend extrapolation essentially involves two steps: identifying past trends in the variables of interest and using judgment and any hard data that are available to estimate the course of these trends in the future. We present just such a forecast below, performed for the Rochester, Minnesota/Olmsted County urban region in the mid-1960s.[41] Table 3–20 presents the historical growth rates in various industries (in columns 1 and 2) and then moves these growth rates forward based on past experience and judgments about the future (column 3 and the remaining columns, which apply that estimated growth rate in employment to each of the industry groups given the 1960 base level of employment). Most industries are seen as perpetuating their past behavior (such as trade, manufacturing, and services, all of which are predicted to grow as rapidly as they did before 1960).

This presentation is helpful, since it illustrates that many trend "guesstimates" derive from merely plotting past experience and extrapolating these trends graphically. Such an approach is what most people do intuitively when they think into the future. As simplistic and perhaps naive as such an approach may be, it is not at all irrational to forecast in such a manner, particularly to provide a rough first-round

Table 3–20 Employment Projections by Major Industry Group, Olmsted County, 1960–1985

	Annual Rate of Change			Employment				
	1940–60	*1950–60*	*1960–85*	*1965*	*1970*	*1975*	*1980*	*1985*
Agriculture, forestry, and fisheries	−1.7	−2.6	−1.5	2,584	2,399	2,227	2,067	1,918
Construction	2.2	2.7	2.0	1,590	1,757	1,939	2,141	2,364
Manufacturing:								
Food and kindred products	5.5	4.4	3.0	889	1,031	1,195	1,385	1,606
Machinery, except electrical	NA	45.7	5.0	2,124	2,710	3,459	4,415	5,635
Other manufacturing	5.5	7.3	4.0	1,299	1,581	1,923	2,340	2,847
Transportation, Communications and Public Utilities	3.5	2.4	2.5	1,436	1,624	1,838	2,079	2,353
Wholesale and retail trade:								
Wholesale trade	3.4	−0.3	2.0	596	658	727	802	886
Food and dairy products stores	0.4	−0.7	0.5	504	517	530	544	557
Eating and drinking places	1.0	−1.0	0.5	759	778	797	818	838
Other retail trade	3.0	2.1	2.0	2,812	3,105	3,428	3,785	4,179
Finance, insurance, and real estate	4.6	6.4	4.5	1,047	1,305	1,626	2,026	2,525
Business and repair service:	1.3	−2.7	1.0	420	442	464	488	513
Personal services:								
Private households	4.9	1.8	1.5	867	934	1,006	1,084	1,168
Other personal services	−1.5	0.2	0.5	1,256	1,288	1,320	1,354	1,388
Entertainment and recreation services	−0.5	−0.9	0.1	155	156	156	157	158
Medical, professional, and related services:								
Education services	NA	5.5	4.0	1,191	1,449	1,763	2,145	2,610
Other medical, professional, and related services	2.4	3.6	2.0	7,259	8,015	8,849	9,770	10,787
Public Administration	3.0	3.7	3.0	818	949	1,100	1,275	1,478
Industry not reported	7.1	9.4	3.0	1,091	1,265	1,466	1,700	1,970
Total Employed	2.4	2.8	2.3	28,697	31,973	36,088	40,375	45,780
Population Forecast, Economic Analysis				71,734	79,933	90,220	100,938	114,450
Population Forecast, Demographic Analysis				72,351	80,845	90,670	101,854	114,683

Source: Rochester–Olmsted Transportation Planning Study, Economic Base Study Rochester, Minn.: Rochester–Olmsted Transportation Planning Study, 1966.

93

approximation. Victor Zarnowitz of the National Bureau of Economic Research, when analyzing the reliability of various forecasting models, found simple trend extrapolation not without merit in a range of circumstances.[42]

Trend extrapolation such as that discussed above for Olmsted County, Minnesota, basically blends intuition about the past and the future to derive a view of the future in quantitative or graphic terms. It is largely an intuitive and nontechnical approach, and undoubtedly the most widely used form of forecasting, being used daily and unconsciously so frequently its use eludes our knowledge as often as not. Intuition and judgment can also be used outside of a formal trend extrapolation by drawing on local expert knowledge either formally or informally. In reality, we resort to local intuitive knowledge and judgment every time we put a forecast to use in a local area.

Several techniques have been used to incorporate such expert knowledge, judgment and opinion. The most well-known of these is the Delphi Method developed at the RAND Corporation in Santa Monica, California, for use in so-called futures forecasting, wherein technological, social, and political future scenarios are sketched out by panels of experts.[43] The Delphi Method has been applied in a variety of settings, usually for dealing with qualitative issues and their future course. The technique proceeds by bringing together a panel of experts and eliciting their opinions on the future of a given phenomenon, region, etc. These individual opinions are then fed back to all of the other members of the panel in writing, and a second round of opinions is evoked. The procedure continues for at least three rounds (or iterations) until opinions begin to stabilize and some form of synthetic consensus emerges. While not designed specifically for use in forecasting urban economies and urban futures, Delphi studies can be mounted for these purposes and are worthwhile adjuncts to other forecasting approaches.

Delphi studies are the most highly structured means for incorporating subjective and expert knowledge. A slightly less structured but highly useful format involves the creation of lists of experts or key informants knowledgeable about local matters.[44] Such experts include highly focused specialists such as realtors and property managers as well as people with more general local knowledge such as local planners and politicians. These experts are then used to review forecasts and studies made by others, as well as to provide their opinions. The approach differs from the Delphi Method in that it is not iterative and convergence toward a stable set of opinions is not an objective of the approach.

Other approaches to forecasting could have been mentioned here as well. Foremost among these would be the hybrid forecasting models combining econometric and input-output techniques at the national level. However, these techniques are only in their infancy, and their application to urban economic forecasting lies in the future and out-side of our present focus.[45]

Similarly, we could have spent some time discussing the applica-tion of time series concepts and techniques to forecasting urban eco-nomic magnitudes. Here, again, the technique is in its infancy, and the paucity of current urban applications argued for excluding time series forecasts from our current review.[46]

The various methods and examples discussed here represent cur-rent forecasting techniques in relatively wide use for assessing the fu-ture of urban economies. Their frequency of use and reasonably well-established reputations as usable forecasting devices argued in favor of their inclusion here. By the same token, the more exotic and novel na-ture of emerging techniques and their infrequent application (due to their novelty) precluded their inclusion in our survey. However, inde-pendent of the specific approach chosen, whether it was one presented above or one of those currently being developed, *caveat emptor* should be kept firmly in mind. These techniques are only as good as the data and assumptions on which they are based. Exercise care and skepticism about both.

SUMMARY

In this chapter we developed the necessary macroeconomic tools to al-low us to gain the needed perspective on general economic forces and their translation into the demand for and supply of urban land and real property resources. We began our discussion by setting out some concepts and accounting frameworks for the urban economy. In this discussion we drew heavily upon national income accounting concepts. We also developed a simple circular-flow model of urban income de-termination, once again based on national economic concepts.

In the second section of the chapter we turned to a discussion of various models of the urban economy. Included here were economic base, shift-share, input-output, econometric, time series, and hybrid models that combined two or more of these techniques. Details of each model were presented and illustrations were provided using actual studies. Assumptions and weaknesses were also discussed.

The final section turned to questions of forecasting the state of the urban economy. Successful applications of these ideas to metropolitan regions around North America were presented along with the ever-present cautionary words surrounding these forecasting applications. In addition to the formal techniques of urban economic analysis, we also considered less formal approaches to urban economic forecasting, including purely intuitive trend extrapolation.

The range of forecasting techniques available is large. The choice lies with the user and with a sound understanding of the strengths and weaknesses of each approach as well as an equally sound understanding of the particular forecasting or analytic problem facing the potential user. Only through the exercise of informed judgment based on a knowledge of local conditions, the problem to be studied, and the techniques available for studying the problem and the area can we expect to construct and present usable studies of urban economic systems. In this chapter we have attempted to provide some of the background and technical underpinnings.

APPENDIX
THE INPUT-OUTPUT MODEL IN
MATHEMATICAL SUMMARY

As previously shown, the input-output (I-O) model records each sale in the economy as "intermediate" or "final." Total sales or output of any sector of any n-sector model can thus be expressed as follows.

$$\sum_{j=1}^{n} x_{ij} + y_i = x_i \qquad (i = 1, \ldots, n) \tag{A.1}$$

where:

x_{ij} = the value of the output of sector i purchased by sector j,

y_{ij} = the final demand for the output of sector i, and

x_i = the value of the total output of sector i.

The economy is thus conceptualized by n linear equations, each equation expressing the transactions of a particular sector with the processing sectors, and with final demands (sales). Equation (A.2) represents the major portion of our first table, the Transactions Table. As such, it is merely a set of balance equations or accounting identities. To complete the mathematical description of the Transaction Table, we write

$$\sum_{j=1}^{n} x_{ij} + p_j = x_j \qquad (j = 1, \ldots, n) \tag{A.2}$$

where p_j = final purchase (purchases of imports and other factors) by sector j.

$$x_i = x_j \qquad \text{for all } i = j \tag{A.3}$$

The second table of the I-O model, the Table of Direct Requirements, can be expressed as the matrix (a_{ij}) where

$$a_{ij} = \frac{x_{ij}}{x_j} \qquad (i, j = 1, \ldots, n) \tag{A.4}$$

Substituting (A.4) into (A.1) yields

$$x_i = \sum_{j=1}^{n} a_{ij}x_j + y_i \qquad (i = 1, \ldots, n) \tag{A.5}$$

97

which may be expressed more compactly as

$$X = AX + Y \tag{A.6}$$

where:

$$x = \begin{pmatrix} x_1 \\ x_2 \\ x_n \end{pmatrix} \qquad A = \begin{pmatrix} a_{11}a_{12} \dots a_{1n} \\ a_{21}a_{22} \dots a_{2n} \\ a_{n1}a_{n2} \dots a_{nn} \end{pmatrix} \qquad Y = \begin{pmatrix} y_1 \\ y_2 \\ y_n \end{pmatrix} \tag{A.7}$$

It may now be shown that total output minus intermediate demand equals the net output of the system or final demand.

$$X - AX = (I - A) X = Y \tag{A.8}$$

where I is an $n \times n$ identity matrix. Given the exogenous or final demands on the economy, it is possible to solve the system for total outputs.

$$X = (I - A)^{-1}Y \tag{A.9}$$

where $(I - A)^{-1}$ is the third table of the I-O model, the Table of Direct Plus Indirect Requirements, which is customarily written in transposed form, $(I - A)^{-1}T$, for convenience of reading tabular information.

Footnotes

1. This excellent point is developed at some length in N. H. Lithwick and Gilles Paquet, eds., *Urban Studies: A Canadian Perspective* (Toronto: Methuen), Chapter 2.

2. Charles L. Leven, "Regional Income and Product Accounts: Construction and Application," in W. Hochwald, ed., *Design of Regional Accounts* (Baltimore: The Johns Hopkins University Press), 1961, pp. 148–195.

3. For a discussion and illustration of some of the more technical issues relating to urban and regional income and product accounts, see: Werner Z. Hirsch, ed. *Elements of Regional Accounts* (Baltimore: The Johns Hopkins University Press), 1964; Werner Z. Hirsch, ed., *Regional Accounts for Policy Decisions* (Baltimore: The Johns Hopkins University Press), 1966; and Stan Czamanski, *Regional and Interregional Social Accounting* (Lexington, Mass.: D. C. Heath), 1973. Finally, for a more complete introduction to some of the elements of urban macroeconomics, many of which could not be covered adequately here, see: Werner Z. Hirsch, *Urban Economic Analysis* (New York: McGraw-Hill Book Co.), 1973, especially Chapters 6, 7, and 8; Alan R. Winger, *Urban Economics* (Columbus, Ohio: Charles E. Merrill), 1977, especially Chapter 4; and James Heilburn, *Urban Economics and Public Policy,* 2nd edition (New York: St. Martin's Press), 1981, especially Chapter 7.

4. See footnote 3 for details.

5. The best one-step introduction to economic base is still Charles M. Tiebout, *The Community Economic Base Study* (New York: The Committee for Economic Development), 1962. For a good critique of the concept, see Heilbrun, *op. cit.*, Chapter 7.

6. H. C. Davis, *Regional Economic Base Analysis* (Vancouver, B.C.: School of Community and Regional Planning, University of British Columbia), unpublished monograph, 1973.

7. See Davis, *op. cit.*, and Tiebout, *op. cit.*, for details on technique, applications, and assumptions.

8. Edward L. Ullmann, Michael F. Dacey, and Harold Brodsky, *The Economic Base of American Cities*, revised and enlarged edition (Seattle, Wash.: The University of Washington Press), 1971.

9. See Tiebout, *op. cit.*, Chapter 5, for details.

10. Tiebout, *op. cit.*, p. 49.

11. Ullman, Dacey, and Brodsky, *op. cit.*

12. Tiebout, *op. cit.*, p. 33.

13. The shift-share literature is very extensive at the present time and still growing rapidly. The interested reader is directed to the following papers, which are frequently quoted and, together, cover virtually all of the essential issues that have been raised to date. Lowell D. Ashby, "The Geographical Redistribution of Employment: An Examination of the Elements of Change," *Survey of Current Business* 44(1964):13–20; H. James Brown, "Shift-Share Projections of Regional Growth: Am Empirical Test," *Journal of Regional Science* 9(1:1969):1–18; James A. Chalmers and Terrance L. Beckhelm, "Shift and Share and the Theory of Industrial Location," *Regional Studies* 10(1976):15–23; J. M. Estaban-Marquillas, "A Reinterpretation of Shift-Share Analysis," *Regional and Urban Economics* 2(3:1972):249–255; Michael R. Greenberg, "A Test of Alternative Models for Projecting County Industrial Production at the 2, 3 and 4-digit Standard Industrial Code Levels," *Regional and Urban Economics* 1(4:1972):397–417; Franklin James Jr. and James Hughes, "A Test of Shift and Share Analysis as a Predictive Device," *Journal of Regional Science* 13(2:1973):223–231; H. S. Perloff, E. S. Dunn, Jr., E. E. Lampard, and R. F. Muth, *Regions, Resources and Economic Growth* (Lincoln, Neb.: University of Nebraska Press), 1960; and Benjamin H. Stevens and Craig L. Moore, *A Critical Review of the Literature on Shift-Share as a Forecasting Technique* (Philadelphia, Pa.: Regional Science Research Institute), 1979. In the discussion which follows, we have chosen to use the notation given in Bruce E. Lindsay and Susan E. Martin, "Employment Changes Via Shift-Share: The Southern New Hampshire Experience," *The New England Journal of Business and Economics* 5(1:1978):110. Their notation is among the clearest amidst a multitude of rather confusing representations that have clouded much of the shift-share discussion.

14. Lindsay and Martin, *op. cit.*

15. The debate about the stability of the regional competitive share component is very much related to this issue. See H. J. Brown, *op. cit.*; Daryl A. Hellman, "Shift-Share Models as Predictive Tools," *Growth and Change* 7(3:1976):3–8; Henry W. Herzog, Jr. and Richard J. Olsen, "Shift-Share Analysis Revisited:

The Allocation Effect and the Stability of Regional Structure," *Journal of Regional Science* 17(3:1977):441–454; Christos G. Paraskevopoulos, "The Stability of the Regional Share Component: An Empirical Test," *Journal of Regional Science* 11(1:1971); and, finally, Stevens and Moore, *op. cit.*

16. H. Craig Davis, *An Interindustry Study of the Metropolitan Vancouver Economy* (Vancouver, B.C.: Faculty of Commerce and Business Administration, Urban Land Economics Division, University of British Columbia), 1974.

17. For additional detail about input-output analysis and its various applications, see: H. B. Chenery and P. G. Clark, *Interindustry Economics* (New York: John Wiley and Sons), 1966; W. W. Leontief, "Input-Output Economics," *Scientific American* 185(4:1963):15–21; H. W. Miernyk, *The Elements of Input-Output Analysis* (New York: Random House), 1965; W. H. Miernyk and J. T. Sears, *Air Pollution of Abatement and Regional Economic Development* (Lexington, Mass.: D.C. Heath), 1974: Harry W. Richardson, *Input-Output and Regional Economics* (New York: John Wiley and Sons), 1972; P. A. Victor, *Input-Output Analysis and the Study of Economic and Environmental Interaction* (Vancouver, B.C.: Department of Economics, University of British Columbia), unpublished Ph.D. thesis, 1971; and R. W. Williamson, "Simple Input-Output Models for Area Economic Analysis," *Land Economics* 46(3:1979):333–338. The foregoing is by no means an exhaustive list but does give the reader a range of detail from rather introductory material (Miernyk [1965]) to more advanced studies (Leontief [1966]), on to applications (Miernyk and Sears [1974]).

18. H. Craig Davis, *op. cit.*

19. Lawrence Klein and Norman J. Glickman, "Econometric Model-Building at Regional Level," *Regional Science and Urban Economics* 7(1:1977):3–23.

20. *Ibid.*, p. 15.

21. For more information about the details and techniques of regional econometric model building, see Norman J. Glickman, *Econometric Analysis of Regional Systems: Explorations in Model-Building and Policy Analysis*, (New York: Academic Press), 1977; Frederick W. Bell, "An Econometric Model for a Region," *Journal of Regional Science* 7(2:1967):109–127; and S. Saltzman and H-S Chi, "An Exploratory Monthly Integrated Regional National Econometric Model," *Regional Science and Urban Economics* 7(1:1977):49–81. Finally, for an excellent general introduction to econometric model building and its associated techniques, see Robert S. Pindyck and Daniel L. Rubinfeld, *Econometric Models and Economic Forecasts* (New York: McGraw-Hill Book Co.), 1976.

22. The present discussion follows closely the highly intuitive and lucid discussion in E. F. Beach, *Economic Models* (New York: John Wiley and Sons), 1957, Chapter 3.

23. Beach, *op. cit.*, p. 35.

24. Norman J. Glickman, *An Econometric Forecasting Model for the Philadelphia Region* (Philadelphia, Pa.: Regional Science Research Institute), 1970, Discussion Paper Series, no. 39.

25. The simulation modeling literature is extensive and no attempt can be made here to even begin to review. However, a number of overview papers may be of help to the interested reader to get more of the flavor of these models as well as to help to identify some of the specific models and studies that might be of interest. The following half-dozen or so references should provide a good starting

point. Michael Batty, "Recent Developments in Land Use Modelling: A Review of British Experience," *Urban Studies* 9(1:1972):151–177; D. E. Boyce, N. Day, and C. McDonald, *Metropolitan Plan-Making* (Philadelphia, Pa.: Regional Science Research Institute), 1970; G. D. Brewer, *Politicians, Bureaucrats and the Consultant* (New York: Basic Books), 1973; M. A. Goldberg, "Simulating Cities: Process, Product, and Prognosis," *Journal of the American Institute of Planners* 43(2:1977):148–157; William Goldner, "The Lowry Model Heritage," *Journal of the American Institute of Planners* 37(2:1971):100–111; Britton Harris, "Quantitative Models of Urban Development: Their Role in Metropolitan Policy-Making," in Harvey S. Perloff and Lowdon Wingo, eds., *Issues in Urban Economics* (Baltimore: The Johns Hopkins University Press), 1969; Douglass B. Lee, "Requiem for Large-Scale Models," *Journal of the American Institute of Planners* 39(2:1973):163–178; Janet R. Pack, *Urban Models: Diffusion and Policy Application* (Philadelphia, Pa.: Regional Science Research Institute), 1978; Stephen H. Putman, "Urban Land Use and Transportation Models: A State of the Art Summary," *Transportation Research* 9(2:1975):187–202; and Alan G. Wilson, *Urban and Regional Models in Geography and Planning* (London: John Wiley and Sons), 1974.

26. Donella H. Meadows, Dennis L. Meadows, Jorgen Randers, and William W. Behrens III, *The Limits to Growth* (New York: Universe Books), 1972. Also see the criticisms of this work that appears in H. S. D. Cole, C. Freeman, M. Jahoda, and K. L. R. Pavitt, eds., *Models of Doom: A Critique of The Limits to Growth* (New York: Universe Books), 1973.

27. Jay Forrester, *Urban Dynamics* (Cambridge, Mass.: M.I.T. Press), 1969. For an interesting collection of papers extending and criticising the Forrester urban model, see Kan Chen, ed., *Urban Dynamics: Extensions and Reflections* (San Francisco, Ca.: San Francsico Press), 1972.

28. For an excellent overview of the issues involved in time series modeling, see Gordon L. Clark, "Awkward Problems with Large-Scale Econometric Models and Regional Forecasting Tools: A Commentary on Two Recent Issues of Regional Science and Urban Economics," (Cambridge, Mass.: Department of City and Regional Planning, Harvard University), mimeographed, 1979. For the technical details of the approach, see C. Granger and P. Newbold, *Forecasting Economic Time Series* (New York: Academic Press), 1977.

29. Clopper Almon, Jr., et al., *Interindustry Forecasts of the American Economy* (Lexington, Mass.: D. C. Heath), 1974.

30. For interesting developments in this area using statistical techniques to explain the regional share component and thus remove its variability, see: Rae Zimmerman, "A Variant of the Shift and Share Projection Formulation," *Journal of Regional Science* 15(1:1975):29–38; and also Benjamin H. Stevens, Glynnis A. Trainer, and Marguerite D. Woelfel, *Industrial Growth in Massachusetts: Some New Perspectives* (Philadelphia, Pa.: Regional Science Research Institute), 1978.

31. Metropolitan Area Planning Council, *Economic Base and Population Study for Eastern Massachusetts* (Boston: Metropolitan Area Planning Council), 1967.

32. *Ibid.*, but volume I, which deals with methodological issues, in particular.

33. See footnote 13 above, especially the papers by Brown; James and Hughes; and Stevens and Moore for the essence of the debate.

34. See footnote 15 above, particularly Brown and Paraskevopoulos.

35. Zimmerman, *op. cit.*

36. Walter Isard and Thomas Langford, *Regional Input-Output Study* (Cambridge, Mass.: M.I.T. Press), 1971, especially Chapter 14.

37. Philip J. Bourque, "An Input-Output Analysis of Economic Change in Washington State," *University of Washington Business Review* (1971):5–22.

38. Glickman, *An Econometric Forecasting Model for the Philadelphia Region.*

39. *Ibid.*, pp. 43–45.

40. See only introductory econometrics text such as Pindyck and Rubinfeld, *op. cit.*; N. R. Draper and H. Smith, *Applied Regression Analysis* (New York: John Wiley and Sons), 1966; or C. F. Christ, *Econometric Models and Methods* (New York: John Wiley and Sons), 1966.

41. Rochester-Olmsted Transportation Planning Study, *Economic Base Study* (Rochester, Minn.: Rochester-Olmsted Transportation Planning Study), 1966.

42. Victor Zarnowitz, *An Appraisal of Short-Term Economic Forecasts* (New York: National Bureau of Economic Research), 1967.

43. Bell Canada, *Delphi: The Bell Canada Experience* (Montreal: Bell Canada), 1972; N. Dalkey and O. Helmer, "An Experimental Application of the Delphi Method to the Use of Experts," *Management Science* 9(3:1963); T. J. Gordon and O. Helmer, *Report on a Long Range Forecasting Study* (Santa Monica, Ca.: The RAND Corporation), 1964 (this is the classic Delphi study); and H. A. Linestone and M. A. Turoff, eds., *The Delphi Method: Techniques and Applications* (Rading, Mass.: Addison-Wesley), 1975.

44. For an excellent applicaiton of the key informant approach, see Metropolitan Transportation Commission, *BART Impact Studies—Land Use and Urban Development Task* (Berkeley, Ca.: Metropolitan Transportation Commission), 1978.

45. See Almon et al. *op. cit.*, and Roger Bolton, "Multi-regional Models in Policy Analysis" (mimeographed), a paper presented at the Conference on Modeling the Multi-Region Economic System, held in Philadelphia, Pa., June 14–15, 1979. The paper by Roger Bolton presents an interesting review and critique of emerging techniques of regional economic forecasting and is an excellent overview source.

46. For one of the few applications of time series modeling to urban and regional forecasting, see Gordon L. Clark, "Predicting the Regional Impact of a Full-Employment Policy In Canada: A Box-Jenkins Approach," *Economic Geography* 55(1979):261–273.

4

THE DEMAND FOR
URBAN LAND

INTRODUCTION

Economics is said to be the study of the optimal allocation of scarce resources among competing uses.[1] This obtains as much with land as with any other commodity. For instance, in agricultural production land is used for various crops while in urban areas land can be used for commercial, industrial, or residential purposes. There may be demand for land simply as a store of value and not for any inherent productive characteristics. This includes the possibility of using land for speculation or as a hedge against rising prices.[2]

The basis for allocating land between various uses derives from the prices and incomes obtainable from the alternative uses, and also from the legal structure and constraints such as zoning and restrictive convenants. In a competitive market economy, urban land is allocated according to its highest and best (most profitable) use.

Some idea of the basic allocational problem of urban land markets is indicated in Table 4–1, an historical description of growth in Chicago. Over time, development of urban Chicago extended further away from the central business district, with an accompanying increase in the relative proportion of single-family versus multiple-family housing. A theory of the demand for urban land should be able to explain, among other phenomena, why apartments constitute the bulk of housing nearer the center of the city, and also why agricultural production does not occur in downtown areas.

The underlying economic theory for explaining this allocation of land is based on the willingness of a farmer, homeowner, or businessperson to pay for the land, given economic and social conditions and institutional arrangements. This theory of bid rents has its historical origins in the work of Johann von Thünen.[3] The theory has

103

Table 4–1 Urban Land Use (Residential) and Population Density Chicago Pre-1879 to 1955–60

(1) Period	(2) Proportion of single-family Dwellings in Total Housing Constructed	(3) Incremental Population Density (persons/ square mile)	(4) Total Area Developed (square miles)	(5) Midpoint—New Development (miles)
Pre-1879	21.2	6.8	15,505	1.0
1880–89	16.2	16.1	16,494	2.9
1890–99	18.1	37.0	16,123	4.9
1900–09	25.3	51.7	14,676	7.1
1910–19	36.0	68.5	12,514	9.3
1920–24	47.1	53.9	10,281	11.2
1925–29	50.5	90.1	9,584	12.9
1930–34	58.5	13.6	7,996	14.1
1935–39	64.1	15.2	6,850	14.4
1940–44	55.2	24.7	8,653	14.8
1945–49	67.0	55.7	6,260	15.6
1950–54	71.3	121.5	5,403	17.2
1955–60	72.0	160.6	5,652	19.5

Source: D. Harrison, Jr., and J. F. Kain, "Cumulative Urban Growth and Urban Density Functions," *Journal of Urban Economics* 1 (1974): 73-74.

been elegantly formalized by Alonso, and it is Alonso's development which is presented here. At first, the simplest version is developed.[4] This is then extended to indicate how land is allocated under more reasonable and realistic assumptions.

BID RENTS FOR LAND

The Agricultural Base—One Commodity

To commence, it is useful to define various types of rent as they arise in application to urban land. The types used are as follows:

1. *Land rent* is any payment for the use of the services of land for a period of time. An example is the rent payment per month on an apartment lease.

2. *Economic rent* is any payment to a productive factor in perfectly inelastic supply. This payment is in excess of that required to maintain land in its current use.

3. *Bid rent* is the maximum amount someone is willing to pay for land at various locations, representing the maximum amount that the bidder is willing to pay to obtain the land for the given use.

It is possible for land to obtain both land rent and economic rent at the same time. Bid rents arise from the competition for land from various sources. The bid rent model developed by von Thünen assumes the following:

1. There is a single, isolated city situated on a flat, featureless plain. Agricultural produce is shipped from points on the plain to the city center.

2. The land has only agricultural uses and is in perfectly inelastic supply.

3. Transportation costs are proportional to distance from the city center (they have a constant cost per mile).

4. Production for agriculture involves fixed proportions of capital and labor.

These assumptions rule out differential intensity of cultivation, increasing or decreasing per mile transport costs, and differences in the quality and fertility of land.[5]

Suppose a farmer is growing corn. The yield of corn is 50 bushels per acre, and the cost of this yield is $120 for labor and machinery services (the labor costs include imputations for the time the farmer and family expend in production, and for the opportunity cost of not using capital investments elsewhere). The price of a bushel of corn is $4, so one acre of product sells for $200. If corn were produced at the city center, where the market is located, there would be a net return per acre of $80, or the value produced less costs of production excluding land payments. However, transportation charges do apply, and let these be $0.20 delivered cost, insurance, freight (c. i. f.) to the market per bushel per mile, or $10 per acre per mile away from the center. The net revenue from the land, or gross revenue less labor and capital costs, is $80 per acre. Since transport charges are $10 per acre of output for each mile of distance from market, land up to 8 miles away can be used for corn growing. This implies that any land more than 8 miles from the city center cannot produce corn economically for the market, and no corn is produced farther away than this.

Returning to the definition of economic rent, the difference between total revenue and cost provides a relevant example, for the land has no alternative use. The farmer is facing a simple decision, namely, whether to grow or not to grow corn. All land is earning economic rent (assuming initial land costs were zero), but land closer to the city center is more profitable. Hence, farmers compete for land closer to the center, bidding up its price, and economic rent becomes land rent. Ultimately, if there is perfect competition, the land rent is bid up to the point where the farmer receives only normal profit, or the return on capital and labor invested that covers the opportunity cost of not using these resources elsewhere.[6]

This may be examined in mathematical terms. Let d be the distance from the city center, p the price per bushel, c the average cost of production per bushel (here $2.40 per bushel), and q the yield per acre. Then the land rent $r(d)$ per acre, a function of distance, is

$$r(d) = q[p - c - t(d)] \qquad (4.1)$$

where $t(d)$ is the cost of transporting one bushel to market at distance d. It is assumed that marginal costs are constant in the relevant range of production, so average and marginal costs are equal.

Since transport costs are linear, $t(d) = fd$ where f is the c. i. f. cost, or cost, insurance, freight charge, per bushel per mile. In this case,

$$r(d) = a - bd \qquad (4.2)$$

where $a = q(p - c)$ or the rent, per acre, in absence of transport costs, and $b = qf$, the freight charge application per acre. Yield per acre, price of corn, production costs, and freight charges are all constant, so a and b are parameters and the land rent is linear in distance. For the corn example, $a = \$80$, or the economic rent applicable to land in the absence of transport costs. The slope of the rent with distance is $b = \$10$, the units being rent per mile. Here is the rent gradient, and the situation is indicated in Figure 4–1, where the downward-sloping curves are termed "bid rent curves." The intercepts in Figure 4–1 are a and d^*, with d^* being the distance beyond which land rent is zero, or 8 miles from the center in the present corn example. Comparative statics can be examined. In equation (4.2), b depends only on the yield per acre and transport costs, while a depends on the price of corn and cost of production, and is linear in both. As an example, suppose corn increases in price to \$5 per bushel. Therefore, at an ouput of 50 bushels per acre, total revenue is \$250 per acre. Labor and machinery production cost per bushel, c_j, is \$2.40 per bushel, or \$120 per acre given a yield of 50 bushels per acre. Transport costs per mile per bushel are \$0.20 and yield per acre is 50 bushels, so that transportation cost per

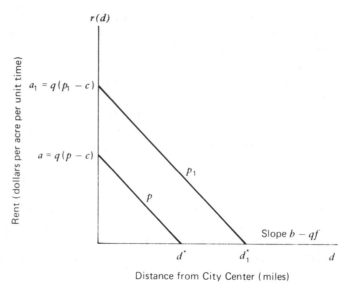

Figure 4–1. Agricultural land rent: bid rent curves.

mile, per acre of output, is $10. So, $q[p − c − t(d)] = 50$
$[5 − 2.4 − 0.2d]$ where d is distance from the center, which equals
$130 − 10d$.

Now $a = q[p − c]$, or rent in a no-transport cost case. Using our
example, this equals $50 [5 − 2.4] = 130$. Then $a = \$130$ and b remains
at $10. Thus, the economic rent declines to zero in (4.1) at a distance of
$r(d) = 130 − 10d = 0$, or $d^*_1 = 13$ miles, with transport costs absorbing all economic rent at this distance. The conclusion is that land up to
13 miles from the city center is profitable for corn growing. If the price
of corn increases, the distance for growing also increases.
    When $r(d) = 0$,

$$d^* = \frac{a}{b} \text{ and } q > 0 \qquad (4.3)$$

Thus, the critical distance is the ratio of the economic rent to the transport cost gradient. If q is positive, corn is grown at that distance. This
follows from (4.2), since the last mile where corn is grown is where $r(d)$
$= 0$, or $a − bd = 0$. If the solution to this is $d = d^*$, then $d^* = 1/b$ is the
critical distance. For distances where d is greater than a/b, $q = 0$ and
thus no corn is grown. Corn will continue to be grown at a 13-mile radius (i.e., d^*_1 in Figure 4–1) from the center of the city when it sells for
$5 per bushel, and at an 8-mile radius for a $4-per-bushel price. Competition will ensure that all the economic rent is converted to bid land
rent as farmers bid for the right to earn economic rents at each distance. Landowners up to each critical distance will be able to charge the
relevant land rent, $r(d)$, while those beyond our critical distances (8 and
13 miles in the above cases) receive no land rent as there is no economic rent for farmers to bid with beyond these distances. The existence of positive economic rent is a necessary condition for farmers to
bid for land and create positive land rents in the bidding process.
    It is now possible to examine responses to the various components
of bid rents, namely, prices, costs of production, freight charges, and
yield per acre. An increase or decrease in the price or cost of production causes a parallel shift of the bid rent curve. This is analogous to an
increase or decrease of income in the theory of consumer demand.
This derives from the definition of bid rent, $r(d)$, as $q[p − c − t(d)]$. Price
is p, so an increase in this (Δp) with the yield q constant will change the
bid rent by Δp_8. This is constant, so the shift is outward and parallel.
The slope depends on q, yield per acre, and f, freight costs.
    An increase in freight costs is illustrated in Figure 4–2. For the
corn example, suppose costs rise from $0.20 to $0.30 per bushel, or
from $10 to $15 per mile per acre of output. Then b becomes $15, and
the critical distance for growing is 80/15, or 5.33, miles. In Figure 4–2,
a rotation of the bid rent curve around a, analogous to a price change
in consumer theory, is indicated. A change in transport cost increasing

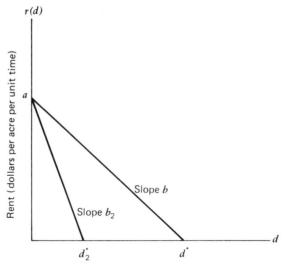

Figure 4–2. Bid rent curve: increase in freight costs.

the slope of b_2 to -15 reduces the critical distance to d^*_2 or 5.33 miles in this example, and no corn is grown farther away than this.

The theory of bid rents indicates that where transport costs rise, a gradient of declining land prices develops for land farther away from the city center.[7] The slope and location of this gradient determines the margin beyond which it is not profitable to engage in agricultural production. Competition among farmers implies that the economic rent paid to a factor in perfectly inelastic supply (i. e., agricultural land) becomes land rent, so that the site or land rent here exactly equals the economic rent that competitive bidding has eliminated for farmers. The economic rent is captured in the site rent and goes to landlords.

Finally, the total production of corn can be calculated. The land is located on a flat, featureless plain and d^* is the most distant location. Total production by all farmers is:

$$Q = qS(d) \qquad (4.4)$$

where the supply function $S(d)$ for the featureless plain is output per acre at various distances less than our critical distance d^* beyond which no production occurs. $S(d)$ is the area of a circle of radius d^*. Thus, $Q = q\pi d^2$ is the total supply. For corn, the critical distance d^*, was 8 miles, yielding a supply of $50 \times 3.142 \times 8^2 \times 640 = 6,434,816$ bushels. The last factor is the number of acres per square mile.

The Agricultural Case—Two Commodities

Suppose there is a second alternative crop that farmers can grow, say, wheat. For wheat the yield per acre, costs of production, and cost of transportation all differ from those for corn. Suppose that transport costs for wheat are $0.15 per bushel per mile, the yield is 40 bushels per acre, and production costs are $1.00 per bushel. Then $b = qf$ or $6 per acre per mile, and this is the slope of the rent gradient.

The situation is illustrated in Figure 4–3 for two crops with differing transport costs. The two bid rent curves are shown with intersection at b. Note that even though the slopes are different, the bid rent curves do not have to intersect. If the price of wheat were to rise sufficiently to yield a rent curve with economic rent above a_c, all the land would be allocated to wheat and none to corn. This is under the assumption that wheat and corn are the only two commodities grown.

Up to d_B all the land is rented for corn production, since the bid rent is higher than for wheat. After d_B land is used for wheat, up to the critical level d^*_w. The bid rent function when there are two commodities becomes $a_c B d^*_w$, indicated by the shaded frontier in Figure 4–3. Corn growers are unsuccessful at obtaining land closer to the city center than d_B, so the portion $a_w B$ will not be observed in the marketplace. The bid rent function for corn remains of the form $q[p - c - t(d)]$, but bids are successful only if d is less than d_B.

Suppose that for wheat the yield per acre is 40 bushels, and it can be sold for $2 per bushel. The labor and capital costs of production, including the opportunity costs to the farmer, amount to $40 per acre, or $1 per bushel. As before, average and marginal costs are equal in the relevant range. Then $A = q(p - c) = 40$. Let transport cost 5 cents per mile. At 40 bushels per acre, the cost of moving the output of one acre one mile is $2, and $= qf = 2$. This gives us $r(d) = 40 - 2d$ for wheat, and $r(d) = 80 - 10d$ for corn. Where the two bid rent curves

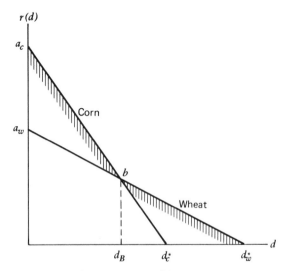

Figure 4–3. Bid rent curves for two commodities.

cross is where $40 - 2d = 80 - 10d$, or $8d = 40$. At a distance of 5 miles, the farmer is indifferent. This is d_B.

The analysis can be extended to any number of agricultural crops. For each there is a bid rent curve, with the successful bid being the highest rent on the $r(d)$ axis paid at each distance. Hence, agricultural land is allocated under competitive conditions to the user willing to pay the highest price. The observed rents paid for land constitute the set of highest bids over each usage. At each location, this is the market equilibrium rent.

URBAN COMMERCIAL LAND

Although the previous examples pertain to agriculture, the general principle remains that land is allocated to the highest bid rent at each location. The discussion is now extended to treat urban commercial land. Location now becomes a characteristic of the land that affects its productivity, a situation that was assumed away earlier.[8]

A common saying in retailing notes that success depends on "location, location, and location." The retailer pays for the selling ability of land rather than its fertility. While the farmer sells in a perfectly competitive market and faces a perfectly elastic demand curve, the retailer has a downward-sloping demand curve for services because of monopoly power arising from location. Isard's determinants of urban land rents clearly reinforce the importance of location:

1. distance from the central business district (CBD)

2. accessibility of the site to customers

3. number of competitors and their location

4. external effects in lowering other costs[9]

To place this in mathematical terms, suppose the firm sells its output in the CBD and bears the costs of transportation to market. Production costs for the retailer on labor, family time including opportunity costs, and capital services are $c(d)$. The profit at location d is:

$$\pi(d,p) = p \cdot q - c(d) - r(d)n(d) - f(d)q \qquad (4.5)$$

where p and q are the price and quantity of output, and $n(d)$ the number of land units rented at distance d. Land rent is $r(d)$ and freight costs $f(d)$. Profits depend on d, the distance from the CBD and the price of output p. The cost of labor and capital inputs may vary with location. For example, wages may be higher in the central city than in the suburbs.

For a given profit level $\pi(d,p) = \bar{\pi}$, the total payment for land is $r(d)n(d)$, which is:

$$r(d)n(d) = p \cdot q - c(d) - f(d)q - \bar{\pi} \qquad (4.6)$$

and the rent per unit of land is:

$$r(d) = [p \cdot q - c(d) - f(d)q - \bar{\pi}]/n(d) \qquad (4.7)$$

being total revenues $p \cdot q$ less labor and capital costs $c(d)$ and total freight charges $f(d)q$ divided by land used $n(d)$. If all land is of uniform quality in that building and construction conditions are identical, the rent measure $r(d)$ becomes the land rent per square foot. Land may not necessarily be of uniform quality, however, even for commercial purposes. For example, drainage and building conditions may vary, even at adjacent locations. A quality index for land can be constructed to adjust for these various factors, allowing the use of land rent per square foot of a standard-quality land. As an example, let us assume that output measured as an index is 50, with a price of $4; labor and capital costs are $100; and revenues and costs are measured on a daily basis and do not depend on location. Transport costs are 2 cents per mile per unit. Then $p \cdot q = \$200$ and $c(d) = \$100$, with $f(d)q = d$. For a given excess profit of $50, $r(d) = 200 - 100 - d - 50$, or $50 - d$. If $n(d) = 1$, and the rent is on a square-foot basis, the rent is $50 - d$. Thus, those at the center pay $50 per square foot in rent.

Notice that the bid rent function (4.7) is only a general case of the bid rent function (4.1), where $r(d) = q[p - c - t(d)]$. If $c(d) = c$, labor and capital costs are the same at all locations. Suppose that all firms use the same quantity of land, and that $n(d)$ is normalized at $n(d) = 1$. Recall that normal profits include the opportunity costs of using the labor and capital resources elsewhere, so the cost definition can include profits $o - \pi$. In this case, (4.7) is exactly the von Thünen bid rent in (4.1).

However, the bid rent curve in (4.7) contains some important differences in comparison with the von Thünen formulation. First, there is the flexibility in c to vary with distance, or $c(d)$. This is an expenditure, and:

$$c(d) = w_i(d)x_i(d) + \ldots + w_N(d)x_N(d) \qquad (4.8)$$

where $w_i(d)$ is the price of the ith input, and $x_i(d)$ its quantity, $i = 1, \ldots, N$ at distance d. For example, if the firm is a restaurant, where location will be an important characteristic, $w_i(d)$ could be the wages of waiters and waitresses, and $x_i(d)$ the number of hours they are employed, all at distance d. The wages and hours for cooks could be represented by $w_i(d)$ and $x_2(d)$, and those for buspersons by $w_3(d)$ and $x_3(d)$. The wages and number of hours worked could vary with distance from the CBD. If workers do not live at the CBD and must be compensated for commuting time and transport costs, wages could be higher for closer locations.

The bid rent curve for the firm considering the commercial land

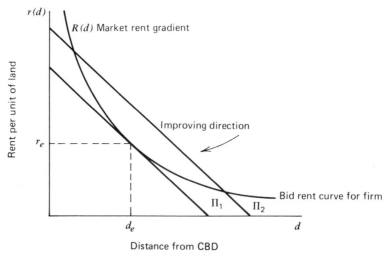

Figure 4–4. Bid rent curves for urban commercial land.

market is indicated as in equation (4.7). With $n(d) = 1$, $c = c(d) - \bar{\pi}$, the bid rent curves are linear, the economic rent and slope as derived in Figure 4–1. In Figure 4–4, a bid rent curve in linear form for such urban commercial land is indicated. Here $r(d)$ is the rent per unit of land and d the distance from the CBD. The market rent gradient is $R(d)$ and Π_1 and Π_2 the profits obtainable at two alternative locations. Note that if $n(d)$ is not equal to one, and c varies with distance, the bid rent curve is not linear. This is a likely occurrence. Suppose, in the restaurant example, operating costs are higher in the CBD, but the same amount of land is being examined at different locations, with $n(d) = 1$. Then $c(d)$ decreases with distance and bid rent increases with distance. This is because the bid rent function for the restaurant is in this case:

$$r(d) = p \cdot q - c(d) - f(d)q - \bar{\pi} \qquad (4.9)$$

with $n(d) = 1$. Let freight costs be constant, at $f = f(d)$.[10] As the constant level of profits increases, the bid rent decreases. So, in Figure 4–4, π_1 is larger than π_2 bur corresponds to a lower bid rent.

Although there is no necessity for the bid rent functions to be linear, in Figure 4–4 they are so illustrated for convenience. We are considering a single firm, a restaurant, and perfect competition is assumed to prevail. Suppose this structure is represented by $R(d)$ drawn as a negative exponential form (i.e., a nonlinear negatively sloped rent structure), shown in Figure 4–4. Then the location that maximizes profits for the firm is the one where the market rent gradient is tangent to the lowest possible bid rent curve. The arrow indicates the improving direction, which results in an increase in profits to the firm. Equilibrium is indicated at distance d_e from the CBD with rent r_e.

This is analogous to the maximizing position of a consumer or firm. Here the firm is minimizing the rent to be paid at the location, subject to the existing structure of rents charged at different locations. Hence, the market for urban commercial land for a firm can be derived by knowing the market rents by location, whose graph yields $R(d)$, and the cost structure faced by the firms, yielding the bid rent curves.[11]

URBAN RESIDENTIAL LAND

To examine the residential land example, suppose a household is located in a city where the costs of transportation and commuting to work are positive. The household derives utility from the consumption of housing and all other goods.[12] One period of decision making is considered at first and total income for the household is fixed. The utility level obtained from housing is $h(d)$ based on distance d and from other goods $g(d)$. The utility function is $u(h(d),g(d))$. Consumption of both housing and other goods varies with location d. Prices in some locations differ from others. At the center, for example, congestion and restricted parking, together with higher labor costs in production, make goods more expensive. Higher transport costs increase the prices of goods at remote locations, and construction costs or building codes and restrictions such as zoning bylaws may make housing vary in price across locations.[13]

For our example, let us assume that the rent per unit of land is $r(d)$, as above, and $c(d)$ is the cost of commuting to the CBD, both dependent on d. Let the price of other goods be p_g. The budget constraint facing the household is:

$$y - c(d) = p_g g(d) + r(d)h(d) \qquad (4.10)$$

stating that gross income less commuting costs is equal to expenditure on goods other than housing $p_g g(d)$ and expenditure on housing services $r(d)h(d)$. The expenditure takes place in a given period, such as one month. Owner-occupiers rent to themselves at the prevailing market rent. The two items not dependent on location are income and prices of other goods.[14]

At location d_2, with the price of other goods fixed at p, the quantity of goods purchased if no housing at all were purchased is $g_2 = [y-c(d_2)]/p_g$. This represents the intercept of the budget constraint on the vertical axis. Suppose this household allocated all of its income to housing services, setting $g = 0$. Then $y-c(d_2)$ is total housing expenditure. Taking an arbitrary rent $r_2 (d_2)$ at this distance, so the intercept on the horizontal axis becomes $h_2 = [y - c(d_2)]/r_2/d_2)$, as indicated in Figure 4–5. The line g_2h_2 is the standard budget constraint of consumer theory.

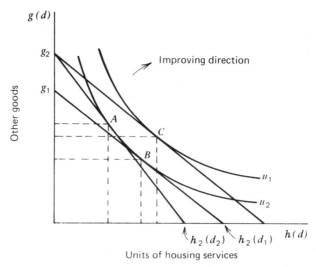

Figure 4–5. Household equilibrium in demand for housing and other goods.

The household maximizes utility subject to its budget constraint, yielding the following problem:

$$\text{maximize} \quad u(h(d), g(d))$$
$$\text{subject to} \quad (y - c(d) \geq p_g g(d) + r(d)h(d) \tag{4.11}$$

As in the traditional case, the household maximizes utility where the highest indifference curve u_2 is tangent to the budget constraint. Equilibrium occurs at point A, indicating the level of housing services and other goods consumed. An alternative way of formulating the household problem is to state that expenditure on housing and other goods is to be minimized subject to the constraint that utility not exceed a reference level. This yields:

$$\text{minimize} \quad p_g g(d) + r(d)h(d)$$
$$\text{subject to} \quad u(h(d), g(d)) \geq \bar{u} \tag{4.12}$$

and an expenditure function $e(p_g, r(d), \bar{u})$. Here the reference utility level is $\bar{u}$.

Returning to Figure 4–5, consider the household at another location, d_1. The vertical intercept is known, and this must be $[y - c(d_1)]/p_g$, or g_g. The problem is to select the rent that produces the same level of utility for the household, so it must be tangent to the same indifference curve, u_2. Knowing the intercept g_1 and the tangency, this indifference curve can be drawn, with the tangency occurring at B. The rent at location d_1 can now be calculated, because the intercept $h_2(d_1)$ is known. The rent is:

$$r_2(d_1) = [y - c(d_1)]/h_2(d_1) \tag{4.13}$$

so two different rents at alternative locations are derived, but for households at the same utility level.

The interpretation of this is as follows. Suppose a household locates at d_2 and is maximizing its utility in Figure 4–5. Housing services are functions of distances. Then point A is achieved, with the coordinates indicating the quantity of other goods and housing services consumed. If that household were to relocate because of a job transfer or change in locational preference, but was to remain as satisfied in the new location, d_1, as at d_2, the new equilibrium would occur at B in Figure 4–5. For this case, the rent, $r_2(d_1)$, is less than at $r_2(d_2)$, so relatively more housing services are consumed. The household locating at d_1 consumes more housing at point B than that locating at d_2 and consuming at A. Rent is cheaper with respect to other goods. Other goods are relatively more expensive, so their consumption declines. The slope of the line from g_2 to $h_2(d_2)$ is the negative of the relative price of housing $r_2(d_2)$, with respect to the price of goods. At d_1, the price of housing is lower. The slope is $- r_2(d_1)/p_g$, and this is smaller in absolute value than before.

A similar analysis could be performed for any number of locational alternatives, all yielding the utility level u_2. For locations d_1 and d_2, the rents $r_2(d_1)$, and $r_2(d_2)$, were constructed. If locations $d_3, \ldots, d_N$ were alternatives for the household rents, $r_2(d_3), \ldots, r_2(d_N)$ would be derived. This implies a set of rents for different locations but yielding the same level of utility, the definition of a bid rent function. Consequently, the bid rent function for residential urban land is the set of rents yielding the same utility to a household, given income and the prices of other goods.

There is one bid rent function for each indifference curve. The bid rent structure is indicated in Figure 4–6. The curve for utility u contains $r_2(d_1)$ and $r_2(d_2)$. It is drawn to be linear, but this is not a requirement. As before, the market rent structure or rent gradient is $R(d)$, unaffected by the behavior of any one household.

For utility level u_1 another bid rent curve exists, and the improving direction is toward the origin. The intersection of the rent gradient with u_1 yields r^* and d^*, the equilibrium rent and location. For every utility level there is a separate bid rent function. At location d_1, the rent for the utility level u_2 is $r_2(d_2)$. For utility level u_1, following the dotted line on the d_2 coordinate downward, the bid rent is $r_1(d_2)$. This rent is lower, enabling the household to purchase more housing services and achieve a higher utility level.

The household will locate at d^* and pay r^* rent, for the market rent gradient remains fixed and the household will move to the higher indifference curve. Hence, the demand for urban residential land, used in the production of housing services, is derived. The household maximizes utility, given income and the price of other goods. This yields a demand for housing services and other goods. From this is ob-

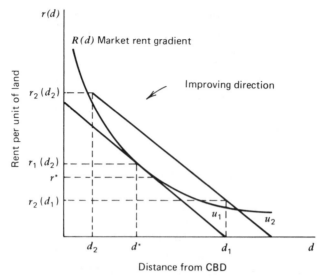

Figure 4–6. Bid rent curves for urban residential land.

tained the bid rent curves for each utility level. By seeking the most favorable bid rent, given the market rent gradient, the location can be derived. It should be noted that housing services are produced by land and structures, and unless the land directly enters the utility function, its demand must be derived from that for housing. Residential land demand involves two stages. In the first, housing demand is determined. In the second, the demand for land can be calculated. The above processes of market behavior generate population density gradients such as those in Figure 4–7. As distance from the CBD increases, population density decreases. The trend over time appears in the gradients to flatten.

THE DEMAND FOR URBAN AGRICULTURAL, COMMERCIAL, AND RESIDENTIAL LAND SUMMARIZED

We have derived the demand for land as resulting from competition between three main uses: agricultural, commercial, and residential. Also, within each main use there will be competition for land (e.g., offices and retail outlets compete for commercial land). A comparison among the three is indicated in Table 4–2.

The price of the commodity in the agricultural case is variable, with the bid rent curve determined by price movements. The commodity here is the output of the producer. The mechanism of adjustment will be detailed further when the behavior of the entire land market is explained. For the analysis of this chapter, an increase in the price of an agricultural commodity changes the bid rent function. New farmers enter without restriction until these economic rents are com-

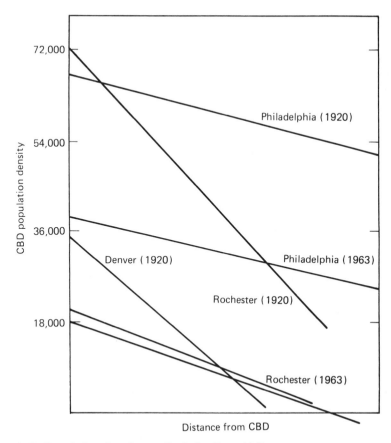

Figure 4–7. Population density gradients for three U.S. cities in 1920 and 1963. [*Source*: From Mills, *Studies in the Structure of the Urban Economy* (Baltimore, Md.: Johns Hopkins University Press), 1972, p. 45.)

Table 4–2 Comparison of Market Mechanisms and Structures Between Agricultural, Commercial and Residential Land

| Land Use | Variables | | | Mechanism of Adjustment | | |
	Price (Commodity)	Profits	Utility	Entry/Exit	Preference Among Curves	Preference Along Curves
Agriculture	variable	constant	n.a.	unlimited	none	none
Commercial	constant	variable	n.a.	limited	lower curve	none
Residential	not applicable (n.a)	n.a.	variable	none	lower curve	none

Source: William Alonso, *Location and Land Use* (Cambridge, Mass.: Harvard University Press), 1964, p. 74.

peted away. The reverse operation, with free exit, applies if the price falls. Agricultural profits are held constant at "normal" levels, including opportunity costs of the capital and labor employed. This obtains over all the bid rent curves; hence, farmers have no preference in this regard.

The same does not apply for residential land use, for the total population of the urban area is assumed to be given. Entry or exit of population is not a variable. Market adjustment arises through the preference of the individual for lower bid rent curves, yielding greater satisfaction.

The case for the commercial or industrial firm is intermediate. The number considered is limited. Some firms do not enter a market unless they can bid successfully for land and remain below their zero profit bid rent curve, so there is limited entry and exit. Again, adjustment arises through a preference for lower bid rent curves.

THE DEMAND FOR LAND FOR SPECULATIVE PURPOSES

There may also be a demand for land that is independent of the productivity of its use for either agricultural, commercial, or residential purposes. This demand may potentially arise from distortions created by the tax system or from the effects of inflation.[15]

In the previous analysis, the household has an income of y after tax, and must allocate this between housing and other goods. Let τ be the marginal rate of personal income taxation, and let z be the before-tax income of the household. The household has two periods under consideration, say, t and $t+1$, with $t+1$ occurring a year after t.

Suppose the land is acquired by the household purely for investment purposes, with no consumption objective. Let the rate of expected inflation be p^e, and let r be the rate of interest on investments other than land, which could be exemplified by savings accounts or other financial deposits.

If r_n is the net return to these savings deposits after tax, then:

$$r_n = (1 - \tau)r - p^e \tag{4.14}$$

where the expected inflation is not deductible in calculating tax liability. The interest rate on other investments is r, but this would be subject to tax. So $(1-\tau)r$ is the after-tax rate of interest; subtracting expected inflation p^e yields the real after-tax returns from these investments. Were this the case, r_n would be equal to $(1-\tau)(r-p^e)$. If the rate of interest is 12 percent and expected inflation 10 percent, an investor in the 40 percent marginal tax market receives -2.8 percent return on investment.

The alternative investment is in land, which has no cash return but increases with the rate of inflation expected at p^e. Capital gains on land are taxed at half the regular rate in both the United States and Canada, so $r_L = (1-\tau/2)p^e - p^e$. This assumes that the land has no marginal product. If the land has a positive marginal product, the results are changed to increase the return, but the qualitative effect is similar. To indicate this, suppose the real marginal product of land is k. Then the real return is the marginal product plus inflation, or $p^e + k$ before tax. The tax rate on capital gains is $\tau/2$, so the after-tax rate is $(1-\tau/2)*(p^e + k)$. Finally, r_L is obtained from the real return after inflation and taxes by subtracting p^e. Then

$$r_L = (1 - \tau/2)(p^e + k) - p^e \qquad (4.15)$$

and if k is 2 percent, $r_L = .096 - 0.1$, or -0.004 percent. Both returns after inflation are negative, but that for land is smaller. The lower tax rate on land leads to a larger investment in an inflationary environment.

SUMMARY

It is important to discuss where limitations exist in the bid rent model of the demand for urban land. In the agricultural case, the production technology may involve fertilizer, seed, machinery, and labor, as well as land, with several outputs. An intricate pattern of substitution between land and other inputs and outputs arises. The type of competition for land between uses may be unrealistic. Land close to urban areas and used for agricultural purposes tends to be allocated to market gardening or stabling of horses, where the unmeasured income of landownership will enter the equation.

Land does not have equal fertility or productivity in agriculture, nor is it a flat, featureless plain. This problem requires adjustment, but some of the qualities may not be readily apparent to potential landowners. The potential owners may have differential expertise in evaluating soil conditions and fertility. This may bring uncertainty into the purchase of land for agricultural purposes. Similar arguments also apply to commercial, industrial, and residential uses. All contractors, developers, and architects differ in their ability to evaluate the profitability of a project, particularly as the returns are made in the future.[16]

Uncertainty also enters the demand for land through the price of the commodity. If the price of agricultural output is unpredictable, then the demand for land reflects this uncertainty. Where agricultural prices are stabilized by marketing boards or planting restrictions, entry is restricted and the bid rent model must be adapted to include monopolistic considerations.

In the commercial and industrial sector, the profit relation is determined by the interaction of land rent and a number of prices for inputs and outputs. These prices may be random, affecting the demand for land. The examples used yield linear bid rent curves, but this may not always be the case. More complicated forms may not yield a market equilibrium.

No role for speculation or expectations enters the model, despite the possibility that land purchasers may have no short- or long-term intention of engaging in production. To include speculation involves dealing with inflation and how presumed knowledge of future land demand affects current land demand. The model used has only one time period, but a generalization to many periods would involve the consideration of speculation and greatly increase the complexity of the model.

The regulatory environment, particularly at the municipal or county level, affects the demand for land. A greenbelt area or land reserve, where government controls restrict land usage, clearly influences the bid rent model.[17] Zoning restrictions generally reduce the competition for land. Some restrictions can be included in the model, but "quantitative" limits such as height or floor space restrictions on apartment buildings may not easily yield a price for rent calculations. Environmental and growth controls further complicate the analytical situation.

This is not an exhaustive list of limitations, nor do these render the bid rent model necessarily less useful. While many limitations could be included, the resulting model would be cumbersome, albeit more realistic. However, the essence of the model remains: The demand for urban land is determined by the bid rents alternative purchasers are willing to pay, the land going to the highest bidder.[18]

APPENDIX: DERIVATION OF COMPARATIVE STATISTICS OF BID RENT CURVES

Following Equation (4.1), the rent function is:

$$r(d) = q[p - c - t(d)]$$

and the linearity assumption on freight costs may be relaxed. Now $\partial r/\partial q = p - c - t(d)$, which is non-negative up to the critical d where $p - c - t(d) = 0$. So rent is increasing in yield. Also, $\partial r/\partial(\text{ip} - c) > 0$, that is, increases in prices or reductions in production costs increase rents.

Now $t(d)$ is the incremental transport cost, and $\partial r/\partial d = q \partial t/\partial d$. If $\partial t/\partial d > 0$, or incremental transport costs increase with distance, then the rent increases with distance. In the case where $\partial t/\partial d < 0$, the rent decreases with distance.

Footnotes

1. See Lionel (Lord) Robbins, *An Essay on the Nature and Significance of Economic Science* (London: Methuen) 1932.

2. This problem has become more acute whenever prices generally are rising, and distortions exist in the tax system which provide incentives for people to hold land. The focus here is largely on the productive demand for land, but the speculative aspect will also be examined. More detail on land speculation, as well as demand for other stores of value such as gold, is contained in Martin Feldstein, "Inflation, Tax Rules and the Prices of Land and Gold," *Journal of Public Economics* 14(1980): 309–318.

3. J. H. von Thünen, *Der isolierte Staat* (Hamburg), 1826.

4. These assumptions are discussed in William Alonso, *Location and Land Use* (Cambridge, Mass.: Harvard University Press), 1964. The reader is also directed to Michael Chrisholm, *Rural Settlement and Land Use* (London: Hutchinson and Co.), 1962.

5. See Alonso, *op. cit.*, p. 37. The discussion in this section is based on his Chapter 3. Further developments are contained in William Alonso, "A Theory of the Urban Land Market," *Papers and Proceedings of the Regional Science Association* 6(1960): 149–157.

6. Robert E. Schenk, "A Theory of Vacant Urban Land," *AREUEA Journal (Summer 1978): 153–163.*

7. Roger E. Alcaly, "Transportation and Urban land Values: A Review of the Theoretical Literature," *Land Economics* (February 1976): 42–53.

8. For a case study analysis of the importance of location, see Philip David, *Urban Land Development* (Homewood: Richard D. Irwin, Inc.), 1970.

9. Walter Isard, *Location and Space Economy* (New York: John Wiley and Sons), 1956, p. 200.

10. For a restaurant, freight costs would include delivery charges of meals.

11. David Whitaker, "Bidding for Land Development," *AREUEA Journal* (Fall 1981): 223–233.

12. Louis Winnick, *American Housing and Its Use: The Demand for Shelter Space* (New York: John Wiley and Sons), 1957.

13. G. Johnson and A. Schmid, *The Impact of Suburban Land Conservation Policies on Land Price Appreciation* (East Lansing: Department of Agricultural Economics, Michigan State University), 1983.

14. Income and the prices of other goods may themselves vary with location. The costs of commuting to jobs in the CBD may entail higher wages for these jobs. The cost of transport, freight, and taxes, in addition to land rent itself, may imply that the price of goods, p_g, also differs across locations.

15. See Thomas Boehm and Joseph McKenzie, *The Investment Demand for Housing* (Washington, D.C.: Office of Policy and Economic Research), 1981.

16. See Simon Chamberlain, *Aspects of Developer Behavior in the Land Development Process* (Toronto: Centre for Urban and Community Studies, University of Toronto), 1972.

17. See David Dowall, *The Suburban Squeeze* (Berkeley: Institute of Urban and Regional Development, University of California), 1981.

18. See David Scheffman, "Some Evidence on the Recent Boom in Land and Housing Prices," in Larry Bourne and John Hitchcock, eds., *Urban Housing Markets* (Toronto: University of Toronto Press), 1978, pp. 57–85.

5

THE SUPPLY OF LAND AND IMPROVEMENTS

INTRODUCTION

The market for land involves both the demand and supply sides. The supply side would appear at first glance to be less interesting than the demand side we have just studied, since intuitively the supply of land appears fixed and therefore perfectly inelastic. For a variety of reasons, this is not the case in practice. For example, land can be "reclaimed" from the sea, from steep mountainsides, and literally from the air through the construction of multi-storied buildings. For these examples, time plays a key role in determining the supply of land; no additional supply may be forthcoming in the short run, and land supply may indeed by inelastic; however, with a longer time frame, there may be increases in the supply of land.

Land supply also depends on government regulations. For instance, zoning, which may prevent land from being allocated to its highest and best use, restricts the supply. Similarly, restrictions on flood plain or mountainside development also limit usable urban land supplies.

The present chapter commences with an examination of the urban development process and how land comes to be supplied. The land improvement process is explored, where the various stages of construction are specified. Next, a model of the urban land and housing markets is discussed, based on a production function for structures, where land and construction services are substitutes.

THE URBAN LAND DEVELOPMENT PROCESS

Ultimately, the supply of land to the urban land market cannot be developed without being completely integrated with land use regulations.

Consider a landowner holding a parcel of land for development. To supply this land in developable form requires subdivision and servicing. This usually entails the provision of utilities, roads and other forms of infrastructure.

Zoning regulations affect the type of subdivision developed, and other regulations require approval by a local permit-granting body. The typical steps in a development process start with an analysis of market conditions. Steps following this involve the selection of an appropriate site, a site survey, acquisition of land, and arrangement of a financing package and the design and physical planning of the site into marketable parcels.[1]

It is at this last stage that government regulations typically must be met and approvals obtained. Finally, the improved lots may be sold as is, or construction of buildings could be undertaken. We will look at these steps in detail.

Market Analysis

Market analysis begins with an assessment of the level of local business activity. Such aggregate economic variables as (1) expected inflation in all goods and services, (2) changes in real output per capita in aggregate incomes, and (3) population and employment may all be relevant here.

As part of the market analysis, models of construction and land supply involve a specification of current and future interest rates. In an inflationary environment, holding land and not supplying it to market may yield capital gains to the holder. Supply of land is thus levered on these expectations.

Suppose land is measured in $1 units. A parcel of land with a value of $100,000 can be interpreted as 100,000 land units. This abstracts from quality differences in the land. This is an asset price, as it pertains to land at a given point in time.

The potential developer, now a landholder, must calculate the user cost of land, or the cost of the flow of services during one period. One such cost is the interest rate, or mortgage rate, which may be denoted by r. The effective annual property tax rate is τ_e in percentage terms, and the cost of insurance and other services per annum is s. Let all these be proportions of $1, so the user cost or cost of service flow, is $r + \tau_e + s$. If the interest rate per $1 is .10, taxes are .01 and insurance is .01, the user cost is .12, or 12 percent annually.[2] This excludes the potential of capital gains to the landholder. If land increases at rate p, then the user cost of $1 of land services is:

$$U_L = r + \tau_e + s - p \qquad (5.1)$$

and if p is .1, then $U_L = .02$ for the above figures. This is the sum of all percentage carrying charges during the period. This is positive, so there is a net cost during the period to holding one unit of land, even after the subtraction of p, potential capital gains.

Assume our landowner is an individual investor and faces no taxation on capital gains but deductibility of carrying charges, as in the United States.[3] The marginal tax rate of the individual investor is τ. If U_L (taxes) is the cost net of taxes, then:

$$U_L \text{ (taxes)} = (1 - \tau)(r + \tau_e + s) - p \qquad (5.2)$$

and if τ is .4, in the example, U_L becomes .072 − .10, or −.028. This means that the investor earns a return from holding the land without providing any improvement services and is less likely to supply it to market. Including taxes, the cost per unit of holding land is reduced.

Note that the decision to supply the land does not strictly depend on the sign or magnitude of the user cost U_L. Rather, it depends on the opportunity cost of holding the land versus the next best alternative. What (5.1) and (5.2) suggest is that as inflation and the expectation of inflation accelerate, and if there are distortions in the tax system, there may be incentives to hold land rather than supply it. With the preferential tax treatment accorded capital gains, and the ability to deduct carrying charges on property against other income, it may be optimal to hold land for speculative purposes.

There is an additional aspect to the problem that concerns the transaction cost of supply. If sales commissions and legal fees are large, turnover and supply may be reduced. The higher the transaction costs, the less likely a person is to put property on the market. In essence, both economic and institutional considerations determine the desirability of holding land in raw form versus supplying it to the market.

Expectations play a significant role in the analysis of market conditions. Participants require accurate information on land-use controls and the probability of affecting changes in designated land uses. In a given use, for example, single-family residential, a parcel of land has a particular market value. However, there may be a nonzero probability of rezoning to another more valuable category, for example, for duplex use. This may increase the market price of the land. Such probabilities depend on political, economic, and demographic patterns. There is a set of probabilities of rezoning from one use to another, and assessing accurately this set is part of the developer's "art."

Ultimately, the research effort placed in market analysis yields information on land uses and their spatial distribution. Individuals vary with regard to their expectations of market behavior of prices and of the future course of land use and development regulations. These different expectations must be accounted for before making the commitment to buy raw land for development. Hence, in determining the supply of land, regulations and expectation are important determinants.

Site Surveying and Planning

Surveying requires data collection in and around the proposed development. Planning involves the binding of the structure, improvements, and site with the surrounding environment.[4] Planning under governmental authority nominally has the focus of protecting the local environment and residents. For example, there may be a positive externality to residents from having a city park. However, no one is willing to pay the individual price for parkland, while a developer may be willing to pay the price for another use. Here, there may be a role for planning. It may, however, also serve to increase the user cost or unit cost per time period of developing land, as opposed to maintaining it in an unserviced state. With the increase in such costs, the supply of land to the market may shift backward, resulting in price increases. In calculating the economic balance sheet for planning activities, any benefit from land and planning regulation therefore must be reduced by this higher price.

The situation is depicted in Figure 5–1. The demand for land services is downward sloping and the supply of land services is upward sloping and dependent on the unit cost to the owner. The regulations cause the supply to shift from S to S'. The user cost rises from u to $+u'$, and the quantity of land transacted on the market falls from L to L'. If planning regulations impose a cost of c per unit of land held per period, then:

$$U_L = r + \tau_e + s + c - p \qquad (5.3)$$

Further, planning restrictions may take the form of fixed costs. Examples are the submission of environmental and social impact statements for development. Other examples are the costs of conformity with the planning process, including possible delays and holding costs on the land. The urban land economist can attempt to quantify these costs. Whether these costs outweigh the planning benefits depends on societal preferences and evaluation of the regulation benefits.

More pragmatically, site surveying involves taking an inventory of site features. From a *topographic survey* one can obtain data on soil types, their location, and erosion aspects. Vegetation types, their location, and measures to ensure species stability are also relevant. A *landform survey* depicts geological features,[5] and the hydrology and climate of the area also need to be inventoried.

Site planning proceeds first with reference to a site map. This indicates the relative location of the site with regard to existing and proposed streets and highways leading to the site. The site map reports on major land uses adjacent to the site, for example, existing public facilities such as schools and community centers. Access to transportation facilities is also included.

Another survey typically performed in this step-by-step approach to development is a *boundary survey*. This includes bearings in degrees,

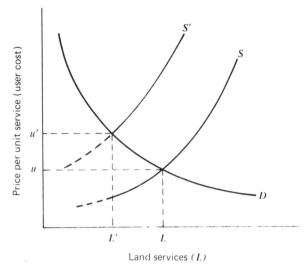

Figure 5–1. Effect on land market (supply) of planning regulation.

distances, and angles of outside boundaries. The location of connecting streets on the boundary are also included, as are any encroachments. The owners of adjacent properties are recorded, as are corner markers. Triangulation squares provide a technique for measuring the distance between two points, so that the computed area of all parcels in square feet can be included. The true meridian and the magnetic meridian are also recorded with the date of survey.

The *utilities survey* details all existing easements, the location and size of existing water, gas, electric, and steam mains and underground conduits. Also included are sanitary and storm sewer locations, rail lines, and police and fire service boxes. The planning stage involves bringing together socioeconomic and engineering data, with the analysis of market demand and architectural creativity to produce the plan.

Approval Process

The approval process is divided into a number of stages. The application process involves meetings with municipal planners to determine whether the development is feasible in principle.[6] The preliminary application for a subdivision involves a formal application, the engineering layout of site plans, maps of the area and proposed plan, legal documentation, certificates of encumbrance to show claim to the property, and, in some jurisdictions, an environmental impact study. The developer typically submits a schedule of development, number of proposed dwelling units, lot coverage and density statement, together with a legal description of the site.

Conformity with zoning and building regulations is examined.

Any rezoning application or request for a variance occurs here. Rezoning involves research and approval by municipal authorities, public hearing, and, ultimately, approval by the municipal council. If this preliminary application is approved by the municipality after on-site inspection, the developer can proceed to final approval.

The final approval stage requires detailed drawings of each phase of the development. Often, the municipality also must receive approval from state or provincial departments such as highways, where such departments may have relevant jurisdicton. A servicing agreement is reached between municipal and development engineers. This involves posting of bonds to ensure that the appropriate servicing is performed.

The final plans are then submitted for approval. The developer must certify that taxes and carrying charges are paid. If approved, the subdivision must be registered and certificates of landownership are submitted for endorsement or cancellation. Upon registration, a prospectus must be issued, outlining in legal terms the main features of a development. This must be presented to any prospective purchaser or agent.

The approval process outlined above applies to local government.[7] It may also be necessary to receive approvals from state or provincial and federal governments on such items as water and sewage plans and installations. If financing is obtained from some public or publicly guaranteed source, further approval of development standards may be required.

Financing and Installation of Site Services

Financing such "front end" costs as land acquisition, planning, and site improvement typically involves large demands for credit.[8] There are various financing options available. A *joint venture* agreement between landowner and developer reduces developer financing requirements in return for giving the landowner equity participation in the development. Additional forms of financing include: A *ground lease* providing for a long-term lease reduces the initial financing requirement. *Deferred financing* provides for a holdback on the land payment until the developer has received approvals and completed financing arrangements. This allows the developer to avoid carrying charges on a property until development is possible. It also reduces the risk of the developer. *Land syndication* involves a large number of small investors to reduce investment by the developer. The syndicate members are usually individuals seeking tax shelter. A *deed* and *purchase money mortgage* involve financing by the landowner, with this party retaining the right of foreclosure. A *land contract* is similar, except that title remains with the landowner.

Site services, including improvements such as roads and water and sewage lines, may be provided directly by the municipality via the creation of local improvement districts, to be repaid by specific tax levies against the subdivision. If the developer provides these services, they are naturally subject to conformity with municipal inspection and the cost is covered by sales revenues.

With water and sewage, an important issue is whether the developer is able to connect to the existing public systems, and the effect on capacity. As additional people are connected, capacity is strained. One solution is to create excess capacity in the short run, chargeable to the developer.

Site-improvement financing typically involves an interim or construction loan. This is a short-term loan to finance design and construction expenses. Conventional financing sources are banks, trust companies, pension funds, and government agencies. Another source in the United States is the Real Estate Investment Trust (REIT).[9] Legislation in 1960 had the objective of providing the small investor with access to investment funds. The REITs include short-term trusts providing interim financing, long-term trusts for commercial or apartment mortgages, and equity trusts involving real property ownership and combination trusts. The two alternative financing mechanisms involve debt and equity. In the latter case, this may be the only viable alternative for the small developer. Institutions such as life insurance companies and pension funds have more recently been interested in taking an equity position in real estate ventures.

Marketing and the Supply of Improvements

The supply of serviceable sites requires a marketing function. With predevelopment land sales, the buyer takes delivery prior to the installation of services. With developed land sales, owner-builders may purchase from the developer. A typical pricing structure involves a discount for early buyers to account for risk, although this depends on the market expectations.[10]

The design phase between the developer and architect commences with space planning and involves the placement of the structure on the site and the design and distribution of space within the structure. The engineering design phase emphasizes building features, wall and floor construction, and footings.

The approval process follows and requires submission of site and building plans and their compliance with codes. In the United States there are various building codes and Model Code Associations. These are summarized in Table 5–1. In Canada there is a uniform National Building Code. The advantage of having a uniform building code is that builders and architects can become familiar with the specifications, and prevents local workers and suppliers from establishing monopoly profits. The disadvantage is that it does not permit the flexibility afforded by local factor proportions, varying environmental conditions, and local and regional tastes.

Table 5–1 Major Building Code Forms in the United States

Structural:	(1)	Basic Building Code
	(2)	Southern Standard Building Code
	(3)	National Building Code
	(4)	Uniform Building Code
Plumbing:	(1)	Building Officials and Code Administrations International Plumbing Code (BOCA)
	(2)	Southern Standard Plumbing Code
	(3)	Uniform Plumbing Code
Electricity:	(1)	National Electrical Code
Model Code Associations:	(1)	Building Officials and Code Administrators International (BOCA)
	(2)	Southern Building Code Congress (SBCC)
	(3)	American Insurance Association (AIA)
	(4)	International Conference of Building Officials (ICBO)
	(5)	International Association of Plumbing and Mechanical Officials (IAPMO)
	(6)	National Fire Protection Association (NFPA)

Building codes are drafted to regulate safety, fire hazard, and sanitation. They control wall thickness, beam spacing, and electrical, plumbing, and ventilation installation. Insulation and seismic controls are also included. Elsewhere in this book the costs and benefits of regulation in the building code are studied. At this juncture we merely present them descriptively as part of the development process.

Typical costs in the supply of structures include materials, architectural fees, permits, labor costs, and equipment services. The financing vehicle is usually through debt, with an interim loan to cover the construction costs that are advanced by the financial institution. These are released in installments, or "draws," during the period of construction.[11] This provides for monitoring during construction by the financial institution to ensure that funds are not diverted or provided in advance of need. At completion, the interim is usually converted to a conventional mortgage.

The Construction Process

A possible sequence of steps in a construction process begins with a call for bids from contractors by the owner and architect. Bids are made on cost and time of completion. The selected general contractor then may subcontract some of the work to various trades such as plumbing, roofing, electrical, painting, and heating. The labor force for each subcontracted job is usually hired on a piece basis, frequently through union hiring halls. Alternative construction forms are of the on-site specialized type and prefabrication. In the latter case, major portions are constructed off the site in a factory.

This section has indicated the process by which land is converted to usable supply, including its improvements. It provides an indication of the range of issues and problems faced in the development process.[12] These are the main institutional factors involved. It remains to examine the theory of the supply of land and improvements to which we turn next to provide conceptual underpinnings for the process we have just described.

MODELING THE URBAN LAND AND HOUSING MARKETS

Though very few models deal with the supply of land alone, extensive work has been done on the supply of improvements. To indicate an example of a land development model, one is summarized. In the land development model discussed here, based on Davies,[13] there is a separate land equation, in addition to interactions between land and housing and the treatment of housing as a consumption and investment good. It indicates that housing can be used both to provide shelter and as an investment. It is also a model that develops the supply of lots, and shows the effect of taxes and government policies.

Builders augment the stock of housing units in response to profitability conditions.[14] House prices and rents change in response to changes in the respective stocks of rental and ownership housing. The stock of lots changes with respect to the stock of lots per household, expected profitability of constructing single-family homes, and the prime interest rate.

For single-family units, the stock of lots at the end of a given period is the sum of the stock at the beginning of the period, minus the number of housing starts, plus the number of additional lots created by legal registration of subdivision plans and agreements. In practice, estimating and applying this model requires examination of all plans, and potentially of city maps as well. Other sources of lot creation include demolition, with or without rezoning, rezoning of vacant land, and subdivision of existing lots into smaller ones.

The price of lots arises from the profitability of housing construction. At any given point in time the stock is fixed, so the price depends on demand, as in Table 5–2. Let P be the asset or purchase price of a lot, as distinct from the price of lot services. The stock of lots at any given time is L. Demand at D_1 implies the presence of an equilibrium price at P_1. Should demand increase to D_2, for example, the price of lots increases to P_2. In general, a pricing equation for lots may be constructed as:

$$P = P(r, \pi, L) \qquad (5.4)$$

where r is the interest rate, π the profitability of housing, and L the stock of lots. Now land is an asset earning no interest. If interest rates rise, the opportunity cost of holding land versus other alternatives, such as money market funds or term deposits, rises, so the price of land falls.[15] As the profit per unit of housing increases, lot prices in-

Table 5–2 Model of the Land and Housing Market (effect of a change in variable on right on variable on left is given in parentheses

Lot prices (Land)	Dependent on Interest rates (decreases) Housing profits (increase) Lot stock (increase)
Housing starts	Interest rates (decrease) Housing profits (increase) Vacancies (decrease)
Housing completions	Housing starts (increase)
Housing stock	Depreciation/demolition (decrease) Logged housing stock (increase) Housing completions (increase)
House prices	Unit price of (decrease) Income (increase)

crease. From Figure 5–2, any increase in the stock of lots reduces prices.

The number of housing starts may similarly depend on profitability of constructing housing, interest rates, and housing vacancies.[16]

Other potential equations may arise for repair and maintenance and the supply of existing houses. In this more extended version, the price of lots depends on the unit or user cost of lots, profits in housing, and the stock of lots. Variables sometimes included are vacancies, or the stock of unoccupied units, and the price of housing. The number of housing starts can then be plausibly assumed to depend on interest rates, housing profits, vacancies, and the price of housing. Of course, various lag structures may arise on these variables. Housing starts do

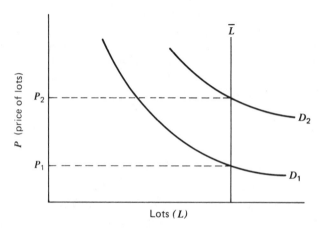

Figure 5–2. Price of lots in short-run market.

not immediately respond to changes in interest rates, for example. Davies finds that a three-month lag on interest rates is normal.[17] Thus, current interest rates will affect starts three months hence.

Completions are specified as being a lagged weighted function of previous housing starts. Starts are completed in the future. Nominally, these weights must sum to one, reflecting the fact that starts ultimately are completed. For example, if half of current starts are completed in the current period and if half are completed the following period, housing completions are the sum of half of the starts this period and half of the starts in the previous period.

More plausibly, completions also have a seasonal component. At the end of the period, the housing stock consist of the previous stock adjusted for demolitions plus those completed. The stock of houses in any period is the sum of those existing in the previous period, less those demolished and plus those added through new construction. The demolition rate is typically small, but can be quite large in older cities such as Chicago and St. Louis.

The price of houses depends on two motives. One is for consumption; the other is for investment. The appropriate specification is for the user cost of housing to affect demand. The user cost of one unit of housing is the sum of the interest rate, property tax rate on housing, and maintenance rate, less any capital gains. The price of housing depends on income and this user cost. As the former increases, the price of housing declines. There is a crucial difference between the user cost and the price of housing: The former is the user cost of the flow of one unit of housing services per period; the latter is the asset price of one unit of housing stock. The user cost would be the cost of renting one unit of housing one period, while the price is the cost of purchasing it. As income increases, the price of housing increases. The above completes a possible model of the market for single-family homes. It is summarized in Figure 5–3.

The model may be embellished in several ways. First, the supply may be increased by improving the quality of the existing stock by renovation and refurbishing. Repair and maintenance is a large component, since new construction is typically less than five percent of total stock. Second, a decision to supply existing houses differs from one to construct new ones. The supply of existing houses depends on the transaction costs of offering them to market, such as real estate commissions and legal fees.

The model sketched in Table 5–2 is estimated by Davies for the city of London, Ontario. A simulated increase of 250 units in the supply of lots is effected, by legal alteration. This is fed through the model and the stock of houses estimated. The results show that an increase in supply of lots, from legal redefinitions or rezoning, has a substantial effect in reducing house prices and rents.

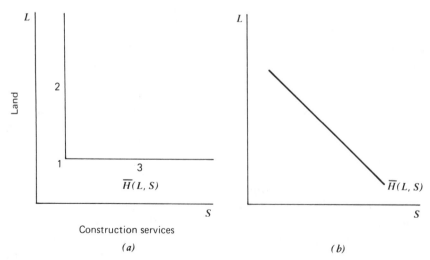

Figure 5–3. Substitution between land and construction services. (a) No substitutability. (b) Perfect substatutability.

SUPPLY OF IMPROVEMENTS: PRODUCTION FUNCTIONS

Extensive literature exists on the supply of improvements, usually focused on housing. This section develops the supply of housing, expressed as a function of land and construction services. This yields a derived demand for land from the supply of housing or other improvements.

The crucial variable in this estimation is the elasticity of substitution, a measure of the flexibility with which construction services and land can be interchanged. In Figure 5–3a, where L denotes land and S is construction services, the isoquant is $\bar{H}$. This represents the combinations of land and construction services yielding the same supply of output, called housing, here $\bar{H}$.

One problem arises with defining construction services. These include raw materials and supplies, labor, and the services of equipment used in construction. It would be appropriate to test for whether these heterogeneous goods and services can be aggregated. However, an index of construction services can only be formed under very restrictive and unrealistic assumptions, given the heterogeneity of construction inputs.

In figure 5–3a, the implication is that there is no substitutability between land and construction prices. Intuitively, one might argue that there is a given land requirement for a house, and substitution by labor or materials is impossible. At point 1 in the figure, the least amount of both factors used to produce housing $\bar{H}$ is attained. By comparison, at point 2 there is an additional amount of land available, but no additional housing can be produced (i.e., construction services are a "binding" constraint). The reverse obtains at point 3, where more than the minimum amount of construction services is available. However, the absence of additional land renders it impossible to produce more housing (i.e., land is a "binding" constraint).

This argument is not watertight, and indicates one of the problems with this approach to estimating the supply of housing. Presumably, all else being equal, a house built on a larger lot will be more valuable. The package of construction services and land produced is more expensive, and effectively produces a more valuable house. This is a violation of the production function argument for the isoquant in Figure 5–3a, suggesting that the procedure may not be automatically applicable to housing.

In Figure 5–3b, there is a linear isoquant. This indicates that land and construction services are perfectly substitutable. Any change in the price of one causes a shift to the other completely. However, the actual substitution between land and services depends on technical and institutional factors.

Prior to reporting on estimates of the construction technology, the various arguments and problems that follow from the foregoing model may be summarized.

1. Construction services are viewed as an index of nonland commodities. Such an aggregate should be tested for, since it contains labor, materials, and equipment and capital.

2. The value of construction services is usually the value of the house less the value of land. This involves "adding-up," or total revenue equals total costs, and may impose an implicit assumption of constant returns to scale on the construction technology.

3. Land is not obviously an input in the construction process. It may be both an input and an output. Additional lot size makes a house more valuable, all else being equal, but additional labor input in house production only may be an indication of inefficiency.

4. The technology may vary across geographical regions and across builders.

5. Building codes, zoning, and other restrictions impose constraints on the efficient production of housing. [18] These affect substitution possibilities by making the isoquants more L-shaped. [19]

The production function for housing services can be expressed in land and construction services:

$$H = H(L, S) \qquad (5.5)$$

The elasticity of substitution between L and S indicates the degree to which land can replace construction in production. It is the percentage increase in the ratio of construction services to land, or S/L, divided by the percentage increase in the relative user cost of land to construction, or U_L/U_S where U_S is the price of construction services. Suppose property taxes increase and they are properly accounted for in the user cost framework. As these increase, U_L also increases, making land relatively more expensive.

By assumption, housing is produced by only two goods, land and construction. Since the isoquant is convex to the origin, indicating a diminishing marginal rate of technical substitution, the elasticity of substitution is positive. Hence, S/L increases, and the industry substitutes construction for land.

In terms of estimation, a common data source is that for new single-family houses sold under the Federal Housing Administration (FHA) and United States Department of Housing and Urban Development (HUD) 203 program. In this sample, information for individual new homes is recorded concerning selling price, characteristics of construction, and appraised or assessed lot value. For Canada, Statistics Canada publishes a price index on new single-family houses, while CMHC publishes price indices for housing built under the National Housing Act.

The U.S. FHA–HUD data base suffers from a truncation problem. A price limit on houses is introduced, so that expensive houses are excluded. Since this is the dependent variable in the production function, there is likely to be some bias in estimation. Some studies also use aggregate data rather than individual housing transactions, so further distorting results.

An example of such estimates is reported in Table 5–3, from Robert Edelstein.[20] The FHA–HUD data were used, and the first column indicates the elasticity of substitution. Below the elasticity is its standard error. This is an indication of the variability of the estimate.

Table 5–3 Estimates of Elasticity of Substitution Between Land and Construction

Geographic Area	Elasticity	Land Share	Construction Share
Los Angeles–Long Beach SMSA	.58 (.15)	.24	.76
Three New Jersey counties in Philadelphia–Camden SMSA	1.43 (.17)	.16	.84
Two San Bernardino SMSA counties	.38 (.11)	.21	.79
San Diego SMSA	1.19 (.06)	.27	.73
Two San Francisco SMSA counties	.90 (.07)	.22	.78
Nine-county aggregate estimator	.31 (.33)	.21	.79

Source: R. H. Edelstein, "The Production Function for Housing and Its Implications for Future Urban Development," in G. W. Gau and M. A. Goldberg (eds.), *The Future of North American Housing Markets* (Cambridge, Mass.: Ballinger), 1983.

The ratio of the estimate to its standard error is a measure of statistical significance. If this ratio exceeds 1.96, one can say with 95 percent confidence that the estimate is not zero. If the elasticity is less than one, there is relative difficulty in substituting construction services for land. If it is greater than one, the reverse conclusion obtains. The results appear to have substantial regional variation. In the San Diego area, the elasticity of substitution is greater than one, but in Los Angeles it is 0.58. The results suggest that estimates of substitution remain unsettled. The last column indicates the share of construction costs in the total of construction and land costs. These typically appear to be at least 70 percent of the total.

SUMMARY

This chapter has developed concepts dealing with the supply of urban land and with improvements to the land. Expectations about future prices and interest rates were seen to affect the decision to offer land to the market. The supply of land also depends on government regulations. The supply side of the land market is not perfectly inelastic. This inelasticity affects the development of models of the land market. Finally, the supply of improvements was discussed and also shown to depend on interest rates and expectations, and additionally on taxes and the technology of production.[21]

Typically, the approval process is complex, with a series of stages. As an example layout, that for Halifax is indicated as Figure 5–4. The stages through which a developer must pass are many, and they cannot be completed in a short period. This required holding period increases the price of land and housing to the developer.

Footnotes

1. A. M. Weimer and H. Hoyt, *Principles of Real Estate,* (New York, Ronald Press Co), 1960, pp. 124–125; and M. A. Goldberg and B. Allan, "Urban Growth: A View from the Supply Side," *AREUEA Journal* (Fall 1978): 247–270.

2. If a mortgage is held, an adjustment is required over the term of loan.

3. In the United States, capital gains taxes exist but they may be deferred almost indefinitely.

4. J. de Chiara and L. Koppelman, *Site Planning Standards* (New York: McGraw-Hill), 1978, Section 1. Site surveying and planning is also discussed in Urban Land Institute, *Residential Development Handbook* (Washington, D.C.: Urban Land Institute), 1978, pp. 148–153: and R. Unterman and R. Small, *Site Planning for Cluster Housing* (New York: Van Nostrand Reinhold), 1977.

5. Site planning is discussed in K. Lynch, *Site Planning,* second edition (Cambridge, Mass.: MIT Press), 1971. An analog for Canada is Canada (Central) Mortgage

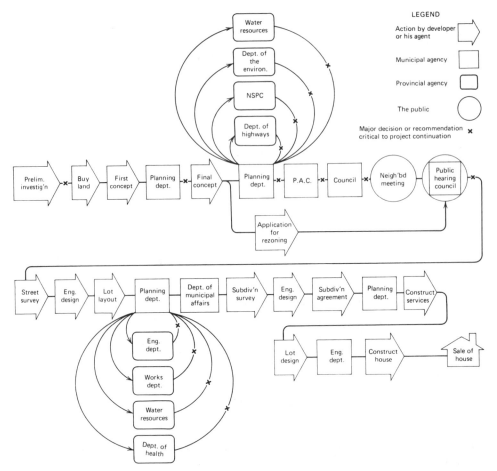

Figure 5–4. Development approval process, Halifax.
(Based on flow diagram by M. E. Lloyd & Assoc.)

and Housing Corporation (CMHC), *Site Planning Handbook* (Ottawa: Ontario, CMHC), 1978.
el72

6. The approval process is well discussed in the *Residential Development Handbook, op. cit.*

7. Albert F. Eger, *Subdivision Approval Time and the Supply of Subdivision Approvals: The Case of Ontario* (Montreal: Faculty of Management, McGill University), 1979.

8. Site servicing is discussed in the *Residential Development Handbook, op. cit.* See also the National Association of Home Builders, *Land Development Manual* (Washington, D.C.: National Association of Home Builders), 1974.

9. While the services are provided by the firms, the more relevant consideration is the incidence: Who ultimately pays depends on relative elasticities.

10. David E. Mills, "Market Power and Land Development Timing," *Land Economics* (February 1980): 10–20.

11. See the *Residential Development Handbook, op. cit.*

12. Michael E. Gleesan, "Effects of an Urban Growth Management System on Land Values," *Land Economics* (August 1979): 350–365; and David Dowall, "Reducing the Cost Effects of Local Land Use Controls," *Journal of the American Planning Association* (April 1981): 145–153.

13. See G. W. Davies, "A Model of the Urban Residential Land and Housing Markets," *Canadian Journal of Economics* (1977): 392–410.

14. See Michael A. Goldberg and Daniel Ulinder, "Residential Developer Behavior 1975: Additional Empirical Findings," *Land Economics* (August 1976): 363–370.

15. There may also be a speculative demand for land. As interest rates rise, more people expect them ultimately to fall. Those who buy land at the time of high rates may then gain as interest rates fall.

16. See, for example, L. B. Smith, "A Model of the Canadian Housing and Mortgage Markets," *Journal of Political Economy* 77 (1969): 795–816.

17. See Davies, *op. cit.*, p. 400.

18. The requirement is that relative prices are constant.

19. Additional issues on the substitution between land and construction services are raised in J. McDonald, "Capital-Land Substitution in Urban Housing: A Survey of Empirical Estimates", *Journal of Urban Economics* 9 (1980): 190–211.

20. Robert H. Edelstein, "The Production Function for Housing and Its Implications for Future Urban Development," in George W. Gau and Michael A. Goldberg, eds., *The Future of North American Housing Markets* (Cambridge, Mass.: Ballinger Books), 1983.

21. For a more comprehensive treatment, see John McMahan, *Property Development* (Toronto: McGraw-Hill Book Company), 1976.

6

FINANCING URBAN DEVELOPMENT: FINANCIAL MARKETS, ANALYTICAL TOOLS, AND THE PRIVATE SECTOR

FINANCING AND THE URBAN DEVELOPMENT PROCESS

Urban development is costly. Its capital requirements are enormous. To construct additional housing, shopping facilities, office buildings, and the infrastructure to support these developments requires massive expenditures by developers and governments. In this chapter and the one immediately following, we shall focus our attention on the financing of urban development. In this chapter our attention is directed toward private sector financing as we address questions related to capital markets and mortgage finance, and their interaction with the development process. In Chapter 7 we will look at public sector finances, with particular emphasis on local levels of government.

In the preceding chapter we explored the supply side of the market. Our discussion quickly turned to the urban development process and to the creation of new supplies of urban land and buildings. That discussion took place on the assumption that adequate financial resources were available to pay for new development (including redevelopment). In this chapter, we look at the conditions that give rise to adequate funding of urban development. We do this both from a macro point of view, looking at mortgage and capital markets and the availability of funds generally, and from a more micro point of view, focusing on the elements that comprise the financial decision-making process of both borrowers and lenders. This micro view necessarily takes us into the field of financial analysis with specific reference to the application of financial tools to real estate decisions. The focus is on private sector sources and uses of funds in the development process. The objective is to provide an understanding of the forces and factors that bear on the development process. A proper understanding of the private sector financing of urban development will significantly enhance our understanding of the supply of, and demand for, urban land and real property; it provides insights into the cyclical nature of the urban development process, and it will also provide a basic understanding of the financial environment within which the urban development process functions, and of the influence that this financial environment can exert. Without a proper appreciation of this financial environment and its workings, neither developers nor public policymakers can be expected to be able to make viable and economically sound decisions.

The Urban Development Process: A Review

The following stages have generally been identified as comprising the urban development process[1]

1. Site selection and locational analysis

2. Land assembly

3. Site planning, subdivision, and site servicing

4. Building construction

5. Selling and/or leasing land and/or buildings

6. Property management

All of the initial stages of the process require varying amounts of cash outlay, with longer-run returns as the lure. As the developer progresses through stages 1 to 4, the eventuality of receiving cash returns gets closer, but so do the magnitudes of the cash required.

For example, the site selection and locational analysis phase requires modest outlays for most residential subdivisions, usually on the order of several thousands of dollars, though the size of the outlay increases dramatically as the scale of the project grows. Thus, for large mixed-use projects the cost of preplanning and financial analysis can run into the millions of dollars, a significant outlay when the marketable product can be several years or even a decade or more away. Land assembly is considerably more expensive, running into the tens of thousands of dollars for smaller developments and perhaps tens of millions for large central-city and suburban sites.

In addition to these costly outlays, developers need significant staying power, since they find themselves in large negative cash flow positions until they can market the product, be it the finished lots or the finished building.[2] This requirement of staying power has grown in importance as approval and subdivision processes have grown increasingly complex in the quest for environmental quality and protection, placing additional burdens on the development industry.[3]

In view of both the magnitudes of the funds required and the long drought before these funds bear financial returns, we can begin to appreciate the economics of the urban development industry, based heavily on borrowed capital and significant waiting times before the capital earns a cash return. These twin forces of heavy capital outlays and cash flow shortages combine to put the development industry in the position of heavy borrowers, usually secured through placing mortgages on land and buildings. Debt is preferred to equity financing (except for the larger public real estate companies) because developers are famous (or notorious) for their entrepreneurial spirit, a spirit that resents the loss of control invariably associated with equity participation.

The Mortgage Market in Capsule Form

Having established the needs of the various stages in development for capital, we can examine the principal borrowers who participate in the development process, as well as the lenders.

The Borrowers   There are three primary borrowers:

1. Subdividers and land developers

2. Developers of built form

3. Final consumers

Subdividers and Land Developers   We will exclude from this group the pure speculator who merely purchases raw land for speculative purposes, with no intention of servicing or improving it. While an important element in the development process, these so-called pre-development landholders have more modest capital requirements and can often pay for their holding costs through agricultural rents, in the case of rural/urban fringe land, or through such underdeveloped uses as parking lots in the case of urban land. The first people who need to expend significant sums are the subdividers and land developers who must purchase the land and pay for planning and subdividing it as well as for the engineering services that enable the land to be occupied for urban uses (assuming it is undeveloped fringe land initially). As a minimum, these would include roads, sewers, water, and utilities. The precise level of these site services varies from jurisdiction to jurisdiction, and as servicing standards increase, so do the costs of development, the gestation period of the development, and the need for additional financial resources.[4]

Developers of Built Form   Here we are including all those developers who begin with vacant or underutilized land or buildings and who bring their entrepreneurial skills to bear on the site to end up with either new or improved buildings. This phase of the development process can require extraordinary amounts of capital when one considers that central-city land can sell for as much as $5000 per square foot in cities such as Hong Kong and Tokyo, and that buildings can cost more than $100 per square foot (in 1983 dollars) to construct. In the case of a central-city office building of perhaps 100,000 square feet on a site of 10,000 square feet, the developer might spend $10 million on the building and another $5 million on the land and have to wait several years for tenants to move in and begin to receive a return. Larger projects can run into the hundreds of millions of dollars with correspondingly long waits until rental or sales income begins flowing. Developers seldom have cash resources even approximating as much as 25 percent of the cost of these developments and must resort to debt financing, through bank loans and/or mortgages.

Consumers   The final user of such built form can be a large corporation occupying offices, small merchants occupying retail space in a shopping mall, or households occupying apartments or condominiums or engaged in traditional outright ownership of a house and its land. Large businesses seldom have to borrow to occupy their premises: They either pay rent or use cash from normal business activity. Smaller merchants often must resort to debt financing to improve their premises. However, with a growing trend toward condominium ownership of stores and offices, increasingly smaller businesses must resort to mortgage financing. Housing consumers, in contrast, virtually always must resort to mortgage financing, the largest single form of debt financing in either Canada or the United States.

Summary   Financing, usually through debt, of the development of real property has been common practice, necessitated by the large outlays required in the development process and the waiting time until they bear cash returns. Mortgage financing has also been commonplace for the purchaser of housing as few households can afford to buy housing outright, given the magnitude of the purchase relative to annual incomes of households. However, with the trend toward nonresidential condominium development, we can expect to see small business consumers of real property added to households as demanders of mortgage financing. Developers have been shifting to eventual consumers the problem of financing the final product in the long run.

The Lenders   The largest lenders include

1.   Banks (national in Canada; national and state in the United States)

2. Thrift institutions (credit unions and trust companies in Canada; savings and loan associations and mutual savings banks in the United States)

3. Life insurance companies

4. Government (primarily federal governments, with growing state and provincial governmental involvement)

In addition to these institutions, private individuals, pension funds, and mortgage loan companies contribute funds to the mortgage markets of the United States and Canada.

REAL ESTATE CREDIT

In the preceding discussion we identified two quite different users of credit in the urban development process: those in need of capital to improve the land and/or build or rebuild structures on the land, and those who are final purchasers of this developed real property. In the above dichotomy, developers who keep their developments for long-term rental income are also the ultimate purchasers, and thus appear in both groups.[5]

The two forms of credit break down into credit required to develop real property and credit required to purchase or prepay long-term leases for this developed property. The first form of credit is called interim financing and revolves around the construction and development process (often called C & D loans). This short-term credit enables the developer to assemble and service the land or build the buildings. The second kind of credit is needed for the longer-run purchase or lease of the developed property and is referred to as permanent, or takeout, financing, usually done through a mortgage on the finished property.

Interim Financing

In their book, *Real Estate Financing*, Fred Case and John Clapp define interim financing as "short term loans designed to bridge the gap between the time money is needed (e.g., for construction) and the time a permanent debt or equity investor is found (e.g., the completed property is sold)."[6] Interim financing provides the working capital with which the developer can bring a project from an idea through to a marketable, finished product. Because a finished product is obtained only at the end of the process, these loans are also riskier (and costlier), since half-finished office buildings do not have the same value as completed and occupied buildings, even when adjusted for proportion completed.

Developers must rely on this more costly interim financing (often 2 to 3 percentage points higher than mortgage rates) to buy land, service it, and buy building materials, architectural and engineering services, and construction labor, all required by the development process. Interim funds are used to finance all of the interim stages of the process leading up to and including the finished product, be that product a residential lot or a large shopping center.

To see where these funds come from, we can look at Tables 6–1 and 6–2 based on U.S. data for 1970–74 and 1977 (in order). Unfortunately, no similar Canadian data exist on interim financing, though these exist for long-term mortgage financing.

Forms of interim financing exist other than financing for construction *per se*.[7] Many land loans are made to nondevelopers and thus cannot be construed as interim financing. Tables 6–1 and 6–2 give us some insights into the sources of credit for other phases of the development process than the finished product. In the case of land loans, the commercial banks dominated the market with over 45 percent of the loan originations in 1974. Savings and loans and mutual savings banks together accounted for 16 percent of the originations, in marked contrast to the picture that emerges from Table 6–2, where thrift institutions accounted for 39 percent of the construction loans outstanding. Commercial banks still held the lion's share of construction loans with nearly 42 percent of the outstanding loans. If there is one common theme from these two tables it is that commercial banks play an extremely important role in the provision of funds for the early stages of the development process (e.g., land acquisition and construction). A very different picture obtains in the distribution of permanent mortgage financing.

Long-Term Mortgage Financing

Having obtained sufficient interim financing to complete a development, the developer must find a longer-term source of funds to finance the completed project.[8] This long-term financing usually takes the form of a mortgage loan from a financial institution, where the finished development is the collateral for securing the loan.[9]

Since the mortgage loan is a long-term commitment compared with the short-term nature of interim loans, we should expect that different lending objectives would be fulfilled by mortgage loans and, correspondingly, that a different mix of lenders would be apparent than in the case of interim financing. This is borne out by looking at the data in Table 6–3. Commercial banks are no longer the dominant lenders. In 1977 commercial banks in the United States held $129.5 billion in outstanding mortgages, compared with the $386.9 billion held by thrift institutions (savings and loan associations and mutual savings banks). Of the total $754.6 billion in outstanding long-term mortgage loans, thrift institutions held over 50 percent of these mortgages in their portfolios, commercial banks accounted for roughly 17 percent of the total, life insurance companies just under 12 percent and federal credit agencies held just under 10 percent.

Table 6–1 Origination of Land Loans (dollars in millions)

Year	Commercial Banks	Mutual Savings Banks	Sales	Insurance Companies	Mortgage Companies	Investment Trusts	Misc. Lenders	Total
1970	$1006	$ 80	$ 505	$103	$ 294	$ 563	$ 9	$2560
1971	2273	80	763	61	728	865	25	4795
1972	2449	173	1188	71	1062	1588	1	6532
1973	3552	144	1128	75	1572	2486	5	8962
1974	3143	129	1019	106	1385	1150	2	6934

Source: Arnold Diamond, *The Supply of Mortgage of Credit, 1970–1974* (Washington: U.S. Department of Housing and Urban Development), 1975, p. 121.

Table 6–2 Construction Loan Holdings, by Type of Property and Lender, End of Second Quarter, 1977 (percent of total dollar amount)

Type of Property	Commercial Banks	Savings and Loan Assns	Mortgage Investment Trusts	Mortgage Companies	Life Insurance Companies	State and Local Credit Agencies	Mutual Savings Banks	All Others[a]
1–4 Family	28.8	56.8	2.6	9.3	0.1	0.1	2.3	—
Multifamily	36.4	25.3	11.8	9.2	0.4	13.5	3.0	0.4
Nonresidential	61.0	18.9	7.4	7.9	2.3	—	2.0	0.5
Total	41.8	36.7	6.2	8.8	0.9	2.9	2.3	0.4

Source: U.S. Department of Housing and Urban Development, *HUD News*, December 12, 1977, Table 24.
[a]All other groups include noninstitutional pension funds, state and local retirement funds, and federal credit agencies.

Table 6–3 Holdings of Construction, Long-Term Mortgage, and Land Loans, by Type of Loan 1970 to 1980, and by Lender (in billions of dollars, as of end of year)

Type of loan	1970	1975	1976	1977	1978	1979	1980	Total (1981)	1981 — Lender					
									Savings and loan Assn.	Commercial banks	Mutual savings banks	Life insurance companies	Federal credit agencies	Mortgage pools
Mortgage credit, total	422.0	731.3	805.2	925.8	1064.8	1214.1	1317.4	1399.0	517.9	282.7	99.3	135.6	140.2	149.6
Construction Loans	18.3	41.4	37.2	45.0	54.2	59.4	62.6	67.8	18.3	39.9	1.9	.8	2.6	—
1–4 unit family homes	5.4	12.9	15.3	22.0	26.2	26.6	26.4	5.5	11.5	2.6	.6	—	—	—
Multi family residential	6.2	11.6	9.4	9.4	11.0	12.7	13.8	4.5	.2	6.9	.7	—	2.6	—
Non residential	6.5	16.9	12.5	13.6	16.9	20.1	22.4	7.8	4.6	20.4	.6	.8	—	—
Farm properties	.1	—	—	—	—	—	—	—	—	—	—	—	—	—
Long-term mortgage loans	399.5	678.8	757.3	871.0	999.8	1140.7	1241.8	1319.0	493.4	237.7	97.1	134.5	137.7	149.6
1–4 unit family homes	266.9	434.5	493.0	578.7	677.6	786.1	857.2	908.9	424.6	155.0	67.9	16.9	70.7	134.2
FHA-insured	61.9	67.8	71.5	74.6	80.8	95.3	104.9	112.8	10.7	4.1	9.7	4.1	23.4	51.7
VA-guaranteed	37.2	56.8	61.7	69.1	75.3	85.8	91.1	94.6	14.2	2.4	10.3	2.6	12.8	48.9
Conventional	167.8	309.9	359.8	434.9	521.5	605.3	661.2	701.5	399.7	148.5	47.9	10.2	34.5	33.6
Multifamily	45.8	81.9	87.4	93.8	100.9	108.4	113.9	118.1	35.8	7.1	14.2	18.9	6.4	.1
Nonresidential	66.4	128.4	139.0	154.8	171.3	188.5	204.9	217.7	32.6	67.3	15.0	85.7	16.7	.1
Farm properties	20.3	33.8	37.9	43.7	49.9	57.7	65.7	74.3	.4	8.3	13.1	43.8	7.2	
Land loans	4.2	11.1	10.7	9.8	10.9	11.7	13.0	12.2	6.1	5.0	.2	.3	—	—

Source: U.S. Dept. of Housing and Urban Development, *The Supply of Mortgage Credit, 1970–1979,* and monthly and quarterly press releases based on Survey of Mortgage Lending Activity. Also in U.S. Bureau of the Census, *Statistical Abstract of the United States 1982,* (Washington: Government Printing Office) Table 841, p. 511.

Table 6–4 provides an analogous view of the distribution of Canadian mortgage loans. In sharp contrast with the U.S. situation, no single financial institution or sector dominates. Trust companies and chartered banks held about 20 percent of the stock of outstanding mortgages each in 1981 and were the largest holders of mortgage loans, while life insurance companies, credit unions, and government each held about 15 percent of the stock. It appears from these data that the stock of outstanding mortgages is much more diffused in Canada than in the United States.

MORTGAGES AND MORTGAGE MARKETS

Our discussion of mortgages and mortgage markets requires significant institutional knowledge and represents the first point at which institutional details become critical. Of direct concern are the workings of the financial institutions that provide credit to the urban development process, as well as the government policies and rules that affect the provision of credit, including direct government involvement in mortgage and mortgage-related capital markets. The following analysis, with its emphasis on financial and government institutions, is therefore intended to provide specifics on the mortgage market and also to introduce the importance of this kind of institutional analysis in the understanding of market function.[10]

In a most thought-provoking essay on "Institutionalism and Urban Land Economics," Richard Ratcliff observed that there is an essential need to consider both institutions and economic abstractions when confronting actual decisions.[11] He concludes by stressing the need to consider institutions both in time and place explicitly: Institutions change over time and from place to place. We are frequently blind to the very significant impacts that institutions, often hidden from view by their very familiarity, have on the day-to-day functioning of our lives.

Fortunately, the comparison employed here helps to make institutions and their roles explicit. By observing how real property markets function in two very different institutional settings we can better appreciate both the general market forces and the specific institutional forces that shape those markets. This point will become clear immediately when we look at the mortgage markets in the United States and Canada and see two very different sets of institutional arrangements and forces. In the first case explored below, the problem is to provide adequate financial resources to the urban development process. Canadian and U.S. mortgage markets and government policies have evolved quite different means for realizing this goal, these differences flowing from deep-seated underlying institutional variants.[12]

Our comparative view meshes neatly with our institutional analyses to yield a powerful approach to defining and treating urban issues.

Table 6–4 Mortgage Loans Outstanding by Holder of Loan, 1934–1980 (millions of dollars), CANADA

Period	Lending Institutions					Governments and Government Agencies	Corporate Lenders	Other Companies	Pension Funds	Estates, Trusts, and Agency Funds of Trust	Total
	Life Insurance Companies	Chartered Banks	Loan Companies	Trust Companies	Credit Unions						
1934	420	—	190	99	—	164	76	28	—	—	977
1935	405	—	183	97	—	155	69	26	—	—	935
1936	393	—	177	98	—	160	66	24	—	—	917
1937	390	—	172	98	—	169	65	23	—	—	917
1938	393	—	172	91	—	180	62	21	—	—	919
1939	401	—	174	89	—	189	61	14	—	—	928
1940	412	—	169	86	—	193	59	14	—	—	933
1941	404	—	164	77	—	193	58	14	—	—	910
1942	396	—	158	80	—	185	57	14	—	—	890
1943	374	—	149	75	—	170	53	13	—	—	834
1944	360	—	139	69	—	151	45	13	—	—	777
1945	339	—	137	66	—	151	39	14	—	—	746
1946	372	—	152	70	—	189	34	16	—	—	833
1947	456	—	173	77	—	248	34	19	—	—	1,007
1948	591	—	201	87	—	276	34	17	—	—	1,206
1949	729	—	232	99	—	350	35	21	—	—	1,466
1950	901	—	265	113	—	459	38	24	—	—	1,800
1951	1,077	—	289	128	111	595	42	26	—	—	2,268
1952	1,214	—	314	136	129	674	46	29	—	—	2,542
1953	1,402	—	352	149	155	768	49	33	—	—	2,908
1954	1,658	74	396	178	171	850	49	42	—	—	3,418
1955	2,016	294	444	228	211	868	66	43	—	—	4,170
1956	2,408	493	497	268	236	893	85	57	—	—	4,937
1957	2,660	586	521	275	262	973	114	70	—	—	5,461
1958	2,875	790	569	343	295	1,337	125	80	—	—	6,414
1959	3,140	968	629	409	341	1,681	326	88	—	—	7,582
1960	3,412	971	698	472	390	1,995	524	97	299	534	9,392
1961	3,710	953	815	622	426	2,229	759	119	341	667	10,641

Table 6-4 (Continued)

Period	Lending Institutions					Governments and Government Agencies	Corporate Lenders	Other Companies	Pension Funds	Estates, Trusts, and Agency Funds of Trust	Total
	Life Companies	Chartered Banks	Loan Companies	Trust Companies	Credit Unions						
1962	4,142	921	989	845	479	2,410	989	144	414	865	12,198
1963	4,560	885	1,118	1,103	549	2,531	1,371	175	479	1,069	13,910
1964	5,094	846	1,492	1,449	622	2,823	1,642	210	542	1,307	16,027
1965	5,662	810	1,839	1,975	695	3,222	1,930	276	623	1,586	18,618
1966	6,248	778	1,949	2,169	883	3,879	1,998	310	676	1,817	20,707
1967	6,636	840	2,073	2,414	1,060	5,006	1,989	319	724	1,966	23,027
1968	7,107	1,057	2,235	2,727	1,105	5,732	2,068	335	776	2,133	25,275
1969	7,490	1,324	2,508	3,264	1,202	6,400	1,980	343	863	2,555	27,929
1970	7,723	1,481	2,868	3,829	1,353	7,221	2,052	382	1,022	2,714	30,645
1971	7,880	2,338	3,152	4,480	1,660	8,183	2,079	400	1,169	2,768	34,109
1972	8,145	3,508	3,749	5,462	2,391	8,865	2,186	387	1,296	2,886	38,875
1973	8,768	4,713	4,753	7,194	3,360	9,500	2,416	438	1,551	3,390	46,083
1974	9,569	6,307	5,509	8,846	4,175	10,300	2,098	506	1,926	4,386	53,622
1975	10,364	8,039	6,560	10,542	5,205	11,100	2,518	581	2,479	4,983	62,371
1976	11,494	9,385	7,452	13,170	6,821	12,073	2,208	791	3,216	6,288	72,898
1977	12,916	12,089	7,707	16,938	9,167	12,868	2,741	909	4,005	7,050	86,390
1978	13,187	15,569	8,297	20,479	11,653	13,104	3,287	996	4,748	9,605	100,925
1979	14,811	18,580	9,976	24,384	13,982	13,114	3,477	1,129	5,320	9,997	114,770
1980	16,319	19,105	12,956	26,814	15,619	13,698	3,543	1,192	5,821	10,525	125,592
1981	17,792	30,901	17,311	27,888	16,321	14,782	2,972	3,014	6,208	11,359	148,548

Source: Canada Mortgage and Housing Corporation, *Annual Housing Statistics* (Ottawa, Ont.: CMHC), 1982, Table 74, p. 64.

It is a view considerably richer and potentially much more productive than one based on economic analysis and knowledge of only one institutional setting. Accordingly, we begin by applying this comparative institutional method to our study of workings of mortgage markets.

The Importance of Mortgage Markets in North America

Mortgages represent a massive portion of the capital markets of the United States and Canada, exceeding in magnitude much more highly touted corporate and consumer debt. Tables 6–5 and 6–6 give us some idea of the scale of the mortgage markets in both Canada and the United States.

Mortgage debt is enormous in both countries. In the United States, where public concern is often expressed about the size of the national debt, we see that total government debt outstanding for all levels of government does not equal mortgage debt outstanding. In 1981 total government indebtedness represented only about two-thirds of the mortgage debt outstanding in the United States. Table 6–6 presents analogous data for Canada, where the picture is equally dramatic: Mortgage debt greatly exceeds all government outstanding debt, and in 1981 government debt was only 63 percent of mortgage debt.

If we compare the importance of mortgage debt for the major lending institutions in Canada and the United States, mortgages represent an important investment. Tables 6–7 and 6–8 compare the financial structure of the major mortgage lending institutions. For example, in 1980 mortgages represented 17 percent of commercial bank assets and 80.0 percent of of savings and loan association assets in the United States. In Canada, where all banks are federally chartered and where there are no savings and loan associations, we see a somewhat different pattern. For 1981, chartered banks had just 8.8 percent of their assets in mortgages, with a legal limit of 10 percent, while trust companies and credit unions had 63.9 percent and 40.9 percent of their assets, respectively, in mortgages. The only financial institutions that are not heavily dependent on mortgage loans are banks. For the remaining institutions, mortgages represent a large and very important component of their loan portfolios and assets.

The interdependence of mortgages and other financial instruments is illustrated by Tables 6–9 and 6–10, which present interest rate movements over the past 17 years for major financial instruments in the United States and Canada. From both tables, mortgage rates move in concert with other interest rates, though there are some noticeable lags in interest rates for mortgages in both the United States and Canada, a phenomenon that has attracted the attention of researchers trying to ascertain the reasons for this observed *stickiness* in mortgage rates.[13]

Table 6-5 Mortgages, Government and Corporate Debt, United States, 1961–1982

Year	%	Securities Outstanding[a]	%	Total Mortgages Outstanding[b]	%	New Corporate Bonds Issued[c]	%	New Preferred Stock Issued[c]	%	New Common Stock Issued[c]	Gross National Product[d]
1961	59	305066	37	190400	1.8	9420	.09	450	.6	3294	518700
1962	56	312845	38	210600	1.6	8969	.08	422	.2	1314	560300
1963	54	320638	40	234000	1.8	10872	.06	342	.2	1022	590500
1964	52	329547	41	259800	1.7	10865	.07	412	.4	2679	632400
1965	49	332229	48	325800	2.0	13720	.05	360	.2	1438	683900
1966	46	340705	47	347000	2.1	15561	.08	574	.3	1939	743300
1967	45	359466	47	369800	2.8	21954	.1	885	.2	1595	793900
1968	45	384796	46	396900	2.0	17383	.07	637	.5	3946	864200
1969	41	380081	46	450000	2.0	18348	.07	682	.8	7714	929100
1970	43	407364	49	452000	2.5	24365	.1	1310	.7	6849	982400
1971	43	449063	48	500000	3.1	32129	.4	3670	.9	9291	1046800
1972	40	472953	48	565000	1.4	16921	.2	2411	.9	10328	1171100
1973	38	493869	47	618000	1.0	12899	.2	2398	.6	7606	1306300
1974	37	517015	48	673500	1.8	25335	.1	1745	.3	3947	1406900
1975	41	607207	49	727600	2.1	31492	.2	3088	.5	7179	1498900
1976	41	688813	47	806100	1.5	25263	.1	2353	.5	8296	1700100
1977	41	765669	54	1020000	1.2	21929	.1	2421	.4	7857	1887200
1978	39	837807	54	1169000	.8	18881	.08	1759	.35	7760	2156100
1979	37	888590	55	1327000	1.1	26468	.08	1965	.35	8581	2413900
1980	37	978662	55	1452000	1.6	44110	.12	3195	.7	18717	2626100
1981	37	1076032	53	1545000	1.3	38615	.06	1633	.84	24716	2925500
1982	—	—	—	1560000	—	—	—	—	—	—	—

Source: [a]Board of Governors of the Federal Reserve System, *Federal Reserve Bulletin* (Washington: Board of Governors of the Federal Reserve System), Tables 1.41 and 1.46.
[b]U.S. Bureau of the Census, *Statistical Abstract of the United States, 1982,* Table 842, p. 512.
[c]U.S. Bureau of the Census, *Statistical Abstract of the United States, 1982,* Table 858, p. 518.
[d]Board of Governors of the Federal Reserve System, *Federal Reserve Bulletin,* Table 2.16.

Table 6–6 Mortgages, Government and Corporate Debt, Canada, 1961–1982

Year	%	Gov't Securities Outstanding[a]	%	Total Mortgages Outstanding[b]	%	New Residential Mortgages Approved[c]	%	New Corporate Bonds Issued[c]	%	New Preferred Stock Issued[e]	%	New Common Stock Issued[e]	Gross National Product[f]
1961			27	10641	2.7	1086							39646
1962			28	12198	2.8	1221							42927
1963			30	13910	3.2	1468							45978
1964	41	20733	32	16027	3.6	1805	2.7	1373	.2	115	.8	409	50280
1965	37	20681	34	18618	3.6	1971	3.5	1963	.5	255	.5	293	55364
1966	34	21011	33	20707	2.0	1236	2.7	1672	.4	238	.6	389	61828
1967	33	22011	35	23027	2.6	1756	2.2	1479	.3	180	.4	269	66409
1968	32	23556	35	25275	3.3	2367	2.0	1444	.2	122	.6	448	72586
1969	30	23902	35	27929	3.0	2362	1.9	1547	.2	143	1.1	852	79815
1970	30	25746	36	30645	2.5	2120	2.6	2196	.2	101	.3	251	85685
1971	30	28277	36	34109	4.1	3829	2.8	2687	.2	111	.2	230	94450
1972	28	29873	37	38875	4.7	4901	2.3	2473	.2	199	.5	420	105234
1973	24	29737	37	46083	5.6	6971	1.9	2295	.1	84	.4	527	123560
1974	23	33947	36	53622	4.0	5954	1.9	2819	.3	475	.2	318	147528
1975	23	37920	38	62371	5.4	8972	2.4	4027	.4	710	.3	547	165343
1976	22	42152	38	72898	5.3	10201	2.7	5228	.4	684	.3	591	191031
1977	24	50172	41	86390	7.0	14609	3.1	6570	1.1	2445	.3	697	208868
1978	28	64310	44	100925	6.0	13887	2.7	6242	2.6	5886	.5	1097	230490
1979	27	70600	44	114770	5.4	14049	1.7	4405	.6	1648	1.1	2862	261576
1980	28	82659	43	125581	4.1	11988	2.0	5736	3.9	2559	1.0	2814	291869
1981	28	94148	45	148548	2.7	8971	2.6	8459	1.1	3521	.8	2643	331338
1982	32	112434	—	—	3.1	10673	2.1	7308	.8	2736	.3	1137	348925

Sources: [a]*Bank of Canada Review* (Ottawa, Ont.: Bank of Canada), 1983, Table 21.
[b]Central Mortgage and Housing Corporation, *Canadian Housing Statistics, 1983*, Table 74.
[c]Central Mortgage and Housing Corporation, *Canadian Housing Statistics, 1983*, Table 33.
[d]*Bank of Canada Review*, March 1983, Table 33.
[e]Statistics Canada, *Canadian Statistical Review* (Ottawa, Ont.: Statistics Canada), May 1982, Table 1.2.
[f]*Bank of Canada Review*, March, 1983, Table 52.

Table 6-7 U.S. Assets and Mortgage Loans of Lending Institutions (in millions)

Year	Commercial Banks[b,e]	Savings & Loans Associations[a]	Mutual[a] Savings	Credit[a] Unions	Life Insurance Companies[a]	Finance Companies[c]
			Cash Disbursements			
1968	265259	140373	54693		92236	
1969	295547	148838	57605		95816	
1970	313334	159657	60030		101348	
1971	320900	184981	64877		104393	
1972	378900	218772	70542		108078	
1973	449000	250850	77102		115625	67700
1974	500200	272284	78703	24432	124481	73300
1975	496900	307380	81244	28169	130605	75300
1976	578734	356183	86813	34384	135888	83400
1977	657513	420091	94405	42055	145455	99200
1978	695443	478794	102352	51807	160324	116000
1979	na	532621	108161	53125	170809	136000
1980	na	572784	111598	47774	204193	145900
1981	na	601088	114750	50448	221909	166100
		All Mortgages as Percentage of Total Assets				
1968	7.4	85	75		37	
1969	14	87	76		37	
1970	13	85	73		35	
1971	13	85	69		34	
1972	14	85	67		32	
1973	15	85	69		32	
1974	15	84	68		33	
1975	15	82	64		31	
1976	15	82	61		28	
1977	16	83	60		28	
1978	18	83	60		27	
1979	18	82	61		27	
1980	17	80	58		27	
1981	na	78	57		27	
		All Mortgage Loans Outstanding				
1968	65700	130802	53456		69973	
1969	70700	140347	56138		72027	
1970	73300	150331	57948		73227	
1971	82500	174250	62069		75496	
1972	99300	206182	67563		76948	
1973	119100	231733	73231		81369	
1974	132100	249293	74891		86234	
1975	136500	278590	77221		89167	
1976	151200	323005	81630		91552	
1977	179000	381163	88195		96848	
1978	214000	432808	95157		106167	
1979	245200	475688	98908		118421	
1980	263600	503192	99865		131080	
1981	na	518350	99997		139046	

154

Table 6–7 (Continued)

Year	Commercial Banks[b,e]	Savings & Loans Asso- ciations[a]	Mutual[a] Savings	Credit[a] Unions	Life Insurance Companies[a]	Finance Companies
			Total Assets* (D = December; Q4 = 4th quarter)			
1968	500,657	154451	71153		187695	
1969	530,665	162149	74144		197208	
1970	576,242	176183	78995		207254	
1971	640,225	206023	89370		222102	
1972	739,033	243127	100592		239730	
1973	835,024	271905	106650		252436	72200
1974	919,600	295524	109550	31948	263349	79600
1975	964,900	338233	121056	38037	289304	81600
1976	1,030,700	391907	134812	45225	321552	89200
1977	1,145,400	459241	147287	54084	351722	104300
1978	1,303,900	523542	158174	62348	389924	122400
1979	1,480,300	578962	163405	65854	432282	140900
1980	1,702,700	630712	171564	71709	479210	150100
1981	1,765,800	663844	175728[D]	77682[D]	521354[D]	1714000[Q4]

*Credit Union total assets are "Total Assets/Liabilities Capital"; Commercial Bank total assets are "Total Assets/Total Liabilities."

Sources: [a]Board of Governors of the Federal Reserve System, *Federal Reserve Bulletin,* Table 1.38 (Table 1.37 for 1978–81).
[b]Board of Governors of the Federal Reserve System, *Federal Reserve Bulletin,* Table 1.24 (Table A–14 for pre-1976).
[c]Board of Governors of the Federal Reserve System, *Federal Reserve Bulletin,* Table 1.521.
[d]U.S. Bureau of the Census, *Statistical Abstract of the United States, 1981,* Table 847 (1979-81), p. 511.

Finally, to put mortgage debt in a more global perspective, compare mortgage debt and the gross national product over the post-1960 period (see Tables 6–5 and 6–6). In 1960 mortgage debt represented 40.9 percent of U.S. GNP and only 24.5 percent of Canadian GNP. Admittedly the former is a stock concept, while the latter represents a flow. By 1981 the figure for the U.S. had risen to 58.0 percent of GNP, while for Canada, in 1981, mortgage debt had grown to 38.5 percent of GNP. The growth in Canadian mortgage debt is entirely consistent with the boom in housing prices that occurred in Canada during the 1970s. If we assume that the mortgages in force have an average rate of interest of 10 percent in the United States and 12 percent in Canada, we see that servicing these mortgages only requires about 5 percent of GNP in each country.

Development of U.S. and Canadian Mortgage Markets

It is the function of capital markets to transfer capital from those sectors in society with excess funds (typically, households through savings, businesses through retained earnings and positive net cash flows, and financial institutions) to those sectors that require funds for continuing their operations or for expanding their physical capital stock (housing

Table 6–8 Assets and Mortgage Loans of Lending Institutions, 1972–1981

Period	Life Insurance Companies		Chartered Banks[b]	Loan Companies[c]	Trust Companies[d]	Credit Unions	All Lending Institutions	Other Lending Institutions[e]	Estate Trust & Agent Funds & Trust Co.'s[f]
	Sample of 16 Companies	All Life Companies							
Cash Disbursements (millions of dollars)									
1972	777	810	1,401	1,277	1,426	**	4,914	40	**
1973	1,123	1,184	1,956	1,625	2,922	**	7,687	61	**
1974	1,144	1,297	1,858	1,899	2,865	**	7,919	52	**
1975	1,149	1,327	2,150	2,253	2,917	**	8,647	153	**
1976	1,320	1,529	2,518	1,845	3,757	**	9,649	224	**
1977	1,866	2,204	4,207	2,473	4,725	**	13,609	205	**
1978	1,912	2,023	4,685	2,728	5,867	**	15,303	339	**
1979	2,208	2,367	5,175	3,196	6,344	**	17,082	318	**
1980	1,903	2,185	4,057	2,595	5,197	**	14,034	225	**
1981	1,768	2,170	2,337	3,916	4,174	**	12,597	257	**
Repayments (millions of dollars)									
1972	553	590	304	431	563	**	1,888	24	**
1973	607	623	448	590	884	**	2,545	24	**
1974	592	587	567	606	896	**	2,656	26	**
1975	588	628	734	605	911	**	2,878	81	**
1976	615	735	861	498	979	**	3,073	75	
1977	768	866	1,404	944	1,404	**	4,618	78	
1978	888	848	1,825	1,277	2,104	**	6,054	181	**
1979	891	854	1,995	1,206	2,337	**	6,392	152	**
1980	867	759	1,677	1,107	2,688	**	6,231	163	**
1981	854	793	1,226	1,344	3,135	**	6,498	198	**
All Mortgage Loans Outstanding (millions of dollars)[a]									
1972	6,179	8,145	3,508	3,749	5,462	2,391	23,255	387	2,866
1973	7,221	8,768	4,713	4,753	7,194	3,360	28,788	438	3,390
1974	7,754	9,569	6,307	5,509	8,846	4,175	34,406	506	4,386
1975	8,315	10,364	8,039	6,560	10,542	5,205	40,710	581	4,983
1976	9,020	11,494	9,385	7,452	13,170	6,821	48,322	791	6,288
1977	10,117	12,916	12,089	7,707	16,938	9,176	58,817	909	7,050
1978	11,141	13,187	15,569	8,297	20,479	11,653	69,185	996	9,605
1979	12,459	14,811	18,580	9,976	24,384	13,982	81,733	1,129	9,997
1980	13,494	16,319	19,105	12,956	26,814	15,619	90,813	1,192	10,525
1981	14,409	17,792	30,901	17,311	27,888	16,321	110,213	3,014	11,359

Total Assets (millions of dollars)[b]

Year									
1972	15,103	63,222	18,037	4,778	8,601	8,364	103,002	935	27,667
1973	16,317	79,754	19,681	5,913	10,509	10,425	126,282	1,044	29,454
1974	17,536	97,015	21,038	6,743	12,443	12,235	149,474	1,155	30,121
1975	19,183	108,378	23,531	8,017	14,604	15,393	169,923	1,232	34,443
1976	21,212	126,403	26,462	9,226	18,335	18,847	199,273	1,516	38,217
1977	23,677	150,447	29,776	9,274	23,203	23,856	236,586	1,763	44,011
1978	26,307	189,100	33,485	10,285	27,906	28,892	289,668	1,706	53,241
1979	29,183	229,151	37,864	12,330	33,373	32,567	345,285	1,972	60,636
1980	32,378	281,244	43,172	16,075	38,968	37,010	416,469	2,104	69,399
1981	36,494	349,741	55,613	20,691	43,641	39,864	509,510	4,652	78,584

All Mortgages as Percent of Total Assets

Year									
1972	44.5	5.5	78.5	63.5	28.6	22.6	41.4	10.4	45.2
1973	44.3	5.9	80.4	68.5	32.2	22.8	42.0	11.6	44.6
1974	44.2	6.5	81.7	71.1	34.1	23.0	43.8	14.6	45.5
1975	43.3	7.4	81.8	72.2	33.8	24.0	47.2	14.5	44.0
1976	42.5	7.4	80.8	71.8	36.2	24.3	52.2	16.5	43.4
1977	42.7	8.0	83.1	73.0	38.4	24.9	51.6	16.0	43.4
1978	42.3	8.2	80.7	73.4	40.3	23.9	58.4	18.0	39.4
1979	42.7	8.1	80.9	73.1	42.9	23.7	57.3	16.5	39.1
1980	41.7	6.8	80.6	68.8	42.2	21.8	56.7	15.2	37.8
1981	39.5	8.8	83.7	63.9	40.9	21.6	64.8	14.5	32.0

[a]Bank of Canada Review.

[b]Mortgage Loans of Chartered Banks exclude any reserves or appropriations for losses.

Source: Banks of Canada Review.

[c]From 1976 on, figures have been revised to exclude Mortgage Investment Corporations.

Source: Statistics Canada, Financial Statistics, Cat. No. 61-006.

[d]Source: Statistics Canada, Financial Statistics, Cat. No. 61-006.

[e]Includes Quebec savings banks, mutual benefit and fraternal societies.

From 1976 on, figures have been revised to include Mortgage Investment Corporations, and from 1978 on, figures include Quebec savings banks and Mortgage Investment Corporations.

Source: Statistics Canada, Financial Statistics, Cat. No. 61-006.

[f]Include funds administered for trusteed pension plans.

[g]Includes agreements for sale.

[h]Excludes companies without mortgage loans outstanding except in case of estates, trust and agency funds.

Canada Housing Statistics, 1982, table 71, page 61.

Sources: Central Mortgage and Housing Corporation, Canadian Housing Statistics, Table 71, p. 61

Table 6–9   Bond Yields, Stock Yields, Mortgage Rates (U.S.)

Year	Long-term Federal Gov't Bonds	Long-term Corporate Bonds 5 yr	10 yr	20 yr	30 yr	Conventional Mortgage Loans New Home	Exciting Home	Interest Rate (maximum) on FHA-Insured Mortgage Loans
1961	3.90	3.75	4.00	4.12	4.22	—	—	5 ¾–5 ¼
1962	3.95	3.97	4.28	4.40	4.42	—	—	5 ¼
1963	4.00	3.77	3.98	4.10	4.16	—	—	5 ¼
1964	4.15	4.15	4.25	4.33	4.33	—	—	5 ¼
1965	4.21	4.29	4.33	4.35	4.37	5.83	5.89	5 ¼
1966	4.66	4.97	4.91	4.80	4.75	—	—	5 ¼–6
1967	4.85	5.28	5.23	5.00	4.95	—	—	6
1968	5.25	6.24	6.20	6.00	5.93	—	—	6–6 ¾
1969	6.10	7.05	7.05	6.77	6.54	—	—	6 ¾–7 ½
1970	6.59	8.10	8.00	7.60	7.60	8.52	8.56	7 ½–8
1971	5.74	5.85	7.05	7.12	7.12	7.75	7.83	8–7
1972	5.63	6.50	7.05	7.05	7.01	7.64	7.70	7
1973	6.30	6.85	7.05	7.20	7.20	8.30	8.33	7–8 ½
1974	6.99	7.47	7.67	7.80	7.80	9.22	9.23	8 ½–9
1975	6.98	7.70	8.00	8.35	8.35	9.10	9.14	9
1976	6.78	7.96	8.18	8.30	8.30	8.99	9.04	8–9
1977	7.06	7.25	7.60	7.75	7.95	8.95	9.00	8–8 ½
1978	7.89	7.75	7.98	8.20	8.25	9.68	9.70	9.70
1979	8.74	9.40	9.35	9.08	9.10	11.15	11.16	10.87
1980	10.81	12.80	12.40	12.30	12.30	13.95	13.95	13.44
1981	12.87	13.25	13.00	13.00	13.00	16.52	16.55	16.29

Source: U.S. Bureau of the Census, *Statistical Abstract of the United States, 1982,* Table 855, p. 517 (1981).

for households, plant and equipment for businesses and government, and operating capital for both the private and the public sectors). The terms on which these flows of capital occur depend in part on the risks, the returns, and the liquidity of the transfer mechanism such as bonds, stocks, or mortgages. The higher the yield and the lower the risk, the more available is the supply of capital.

The policy problem facing governments in both the United States and Canada with respect to mortgages has been, how can mortgages be made more attractive financial instruments so that they can compete successfully for scarce capital resources with other financial instruments? Of the various financial instruments, mortgages are singled out for attention because of the special place held by housing in the economy and in the political arena. Housing is a particularly important economic and social good, occupying a unique position in the typical household's budget and priorities. The problem of providing adequate mortgage funds to households is related to the problem of making mortgages competitive in capital markets and has inspired quite diverse solutions in Canada and the United States.

Table 6–10 Bond Yields and Mortgage Interest Rates (Canada)

Year	Long-term Federal Gov't Bonds	Long-term Corporate Bonds	Conventional Mortgage Bonds	Interest Rate (maximum) on NHA-Insured Mortgage Loans
1961	4.95	5.31		6.50
1962	5.12	5.31		6.50
1963	5.17	5.45		6.25
1964	5.03	5.48		6.25
1965	5.44	6.03	7.40	6.25
1966	5.76	6.77	7.95	7.25
1967	6.54	7.52	8.52	8.25
1968	7.30	8.11	9.10	8.75
1969	8.33	9.32	10.50	9.375
1970	6.99	8.87	10.16	9.79
1971	6.56	8.30	9.10	8.91
1972	7.12	8.17	9.22	9.00
1973	7.70	8.85	10.02	9.88
1974	8.77	10.76	11.88	11.75
1975	9.49	11.02	11.89	11.89
1976	8.47	9.80	11.27	11.18
1977	8.77	9.64	10.33	10.16
1978	9.68	10.35	11.53	10.97
1979	11.33	12.06	13.58	12.93
1980	12.67	13.62	15.60	14.07
1981	15.27	16.54	17.79	Figure noncomparable

Source: Central Mortgage and Housing Corporation, *Canadian Housing Statistics,* Table 75.

U.S. Mortgage Market Development[14]

The development of the U.S. mortgage market is closely tied to the evolution of the mortgage instrument, thus, the market and the instrument must be discussed in parallel. In the early part of this century, mortgage loans differed dramatically from their present form. Mortgages were typically 3 to 5 years in length. Loan-to-value ratios rarely exceeded 50 to 60 percent. At the end of the mortgage term the entire mortgage balance was due, since borrowers paid interest only during the term of the mortgage. There was no mortgage insurance to protect lenders. Property taxes were seldom collected to protect lenders from property tax defaults and resulting tax sales. Refinancing of mortgages at the end of their term was relatively easy and there were few defaults.

With growing unemployment and declining overall economic activity during the Depression, homeowners found it increasingly difficult to borrow the needed funds to repay mortgage principal at the end of the mortgage term. Property tax payments also represented a hardship. Moreover, down payments were difficult to accumulate, and purchasers were scarce. Not surprisingly, foreclosures soared and property markets crumbled, as did financial institutions. It is estimated that between 1931 and 1934 250,000 foreclosures took place per year in the United States. By 1933 the President of the United States closed 14,000 of the nation's 33,000 banks. The above circumstances led to the development of the standard mortgage contract.

Federal involvement began with the creation of the Home Owners Loan Corporation (HOLC) in 1933 for homeowners obliged to refinance their homes (and pay off the existing mortgage loan principal as mortgage loans terminated with a so-called "balloon payment" to the mortgagee (lender). HOLC was financed through the issue of government-guaranteed bonds and was responsible for refinancing more than one million homes.

In 1934 the Federal Housing Administration (FHA) was created. FHA was not a mortgage lender, but rather an insurer of mortgages originated by other financial institutions. It provided added security, which enabled risk-averse financial institutions to increase their participation in the mortgage market. It also provided for certain minimal construction standards and paved the way for a national mortgage market by standardizing the mortgage contract and by guaranteeing the loan.

Prior to HOLC and FHA it was uncommon to amortize principal over the life of the loan. Terms were short and loan-to-value ratios low. With the advent of these two federal programs, fully amortized loans became standard. Initial loan terms were for 20 years, and loan-to-value ratios were 80 percent. Such fully amortized, high-ratio, long-term mortgages led to a revolution in mortgage lending. They significantly reduced the risk to lenders and to borrowers by ensuring that over the life of the mortgage the entire principal balance would be repaid in a series of equal monthly payments. This combined with FHA mortgage insurance to increase greatly the attractiveness of the mortgage instrument as an investment.

This attractiveness was further increased by the creation of the Federal National Mortgage Association (FNMA or "Fannie Mae") in 1938 to buy FHA-insured mortgages and sell them in the open market when times allowed such sales. This greatly increased the liquidity of the mortgage instrument, reducing risk to the lender and making FHA-insured mortgages a very competitive financial instrument. As a result of these federal programs, real property markets and mortgage markets experienced a significant turn around during the 1930s and developed stability.

As the end of World War II approached, Congress passed the Servicemen's Readjustment Act of 1944 to provide for adequate mortgage financing for returning veterans. The original act was amended subsequently in 1945, 1946, and 1950, each time with the goal of broadening the terms and making mortgage funds more readily available to returning veterans. Such financing to veterans was administered by the Veterans' Administration and, while it did not introduce any new concepts, it significantly expanded the federal role in residential mortgage financing. In 1955 VA lending activity reached its peak with a total of 643,226 loans closed, which accounted for nearly 25 percent of all housing starts during that year.

The basic pattern of mortgage lending was thus firmly established by the end of World War II. The standard mortgage instrument and federally sponsored mortgage insurance and secondary markets for these insured loans enabled mortgage markets to attract sufficient funds for the financing of urban development under normal economic conditions.

Flows of mortgage funds are notoriously unstable.[15] This instability derives from several sources. First, monetary policy has a very significant impact on the mortgage sector, and therefore on the housing and construction industries, which are so dependent on mortgage financing for their operations. As monetary authorities move to regulate the money supply, they affect the supply of mortgage credit at the same time. A second instability faced by U.S. mortgage markets is the phenomenon of *disintermediation.* Disintermediation occurs during periods of rising interest rates that attract funds away from financial intermediaries such as thrift institutions and banks and into bond and short-term money markets where advantage can be taken of these high rates. The result is that financial intermediaries experience a net outflow of funds that prevents them from lending in mortgage markets. This disintermediation process is engendered by the existence of institutional rigidities that limit the interest rates that can be paid to passbook savers.

Regulation Q of the Federal Reserve Board regulates the maximum rate that can be paid by banks, and the Interest Rate Adjustment Act of 1966 limits the passbook rates that can be offered by thrift institutions. These rates have been deregulated with legislation passed in 1980. The original intent of such *deposit rate ceilings* was to protect the ability of thrift institutions to attract ample funds in the face of competition from commercial banks, since thrift institutions are major sources of mortgage credit and it was determined that it was socially desirable to maintain adequate supplies of residential mortgage credit. The deposit rate ceilings have the reverse effect in periods of rising interest rates, as they inhibit thrift institutions from competing for savings funds by limiting the amount of interest that can be paid, thus making other vehicles such as bonds and certificates of deposit attractive even to relatively small savers. In Canada, where such interest rate ceilings have not been present in the post-World War II era, the disintermediation problem is virtually nonexistent.

A third source of cyclical instability in the supply of mortgage credit comes from the existence of usury laws in 48 of the 50 states that limit the contract rate of interest that can be charged.[16] As interest rates rise above these legislated maxima, the supplies of mortgage (and other consumer credit) dry up, unless of course other means are employed to raise the effective rate to the prevailing market rates. This can be done by charging finder's fees or by requiring other forms of cash bonuses to be paid by the borrower for the right to borrow at the stated interest rate limit. There are distortions in such arrangements, for existing borrowers are generally protected at the expense of new borrowers.

One last facet of mortgage markets relates to the view that mortgage loans represent a residual lending activity after other loans are made. If funds are ample for all types of loans, then mortgage lending proceeds. However, if credit conditions tighten, then mortgage lending is reduced as lenders adjust their portfolios to accommodate tighter monetary conditions. Commercial banks in particular exhibit such residual lending behavior. The impact on the mortgage market is considerable, since residual lending tends to accentuate cyclical instability of real estate markets. Mortgage credit has also been adversely affected by continued and volatile high rates of inflation. The high level of uncertainty engendered in such a climate has prompted lenders and borrowers alike to opt for more flexible instruments. The standard mortgage instrument with its fixed interest rate, its long term, and its unchanging return is poorly suited to the needs of lenders in inflationary periods. This inflexibility limits the desirability of holding such standard mortgage contracts as assets.

Despite the great improvements that were made during the 1930s and the immediate post-war period, mortgage markets continued to be plagued by cyclical instabilities in the 1960s and 1970s, and increasingly by inflation and the inflexibility of the standard mortgage contract during the rapid and unanticipated inflation of the 1970s and early 1980s.

To overcome these difficulties, a number of innovations were introduced into the U.S. mortgage during the 1960s. The pace of innovation quickened during the 1970s and continued into the early 1980s as the growing inadequacy of the standard mortgage contract in an inflationary and volatile environment became apparent. Many of the developments in the U.S. mortgage market were necessitated by the particular set of institutional arrangements that exist in the United States, such as Regulation Q, the Interest Rate Adjustment Act, and the dominance of the thrift institutions as suppliers of residential mortgage credit. In Canada, where these institutional details differ dramatically, a different set of policies was employed to maintain the viability of the mortgage sector, though the quest for alternative mortgage instruments to cope with the recent volatile inflation rates has been just as vigorous.

Disintermediation and cyclical instability typified the availability of mortgage credit after the middle 1960s. Lenders in the United States found themselves in severe liquidity squeezes with long-term assets (mortgage loans based on the standard mortgage contract) and highly volatile short-term liabilities (passbook savings deposits). Accordingly, during the 1960s the U.S. government acted to improve the marketability of mortgages through the development of secondary markets for mortgages, improving the liquidity position of mortgage lenders, especially the thrift institutions. First, 1968 saw the creation of the Government National Mortgage Association to increase the liquidity of mortgages through issuance of highly liquid securities backed by pools of FHA, VA, and Farmer's Home Administration mortgages. The so-called "Ginnie Mae" pass-through securities provide lenders with the ability to issue securities guaranteed by the U.S. government and backed by pools of mortgages.[17]

At the same time that Ginnie Mae was created, Fannie Mae was moved into the private sector. Fannie Mae's sales and purchases of FHA-insured mortgages must be profitable enough to keep Fannie Mae in business. Fannie Mae provides added liquidity by being an important participant in the market, though it no longer subsidizes such secondary market activities, subsidies being provided through Ginnie Mae, which is government-owned. Taken together, Ginnie Mae and Fannie Mae have increased the liquidity of the standard mortgage contract insured under various government programs, though the S & L industry still faced a liquidity crisis in the late 1970s and early 1980s, a crisis related directly to the protective measures such as Regulation Q.[18] This crisis has been eased through the introduction by financial institutions, in late 1982, of money market accounts paying market interest rates.

Another vehicle for increasing liquidity is the Federal Home Loan Mortgage Corporation ("Freddie Mac") established in 1970 by the Emergency Home Finance Act. Freddie Mac, like Ginnie Mae, is government-owned, but unlike Ginnie Mae, the mortgaged-backed securities Freddie Mac deals in are not federally insured. Freddie Mac securities are backed by conventional home mortgages, which may or may not be privately insured.[19]

Taken together, Fannie Mae, Ginnie Mae, and Freddie Mac have taken an essentially local financial instrument (most savings and loan associations are geographically restricted in their lending area) and have enabled it to be traded on national markets. Areas of surplus savings such as the U.S. Northeast can then purchase mortgages from areas of surplus mortgage demand, such as the fabled Sun Belt, thus increasing the liquidity of the deficit Sun Belt while increasing yields on surplus funds in the excess-cash Northeast.

To understand better the nature of past and proposed mortgage innovations, we move on to consider the various components of a mortgage contract.

Amortization Period: the length of time over which the principal is to be repaid in full.

Contract Rate of Interest: the nominal rate of interest specified in the contract; not to be confused with the effective rate (see appendix at the end of this chapter).

Term of the Mortgage: the length of time over which the contractual terms of the mortgage remain in force.

Prepayment Provisions: the terms under which all or part of the mortgage may be repaid prior to expiration of the mortgage contract.

Assignability of the Loan: the ability to assign a mortgage to a house purchaser by the mortgagor. Such assignability is frequently obviated by the "due on sale" clauses wherein the mortgage is due in full on sale of the house. Such due on sale clauses have been struck down recently in many U.S. courts. Canadian mortgages are generally assignable in contrast.

Monthly Payments: the payments needed to amortize completely the mortgage loan over the amortization period.

Loan-to-Value Ratio: the percentage of the purchase price that is covered by the mortgage loan. The down payment is inversely related to the L/V ratio.

Finder's Fees and Other "Bonuses" to the Lender: fees that constitute additional costs to the borrower over and above the contract rate of interest and are usually payable in advance at the time of signing the mortgage contract.

Households and mortgage lenders combine these various terms to create a specific mortgage that satisfies the monthly payment ability of the household and the security of the lending institution. In addition, mortgage lenders are interested in several other variables, aside from the foregoing mortgage terms, in reaching their mortgage loan decision. The two principal variables are:

Borrower Characteristics   Of particular concern here is the ability of the borrowing household to meet the monthly mortgage payments for principal and interest, and also the ability to pay for property insurance and taxes. Measures of monthly debt service divided by monthly income are used here, with a ratio of ± 30 percent being common today (that is, principal, interest, and taxes should not exceed ± 30 percent of monthly gross household income). The previous credit history of the household is also important.

Housing Unit Characteristic   Since the housing unit is the ultimate collateral for a residential mortgage loan, the value and characteristics of the unit are of central importance to the lender. Is the structure sound and in good condition? Is the neighborhood good and stable? Are there any mortgage, tax, or mechanic's liens against the title?

The standard mortgage contract represents an imperfection in the mortgage market, impeding the flow of funds into the mortgage sector during periods of rising inflation. This stems from the contract terms of the standard mortgage, wherein the term and amortization are identical and can range up to 40 years. Moreover, the contract rate of interest is fixed over the entire term of the mortgage. In an inflationary environment, this can lead to significant losses to mortgage lenders, particularly if the lenders have short-term liabilities such as passbook accounts or certificates of deposit. Lenders can encounter difficulties in matching the yield spreads between their assets (the mortgages), which are long-term and fixed in nature, and their liabilities, which are short-term and highly volatile. Several approaches exist to overcome such mismatching. First, we can restructure the mortgage contract so that the terms can be renegotiated more frequently, allowing lenders to adjust periodically their assets and liabilities to help solve this matching problem. A second approach is to vary the contract rate of interest to maintain profitable "spreads" between mortgage interest rates and the interest rates at which financial institutions must borrow from the public and from capital markets.[20]
Both of the foregoing approaches aid the lender by transferring greater interest rate risk to the borrower. However, whereas continued inflation represents a potential cost to lenders, it is a benefit to borrowers who repay constant monthly amounts over the term of the mortgage with cheaper dollars. However, the standard mortgage contract is not without its problems for the typical household preparing to purchase its first house in an inflationary environment where house prices are significant contributors to the inflation. These households, usually young, have relatively limited current incomes yet relatively buoyant expectations about their future and long-term incomes. Thus, the standard mortgage contract with its constant monthly payments can represent a severe burden to young households attempting to purchase housing with their minimal down payment during periods of general inflation and rapid house-price appreciation. The resulting high monthly payments present little difficulty in the longer run as incomes are expected to rise, but they can present critical cash flow problems in the shorter run. A preferable payment alternative may involve rising monthly payments in keeping with anticipated rising household incomes. Such schemes overcome the "tilt problem" wherein under high nominal interest rates real monthly payments are high initially and decline over time (e.g., they are "tilted" toward the present).
One final problem presented by inflation is its particularly harsh impact on households with relatively low incomes. Such households might own a home free and clear of any debt yet still find it difficult to

maintain the home in the face of rising property taxes and energy costs. Such a situation is becoming increasingly common as North America's population ages and more households find themselves on relatively low incomes and occupying the family home. A reverse mortgage permits such households to borrow against equity in the home. Title may pass to the lending institution at some future date.

These four situations (shorter term, variable rate, increasing payment and reverse and/or equity participation mortgages) account for the vast bulk of suggested and newly implemented variations in the standard mortgage contract, all of them intended to overcome shortcomings of the standard mortgage either to lenders or borrowers during periods of rapid inflation. The variants that have been experimented with to deal with these situations include the following

1. *The "Canadian" Mortgage:* This is only one of many possible variations of the standard mortgage contract so that the contract period is considerably shorter than the amortization period. In the specific case of the so-called Canadian mortgage, the term is set at a maximum of five years and the amortization period is specified separately. Every five years the borrower must renegotiate the terms of the mortgage. This five-year term was chosen because of changes in the Canada Interest Act in 1969. The important point is that it is possible to have shorter periods over which the mortgage is in force. In addition, many Canadian mortgages are "open" even within the five-year period, implying that borrowers can repay if interest rates fall. The short period also reduces the liquidity risk to the lender.

2. *The Variable-rate Mortgage (VRM):* The VRM attacks inflexibility by providing for a variable interest rate over the life of the mortgage. The variations are numerous, with the interest rate being tied to everything from prevailing mortgage rates each month or year, to being indexed to central bank interest rates set by the Bank of Canada or the United States Federal Reserve Board. The notion is always the same: Provide the lender with a variable interest rate so that losses due to interest rate risk are reduced significantly. Varying the interest rate that lenders charge allows them to maintain a spread between the mortgage rate and the interest rate they must pay for deposits.

3. *Graduated-payment Mortgages (GPM): and Price-level Adjusted Mortgages (PLAM):* The general idea is that monthly payments in the early years of the mortgage are low and within the budget of the young household purchasing its first house, usually with a minimum down payment. Over time, the level of monthly payments rises in concert with assumed increases in monthly household incomes. The rate of increase of the payments can either be specified in advance (the graduation rate in the GPM) or tied to some index such as the Consumer Price Index (CPI) (the price level in the PLAM). Lower monthly payments initially must be repaid through higher monthly payments at the close of the mortgage. The borrower borrows additional principal at the beginning and must pay back these additional sums plus interest by the termination of the mortgage).

4. *Reverse Annuity Mortgages:* These mortgages were designed to ease the burden of home maintenance for households on fixed income and who already owned

their homes, in contrast to the previous designs which sought to improve access to homeownership. The household functionally borrows money from a financial intermediary using the built-up equity in the house as collateral. The money is disbursed monthly as an annuity until the total principal has been exhausted by the monthly payments. The lender is repaid on sale of the house or death of the household members.[21]

5. *Mortgage-backed Futures Contracts and Mortgage Options:* The preceding variations on the standard mortgage contract all represent institutional adaptations to persistent and unanticipated inflation. In general, they shift interest rate risk to borrower households. Mortgage-backed futures contracts and mortgage options provide a means for hedging against unanticipated inflation and are based on the standard mortgages that comprise the Ginnie Mae mortgage-backed security.[22] They provide a means for shifting such interest rate from households and institutions unwilling or unable to bear such risks to markets where risktakers are willing.

Trading in mortgage futures commenced in October 1975 on the Chicago Board of Trade. Traders can buy and sell futures contracts for delivery up to one year in the future. These contracts are based on $100,000 Ginnie Mae pass-through certificates yielding 8 percent.

By using mortgage-backed futures contracts lenders, mortgage brokers, and borrowers can protect themselves against adverse movements in mortgage interest rates up to 12 months in the future. Sellers of mortgages can protect themselves against possible declines by contracting forward at a fixed rate. Similarly, buyers of mortgages can also contract forward to ensure the purchase of mortgages at known rates also up to 12 months in the future.

The great virtue of such a market is that it provides a formal means for protecting oneself against mortgage interest rate changes. Since it is based on the standard FHA-insured mortgage that is the basis for the Ginnie Mae pass-through certificate, it builds directly on the standard mortgage. The Board of Trade mortgage-backed futures market allows lenders and big borrowers alike to lay off some of the interest rate risk inherent in the standard mortgage. The use of financial options markets on mortgages also presents an effective means for moving interest rate risk from households to risktakers who are willing (for a price) to bear these risks. Moreover, such a mortgage option market opens the possibility for mortgage renewal insurance for households facing mortgage renewals in volatile times.[23]

6. *The Shared Appreciation Mortgage (SAM):* Another means for lowering initial monthly payments during inflationary times is to give the lender a share of the appreciation in house value in return for a lower nominal interest rate. What the homeowner gives up in potential capital gain can be made up through lower monthly payments[24] as lenders pass on lower contract interest rates for a share of the anticipated capital gain.

Discussion of Alternative Mortgage Instruments

Changing the term of the mortgage or varying the rate of interest over the term makes mortgages much more attractive investment vehicles by reducing interest rate risk and making it easier for financial institutions to match the rates on assets and liabilities. These gains are being achieved at the expense of the borrower, who must share some of the interest rate risk with the lender. Previously, borrowers absorbed almost no interest rate risk because they were protected against interest increases through the long term of the standard mortgage contract. If interest rates decreased, borrowers usually had the option (in the United States) of refinancing their mortgage (i.e., paying off the old mortgage at high interest rates and taking out a new mortgage at prevailing lower rates). Despite having to absorb interest risk, the consumer also benefits since the heightened attractiveness to lenders of short-term and VRM mortgages increases the flows of capital into mortgage markets, keeping interest rates down and helping to ensure adequate mortgage credit.

The GPM and PLAM make it easier for borrowers to make monthly payments initially and purchase more housing for the same down payment than would otherwise be possible. However, they do expose the lender to greater default risk, since the early years of the mortgage are typified by negative equity buildup (i.e., the principal is increasing not decreasing, as would be the case in the standard-level payment mortgage). The increased outstanding balance means that lenders have more of their capital at risk and that borrowers have no significant increase in equity. This leads to the final weakness of the scheme from the lender's point of view. What happens if household incomes do not increase at the anticipated rate and thus the household cannot meet the gradually rising monthly payments? Under a normal mortgage, the growing equity interest in the home acts as a significant disincentive to default. However, with GPMs, the outstanding balance grows, and should the household encounter financial difficulties, there is actually some added incentive to default in the early years. Stagnating household incomes and house prices can both occur in recessions, and institutions could face much greater risk of loss. Tables 6–11 and 6–12 provide a summary comparison of the characteristics of the GPM, PLAM, and the standard-level payment mortgage and illustrate the preceding points.

The reverse annuity scheme is also not without problems. Foremost among them is that posed by the household's living past the termination of the reverse annuity mortgage and not being able to repay the mortgage without selling the home. Since RAMs were devised to help older households avoid the traumas of selling their home and relocating, this is a significant problem for the household. Also, the inherent conservatism of financial institutions has led them to provide RAMs for relatively small proportions of the market value of the house, and for relatively short periods of time, thus defeating the initial purpose of the RAM.

One final point should be made about these recent variations on the standard mortgage contract, and this relates to their effects on the secondary mortgage markets. One of the virtues of the standard mort-

Table 6–11 Comparison of Mortgage Payments and Payment-to-income Ratios Under a Level-payment Mortgage (LPM) and a Graduated-payment Mortgage (GPM)

(Calculations based on a $50,000 mortgage, amortized over 25 years, assuming a 5 percent real rate of interest, a 10 percent inflation rate, and a 15 percent nominal mortgage rate; and initial borrower income of $25,000, assumed to increase at the rate of inflation of the previous year plus 2 percent.)

Year	Beginning Principal	Interest Amount Real Component	Inflation Component[a]	Annual Payment	Ending Principal	Annual Mortgage Payment-to-Income Ratio (current dollars)
Level-Payment Mortgage (LPM)						
1	$ 50,000	$7,465	$ 7,685	$ 49,800	30.74	
2	49,800	7,435	7,685	49,550	27.45	
3	49,550	7,385	7,685	49,250	24.51	
4	49,250	7,335	7,685	48,900	21.88	
5	48,900	7,285	7,685	48,500	19.54	
10	46,300	6,885	7,685	45,500	11.09	
15	40,900	6,085	7,685	39,300	6.29	
20	29,800	4,335	7,685	26,450	3.57	
25	6,900	785	7,685	0	2.03	
Graduated-Payment Mortgage (GPM)						
1	$ 50,000	$2,500	$5,000	$3,490	$54,010	13.96
2	54,010	2,700	5,400	3,850	58,260	13.75
3	58,260	2,913	5,826	4,247	62,752	13.54
4	62,752	3,138	6,275	4,687	67,478	13.34
5	67,478	3,374	6,748	5,173	72,427	13.15
10	93,636	4,682	9,364	8,483	99,198	12.24
15	119,570	5,979	11,957	14,119	123,387	11.56
20	124,059	6,203	12,406	24,406	118,228	11.35
25	41,513	1,038	2,076	42,076	0	11.21

Note: If the initial payment were based on the amount necessary to amortize a 25-year mortgage at a 3 percent interest rate (5 percent real rate minus 2 percent real increase in income), the annual mortgage payment to income ratio would remain constant over the 25-year term.
[a]Inflation component based on the actual rate equalling the expected rate of 10 percent.

gage was uniformity, permitting easy sale on secondary markets. The same does not hold for VRMs, GPMs, RAMs, and PLAMs (though five-year mortgages really present no difficulties in this area). Given the tremendous variation in terms that are possible under these innovative mortgage instruments, it is unlikely that lenders could package the homogeneous bundles of mortgages needed to make the secondary market work. The added flexibility is likely to be purchased at the cost of diminished liquidity, which tends to make these mortgages less attractive.

All of these innovations have been in response to rapid and often unanticipated inflation. The lingering question that is largely unasked is, how will these instruments affect the attractiveness of mortgages to both borrowers and lenders should more stable and/or lower interest rates return? Do they build in inflation in such a way that these mortgages will themselves represent significant rigidities in less uncertain

Table 6-12 Comparison of Mortgage Payments and Payment-to-Income Ratios Under a Graduated-Payment Mortgage (GPM) and Price-Level-Adjusted Mortgage (PLAM) With Variable Inflation

(Calculations based on a $50,000 mortgage, amortized over 25 years, assuming a 5 percent real rate of interest, an expected inflation rae of 10 percent when the mortgages are contracted, an actual inflation rate of 10 percent for years 1 and 2, 15 percent for years 3 to 5, and 3 percent for years 6 to 8, and an initial nominal mortgage rate of 15 percent. Borrower income is initially $25,000 and assumed to increase at the rate of inflation of the previous year plus 2 percent.)

| Year | Inflation Rate | Beginning Principal | Interest Amount | | Annual Payment | Ending Principal | Borrower Income | Annual Mortgage Payment-to-Income Ratio (current dollars) |
			Real Component	Inflation Component				
Price-Level-Adjusted Mortgage (PLAM)								
1	10	$50,000	$2,500	$ 5,000	$3,490	$54,010	$25,000	13.96
2	10	54,010	2,700	5,400	3,850	58,260	28,000	13.75
3	15	58,260	2,915	8,739	4,247	65,667	31,360	13.54
4	15	65,667	3,283	9,849	4,905	73,894	36,691	13.27
5	15	73,894	3,695	11,084	5,665	83,008	42,929	13.20
6	3	83,008	4,150	2,490	6,546	83,102	50,227	13.03
7	3	83,102	4,155	2,493	6,756	83,210	52,738	12.81
8	3	83,210	4,161	2,496	6,993	82,884	55,375	12.63
9	3	82,884	4,144	2,487	7,221	82,294	58,144	12.41
Graduated-Payment Mortgage (GPM)								
1	10	$50,000	$2,500	$5,000	$3,490	$54,010	$25,000	13.96
2	10	54,010	2,700	5,400	3,850	58,260	28,000	13.75
3	15	58,260	2,915	8,826	4,247	62,752	31,360	13.54
4	15	62,752	3,138	6,275	4,687	67,478	36,691	12.77
5	15	67,478	3,374	6,748	5,173	72,427	42,929	12.05
6	3	72,427	3,621	7,243	5,712	77,579	50,227	11.37
7	3	77,579	3,879	7,758	6,307	82,909	52,738	11.96
8	3	82,909	4,145	8,290	6,967	88,378	55,375	12.58
9	3	88,378	4,419	8,838	7,699	93,636	58,144	13.24

Note: PLAM mortgage payment-to-income ratio approximately equals GPM ratio when actual inflation equals expected inflation.

times? With the rapid decline in interest rates in 1982 and 1983, standard mortgages have become popular again and alternative mortgage designs increasingly relegated to bookshelves for future use, should inflation pick up again.

Remaining Difficulties

While the foregoing innovations have helped the mortgage instrument remain competitive with other financial instruments during a period of rapid inflation, a number of other problems linger. First, cyclical instability is likely to remain an issue because of the great interest sensitivity of the construction sector and of household demand for mortgage funds. Thus, monetary policies will quickly be translated into changes in the demand for and supply of mortgage funds. Second, inflation continues to lurk as a potential problem for virtually all developed economies and could continue to wreak its own particular hazards on the mortgage sector. Third, institutional rigidities such as Regulation Q, the Interest Rate Adjustment Act and state usury laws all create major imperfections in the mortgage market that put it at a sufficient disadvantage when competing against other financial markets.

In the longer run, either these imperfections will have to be systematically removed or else more elaborate devices than Fannie Mae put in place to enable additional funds to be pumped into the mortgage market. Greater flexibility in the standard mortgage contract will also be needed to allow it to be competitive with other financial instruments. Care must be taken that this added flexibility does not hamper the functioning of the secondary mortgage markets, which are needed to provide additional liquidity to mortgage lenders who face the prospect of disintermediation brought on in part by government policies designed to assist the flow of mortgage funds.

Fourth, and finally, in order to enable mortgage lenders to match assets and liabilities properly, for each alternative mortgage instrument cited above (and for any others one could devise as well) there must be created a corresponding "alternative deposit instrument." Thus, corresponding to the GPM must be a "graduated payment deposit" that increases as the graduation rate in the GPM increases. The same would hold for PLAMs and SAMs.[25] Moreover, such new deposit instruments would need to be marketed to, and accepted by, the general public if the alternative mortgage instruments would have any chance of working. The popularity of the VRM in Canada stems in part from the perfect match with variable deposit interest rates paid on passbook accounts in Canada. In the future, therefore, any push for alternative mortgage designs must be matched by corresponding deposit designs and government policies to promote both.

Canadian Mortgage Market Development[26]

Canadian mortgage markets faced a similar problem to those discussed above: how to ensure that adequate funds flow into the mortgage market. However, the solution to this problem has taken a very different tack in Canada from that taken in the United States. As a generalization it is safe to assert that Canadian government policy has evolved so as to minimize institutional restrictions.

Canadian Mortgage Markets to 1960   While the roots of the problem were very similar, Canadian government policies to improve the flow of funds into the mortgage market followed a different course from that in the United States. Plagued by massive foreclosures and collapsing housing and real property markets, the government of Canada passed the Dominion Housing Act in 1935, more to create employment and stimulate aggregate demand than to build housing. This act was extremely limited in its scope and was confined to the direct financing of limited numbers of housing units by the Canadian government.

Canadian government involvement in mortgage markets did not begin in earnest until the passage of the National Housing Act (NHA) in 1944 and the Central Mortgage and Housing Act in 1945. It was through these acts that the government of Canada started the movement toward a competitive and active mortgage sector.

The National Housing Act of 1944 embodied the following programs

- joint federal-private mortgage lending

- federal guarantees of home improvement loans

- low-interest loans for low-cost limited-dividend housing

In 1945 the Central Mortgage and Housing Corporation (CMHC) was created as a Crown Corporation, or corporation owned directly by the federal government, with responsibility for implementing the National Housing Act provisions. Between 1945 and 1954 the federal government added a number of lending programs to the NHA, all of which involved it in mortgage lending directly.

It was not until the National Housing Act of 1954 that Canadian government mortgage lending moved away from direct involvement in mortgage markets as a lender or joint lender and toward the role that FHA had been playing in the United States for two decades as an insurer of loans. Central Mortgage and Housing Corporation thus became a large mortgage insurer. With NHA mortgage insurance available to lenders who had been approved by CMHC, and to housing units that met specified construction standards, the risks involved in residential mortgage lending declined significantly and mortgages became increasingly attractive. Chartered banks were permitted to hold NHA mortgages by revision of the Bank Act.

This was the general pattern of government involvement through the 1950s: mortgage insurance for approved lenders and for households and housing units meeting certain NHA criteria. A minor secondary market developed as CMHC packaged and sold NHA mortgages at public auction. Between 1954 and 1960 NHA was modified only slightly on the foregoing pattern, and CMHC remained as a lender of last resort to households that had been denied a mortgage loan by at least two lending institutions.

Problems Arising in Mortgage Markets By the 1960s the pattern of mortgage lending based on both NHA and conventional mortgage loans had adjusted to the changes in the NHA in 1954. The pattern differed significantly from that in the United States. For example, where thrift institutions play an important role in U.S. mortgage markets, as we saw, the sources of mortgage credit in Canada are more diverse and consist of life insurance companies, trust companies, mortgage loan companies, chartered banks, credit unions, and the Canadian government.

While the idea of NHA insurance appears to have worked in broadening the sources of funds, problems arose during the 1960s that necessitated a series of government actions to increase the efficiency of the mortgage market. The first problem to surface became apparent in 1961 when mortgage interest rates rose above 6 percent. Under the Bank Act at the time, chartered banks were not allowed to lend at rates in excess of 6 percent. As the mortgage rate rose above 6 percent, it precluded banks from lending in mortgage markets. The gains that had been achieved with the changes in NHA in 1954 were quickly lost as banks had to drop out of the mortgage market. A second problem related to ceilings on interest rates on NHA-insured mortgage loans. These made NHA mortgages increasingly unattractive to lenders during the 1960s. Trust companies were also experiencing problems in matching their generally short-term liabilities (usually in the form of passbook accounts, or five-year Guaranteed Investment Certificates (GICs) with long-term fixed assets, mortgages.

These problems were unique to Canadian mortgage markets, being tied to the particular mortgage market institutions that were evolving in Canada. Canadian mortgage markets also suffered from some of the general difficulties that plague mortgage markets such as cyclical instability from changing monetary policies and the interest sensitivity of mortgage demand. By the end of the 1960s inflation was also beginning to take its toll by making mortgage lenders increasingly aware of interest rate risks associated with holding a long-term asset with fixed financial terms.

Mortgage Market Developments in Canada During the 1960s and 1970s

A number of very significant changes across a range of government policies affected mortgages and mortgage markets in Canada. First, NHA mortgages were made more attractive to private lenders. Beginning in 1967, the NHA interest rate was tied to the Government of Canada bond rate, thus allowing the NHA rate to move in tandem with the market, though not allowing it to move completely freely subject to demand and supply pressures. Also, the 1967 Bank Act removed the 6 percent lending rate ceiling for chartered banks. In response to this change, chartered bank holdings of mortgages grew from $840 million in 1967 (or 3.6 percent of the mortgages outstanding) to $30,901 million in 1981 (or 20 percent of the mortgages outstanding).[27]

In 1969 the NHA rate was finally freed completely and allowed to be completely market-determined, removing the last significant barrier to full competitiveness for NHA mortgages. The Interest Act and the NHA also were changed in 1969 to allow borrowers to refinance loans after 5 years without any prepayment penalty. This seemingly innocent provision had extremely important consequences for the standard mortgage document and for Canada's mortgage markets.

First, the term of mortgages in Canada immediately dropped to five years. Amortization periods and terms no longer coincided. The "Canadian" mortgage mentioned earlier was thus born. Mortgages were to be amortized over periods ranging up to 40 years, but the terms of these mortgages were to be renegotiated every five years. Second, these five-year-term mortgages allowed trust companies and the rapidly growing credit unions to begin to match liabilities (frequently in the form of five-year-term deposits such as the GICs noted previously) with their assets (now largely comprised of five-year-term mortgages). The five-year-term mortgage significantly reduced the risk of holding mortgages, as it reduced the matching problem and increased liquidity.

Finally, in the 1970s allowance was made for the creation of forms of mutual funds that would invest almost exclusively in mortgage loans. Mortgage Investment Companies (MICs) and Real Estate Investment Trusts (REITs) were allowed to pass through their mortgage interest earnings directly to holders of units in these trusts, providing that the vast majority of their assets were held in residential mortgages and that several other less stringent conditions were met. This increased the flow of mortgage funds as well, though only in a minor way since MICs and REITs together hold less than 5 percent of the mortgages outstanding in Canada at present.[28]

The developments in the late 1960s achieved their objectives: The major imperfections that existed in Canadian mortgage markets were almost all removed, making both NHA and conventional mortgages more liquid. Canada experienced a boom in house prices and housing construction during the 1970s that would have been difficult to contemplate in the absence of a smoothly and efficiently functioning housing market.[29] Mortgages outstanding grew more than sixfold, from $23.0 billion in 1967 to $148.5 billion in 1981.

Looming Problems for the Future Canadian mortgage markets are likely to be plagued by the same global problems that we found in the U.S. mortgage and capital markets. Inflation, cyclical instability, and close dependence on monetary policy and monetary instruments will continue to challenge the ability of the Canadian mortgage market to attract and hold mortgage funds into the future.

The Canadian market has evolved to the point where there are few remaining imperfections, and few impediments to the orderly flow of funds. Government imperfections such as restrictions on bank mortgage lending and regulated ceilings for NHA mortgages have all disappeared. This stands in marked contrast to the situation in U.S. mortgage markets, where Regulation Q, the Interest Rate Adjustment Act, state usury laws, and restrictions on thrift institution lending all combine to introduce and maintain barriers to efficient mortgage market operation. A striking example is provided by the phenomenon of disintermediation wherein financial institutions suffer outflows of funds during periods of rising interest rates. This problem exists to a minor degree at worst in Canada, since financial institutions are free to attract savings from the general public at whatever rates they can afford to pay and still make a profit. Savings interest rates move freely with general capital market conditions.

The absence of disintermediation in Canada is an important adjunct of the institutional measures in Canada to deregulate the mortgage market. This absence explains the lack of a need for an organized secondary mortgage market. Without disintermediation there are significantly easier ways to ensure liquidity (and solvency) of financial institutions and the viability of the mortgage market than the development of such large-scale institutions as Ginnie Mae, Fannie Mae, and Freddie Mac.

There is another reason for the absence of organized secondary markets worth discussing and this relates to the great flexibility that has been built into the mortgage contract itself. Beginning with the five-year term in 1969, Canadian lenders have been able to offer mortgages that allow them to match the term of their assets (mortgages) and liabilities (passbook accounts, five-year GICs, certificates of deposit). During the late 1970s, borrowers were able to obtain terms ranging from one month to five years from most chartered banks, trust companies, and credit unions. Further developments have led to prime rate-based mortgages with a one-month term. The added flexibility that goes with such short-term mortgages obviated the need for secondary mortgage markets, since there were only minimal mismatches between assets and liabilities and thus no major cash (liquidity) squeezes were placed on lenders.

The other new mortgage instruments we discussed previously have also been tried in Canada. Only the graduated-payment mortgage seems to have attracted much enthusiasm, and that largely because of CMHC experimentation with a form of GPM and its willingness to insure such a risky innovation. Variable-rate mortgages have not received nearly the attention in Canada that they have in the United States perhaps because the short term available in Canada can accommodate unanticipated inflation. A one-month mortgage term is essentially a VRM. Reverse annuity mortgages (RAMs) have been accepted slowly, perhaps because of the inherent conservatism of both the financial community and the likely demanders of such mortgages (older households).

A very different set of institutional constraints and developments has allowed the Canadian mortgage market to deal with problems of inflation, instability, and liquidity in ways that are very different from those that have been necessary in the United States, where its institutional arrangements necessitated further government involvement through secondary markets. There is one recent innovation of potential benefit to Canadian mortgage and financial markets and that is the futures and option market notions pioneered by the Chicago Board of Trade beginning in 1975. Many of the conditions that led to the founding of the futures and options markets in Chicago do not exist in Canada (for instance, the mortgage banking industry and its commitment process). However, the underlying need for a mechanism to hedge interest rate risk during periods of high inflation does apply to the Canadian situation as well as to that in the United States. Given the significant increases in efficiency that have been observed as a result of the existence of the mortgage-backed futures market, the concept appears to have sufficient merit and relevance that it can be reasonably expected to see a similar hedging mechanism at work in Canada. It is significant to note that CMHC has recently announced the development of mortgage renewal insurance that will use options markets to shift interest rate risk from borrowers.[30]

SUMMARY

This chapter has served a number of purposes. First, it has demonstrated the importance of mortgage financing not just in the urban development process, but in the capital markets of Canada and the United States as well. Mortgage markets are enormous users of capital in both countries, considerably outstripping other forms of private debt in size and importance.

Having established the importance of mortgages in capital markets, we went on to explore some of the differences that exist in means for financing urban development. Both interim and long-term financing were discussed.

Finally, we traced through the development of the mortgage instrument and the mortgage markets in both the United States and Canada. The discussion pointed up the very significant institutional differences that exist in the countries that both caused and effected very different patterns of mortgage market development in the two countries. Most striking perhaps was the absence of any secondary market activity in Canada and the related absence of any significant degree of disintermediation and liquidity problems. This discussion highlighted the need to explore institutional arrangements if we are to fully understand the workings of real property (and mortgage) markets. For example, trying to implement the Canadian short-term mortgage in the United States as a solution to liquidity problems and rigidities in the market would be pointless (and bound to fail) if we did not have an understanding of the institutional concomitants of the liquidity problem such as Regulation Q and the Interest Rate Adjustment Act.

APPENDIX: SOME MATHEMATICS OF MORTGAGE FINANCE

In this appendix we turn from the macro environment of mortgage markets to cover some of the essential technical ideas in mortgage finance. These are micro issues at the level of the individual firm and are best dealt with separately. The discussion is intended to provide an intuitive and brief introduction to these ideas, leaving for more advanced courses and more specialized texts the task of developing greater sophistication and detailed working knowledge. The purpose of this introduction to mortgage finance is to develop some understanding of the analytical tools that have been developed to help us better comprehend the impacts of various public and institutional policies on mortgage yields, profitability, and the availability of mortgage credit.

The discussion proceeds from the relatively straightforward notion of compound interest up through the potentially complex concepts of net present value and internal rate of return. Along the way, numerous examples will be used to illustrate the workings of each concept.

SIMPLE AND COMPOUND INTEREST

Consider an investment of $1000 that earns 10 percent *simple* interest per annum. Such an investment will yield interest income of $100.00 per annum over its life (assume, for simplicity, the investment lasts for 10 years). To calculate the interest income due each year, one merely multiplies the original principal (the $1000) by the annual interest rate. Most long-term bonds earn simple interest payable annually. Simple interest is conceptually and mathematically quite uncomplicated, as shown below.

$$I = Prn \qquad\qquad (A.1)$$

where:

I = interest

P = principal

r = the interest rate per period

n = the number of time period over which the investment earns interest

Using the above example:

$$I = \$1000 \times 10\% \times 10 = \$1,000$$

If the investment lasted for only 7 years and 183 days (e.g., one-half year), then I would be:

$$I = \$1000 \times 10\% \times 7.5 = \$750$$

So much for the case of simple interest. Now let us consider the case where our interest income is automatically added to the principal so that the principal grows each year. This is the case of compound interest. Using the same assumptions as above, but this time compounding each year's interest income by adding it to the principal balance, we have the following.

Year 1:

$$I_1 = P_0{}^r$$
$$= \$1000 \times 10\% \times 1 = \$100$$

where:

I_1 = interest earned at end of first period
P_0 = initial starting principal balance
r = periodic rate of interest

Year 2:

$$I_2 = P_1 r$$
$$I_2 = (P_0 + I_1)r$$
$$I_2 = (P_0 + rP_0)r$$
$$I_2 = (P_0(1 + r))r$$
$$I_2 = (\$1000 \times (1 + 0.10)) \times 0.10$$
$$I_2 = (\$1000 \times 1.10)) \times 0.10$$
$$I_2 = (\$1,000) \times 0.10$$
$$I_2 = \$121.00$$

where:

I_2 = interest earned at end of second period
P_0 = starting principal investment
I_1 = interest earned at end of first period
r = periodic rate of interest
P_1 = principal at end of first period (beginning of second period)

Year 3:

$$I_3 = P_2 r$$

$$I_3 = (P_1 + I_2)r$$
$$I_3 = ((P_0 + I_1) + rP_1)r$$
$$I_3 = ((P_0 + rP_0) + r(P_0 + I_1))r$$
$$I_3 = ((P_0 + rP_0) + r(P_0 + rP_0))r$$
$$I_3 = (P_0 + rP_0 + rP_0 + r^2P_0)r$$
$$I_3 = (P_0 + 2rP_0 + r^2P_0)r$$
$$I_3 = (P_0(1 + 2r + r^2)r$$
$$I_3 = (P_0(1 + r)^2)r$$

where:

I_3 = interest earned at end of third period

P_2 = principal at end of second period

other variables defined as before

Inserting the figures from our example into this equation yields

$$I_3 = (\$1000(1 + 0.10)^2) \times 0.10$$
$$= (\$1000(1.10)^2) \times 0.10$$
$$= (\$1000(1.21)) \times 0.10$$
$$= (\$1210) \times 0.10$$
$$= \$121.00$$

Unlike the simple-interest case, interest earned rises by increasing amounts because the principal on which this interest is being earned is growing.

	<Simple Interest>		<Compound Interest>	
Period	Principal	Interest	Principal	Interest
1	$1000	$100	$1000	$100
2	1000	100	1100	100
3	1000	100	1210	121
.	.	.	.	.
.	.	.	.	.
.	.	.	.	.
10	1000	100	2358	236

A pattern emerges in the examples that allows us to generalize the compounding process and develop a general formula for calculating compound interest and principal.

Remember from above that,

$$I_3 = P_2r$$
$$I_3 = (P_0(1 + r))^2r$$

Thus, in general we have the following relationship.

$$I_n = (P_0(1 + r)^{n-1})r \qquad \text{(A.2)}$$

$$P_n = P_0(1 + r)^n \qquad \text{(A.3)}$$

Equation (A.2) allows us to calculate the interest earned in period n given a starting principal balance of P and a periodic rate of interest of r. Equation (A.3) tells us how big our ending principal balance will be if it grows at a rate of r per period over n time periods.

This procedure, whereby we compounded an initial principal balance, allows us to calculate the future value of that principal over n time periods earning an interest rate of r per period. However, for many investment problems we will want to work in the opposite direction, and instead of compounding our principal to find its future value, we will want to find the present value of some future sum.

For example, an investment opportunity might arise that promises the potential investor the rights to the gains from the sale of an office building. The sale in year 10 is expected to net $100,000. In order to evaluate the value of this investment, the potential investor must convert this future value to a present value through the process of discounting (the inverse of compounding). We can make use of equation (A.3) to help us solve this problem as follows.

$P_{10} = \$100,000$

$r = 12\%$ (the rate of interest that the investor wants to earn per year on the investment)

$P_0 =$ the unknown present value of the future gain at 12 percent interest

$$P_{10} = P_0(1 + 0.12)^{10}$$
$$\$100,000 = P_0 (3.1058)$$
$$\text{Hence } P_0 = \$32,197$$

More generally, we can rewrite (A.3) to solve for present values instead of the future values represented by P in that equation. Such a rewritten equation appears below.

$$P_0 = \frac{P_n}{(1 + r)^n} = P_n(1 + r)^{-n} \qquad \text{(A.4)}$$

Another way of looking at discounting is the following. What principal sum do we have to invest in the present to accumulate a given future value in year n at interest rate r? Taking another example, if we can accumulate $10,000 5 years hence to pay for university tuition, and current interest rates are 13 percent, how much do we have to put away today (the present value) to accumulate that future value? Using (A.4),

$$P_5 = \$10,000$$
$$r = 13\%$$
$$n = 5$$
$$P_0 = \$10,000 \times (1 \times 0.13)^{-5}$$
$$= \$5427.60$$

In other words, if we want to have $10,000 available 5 years hence, and if we can earn 13 percent on our investment, we need $5427.60 today (e.g., the present value of $10,000 at 13 percent for 5 years is $5427.60). To check out this answer we can use equation (A.3), where

$$P_0 = \$5427.60$$
$$r = 13\%$$
$$n = 5$$
$$P_5 = \$5427.60(1 + 0.13)^5$$
$$= \$5427.60(1.842)$$
$$= \$10,000.00$$

Compounding, discounting, present value, and future value represent the building blocks for the more complex calculations.

Effective and Equivalent Rates

A problem that immediately confronts the financial analyst when dealing with mortgages and real estate finance is the determination of the effective rate of interest as opposed to the stated nominal rate of interest. For example, mortgage loans in Canada and the United States which bear an interest rate of 12 percent have significantly different effective annual rates because of the method of calculating the interest. In the United States, savings and loan associations typically compound the interest monthly, whereas in Canada chartered banks and trust companies typically compound the interest semiannually. The effective rate of a 12 percent mortgage in the United States compounded monthly is 12.68 percent per annum, while the effective rate of a 12 percent mortgage in Canada compounded semiannually is 12.36 percent. This stated difference of 0.32 percent per annum appears small but implies that annual interest payments will be 2.6 percent greater in the United States than in Canada (12.68/12.36 = 0.026).

Converting nominal rates to effective annual rates is relatively straightforward and follows the formula set out below.

$$r = (1 + i)^m - 1 \qquad (A.5)$$

where:

r = the effective annual rate

i = the stated periodic rate being equal to j_m/m

where j_m is the stated nominal rate and m is the number of times the rate is compounded per year.

We can thus rewrite equation (A.5) in the following form.

$$r = \left(1 + \frac{j_m}{m}\right)^m - 1 \tag{A.6}$$

An example should serve to demonstrate how the formula works. Consider two mortgages, one being offered by a bank and carrying a nominal rate of 13 percent semiannually, and the other mortgage being offered by a thrift institution (e.g., a credit union, savings and loan association, or mutual savings bank) at a nominal rate of 12.75 percent but compounded daily. Which mortgage should a prudent consumer (or investor) choose, all else being equal?

Case 1: Bank Mortgage

$j_m = 13.00\%$

$m = 2$ (semiannual compounding)

$$r = \left(\frac{13\%}{2}\right)^2 - 1 = \left(\frac{0.13}{2}\right)^2 - 1 = (1.065)^2 - = 1.342 - 1$$

$$= 13.42\% \text{ per annum}$$

Case 2: Thrift Institution

$j_m = 12.75\%$

$m = 365$ (daily compounding)

$$r = \left(\frac{1 + 12.75\%}{365}\right)^{365} - 1 = \left(\frac{1 + 0.1275}{365}\right)^{365} - 1$$
$$= (1 + 0.0003493)^{365} - 1 = (1.0003493)^{365} - 1$$
$$= 1.1360 - 1$$
$$= 13.60\% \text{ per annum}$$

This example demonstrates that even though the thrift institution mortgage carries a lower nominal rate (12.75 percent vs. 13.00 percent), it is the more expensive of the two mortgages, having an effective annual rate of 13.60 percent vs. the 13.42 percent being charged by the bank. Assuming that all other terms of the mortgage are identical (e.g., the term, amortization period, down payment, and repayment provisions), the bank mortgage is preferable. The interested reader should practice the foregoing computation using a range of nominal rates and compounding frequencies.

To conclude this section, interest rates are typically stated in terms of some nominal interest rate compounded so many times per year, monthly and semiannual compounding being the most common. Before any comparison of investments or loans can be made, these nominal rates must be converted to their equivalent effective annual rate, in essence, the rate at which interest would be calculated to yield the same interest if compounding were to take place only once a year.

Interest Calculations: A Summing Up and Comparison

There is one other calculation related to nominal and effective rates that needs discussion before we can summarize the differences among various interest rates. This is the equivalent rate, and it builds directly on the previous work we did in calculating effective rates. The problem is as follows. How can we convert one nominal rate into an *equivalent* nominal rate with identical effective rates of interest. For example, what is the equivalent nominal rate of interest compounded monthly for a 12 percent nominal mortgage compounded semiannually. We proceed in two steps: First we convert the known nominal rate to an effective rate; then we convert this effective rate into the unknown nominal rate.

Rate 1: 12 percent compounded semiannually

First we must find the effective annual rate of interest, r. Returning to (A.6),

$$r = \left(\frac{1 + 12\%}{2}\right)^2 - 1 = \left(1 + \frac{0.12}{2}\right)^2 - 1 = (1.06)^2 - 1 \qquad \text{(A.6)}$$

$$= 12.36\%$$

Rate 2: Unknown, compounded monthly with a 12.36 percent effective rate

To find our unknown rate, we must work through equation (A.6) in reverse order. In equation (A.6) we had

$$r = \left(1 + \frac{j_m}{m}\right)^m - 1$$

where j_m and m were known and we wanted to find the effective annual rate, r. In the present case r is known and so is m (monthly $= 12$). Now we want to find j_m. We can do this by solving equation (A.6) in terms of j_m instead of in terms of r, as it is presently stated.

$$r = \left(1 + \frac{j_m}{m}\right)^{m} - 1$$

$$1 + r = \left(1 + \frac{j_m}{m}\right)^m$$

$$(1 + r)^{1/m} = \left(1 + \frac{j_m}{m}\right)$$

$$(1 + r)^{1/m} - = \left(1 + \frac{j_m}{m}\right) = i$$

In the present case we have, $r = 12.36$ percent and $m = 12$, so

$$(1 + 0.1236)^{1/12} - 1 = i$$
$$(1.1236)^{1/12} - 1 = i$$
$$(1.1236)^{0.08333} - 1 = i$$
$$1.0097588 - 1 = i$$
$$0.0097588 = i$$
$$11.71055\% = j_{12}$$

We can now state that an interest rate of 12 percent compounded semi-annually ($m = 2$) is equivalent to an interest rate of 11.71055 percent compounded monthly ($m = 12$), since both have an effective annual rate of 12.36 percent.

To summarize these ideas, we have compiled the following tables. Table A1 sets out periodic, nominal, effective, and equivalent interest rates over a range of periodic rates and compounding periods. Table A2 shows how increasing the compounding period leads to systematically higher interest payments, which is intuitively sensible since larger compounding periods imply higher effective interest rates.

Table A–1 Comparison of Periodic, Nominal, Effective, and Equivalent Interest Rates

Periodic Rate i %	Number of Compounding Periods m	Nominal Rate per Annum j_m %	Effective Annual Rate r %	Equivalent Semiannual Rate i_{SA} %	Equivalent Nominal Rate for Semiannual Compounding j_2 %
i	m	$(j_m = i \times m)$	$r = (1+i)^m - 1$	$i_{SA} = (1 + i)^{m/2} - 1$	$j_2 = 2 \times i_{SA}$
1	1	$j_1 = 1\%$	1%	0.50	$j_2 = 1.00$
1	2	$j_2 = 2\%$	2.01%	1.00	$j_2 = 2.00$
1	3	$j_3 = 3\%$	3.03%	1.50	$j_2 = 3.00$
1	4	$j_4 = 4\%$	4.06%	2.01	$j_2 = 4.02$
1	6	$j_6 = 6\%$	6.15%	3.03	$j_2 = 6.06$
1	12	$j_{12} = 12\%$	12.68%	6.15	$j_2 = 12.30$
2	6	$j_6 = 12\%$	12.61%	6.12	$j_2 = 12.24$
3	4	$j_4 = 12\%$	12.55%	6.09	$j_2 = 12.18$
4	3	$j_3 = 12\%$	12.49%	6.06	$j_2 = 12.12$
6	2	$j_2 = 12\%$	12.36%	6.00	$j_2 = 12.00$
12	1	$j_1 = 12\%$	12.00%	5.83	$j_2 = 11.66$

Source: Executive Programs, Faculty of Commerce, U.B.C., *Technical Aspects of Real Estate and Mortgage Finance,* page II-29, interest rate calculations and concepts.

Table A–2 Interest Costs, Compounding Period, and the Duration of the Loan *(Amount of Interest Due as a Function of Duration of Loan—*Loan amount = $1000.00; Interest Rate = 12 percent)

Length of Loan (months)	Simple Interest (assume 12 mos. of equal length)	Compound Interest Monthly	Quarterly	Semiannual	Annual
1	$ 10.00	$ 10.00			
2	$ 20.00	$ 20.10			
3	$ 30.00	$ 30.30	$ 30.00		
4	$ 40.00	$ 40.60			
5	$ 50.00	$ 50.01			
6	$ 60.00	$ 61.52	$ 60.90	$ 60.00	
7	$ 70.00	$ 72.14			
8	$ 80.00	$ 82.86			
9	$ 90.00	$ 93.68			
10	$100.00	$104.62			
11	$110.00	$115.67			
12	$120.00	$126.82	$125.51	$123.60	$120.00
13	$130.00	$138.09			
14	$140.00	$149.47			
15	$150.00	$160.97	$159.27		
16	$160.00	$172.58			
17	$170.00	$184.30			
18	$180.00	$196.15	$194.05	$191.02	
19	$190.00	$208.11			
20	$200.00	$220.19			
21	$210.00	$232.39	$229.87		
22	$220.00	$244.72			
23	$230.00	$257.16			
24	$240.00	$269.74	$266.77	$262.48	$254.40

Source: Executive Programs, Faculty of Commerce, U.B.C., *Technical Aspects of Real Estate and Mortgage Finance,* page II-29, interest rate calculations and concepts.

SIMPLE ANNUITIES: THE BASIS FOR MORTGAGE LENDING

An annuity is an investment that provides for the periodic payment of a monetary sum. The variable elements of annuities include:

1. *Term:* the period over which the payments are to be received, from the initial payment date to the terminal payment date.

2. *Payment period:* the interval of time between the payments.

3. Compounding period: the time interval over which the interest due on the principal is calculated. There are m compounding periods in one year and n compounding periods in the term of the loan. The number of compounding periods per year may (in the case of ordinary simple annuities) correspond to the number of payment periods in a year, or it may not (as in the case of ordinary general annuities).

One other distinction should be made between *annuities* and *annuities due*. In the case of an annuity, the payment takes place at the end of each payment interval (as in residential mortgages, where the first payment is not made until the end of the first month). In the case of an annuity due, the payment is due at the beginning of each payment interval (as in monthly apartment rents).

A typical credit union or savings and loan association mortgage is a good example of an ordinary simple annuity where payments are made monthly and interest is calculated monthly. (Note that the typical chartered bank mortgage in Canada is not an ordinary simple annuity, since interest is generally calculated semiannually—a compounding period of $m = 2$—and payments are made monthly. Such an annuity is more complicated and represents an ordinary general annuity wherein the semiannual interest rate must be converted to its equivalent monthly rate before the calculation of payments can be determined.)

We begin by considering an example of a mortgage with the following conditions and contract terms.

Term: 5 years ($n = 60$ monthly payments)

Interest Rate: 12 percent compounded monthly ($m = 12$)

Principal: $50,000.00

Problem: What is the monthly payment that is required to repay fully the principal and meet all interest payments over the term of the mortgage?

This problem summarizes the issues in mortgage calculations.

We can envision an annuity as a stream of payments, each being discounted back to the present as follows.

$$\text{Present Value of Annuity } (PV) = R(1 + i)^{-1} + .R(1 + i)^{-2} + R(1 + i)^{-3} + \ldots + R(1 + i)^{-n} \qquad \text{(A.7)}$$

where:

R = periodic payment

i = interest rate per period

n = number of periods (term of the annuity)

When dealing with mortgages that run for 35 or 40 years (i.e., 420 or 480 monthly payments), calculating each discount factor and then adding up all of the discount factors and multiplying them by the periodic payment could become an incredibly time-consuming and error-laden chore. Fortunately, there is a concise mathematical formula that gives us the sum of the various discount terms in an easily calculated and compact form. Using this formula, we can restate equation (A.7) as follows

$$PV = R \left[\frac{1 - (1 + i)^{-n}}{i} \right] \tag{A.8}$$

where all the terms in this equation are as previously defined. We can now return to our original mortgage problem and find the monthly payments needed to completely amortize a mortgage of $50,000.00 at 12 percent per annum compounded monthly for 5 years.

Using equation (A.8)

$$\$50,000 = R \left[\frac{1 - (1 + 0.01)^{-60}}{0.01} \right]$$

$$\$50,000 = R \left[\frac{1 - 0.5504496}{0.01} \right]$$

$$\$50,000 = R \left[\frac{0.4495504}{0.01} \right]$$

$$\$50,000 = R \, (44.955033)$$

$$\$1112.22 = R$$

Thus, 60 monthly payments of $1112.22 completely amortize a $50,000 mortgage at 12 percent (1 percent per month) compounded monthly.

Equation (A.8) is straightforward and easily applied. It can be used to solve for the present value of a stream of annuity payments, given the interest rate and the value of each payment. It can also be used to solve for the periodic rate of interest, given the present value (or principal balance) and the periodic payments. Given any two of the three unknowns in equation (A.8), the third can be calculated. The only calculation that presents any difficulty is solving for the periodic rate, since there is no method other than trial and error to find the rate at which the stream of periodic payments exactly equals the present value. There is no conceptual difficulty involved, only a series of trial-and-error calculations until the appropriate rate is found.

There is only one additional calculation that we need to cover at this point, and that is deriving the future value of a stream of annuity payments (in essence, the inverse of the problem that we have just considered). Let's start with an example again.

Consider a household that wants to purchase a house 2 years hence and requires at that time a down payment of $20,000. If it earns 10 percent per annum on a savings account where interest is calculated monthly, how much must be saved each month to accumulate the desired down payment?

Term: 2 years (24 months)

Interest Rate: 10 percent per annum (0.833 percent monthly)

Future Value: $20,000

We can begin to solve this problem by setting out a stream of payments and the interest earned in each period. (Note that this is conceptually identical to the earlier problem summarized in equation (A.7), except that this time we are not discounting the payments but are earning interest on them instead, with the greatest interest earned on the first payment, since it earns interest the longest, and so on.)

$$\text{Future Value of Annuity (FV)} = R(1 + i)^n + R(1 + i)^{n-1} +$$
$$R(1 = i)^{n-2} + \ldots + R(1 + i)^1 \quad \text{(A.9)}$$

There is also a formula available which allows us to calculate the sum of these compounding elements.

$$FV = R\left[\frac{(1 + i)^n - 1}{i}\right] \quad \text{(A.10)}$$

Returning to our household trying to accumulate a down payment, we have the following.

$$\$20,000 = R\left[\frac{(1 + 0.00833)^{24}}{0.00833} - 1\right]$$

$$\$20,000 = R\left[\frac{1.2202941}{0.00833} - 1\right]$$

$$\$20,000 = R\left[\frac{1.2202941}{0.00833}\right]$$

$$\$20,000 = R\,(26.435401)$$

$$\$756.56 = R$$

Assuming that interest can be earned at a rate of 10 percent per annum compounded monthly (e.g., 0.00833 per month), monthly payments of $756.56 must be made for 24 months to accumulate the required $20,000 down payment.

As was the case with discounting and present value calculations, knowing any two of the terms in equation (A.10) allows us to calculate the third term. Once again, calculating the rate of interest required to balance the two sides of the equation is the most time-consuming task, being based again on trial and error. There are no conceptual difficulties involved in any of these calculations, however.

Among the texts that a reader might consult, the following should all provide the necessary technical details to probe more deeply into the subject of real estate finance: James H. Boykin, *Financing Real Estate* (Lexington, Mass.: D. C. Heath), 1979; William B. Brueggeman and Leo D. Stone, *Real Estate Finance*, 7th edition (Homewood, Ill.: Richard D. Irwin), 1981; Sherman J. Maisel and Stephen E. Roulac, *Real Estate Investment and Finance* (News York: McGraw-Hill Book Co.), 1976; Paul F. Wendt and Alan R. Cerf, *Real Estate Investment Analysis and Taxation* (New York: McGraw-Hill Book Co.), 1978; S. A. Pyrrh and J. R. Cooper, *Real Estate Investment* (Boston, Mass.: Warren, Gorham and Lamont), 1982; D. R. Epley and J. A. Millar, *Basic Real Estate Finance and Investments* (New York: John Wiley and Sons), 1981; and A. J. Jaffe and C. F. Sirmans, *Real Estate Investment Decisionmaking* (Englewood Cliffs, N.J.: Prentice-Hall), 1982.

Some Additional Complexities

We have learned virtually all of the essentials needed to assist us in understanding most of the technical aspects of mortgage financing. Some of the wrinkles that one commonly encounters include the following.

Balloon Payment This is a sum equal to the unpaid balance on a mortgage that is paid in a lump sum before the mortgage is fully amortized. This can happen as a result of prepayment of fully amortized mortgage or when the term of the mortgage is less than the amortization period, as is common in Canada, where there is a five-year rollover and renegotiation of contract terms.

Ordinary General Annuities Here the compounding period differs from the payment period. To solve the problem one merely finds the effective rate and converts it to the equivalent rate, which is consistent with the frequency of the payment period.

Outstanding Balances If the term of the mortgage is less than the amortization period, there will be an outstanding balance at the end of the term since the mortgage will not be fully amortized. More generally, the outstanding balance is the amount of principal the borrower has not repaid at any given point of time during the loan. Outstanding balances can be calculated using the future value calculations just discussed by subtracting the future value of the stream of monthly payments from the future value of the principal, both as at the time period of concern.

Discounts, Bonuses and Trading Mortgages In each of these instances the face value of the mortgage at the contract rate of interest differs from the prevailing rate of interest. If interest rates have fallen, the holder of a mortgage can sell it with a bonus. Conversely, if current rates have risen above the contract rate in a mortgage, the mortgagee (the mortgage owner or lender) must discount the mortgage if selling it.

NET PRESENT VALUE AND INTERNAL RATES OF RETURN: THE BOTTOM LINE

Ultimately, the investor in a real property development wants to know the level of return that is being earned—the so-called bottom line. Many of the techniques discussed at the beginning of this book, such as urban economic analysis and forecasting, provide the real-property analyst with the necessary background to begin to estimate the income stream that is likely to flow from a development. Information on the future of the urban economy (on both the demand and supply sides) can be combined with local knowledge about political and social change to yield an estimate of the likely productivity of the real property investment. This productivity includes estimates of income streams from the project but also estimates of future costs, resulting in an estimate of net cash flow over a reasonable investment horizon. However, the investor requires some means for comparing among alternative investment opportunities, since the cash flows themselves might result from dramatically different-sized investments.

Two commonly used approaches to net out this scale effect to enable different developments to be compared are the net present value approach (NPV) and the internal rate of return (IRR) approach. Under certain circumstances, they are equivalent.

Net Present Value

This approach takes as given the discount rate used by the investor, perhaps the investor's actual cost of captial, or some proxy such as the prevailing mortgage rate. It also assumes that the net cash flows are known over the investment period (e.g., the gross income stream net of maintenance, interest, and property tax costs). It then compares the discounted present value of these net cash flows with the initial capital cost of the project in question. The object is to maximize the difference between the net present value of these income flows and the initial outlay, as follows.

Net Present Value = (Discounted Present Value of Net Income Stream) − (Initial Capital Outlay)

Using our earlier notation, we have:

$$NPV = R_1(1 + i)^{-1} + R_2(1 + i)^{-2} + \ldots + R_n(1 + i)^{-n} - ICO \quad (A.11)$$

$$NPV = \sum_{n=1}^{N} R_n(1 + i)^{-n} - ICO \quad (A.11a)$$

where:

R_1 = net cash flow during period n

i = investor's cost of capital or discount rate

N = investment duration

ICO = initial captial outlay

Internal Rate of Return

The internal rate of return is conceptually similar to the NPV method, except here the object of the exercise is to find the internal rate of return r that makes the stream of net cash flows equal the initial capital outlay.

Initial Capital Outlay = (Stream of Net Cash Flows Discounted at Internal Rate of Return r)

Again, turning to our mathematical shorthand,

$$ICO = R_1(1 + r)^{-1} + R_2(1 + r)^{-2} + \ldots + R_n(1 + r)^{-n} \qquad (A.12)$$

$$ICO = \sum_{j=1}^{n} R_j(1 + r)^{-j} \qquad (A.12a)$$

We can see from equations (A.11a) and (A.12a) that when $NPV = ICO$ (i.e., the discounted stream of benefits exactly equals the initial capital outlay), the internal rate of return and the discount rate in the NPV method will be identical and the approaches will yield equivalent results. This is not an especially likely occurrence, however, and the two approaches may yield quite different rankings of projects. In the IRR approach, that investment is preferred which yields the highest expected IRR, while in the NPV method it is the NPV which is to be maximized. The NPV approach suffers because it does not account for the scale differences that might exist among projects (e.g., the largest and most costly project might have the largest NPV but the lowest return on equity). The IRR approach suffers because it assumes implicitly that the incomes can be reinvested at the constant rate r, which is a weak assumption over the long run and where one can reasonably expect that more marginal projects will enter the market, thus lowering the return that could be realized on these income flows. These are very technical side issues that need not concern us at this point. Again, the interested reader is directed to the readings cited earlier for greater discusson of the realtive virtues of the two approaches for calculating investment return.

One last point needs to be made about both of these techniques. Despite their sophistication, they are well within the reach of the tools presented earlier in this appendix. The NPV method merely requires the use of the discounting technique. The IRR approach requires the user to solve through trial and error for the unknown rate r. This is exactly the same as the earlier problem of solving for a rate on a mortgage or other loan or annuity.

In addition to these more elegant approaches to evaluating real property investments, there are a host of rules of thumb that are in common use. Foremost among these are measures of net cash flow divided by equity or purchase price. These rule-of-thumb approaches are very straightforward and provide investors with the means for comparing among alternative investment opportunities without having to resort to the more sophisticated NPV and IRR approaches and their recent variants. Since these measures are intuitively obvious and present no difficulty at all in their application, the reader is urged to consult some of the more professionally oriented journals, such as the *Appraisal Journal,* the *Real Estate Review,* and *The Appraiser,* for current rules of thumb used by practicing professonals. There are far too many such rules for us to go over them in detail here, and because of their simplicity there is really no need to discuss their use at any length. One excellent reference that readers might want to consult, however, is David Arthur, *Real Estate Investment Analysis: Current Practice* (Vancouver, B.C.: The Urban Land Economics Division, Faculty of Commerce and Business Administration, University of British Columbia), 1977. This paper discusses the use of a range of rules of thumb and more sophisticated analytical tools and provides some interesting guidelines for using these alternative techniques.

The point to stress from all of the foregoing discussion of investment return calculation is the need to provide the investor with a consistent measure with which to compare alternative investment opportunities. The bottom-line answer derived from each technique is likely to differ considerably, and the potential user of these techniques is once again warned to understand fully the assumptions that are implicit in each approach. From our perspective, all current techniques build on the concepts we have been discussing in this appendix and represent a kind of focal point for the real estate analyst to bring his or her tool kit to bear on an investment problem. That tool kit will include our urban economic tools as well as the more microeconomic tools of finance and investment analysis.

Footnotes

1. For greater detail on the various stages of the urban development process, see: Michael A. Goldberg and Daniel D. Ulinder, "Residential Developer Behaviour 1975," *Land Economics* 52(3:1976):363–370; Edward Kaiser and Shirly F. Weiss, "Public Policy and the Residential Development Process," *Journal of the American Institute of Planners* 36(1:1970):30–37; and Marion Clawson, *Suburban Land Conversion in the United States,* (Baltimore: The Johns Hopkins University Press), 1971.

2. Negative cash flows are the large cash outflows that result from the need to pay for labor, land, and materials well before any income can be derived from a real estate development. The cash outflows can be enormous, and thus the developer requires a line of credit to finance the early stages of development before any cash inflow can be expected.

3. Holding periods have been increasing steadily in both the United States and Canada. See, for example: Goldberg and Ulinder, *op. cit.,* and *Management and Control of Growth, Volume III* (Washington, D.C.: The Urban Land Institute), 1975, especially Chapter 19. Also *Management and Control of Growth, Volume V* (Washington, D.C. The Urban Land Institute), 1980, Chapter 38.

4. These large front-end costs of development, coupled with growing delays in approval processes, put added drains on developer cash reserves, which tend to be tightly stretched in any case. Thus, any move by any of the several levels of government to delay development or add costs through higher servicing standards meets great resistance from developers as it raises their cash requirements and their need for additional debt financing.

5. More specifically on this point, many large development companies do actually sell finished developments to operating subsidiaries charged with maintaining and operation of these investments.

6. Fred E. Case and John M. Clapp, *Real Estate Financing,* (New York: John Wiley and Sons), 1978, p. 404.

7. See James H. Boykin, *Financing Real Estate* (Lexington, Mass.: D.C. Heath), 1979, Chapter 13.

8. Developers often find themselves in a potentially precarious double-bind situation vis-à-vis long-term take-out financing and short-term interim financing. Frequently, short-term loans will not be available unless the developer can come forward with a long-term take-out commitment.

9. Sometimes, however, developers will place a mortgage on part of the development (the land underneath the buildings, for example), or they may pre-sell some of the development to provide themselves with the necessary longer-term financing, or part of it, anyway.

10. We will be covering these institutional details below. At this point it is important to stress their importance, and that they are likely to differ significantly between the United States and Canada, as they in fact do.

11. Richard U. Ratcliff, "Institutionalism and Urban Land Economics," in Michael A. Goldberg, ed., *Recent Perspectives in Urban Land Economics* (Vancouver, B.C.: Urban Land Economics Division, Faculty of Commerce and Business Administration, University of British Columbia), 1976, pp. 4–5.

12. Throughout our discussions we will be taking the term "institutional" in its broadest possible context to include relevant legal, political, cultural, and social phenomena as well as formally constituted "institutions" such as banks, the Federal Reserve System, city councils, etc.

13. See Lawrence B. Smith, *The Postwar Canadian Housing and Residential Mortgage Markets and the Role of Government (Toronto, Ontario: University of Toronto Press), 1974, Chapter 5, on stickiness of rates.*

14. Excellent discussions of the development of the U.S. mortgage market can be found in a number of introductory books on real estate finance. See, for example: Boykin, *op. cit.;* Case and Clapp, *op. cit.;* (Homewood, Ill.: Richard D. Irwin), 1977; Maurice A. Unger and Ronald W. Melicher, *Real Estate Finance* (Cincinnati, Ohio: South-Western Publishing Co.), 1978; John P. Wiedemer, *Real Estate Finance, 2nd edition* (Reston, Va.: Reston Publishing Co.), 1977 and William B. Brueggeman and Lee D. Stone, *Real Estate Finance,* 7th edition, (Homewood, Ill.: R.D. Irwin), 1981, Part Four.

15. This instability underlies a great deal of the government policy aimed at ensuring adequate supplies of mortgage funds, especially for the residential mortgage market. This instability has also attracted the interest of academics trying to model and explain mortgage market behavior. See, for example:

Lawrence B. Smith, *op. cit.*; Jack M. Guttentag, "The Behavior of Residential Mortgage Yields since 1951," in Jack M. Guttentag and Philip Cagan, eds., *Essays on Interest Rates, Volume 1* (New York: National Bureau of Economic Research), 1969; Dwight M. Jaffee, "An Econometric Model of the Mortgage Market: Estimation and Simulation," in E. Gramlich and D. Jaffee, *Savings Deposits, Mortgages and Residential Construction* (Lexington, Mass.: D.C. Heath), 1972. The resulting plight of savings and loan associations in particular has attracted much interest, given their difficulties as a result of mortgage market instabilities, especially during the period 1978–1983. Regulation of the industry is closely related to the instability. See P. H. Hendershott and K. E. Villani, *Regulation and Reform of the Housing Finance System* (Washington, D.C.: American Enterprise Institute), 1978, and E. J. Kane, "S&L's and Interest-Rate Reregulation: The FSLIC as an In-Place Bailout Program," *Housing Finance Review* 1(3: 1982):219–243.

16. Boykin, *op. cit.*, has a complete inventory of state usury statutes.

17. Case and Clapp, *op. cit.*, in Chapters 8 and 9, have an excellent discussion of these pass-through securities and related federally backed or initiated financial instruments.

18. See Paul F. Wendt and Richard R. Haney, Jr., "Secondary Mortgage Market Performance Under Pressure," *American Real Estate and Urban Economics Association Journal* 3(2:1975):31–41.

19. Once again, see Chapters 8 and 9 in Case and Clapp, *op. cit.*, for excellent discussions of the Fannie Mae, Ginnie Mae, and Freddie Mac instruments and some of their intricacies.
    This concern with neighborhood has led to the practice of "red-lining" whereby certain neighborhoods are deemed too risky to lend in. Such spatial discrimination has led to vigorous debate in the literature as well as a great deal of investigation and legislation at the state and federal levels in the United States. For details, see Peter M. Hutchinson, James R. Ostas, and J. David Reed, "A Survey and Comparison of Red-Lining Influences on Urban Mortgage Lending Markets," *Journal of the American Real Estate and Urban Economics Association* 5(4:1977):463–472, and C. Duncan MacRae, Margery A. Turner, and Anthony M. J. Yezer, "Determinants of FHA Mortgage Insurance in Urban Neighborhoods, *Housing Finance Review* 1(1, 1982):55–71.

20. An excellent volume on alternative mortgage instruments (AMIs) is Franco Modigliani and Donald Lessard, eds., *New Mortgage Designs for an Inflationary Environment (Boston: The Federal Reserve Bank of Boston), Conference Series No. 14, 1975. See especially the paper by Richard A. Cohn and Stanley Fischer, "Alternative Mortgage Designs," p. 47–69, in the Modigliani–Lessard volume. Also see Jack L. Carr and Lawrence B. Smith, "Inflation, Uncertainty and Future Mortgage Instruments," in George W. Gau and Michael A. Goldberg, eds., North American Housing Markets into the 21st Century* (Cambridge, Mass.: Ballinger Publishers), 1983, pp. 203–231.

21. For details of the RAM concept, see Jack M. Guttentag, "Reverse Annuity Mortgages: How S&L's Can Write Them," in *Alternative Mortgage Instruments Research Study, Volume III,* November 1977.

22. For an introduction to mortgage-backed futures markets, see: Richard L. Sandor, "Trading Mortgage Interest Rate Futures," *Federal Home Loan Bank Board Journal* (September, 1975): 2–9; and Neil A. Stevens, "A Mortgage Futures Market: Its Development, Uses, Benefits and Costs," *Federal Reserve Board of St.*

Louis Review (April 1976):pp.12–19. For an analysis of their utility in shifting interest rate risk from households to appropriate risk markets, see George W. Gau and Michael A. Goldberg, "Interest Rate Risk and Residential Mortgages: Efficient Allocation of Risk Through Financial Futures Markets" (Vancouver, B.C.: Faculty of Commerce and Business Administration, University of British Columbia), 1982, mimeographed working paper.

23. The idea of extending financial futures instruments (such as mortgage options and mortgage-backed futures) to develop mortgage renewal insurance to protect households against adverse interest rate changes when they renew their mortgages is explored in great depth in George W. Gau and Dennis R. Capozza, "Mortgage Rate Insurance" (Ottawa, Ontario: Canada Mortgage and Housing Corporation), August 1982.

24. For details on the shared appreciation mortgage and its relationship to the other alternative mortgage instruments being discussed here, see George W. Gau, "An Examination of Alternatives to the Rollover Mortgage" (Ottawa, Ontario: Canada Mortgage and Housing Corporation), 1981, discussion paper, especially pp. 25–28. Also see Lewis Freiberg, "The Problem with SAM: An Economic and Policy Analysis," *Housing Finance Review* 1(1:1982):93–102.

25. For a discussion of the need for alternative liability instruments, which are necessary to allow lenders to match their assets (the proposed alternative mortgage instruments) with their liabilities (the required new liability and deposit designs), see Michael A. Goldberg, "Price Level Adjusted Mortgages" (Ottawa: Canada Mortgage and Housing Corporation), 1982, a paper presented to a CMHC conference on Mortgage Instruments for the 1980, pp. 8–10.

26. Some excellent references exist on the Canadian mortgage market. See, for example: Lawrence B. Smith, *op. cit.;* James E. Hatch, *The Canadian Mortgage Market* (Toronto, Ontario: The Queen's Printer for Ontario), 1975; and J. V. Poapst, ed., *Developing the Residential Mortgage Market,* 3 volumes (Ottawa, Ontario: Central Mortgage and Housing Corporation), 1973.

27. *Canadian Housing Statistics, 1978,* (Ottawa, Ontario: Central Mortgage and Housing Corporation), 1979.

28. Poapst, *op. cit.,* argues strongly in favor of the creation of a secondary mortgage market in Canada based on his perceived need for massive flows of mortgage funds during the 1970s. He argues for the creation of Mortgage Investment Companies (MICs) and Real Estate Investment Trusts (REITs), both of which have come to pass but occupy miniscule positions in the Canadian mortgage market, as a review of Table 6–4 will quickly demonstrate. His argument was based on the need for such markets and institutions in the United States, but, as we have seen, the lack of deposit rate ceilings and the relatively greater degree of flexibility in the Canadian mortgage instrument have allowed Canadian mortgage markets to provide record flows of funds using extant instruments and institutions.

29. While Canadian capital markets and their mortgage submarkets may be functioning efficiently, there is some reason to believe that government programs have tended to distort things by making housing more attractive than it otherwise would have been, therefore attracting more capital into housing markets than would be the case without government efforts. See Lawrence B. Smith, "Federal Housing Programs and the Allocation of Credit and Scarce Resources,"

in James E. Pesando and Lawrence B. Smith, *Government in Canadian Capital Markets: Selected Cases* (Montreal: C. D. Howe Research Institute), 1978.

30. See Gau and Capozza, "Mortgage Rate Insurance," *op. cit.,* and also Dennis R. Capozza and George W. Gau, "Expected Risk Premiums and Mortgage Rate Spread Options" (Ottawa, Ontario: CMHC and Toronto Stock Exchange), October 1982.

7

THE LOCAL PUBLIC SECTOR

INTRODUCTION

The local public sector includes municipalities, counties, school and special-purpose districts, and metropolitan governments. These levels of government have profound effects on urban land markets. The provision of services by the local public sector, in theoretical work on public finance, has been found to be similar to the private sector. People have choices on location within a metropolitan community, that is, they can choose their optimal mix of taxes and service levels. If they are not satisfied with the level of service, they can relocate to another jurisdiction. In the classic article by Tiebout, it was found that those not satisfied vote with their feet.[1]

Part and parcel of the issue of the local public sector economy relates to the problem of local public goods: police and fire protection, educational services, sanitation and park services. Provision for attendance at a given school may depend on residency within the local municipality. The difference between public goods provided by local government and those provided by higher levels of government is that people can be excluded from the consumption of local public goods. One citizen cannot prevent another from consuming services of the Defense Department, but the same cannot be said for schools or community centers servicing local districts.

The exclusion principle for local public goods does not necessarily imply that new residents must pay higher prices to take advantage of extant local services. In some cases, however, marginal entrants such as developers of new housing, must provide ancillary roads and sewer connections substantially in excess of the prevailing average. Goldberg (1980) has discussed the controversy arising from the municipalities requiring higher servicing standards on new entrants, and concludes there may be sound economic reasons for such standards.[2] In other cases new entrants automatically receive the same levels of service as existing residents at the same cost. However, nonresidents are excluded in both cases. A final issue is the question of congestion that is ultimately imposed on existing residents by new in-migrants.

Later in this chapter the effect of local public goods on land prices is considered. Suppose one municipality has school facilities perceived to be of better quality than those of its neighbors. Only residents of the municipality qualify, so the demand, and the assumed constant supply of land increases the price. The degree of capitalization is to the extent that prices increase as a consequence of this in-migration. An analogous argument obtains with local taxation. For no increase in the supply of local public goods, higher taxes are capitalized into reduced land prices.

There are some assumptions in research on capitalization. First, all residents of a given municipality are assumed to consume the services equally. This need not necessarily obtain. Further, the empirical research is divided on whether tax capitalization occurs. The range is from no capitalization, or no reduction in property prices if taxes increase, to full capitalization, where prices fall by the present value of the increase in the tax bill.

The local public sector can also affect location and construction decisions through examples such as exclusionary zoning. Zoning regulations restricting land use to single-family residential, when multiple-family usage would obtain in the market, cause land prices to fall.

A further section of this chapter, "Local Taxes," discusses the revenue side of local public finance. The main revenue source is the property tax, levied by assessments on various categories of property. Other revenue sources are user fees such as entry fees to public parks and swimming pools, and sales tax. In addition, some local municipalities are permitted to charge income taxes on residents.

The final section, "Local Expenditures," explores expenditures at the local level in some detail, focusing on specific individual local public goods such as schools and fire protection.

THE THEORY OF LOCAL PUBLIC GOODS

Metropolitan areas are divided into a large number of separately governed communities and special-purpose districts. An individual may have the choice of several communities, with location and distance to work being factors in the decision. Tiebout argues that if there is a sufficient number of communities, a consumer can reveal his or her preferences on desired police and fire protection and schooling by selecting among these locations.[3] Hence, the demand for local public goods may be derived similarly to that for private goods such as cheese, beer, or housing services.

However, competitive analogs depend on the presence of a large number of communities, the "firms" supplying local public goods. Since this is not the case in practice, monopolistic competition may arise, with communities attempting to attract or discourage new residents.

The observed case in local communities, particularly in the United States, suggests that competitive conditions with free entry to municipalities have failed. Instead, monopolistic entry restrictions have been imposed, with those inside the community having privileged access to educational and other services. Examples are zoning restrictions with large lot sizes, and restrictions on the availability of industrial and commercial land. An appropriate comparative theory may be that developed for clubs, as suggested by Buchanan.[4] Clubs can impose exclusionary entrance requirements.

The benefits of local public goods are spatially restricted, which immediately raises the following issues.

- If the public goods are "pure" in the sense that consumption cannot be excluded, then metropolitan consolidation with one community is appropriate. This is because there are economies of scale in the provision of these services. However, land size is fixed and there may be spatial components to the public good. For example, a park in a given location will be closer in distance to some residents than to others. To compensate, people travel to the park; as a result, congestion in the given community increases, leading to a situation where both park users suffer and more than one jurisdiction is preferable.

- There are increasing returns in the provision of the public good, but the fixed land supply (e.g., spatial scale) implies that there are decreasing returns to labor for the population in any one community. Each additional worker is assigned to the fixed land, so there are decreasing returns in labor. For example, garbage collection for one additional resident may be possible at below the existing average cost for current residents. However, employment of the new in-migrants yields a marginal product below that for existing residents. With fixed land, resources, and densities, a trade-off exists between allowing and not allowing increased density.

The Equilibrium Popluation Level in a Community

To develop an analysis of the provision of local goods, consider the following.[5] Let total output of goods and services in the municipality be Y, and this can be allocated either to private or public consumption. There are L residents in the community, and each consumes the same amount of private output C. The rest of total output is produced by the government, G. Government output is provided through water, fire, police, and sanitation services as well as schools. These do no necessarily have to be provided by the public sector, and some may well lie in the private consumption level C. Total demand equals total supply, or the income and expenditures sides of local acounts balance. So:

$$Y = CL + G = f(L:A) \qquad (7.1)$$
$$\text{(demand)} \quad \text{(supply)}$$

where $f(L:A)$ is the aggregate supply of goods coming from the production function. Output produced depends only on land and labor. Land (A) is fixed in the short run.

Equation (7.1) is an analog of the two approaches to measuring national output developed in Chapter 3, except that the application is now to the local level. Total expenditure on private goods and public goods, the left side, is equal to total income received. Suppose each resident has indifferences curves $\bar{U}(C,G)$ defined for given $\bar{U}$. The situation is depicted in Figure 7-1, and C^* and G^* represent the equilibrium quantities of private and public goods consumed.

Equilibrium occurs where the indifference curve is tangent to the budget constraint (7.1). To determine the slope, hold population in the community and output fixed. So:

$$0 = L\Delta C + \Delta G \qquad (7.2)$$

for ΔC and ΔG changes in private and public goods consumed. Rearranging:

$$\frac{\Delta C}{\Delta G} = -\frac{1}{L}$$

or one unit increase in the public good decreases private consumption by the inverse of the population (a trade-off). This is a measure of the crowding out associated with local expenditures. This crowding out arises when, for example, the government increases spending on

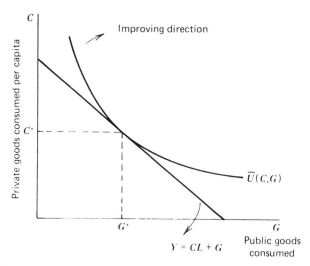

Figure 7–1. Local public goods demand, fixed population.

schools, and income is fixed by the capabilities of the production function, the local citizenry must spend less on food, housing, and private goods. Suppose there are 10,000 inhabitants of the municipality and they each spend $10,000 on units of private goods, each of which cost $1. Suppose further that the local government is spending $40 million. Goods can be considered measured in units priced at one dollar. So, total income Y is $(10 \times 10) + 40$, or $140 million. If supply is fixed and the government embarks on a road development program costing $5 million, private resources available for spending must fall by the same amount, to $95 million. However, the population is still 10,000, so on average each has seen purchasing power decline in private goods from 10,000 to 9500, or 5 percent. This is the essence of (7.3). An increase in government spending has an effect on each member of the municipality.

The slope of the indifference curve is $\Delta C/\Delta G = -MU_G/MU_C$, the ratio of the marginal utilities, or marginal rate of substitution. So:

$$-\Delta C/\Delta G = \frac{MU_G}{MU_C} = \frac{1}{L} \tag{7.4}$$

yielding

$$MU_C = L \times MU_G \tag{7.5}$$

or:

$$1 = \frac{L \times MU_G}{MU_C} \tag{7.6}$$

If G increases by one unit, C must decrease by one, so the marginal rate of transformation is unity. The expression $L \times MU_G/MU_C$ is the sum of the marginal rates of substitution. Each person has a marginal rate of substitution between public and private goods of MU_G/MU_C, say, between roads and car services. The condition of equilibrium is that the marginal utility of car services to one motorist is equal to the marginal utility of road services over all consumers. Consider the road program again. It has been determined that the change in government spending to pay for the program is equal to the change in private spending per capita times the population, a definition, from $\Delta G + L\Delta C = 0$. However, each consumer also has a trade-off between evaluating roads and private goods, given by the slope of the indifference curve. Now the amount of road building each person is willing to give up to obtain more consumption (and vice versa) at the margin is $\Delta C/\Delta G = -MRS$ where $MRS = MU_G/MU_C$, the marginal rate of substitution between private and public goods. But the government constraint means $\Delta C\Delta G = -1/L$, so $MU_G/MU_C = 1/L$. The left side is each individual's willingness to trade off one good for another.

Further problems arise when there are widely different valuations of local public goods. School improvements may not be valued the same.

This is a problem with public goods. One must determine each person's demand in order to pay for the good, yet no person can be denied access. Thus far, no derivation has been made of the effect on the land market of these local expenditures. Suppose the community or municipality now decides to expand and admit more people. Returning to Figure 7–1, the public goods intercept, where there is no private consumption, is:

$$Y = G = f(L{:}A) \tag{7.7}$$

and for private goods, with $G = 0$:

$$Y = CL = f(L{:}A) \tag{7.8}$$

So:

$$C = f(L{:}A)/L \tag{7.9}$$

which is output per resident.

Now comes the population increase, for example, with a new subdivision. Population increases from L_1 to L_2 in Figure 7–2, and the level of public goods produced becomes a maximum of $G_2 = f(L_2)$. Because the production function has decreasing returns to scale, the maximal level of private goods per capita declines.

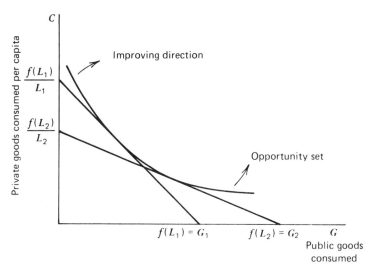

Figure 7–2. Population increase in municipality: land fixed.

The amount of private goods produced is:

$$C = \frac{f(L) - G}{L} \tag{7.10}$$

or $CL = f(L) - G$. Suppose G is held constant and the population size is varied to maximize private goods. As a real-world analog, the size and the quality of the school system is fixed. The municipality then faces the problem of how many residents to admit to maximize private consumption. The problem is indicated in Figure 7–3. The maximum is achieved where consumption of private goods is the marginal product of labor. So:

$$C = \frac{f(L) - G}{L} = MP_L \tag{7.11}$$

where MP_L is the marginal product of labor.[6] The level of private consumption at the margin is the amount produced by the last resident. So:

$$G = f(L) - LMP_L \tag{7.12}$$

or the public output is total output, minus employment, times the marginal product of labor. Since MP_L is equal to the wage W:

$$G = f(L) - LW \tag{7.13}$$

or output less wage costs.

The interpretation of this is important. If a municipality has fixed land and wants to determine the population size that maximizes per

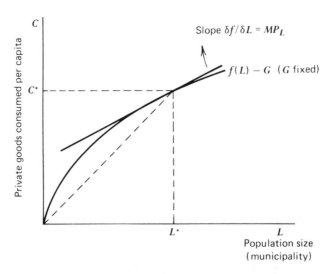

Figure 7–3. Determining optimum population.

capita consumption, the rule is to provide public goods equal to the amount of economic rent, $f(L) - LW$. This provides a rule for determining the size of the local public sector.

For any municipality, the issue is to determine what size the local public sector should be. Total output produced is paid to only two factors, land and labor, and the former is fixed. It thus earns economic rent. For our exemplary municipality with 10,000 people, let the average income be $12,000. Total income paid to people is then $120 million. The value of total output in the municipality is $140 million. The total land rent is the difference between the two, or $20 million.

If the municipality provides schools, safety, and utility services totaling the economic rent on land, or $20 million, the per capita consumption of private goods is optimized. In Chapter 4, economic rent was converted to market rent by the competitive bidding process. Economic rent on land provides a measure of how far the municipality should expand in offering public goods. This is another indication of the usefulness and importance of economic rent.

Economic rent accrues to the fixed land. A century ago Henry George, with this situation in mind, advocated a single tax on land use. This is the only tax necessary here to finance the purchase of the public good, and it is nondistortionary in that it falls on rent. However, the point remains that there exists in a municipality an optimum population where the benefits in additional output are balanced by congestion on the given land base.

Economic rent on land yields the exact quantity of municipal revenue required to finance the municipal budget. If taxes on land were the only source of revenue, a single tax would determine the amount of expenditure. This budget maximizes private consumption. The tax falls on a factor in perfectly inelastic supply, and nominally there are no distortions. Landowners cannot move their property out of the municipality. It is this notion that underlies local property taxes, which account for almost two-thirds of municipal revenues. There is an economic argument in its favor, as has been indicated.

Land Values and Capitalization

The conclusion is that there are no distortions in the tax system, where land rent is used exclusively to provide public goods. In practice, taxes are not levied to the point where they exhaust economic rent. Political pressures are against a single land tax. Also, land may not be in perfectly inelastic supply.

Since economic rent taxes are now at some rate t less than 100 percent, public sector deficits must be financed by alternative means. Suppose this is done by a fixed lump-sum tax T on each resident. Examples are business license fees, but here T represents a poll tax.

Some of the economic rents now are collected by the landowners, since the municipality is not collecting them all. Hence, the quantity of schooling, fire services, and other local public goods affects rents. For each community, as before, per capita consumption C is the marginal product of labor MP_{Li} ($i = 1, 2$) before the payment of property taxes. Each citizen must pay taxes required for the local public goods, comprising the following:

1. fixed assessment T_i

2. land rent taxes tR_i

where R_i is the amount of land rent per unit of land, and each person has one unit. So the budget constraint for each resident is:

$$C = W_i + (1 - t) R_i - T_i \qquad i = 1, 2 \qquad (7.14)$$

or consumption is gross income from work, plus the land rent the resident is permitted to keep, less the per capita tax. Here W_i is the gross wage each person obtains from work, $(1 - t)R_i$ is the portion of the land rent he or she retains after paying property tax, and T_i is the fixed lump-sum tax. This varies across the two communities. So there are three components of consumption. These may be discussed separately. This indicates the response in the local public sector if there is an increase in population or migration.

Labor market The effect in the labor market is given by the marginal product of labor equal to the wage. It is assumed that there are diminishing marginal products for labor. Since the wage is equal to the marginal product, each new resident increases competition in the labor market, reducing wages for those already there. If this is a pure "bedroom community" where there are no employment opportunities and people must commute to work, then this effect is zero. However, in general, a population influx reduces per capita consumption somewhat as in Figure 7–4a.

Land Rent Land rent is affected by the arrival of new people. Total rent is AR_i, with A fixed; and, from (7.12), the economic rent is $f(L_i) - L_iW_i$, or output less labor costs. So:

$$R_i = [f(L_i) - L_iMP_L]/A \qquad (7.15)$$

and this is indicated in Fig. 7–4a. Output $f(L_i)$ is the total area under the wage curve.[7] As the population increases, for example, from L_1 to L_2, the land rent also increases, as given by the shaded area of Figure 7–4b. The arrival of new potential members of the community increases the demand for land, increasing land rents for those already in the community. Total land rent is the area under the curve $f(L_i)$ less

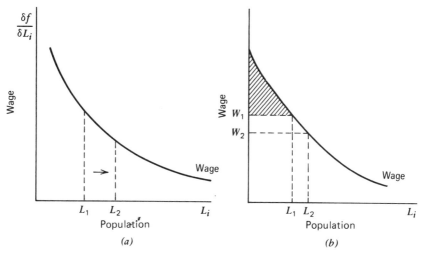

Figure 7–4. Effect of migration on resident of given community.(a) Effect from the labor market. (b) Effect in land rent.

the payments to labor $W_i L_i$, since W the wage is equal to the marginal product of labor.

Per capita taxes Thus far, the effect of increased migration in a municipality has been analyzed. The effect on the labor market is to depress wages, while the land rent increases when new people arrive. Public goods expenditure is G_i, and tax collections on land is tAR_i, where A is the land mass. This leaves the per capita tax as:

$$T_i = (G_i - tAR_i)/L_i \tag{7.16}$$

Suppose the addition of more residents has no effect on the local public goods provided, G_i. Then, whether the head tax must be increased depends on the response with respect to rents. From the above this is positive, so the effect on $-tAR_i$ is negative, reducing taxes for the existing residents.

Hence the tax and land rent effects are beneficial, and the labor market effect is negative for residents. Since the public goods such as the school system are financed by methods other than the single 100 percent rent tax, the additional demand increases land prices. The point is that, with a Henry George model, where the only local tax is one on property and all land economic rents are taxed away by the municipality, increased migration does not pump up land prices. However, if all land rents are not taxed away, the rule applies. This is the issue of property tax capitalization, where the benefits of these services are ultimately reflected in land prices, to the benefit of the existing owners. Further, the theory indicates that, to determine the size of the local public sector and goods provided by it, people must determine not only their own utility but the in-migration decisions of others. There is empirical controversy on whether tax capitalization occurs, but the crucial issue here is that exogenous migration decisions are important and intimately affect local taxes, services, and rents. As seen here, new arrivals affect both the land and labor markets.

The considerations here apply to suburban communities in the United States, which frequently are organized as clubs. Low-density zoning, such as single-family residential with large minimum lot sizes, increases the entry fee for the potential in-migrant, as land prices and job opportunities are affected. Local regulation may affect many of the market factors discussed in Chapters 4 and 5.

These clubs cater to differing preferences individuals have when trading off private goods for local public goods. Within the latter, some citizens may value parks more than schools. If there are consumers who place a zero price on all public goods, a community may offer low taxes and no services. Paradoxically, both rich and poor communities may evolve to such a state. A ghetto with no tax base may be forced to offer no services.

Allocating Public Land

Another issue at the local level is the allocation of public land among competing users. Extensive models of the allocation of private land have been presented, but it is also relevant to examine public land. Considering purely recreational uses, an area may be used as a wildlife sanctuary or upgraded to a playground for children. Locally owned land can be assigned to commercial or industrial uses. Here we are concerned with land owned by the municipality, and it is constructive to retain the recreation example.

Where the majority of landowners in the municipality are not direct consumers of the parkland, they will vote to maximize the number of entrants into the community, since their objective is to maximize land value and their rents. This in turn may lead to increased migration and decreasing wages.

Rich and Poor Communities

As peviously noted, some communities have restrictions that act as barriers to entry, but not for the wealthy. This introduces the further question of rich and poor municipalities and their treatment of public goods.

There are two types of public goods of interest. The first is a publicly provided private good, such as schooling. This is a private good because access to education can be limited. If the educational system provides the same standard to all, and is financed by a property tax, the redistribution can be considerable.[8] A community with expensive houses and land may be able to provide expensive schooling. Access to the community yields high-quality schooling as a benefit, but the entry fee is higher, assuming some capitalization. It is thus possible for the rich to afford higher-quality schooling even where there is no nominal tuition. In terms of redistribution, since the rich own more expensive property, their share of the tax load is higher, however, the equalizing or leveling of income groups as a goal of education is short circuited.

The second type of public good may be "pure" in that access is not deniable. However, preferences for this good by rich and poor may not be similar, and the rich may object to redistribution. For example, local government at the county level is partially responsible for welfare costs in the United States. The rich are likely to oppose this on the basis that they both contribute a larger share and receive no benefits.

Suppose there are two groups of people, with utility defined by U_R and U_P for rich and poor, respectively.[9] These people all live in separate rich and poor municipalities. Under the previous set of assumptions, equilibrium is defined in Figure 7–5a. This solution involves substitution between private and public goods equal to the inverse of the population as before, yielding G_R in Figure 7–5a. A similar problem confronts the poor where Y_P is the income of a poor person, and this yields the level of public goods demand, GP, in the poor municipality.

Now suppose the two groups want to form one community. The total income of all rich people is $L_R Y_R$, and the corresponding total for poor people is $L_P Y_P$. So total income is now $L_P Y_P = L_R Y_R$, and if all of this is spent on local public goods, it is possible to achieve G max shown in Figure 7–5b.

The representative rich person now has a budget constraint shown by the higher dotted line in Figure 7–5b, while the poor person

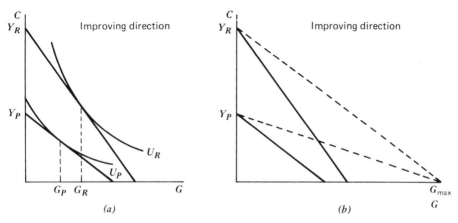

Figure 7–5. Rich and poor communities. (a) Rich and poor communities separate.(b) Rich and poor communities mixed.

has a constraint indicated by the lower dotted line. In either case, both are better off. However, in practical terms there remain problems with any redistribution involved.

The theory of local public goods indicates that spillovers are present, and the demand for them depends on the utility of all members of the community, not just those in one jurisdiction. Also, migration decisions must be included in any demand for local public goods. The theory also explains why rich and poor may cluster separately, and in the case where local taxes fall below economic rents, land values increase to capitalize these benefits. It remains to examine the practical considerations of taxes and expenditures at the local level as they affect land prices. Government policies on taxes and the level of local public expenditures affect land prices.

Local Taxes   The major component of local government revenue is the property tax. Theoretically, taxation on land is argued as being appropriate on efficiency and equity grounds, if the land is earning economic rent.[10] Increased taxation does not alter the supply of land, since it is perfectly inelastic, and hence the output produced is unchanged. Land rents are converted to tax revenue. It may be the case that the land is not in perfectly inelastic supply, in which case the rule loses some validity.

In 1972, in the United States, taxes on property accounted for 83 percent of local tax revenue. For school districts, it accounted for 98 percent; townships, 91 percent; and counties, 86 percent, though for municipalities it was "only" 64 percent.[11] In 1978 total revenue of Canadian local governments from own sources, or excluding transfers from higher levels of government, was $10.4 billion, of which 6.7 billion came from property taxes.[12] In both the United States and Canada, tax rates and assessments are made at the state or provincial and local levels, though in other countries, notably Britain, rates are set by a national authority.

The local levy of property taxes in the United States and Canada is based on two factors.

1. The assessment level for property taxes is an amount for valuation purposes on which the tax is levied.

2. The nominal property tax rate, or mill rate, is the rate of tax levied on the assessment level. The term "mill rate" applies because the tax is frequently expressed per $1000 of assessment.

Suppose a property owner has a house of market value V, with assessment A and nominal property tax rate t_n. Then the effective property tax rate is:

$$t_e = \frac{At_n}{V} \qquad (7.17)$$

If $A/V = a$, then the assessment-market value ratio $t_e = at_n$, (i.e. the product of the assessment ratio and the nominal tax rate). Consider a house with a market value of \$100,000 and an assessed value of \$50,000, with a nominal property tax rate of 94 mills, or \$94 per \$1000 of assessment. Then a is 0.5 and t_n is .094, so the effective property tax rate is 4.7 percent.

The average property tax rate in the United States in 1972 was 1.6 percent in effective terms.[13] This is prior to the savings arising because property taxes are deductible against other income in computing federal tax liability. This leads to further issues in constructing the effective rate of taxation. To the owner of a property, this reduces his or her user cost of operating the property per unit of time. In the United States, residential property taxes are so deductible, but this provision does not exist in Canada. If the marginal tax rate of the individual is t, then the effective property tax rate is:

$$t_e = (1 - t)at_n \qquad (7.18)$$

for the United States, further lowering the effective rate.

Since the tax parameters, the mill rate, and assessment levels are set locally, or in conjunction with states and provinces, there is scope for variation across jurisdictions. Some jurisdictions have instituted a program of market value assessments. This involves frequent, usually annual, reassessment of every property in the jurisdiction. If complex market value assessment obtains, then $a = 1$. Naturally, the imposition of market value assessment involves substantial costs of assessment and establishment of appeals procedures. There are costs involved in carrying out the annual assessment and in establishing an appeals procedure. These are administrative costs in creating an equitable property tax structure.

Since the effective property tax is at_n prior to deductibility, a given tax rate can be achieved by altering the mill rate t_n. The problem here is that the mill rate is typically set at the same level over all property in a given category, and does not reflect relative market value movements. Although commercial, industrial, and residential property may have separate mill rates, all residential property may be subject to the same rate. Hence, if certain residential areas are increasing in value faster than others, mill rates will not sufficiently alter relative tax loads in the absence of annual reasssessments with no error, or if market values change substantially within one year. This phenomenon may arise as a consequence of the decay of urban centers. As a solution to the problem, property assessments could initially be set at zero. If the area recovered, subsequent repeated market value reappraisals could result in positive tax revenues.

In terms of the competition among "firms" or jurisdictions to attract citizens, what is relevant is at_n and not either component. Further, marginal tax rates are important. As discussed earlier, there may be differences in strategic behavior between rich and poor communities in attracting new residents. Suppose two jurisdictions have the same assessment-market value ratio a and nominal tax rate t_n, but property taxes are deductible from other income for tax purposes. Then, due to higher marginal tax rates, the effective tax rate facing buyers of the services in the rich community is lower than that in the poor community. The municipality in each case has the same tax rate for revenue raising, since at_n is the same.

Suppose a person has a marginal tax rate of 40 percent, and at_e is 1.6 percent, the average in the United States. Then the effective tax rate is 1.6 × 0.6, or 0.96 percent. This is the effective tax rate for the individual taxpayer. To the municipality, the tax rate naturally excludes the marginal personal rate. The subsidy is effectively provided by the federal government.

States and provinces have attempted to impose some form of standard assessment procedures. As one option, the entire assessment function can be assumed by the state or provincial government, with the municipalities retaining control only over the mill rate. There may be economies of scale in carrying out and administering the assessments. Nevertheless, the existence of a personal tax structure with progressively higher marginal rates on higher incomes, the deductibility of property taxes, and differing mill rates all militate against uniformity in property taxes. In a sense, this diversity permits consumers a more effective choice on taxes and services, in conformity with the Tiebout hypothesis. (Note that this will tend to be truer in the United States, which has property tax deductibility, than in Canada which does not.)

Problems in Assessments

The market value assessment procedure has already been examined. An alternative is the use of rental income value. The United States and Canada use the former procedure, even if imperfectly, and the latter is sometimes used for income properties. In Britain, the latter procedure is used exclusively. The rental income procedure is to levy the tax on the flow of rental services from a property. However, if land is held for speculative purposes or in undeveloped form, there may be no cash flow and no tax liability, yet such properties possess a market value.[14] In an era of speculation where individuals hold land as a store of value, the rental income procedure leads to the absence of horizontal equity, or equal treatment of similar types of wealth. One property owner may have an empty lot valued at $100,000 but generating no current income, while another may possess a rental house worth \$100,000 and yielding \$20,000 annually, for example, as student housing. The latter would be subject to taxation on the revenue or income method and the former would not. The famous case of London's Centre Point office tower, which remained vacant and untaxed for years, highlights the difficulties in rental-based taxing methods. Some property owners generate no cash flow, so the rental-based method may create financial difficulty.

Part of the reason for the different asset values of property is the risk and uncertainty involved. An empty lot, or "raw land," is more risky and less liquid than a rental house. However, an empty lot has value and the taxation on market value is more appropriate here. This is not to minimize the problems with assessment procedures. First, market value is difficult to determine, particularly where transactions are infrequent and irregular. Second, some property owners have characteristics such as low income which make it difficult to pay taxes. Groups in this category include the elderly and the handicapped. Yet there may be social savings in reduced care costs through keeping these groups in their homes.

Taxing Land Versus Taxing Improvements

The Henry George model argues that since land is in perfectly inelastic supply, it can earn an economic rent. This assumes demand is such that supply and demand intersect at a positive price. If not, the land is vacant and earns no rent. This forms the basis of the argument for a single tax on land. In practice, the property tax is levied not only on land but also on site improvements, where they exist. Buildings or structures bear a part of the property tax. With the land tax there are no distortions, provided perfectly inelastic supply obtains. Taxes on buildings reduce the amount of construction and improvements. One effect, it has been argued, is to reduce construction of low-income dwellings; and it would be preferable, it is suggested, to increase the relative share of property taxes borne by land. The tax reallocation would shift the burden toward land, where allegedly no distortion arises.

Property Tax Capitalization

A further theoretical issue, also discussed above, is the degree to which property taxes are capitalized in the prices of property in the municipalities. One model used to test for this phenomenon is to determine the correlation between house prices in the municipality and the rate of property taxes. Presumably, the higher the taxes, the lower the value of houses, all else being equal.[15]

The problem with this formulation is that no imputation is made for the expenditure levels and quality of services by local governments. Often, however, some municipalities spend more than others, or provide a more attractive package of local public goods. To eliminate this problem, one procedure is to confine the study to property within a given municipality, but here there may not be substantial variation in property taxes. Some municipalities have the same tax rate on all property, so no capitalization effect can easily be measured.

The motivation for the research is to determine to what extent people "vote with their feet" in selecting a municipality. Studies for suburbs of New Jersey suggest that property taxes are capitalized, in that higher taxes reduce property values. However, when the data are restricted to members of a given municipality, the results are less clear, and no capitalization emerges.[16]

The precise magnitude of tax capitalization can be obtained by considering a specific example. Suppose the actual tax rate for a house worth $20,000 increases from 0.02 to 0.03 and has an incremental life for the house of 40 years. Also, the tax increase is assumed to be permanent. At a discount rate of 5 percent, the value of the house would decline to $17,740 under full capitalization. The calculation is:

$$e^* = \frac{[e(1 + \theta p)]}{[1 + (\theta + \Delta)p]} \tag{7.19}$$

where e^* is the capitalized value of a house currently worth e, and θ is the actual tax rate. The incremental change in the tax rate is Δ, and p is the present value of a $1 annuity discounted at the given rate and over the incremental house life. The present value of $1 annuity over 40 years at 5 percent is $p = \$17.16$. Consequently:

$$e^* = \left\{ \frac{20{,}000\ [1 + (0.02 \times 17.16)]}{1 + 0.03 + 17.16} \right\}$$

yielding $17,740 and $e - e^*$ is $2260, the capital loss.

Distribution and Burden

There has been extensive discussion as to the high level and rapid rate of growth of property taxes. The problem derives from the fact that the property tax is more visible than other forms of taxation, and therefore more subject to taxpayer protest than weekly or even monthly income tax withholding.

Turning to some empirical evidence, based on an individual sample, for the Canadian city of London, Ontario, average effective property taxes are indicated in Table 7–1 by both income class and house value. As far as income class is concerned, the effective property tax prior to the calculation of a tax credit is regressive, with lower rates applying to higher-income earners. Even with the provincial property tax credit, which is a constant dollar amount, a proportional effect ap-

Table 7–1 Property and Personal Income Tax Rates
Distribution of properties and personal income tax rates by income class and house value,
London, Ontario 1973 (sample means)

	Number in Sample	Effective Properties Tax Rate	Marginal Tax Rate, Household Head	Property Tax Credit	Net Property Tax Rate
Income class ($)					
<3,000	171	0.0105	0.1979	0.0050	0.0055
3,001– 6,000	133	0.0096	0.2475	0.0045	0.0051
6,001–10,000	368	0.0079	0.2939	0.0019	0.0060
10,001–15,000	384	0.0060	0.3434	0.0007	0.0054
15,001–25,000	136	0.0060	0.4334	0.0001	0.0059
<25,000	32	0.0069	0.4531	0	0.0069
House value ($)					
<20,000	72	0.0124	0.2594	0.0064	0.0060
20,001–30,000	278	0.0105	0.2801	0.0035	0.0069
30,001–40,000	378	0.0077	0.3048	0.0016	0.0061
40,001–50,000	297	0.0053	0.3201	0.0009	0.0044
50,001–60,000	99	0.0038	0.3645	0.0003	0.0035
> 60,000	100	0.0065	0.3731	0.0004	0.0060
Aggregate sample	1224	0.0076	0.3106	0.0020	0.0057

Source: P. Chinloy, "Effective Property Taxes and Tax Capitalization," *Local Economics* (May 1982): 744.

pears to arise. By contrast, the personal income tax rate is progressive, increasing with income.

The results are similar to house value. The least expensive houses appear to bear the highest property tax rates prior to the application of the credit. When the tax credit is applied, this regressive aspect is neutralized slightly.

For the United States, some similar data are reported in Table 7–2. Low-income households pay a relatively high percentage of total income in property taxes, and this percentage falls as income increases. The regressive conclusion may be strengthened when it is realized that imputed income from housing services is not included in the income definition, and higher-income households will enjoy even higher inputed rents, tax free.

To summarize, the property tax remains the most important source of local revenues. Excluding transfers from federal and state or provincial governments, municipalities receive about three out of every five dollars from this source. Controversy arises as to the mode of assessment and whether improvements as well as land should be taxed.

LOCAL EXPENDITURE

The definition of local public goods holds that exclusion may be possible under certain circumstances, with the municipality operating, in ef-

Table 7–2 Burden of Real Estate Tax on Low-Income Households and Elderly Single-Family Homeowners, 1970

| Family Income[a] | Real Estate Tax as Percentage of Family Income | | | Percentage of Homeowners | |
	All (I)	Elderly[b] (II)	Nonelderly (III)	Elderly[b] (IV)	Nonelderly (V)
Less than $2,000	16.6	15.8	18.9	74.5	25.5
$ 2,000–2,999	9.7	9.5	10.1	70.3	29.7
$ 35,000–5,999	5.5	6.2	5.1	32.0	68.0
$10,000–14,999	3.7	3.9	3.7	6.4	93.6
$25,000 or more	2.9	2.7	2.9	9.8	90.2
All groups	4.9	8.1	4.1	20.2	79.8

[a]Census definition of income, which excluded imputed rent.
[b]Age sixty-five and over.

Source: Advisory Commission on Intergovernmental Relations, *Federal-State-Local Finances: Significant Features of Fiscal Federalism,* 1973-74 (Washington), p. 201, as reprinted in R. A. Musgrave and P. Musgrave, *Public Finance in Theory and Practice,* 2nd edition (New York: McGraw-Hill), 1976.

fect, as a club. It remains to discuss the various forms of expenditures on these local public goods, and the effect of their provision on urban land markets.

Schools and Education

Education is the largest single component of local expenditure, accounting for almost half the total. Since the bulk of school financing comes from the property tax, jurisdictions possessing more property tax resources can offer better educational facilities.

There are several issues regarding the treatment of education in the local public sector. The first is the base for support of the system. The usual level applies to commercial, industrial, and residential property. Whether users of commercial and industrial property benefit from the local school system depends on spillovers, or on external effects of education. To the extent that such users do not benefit from the educational services, these are distortions. If there is no benefit to commercial users, then the property tax for schools is a pure tax on land and improvements, resulting in a reduction in the quantity of commercial construction and of commercial services delivered.

A second issue is whether the private or public sector should be providing the education. Since the public sector is relying on land and improvements taxes, there is the additional issue as to whether this is an appropriate financing vehicle. The case hinges on whether there are substantial social returns on education, as distinct from the returns to the individual student. If there are social returns, there is an argument for education to be provided in the public sector, though the method of taxation is still in question.

The above neglects some important factors, including the benefit of learning for its own sake and whether schools foster or reduce racial discrimination. In any event, the analysis does not change the fact that land and improvements taxes as financing vehicles introduce distortions.

Police, Fire and Other Services

The same rule for evaluating benefits can be applied to other services. In the education context of (7.21), the first component is the benefit, and the second and third, the cost. If the benefit exceeds the cost, then there may be an argument for intervention. The problem is that costs and benefits of these services cannot easily be measured.

In the case of security services for police and fire protection, a pure public goods argument can be made. Here, the consumption of additional services by one person does not reduce those of another. Yet the theoretical arguments of congestion may also apply, with each additional entrant reducing the wage and decreasing the effectiveness of protective services but increasing the property values.[17]

However, there are other problems with police and fire protection. First, communities with higher property values can afford higher levels of security services, with the converse obtaining in communities with lower property values. If the latter communites also have higher crime rates, then the requirement for protection is higher there. The solution may involve converting police and fire to a metropolitan basis, but there may be opposition to the implicit redistribution involved, an issue discussed in Chapter 15.

Second, in the case of fire services, there remains the issue of efficiency of the public sector. Several communities operate volunteer fire services as an alternative. Analogously, many communities purchase from private suppliers garbage collection, park maintenance, and other private goods normally delivered by the public sector in other communities.

SUMMARY

Our primary interest here has been on the effect of the local public sector on urban land markets. The basic use of a pure land tax in the Henry George sense is nondistortionary, but even then only under some very restrictive assumptions. In the usual case, the property tax on land falls on land and its owners and is not shifted into costs of housing or property services.

Feldstein has presented an alternative scenario.[18] Suppose the land is used for agricultural purposes and the owner is a self-employed farmer. The imposition of a tax, albeit on economic rent, reduces the farmer's return on investment. To compensate, there may be an income effect. As an example, the farmer may now work harder on the land, to increase its productivity and restore the earlier return. However, the labor-land ratio would now rise, implying that, for many production technologies, the ratio of wages to land rent would fall, as land is used relatively more scarcely. The ultimate effect is to alter relative prices and increase land rent.

There is less controversy on the application of the tax to improvements. A distortion arises, reducing the quantity of housing and commercial property services.

A number of issues on local government have not been dealt with here, being reserved for a later chapter. Included here, but to be discussed in detail later, are such issues as the property tax revolt and the crisis in the delivery of public services. The ultimate issue is that if people consume local public goods, it is not easy to explain why land should pay for them.

Footnotes

1. See C. M. Tiebout, "A Pure Theory of Local Expenditures," *Journal of Political Economy* 64: (1956) 416–424. Of course, consumers can also express their preference at the aggregate level. Those unhappy with the government of one country can leave for another. The theory is usually applied to local jurisdictions, however.

2. As an example, see M. A. Goldberg, "Municipal Arrogance or Economic Rationality: The Case of High Servicing Standards," *Canadian Public Policy—Analyse de Politiques* 6: (1980) 78–87. It is argued that there is justification in imposing high servicing standards because of the externality associated.

3. Tiebout, *op. cit.*, p. 422.

4. J. M. Buchanan, "An Economic Theory of Clubs," *Economica* 32: 1964 1–14.

5. The model relies on Buchanan, *op. cit.* + r A. B. Atkinson and J. E. Stiglitz, *Lectures on Public Economics* (New York: McGraw Hill), 1979, Lecture 17; and J. E. Stiglitz, "The Theory of Local Public Goods," in M. S. Feldstein and R. P. Inman, eds., *The Economics of Public Services* (London: Macmillan), 1977.

6. Private goods output is:

$$C = \frac{(f(L) - G)}{L}$$

Fix G, the level of local public goods, and choose the size of population in the municipality L_2 to maximize private consumption C. So:

implying:
$$\frac{\partial C}{\partial L} = \frac{\left[L_k \frac{\partial f}{\partial L} - (f(L) - G) \right]}{L^2} = 0$$

$$L \frac{\partial f}{\partial L} = f(L) - G$$

or:

$$\frac{\partial f}{\partial L} = \frac{[f(L) - G]}{L} = C$$

7. Now:

$$R_i = \frac{[f(L_i) - L_i \, \partial f/\partial L_i]}{A}$$

and A can be set at unity for convenience.
Also:

$$\frac{\partial R_i}{\partial L_i} = \frac{\partial f}{\partial L_i} - L_i \frac{\partial^2 f}{\partial L_i^2} - \frac{\partial f}{\partial L_i} = -L_i \frac{\partial^2 f}{\partial L_i^2} > 0$$

given decreasing returns in labor.

8. See Stiglitz, *op. cit.*

9. See Atkinson and Stiglitz, *op. cit.*, pp. 548–549.

10. The original discussion is contained in Henry George, *Progress and Poverty,* (New York: Appleton), 1882.

11. See U.S. Bureau of the Census, *Government Finances in 1971–72* (Washington: Government Printing Office), p. 30.

12. Statistics Canada, Public Finance Division, *General Revenue of Local Governments,* 1976.

13. U.S. Bureau of the Census, *Taxable Property Values and Assessment—Sales Ratios, Part 1, Taxable and Other Property Values,* 1972 Census of Governments (Washington, D.C.), 1973.

14. Albert M. Church, "The Effects of Local Government Expenditure and Property Taxes on Investment," *AREUEA Journal* (Summer 1981): 165–180.

15. Residential capitalization is explored in Diane Krantz et al., "Residential Property Tax Capitalization: Consistent Estimates Using Micro-Level Data," *Land Economics* (Nov. 1982): 488–497; and D. Kohlhepp and C. Ingene, "The Effect of Municipal Services and Local Taxes on Housing Values," *AREUEA Journal* (Fall 1979): 318–343.

16. See W. E. Oates, "The Effects of Property Taxes and Local Public Spending on Property Values: An Empirical Study of Tax Capitalization and the Tiebout Hypothesis," *Journal of Political Economy* 81: (1969) 957–971; H. Rosen and D. Fullerton, "A Note on Local Tax Rates, Public Benefit Levels and Property Values," *Journal of Political Economy* 85: (1977) 433–440: and A. T. King, ;"Estimating Property Tax Capitalization: A Critical Comment," *Journal of Political Economy* 85: (1977) 425–432. All of these studies find that there is a considerable degree of house price reduction from property taxes in the United States. Confining themselves to residents of a single jurisdiction are two studies that fail to produce evidence of capitalization. These studies for Canada are by T. J. Wales and E. Wiens, "Capitalization of Residential Property Taxes: An Empirical Study," *Review of Economics and Statistics* 56: (1974) 329–333, for Surrey, British Columbia; and P. Chinloy, "Effective Property Taxes and Tax Capitalization," *Canadian Journal of Economics* 11: (1978) 740–750, for London, Ontario.

17. See M. S. Johnson and M. J. Lea, "Differential Capitalization of Local Public Service Characteristics," *Local Economics* (May 1982): 189–203.

18. See M. S. Feldstein, "The Surprising Incidence of a Tax on Pure Rent: A New Answer to An Old Question," *Journal of Political Economy* 85: (1977) 349–360.

8

POLITICAL, LEGAL, AND OTHER INSTITUTIONAL PREREQUISITES TO AN UNDERSTANDING OF URBAN LAND MARKETS

INTRODUCTION: THE POLITICAL NATURE OF THE URBAN DEVELOPMENT PROCESS

Even in the United States, where the rights of the individual to pursue economic goals are highly prized, touted, and protected, one cannot imagine any longer the unfettered pursuit of private economic gain at the expense of others. Perhaps in no other market is the allocation of society's scarce resources influenced as much by the actions of government as is the urban land market. Politics, in a very real sense, is where the study of institutional factors affecting urban land markets must begin. It is the political process that establishes the laws, rules, and conditions under which urban real property markets must operate. It is the political process that mediates private gain and use through real property investment and the greater public interest that is often called on to bear the external costs of such private actions. In addition, as in the case for instance, of racial discrimination, the political process is asked to remove or overcome an imperfection in the market allocation process.

However, it is not our purpose here to get into a detailed analysis of the politics of urban development in the United States and Canada. It is merely our purpose to point out that allocation decisions in urban land markets are governed by much more than the laws and tenets of microeconomics.

The political process and the legislation produced by it buffer the purely economic considerations that are the concern of developers and urban economic analysts. Legislation allocates funds to pay for highways, trunk sewers, and water supplies. Legislation also allows certain uses and disallows others. Legislation establishes rules for subdividing raw land, for building structures on suitably zoned and subdivided land, and for maintaining or demolishing these structures. Legislation (and the political process) ultimately place limits on rights to develop or use land. Accordingly, we will begin our discussions with the key institutional concept of real property rights, for these rights and their evolution over time determine the course of urban development. It is these rights, after all, that are bought and sold in urban land markets and greatly influence market price.

After having discussed property rights and their dynamic and rapidly changing nature, we can go on to survey the different forms that the regulation of urban development has taken in Canada and the United States in light of very different institutions of real property and of means for regulating it. Once again, the value of the comparative institutional approach will become clear as we proceed.

THE LEGAL BASIS FOR URBAN DEVELOPMENT

It is not land that is traded in urban land markets but rather bundles of rights to the use of specific parcels of land and the improvements that have been constructed on them. These rights are defined in law and in practice and are very much culturally dependent.[1]

Richard T. Ely, one of the pioneers in the study of urban land economics and one of the founders of the so-called institutionalist school of economics, defined property rights in the following way.[2]

By property we mean an exclusive right to control an economic good. By private property we mean the exclusive right of a private person to control an economic good. By public property we mean the exclusive right of a political unit (city, state, nation, etc.) to control an economic good.[3]

Elaborating on Ely's concept, Herbert B. Dorau and Albert G. Hinman noted, "The essentials of property are, thus, *an exclusive right, an economic good, a legally created or recognized person* to exercise the right over the good, and *organized authority.*"[4]

That property is a socially based and dynamic construct is the basic tenet of the so-called *social theory of property.*

Thus we arrive at the social theory of property, which explains the institution as having evolved as a medium for the promotion of the general welfare. It follows then, that since society is dynamic, so must be the institution of property, to be subjected to constant alteration as man's notions of the general welfare shift and evolve and as technological advance calls for new patterns of social organization.[5]

Given this culturally based and dynamic view of the institution of property (and property rights), it should not be at all surprising to find that different cultures mean quite different things when speaking of the institution. An example is the right to develop a parcel of land that is normally assumed to go hand in hand with ownership. Such development rights are explicitly acknowledged as residing with the government (the Crown) in Canada, whereas in the United States such rights in varying forms are seen as being part of the ownership rights of the individual property owner. Clearly, in view of such different perceptions about the bundle of rights that go with land ownership, we should expect quite different approaches to land development and the control of land development between Canada and the United States.

Forms of Ownership and Other Common Interests in Real Property

Over the centuries, real property has become more broadly held. Initially, under feudal forms of ownership all land and fixtures on the land were owned by the king. These interests in real property slowly became vested in nobles in return for various services and obligations given the king. From these beginnings have evolved our present system of real property ownership and related rights, where such rights, in theory at least, are accessible to any member of society willing and able to purchase the rights.[6]

Ownership of, or interests in, real property is governed by real property law, which has several unique features.[7]

1. Transfer of interests in real property is usually in writing, whereas personal property (personalty) is usually transferred on delivery.

2. Concept of *curtesy* (a widower's right to real property owned by deceased wife) and *dower* (similar rights for a widow) apply to realty but not to personalty in general.

3. Disposition of property on death of the owner differs substantially between realty and personalty.

4. Realty cannot in general be seized by creditors until personalty has been completely exhausted.

5. The relevant laws of the state or province in which realty is located regulate the rights and interests in the realty, whereas the state or province in which the owner resides governs the personalty.

These differences are acknowledged in law and flow directly from the unique characteristics of land and improvements. Because of these differences, unique forms of ownership and related interests in real property have evolved. We will be discussing the most common and important interests (including several forms of ownership), and refer the interested reader to more specialized books for greater detail about real property law.[8]

Forms of Real Property Ownership

Ownership can be immediately broken into two subclasses.

1. Freehold estates provide both the legal title to the land and the exclusive right to possession and use.

2. Leasehold estates provide rights to use and enjoy the land, but do not convey the title.

Within each of these broad classes of ownership there are a number of subclasses with somewhat differing rights.

Freehold Estates   There are two principal freehold estates.

1. *Fee-simple* or *fee-simple absolute estates* confer rights to use and occupy the land without limit (subject to the overriding powers of the various levels of government).

2. In *life estates,* such as dower and curtesy, the owner in fee simple bestows rights of ownership on a second party as long as the party lives, after which time these rights either revert to the original owner or to his/her designee.

In either of these cases, there are numerous terms and conditions that can be attached to the fee-simple estate. We will explore some of these later. For present purposes it should be remembered that property is a complex bundle of rights. The highest form of ownership with the most broadly encompassing set of rights is contained in the fee-simple estate with no other restrictive terms and conditions. The types of terms and conditions that a property owner can attach are unlimited. The unfettered fee-simple estate can be constrained in numerous ways, however, and the prospective buyer must be aware of the bundle of rights embodied in the contemplated purchase. Fortunately, since property rights are defined in law and restrictions must be set out in registered written documents, purchasers can, and should, carefully check the restrictions accompanying the fee-simple estate.

Leasehold Estates   Under a leasehold estate the right to possession and use passes from the property owner to the tenant for a specified period of time, in return for which the tenant agrees to pay the landlord rent. As with freehold estates, the variations are essentially limitless. The principal terms in a leasehold estate are the term of the lease, the rights, restrictions, and conditions that are assigned by the landlord to the tenant, the rent, and the conditions for enforcing the terms and conditions of the leasehold. The leasehold interest can be for a fixed period of time such as one year, which is typical for residential properties, to 22 years for commercial properties, and 99 years for land leases. Leases where no termination date is specified are referred to as *periodic tenancies* and renew themselves automatically on an annual, monthly, weekly, or even daily basis subject to termination by one of the parties.

Terms, Conditions, and Restrictions on Ownership The restrictions that can be placed on the rights to use real property are highly varied. Over time, a number of limitations on the property right have come to be used with some frequency. We will briefly examine the more common terms, conditions, and restrictions that can be placed on the unfettered property right. Less common and more esoteric vehicles will not be explored, but the interested reader is directed to any of the widely used texts on real property law for information on such details.[9]

Incorporeal Rights These do not represent an estate or ownership interest in land or improvements, but rather represent privileges to use another person's property. The most common incorporeal right is an *easement* which is an irrevocable right to use someone else's land. Granting a right-of-way to a utility for its placing of overground or underground wiring is a common form of easement and is usually done in return for a fee. Easements differ from licences, which may grant identical rights in that licences run for a term, whereas easements run in perpetuity.

Liens These represent rights, held by creditors, that are secured by a piece of real property. The most common forms of liens are mortgage liens held by mortgagees as collateral for a mortgage loan; tax liens placed by taxing authorities such as local governments to obtain back taxes; and mechanics' liens placed by tradespeople to ensure payment for work done to maintain or construct improvements.

Deed Restrictions or Reservations These limitations are placed on the property by the property owner, either voluntarily or in consideration of some form of payment. *Restrictive covenants* are restrictions that limit the uses to which a property can be put. They run with the title to the property. A common form of restrictive covenant limits the use of a single-family home to that of a residence for only one family and may further restrict the owner from redeveloping the land as long as the covenant remains in force. Failure to comply with a restrictive covenant can result in court-ordered compliance. In contrast, restrictions placed on properties at the time of transfer from one owner to another as *conditions of sale* lead to forfeiture of the property and return to the original owner, or his or her designee, should the conditions not be met. One final restriction is a *reservation* where a selling party may reserve certain rights such as an easement or other forms of incorporeal rights, for example. The essential point to note in all of the above is that they restrict property rights and therefore place limitations on use and value.

Title Up to this point we have discussed the various forms of ownership and restrictions on ownership. We have not, however, discussed the documentation that confers, conveys, and allows a property owner to verify ownership. Property rights and restrictions are concepts. They are made concrete in the *title* to the land and buildings. The most valuable title is one that is free and clear of any and all restrictions (i.e., no mortgage or other lien, no covenants or restrictions, and no leases registered against the title). This form of a fee-simple ownership represents the highest form of ownership and is symbolized in the free and clear title to a piece of property that gives the owner the unfettered right to use, subject to local planning restrictions, and sell the property. It is the title to the land and buildings (and therefore to the "rights" to use these lands and buildings) that is actually bought and sold in the marketplace.

Accordingly, buyers must be aware of the exact bundle of rights that are included in the title and, more precisely, which rights are excluded through deed restrictions, liens, and leases. This indicates the importance of searching the title as registered in the state, provincial, or county registry office to ascertain which rights are included and which ones are excluded through the registration of liens, leases, and other restrictions against the title. In some jurisdictions the state, province, or county will guarantee that all rights and restrictions are recorded and that any unrecorded rights and restrictions are not the responsibility of the purchaser (the so-called Torrens System of title registration). In other jurisdictions no such guarantee is offered and buyers must purchase title insurance to provide such a guarantee. Hence, lenders are willing to provide mortgage funds without fear that a prior owner with an interest in the property may come forward to claim that interest.

Emerging Trends in Property Rights in the United States and Canada

Property rights are social constructs. They are dynamic and reflect the changing nature of society. This implies that we should expect to see property rights changing over time in both the United States and Canada, and between the United States and Canada, given their different social, economic, legal and cultural basis.

In the early 20th century, fee-simple ownership conveyed virtually complete control over one's land and improvements. Zoning laws had not yet come onto the scene, nor had any of the other common forms of government regulation such as environmental controls. Private property markets operated in an Adam Smith-like fashion, with essentially no government limitations on their functioning; building and fire codes being the only significant exception circa 1900. Adjacent property owners who were injuriously affected by traffic, noise, soot, or noxious odors did have recourse through the English common law notion of nuisance, but such recourse was limited and had to be sought case by case, property by property, owner by owner.

The passage of this century has seen dramatic changes in such *laissez faire* notions of private real property rights. It is virtually inconceivable today that developers would be allowed to put up unsafe buildings that imposed excessive traffic and noise burdens on neighboring properties. Automobile and steel factories cannot be imagined in single-family residential areas.[10]

Inroads which have been made on the freedom of owners of private property and which are now accepted as commonplace would have been unthinkable to our grandfathers, and it is within the realm of possibility that inroads which are unthinkable to us now may be commonplace to our grandchildren. Time will tell. As our society develops and changes, the test should be what is necessary in order to do the greatest good for the greatest number. One thing to keep uppermost in your mind when traveling down this road of curtailing a man's freedom of action is the basic belief that the greatest good for the greatest number comes from making men free and while some regulation is justified because it enables men to enjoy their freedom, too much regulation may destroy the freedom entirely. Keeping the proper balance in this regard should guide the development of the law.[11]

The balance since 1900 has shifted away from unfettered property rights toward greater societal control and modification of those rights. This process has been a relatively continuous one, with some critical decisions paving the way. Since the situation on these issues of property is so different in the United States as compared to Canada, we must at this point divide our discussion.

Evolution of Property Rights in the United States in the 20th Century

Cassner and Leach sketch out a hierarchy of limitations of property rights that provides a convenient framework for looking at the evolution of property rights in the United States during the present century.

Legislation or other governmental action designed to control the use of land fits into a rather clearly defined pattern. First, you have the attempts to exclude from the land certain groups of people, such as those of a certain race or aliens. Second, you have the attempts to restrict the use of the land to certain purposes, such as a zoning act which permits the land to be used only for residential purposes. Third, you have the attempts to regulate the extent of the use of the land, such legislative action being taken in the interest of conserving the natural resources of the country. Finally, you have the attempts to deprive the owner entirely of the use of his land, such as when the land is taken under eminent domain.[12]

Standing in opposition to the ability or desires of governments in the United States to limit property rights is the Constitution of the United States, which protects property rights directly. In the Fifth Amendment to the Constitution, a person cannot "be deprived of life, liberty, or property, without due process of law; nor shall private property be taken for public use without just compensation."[13] Property rights are also protected in the 14th Amendment where it is affirmed that

No State shall make or enforce any law which shall abridge the privileges or immunities of citizens of the United States; nor shall any State deprive any person of life, liberty, or property, without due process of law; nor deny to any person within its jurisdiction the equal protection of the laws.[14]

The Fourteenth Amendment is one of the so-called Civil War amendments that extended all rights in the Constitution to all people of the United States and protected these rights from state encroachment. It has provided the basis for most of the civil rights suits of the past three decades and has been the foundation for many recent suits against municipalities that employ zoning restrictions to keep out poorer households.

The substance of these constitutional provisions is that no government can make any law that denies a person their right to "life, liberty, or property." Two conflicting forces arise in the area of property rights: On the one hand, there is a need to provide for the greatest good for the greatest number; on the other hand, there is the need to protect the rights of individuals against government encroachment. The courts have ruled in favor of individual rights, as opposed to those of governments to infringe on those rights, unless governments can show that the general welfare is being significantly and adversely harmed by the continued exercise of private rights.

The first attempts to limit property rights were those passed by state and local governments to prevent nonwhites and immigrant groups from purchasing and enjoying residential properties. These ordinances were struck down by the U.S. Supreme Court as conflicting with the Fourteenth Amendment, primarily, but also with the Fifth Amendment. These attempts to deprive nonwhites and aliens of their property rights were begun at the turn of the century and continued up through the 1970s, though in much more disguised and sophisticated form since the 1954 *Brown* v. *Topeka Board of Education* landmark civil rights case.

Zoning and Related Land Use Controls

Unfettered enjoyment of property rights did not fare so well in the second class of government actions: those designed to limit land uses through zoning and other planning legislation. The landmark case here was, and still is, the *Village of Euclid* v. *Ambler Realty Company* wherein the U.S. Supreme Court found in favor of the village of Euclid (Ohio) in its attempt to enforce a zoning ordinance that it had passed, with due process, in 1922. This 1922 decision is the basis for much, if not all, of the land-use controlling legislation that has been passed since 1926 in the United States. The issues are sufficiently general that a brief look at *Euclid* v. *Ambler* is in order.

The Supreme Court dealt directly with the trade-off between the individual's right to property and the community's right to a sound and healthy environment for its citizens to enjoy their constitutionally protected freedoms. After discussing these issues at some length, the Court found,

In light of these considerations, we are not prepared to say that the end in view was not sufficient to justify the general rule of the ordinance . . . . It can not be said that the ordinance in this respect "passes the bounds of reason and assumes the character of merely arbitrary fiat."[15]

Thus, the way was opened for local areas, seeking to provide for the general welfare (the greatest good for the greatest number), to pass legislation regulating the use and intensity of use of lands falling within their jurisdiction. The impact of *Euclid* v. *Ambler* can begin to be gleaned from the following.

In 1922 the U.S. Department of Commerce issued the Standard State Zoning Enabling Act, which provided a model act through which states could delegate the zoning power, inherent in their police powers, directly to cities and counties. This was followed by the issue, again by the U.S. Department of Commerce, of the Standard City Planning Enabling Act in 1928.[16] The popularity of zoning can be seen from the fact that by 1930 29 states had adopted the State Zoning Enabling Act, and by 1946 all 48 states in the Union had adopted the act, and some 1500 zoning ordinances were the result.[17] The idea that states and local governments could so restrict property rights did not gain acceptance very readily among property owners, as it is estimated that between 1920 and 1970 state courts heard over 10,000 zoning cases.[18]

Zoning is a field of study in itself. It is becoming increasingly more complex as local, county, and state governments seek to protect residential, industrial, commercial, and natural environments through its use. At the present time zoning not only regulates use and intensity, but in many jurisdictions it also regulates setbacks, shadows, height, and aesthetic considerations such as facing materials, colors, lighting, and planting of trees and shrubs. It has come a long way from its initial objectives of health and safety, narrowly conceived as the separation of incompatible land uses. The variants of the basic zoning code, originated in New York City in 1916, are enormous and changing daily. Zoning is one of the major limitations placed on private property rights.[19]

As prevalent as zoning has become, it is being challenged by a new set of limitations of property rights based on our third component of property right restrictions: protection of our natural resources. The field of environmental protection, and its closely allied area of urban and rural growth controls, exploded during the 1970s the way zoning did during the 1930s. The U.S. government, absent from local land use matters through constitutional prohibitions, has moved into the environmental protection area in an attempt to take up some of the slack left by overlapping state jurisdictions and by the need to overcome spillover problems and environmental externalities that effect more than one state. As with zoning, any attempt at a comprehensive review is impossible because of the magnitude of the legislation, court decisions, and administrative regulations.[20] We will look at land use controls in more detail in a later chapter.

We can divide our task by level of government. Beginning with the U.S. federal government, the first major thrusts into environmental protection are the 1969 National Environmental Policy Act, the Clean Air Act Amendments of 1970, and the Federal Water Pollution Control Act Amendments of 1972.

National Environmental Policy Act of 1969 (NEPA) The enormous environmental concern that arose in North America during the 1960s in response to polluted air and water and a degraded natural environment culminated in the passing of the National Environmental Policy Act of 1969. As stated at the outset of NEPA,

The purposes of this Act are: To declare a national policy which will encourage productive and enjoyable harmony between man and his environment; to promote efforts which will prevent or eliminate damage to the environment and biosphere and stimulate the health and welfare of man; to enrich the understanding of the ecological systems and natural resources important to the Nation; and to establish a Council on Environmental Quality.[21]

The Council on Environmental Quality (CEQ) was to be located in the Executive Office of the President and basically modeled after the Council of Economic Advisors. It was to report annually to the president and the Congress on the general state of the natural environment and to undertake necessary environmental studies and advise the president on environmental matters.

However, the most far-reaching of the provisions of NEPA was for the inclusion of an environmental impact statement (EIS) in any "recommendation or report on proposals for legislation and other major Federal actions significantly affecting the quality of the human environment."[22] The requirements of an EIS to accompany proposed private and public actions has led to a revolution in the development process, particularly for large-scale projects with environmental consequences. Moreover, NEPA has provided a lead and an example that has quickly spread to the state and local level and to the proliferation of EIS requirements and other environmental protection state and local legislation.[23] It has also led to a bevy of legal suits and countersuits by governments, developers, industrial corporations and trade groups, and by special-interest citizen and environmental protection organizations.[24]

The Clean Air Act Amendments of 1970   The act, building on the original act of 1955 and amendments in 1963, 1965, and 1967, established the need for state implementation plans (SIPs). Each state in turn was broken into Air Quality Control Regions (AQCRs) and states were required to meet standards for both mobile and stationary air pollution sources through the development of the SIPs, submitted to the Environmental Protection Agency (EPA).

The Clean Air Act Amendments of 1970 have significant implications for land use, and therefore for property rights. By imposing standards on both mobile and stationary air pollution sources, EPA has the authority to affect urban form through the discouragement of automobile use, freeway development, and urban dispersal as well as through limiting industrial air pollution and therefore placing an essential and new parameter into the industrial (and commercial) location decision. In its quest to force compliance with its standards of air quality, EPA has restricted parking in downtown areas, limited highway construction, and placed limits on industrial development and airborne effluent.

The Federal Water Pollution Control Act Amendments of 1972   These amendments brought general environmental concerns to bear very specifically on questions of water quality and effluent discharges. The amendments prescribed specific limitations in effluent discharges and set out schedules for adherence.[25] Analogous to the Clean Air Act Amendments, geographic areas are defined for closer scrutiny and states are asked to put forward plans for dealing with these problems. Again, the philosophy inherent in these acts is that such highly localizable problems as air and water pollution should be treated at source by state and local government. Federal funds are available to states and local areas for developing pollution control and abatement programs and for aiding severely affected sectors.

There are significant potential impacts for land use and urban development, as water quality control considerations can play a central role in allowing a developer to carry out a project. The economic base of communities with large water users and/or polluters can be very seriously affected. Federal standards and procedures must be met, potentially lengthening the time and cost for carrying out a planned development, as well as eliminating polluting activities from the urban economy and from urban land markets.

Environmental Protection Agency (EPA) The EPA came into being in 1970 as a reorganization of a range of existing government departments and regulations. Bureaus, programs, regulations, and responsibilities for environmental protection were put under the aegis of EPA for more effective coordination and implementation of existing and planned programs. Since its inception EPA has grown in importance. The Clean Air Act Amendments of 1972, the Federal Water Pollution Control Act Amendments of 1972, the Noise Control Act of 1972, and the Safe Water Drinking Act of 1974 all fall under the domain of the EPA for their enforcement and administration. All have implications for land use and urban development, and thus for our central concern here with real property rights.

The federal government thus has become involved in the land use and urban development process that constitutionally and traditionally has been the exclusive purview of the states and its agents, the counties and cities. The enjoyment of unencumbered property rights has been curtailed further by zoning and land use controls at the local level and by federal actions, primarily in the area of environmental quality legislation.[26]

State and Local Controls of Land Use and Urban Development

The *Euclid* v. *Ambler* case established the rights of state and local governments to curtail property rights in the interest of the general societal welfare. Recently such curtailment has broadened, spurred by federal initiatives in the environmental area and by local citizen concerns about the declining livability of their communities in the face of urban growth pressures.

By recent count, roughly half of the 50 states had environmental protection acts with some form of environmental impact statement or administrative requirement.[27] Table 8–1 summarizes the activities of the 50 states in the area of environmental protection. It shows which state agency has primary responsibility for environmental protection and lists the states with environmental plans or impact requirements as of 1975. The list is impressive. However, it refers only to environmental management programs. Superimposed on these are managed growth programs, tied principally to coastal zone management but also related to broader areas of land use management. These growth management programs are summarized in Table 8–2, and are indicative of the activities in place up to late 1975.

Combining state programs in environmental management with

those in the growth management area leads to a complex and highly diversified system for managing land resources and, for our present focus, implies significant changes in the ways in which property rights can be exercised.[28] The introduction of statewide land use and growth management schemes, invariably over and above local schemes, has been dubbed the "quiet revolution" in land use controls.[29] The interjection of other levels of government encroaches on the right to use property to its highest and best use, and such encroachment is growing.[30] In addition to local zoning and subdivision regulations and federal environmental programs, state requirements now must often be met before development can take place, infringing on property rights but also protecting the greater public welfare and the environments on which it is dependent for health and enjoyment. Ultimately, the degree of environmental regulation depends on some measure of the net present social value of such activity. The benefit includes the social valuation of environmental quality. The cost is that for compliance with the regulations.

If we can extend the "quiet revolution" in statewide land use controls to statewide growth and environmental management schemes, then we could reasonably typify local land use and growth management as the "loud revolution." The veritable explosion in locally based growth management and environmental quality policies since the late 1960s has filled countless volumes on law, land use planning, trade publications from both the planning and development professions, and—last, but by no means least—the courts. The perceived assault on property rights represented by the "loud revolution" in local land use and growth management policies has brought vigorous action on the part of land and property owners to protect the rights they feel are vested in their lands, historic buildings, farms, and new structures.[31]

The enormous number, great diversity, complexity, and rapid change of such controls at the local level defy any summary measures and tables such as those we presented above for the states. We leave for a later chapter (Chapter 11) to treat such local land use control and growth management techniques at the required depth.

The following areas are all subject to local government control in attempts to enhance the qualities of economic, fiscal, physical, and social environments. Developers have been required to post performance bonds or agree to reimburse the municipality or county for site servicing. Historic structures have been declared landmarks and the rights to demolish and reuse them severely restricted. Dedications of lands for public parks and recreation areas are becoming commonplace. Schedules of development charges to cover off-site costs induced by new developments are gaining in popularity at the local level. Moratoria in the extension of sewers and waterlines have been declared, effectively curtailing the use of lands not served by existing or planned sewer and water services. Sewage treatment facilities have also

Table 8–1 State Environmental Protection Activities
(* = yes; — = no)

State	Consolidated Organization			Environmental Policy			Inter-agency Environ-mental Coordinating Council	Citizen Environ-mental Policy Council	Compre-hensive Environ-mental Plan	State Environ-mental Impact Require-ment	Environ-mental Informa-tion System
	Health	EPA	Super	Constitu-tional Amend-ment	Policy Act	Executive Order					
Alabama	*	—	—	—	—	—	—	—	—	—	*
Alaska	—	—	*	—	—	—	—	—	—	—	—
Arizona	*	—	—	—	—	—	*	—	—	—	*
Arkansas	—	*	—	—	*	*	*	—	—	—	—
California	—	—	—	—	—	*	—	—	—	*	*
Colorado	*	—	—	—	*	*	—	—	*	*	—
Connecticut	—	—	*	—	*	*	—	—	*	—	*
Delaware	—	*	*	—	*	*	—	—	*	—	*
Florida	—	*	—	*	*	*	—	—	*	—	*
Georgia	—	—	*	—	*	*	—	*	*	—	—
Hawaii	*	—	—	—	*	—	—	—	*	*	*
Idaho	*	—	—	*	*	—	—	—	—	—	—
Illinois	—	*	—	—	*	—	—	—	—	—	—
Indiana	*	—	—	—	*	—	*	*	—	—	*
Iowa	—	*	—	—	—	—	—	—	—	—	*
Kansas	*	—	*	—	—	—	—	*	—	—	—
Kentucky	—	—	—	—	—	*	—	—	—	—	—
Louisiana	—	—	—	—	*	*	—	*	*	—	*
Maine	*	*	—	—	—	*	—	—	*	*	*
Maryland	—	—	*	*	*	*	*	—	*	*	*
Massachusetts	—	—	—	*	*	—	*	—	—	*	—

State										
Michigan	—	—	*	—	*	*	*	—	*	—
Minnesota	*	*	—	*	*	*	*	—	*	*
Mississippi	—	—	—	—	—	—	—	—	*	—
Missouri	—	*	—	*	—	—	—	—	—	*
Montana	*	—	*	—	*	*	*	*	*	—
Nebraska	*	—	—	—	*	*	—	—	*	*
Nevada	*	—	—	—	—	—	—	—	—	—
New Hampshire	—	*	—	*	*	*	—	—	*	*
New Jersey	*	—	*	*	—	—	—	—	—	*
New Mexico	*	*	*	*	—	—	—	—	—	*
New York	—	*	*	*	*	—	—	—	—	*
North Carolina	—	—	—	—	—	—	—	—	—	*
North Dakota	*	—	—	—	*	*	*	—	*	—
Ohio	—	*	—	—	—	—	—	*	—	—
Oklahoma	*	—	—	—	—	—	—	—	—	—
Oregon	—	*	—	*	*	—	—	—	—	—
Pennsylvania	—	*	*	*	—	—	—	—	*	*
Rhode Island	*	—	*	*	*	*	—	*	—	*
South Carolina	*	—	—	—	—	—	—	—	—	—
South Dakota	*	—	—	—	*	*	—	*	*	—
Tennessee	*	—	—	—	—	—	—	—	—	—
Texas	*	—	—	*	*	*	—	—	—	—
Utah	*	—	—	*	—	—	—	—	*	—
Vermont	—	*	—	—	—	—	—	—	*	—
Virginia	—	—	*	*	*	—	—	—	*	—
Washington	—	*	*	—	*	—	—	—	*	—
West Virginia	—	—	—	—	—	—	—	—	—	—
Wisconsin	—	*	*	—	*	*	—	*	*	*
Wyoming	*	—	—	—	—	—	—	—	—	—

Source: Council of State Governments, *Integration and Coordination of State Environmental Programs* (Lexington, Ky: Council of State Governments), 1975, p. 99.

235

Table 8–2 Summary of Growth Management Programs

Organizational Location	Program Area (Percent of States)		
	Land Use Management	Coastal Zone Management	Critical Areas Management
State planning agency	32	33	20
Pollution control agency	0	30	0
Natural resources or other agency	15	17	20
Independent Board or Commission	15	20	50
Joint planning agency and pollution control agency	23	0	0
Joint planning agency and other agency	15	0	10
Total	100	100	100
	(N = 13)	(N = 30)	(N = 10)

Source: This table was adapted from The Council of State Governments, *Integration and Coordination of State Environmental Programs* (Lexington, Ky: The Council of State Governments), 1975, p. 81.

been scaled or slowed down, again in an attempt to slow or limit growth. Outright refusal to grant building and development permits outside certain specified height or density limits have adversely affected the ability of land and property owners to develop or redevelop their properties. Zoning codes have become more complex and restrictive, at times specifying a variety of design and architectural elements as well as height, site coverage, and use. Prime agricultural and ecologically sensitive wetlands, marshes, forests, and unique vistas and formations have also been protected at the local level with state help.[32]

The growth in concern for the quality of the urban environment has led local governments to expand the range of policy instruments at their disposal well beyond simple zoning controls of land use and intensity. As historic preservation, growth management, farmland, and other unique ecological habitat concerns become part of the local government planning agenda, the diversity and complexity of locally based limitations on property rights and on the urban development process expanded enormously. The result was a diminution of classical property rights to protect and promote the general health and welfare of local residents. A further result has been an unparalleld eruption of lawsuits by developers and other property owners seeking to maintain and preserve those property rights that they feel are rightfully theirs under the Constitution of the United States. Local governments simultaneously are seeking to maintain and preserve the livability of local environments for all local residents. The courts, as arbiter, are swamped in the process. However, one trend is clear: Local governments are slowly but surely winning, and private property rights are becoming increasingly public property rights.

Summing Up Property Rights Evolution in the United States

From the advent of the 20th century to the present time there has been continuous change in the concept of private property in the United States. The change has been from unencumbered private enjoyment of property, including the right to develop that property at its highest, best, and most profitable use, to more constrained property-use rights.

The constraints arise from all levels of government. The U.S. federal government has become involved since the 1960s in environmental protection and management, using both "carrots" (grants for planning, sewage and water treatment, and other pollution control developments) and "sticks" (strictly enforced standards on air and water pollution and limitations on the generation and emission of pollutants).

At the state level, environmental management and protection agencies have sprung up in virtually every state to deal with federally mandated pollution controls and management plans. States have also chosen frequently to extend federal provisions to areas of their own jurisdiction, setting up their own environmental management agencies to deal with statewide (as opposed to national) environmental concerns.

Finally, at the local level, these general environmental concerns have translated themselves into a vast and staggering array of land use, subdivision, and growth management tools and regulations. Not only are the limitations on the use and development of private property greatly expanded, but the processes, approvals and permits required to exercise these limited rights have become in concept, significant stumbling blocks and limitations in their own right. We need not view these changes in the rights of real property owners to use and develop their properties as disastrous and calamitous. Rather, they are changes in land-use institutions to reflect changes in societal needs and values. As such, they are just as natural and adaptive as were earlier laissez faire conceptions when society was more dispersed, less complex, and significantly less interdependent.

Property Rights in Canada: Their Status and Evolution

Standing in marked contrast to the constitutional protection of real property in the United States is the absence of such protection in Canada. This has implications and consequences for the course of property rights in Canada, and leads to a dramatically different set of rights. The regulation of urban development is markedly different in Canada when compared with the United States. We must start at the top as we did in the United States and look to the Canadian "constitution" for clues and guidelines about property and property rights.

The Canadian "constitution" is not a constitution at all in the usual sense of the word, since it is not Canadian in origin, nor has it traditionally embodied the usual guarantees and protections of rights that we have come to associate with constitutions and their almost axiomatic "constitutional rights." Rather, the Canadian "constitution" was, until 1982, an act of the British Parliament and not of the Parliament or people of Canada. This act, entitled the British North America Act, 1867, with subsequent amendments, is "An Act for the Union of Canada, Nova Scotia, and New Brunswick, and the Government thereof; and for Purposes connected therewith."[33] Its primary purposes were to establish procedures for enacting laws at both the national and provincial levels; to establish procedures for electing legislators and for carrying out the laws of the land; and, most importantly for our purposes, to allocate powers to the Parliament of Canada (Section 91) and to the provincial legislatures (Section 92). The BNA Act also established the judiciary and set out its areas of jurisdiction. Finally, and also of importance to the conduct of local government, the BNA spells out in some detail the means by which the two senior levels of government are allowed to finance their activities. The recently enacted "made in Canada" constitution, The Canada Act of 1982, while creating the Canadian Charter of Rights and Freedoms, has not altered the allocation of powers between the federal and provincial legislatures.

Nowhere in the BNA Act were questions of individual civil or property rights raised or discussed. Questions of civil and property rights do concern the BNA Act and are dealt with in some detail in Section 92, where governance of "all Matters of a merely local or private Nature in the Province" are set out. It was not until the 1982 Canadian Charter of Rights and Freedoms that civil liberties were protected.[34] The specific areas delegated to the provinces in Section 92 that are of interest of us here include the following.[35]

1. Section 92(8). "Municipal Institutions in the Province."

2. Section 92(9). "Shop, Saloon, Tavern, Auctioneer and other Licences in order to the raising of a Revenue for Provincial, Local, or Municipal Purposes."

3. Section 92(10). "Local Works and Undertakings . . . . "

4. Section 92(11). "The Incorporation of Companies with Provincial Objects."

5. Section 92(13). "Provincial and Civil Rights in the Province."

6. Section 92(14). "The Administration of Justice in the Province . . . and including Procedure in Civil Matters in those Courts."

Moreover, the preamble to Section 92 observes the following concerning these enumerated provincial powers: "In each Province the Legislature may exclusively make Laws in relation to Matters coming within the Classes of Subject next herein-after enumerated." For our present interest in real property rights, therefore, we must look exclusively to the provinces. There are no federal or constitutional protections of property rights. Even the new Canadian Charter of Rights and

Freedoms significantly excludes property rights from protection, much to the chagrin of organized real estate groups.

One other essential point needs to be made relating to real property in Canada as distinct from real property in the United States. The historical evolution of real property under the English common law system used in English-speaking Canada places significant limitations on property ownership from the outset. Foremost among these is the concept of ownership. Under the Constitution of the United States, an individual's property rights are acknowledged and protected. An individual has such rights and in essence can *own* land. In Canada, strictly speaking, people do not own land. In the United States the fee-simple estate implies ownership of the land as well as of the rights to use the land (subject, of course, to compliance with local, state, and federal statutes). In Canada fee-simple estates in land imply ownership of the rights to use but not ownership of the land itself *per se*. Ownership of the land remains with the Crown or government.[36] The above provisions remain intact with the 1982 Canada Act.

The implications of these differences for real property rights and for the urban development process are enormous. First, the government does not have to expropriate land, since it already owns it. In practical application, both the federal and provincial governments have seen fit to encumber themselves with expropriation acts guaranteeing owners rights and procedures for compensation in the event of expropriation. Thus, there are 11 sets of expropriation acts in Canada: one in each of the ten provinces and one for the federal government. The federal act was significantly changed in 1970, and most provincial expropriation statutes have been recently revised.[37] Just as the Crown has chosen to encumber itself with such acts, it can unencumber itself and revoke the expropriation acts or alter them dramatically. The land belongs to the Crown and the initiative lies with the Crown as well on how to treat property rights.

We now have to ask how these differences work. Do they produce radically different rules of the game for urban development and have they led to radically different conceptions of property rights in the two countries? Somewhat surprisingly, the differences are not as great as one would expect *a priori*. Expropriation in Canada operates along principles very much like those used in the United States. The urban development process operates in a very similar manner in both countries, though here we can see some important differences that reflect the differences in the underlying property rights in the two countries.

In both countries, regulation of real property markets, title registration, and municipal institutions are vested with the states or provinces. The states or provinces have delegated their powers to local governments. Similar zoning statutes and subdivision practices are at work.

In Canada, as opposed to the United States, the provinces and their agents, the cities, have significantly greater regulatory powers over property because of the absence of any constitutional protection of property rights and because of the ultimate ownership by the Crown of all land in Canada. A striking example will highlight these differences.

In August 1972 the New Democratic Party (a socialist democratic party) was elected to power in British Columbia. One of its campaign promises was the protection of farmlands from urbanization and from the alienation of food-growing capacity for the province. In December 1972 the Provincial Cabinet "froze" all farmland in agricultural use pending legislation. This freeze prevented any land, either in farm use or with good farming potential from being converted to nonfarming use. It was made permanent in the early spring of 1973. The law required the registrar of land titles to note permanently on all parcels of land falling within the so-called Agricultural Land Reserves (ALRs) that they were protected and could only be used for farming (including letting them lie fallow). All such titles are marked "ALR," informing prospective buyers that the bundle of rights that accrue to the owner of a fee-simple estate does not include the right to develop the land for urban purposes or to otherwise alienate its food-growing capacity.[38] There is an appeal procedure and a Land Commission established to hear appeals from owners whose land had been incorrectly classified, but no compensation was to be paid to affected landowners.[39] In 1975, 1979, and again in 1983 the NDP lost provincial elections to a "free enterprise" party, the Social Credit Party, yet virtually no changes have been made to the act or to the concept.

This contrasts markedly with attempts in the United States to preserve farmland, where constitutional guarantees have precluded zoning land for farm use without compensating owners. To get around obstacles posed by these constitutional guarantees, such convoluted schemes as Transferrable Development Rights (TDRs) arose to enable farmland owners to be compensated for development rights, while protecting and preserving the land.[40] Other involved schemes work through the purchase of easements from farmers or through the outright purchase and leaseback of the lands.[41] The attempts to save prime agricultural land in the United States, of necessity, must be considerably more elaborate and less direct than similar attempts in Canada.

These significant powers over property use show up in the urban development process. For example, Canadian municipalities have shifted costs of suburban development onto the developers by requiring very high levels of site servicing, compliance with stringent building and subdivision codes, and by requirements of cash payments for off-site costs that new developments impose on a municipality. Developers have been required to widen major traffic arteries, to put in traffic control devices, to dedicate significant portions of their lands for parks (10 percent or more), and to build community centers and recreation facilities.[42] It was even the case in British Columbia during the 1970s that municipalities could in essence sell rezonings to developers in exchange for certain considerations such as cash payments, public parks, and ice rinks.[43] These practices came to a halt when the province of British Columbia changed the Municipal Act, which provides the ground rules under which municipalities operate.[44] This stands in contrast with the U.S. case where all levels of government are constrained by the Constitution and must demonstrate that limitations of property rights are not unreasonable, are not arbitrary, and are motivated by concern for promoting the general health and welfare of the citizenry.

Apparent similarities between U.S. and Canadian urban development processes and rights derive from very different powers. Such an understanding can also serve to promote an appreciation for the problems faced in each society and for the specific remedies taken (e.g., TDRs in the United States versus the Agricultural Land Reserves in British Columbia). We can also understand why local authorities in Canada can exercise seemingly unconstitutional powers (from the U.S. perspective) or, alternatively, why local authorities in the United States are relatively helpless (from the Canadian perspective).

What is the status of real property rights in Canada today? First, Canadians are protected against expropriation of their real property by the existence of fair expropriation statutes at the federal and provincial levels. Their rights are similar to those granted by the U.S. Constitution. Second, rights to use and develop real property are being increasingly curtailed by the existence of more demanding land-use and subdivision control legislation at the local level, reflecting public concern over decreasing urban environmental quality. Two differences are worth stressing.

First, in Canada there is no significant federal presence in the land-use and environmental management field. This derives directly from the BNA and Canada acts, where such matters are deemed to be a provincial responsibility exclusively. The federal government exercises some control over rivers and harbors, but lacks, for example, the widespread authority granted to the EPA by the several environmental protection statutes of the 1970s in the United States.[45]

Second, and of equal importance, property rights of individuals came to their present status in Canada by a very different route than did those in the United States. In the United States individual property rights have slowly been narrowed by judicial rulings favoring the need to protect the general welfare at the expense of individual property rights. In Canada almost the reverse has happened: Property rights originated with the king and slowly devolved to lords, knights, and later the masses.[46] Ownership has always been vested in the Crown. Rights to occupy and use the land passed to the population-at-large, with a clear understanding that what the Crown granted, the Crown could take back.

Property rights in both Canada and the United States are being subjected to increasing limitations by virtually all levels of government. Canadian and U.S. property "owners" appear to have the same rights and responsibilities when developing or using land. These similarities mask the essential underlying difference that in Canada property rights are defined by the Crown through legislation over time, while in the United States, in contrast, it is the courts that have been reinterpreting competing sections of the U.S. Constitution in favor of the general welfare at the expense of individual property rights. These rights are taken as a given (by the Constitution), which is not the case in Canada.

One overlapping element does unite property rights in both nations: They are both dynamic concepts, continually being reinterpreted in light of contemporary needs and values. In Canada this is done directly through legislation, while in the United States it is achieved through testing legislation in the name of the common good against constitutional property-rights guarantees.

An additional trend warrants mention, and that is the existence of the "quiet revolution in land use controls" in Canada as well as in the United States. Several provincial governments during the late 1970s moved to redefine the terms under which they delegate land-use and subdivision authorities to their municipalities. The province increased its role with an eye toward streamlining and rationalizing urban development procedures.

SUMMARY

The social theory of property rights discussed at the beginning of this chapter implied a dynamic concept of property, changing as societal needs and values change. Such needs and values are expressed in North America through the political and legal process.

Property rights and the ability to put them to use to build and alter human settlements evolve daily as a result of the political interaction of three principal sets of actors: the public, politicians, and technicians. Property rights are not rigid, absolute, or cast in concrete. One trades rights in urban land markets, not properties *per se*. It is imperative that buyers and sellers in urban land markets understand the context within which such rights exist and are traded.

Other relevant institutional factors could have been the focus here. For example, development approval processes and the role of banking and financial institutions in the urban land marketplace could have provided the institutional bases for our discussion. We also could have looked into the nature and degree of involvement in the urban development process of public utilities such as water, sewage, and power providers. Such explorations would have pointed up major differences among markets. It would have lent additional support to the assertion that institutional factors matter and are central components of the urban land market process.

Such an exploration would have been lengthy and rooted in masses of detail. Instead we chose to sketch out some general principles for looking at urban land market institutions. We focused on the most important of these: the concept of property rights and its social basis. Similar points could have been made about these other institutions that play important roles in urban development.

We can now put our various analytical tools together to deal with urban land markets as a whole. The economic, financial, and institutional constructs in the previous chapters can be brought to bear on discovering how the urban land market functions to determine price and quantity and, by so doing, allocates society's scarce urban land resources in an efficient and productive manner.

Footnotes

1. Some cultures do not have the concept of private property at all. In these traditional cultures, private ownership of resources proved maladaptive and the property concept did not develop. See, for example, Harold Driver, ed., *North American Indians* (Norman, Okla.: University of Oklahoma Press), 1968.

2. For an excellent discussion of institutionalists and institutionalism in urban land economics, see Richard U. Ratcliff, "Institutionalism in Urban Land Economics," in Michael A. Goldberg, ed., *Recent Perspectives in Urban Land Economics* (Vancouver, B.C.: Urban Land Economics Division, Faculty of Commerce and Business Administration, University of British Columbia), 1976, pp. 3–9.

3. This quote by Richard T. Ely was taken from Herbert B. Dorau and Albert G. Hinman, *Urban Land Economics* (New York: The MacMillan Company), 1928, p. 259.

4. Dorau and Hinman, *op. cit.,* p. 260.

5. Richard U. Ratcliff, *Urban Land Economics* (New York: The McGraw-Hill Book Co.), 1949, p. 7.

6. For additional details on the evolution of property rights, see Ratcliff, *op. cit.,* Chapter 1; Richard U. Ratcliff, *Real Estate Analysis* (New York: The McGraw-Hill Book Co.), 1962, Chapter 5; Ernest M. Fisher and Robert M. Fisher, *Urban Real Estate* (New York: Henry Holt and Company), 1954, Chapters 4–8; and, for those interested in more detail and history, A. M. Sinclair, *Introduction to Real Property Law* (Toronto, Ontario: Butterworths), 1969, especially Chapters 1 and 2.

7. This discussion is adapted from Ratcliff, *Real Estate Analysis,* pp. 84–85.

8. See references in footnote 6, above, for more detail. For relevant legal background and cases, see: A. James Casner and W. Barton Leach, *Cases and Text on*

Property (Boston: Little, Brown and Co.), 1964; Robert Kratovil and Raymond J. Werner, *Real Estate Law,* 7th edition (Englewood Cliffs, N.J.: Prentice-Hall), 1978; and in Canada see: Frank Taylor, *Cases and Materials on Real Property Law* (Toronto, Ontario: Butterworths), 1977; and J. A. Smyth and D. E. Soberman, *The Law and Business Administration in Canada,* 4th edition (Scarborough, Ontario: Prentice-Hall), 1983, pp. 552–629.

9. See either Casner and Leach, *op. cit.,* or Taylor, *op. cit.,* for needed details for the United States and Canada, respectively.

10. It should be observed that zoning is not present in all cities. The "classic" exception is Houston, Texas, where steel mills and private housing could locate adjacent to each other but, interestingly from an urban land economist's point of view, they do not. In fact, Houston looks remarkably like a zoned city. See Bernard Siegan, *Land Use Without Zoning* (Lexington, Mass.: D.C. Heath), 1972.

11. Casner and Leach, *op. cit.,* p. 985.

12. *Ibid.,* p. 987.

13. Quoted from Edward Conrad Smith, ed., *The Constitution of the United States,* 11th edition (New York: Barnes and Noble Books), 1979, p. 49.

14. *Ibid.,* p. 52.

15. Quoted from Casner and Leach, *op. cit.,* p. 1029.

16. Richard F. Babcock, "Zoning," in Frank So, Israel Stollman, Frank Beal, and David Arnold, eds., *The Practice of Local Government Planning* (Washington, D.C.: International City Managers Association), 1979, Chapter 15. Zoning and other land-use controls are put in the context of real estate law in R. N. Corley, P. J. Shedd, and C. F. Floyd, *Real Estate and the Law* (New York: Random House) 1982.

17. Brian J. Porter, *The Land Use Contract* (Vancouver, B.C.: University of British Columbia), 1973, unpublished M.A. thesis, pp. 8–9.

18. Babcock, *op. cit.,* p. 418.

19. See Babcock, *op. cit.,* and also Michael A. Goldberg and Peter J. Horwood, *Zoning for the 1980s* (Vancouver, B.C.: The Fraser Institute), 1980.

20. For a better idea about the various assaults on zoning and related land-use controls, the interested reader should see the following legal casebooks: Donald G. Hagman, *Public Planning and Control of Urban and Land Development: Cases and Materials* (St. Paul, Minn.: West Publishing Co.), 1973; Bill Shaw, *Environmental Law: People, Pollution and Land Use* (St. Paul, Minn: West Publishing Co.), 1976; and Eva Hanks, A. Dan Tarlock, and John L. Hanks, *Environmental Law and Policy: Cases and Materials,* abridged edition (St. Paul, Minn.: West Publishing Co.), 1975.

21. Quoted from Shaw, *op. cit.,* p. 107.

22. Quoted from Shaw, *op. cit.,* p. 109.

23. For an excellent compilation of articles on the subject of environmental protection and growth management, see Urban Land Institute, *Management and Control of Growth,* Volumes I–V (Washington, D.C.: Urban Land Institute), 1975, 1977, and 1980. Also see the monthly publication from the Urban Land Institute, entitled *Environmental Comment,* for current articles on the evolution of such legislation and practice in this rapidly changing field.

24. See references in footnote 20. Also see Louis L. Jaffe and Laurence H. Tribe, *Environmental Protection* (Chicago, Ill.: The Bracton Press), 1971; and David P. Currie, *Pollution: Cases and Materials* (St. Paul, Minn.: West Publishing Co.), 1975.

25. See Currie, *op. cit.*, Appendix B, for details about the Act. See Currie and Hanks, Tarlock and Hanks, *op. cit.*, for cases.

26. The previously cited Urban Land Institute publications provide insights into the problem. Also see their monthly publication, *Urban Land*, which frequently carries articles dealing with the consequences on development of environmental protection and growth management schemes.

27. See Hagman, *op. cit.*, Chapter XX.

28. This question of integrating these various related environmental, growth management, and land-use programs is the essential focus of the study from which Tables 8–1 and 8–2 are taken. See Thad Beyle, Thomas Peddicord, and Francis Parker, *Integration and Coordination of State Environmental Programs* (Lexington, Ky.: The Council of State Governments), 1975.

29. See Fred Bosselman and David Callies, *The Quiet Revolution in Land Use Controls* (Washington, D.C.: Council on Environmental Quality), 1971.

30. Again, see the Urban Land Institute materials cited in footnote 23, and Hagman, *op. cit.*, Chapter XX.

31. The enormous number of cases bears witness to this point, as does the proliferation of legal casebooks that attempt to keep pace with the explosion in cases. Footnote 20 gave several illustrations but only scratched the surface of the available materials.

32. *Environmental Comment* has featured all of these in their past issues. See, for example, the January 1978 issue, which dealt with farmland preservation.

33. Elmer A. Driedger, *A Consolidation of The British North America Acts, 1867 to 1975* (Ottawa, Ontario: Department of Justice Canada), p. 1. Also, *The Constitution Act, 1982* (Ottawa, Ontario: Ministry of Supply and Services), 1982.

34. This quote comes from Section 92(16) of the BNA Act. See Driedger, *op. cit.*, p. 28. The BNA Act, 1867, became The Constitution Act, 1867, under The Constitution Act, 1982, and its allocation of powers between the federal and provincial legislatures remain unchanged.

35. Driedger, *op. cit.*, pp. 27–28.

36. Sinclair, *op. cit.*, especially pp. 11–12.

37. For an excellent introduction to the 1970 Expropriation Act, see John W. Morden, "The New Expropriation Legislation: Powers and Procedures," in *Recent Developments in Real Estate Law, Special Lectures of the Law Society of Upper Canada* (Toronto, Ontario: Richard De Boo Limited for the Law Society of Upper Canada), 1970, pp. 225–300.

38. For an introduction and early history of the Land Commission Act in British Columbia, which preserves agricultural lands in that province, see David Baxter, "The British Columbia Land Commission Act—A Review," Reprint #8 (Vancouver, B.C.: The Urban Land Economics Division, Faculty of Commerce and Business Administration, University of British Columbia), 1974.

39. such appeals were needed because of the large-scale maps that were used to classify the land in the Canada Land Inventory (CLI). Agricultural lands are defined in the Land Commission Act as being those in Classes I–IV and sometimes Classes V and VI as well as the CLI. However, specific parcels have been found to have soils that differ significantly from the CLI, and where such soils are found to exist and found to be unsuitable for agricultural purposes, property owners can petition the Land Commission to have the parcel removed. Appeals also exist for lands that might be too small or too difficult to farm even though the soils are excellent. The Provincial Cabinet is the ultimate arbiter of such appeals should they need to go beyond the Land Commission.

40. Transferrable Development Rights (TDRs) have been much touted in the United States as a solution to preserving valuable lands and buildings. For an excellent discussion of the TDR concept, see John J. Costonis, "Development Rights Transfer: Description and Perspectives for a Critique," in *Management and Control of Growth*, Volume III (Washington, D.C.: Urban Land Institute), 1975, pp. 92–113.

41. See the aforementioned January 1978 issue of *Environmental Comment*, and also the article by Dallas D. Miner, "Agricultural Lands Preservation: A Growing Trend in Open Space Planning," in *Management and Control of Growth*, Volume III (Washington, D.C.: Urban Land Institute), 1975, pp. 52–60.

42. For a statement of the problem from the developer's viewpoint, see Andrjez Derkowski, *Costs in the Land Development Process* (Toronto, Ontario: The Urban Development Institute), 1976. For a broader statement of the problem and issues, see *Down to Earth, Volumes I and II, The Report of the Federal/Provincial Task Force on the Supply and Price of Serviced Residential Land* (Toronto, Ontario: Federal/Provincial Task Force on the Supply and Price of Serviced Residential Land), 1978.

43. For the details on land-use contracts, a most innovative method of land-use controls, see Porter, *op. cit.*

44. For a discussion of some of the issues involved in these changes, and for additional references, see Michael A. Goldberg, "The BNA Act, NHA, CMHC, MSUA, etc.: 'Nymophobia' and the On-Going Search for an Appropriate Canadian Housing and Urban Development Policy," in Michael Walker, ed., *Canadian Confederation at the Crossroads* (Vancouver, B.C.: The Fraser Institute), 1978, pp. 337–340.

45. U.S. federal powers derive more than anything else from the ability to provide grants in areas of state responsibility. Such "carrots" bring with them the implicit "stick" that they can be withdrawn should the state and local governments not follow federal wishes. In effect, the U.S. federal government can exercise considerable authority in areas intended to be the exclusive responsibility of the states. In contrast, in Canada provincial governments have been wary of such federal grants and have sought to keep them to a minimum and focus them on social programs where there is little room for federal standard setting such as health and hospital cost-sharing, unemployment insurance, and welfare.

46. See Sinclair, *op. cit.*, especially Chapter 1.

9

THE MARKET FOR LAND

INTRODUCTION

Thus far we have developed the demand for land largely by drawing on the theory of bid rents. The demand for land can also be derived from a production function for improvements, and the demand curve is downward sloping. On the supply side we saw that the supply of land is relatively inelastic in the short run, and that, as a result, one useful specification for market equilibrium is that the price of land is determined by demand. We also developed some more complex longer-run supply functions that allowed for more elastic land supplies than the simple short-run model.

The objective of this chapter is to derive and formulate the market for land, accommodating both demand and supply forces. We will first discuss short-run equilibrium where supply is perfectly inelastic and demand depends on current rents, other prices, and tastes. The intersection between supply and demand determines the equilibrium rental price per unit of land services per period. This is for the rental market in land. There is also the issue of land purchases where, even if supply is again perfectly inelastic, demand depends on current and future expectations of land rent per period. For equilibrium, the asset price of land is where supply and expected demand are equated.

The existence of a land market is itself not without controversy. One argument is that the laws of supply and demand cannot operate satisfactorily for land because the supply has a built-in element of monopoly, being fixed by nature.[1] This does not refute the existence of a land market, since markets and equilibrium do exist for goods and services supplied by monopolists. A perfectly inelastic supply is neither necessary nor sufficient for the existence of monopoly because a given stock of land can have diffused ownership.

247

Whether supply and demand both respond to current rents and land prices is examined next. A cobweb model is presented. If supply is not perfectly inelastic for building lots, but depends on economic variables of previous periods, this may lead to either a stable or an unstable equilibrium.

The analysis is then extended to the case where equilibrium is not necessarily assumed to obtain. The asset price of land may not be at the intersection of the demand and supply curves. Rather, excess demand, with frustrated would-be land purchasers, or excess supply, with some landholders unable to sell their property at prevailing prices, are also possibilities. Thus, no inference about whether supply and demand are equal can be drawn from market prices in these disequilibrium models. They have frequently been applied to housing or mortgage markets, but are as applicable in the land market.

There is also the continuing potential for monopoly power in the land market. Controversy arises as to the empirical degree of ownership concentration in local land markets, and whether government intervention is appropriate. These topics are taken up in the last section, entitled "Imperfect Competition."

EQUILIBRIUM MARKET FOR LAND

Single-market Equilibrium

The first part of the analysis develops the market for land under equilibrium, where supply and demand are equal. In the simplest form, there is no distinction between the existing stock of land and the flow of new lots for construction. All lots are homogeneous on a flat, featureless plain.

Assume that there is a fixed supply of land S at any point in time. This applies to the market for a given use of land. To fix ideas, let these be identical single-family residential lots. The demand is downward sloping at D. The demand curve for land is determined by the market price of lots P_L and by other prices such as those for finished lots and improvements. The situation is as in Figure 9–1. The intersection of supply and demand yields the equilibrium price $\bar{P}_L$. If the market is assumed to be self-equilibrating, any instantaneous price dislocation results in a return to $\bar{P}_L$. If the price is in excess of $\bar{P}_L$, there is an excess supply of lots, and the price is reduced. Where the price falls below $\bar{P}_L$, more people are willing to buy lots than there are willing sellers, and the price of lots increases.

The market equilibrium is described by:

$$D(P_L) = S \tag{9.1}$$

whereupon $\bar{P}_L$ solves this equation. If there is an increase in demand to D', for example, through demographic movements, the price increases to $\bar{P}_L'$. This model indicates that government programs or

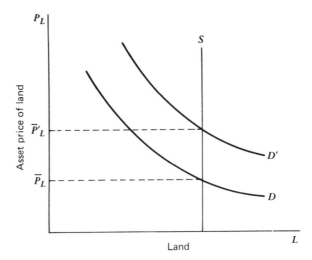

Figure 9–1. Equilibrium in land market (no stocks or flows).

other activities that stimulate demand lead to price increases. As examples, the government could give grants to purchasers of new homes, grants to first-time home buyers or tax credits to individuals purchasing a house and lot. The effect of the government programs is 100 percent capitalized in the increased price. If the shift from D to D' is induced by such a program, the amount of capitalization is $\bar{P}'_L - \bar{P}_L$. It should be noted that this conclusion depends on the inelastic supply assumptions.

As an example, suppose the demand for lots is $D = 500 - 0.01P_L$, and the supply of lots S is 400. For equilibrium, $D = S$, or $500 - .01P_L = 400$, with $P_L = \$10,000$. If there is a shift in demand of a parallel nature, as in Figure 9–1, such that $D = 550 - .01P_L$, P_L becomes $\$15,000$, or price increases by 50 percent. These conclusions rest on the assumption of a perfectly inelastic supply of land, perfect rental markets for land, and response of demand to current prices only. The price of land is entirely demand determined under these assumptions.

The Stock-Flow Model

The model can be expanded to accommodate both stocks and flows.[2] Suppose there are two separate land markets, for lots with existing structures and for lots with new structures. Once built upon, land is placed in a separate market that can be thought of as "existing" with construction improvements. The supply of land in existing form is therefore perfectly inelastic. If this supply is denoted as S_{exist}, then equilibrium for the *stock* of land upon which improvements has been made is characterized by the intersection with the demand curve D_{exist}

for existing land stock. An equilibrium analogous to that in (9.1) arises, with:

$$D_{exist}(P_L) = S_{exist} \qquad (9.2)$$

By solving as before, equilibrium obtains at P_e in Figure 9–2. In this figure the land and improvement stock is indicated on the left side. The quantity of land is measured leftward, or negatively, so the demand curve D_{exist}, having as coordinates a positive price on the vertical axis and a negative quantity on the horizontal axis for land, has the slope indicated. The ratio of these coordinates with a negatively measured demand gives the "positive" slope of Figure 9–2.

The market for new construction—the land that accommodates it may be purchased separately—is indicated on the right side. The supply is not necessarily perfectly inelastic, for as land prices rise, more agricultural or other land is converted to the serviced lots. This yields the supply function S_{new} (P_L, X) where X denotes other variables affecting supply. The demand for lots D_{new} (P_L, Y), from the developer or speculator, depends also on price. Here Y denotes other variables affecting demand.[3]

Supply and demand equilibrium in the market for land on which new housing is built obtains at P_n, the price of such new housing lots. At the equilibrium, the quantity of lots transacted is L_n. As drawn, the price of new lots, P_n, exceeds that of existing lots, P_e. These land types are not necessarily perfect substitutes, so the prices P_n and P_e do not have to be equal. New lots may embody technological change such as improved sewage and underground utility and communications services. Road and service locations may be better designed, and transport facilities more efficiently located.

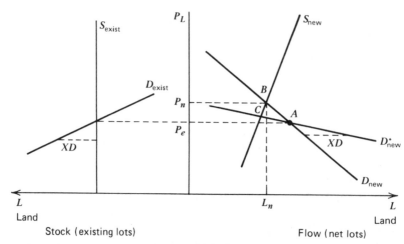

Figure 9–2. Equilibrium in land market (stock-flow model).

In Figure 9–2 the price for new lots is indicated to be above that for existing lots. Suppose that instead of equilibrium occurring at P_e in the existing lot market, there is an excess demand. The excess demand for lots in the existing lot market is XD. This is translated into an increased demand for lots to flow into the market. Demand lies to the right of A, on D^*_{new}. The demand D^*_{new} includes the initial equilibrium plus the excess demand XD. Where price is below equilibrium and $P < P_e$, the demand for new lots increases.

If the price in the existing lot market is above equilibrium, $P > P_e$, then there is an excess supply, with $S_{exist} > D_{exist}$. With an excess supply overhanging the market, there is less incentive to demand lots for new construction or speculation. Demand adjusted for disequilibrium in the existing market, D^*_{new}, falls below D_{new}, to the left of A. Hence, the adjusted demand D^*_{new} is more elastic than D_{new} over this range.

Only at A does the existing lot market demand have no effect on the new market. The price in the existing lot market, P_e, is below P_n, so if there is any interaction, there will tend to be a depressing influence on new demand. This intersection occurs at point C, where the existing market has to affect D^*_{new}. The price is lower than if no existing lot market pressure arose, and the number of new lots brought into service is also lower.

If the price of existing lots is lower than that for new lots, all else being equal, investment in new lots is reduced. There is a theory of investment that depends on the price ratio between existing and new lots. If P_e/P_n is less than unity, then new lot development falls, while if P_e/P_n is greater than unity, investment increases.

Some other aspects of the stock-flow mechanism are worth noting. First, the demand D^*_{new} is always more elastic than D_{new}, the demand unadjusted for the existing market. The supply in the existing market is almost perfectly inelastic. The more elastic the demand in the existing market, the more elastic is D^*_{new}. It is possible for D^*_{new} to be perfectly elastic, whereupon the price of new lots is determined by the supply in the new lot market. Second, in the long run, supply and demand in the new lot market are equilibrated at $D_{new} = S_{new}$ at point B. The presence of the two demands, D_{new} and D^*_{new}, is a short-run phenomenon, solved by shifts of demand in the existing market.

This short-run conflict between stocks and flows has important policy implications. Suppose there is disequilibrium in the market for lots on which improvements already stand. If the price in this market is below equilibrium P_e, then a program to subsidize buyers of existing houses will shift demand upward. This is reflected by an upward and rightward shift of the demand in Figure 9–2. This will reduce excess demand and narrow the gap between D^*_{new} and D_{new}. In such a case the government program may stabilize the market. If the price is below P_e, and there is an excess demand XD, the presence of a government subsidy on purchases of existing units increases the excess demand.

This means that the adjusted demand curve D^*_{new} rotates and becomes more elastic as new construction increases to reduce the excess demand.

On the supply side, a change in zoning regulations that affects the existing stock of lots, for example, through legalization of smaller lots or basement rental units, shifts supply to the right. Where there is an excess demand, this can serve to equilibrate the market. The alternative is to subsidize new construction, shifting the new supply to the right. Thus, policy initiatives need to consider the elasticities of supply and demand in both the new and existing lot markets.

In addition to the argument about whether markets are efficient allocators and whether housing and land markets are competitive, there is the problem of inertia. The stock-flow model has time as an integral element. A government program announced to subsidize supply in a market with excess demand may come on stream during a period of excess supply, thus worsening the excess supply and disequilibrating the market further, instead of its intended equilibrating effect. An example is that of land banking. The purchase of land at a time of excess demand contributes only to further increases in price. If this land is then released in a slow or declining market, it contributes to the deterioration. A second example is government grants, which may come on stream only during periods of excess demand.

Another issue in the supply and demand for land is that of speculation. Demanders of land include both those who hold land for current construction purposes and those who are speculators. For these purposes, speculators are defined as those with no intention of building or developing in the short run. Speculation may shift the demand upward or downward, depending on price expectations of the speculators. This may stabilize or destabilize the market. If price expectations of speculators are more stable than those of the average player, then the longer-run price fluctuations are reduced. Hence, it cannot be determined immediately whether speculation is a destabilizing phenomenon.

If speculation is stabilizing, the speculator earns profits, and if it is destabilizing, he or she has losses.[4] Suppose the price in a market, such as that in the existing lot sector of Figure 9–2, is below equilibrium. Speculators are correct in expecting that this excess demand in XD can be reduced. The gap between the price at XD and P_e, assuming this is the final and stable equilibrium, represents the speculator profit. This is gross of transaction costs such as capital gains taxes, commissions, and legal fees.

If nonequilibrating forces arise, then the speculator loses. Alternatively, if the speculator expects the excess demand to deteriorate and sells early, prices fall further and the market is destabilized. Since market mechanisms to sell the land and housing markets are limited, the speculator can achieve this only by reducing the existing inventory.

Supply and Demand Factors

In the actual operation of land markets, the supply crucially depends on time. The stages of obtaining financing, land assembly, satisfaction of zoning, planning and environmental regulations and servicing is a processs involving time. During the period when the long approval process by municipalities occurs, the market may change substantially. A market in a boom may reverse to one in decline. Further, land is not a liquid asset in that it cannot readily be converted to cash. The lack of liquidity in the land market creates potential delays in responding to price changes. Landholders cannot hedge their positions in the market by selling land long or short on a futures market. The presence of time lags in the development process, illiquidity and uncertainty on the movement of prices, exposes the developer or landowner to risks. These risks cannot be laid off by purchasing or selling land option contracts. If these markets existed, contracts to buy and sell land in the future would exist. Without such futures markets in land there is a delayed response on the supply side and disequilibrium can occur and persist until the lags work their way through the development process. Were these markets present, a developer who expected prices to fall could purchase contracts to sell land short, by selling land not currently owned and buying back at the expected lower price.

Tax and regulatory policies can also change at short notice. A regime of subsidies for land developers may be replaced by one involving land speculation taxes. Supply also depends on the price of construction materials and services relative to the price for the finished package of site and improvements. The technology of construction likewise influence supply. Precasting concrete off-site, rather than on-site, may reduce costs of columns, beams, and walls. Modular unit construction can further reduce site costs. Such technological change also acts to increase the supply, *ceteris paribus.*

As noted, the demand for land has speculative elements. The speculative demand for land may arise from inflationary expectations or anticipated future urban growth. It was shown in Chapter 4 that perversities in the tax system may create a demand for holding land for purposes other than immediate development. Thus, expected inflation and its interaction with the tax system may create a demand for land, even in the absence of real urban growth.

Demographic factors, including the age and sex composition of households, also influence the demand for land. For land used for residential purposes, demographic factors include the marriage, divorce, and birth rates. In both the United States and Canada, the period subsequent to World War II witnessed a substantial increase in the birth rate. This, "baby boom" reached a peak in the United States in 1957, and in Canada in 1959, to be followed by a sharp reduction in birth rates and, two decades later, by an increase in the demand for housing. These demographic factors presage a reasonably strong demand for housing, and thus residential land, through the late 1980s and early 1990s, to be followed by a sharp decline.

As the birth rate declines, and given a relatively stable death rate, population growth will decline, but other demographic phenomena may also be at work. A large factor is internal migration. Although precise figures on such movements are difficult to construct, such migration from other parts of Canada to British Columbia appears to have been a substantial factor behind the rapid house price increases in 1979–1980. On the other hand, the level of immigration is partly a policy variable, in that the federal governments in the United States and Canada can determine the number of legal immigrants. The problem of illegal immigrants, however, poses severe difficulties in forecasting shifts in urban land demand. This problem is particularly acute in the Southwestern states and large urban centers of the United States.[5]

Another phenomenon is that reduced population growth does not necessarily imply reduced household formation. The declining birth rate has reduced the number of children per household, but liberalized divorce laws have increased the number of single-parent families and the number of households. Each household is smaller, and there is a demand for additional separate and smaller housing units.

Demographic factors impinge substantially on the demand for housing. Alonso cited three factors for the United States.[6] The first is related to the labor market behavior of married women. As more women enter the work force, the cost of having children increases. The cost includes the opportunity cost of not working, the added day-care costs, as well as the traditional costs of raising a child. This reduces the number of births at a given income level. It should be noted that this is a substitution effect in the sense that relative prices of working time are increasing relative to those for day care. As total income increases, however, the number of births may increase because of the resulting income effect.

Alonso's second factor is the change in the definition of a family, with divorces and separations being the largest contributors. The third factor is migration. This further divides into three categories. First, while total demand may be stagnant or declining, there may be shifts in tastes toward older units in central cities. The process of centrification, or renovation of deteriorated central cities by in-migration, may change the slope of the rent gradient. The second category is internal migration. Chapter 1 has indicated a trend of population movement toward rural and nonmetropolitan areas. Even with stagnant population growth, there may be increased demand in specific rural and nometropolitan areas. Third is the previously noted legal and illegal international migration flows.

Also on the demand side, land may be viewed as a normal good. In periods where real incomes are rising, such as from the end of World War II to the late 1970s, the demand for land should also increase, indicating that the demand for land also depends in part on income. Tax and regulatory considerations in landholding, even with no inflation or uncertainty, also affect land demand. Some jurisdictions have imposed restrictions on the sale of land, notably farm and agricultural land to foreigners. Other jursidictions (for example, the province of Ontario during the mid-1970s) have imposed a land speculation tax, depending on the period for which land is held.[7]

Effect of Taxes and Transaction Costs

Tax benefits for various types of land development may become capitalized in land.[8] The degree of capitalization depends on the relative supply and demand elasticities. The situation is depicted in Figure 9–3, where the assumptions of a flat, featureless plain and a large number of homogeneous lots are retained. Initial equilibrium in this market, where there is no distinction between lots for new construction and existing improved lots, is depicted where $D(P_L) = S(P_L)$ or at $\bar{P}_L$. An increase in demand to D' involves a new equilibrium at $\bar{P}'L$. The incidence of the increase is divided between demanders and suppliers. The amount of the demand shift is $\bar{P}'_L - \bar{P}^m_L$, with $\bar{P}'_L - \bar{P}_L$ accruing to the suppliers through higher capitalized land prices and $\bar{P}_L - \bar{P}^m_L$ to demanders. An initial demand subsidy of $\bar{P}'_L - \bar{P}^m_L$ nets the buyer of a lot only $\bar{P}_L - \bar{P}^m_L$.

These factors shift the relevant demand and supply curves in the land market. While our analysis below concentrates on the market response to land prices, it can be generalized to include other factors such as taxes and transaction costs. Even if the only determinant of the

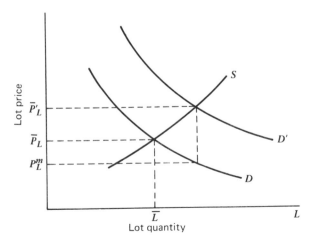

Figure 9–3. Market capitalization.

quantity of lots transacted is price, there still may be differentials between that received by the supplier and that paid by the demander—
so-called wedges.

Suppose the land market is as in Figure 9–3, again with no distinction between new and existing lots. In the absence of any taxes or
transaction costs in land transfer, equilibrium settles at $\bar{P}_L$, and the
number of lots changing hands is $\bar{L}$. As an example, these homogenous lots may sell for $20,000 with no transaction costs. If there are
taxes to be paid by the vendor or title transfer fees, as discussed in
Chapter 6, the net return to the seller is less than $20,000.

Further, the buyer may have costs of transacting, in taxes, legal
fees, and title insurance, in addition to surveys and mortgage charges.
Suppose the sellers must incur costs of $4000 per lot, and buyers are
required to pay $4000. The effective transaction price is no longer
$20,000, even if this is the actual figure agreed on by buyer and seller.
Rather, the buyer is paying $24,000 for access to the lot, and the seller
receives $16,000. There are always costs involved in a transaction; and
intermediation, whether by lawyers or bankers, involves real resources.
The situation is depicted in Figure 9–4. The initial supply curve S
shifts leftward and toward the origin, to S'. The parallel shift is for the
$4000. This can be viewed as an additional marginal cost of supplying
any lot to the market. The demand also shifts downward and to the
origin by a parallel $4000. The intersection between D' and S' occurs
at P^*_L, between the $16,000 and $24,000. The actual point of intersection depends on the relative elasticities of supply and demand.

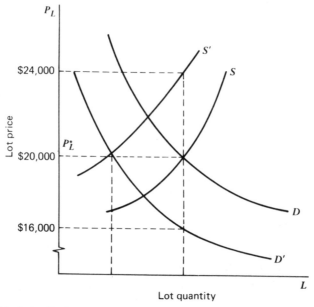

Figure 9–4. Market adjustment to transaction costs.

There is a further issue. If a person, either buyer or seller, can economize on transaction costs by selling the property without a broker or legal costs, some of this saving can be shared. The market need no longer set a unique equilibrium price, even when the lots are homogeneous. There is a trading range between $16,000 and $24,000, providing all costs are potentially avoidable. For example, even for taxes, some provisions may exist for exemptions or nonapplicability. Hence, a distribution of prices arises for homogeneous property in the same location. A competitive market equilibrium for the properties can change significantly once transaction costs are included. What can be said unequivocally is that transaction costs shift demand curves downward and supply curves leftward. Hence, the volume of sales is reduced, although the effect on price is indeterminate.

By contrast, if the supply curve is perfectly inelastic, any shift from taxes or transaction costs comes from the economic rent. A tax implies that the supplier receives less on a net basis, but the quantity transacted is unaffected unless the tax is so large that it exceeds the previous price. In this case, the price and quantity transacted are both zero.

COBWEB (OR LAGGED ADJUSTMENT) MODEL

The previous section suggests a lagged adjustment in housing and land markets. This is likely to occur on the supply side, where responses in permit and approval activity occur as a result of current market conditions, while the production will not be available until a future date. This lagged adjustment has given rise to the "cobweb theorem."

The simplest form of cobweb specification holds that the demand depends only on current land price, while supply depends on the price in the previous period. If there is equilibrium, then:

$$D(P_{L,t}) = S(P_{L,t-1}) \qquad (9.3)$$

where t denotes time. In actual practice there may not be an immediate movement to equilibrium. In Figure 9–5a, initial demand and supply are D and S, respectively, but the supply available in the current period depends on previous prices. If the supply exceeds current demand, such as at A, an excess supply of lots arises and the price falls. In the successive periods there may be iterative movements between excess demand and excess supply, culminating in equilibrium at B. Here the supply is relatively more inelastic than demand, so the equilibrium is stable.

In Figure 9–5b there is no stable equilibrium. Here the demand is more inelastic than supply. More generally, supply may depend on a sequence of lagged prices, or a distributed lag of these. Hence:

$$S = S(P_{L,t}\ P_{L,t-1} \cdots P_{L,t-n}) \qquad (9.4)$$

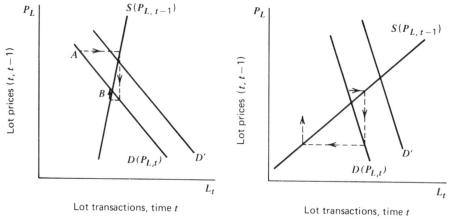

Figure 9–5a. Cobweb models for lots.   **Figure 9–5b.** Unstable cobweb for lots.

where n is an arbitrarily large lag. The current market adjustment discussed earlier depends on current price, and the cobweb model assumes that the lag structure has unit weight on the price in the immediate past period and zero for earlier period prices.

Consider the following example. Suppose a developer assembles a parcel of land for future subdivision when housing markets are prosperous. During the period of subdivision, markets deteriorate and the demand for housing falls. However, the supply is based on the market in the previous period, and the development investment is somewhat irreversible. The demand is based on the market in the current period, and there is a cobweb.

In other models where price adjustments are specified, current price itself may be explained as a weighted average of previous period prices. These models, involving moving averages and lag structures, yield time series predictions of prices. Typically, large sample sizes are required to estimate these functions empirically.

MODELS WITH VACANCIES AND EXCESS DEMAND

Thus far, a stock-flow mechanism has been developed, and various adjustment models have been presented. The issue is whether these adequately and completely represent behavior in the urban land market. It is known that there is always an excess supply of lots on the market, in the sense that there are always empty lots. However, if there is a strict equilibrium, there can be no empty lots. This suggests that the appropriate model for the land market may entail an equilibrium vacancy level.

Consider the total number of lots available for development. In the short run, this is determined by zoning and other restrictions. This may be viewed as the total potential stock of lots, some of which may not be currently actively offered on the market. Let this fixed stock be $\bar{L}$.

On the demand side, if there are temporarily no transactions or intermediation costs, demand depends on the lot price P_L. Supply, or lots actively offered for sale, also depends on P_L. Suppose the price of lots in Figure 9–6 is above equilibrium. If the equilibrium price per lot is $20,000, the market price is $25,000. At $25,000 the actual supply and demand intersect at A. The supply, S, exceeds demand, and the number of lots changing hands is L_A. The total supply of lots is L, so the number of vacant lots is CA in Figure 9–6.

When lot prices are higher than those obtaining in equilibrium, there is an equilibrium vacancy level, BC, and a disequilibrium number of empty lots, AB. The disequilibrium vacancy level arises from the fact that these sellers would be willing to accept $25,000 but are unable to sell at that price. The remainder of lots on the market, or BC, constitutes equilibrium vacancies, because these owners would be unwilling to sell at the prevailing market price. The number of lots transacted is L_A, but there is a distinction between the number of empty lots that would sell at the prevailing price and those that would remain vacant at that price.

If the price is below the equilibrium of $20,000, then the reverse obtains; but there are still some land vacancies. Suppose the price falls to $18,000, as in Figure 9–6. Then those willing to sell lots are fewer than those willing to buy, and there is an excess demand for lots at this price. The number of lots transacted is L_D, the minimum of supply and demand. The excess demand for lots, or those willing to buy at

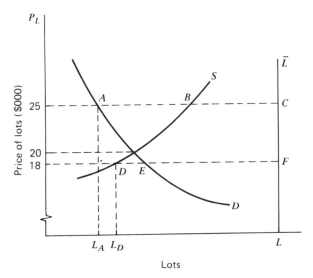

Figure 9–6. Disequilibrium model of land market.

prevailing prices but are unsuccessful, is *DE*, and the equilibrium vacancy level is *EF*.Under these assumptions, there are always some vacant lots on the market. This is the measure of excess supply in the market. The problem is to determine how the market moves toward equilibrium, if in fact this adjustment takes place.

The issue is whether the movement of prices of quantities clears the land market. If there is involuntary excess supply, or the price is above $20,000, one form of adjustment is to assume prices will fall toward equilibrium. Conversely, if there is an excess demand, prices will rise toward equilibrium.

Many models of land and housing markets are formulated on this assumption. The test on direction of price movements is used to classify whether there is excess demand or involuntary excess supply. When prices increase from one period to the next, it is asserted that the market must have been in excess demand. Conversely, when the prices are decreasing, the market must have been in involuntary excess supply. The model is thus reversed. Price changes are used to classify where the market disequilibrium is located.

The idea behind the model is that when prices are increasing for land, demand exceeds supply. The number of lots sold lies on the supply curve, as in *D* in Figure 9–6. For all such periods, the part of the supply curve below the $20,000 price can be distinguished or identified.

Conversely, if prices are falling, supply exceeds demand and the transactions lie on the demand curve above the intersection. This permits a part of each of supply and demand to be distinguished.

The final disequilibrium model of the land market is depicted in Figure 9–7. Here the observations may lie on the curve containing *A* and *D*. Suppose the price is above equilibrium, at *A*. The gap between the actual number of available lots and the demand is *AB*, and excess supply, BC. There are, simultaneously, empty lots and frustrated purchasers, even at relatively high prices. Below equilibrium, at *D*, the excess supply is *DE* and excess demand, *EF*. This permits vacancies and excess demand to exist simultaneously.

The problem with this model is that it is difficult to estimate the excess demand. Typically, the number of potential buyers of a property searching the market is unknown.

Market equilibrium need not be taken for granted in the case of urban land. Prices fluctuate considerably, and there is no reason to believe that they clear the market or lie at the intersection of supply and demand. Any model combining supply and demand in the land market must accommodate the following.

1. *Transaction wedges.* Prices received by the seller on a net basis and paid net by the buyer are typically unequal. The transaction costs or benefits include subsidies paid to buyers, taxes on land transactions, and legal and brokerage fees. These

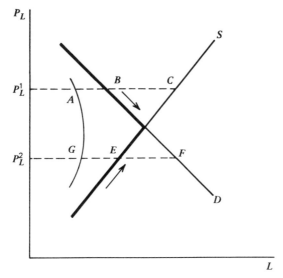

Figure 9–7. Disequilibrium (single market) in lot market, unique supply.

drive a wedge between effective supply and demand price. Who pays these charges depends on the relative elasticities of supply and demand. The sales price does not pass through the intersection of effective supply and demand, even when the land market is in equilibrium.

2. *Disequilibrium.* There is no reason to believe that observed prices pertain to equilibrium. The market may be in a process of adjustment to equilibrium or destabilization. This permits the existence of excess supply, vacant lots, or excess demand.

3. *Vacancies and searchers.* In any land market, there are usually empty lots and people searching. This is taken up more extensively in Chapter 10, but a realistic model must account for these.

4. *Stock-flow differences.* The stock of existing lots is built on, while new supply may be in unserviced form. The price of existing lots relative to "new" undeveloped lots acts as an investment trigger. As this relative price increases, it is more advantageous to increase the flow of lots.

The above define some characteristics of the operation of the urban land market. Further, urban land markets contain the possibilities of imperfect information and gaps in knowledge between buyers and sellers. Lots are not homogeneous, and people differ in evaluating their market potential. Some people have access to preferential financing rates, affecting sales timing. It may not be possible to include all of these factors, but together they form part of the uniqueness of urban land and illustrate why a special body of economic knowledge has grown up to analyze urban land markets.

IMPERFECT COMPETITION

A further complication in the land development process is the potential presence of imperfect competition on the supply side. This occurs if landownership is relatively concentrated. In the Canadian context, this problem, accompanying the rapid increase in land prices in the 1970s, occasioned the establishment of The Federal/Provincial Task Force on the Supply and Price of Serviced Residential Land. This task force, headed by David Greenspan, isolated in its report, *Down to Earth*, a number of factors affecting the land market.[9]

The lot price increases of the early 1970s in Canada were, in the short run, caused by shifts in asset revaluations and demographic factors, the report argues, and not ownership concentration or government restrictions such as slow approvals, high lot servicing charges, servicing requirements on new lots in excess of those on existing lots, tax policies, and zoning restrictions against small lot sizes.[10]

In part the issue arises as to whether asset revaluations were not in turn caused by responses to other government policies. In 1971 the government of Canada introduced capital gains taxes for the first time, on a basis similar to that in the United States: Only half of the nominal capital gains are included in taxable income; the tax is not paid on an annual accrual basis, but only on sale or realization; and no indexing of the base is performed.[11] Exempted were principal residences, of which each individual at the time could be an owner. In the case of a married couple, there could be two owners. The impact of such taxation is to shift consumer demand toward ownership housing and residential land and away from other assets. Hence, government policies may have contributed to the asset revaluation. Second, the tax-free nature of capital gains was fortified by increased inflation occurring during the 1970s.

An additional argument is based on the centralized control of landownership in the hands of a few large landowners. If the supply of land is relatively concentrated, then it is possible, in theory, for owners to exert market power by holding land off the market to restrict supply and raise price. The Greenspan Report argues that this was not the case for the early 1970s, because the production levels of that period were shown to be high and landownership was not concentrated. However, the issue is price change, which may have been caused by large shifts in demand relative to supply. Further, average market prices are determined by the existing stock and not the new flow in the short run, given the supply lags built into the land development process.

An analysis of ownership concentration in the land market needed to be done before reaching firm conclusions on the causes of the Canadian land boom of the 1970s. The supply of land is relatively inelastic, although rezoning and subdivision can increase long-run supply dramatically. If the supply is perfectly inelastic in the short run, one possible explanation for price escalation is the withholding by owners either with or without the exercise of monopoly power. All existing owners may expect continued price appreciation, so their incentives are to delay supply as long as expected price increases exceed carrying charges, including opportunity costs. The Greenspan Report addressed ownership issues and based its approach on earlier work by James Markusen and David Scheffman, which we review here.[12]

Suppose the demand price of housing is growing at x percent (here, the market for residential land is examined, but similar considerations apply to commercial and industrial land). Estimates of the price and income elasticities of demand for housing are both about one in absolute value, though there is considerable controversy on these.[13] They specify that the growth of the demand price, or the price at a perfectly inelastic supply, is approximately the sum of the net growth of families of homeowning age plus the rate of increase of per capita income. This is an approximation for total income growth.

Let the supply increase by y percent (i.e., the vertical supply curve shifts rightward by y percent). If the price elasticity of demand for housing is negative one, this will reduce house prices by y percent. Hence, household formation and income growth of x percent increases housing demand by x percent, because the income elasticity of demand for housing is one. Combining this with the supply, the net effect on prices of household formation of x percent and supply of housing units of y percent is to increase house prices by $(x - y)$ percent.

Now land is only a proportion of housing costs, typically about one-third. Suppose the elasticity of demand for lots with respect to price is also negative one-third. Then a 3 percent increase in the price of land reduces the demand for lots by 1 percent. Alternatively, if the number of lots is reduced by their being held off the market, a 1 percent reduction raises prices by 3 percent.

If y, the lot supply, can increase at a maximum of 5 percent in the short term, then the smallest increase in house prices is $(x - 5)$ percent in equilibrium. It may be possible for lot supply to increase by more than this, but the development delays typically act to limit such activity. This is because construction and approval delay limit increasing the existing housing stock by more than 5 percent annually. This further assumes the market was not previously in excess supply. If the increase in the supply of lots were reduced to zero by witholding land from the market, the largest increase in house prices would be 5 percent. In turn, the maximum increase in land prices under these assumptions would be 15 percent. This is under the assumption of no land being offered for sale.

The above argument is used by Markusen and Scheffman to claim that, in general, supply side imperfections cannot account for a large proportion of observed lot price increases, if these increases are in excess of 20 percent. Some points are worth noting.

1. An observed price change, as demonstrated earlier, is the sum of the adjustments of the supply and demand curves. Suppose the market is below long-run equilibrium, in excess demand. One portion of observed lot price change is the movement of supply toward equilibrium, and this may have occurred in the 1970s. Since the above model is comparing equilibrium points, the ob:-rved price change must be corrected. If between 1970 and 1980 the average lot increased in price by 30 percent, it is possible that 10 percent of that increase is a movement to equilibrium along the existing supply curve, and the equilibrium price may have also increased 20 percent as cost increases pushed the longer-run supply curve up and to the right.

2. If the base is made up of all existing housing units, the supply of housing must include not only new construction but also renovations, additions, remodeling, basement conversions, and in-law suites. The ability to increase total supply under this definition need not be limited to 5 percent in the short run.

3. The assumptions of price and income elasticities of demand for housing must be carefully considered. If the price elasticity of demand for housing is -0.5 instead of -1.0, a reducton of lot supply by 1 percent will raise house prices by 2 percent instead of the previous 1 percent. The effect on house prices can be doubled to 10 percent. "Corrected" price elasticity estimates suggest that the estimate is less than one in absolute value.

The Markussen/Scheffman model also provides qualitative predictions as to the effects of monopoly control on the supply of land. Specifically, the developer must be compensated for development costs plus the agricultural value of the land, if this is the alternative use. The sale in the current period implies that prices do not increase in excess of carrying charges. If landownership is diffused among small holders, none can affect current prices by offering their lots for sale. It is also concluded that under certain assumptions, limitations or deliberate holdbacks on supply cannot contribute to price increases in the lot market.

This differs in imperfectly competitive markets. An increase in supply depresses prices in the current period. Further, this may reduce future demand if some people, who might otherwise have bought in the future, transfer their demand to the current period. The landowner who is a monopolist establishes the condition that marginal revenue from one more current sale equals the marginal costs of development plus the present value of other costs.

Where the developer is a monopolist, the demand being faced is not infinite at the prevailing market price. Rather, the demand faced is downward sloping. The marginal revenue from selling one more unit is less than average revenue. The price is in excess of the marginal revenue. Marginal revenue is price less the reduction in average revenue, because all other units sell for less in order to sell the last unit. A competitive industry will develop more land at a lower average price than a concentrated industry. However, the supply each period depends on expectation of future prices. The overall supply of land is reduced, but not necessarily in each period.

Empirical evidence on landownership and concentration in the previously noted Greenspan study, *Down to Earth*, argues that landownership for residential development is not concentrated. In a sample of undeveloped land in six Toronto suburbs, the following concentration levels are obtained.[14]

	Nominal Ownership	*Effective Ownership*
Top 4	17.5	22.7
Top 6	21.4	30.5
Top 10	27.7	37.1
Top 15	32.6	41.7

The "Top 4," concentration ratio is the share of total undeveloped land owned by the largest four companies. Nominal ownership is based on the firm actually holding the title. Effective ownership is nominal ownership augmented by combining associated companies. Associated companies are those sharing principal officers. The ownership concentration ratios reported are argued to be too low to create "market power" (the ability to influence price significantly).

Some issues arise with this conclusion, obtained across Canada:

1. The concentration ratio method has certain technical flaws. An alternative is to derive a single index of ownership concentration, which introduces other problems of index number construction.

2. A great part of the ownership is vested in municipalities. If there is no short-run intention by municipalities to develop their land, this reduces the effective supply available and may change concentration ratios.

3. The landownership is of lot or land stock. Given approval delays and development costs, the supply of serviced lots, as opposed to raw land, delivered to builders may be extremely concentrated in the short run. Further, there may be differences between large and small developers in response functions with respect to price changes in land. If small developers have higher unit costs of obtaining permits and servicing, they may be slower to respond.

4. Final sales are also important. Builders of speculative houses arrange financing with lot suppliers. They may be more willing to negotiate with large, rather than small, builders.

Bolstering the Greenspan findings is the fact that existing developed lots and developed properties were excluded from the concentration ratios and associated companies were overstated. Thus, controversy exists on the degree of ownership concentration in land markets. Also, while monopoly reduces lot supply and raises prices, additional empirical research is required to determine the magnitude of effects. Existing evidence, however, does not support the view in Canada's urban areas that there is monopoly control of urban land resources.

One remaining issue is the question of public land banking. This has been continually put forward as a policy option during periods when urban land prices increase. Carr and Smith summarize the case both for and against.[15] The arguments for land banking include the following:

1. A publicly owned land bank can eliminate speculative profits.

2. The public land bank can be used as a buffer stock. When prices are high, the land bank sells to reduce prices. With low prices, the public land bank can act to support the market and replenish its supplies.

3. Government land banks can acquire land cheaply using the power of expropriation.

4. Appropriate zoning powers can ensure that all public land is saleable.

5. Public carrying charges are lower because public sector organizations can borrow at lower interest rates.

6. The public land bank may have economies of scale in servicing.

These arguments are subject to some qualifications. In the case of the first two, it is required that the land bank managers have more accurate price expectations than other participants, which is difficult to realize in practice. The public land bank may also contribute to speculative profits if it adds to demand during a period of rising prices. The argument of lower land costs is unclear if the government land bank has higher financing charges. The land bank may not be unconditionally guaranteed. In the United States, municipal bonds are tax-free, so interest rates are lower. Nevertheless, the pre-tax rate, or cost to the economy, is not necessarily lower. Carr and Smith point out that in Canada, where municipal bonds are not tax-free, these securities have yields higher than industrial bonds. This indicates that carrying charges in the municipal sector are not necessarily lower. If economics of scale arise, these would also exist in the private sector. In short, it is highly unlikely that public land banking can achieve its objectives and materially lower land costs without public subsidy.

SUMMARY

This chapter has examined the effects of various policies on land markets. On the demand side, demographic factors and tax changes were seen as being important. Shifts in the size of the population of homebuying age in the 1970s and 1980s have created a large potential demand for housing. The cloud on the horizon is the eventual sharp decline in the number of people of homebuying age in the late 1980s and thereafter, caused by falling birth rates from the 1960s on. Immigration, legal and illegal, is more difficult to predict, but large inflows of immigrants would be required to offset this natural decline.

The supply of land is affected by the time it takes to obtain approval and servicing. This implies that the supply of lots depends on a mixture of previous period prices. More efficient processing of applications would permit the supply to respond to current prices. If monopoly power is present, prices are higher and supply lower. The degree of monopoly power and the magnitude of the price and quantity distortions remain to be determined.

Underlying the market for land is the measurement of transaction costs. Brokerage fees, legal fees, land transfer and development charges all increase the cost of transacting land sales and purchases. Individuals differ in their willingness to search the market and in the degree of information they possess. Hence, some of the transaction costs are related to information services provided. Where this is not the case, a distortion arises.

Footnotes

1. R. W. G. Bryant, *Land: Private Property, Public Control* (Montreal: Harvest House), 1972, p. 150. Also see Ann L. Strong, *Land Banking* (Baltimore: The Johns Hopkins University Press), 1979.

2. For an analogous model of new and existing land markets, see David Nowlan, "The Land Market: How It Works," in M. Walker and L. B. Smith, eds., *Public Property* (Vancouver, B.C.: The Fraser Institute), 1976, pp. 3–37.

3. For identification, or separate distinction, of the supply and demand curves, at least one variable should enter the supply function that does not enter the demand function and vice versa. Variables affecting the supply of land include government regulations on approval and land use, the price of agricultural output, assuming this provides the next best alternative, and the price of servicing per lot. Demand variables include the price of new housing or improvements and the cost per new unit of construction. These additional variables are understood to be included, but are suppressed for notational convenience in Figure 9–2.

4. Price forecasting in speculation is discussed in H. S. Houthakker, "Can Speculators Forecast Prices?" *Review of Economics and Statistics* (1957):143–151. Further analysis of speculation, arguing for no interference with this practise, is in M. Friedman, "In Defence of Destabilizing Speculation," in R. W. Pfouts, ed., *Essays in Economics and Econometrics* (Chapel Hill, N.C.: University of North Carolina Press), 1960. The land market is analyzed in J. Carr and L. B. Smith, "Public Land Banking and the Price of Land," *Land Economics* 51(1975):316–330.

5. W. Alonso, "The Demographic Factor in Housing for the Balance of this Century", in G. Gau and M. Goldberg, eds., *The Future of North American Housing Markets* (Cambridge, Mass.: Ballinger), 1983.

6. Alonso, *op. cit.*

7. For example, in 1979 the state of Iowa limited foreign farmland ownership (*Washington Post,* June 16, 1979). Also see Peter J. Horwood, ed., *Foreign Investment in Land—Alternative Controls* (Vancouver, B.C.: Urban Land Economics Division, Faculty of Commerce, University of British Columbia), 1976. For details on Ontario's speculation tax, see L. B. Smith, "The Ontario Land Speculation Tax: An Analysis of an Unearned Increment Land Tax," *Land Economics* 52(1:1976):1–12.

8. For an excellent review of the literature on capitalization and for a discussion about the extent of capitalization, see George W. Gau, "Tests of Efficiency of Real Estate Investment Markets," presented at the Annual Meeting of the American Finance and American Real Estate and Urban Economics Associations, December 1982.

9. Report of the Federal/Provincial Task Force on Residential Land, *Down to Earth* (Toronto, Ontario), 1979.

10. For an extensive analysis of the land price boom in Canada in the early 1970s, see David T. Scheffman, "Some Evidence on the Recent Boom in Land and Housing Prices," in L. S. Bourne and J. R. Hitchcok, eds., *Urban Housing Markets: Recent Directions in Research and Policy* (Toronto: University of Toronto Press), 1978, pp. 57–85.

11. However, in 1974 the federal government increased the tax brackets for personal income by indexing them to the Consumer Price Index. At the corporate level, a flat tax rate does imply taxes on nominal capital gains.

12. See J. Markusen and D. Scheffman, *Speculation and Monopoly in Urban Development: Analytical Foundations with Evidence for Toronto* (Toronto: University of Toronto Press for Ontario Economic Council), 1978.

13. Part of the difference arises from aggregation bias, in using average data. Also, it depends on whether owners or renters are the unit of observation.

14. See J. Markusen and D. Scheffman, "Ownership Concentration in the Urban Land Market: Analytical Foundations and Empirical Evidence," in L. B. Smith and M. A. Walker, *Public Property* (Vancouver, B.C.: The Fraser Institute), 1976, pp. 147–176. The sample communities are Brampton, Markham, Mississauga, Pickering, Richmond Hill, and Vaughan.

15. See J. Carr and L. B. Smith, "Public Land Banking and the Price of Land," *Land Economics* 51(1975):316–330.

10

THE REAL ESTATE MARKET: MARKET MAKERS, BROKERS, AND OTHER INFORMATION AGENTS

INTRODUCTION

Real estate markets, for both urban land and its improvements, are characterized by uncertainty and incomplete information. Contracts for the use of real estate frequently involve intermediation, where a third party assists in the negotiations between buyer (lessor) and seller (lessee). Negotiations between buyer and seller may also involve additional parties, for each in turn may be represented by an agent, broker, or realtor. For convenience, in the following discussion we will be referring to buyers and sellers though we realize that real property may also be leased or other restrictions placed on its use for financial considerations, such as easements, covenants, and liens.

Intermediation in real estate markets involves more than just brokers. Title search and insurance, legal fees, appraisals, and the negotiations for financing (mortgage brokerage) also involve intermediaries. These services are all important, but the primary focus of this chapter is on real estate agents and on the transaction costs incurred through the use of agents in the trading of real property or real property rights.

Individuals are not typically prohibited from dealing in real estate on their own account. Nevertheless, there remains a large market for real estate agents to negotiate contracts and provide information for buyers and sellers. In theory, such brokerage functions can serve to enhance market efficiency and facilitate transactions. This theoretical result will be subjected to empirical analysis later in this chapter.

Our first objective is to discuss the environment in which real estate transactions are made. Transaction costs on the purchase and sale of real estate are typically large. In terms of application, this chapter focuses on such costs in the market for residential real estate. The arguments are no less applicable to industrial, commercial, and investment property. However, in terms of the brokerage industry, with its agents and salespersons, most emphasis has been placed on the residential market.

The presence of large transaction costs serves to distinguish real estate and its services from other commodities. While the purchase of an apple, for instance, in a store may involve very small search and commuting costs, the costs of facilitating a real estate transaction are significant. Moreover, because some people are more efficient in economizing on transaction costs than others, there can be a wide diversity in prices on otherwise identical properties.

The observation that physically identical commodities may transact at widely different prices underlies Stigler's research, for which he won the 1982 Nobel Prize in Economics. The original research was performed on labor markets, but it appears as applicable to real estate markets.[1] Adopting this analogy, similar sites and their improvements may transact at different prices in the same market. The market contains a large number of buyers and sellers of property services who may not create the usual competitive conditions where only a single price prevails. Thus, as it is possible to obtain property services of the same quality at different prices, a return to information arises. From this return to information arises a market for services of the agents and brokers in real estate.

The real estate market model for brokerage is based on findings by Courant and Yinger.[2] They developed a theory of behavior for agents based on U.S. data. There are costs and benefits of having the typical regulatory structure. These usually involve:

- Regulation by a state or provincially authorized body of licensing requirements;
- Enforcement of education and training requirements;
- Multiple listing service structures, with the regulation here based on brokerage associations.

This chapter focuses on various issues surrounding real estate brokers. Specifically, commission structures and the incentives in listing and selling procedures are examined. The other transaction costs of real estate, such as legal fees, appraisal costs, and taxes and fees imposed in title transfer and insurance, are also discussed. The chapter concludes with a summary of the basic results.

TRANSACTION COSTS AND THE REAL ESTATE MARKET

Without transaction costs, the price of housing services to an owner contains the usual components of interest, taxes, and capital gains. The user cost for an owner is defined as r_o. Suppose a homeowner initially is consuming h^* units of housing. If that owner should decide to move, transaction costs are incurred. On a sale, if a broker or real estate agent is used, the commission typically ranges between 5 and 7 percent. Although the commission rate is only paid by the seller, there is an incidence problem. The supply of houses or real estate offered to the market shifts to the left and the effect on market equilibrium depends on the elasticity of supply and demand. While other transaction costs are incurred on sale, the largest single component is that for the brokerage commission.

In Figure 10–1 the demand curve for housing inclusive of transaction costs is indicated. This is under the assumption that transaction costs are fixed. Between the range of the price of ownership, from a low of r_o to a maximum of $\bar{r}_o$, the household is immobile. Suppose the price of ownership as a percentage rate is defined as:

$$r_O = \mu + d + \tau - p^e \qquad (10.1)$$

where μ is the rate of interest; d, the rate of maintenance and depreciation; τ, the rate of property taxation; and p^e, the rate of expected capital gains increase. Either mortgage interest and property taxes are not deductible, or the marginal rate of personal income taxation is zero.

Suppose the price of ownership is initially r_o^*. Any change in the price of homeownership, for example, through movement in interest rates, that maintains the price of ownership in the range between r_o

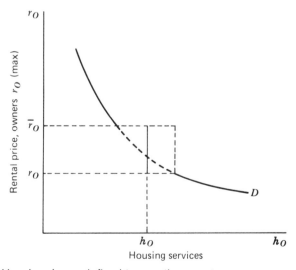

Figure 10–1. Housing demand, fixed transactions costs.

and $\bar{r}_o$ implies that the household does not move. Suppose the interest rate is 10 percent, depreciation and maintenance together account for 3 percent, the property tax rate is 1 percent, and house prices are expected to increase at a rate of 6 percent. The price of ownership of housing is 8 percent, but that is before the application of transaction costs. If these transaction costs are as large as 8 percent of the price of the property, then the cost associated with moving is 16 percent, and that with staying 8 percent. The seller compares the present value of the future earnings stream from the new house with the transaction costs. If these are included, the person tends to be reluctant to move from existing housing.

The person computing the cost of ownership, but not planning to move, has a different cost than one planning to move. The cost of ownership includes all the components of interest rates, depreciation, taxes, and expected capital gains.

Two types of transaction costs are indicated in Figure 10–1 and 10–2. In the former, the transaction costs make the demand for housing become perfectly inelastic in a range around the existing level of housing owned. It takes a large interest rate change, for example, to induce mobility. In the latter, transaction costs are associated with all levels of housing demand except around the initial level.

A 1977 study by Goldberg and Horwood,[3] was conducted in the three largest Canadian cities Montreal, Toronto, and Vancouver and commissioned by the Canadian Department of Consumer and Corporate Affairs in Ottawa. It concluded that closing costs are relatively

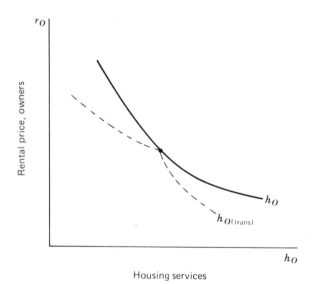

Figure 10–2. Housing demand with variable transactions costs.

large; reported on the extent that certain components are fixed, such as part of title search and appraisal; and found that it is the less expensive properties whose prices are increased more by the cost of the transaction.

There has also been a growing interest in the magnitudes and extent of residential housing transaction costs in the United States. Estimates from *Existing Home Sales, 1981* by the National Association of Realtors indicate that in 1968, in the United States, housing transaction costs amounted to $35 billion, with an average house price of $22,300. In 1978 they were $214.4 billion with an average price of $55,500. Total commissions to realtors in 1968 were estimated to be $2.1 billion, and $12.9 billion in 1978. By 1981, the housing market had declined somewhat under the pressure of higher interest rates. Dollar volume was $184.1 billion in transactions, and commissions were estimated at $11.0 billion, although the average sale price had increased to $78,300.[4] This certainly indicates that transaction costs are a large part of total housing sales.

The relatively high transaction costs have induced a large percentage of individuals in the residential housing market to sell by themselves. Goldberg and Horwood examined the issues of usage of real estate agents and the cost of purchasing their transaction services for a house. The breakdown of the type of agent used in the sample (equally weighted purchases in 1977 in the three cities) is indicated below.

Real Estate Agent Use (%)

	Montreal	*Toronto*	*Vancouver*	*All Sample*
Sale by Owner	38.9	16.4	23.4	26.4
Multiple Listing Service (MLS)	24.2	40.8	29.9	31.5
Exclusive Listing	34.6	37.8	40.3	37.5

The sample was taken retrospectively by examining the *Teela Market Surveys,* which rely on data compiled in Land Registry Offices. Further, the survey indicates that duration on the market is lower for owner-sold properties and that the ratio of transaction price to asking price is higher for owner-sold properties, even without subtracting the commission for those using agents.

The results suggest that individuals have an alternative to retaining an agent. Observed market data for the use of real estate agent services indicated a truncation. There is a distribution of observed commissions, but a large accumulation at zero, for those who sell by themselves.

On the buy side, because people do not pay directly for real estate services, most purchasers use them. Presumably, if a buyer with a realtor deals with an owner-seller, negotiation must arise on payment of a commission to the agent. The distribution of real estate commissions is indicated below, in percent.

	Montreal	Toronto	Vancouver	All Sample
Low (1–4.99%)	10.0	24.3	24.3	20.0
Medium (5–6.99%)	40.0	74.3	52.9	56.5
High (7% and above)	50.0	1.4	22.9	23.5

Real estate commissions are higher in Montreal than in the other two cities, and this is the city with the highest rate of owner selling. This suggests that the demand for real estate services is downward sloping. There is some suggestion of price flexibility, although this is not the perception of the majority of sellers.

Total transaction costs are indicated below for both buyers and sellers. Transaction costs include real estate and brokerage commissions, legal fees, and taxes.

Distribution of Households by Transaction Costs

Sellers (%)				
	Montreal	Toronto	Vancouver	All Sample
Low (0–1.99%)	38.8	10.6	21.8	23.7
Medium (2–7%)	38.8	62.8	54.0	51.9
High (7.1–10.6%)	22.4	26.6	24.1	24.3

This indicates that in Montreal 38.8 percent of people paid 1.99 percent or less in transaction costs.

Again, on the buy side, 54.9 percent of Vancouver buyers paid less than 1 percent in transaction costs.

Distribution of Households by Transaction Costs

Buyers (%)				
	Montreal	Toronto	Vancouver	All Sample
Low (0–0.99%)	8.6	28.3	54.9	29.1
Medium (1–1.99%)	43.1	52.6	32.7	43.0
High (2–8.6%)	48.2	19.1	12.3	27.8

Among sellers, in Montreal there are relatively many who have a low transaction costs to selling price ratio. This is largely accounted for by people selling real estate on their own, without assistance from brokers. By comparison, the majority of sellers in Toronto and Vancouver deal through agents, as indicated by the results. On the buyer side, transaction costs ratios are higher in Montreal than in the other two cities.

Further, the group obtaining low transaction costs were not clustered into those at the expensive part of the market. This may be attributed to low-income consumers having a lower value of time and being more willing to allocate time to this search process, and high-income persons being able to search more efficiently, possibly because they possess better contacts.

The above information points to complexities in the transaction costs for real estate. There is an observed distribution of prices, which may reflect differences in the quality of service. Consumers will have difficulty adjusting to this, given the fact that they are involved in the housing transaction market only infrequently.

The usual explanation of earnings variation between people comes from the theory of human capital, arguing increased earnings derive from increased education and expense. However, in the real estate brokerage industry, this does not always obtain and the potential for being a "superstar" is very real. In this context, such an individual is able to obtain listings and close sales far more efficiently than average. Total earnings are higher even when earnings per transaction may be the same as for other agents. However, the characteristics that determine "superstar" status do not appear to be among those for which measured data are available.

Data have been collected on a survey of British Columbia agents and salespersons in 1981 by Hamilton. Annual earnings are the dependent variable, with a number of explanatory variables included. A regression equation yields the information in Table 10–1.

The dependent variable is annual earnings, with a mean of $29,888, in 1981 dollars, and standard deviation of $27,858. The regression attempts to explain earnings of agents and salesmen. The R^2, a measure of the proportion of variation in earnings attributable to the included characteristics such as sex and job experience, is low at 3 percent.

Table 10–1 Explanation of Annual Earnings, Real Estate Agents/Salesmen, British Columbia, Canada, 1981

Variable Name	Brief Description	Mean	Standard Deviation	Coefficient[b] Dependent Variable
ANNEARN	Annual earnings	$29,888	$27,858	
SEX	Male = 1, Female = 2	1.37	0.48	−7,080 (1,295)
YRSLIC	Years licensed (experience)	4.62	2.71	884 (231)
LICENSEES	Number of licensees in office	16.1	11.35	−147 (72)
OFFICES	Number of offices	8.43	12.24	−40 (70)
FRANCH	1 if a franchise 0 otherwise	0.40	0.49	407 (1326)
RATE	Commission rate[a]	3.67	1.48	−68 (440)
SHARE	Commission split, category=1 if < 51% =2 if 51–55%, =3 if 56–60, =5 if > 65%	3.08	0.97	−91 (664)
CONSTANT	Intercept	1	0	38,567

[a]Rate = 1 if less than 5%, = 3 if 5–6, = if 6–7%.
[b]Standard error in parentheses.
Regression statistics: N Sample size 2032. Regression F for all coefficients. Zero is 10.18 and R^2 is 0.03.

The factors that appear to explain the earnings of salesmen and agents, those with a ratio of coefficient to standard error greater than 2 in absolute value, are SEX (male = 1, female = 2), YRSLIC (years licensed), and LICNSEES (number of licensees in office). Males have higher earnings than females, although the latter may work fewer hours. The average female earns $7080 less than the average male, or about 25 percent less using the mean as denominator. Experience is important, although the variable YRSLIC may in fact be measuring human capital increases acquired through training and experience in the work force, or a sorting process that eliminates the less productive people over time. Experience is a self-selective variable, meaning that only the relatively able survive.

The notable observation is that conventional explanatory variables do not explain earnings. Incentive structures in the commmission RATE and SHARE do not appear to be important explanatory variables. The results confirm that "superstar" status appears to be an unmeasured variable. To construct a model of the market for real estate and brokerage services, both the supply and demand for these is required. The above indicates factors which affect the supply of these services.

ISSUES IN BROKERAGE

A number of issues arise in the modeling of real estate broker behavior. The institutional regulation of the industry, classified as a professional service, varies between the United States and Canada. Regulation is partly internal, administered by real estate brokerage associations, and partly through state or provincial laws. The first leading issue deals with the nature of commissions, the second is the Multiple Listing Service and access to it.

Commission Structures

Commission rates between agents and sellers are typically fixed. For listings on the Multiple Listing Service, a fixed commission structure is required, and superficially there appears to be little commission rate variation on exclusive listings. The real estate brokerage industry operates in the manner of a regulated industry; any competition which occurs is on nonprice matters, such as services. A further adjustment occurs because of the relative ease of entry. Excess profits may well be dissipated by entry into the industry. Service levels rise to meet the commission rate, and there is a larger short-run entry of agents and salesmen that would obtain in the case of unregulated markets. Common commission rates typify competitive markets, so the identification of imperfections becomes problematical. There are two other aspects of fixed commissions. Individuals always have the option of selling their properties themelves and thereby avoid paying any commission. In addition, Goldberg and Horwood discovered that there is some price shading in the commission rate.[5] Almost one-fifth of a sample of sellers in three Canadian cities obtained a reduction in the prevailing rate.

Nevertheless, the regulated fees suggest that any competition occurs primarily in nonprice areas. The typical service is a bundle of commodities, including advertising, searching for and with buyers, Multiple Listing access, negotiation services, appraisal, and transport of potential clients. Services offered may exceed the level that a home seller may have otherwise purchased, and there is no option for taking a subset of these services.

Research by Carroll and Gaston on the earnings of agents shows that where the fail rate on the licensing exam is high, the earnings of brokers is also high.[6] This may mean that either there is restrictive entry or the test is an effective screening device for determining the successful agent, or even that the test score is an accurate reflection of sales skills. The regulated fee rate promotes a larger level of entry to the brokerage industry and overexpansion of firms than would otherwise be the case.

It appears that the demand for brokerage services is downward sloping, though any evidence for this is indirect. In the absence of rate dispersion in any local area, comparisons are required across urban areas, to determine whether those cities with high commission rates have high rates of vendor-sold homes. This appears to obtain. The supply of brokerage services is heterogeneous. Agents are not perfect substitutes, even though they may be receiving the same rate of commission. The higher productivity level of the successful agent may be manifest in a reduced time to sell a given listing. In this sense, agents are imperfect substitutes, even though their market prices are nominally identical. Further, there is imperfect information by home sellers on the quality and productivity of their agent. This is because of their infrequent entry into sales, and partly because there is no rating service on professionals.

On the supply side for these services, experience appears to raise the annual earnings level of a broker. The brokerage industry is highly cyclical. During depressed markets, the less able brokers are forced out of action and the more able survive, a form of Darwinian labor market. Experience is not a credential required for entry in any subfield of brokerage, as education is in other occupations. It appears that there are specific skills associated with the brokerage industry, and that the less able are flushed out. During a slump the less able leave and the relatively skilled workers remain. At the start of an upturn, monopoly rents are earned by the survivors, as the supply of brokers is relatively inelastic; however as the demand for the services shifts upward, this is eventually competed away by new entrants.

Access to Multiple Listing Service

The second area of imperfection is in access to the Multiple Listing Service, which is restricted to real estate agents. An individual wishing to sell a house privately cannot gain access to this larger market. The cost of this policy has been blunted by the growth of franchised firms in the United States and Canada, such as Century 21, which provides a large market in a specific area through computer services. The remaining area where the effect of the Multiple Listing Service has been blunted is with national firms, who have large networks of offices. In Canada, the trust companies also have real estate departments, involving vertical integration of mortgage supply and real estate services. Other options to alter existing commission structures include having a flat fee charged for remaining with the firm on a monthly basis, instead of a commission split. However, alternative contracts on commission structures appear to be the exception rather than the rule in real estate transactions.

MODELS OF REAL ESTATE BROKER BEHAVIOR

The first step in attempting to explain real estate broker behavior is to develop the market scenario. The basic assumption is that properties with apparently similar characteristics sell for different prices in the same market. A graphical indication of this is contained in Figure 10–3. Suppose a property owner is considering offering a unit for sale. Rental price is r, but there is a distribution of potential rent offers that has the form $f(r)$. As is likely in the real estate market, the distribution has a long right tail. This is because the probability of obtaining a very high offer is not zero, but the distribution of prices is limited below by zero. There is a small probability that a high offer may be received. (There is also the possibility that no offers may be received, but this is ignored.)

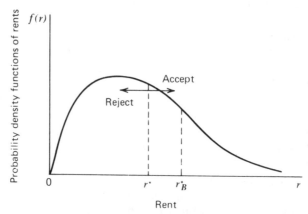

Figure 10–3. Price distribution in a real estate market.

Denote the distribution of the population of price offers as $f(r)$, and suppose that one other offer arrives each period. The searcher, here the owner or seller seeking a buyer, sets an acceptance or reservation price r^*. Any price offer received of at least this level is acceptable, so the unit is transacted, and denoted as the area to the right of r^*. It is possible for two owners listing their property to obtain different transaction prices, for any offer of at least r^* is acceptable. Conversely, two owners of the same type of unit could have differing values of r^*. It would take longer for the person with the higher reservation price to receive an acceptable offer, and the final transaction price could be higher.

The decision rule that follows from this is:

$$\text{accept if} \quad r \geq r^* \tag{10.2}$$
$$\text{reject if} \quad r < r^*$$

and the average rent received can be calculated directly.[7] This all assumes that the owner attempted to sell on his or her own. If a broker were approached, a transaction cost or commission would be involved, and the seller would have to raise the reservation rent to r_B^* to cover the additional cost. Improved knowledge of the real estate market and buyers and sellers means that there may be a better selection of offers. The agent is retained if expected benefits in higher rents exceed costs. A similar calculation occurs if owners are contemplating selling rather than leasing their property.

It is instructive to develop a theory of broker behavior to complement that of seller behavior. As a self-employed businessperson, the broker is engaged in maximizing profits, defined as sales commission revenue less costs. In the following, single-family houses are used as examples, but the model is also applicable to commercial and industrial property as well as condominium units.

Suppose the average house sells for V, and the brokerage commission rate is b. Let variable costs on the sale be k, borne by the broker. So net sales revenue is $bV - k$ on a per house basis.

If the broker sells H houses during the given period, the total sales revenue (R) is:

$$R = (bV - k)H \tag{10.3}$$

The typical broker has three types of costs, related to the information gathering and disseminating activities.[8] These brokerage functions include the following.

1. *Listing services,* or seeking a number of houses for advertising for sale on the market. The broker must search for sellers willing to list with him or her, which involves costs to the broker. These search costs are typically for telephone contact and automobile expenses and time.

2. *Buyer search,* or seeking buyers for houses for which he or she has listings or which are listed through a Multiple Listing Service (MLS). The broker invests in services such as advertising to attract potential buyers.

3. *Showing costs,* or the resources of time and goods expended in showing houses to potential buyers. Examples are "open houses," where the units are available to all comers. A second showing cost is in taking potential buyers to other available houses.

The average income and expenditures for a real estate salesperson in British Columbia are indicated in Table 10–2, based on 1974 survey data. This table lists cash income and expenditures. An economic definition of income should also include an imputation for time spent in search, and the expected benefits from new contacts or listings that have not resulted in current sales. Table 10–3 provides information on the number of real estate salesmen vis-à-vis population in Canadian and U.S. jurisdictions.

In terms of expenditures, let there be a search cost per listing, expressed in both goods and time. It may be the case that some brokers are more efficient in obtaining listings than others, but this is ignored. Analogously, let there be a search cost per buyer. Since showing costs also can be expressed in per buyer terms, total costs are the sum of search costs for listings and for buyers. Consider an example on net

Table 10–2 Average Gross Earnings and Expenses of Real Estate Salesmen in British Columbia, 1974 Monthly

Average Gross Income		$1678
Real estate commissions	$1600	
Property management	8	
Insurance commissions	1	
Appraisal fees	8	
Other real estate income	61	
Average Expenses		$ 306
Automobile	$ 169	
Advertising	45	
Other	92	
Average Net Income		$1372

Source of Commission Income by Type of Sale

Residential	75%
Commercial	9%
Industrial	2%
Farm	7%
Recreational	4%
Other	3%
	100%

Source: G. Rosenbluth, *Real Estate Inquiry,* Government of British Columbia, April 1976, Table 10, p. 42.

Table 10–3 Real Estate Salesmen and Population

Province or State	Real Estate Salesmen	Population (000)	Population Per Salesman
Canada 1971			
Total	21,990	21,568	981
Newfoundland	70	522	7,459
Prince Edward Island	30	112	3,721
Nova Scotia	325	789	2,428
New Brunswick	180	635	3,525
Quebec	2,090	6,028	2,884
Ontario	11,315	7,703	681
Manitoba	795	998	1,243
Saskatchewan	540	926	1,715
Alberta	2,015	1,628	808
British Columbia	4,610	2,185	474
United States 1970			
Total	262,161	203,185	775
California	48,677	19,953	410
Washington	8,510	3,409	401
Oregon	3,967	2,091	527
New York	18,821	16,782	892
Illinois	11,956	10,081	843

Source: G. Rosenbluth, *Real Estate Inquiry Report,* Government of British Columbia, April 1976.

earnings of real estate agents, as drawn from Table 10–2. This indicates the economic cost including opportunity cost, of operating a real estate brokerage. The same survey shows that average hourly net earnings after expenses, but before taxes, were $6.73 in 1974.[9] On a gross tax basis, this may be viewed as the price of time assigned to search.[10] Assume, for convenience, that the average commission of $1600 represents net revenue from the listing and sale of a house, so the number of sales is one. Also, if the broker has six listings and it takes ten hours per month to service each listing, the cost is 10 times $6.73 times 6, or $403.80 per month, including opportunity costs. This is using the estimate of $6.73 as net earnings and the number of listings and hours of service per month per listing. If the "other" costs of $92 are assigned to listings, the total is $495.80.

Let the automobile and advertising expenses, $214, be assigned entirely to sales. If it takes 100 hours of showing and commuting per month to sell one house, the labor expenditure equals $673 plus the $214, or $887. Total expenditures equal the sum of the $495.80 and the $887, or $1382.80 per month. Assume that no benefits for future sales or "goodwill" arise in the month, and that the $78 of other revenue, that is, difference between the $1678 and $1600 in Table 10–2, arises from property sales.

Total monthly revenue is $1678, using estimates of Table 10–2, and expenditures are $1383, rounding to the nearest dollar. This leaves $295 unaccounted for. There are three sources for explaining this "excess profit." First, certain assumptions on efficiency and productivity have been made. Some agents or salespeople may be more productive than others, and will earn an economic rent on their talents. And just as there is a Pavarotti, there may be "star" real estate brokers who are more productive than average, with industry-specific skills that create a net income per hour in excess at the $6.73 which could be received in alternative employment.

Second, the $295 includes the economic rent associated with the holding of a real estate license. Across North America, real estate brokers typically are licensed by a state or provincial authority. Unlicensed individuals are prohibited from selling real estate, except of their own account. Even for those attempting to sell themselves, MLS access, that is, access to a wide market, is typically not available. Further, MLS regulations, analogous to those for stock and securities trading prior to 1975, impose restricted commission structures.

Finally, real estate markets are highly localized and cyclical. As it turned out, 1974 was a good year for both sales volume and prices. As a result, this short-term economic rent may be viewed in a longer-term context as the rent required to keep the salesperson's human capital employed in the industry, acknowledging that there will be years when the economic rent is negative (1982 was such a year in British Columbia, the rest of Canada, and for most the United States as well). The data suggest that real estate agents' income for the United States peaked in 1979.

Hence, the excess profit of $295 per month may be regarded as the price per month of the real estate practice, both for superior skills, for license rents, and to even out longer-term cycles. This $295 monthly is what remains after subtracting all charges. It is a return for having the right to practice in real estate, in addition to a return to any favorable market factors at the times. If all salespeople are equally productive, and there are no cycles, then the $295 is the monthly value of the license. By capitalizing over a long period, the asset price or capitalized price of the license is obtained.

Over a long period, the asset price, again assuming the $295 is entirely asset rent, is $295/$i$, where i is the monthly interest rate. Capitalizing annually, at a 12 percent rate, as a real interest rate in excess of the inflation rate, yields 1 percent monthly, so the value is $29,500. The asset prices of these licenses may rise and fall with the prevailing fortunes of the real estate market.

The objective of the broker is to maximize his or her economic rent, paid to the fixed factors of real estate acumen or skills and license incumbency. These rents may be expressed as the differences between sales revenue and costs of listings and finding buyers. Total revenue is the commission total on one house, less closing costs per house, multiplied by the number of houses sold. Closing costs are exogenous, or not determined by the broker, but commissions may be determined by him. Total expenses, including imputations for time, are listing related and sales related. Let the showing and listing costs also be beyond broker control.

Finally, the number of houses sold can be said to depend primarily on the commission charged, the number of listings, and selling costs. Then house sales can be expressed H (b,L,s) dependent on the commission rate b, number of listings L, and listing and sales costs per unit s. This means that the broker will maximize rents with respect to commission, and listing and sales costs.

Economic theory predicts that lower commission rates in b increase sales. Higher listings in total mean higher sales, and higher sales costs mean lower sales.[11]

To analyze the comparative statics of broker behavior, or what happens when certain variables change, the formulation of Figure 10–4 is used.

Commissions The higher the commission rate, the lower the quantity of sales, holding listing and sales costs constant. This may be viewed as the cost, in lost home sales opportunities, of reducing a commission. The benefit in relative terms is the gain in sales revenue divided by the yield per house $(bV - s)$. Suppose a broker who sells one $80,000 house per month raises his or her commission from 4 to 5 percent. Selling costs per house are $2000. The net yield per house, previously $1200, is now $2000.

An alternative way of viewing the commission structure is as follows. If the broker raises the commission, house sales will fall. The ex-

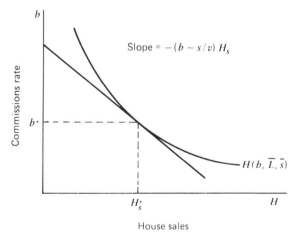

Figure 10–4. Real estate broker behavior—commissions.

tent of the decline depends on the revenues and costs of changing the commission rate. The units of the change are house sales per unit commission. The average return per dollar in percentage terms is $b - V/S$, commission less sales costs. In Figure 10–4 is indicated the equilibrium quantity of house sales and the commission rate.

Frequently, the commission rate is set either through the MLS or through regulation, and the broker cannot alter it at will. It remains exogenous, and the analysis determines exactly how much commission is optimal. The problem is that the set commission may not be b^*, the optimal commission rate.

Listings[12]   The issue here is whether it is profitable to search for more listings. Each listing involves servicing costs, and the return lies only in income generated. Although not considered here, sales price is typically a random variable. If it takes a low value, the broker may lose on the listing. Alternatively, brokers may pay for listings by offering a guaranteed purchase plan, where an undertaking to purchase at a specified reservation price arises.

Suppose a given number of listings produces one more sale, changing H by one. This immediately yields $bV - k$ in revenue to the broker, that is, house commission less variable cost rate. On an $80,000 house at 5 percent commission with $200 for K, $3800 of marginal revenue arises (this also assumes that the agent owns and operates the firm). From this is subtracted s. Suppose this is $1000 per house. Total showing costs are $1000, and assigned to the one house. So net revenue is now $bV - k - s$, or $2800.

The number of listings required was two, costing $100 per month to service, or $200. So the net revenue is reduced to $2600, or $2800 - $200, for two listings, or $1300 per listing, part of economic rent. The broker might be willing to bid $100 for a listing were such direct practices permitted. The change in sales H per listing L may be interpreted as the marginal product of a listing. The marginal product of a listing MP_L reflects the productive efficiency of the broker. The net revenue change from obtaining one more listing is $(bV - k - s)MP_L$, and the cost is s_L. Equating the marginal revenue of a listing with its cost:

$$(bV - k - s)MP_L = s_L \tag{10.4}$$

whereupon

$$MP_L = s_L/(bV - k - s) \tag{10.5}$$

and this is indicated in Figure 10–5. The marginal product of a listing is equated to the ratio of costs to net revenues.

Selling Costs[13]   Selling costs involve the time used showing a property, and advertising and automobile expenses. Analogous to the list-

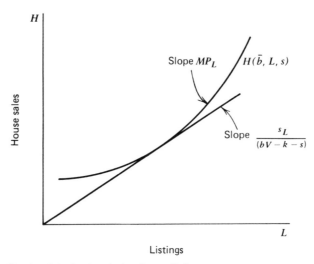

Figure 10–5. Real estate broker behaviour—listings.

ing case, one can define the marginal product of selling costs, in additional houses sold per unit of costs, as MP_s.

Suppose selling costs increase by one unit. Sales revenue increases by $(bV - k)MP_s$. For the case where $bV - k$ is \$3800 let MP_s be .01. Then net revenue is \$38. Marginal costs have two components. The first is the fact that if sales costs increase, for example, because of increases in advertising expenses, all houses are affected. For a one-unit increases in s, all houses involve higher selling costs. Second, the increase affects the likelihood of selling a house, through MP_s, so the total cost increase is sMP_s.

The model describes potential real estate broker behavior. Further embellishment can be added to the specification through modeling how people choose a broker and how a broker makes a sale. Yinger views the selection of a broker as a binary, yes–no process. However, some brokers may engage a different range of services than others. Also, some brokers may engage in a strategy of bidding high for a listing, but then offering a longer duration on the market. In this case, the broker takes a longer time to see the house. The potential seller (buyer of brokerage service) therefore faces a trade-off between speed of sales, sales price, and, in some instances, commission rates. An expanded model of broker behavior and selection is capable of analyzing a broad range of policies and behaviors to determine equilibrium rents and commissions as well as sales and listing volumes.

REGULATIONS ON REAL ESTATE BROKERS

Real estate regulations imposed by state and provincial authorities both limit entry into the brokerage industry and set out rules for the conduct of the industry. The number of salespeople permitted to practice in a jurisdiction varies with regulations, market conditions, and expectations about future market conditions. Some indication of this is contained in Table 10–3, comparing the United States and Canada. In the Canadian context, there are almost 20 times as many sales personnel per capita in rapidly growing British Columbia as there are in stable Newfoundland. The third column of Table 10–3 contains data on the number of people per real estate salesman for various states and provinces. The data indicate that the United States has relatively more real estate personnel than Canada.

In this section, some of the more prominent regulations are discussed; then their impacts, costs, and benefits are developed. Some of the more common regulations include the following.

1. *Own account trading.* Real estate licensees are prohibited from purchasing or selling real estate unless written disclosure of their position is given to a prospective buyer or seller.[14] There may also be further prohibitions on own account activity. Frequently, restrictions are placed on attempts by real estate brokers to use inside information for arbitrage purposes. For example, a broker with better market information that a given listing client could purchase a property and resell in a short time, a practice sometimes termed "flipping." Such practices are discouraged or prohibited outright.

2. *Payments to nonlicensees restricted.* Anyone may act as a real estate agent or salesperson, but the receipt of any fee or commission for doing so is restricted to licensees.[15] Payments of commissions or fees are usually made by the seller to the broker. No restriction is imposed on payment levels to another broker (commission splitting).

3. *Restriction on payment structures.* The common form of payment is by commission, expressed as a percentage of the selling price of the house. Explicitly prohibited in some jurisdictions is what is called a net listing, where the listing agreement between broker and seller calls for payment on the basis of the difference between a guaranteed or target reservation price and the actual transaction price. Fixed fee contracts are also discouraged.

   The above regulations derive directly from legislation. But that is not the only method of imposing limits.

4. *Entry restrictions on licensees.* Educational restrictions or requirements are imposed for entry into the brokerage industry. There may also be requirements on experience. Also, licensees are often divided into agents, who are permitted to operate a real estate firm, manage an office, and list properties directly, and salespeople, who must work for an agent.

5. *Market access limitation through MLS.* Multiple Listing Services act as exchanges, collecting information on local housing markets and facilitating transactions. At the same time, commission rates for MLS listings are set at given levels, and only subscribing licensees may offer properties for sale from MLS. Further, market information on the prices and qualities of houses being bought and sold is available only to MLS members, and not to the general public or nonmember licensees.

Analysis of Restrictions

Legislative   Beginning with own account trading, some argument may be made on behalf of consumer protection. However, the principle of *caveat emptor* presumably applies when a potential seller purchases the services of a realtor and the obligation to know the market value of a property rests with the owner. Ironically, the restriction does eliminate a potential source of market demand, namely, the agents themselves. Ultimately, enforcement difficulties dictate that arbitrage opportunities and price dispersions on similar properties will continue.

Restrictions prohibiting payments to nonlicensees are similar to those in other fields, though they are weaker than those governing law or medicine, where free practice can even be deemed illegal. As in other fields, they serve to create and maintain the economic value of licenses. However, if real estate licensing programs and procedures created sufficient skills so that the costs of acquiring these skills absorbed all the economic rent, then there would be little need for such legislation. An unskilled amateur would be unable to compete effectively. Such is not the case, however, and as a result the primary argument in favor of government regulation derives from the need for consumer protection. A licensed realtor offers services of a given minimum standard. The danger is that restricted entry leads to higher commissions through lack of competition among brokers, making house sales more costly.

Present fee structures distort the market both for brokerage services and for houses. With a commission structured at a fixed rate, the marginal incentives to attract buyers and a higher price for a seller, who is retaining the agent, are weakened. Furthermore, some commission structures have relatively high rates on base amounts, with lower rates above the base. An example is a 7 percent commission on the first $100,000 of transaction price, with 2½ percent on any overage. If the average transaction price is well above $100,000, and in some markets there are few houses selling below this figure, then the commission may act as a fixed cost, possibly reducing broker effort to seek higher offers.

To examine the problem more closely, let us return to the search model. One offer on a house arrives each period.[16] The distribution of offers is as in Figure 10–3, but the broker has to search to obtain an offer. With most of the commission "front-ended" (e.g., paid on the base), the incentive to obtain a high price is reduced.

In Figure 10–6, suppose $f(V)$ is the distribution of offers. This is the distribution of offers without any "effort," or those that would confront any seller attempting to deal on his or her own. The broker, with better information on the market, is able either to eliminate very low offers immediately or, possibly through superior information or access

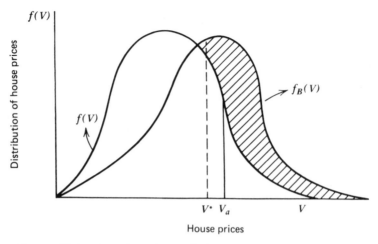

Figure 10–6. Search and commission structures.

to a more restricted market (for example, through MLS), can obtain a more advantageous distribution, $f_B(V)$, with lower variation, and a higher mean or average. In other words, selling on one's own brings $f(V)$, and hiring a broker, $f_B(V)$. The word "hiring" may be a misnomer, for in the usual contract no fee is paid if no sale is made. If the broker feels there is a high risk of no sale, there may be reductions in advertising, selling expenses, and sales effort. Of course, the converse is also true. The broker here faces a potential conflict of interest in wanting to culminate a sale to earn a commission. The broker may not necessarily seek the highest price, if marginal effort is not repaid through marginal gains in commission fees, as in the following case.

Suppose in Figure 10–6 the asking price is V_a, but the seller has a reservation price of V^*, known only to the vendor and possibly his or her broker. A solid line on V_a indicates this information is observable. At any price V, the broker distribution, $f_B(V)$, or prices obtained if a broker is used, brings a higher price than the distribution for own selling, $f(V)$.[17] There is a return to using a broker. To the right of V^*, where the seller is willing to accept offers, the shaded area is the additional probability of selling when a broker is used.

If the commission is at a fixed rate or approaches a flat fee, the broker has a low return to searching for a high offer for the client. Suppose it costs M dollars to search for one offer, and the brokerage commission remains b. The return is only $b(V - V^*)$ if V^* is already obtained. In more concrete terms, suppose the reservation price is $100,000 and the contract is 7 percent on $100,000, with 2½ percent on the balance. On a $100,000 offer the commission is $7000, but on a $150,000 offer, the probability of which is low, given distribution of offers $f_B(V)$, the commission is $8250.

Let the distribution of offers have the discrete form for $f_B(V)$:

$$\text{Probability } (V = \$\ 50{,}000) = .2$$
$$\text{Probability } (V = \$100{,}000) = .4 \qquad (10.6)$$
$$\text{Probability } (V = \$150{,}000) = .2$$
$$\text{Probability } (V = \$200{,}000) = .2$$

and the seller has a reservation price of $100,000. Were the vendor to sell himself or herself, the distribution would be:

$$\text{Probability } (V = \$\ 50{,}000) = .5$$
$$\text{Probability } (V = \$100{,}000) = .3 \qquad (10.7)$$
$$\text{Probability } (V = \$150{,}000) = .1$$
$$\text{Probability } (V = \$200{,}000) = .1$$

so the expected value if a broker is used is $(2 \times \$50{,}000) + (.4 \times \$100{,}000) + (.2 \times \$150{,}000) + .2 \times \$200{,}000)$, or $120,000. If he or she sells without a broker, the expected value is $(.5 \times \$50{,}000) + (.3 \times \$100{,}000) + (.1 \times \$150{,}000) + (.1 \times \$200{,}000)$, or $90,000. The expected return from using a broker is $30,000, and with the commission of $7500 on the contract above, the vendor will retain a broker.[18]

In ten periods, the broker can expect to receive four offers in excess of $100,000. But suppose his or her costs are $500 per period. Suppose also that an offer for $100,000 is already in hand, but the expected value remains at $120,000. Thus, on average, another $20,000 can be expected to be obtained, on which the commission is only an additional $500. The broker is at the margin and obtains no incremental return from additional search.

In fact, since the broker faces the $500 search cost, it is in his or her interest to convince the vendor to accept any price, even the $50,000, for this yields $3500 in commission. The problem, then, is that commission structures may not always be optimal, since they do not reflect vendor and broker utilities simultaneously. Note that the examples of (10.6) and (10.7) show that it remains profitable to hire a broker; however, the appropriate incentive compatible contract needs to be developed.

Educational Requirements and Brokerage Associations The remaining two types of regulations are educational requirements and the presence of the Multiple Listing Service. There are costs and benefits to both types of regulations, and each is considered in turn.

First, consider requirements for education and experience among licensees. The areas of education comprise appraisal, real estate and contract law, financing, and land economics. To the extent that this information better informs consumers, and more rational decisions result, the protection of consumers is facilitated. There are at least three views on education and its supposed benefits.

1. *Human capital.* Education enhances the productivity of each individual, implying that those with education earn more than those without. Alternatively, at fixed commission rates, consumers of brokerage services earn a surplus.

2. *Screening.* Education may not itself be directly productive, but rather serves to distinguish abilities. If potentially able brokers can pass the real estate course, and potentially less competent ones cannot, then the course serves as a screen, whether any useful information is learned or not.

3. *Credentials.* Education is neither productive nor a screening device, but merely a method for discriminating against a group of people not possessing the required credential.

If the real estate courses provide useful training in areas of relevance to the broker, then the education constitutes human capital. In some jurisdictions, however, the licensing courses are seen as not being of sufficient duration, leading to "excessive entry." Since it is difficult to reduce commission rates, marginal entrants tend to work part-time and report low commission earnings, and licensees do not necessarily accumulate human capital nor serve the public with better services.

The second area concerns the Multiple Listing Service. The MLS system is run by the local real estate board and operates a large source of listings for buyers and sellers. Characteristically, these provide for the following.

1. *Pre-determined commission,* usually higher than those involved in listings outside of MLS. However, because the market size is expanded, sellers benefit by a more favorable potential offer

2. *Distribution.* Co-brokerage allocations on how the commission should be split between a listing and selling salesperson and between listing and selling agencies.

3. *Restricted access,* so that the public at large and non-MLS licensees do not have the listing information.

Some further regulations can include a fee for placing a listing and the imposition of residual rights. The latter guards against a seller attempting to deal directly with a buyer once a contract for listing has been signed, to avoid paying a commission.

In terms of the predetermined rates, the person selling a house has three alternatives. Either he or she can sell privately, without a broker; list exclusively with a broker; or list with a broker or MLS. Again, however, the fixed commission structures arise.

Usually there is no local competition to the MLS, implying that some monopoly power exists. Recently, large national brokerage firms and franchises have arisen, often undercutting MLS through providing similar services at similar or reduced fees. Sears in the United States and trust companies in Canada provide examples. An alternative may rest with the possibility of introducing a system where all sellers could list properties merely by paying a fee per period, with access guaranteed to all in the market. This would reduce the arbitrage possibilities and the price dispersion in the offer distribution.

ECONOMIC ISSUES IN BROKERAGE

Several economic issues arise in the area of brokerage. These include the nature of payment contracts, the degree of competition, and deregulation.

Payment Contracts

While payment contracts do not have complete inflexibility, it remains difficult to negotiate a commission directly. The trend has been toward deregulation of fixed commission as when, on May 1, 1975, the U.S. Securities and Exchange Commission eliminated such practices in securities markets. The effect has been to increase the volume of transactions and reduce the effective commission paid on securities transactions.[19] The impact of such deregulation on real estate commissions may be less dramatic because vendors currently have other options and because some negotiation already occurs.

Under existing commission schedules, there is a tendency to engage in "bundling" of services, that is, offering a large number of services, some of which a consumer may not demand. A listing agreement may entitle a vendor not only to sales and closing services, but also brokerage for mortgage, appraisals, relocation planning and assistance, and guaranteed purchase plans. Competition would lead to "no frills" real estate brokerage, with only the basic service offered. Analogs exist with airline and security deregulations.

In terms of the payment contract structures, consider Figure 10–7. Contract I calls for a constant-rate commission, given by the slope of the line. Contract II has a breakpoint, with a higher rate levied on a first level and a lower rate above the threshold. Contract III posits certain fixed charges, but a higher subsequent return. In the low range of the prices, Contract II yields the highest return to the broker and the highest cost to the vendor. Economics usually suggests that incentives be placed at the margin. Under the terms of Contract II, lower transaction prices may result to facilitate the sale. However, as prices rise, the total commission under Contract III is highest, and the marginal incentive to produce a higher price is greatest, benefiting both seller and broker.

Degree of Competition

The nature of the real estate license and the issue of competition is controversial. There are correspondences with the cases of lawyers, notaries public, doctors and chiropractors. The argument in favor of professional regulation is that individuals require protection from unethical and unqualified practitioners in the real estate market. The

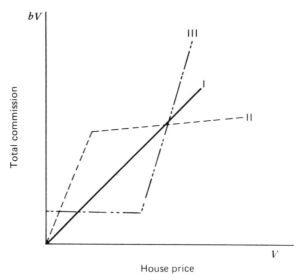

Figure 10–7. Commission payment contracts.

knowledge that a real estate broker has met certain minimum requirements may aid in consumer protection, particularly if there is
reexamination and licenses must be renewed. Nevertheless, there are
drawbacks to the licensing system.

Administrative Costs   Legislation is required, involving resources from
the state or provincial legislature, and also from the civil service, to administer the legislation. Real estate brokers themselves must form
committees or participate in quasi-judicial licensing boards to enforce
discipline and ethical codes. All of these resources are drawn from the
activity of selling property, and potentially add to the costs of buying
and selling real property.

The administrative costs could be partly or completely recovered
by a levy on brokers, but this tax further increases the cost of operation
and may be shifted to clients.

Reallocative Inefficiency   If the licensing structure blocks able people
from becoming brokers, or allows less able brokers to remain, then
there are costs in this misallocation of labor, costs that could be reduced through reduced barriers to entry and exit. By having to obtain
a license prior to practicing, and given the delay in obtaining them,
there is a limit on competition in the industry.

As with any form of licensing, there are costs and benefits. Competition could reduce effective commissions and spur sales, but it could
fail to adequately protect the consuming public.

Effect Of Commissions On Real Estate Markets

The presence of real estate commissions and other transaction costs, such as legal fees, mortgage fees, appraisals, and title search, drives a wedge between the prices faced by buyers and sellers. The analysis is identical to that for a tax. Paul Craig Roberts, in this context, notes the following.

Take the case of a carpenter facing only a 25 per cent marginal tax rate. For every additional $100 he earns before income tax, he gets to keep $75. Suppose that his house needs painting and that he can hire a painter for $20 a day and hire himself out for $100 a day. However since his after-tax earnings are only $75 he saves $5 by painting his own house, so it pays him to choose not to earn the additional $100. In this case, the tax base shrinks by $180, of which $100 is the foregone earnings of the carpenter, and $80 is the lost earnings of the painter who is not hired. (Also the productive efficiency associated with the division of labor is lost.)[20]

If any of the prices in a transaction do not represent appropriate opportunity costs, the same problem arises. For the real estate commission as such, the full effects are indicated in Figures 10–8a and 10–8b.

Figure 10–8a illustrates the market for brokerage services. If commission structures are such that the supply curve is constrained and shifted to the left, the intersection occurs with D and S_1. The incidence of the higher costs (who bears the cost of the restriction) depends on the relevant elasticities of supply and demand. Let the total commission be $u = bV$. With the restrictive supply structure in regulated commissions and closed MLS, the supply curve is S_1 and equilibrium at u_1.

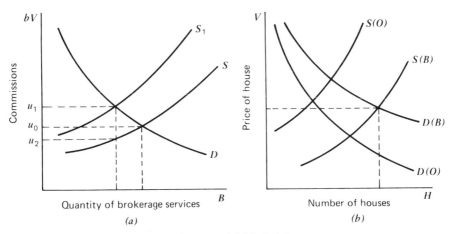

Figure 10–8. The Market for real estate. (a) Market for brokerage services. (b) The market for houses with brokers.

Since in Figure 10–8a the demand is drawn relatively more inelastic than supply, incidence falls on the demand side, or the consumer. Relatively, $u_1 - u_0$ is paid by the demander of brokerage services, both house buyer and seller, and $u_0 - u_2$ by the brokerage industry.

At the same time, it is possible and likely that existing brokerage structures are an improvement over each person selling on his or her own. Without brokers, the intersection occurs as $D(O)$ and $S(O)$. With brokerage, demand for houses increases and the average supply of services also increases. Volume increases, but the average price may also increase, as indicated in Figure 10–8b.

The problem of real estate brokerage and commission is complex. Brokers do facilitate transactions, for otherwise people would engage in transactions on their own. The issue is whether these services are delivered efficiently to consumers. The empirical evidence is mixed, though the theoretical discussion vis-à-vis fixed commissions suggests suboptimal pricing of brokerage services. The issue is further complicated by the trade-off between public protection and allocative inefficiency brought about by entry and exit restrictions.

OTHER TRANSACTION COSTS

There are other transaction costs in the real estate market. Again, if these occur with pricing not equal to the opportunity cost of the resources, distortions arise.

Legal services are purchased by both the buyer and seller. Relatively more of the services are purchased by the buyer, as required by an institution providing mortgage funds. The purchaser must assume the legal costs of the financial institution. These costs are termed "title transfer" or "conveyancing charges."

Legal services are not necessarily provided in a competitive environment. State and provincial licensing is required to be a member of the legal profession. Notaries exist in some jurisdictions, but their numbers are limited.

Some legal fees are related to the value of the transaction, even though costs may not increase proportionately. In this case, the same arguments may apply as in the real estate brokerage situation.

Other transaction costs involved in the transfer of land include registration, title transfer, and insurance. If the fees involved exceed the marginal cost of providing the services, then the resulting tax creates a distortion. Mortgage brokerage or finders fees, appraisals, and surveys are other costs. For these costs, the same conclusion applies. Lower costs facilitate transactions.

SUMMARY

Transaction costs in the context of a search model in real estate markets have been explored. The presence of transaction costs creates an arbitrage opportunity, and real estate brokers are intermediaries facilitating a transaction. Although these services consume resources, and prices or commissions are charged, the more efficient matching of buyers and sellers may reduce real estate prices, facilitating a higher volume of sales.

The issues that arise with brokers are those of regulation, and whether the costs exceed the benefits. Empirical research is required on whether the gain in consumer protection is outweighed by the cost of inflexible commission structures and restricted entry and exit. It is not possible to determine the effects of regulation in the absence of such research.

There are other areas of facilitating market transactions that require further research. These include computer matching, more accessible listing services, and fee-for-services brokerage pricing schemes.

Footnotes

1. On the theory of search, see G. J. Stigler, "The Economics of Information," *Journal of Political Economy* 69, (August 1961): 213–225.

2. The models are in P. N. Courant, "Racial Prejudice in a Search Model of the Urban Housing Market," *Journal of Urban Economics* 5, (July 1978): 309–345; and J. Yinger, "A Search Model of Real Estate Broker Behavior," *American Economic Review* 71 (September 1981): 591–605.

3. M. A. Goldberg and P. Horwood, "Housing Transaction Costs: Evidence from Three Canadian Cities," report submitted to Canadian Department of Consumer and Corporate Affairs, Ottawa, Ontario, 1979.

4. J. H. Crockett, "Prices, Competition, Costs and Efficiency in Residential Real Estate Brokerage," *Journal of the American Real Estate and Urban Economics Association*, forthcoming, Table 1, p. 4.

5. Goldberg and Horwood, *op. cit.*, 5.

6. D. Carroll and G. Gaston, "State Occupational Licensing Provisions and Quality of Service: The Real Estate Business," in R. Zerba, ed., *Research in Law and Economics* (Chicago: JAI Press), 1979.

7. The distribution of rents is $f(\rho)$, with an acceptance if ρ received exceeds ρ^*. The probability of obtaining an acceptable offer is:

$$Pr(\text{accept}) = \int_{\rho^*}^{\infty} f(\rho)\, d\rho = 1 - F(\rho^*)$$

and the expected rent for an acceptable offer is:

$$E(\rho) = \int_{\rho^*}^{\infty} \frac{\rho f(\rho) d\rho}{1 - F(\rho^*)}$$

8. These services are more completely described in Yinger, *op. cit.*, p. 393.

9. E. Rosenbleuth, *Real Estate Enquiry Report* (Vancouver, B.C.: University of British Comumbia), April 1976, Table 8, p. 37.

10. This depends on some assumptions on the amount of time the real estate broker could be spending elsewhere. It may be the case that demand for his or her services is not perfectly elastic, possibly declining rapidly for additional hours. Also, a more appropriate measure of search costs is an after-tax basis.

11. The models become:

$$\text{maximize } R(b,L,s) = (bV - k)H_s(b,L,s) - s_L L - sH_s(b,L,s)$$

$$\text{where} \quad \partial H_s/\partial b < 0, \quad \partial H_s/\partial L > 0 \quad \text{and} \quad \partial H_s/\partial s < 0$$

So:

$$\partial R/\partial b = VH_s + bV\partial H_s/\partial b - s\,\partial H_s/\partial b = 0$$

implying:

$$VH_s = -\,\partial H_s/\partial b[bV - s] \quad \text{(commissions)}$$

The left side, or VH_s, is the gross sales revenue of the broker. On the right, $bV - s$ is per house net revenue, and $-\,\partial H_s/\partial b$ the negative of the change in house sales with commissions. Finally, $-\,\partial H_s/\partial b = VH_s/(bV - s)$, or $\partial H_s/\partial b = -VH_s/(bV - s)$, or $\partial H_s/\partial b = -H_s/(b -- s/V)$.

12. The listing condition is:

$$\partial R/\partial L = (bV - k)\partial H_s/\partial L - s_L - s\,\partial H_s/\partial L = 0 \quad \text{(listings)}$$

in which case

$$\partial H_s/\partial L = s_L/(bV - k - s)$$

13.

$$\partial R/\partial s = (bV - k)\,\partial H_s/\partial s - H_s - s\,\partial H_s/\partial s = 0 \quad \text{(selling costs)}$$

and then:

$$\partial H_s/\partial s = H_s/(bV - k - s)$$

14. As example legislation, we consider the Real Estate Act of British Columbia of 1979 and the Real Estate Amendment Act of 1981, R.S. Chapter 356, 38 Elizabeth 2, Own account trading is discussed in Section 28 of the Real Estate Act.

15. For British Columbia, this is Section 30 of the Real Estate Act.

16. The period may be redefined as the length of time it takes to receive one offer. See Stigler, *op. cit.*

17. Technically, this implies that the expected price from dealing with a broker is always higher. Also, for low V values, the density of $f(V)$ is higher. $Pr(V > V^*) = \int_{V^*}^{} f(V) = F(V^*)$ is greater for nonbroking. In Figure 10–4 the distribution $f_B(V)$ is shown to have less spread than $f(V)$. This need not be the case.

18. Of course, individual vendors differ in their knowledge of the market and com-

petence in sales. It may be possible for an individual to face a similar offer distribution as a broker, but this is difficult without access to MLS information.

19. Between 1975 and 1980, the number of individuals owning stock increased from 25.3 million to 29.4 million as per the annual report of the Securities and Exchange Commission. Commission rates declined substantially for institutions, and marginally for individuals.

20. Paul Craig Roberts, "The Breakdown of the Keynesian Model," *Public Interest, 10* (July 1978):24.

CONTEMPORARY ISSUES OF URBAN LAND ECONOMICS

A RECAPITULATION: THE GROUND ALREADY COVERED

Up to now, we have focused largely on background materials and techniques of urban analysis to provide us with the necessary skills and information to understand the functioning of urban land markets. Accordingly, we began this book by introducing urban land economics as a distinct field of study in its own right. We then went on to see why an urban orientation is called for as we reviewed the evolution of urban areas and looked at some of the emerging trends in urbanization in the United States and Canada.

Given this background, we then moved on to study a number of techniques of urban economic analysis that will enable us to better understand the policy issues that confront us in urban areas, and more importantly that provide us with the necessary understanding to analyze professed solutions and foretell their pitfalls as well as their strengths. To do this we first explored the macroeconomic environment within which urban land markets must function. We discussed a number of techniques for analyzing the urban macroeconomic environment—including input-output, economic base, and shift-share analysis—all of which have been widely used and have been demonstrated to provide useful insights into the relative health or sickness of urban economies.

In the remainder of Part 2 (where we focused on these analytical techniques and concepts) we looked at microeconomics. We studied (in order) the factors that affect the demand for and supply of urban land. We then discussed the financial and institutional environments within which urban land markets must function. Our discussion included analyses of both public and private financial markets. Urban public finance, real estate finance, and mortgage markets were our focus here. We then turned to explore legal and political institutions that affect (and in some cases determine) the course of urban land markets. The institution of property was our principal interest here. As was the case with our review of the financial environment, we found that there were some major differences between the legal and political institutions surrounding urban land markets. This was nowhere as apparent as with the institution of property that has very different rights and meanings attached to it in Canada as compared with the United States. These financial, legal, and political institutional differences between Canada and the United States imply significant differences when we come to discuss policies that affect urban land markets and their operations, and alerted us to the need for understanding the institutional context within which urban land markets function.

In the final portion of Part 2 we brought our various analytical tools and concepts together to enable us to look at urban land market behavior. The result of this synthesis was our ability to determine both the price and quantity of urban land (and real property more generally), thus providing us with a took to analyze policies that affect the price/quantity determination mechanism, all of which brings us up to this third and final portion of the book, where we now turn to examine a range of contemporary issues that relate to urban land markets.

ISSUES AND POLICIES AFFECTING URBAN LAND MARKETS

One of the primary lessons that emerges from the preceding discussion is that urban land markets are highly localized and, as a result, require a good deal of sensitivity to local economic, social, political, and cultural conditions if they are to be well understood. This appreciation of local conditions will become readily apparent below where we will be confronted by two quite different national environments that have created widely different local market institutions and traditions. These environments also imply very different policy solutions as we will see.

First, we will be looking at government controls of land use and urban development, obviously a central input to the understanding of urban land market operations. We will do this in Chapter 11, and will see that Canada and the United States have quite different legal bases for such controls and thus some quite different controls. We will also review the empirical literature that documents the impacts of land use and urban development controls on price and quantity of urban land and real property.

In Chapter 12 our attention shifts to housing, the major single user of land in urban areas: roughly 40 percent of the developed land. We will explore some of the recent policy issues surrounding housing in both Canada and the United States, focusing particularly on price and quantity issues.

Following this discussion, we move on to look at the changing nature of urban economies. In Chapter 13 we look not only at central city economic decline, but more generally at changes in the economies of urban areas, which as we will see includes growth as well as decline. Major trends are discussed and policies to alter these trends are reviewed and subjected to empirical study where possible.

An unstated element in all of the previous issues is the governmental environment within which urban development takes place. Accordingly, in Chapters 14 and 15 we look at major issues relating to the government of urban areas including both financial and organizational issues and suggestions for reform. In Chapter 16 we expand on the interaction of transportation with land uses and markets, a concept first introduced in Chapter 4 in the theory of bid rents. This chapter includes an introduction to the current technology of urban transportation, and draws attention to the empirical research as to its impact.

The foregoing bring us pretty well up to date on the major issues and concerns that confront the analyst of urban land markets. But how will things look in the future? Accordingly, in the final chapter of this book we step back a bit from present conditions to look at some of the unknowns. Chapter 17 introduces some of the current thinking about the future shape of urban areas and some of the social, political, economic, and technological forces that will shape that urban future. An appreciation of the possible and the likely events and conditions that lie ahead will serve to arm the urban land market analyst with an appreciation for the future and for the possible twists and turns it might follow, thus removing some of the surprise (and risk) that awaits urban land markets in the 1980s and 1990s.

CONCLUSION

The prevailing theme is that the student of urban land markets must be firmly rooted in the local conditions that provide the context for the working or urban land markets. The analyst must be wary of simple generalizations from one set of conditions (and particularly from one country to the next) to other conditions in other places. This need for sensitivity derives directly from the local nature of urban land markets and from the institutional basis of land and real property. Land, after all, is a societal based institution as are the rights and responsibilities that accompany the institution of property. Property as a result, and as we have noted above, cannot be separated from the culture, politics, and social values that give it meaning and operationalize it in the everyday workings of urban land markets. It is this cultural or social or political context that must be fully understood if the urban land market analyst is to avoid the trap of local politics and values.

11

MANAGING URBAN LAND RESOURCES: LAND-USE CONTROLS AND LAND POLICY

AN INTRODUCTORY INVENTORY OF ISSUES AND APPROACHES

There are three generally accepted reasons for intervening into the functioning free markets.

1. The *elimination of imperfections* so as to enable the markets to work more efficiently and thus allocate scarce resources better than previously.

2. *Accounting for externalities* so that private and social costs and benefits can be brought into closer correspondence.

3. *Redistributing the scarce resources* of society so that the disadvantaged are provided with a greater opportunity to share in society's output.

The first two objectives of intervention seek to effect *allocational efficiency,* while the third objective seeks to create *distributional equity.* Traditionally, economists have been reasonably effective on the allocation front, but have fared rather poorly on distributional issues.

When transposing these rather general objectives of government involvement in the marketplace into the realm of urban land markets, one of these objectives comes to the fore: the control of externalities. A secondary objective has been the removal of imperfections, particularly in urban housing markets, a subject to be treated in the next chapter. Redistribution of income or resources, however, is not seen as an explicit goal of urban land policy, though there are significant distributional effects of urban land management policies.

We will begin our analysis with the externality issues in urban land markets and focus on the urban land policies designed to minimize or contain the off-site effects of various urban land-using activities. We will then turn our attention to imperfections in urban land markets, most notably with respect to issues of monopolistic and oligopolistic control of urban land resources and the role of land speculators. While not of direct concern, distributional issues will arise as we review some of the work on zoning and other land-use controls intended to control externalities, but shown to have significant redistributional impacts.

We will draw on the tools of analysis set out in Part 2 of this text, particularly those microeconomic tools discussed in Chapters 4, 5, 9, and 10 dealing with markets. We will make frequent reference to the literature to draw some empirically based conclusions to complement our theoretical and conceptual conclusions as to the predicted and observed effects of various urban land management policies and strategies.

Finally, we conclude this chapter with an extension of the analysis into the rapidly growing area of environmental controls and growth management policies, which have sought during the past decade to minimize or even reverse some of the negative external effects that have accompanied urbanization, industrialization, and rapid growth in various regions of North America.

EXTERNALITIES AND URBAN LAND POLICIES TO CONTAIN THEM

Land-use controls date back to the end of the 19th century. The earliest forms of control were zoning ordinances which established exclusive zones for specific types of land-use activities.[1] The fear that adjacent uses and users would devalue properties led to the passage of the first land-use restrictions. The zoning concept has been elaborated significantly over the course of the present century, and land-use controls have burgeoned well beyond the relatively narrow confines of zoning. The desire to protect property values from erosion by negative externalities lies at the heart of land-use controls. As we noted in Chapter 8, limitations on property rights have evolved from protection of property against undesirable individuals all the way to protection against environmental hazard and ecological disruptions.

The earliest land-use control of general interest is most often considered to be that of the city of Modesto, California, which is protection of the first kind observed above.

. . . (it is) unlawful for any person to establish, maintain, or carry on the business of a public laundry . . . within the city of Modesto, except that part of the city which lies west of the railroad tract and south of G street . . .[2]

Here the issue was users more than uses of urban land. The ordinance was a blatant attempt to exclude Chinese from living and carrying out their businesses in certain portions of the city. As such, the Modesto ordinance was a precursor of similar land-use controls that have served as thinly veiled efforts to exclude the poor, blacks, and other minority groups and which have proliferated since World War II.

Modesto therefore provides one source of tradition, that of so-called exclusionary zoning aimed at excluding certain groups in the belief that the presence of these groups will have detrimental effects on property values. However, the more prevalent theme in zoning, that of excluding uses rather than users, is the second step in the hierarchy of limiting property rights as set out in Chapter 8 and can be traced to the New York City landmark zoning bylaw of 1916, an effort spearheaded by merchants and owners of fashionable properties along Fifth Avenue to prevent the spread of the garment industry up that thoroughfare.

Nothing so blasting to the best class of business and property interests has ever been seen or known in any great retail district in any large city as this vast flood of workers which sweeps down the pavements at noontime every day and literally overwhelms and engulfs shops, shopkeepers and the shopping public.[3]

Such concerns by property owners and merchants led the city of New York to form, in 1913, the New York City Advisory Commission on the Height of Buildings, which culminated in the 1916 bylaw that regulated height, area, and use of land and buildings. This law became the model for other legislation and for the U.S. Department of Commerce State Standard Zoning Enabling Act, which was issued in 1924 and adopted by 1929 by 1930. The era of modern land-use controls was under way; the stated objective was to control negative externalities and maintain neighborhood stability and property values.

The Growth and Diversity of Land-Use Controls

The history and substance of land-use controls in Canada and the United States parallel each other quite closely. However, the legal and constitutional bases for controls are sufficiently different that we must look beyond superficial similarities to understand the nature and status of controls in each country. We discussed this point at some length earlier, in Chapter 8, to which the reader is directed for background. Canada followed closely the New York model when Ontario adopted similar legislation in 1921. The municipality of Point Grey, British Columbia, followed suit in 1922, and this traditional form of zoning control was extended to the entire city of Vancouver when it merged with Point Grey in 1927. Other provinces and municipalities picked up on the lead of these areas, so that by the onset of World War II zoning was well established.

One immediate manifestation of the legal differences between Canada and the United States is the absence, in the former, of protracted litigation by private interests challenging the provincial and local government's regulation of the uses of urban land. This is in marked contrast with the United States, where almost every attempt to regulate land use and urban development has been met with court challenges.[4] To highlight this point, we have only to look at the 1950 Alberta Town and Rural Planning Act, closely modeled on the 1947 Town and Country Planning Act of the United Kingdom. These acts separated the notion of development rights from ownership and use, and stated that development rights were the purview of the Crown and that the right to develop or redevelop land or buildings does not go with the land or buildings as a matter of right. The Alberta Town and Rural Planning Act thus opened a new phase in land and urban development controls in Canada, a phase that would have been difficult in the United States, given stringent constitutional protection of private property rights.

Recent Canadian Innovations

The previously cited Alberta Town and Rural Planning Act provided the major departure from previous land-use controls, which were rooted in the 1916 New York City districting ordinance. Recent Canadian innovations build on the underlying idea in the act, namely that development rights are separable from other rights of ownership, use, or occupation. Governments have the legal right, in Canada, to regulate use and development, without such regulation being deemed an expropriation.

Land-use contracts are an excellent case in point.[5] In 1968 the British Columbia Municipal Act gave municipalities in the province the right to enter into contractual relationships with developers, wherein developers were granted the right to develop lands that were either previously zoned for another use or lower density or were unzoned, in return for certain obligations that the developer had to assume. It was amended in 1971 so that land-use contracts had to be treated like zoning bylaws and were subject to the same procedural details, a change in process not in substance. Under these land-use contracts, municipalities could sell zoning. That is, developers were frequently obligated to make cash payments for each lot or housing unit put on the market, service completely their sites, and often provide off-site facilities such as schools, community centers, and parks.[6] Municipalities and developers were thus splitting the profits that accrued from the development of land within the municipality. Such a system allowed municipalities to minimize external effects by writing fairly stringent requirements into the contracts. They also served to promote distributional equity by giving the municipality (and therefore its taxpaying public) access to profits that derived from local public action. This process was significantly more efficient and equitable than previous British approaches,[7] since the Canadian schemes were based on bilateral negotiations rather than arbitrary bureaucratic rules and procedures.[8]

Effective November 1979, land-use contracts were replaced in British Columbia with a more complicated system of development charges intended to curb documented abuses by some municipalities who were seen by the development comnmunity as "blackmailing" developers with excessive demands.[9] While the form has changed under the new system, the principle remains unchanged: To minimize the imposition of externalities on community members, the community has the right to recapture some of the gains that result from public action.[10]

Land-use contracts have their roots in the *development permit system* pioneered by the city of Vancouver in 1956. The development permit system led to the creation of *comprehensive development districts,* which have sprung up in most Canadian cities and in many U.S. central areas.[11] These comprehensive development districts are functionally unzoned areas. They are areas where broad planning guidelines replace use, density, bulk, and other restrictions. Control in such cases is exercised through the development permit process. Development cannot take place until a development permit is issued. Issuance is dependent upon meeting the criteria of the guidelines, which are much more flexible and more subject to bureaucratic interpretation.

Other controls and policies have been used by provincial and local governments in Canada to ensure that external effects of urban land use and development are kept to a minimum. In British Columbia the Health Act forbids the use of septic tanks in developments of less than 5-acre lots in and around urban areas. All lots of less than 5 acres in these areas must be serviced by sanitary sewers.

Perhaps the most elaborate system of controls in North America is at work in Ontario. A hierarchy of controls is provided for by local municipalities, regional governments (for most of the urban areas and all of the large urban areas), the Ontario Municipal Board, and finally the provincial cabiniet.[12] A complex process of public hearings, appeals, and reviews is provided for, with the objective of protecting the public interest and regulating urban land use and development. A major overhaul of the system has just been completed with the 1983 passage of the Ontario Planning Act.[13]

The foregoing represent the major controlling mechanisms at work in Canadian urban areas. Largely absent are many of the more complicated controls existing in the United States, such as water and sewer moratoria, fiscal and exclusionary zoning, and environmental impact statements, since more direct controls can be applied more readily in Canada.

Recent U.S. Innovations

A veritable explosion in land use, urban development, and environmental controls has taken place in the United States during the past decade. We focus here on regulations that seek to protect the public from externalities, reserving for the next section those that have sought to improve market efficiency and overcome the improper pricing of certain land resources such as shoreline, unique ecological zones, farmland, and historic buildings and sites. This improper pricing arises from differentials between private and social cost, the latter including externalities. With the issuance and rapid adoption of the Standard State Zoning Enabling Act by the U.S. Department of Commerce in 1924 and the *Euclid* v. *Ambler* decision (see Chapter 8 for details), zoning bylaws spread rapidly throughout the United States.[14] Zoning controls have been supplemented by a range of federal, state, and local policies and laws intended to further limit the effects of negative externalities deriving generally from continued urbanization, industrialization, and growth.

Beginning with elaborations of the locally based zoning and subdivision ordinance, we have the following extensions, elaborations, perversions, etc.

1. Planned Unit Developments (PUDs)

2. Fiscal zoning

3. Exclusionary zoning

4. Performance zoning

5. Incentive zoning

6. Floating zoning

7. Time zoning

8. Water, sewage, and site service moratoria

9. Building permit and related growth restrictions

10. Official maps

11. Subdivision controls

A brief look at each will serve to illustrate just how much the standard zoning concept has been developed during the past 60 years, often well beyond its initial intent.

Planned Unit Developments (PUDs)[15] PUD's are an attempt to introduce flexibility and creativity into the traditional zoning framework. A PUD allows a developer to cluster buildings and average out densities over an entire project. It is closely related to the average-density zoning, cluster zoning, and comprehensive development zoning concepts. Developers can mix uses, building types, and densities as long as they comply with broad overall density and use concepts.

Fiscal Zoning[16] This is an application of zoning to achieve fiscal, rather than land-use and externality-minimizing, objectives. Fiscal zoning seeks to bar land uses that place burdens on local government expenditures, typically, multifamily housing. Their residents are seen as lower-income families requiring social, educational, and recreational services. Fiscal zoning typically leads to the overzoning of land for light industry such as research and development parks and for high-quality office space, high tax revenue producers with low demands on the public purse.

Exclusionary Zoning[17] Exclusionary zoning returns to the 1885 Modesto ordinance by attempting to exclude certain types of land use and, by extension, land users. It is often closely related to fiscal zoning in appearance, but with exclusionary rather than fiscal objectives. The classic form of such zoning is so-called large lot zoning where 1-, 2-, or even 4- or 5-acre minima are established for single-family lots. Such large lot requirements, frequently coupled with large minimum-size house requirements for these lots, is effective at excluding lower-income (and often nonwhite) households from the municipality. This type of zoning seeks to minimize the perceived negative externality that derives from having people of different races, cultures, or income groups living in proximity to each other. It has been frequently, vigorously, and most often successfully challenged in the U.S. courts.[18]

Performance Zoning[19] This and floating zoning are the most subtle, flexible, and innovative elaborations of zoning. Because of their subtleness and flexibility, they are often difficult to formulate adequately in an acceptable ordinance and, as a result, actual experience with performance zoning is somewhat limited. Rather than regulating land uses and intensities, as does traditional zoning, performance zoning seeks to isolate characteristics of various land-use activities that cause negative externalities and to regulate these characteristics. For example, density in and of itself need not be a problem if there is adequate transportation, water, and sewage capacity. Performance zoning would seek to impose limits in different zones on the traffic and sewage-generating capacities of various uses, instead of on the uses themselves. Thus, a high-rise office building adjacent to a subway station may prove to be no problem to traffic, yet the same building placed in the suburbs or on streets with no subway might cause significant traffic problems.

Incentive Zoning[20]   Whereas traditional zoning is purely negative and seeks to eliminate negative externalities through regulating uses (or use characteristics, as in performance zoning), incentive zoning tries to overcome this by acknowledging that externalities can be positive or negative. Traditional zoning, by too tightly regulating uses, densities, and even building materials, often leads to sterile, unimaginative, and ugly buildings, clearly a negative externality. Incentive zoning attempts to build on positive aspects of built-form such as plazas and open spaces, landscaping, and artwork by giving bonuses or incentives to developers for including such positive elements. New York City has a most imaginative scheme that has served as a successful model of the concept and how it can be implemented.[21]

Floating Zoning   Traditional zoning is implemented through an official plan and a corresponding official zoning map that delimits the various land-use zones permissible under the official plan and the zoning ordinance. Floating zoning builds directly on the official plan but does not specify districts of land use with precisely specified boundaries. Rather, it sets out a functional land-use category such as mixed-income housing or mixed residential-commercial development as well as specifying the purpose (e.g., bring people and jobs, or people and shopping, closer together). At a later, unspecified date, after a developer has brought forward a suitable proposal, consistent with community objectives, the precise boundaries of the zone can be established to permit the developer to move ahead. The concept here is closely aligned with the PUD, mixed-use, and comprehensive development zoning ideas mentioned above.

Time Zoning[22]   This is an innovation that has arisen in response to the demand for controlling urban development in many small but rapidly growing communities. Time zoning can be as straightforward as traditional zoning that is phased in over time on a prescribed schedule. Such timing allows a community to regulate its pace of development to be consistent with its ability to service new land and households. The classic and much heralded example of time zoning is Ramapo, New York, which has been successful in controlling its pace of development through the implementation of a timed sequence of zoning and servicing.[23]

Figure 11–1 indicates a zoning map in the city of Saskatoon, Saskatchewan. The legend rates the large number of alternative types of zoning regulations that can arise in a city. In terms of quality, the zoning ranges the whole gamut from agricultural to different types of high rises. There are also some restricted and less restricted industrial uses. As expected, agriculturally zoned areas of the city are on the

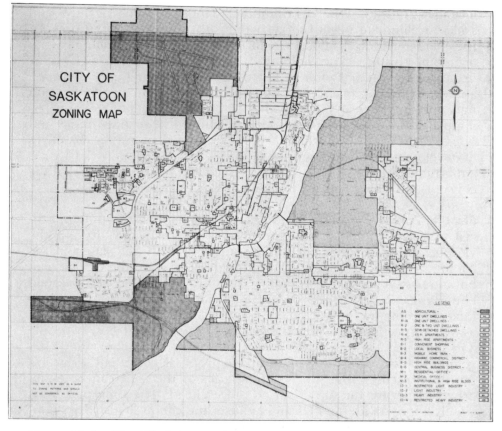

Figure 11–1. City of Saskatoon zoning map.

fringes, and zoning that allows higher density is nearer to the central business district (CBD).

Figure 11–2 depicts the land-use zones in downtown Calgary, Alberta, 1953–1975. The source is the Planning Department of the City of Calgary. Open-space areas are noted on the fringe of the city, and permitted density increases up to high-rise offices in the central portion. The pattern is similar to that exhibited by Saskatoon's zoning map, which begs the question about the efficacy of zoning to create such patterns.

Water, Sewage and Site Service Moratoria[24]   Time zoning opens up the whole subject of growth controls. Where all of the previously discussed controls were placed directly on land, site servicing controls work more indirectly, by controlling the placement, timing, and quantity of basic urban infrastructure such as water, sewage, and road development. Water, sewage, and other infrastructure moratoria attempt to reduce negative effects of growth by directly limiting the urban development

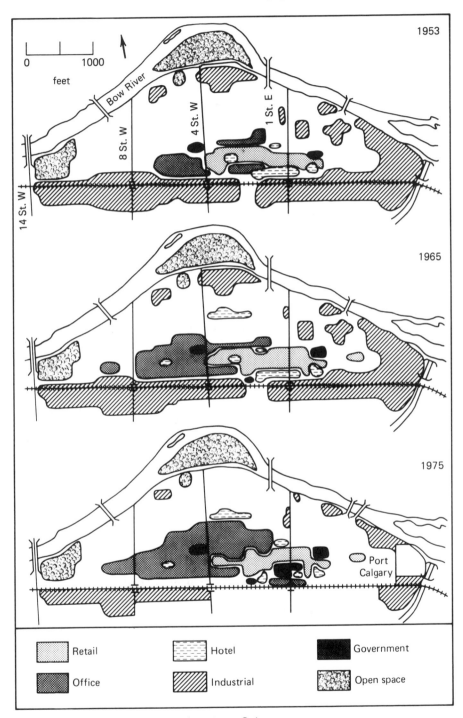

Figure 11–2. Land-use zones, downtown Calgary, 1953–75. (*Source:* City of Calgary Planning Department.)

process. Such measures have been something less that popular with the development industry, and the list of court cases on the subject is lengthy and growing rapidly.[25] The cost of such growth controls lies in ultimately higher land and improvement prices.

Building Permit and Related Growth Restrictions[26] While moratoria on infrastructure limit the amount of serviced land available for urban growth, building permit restrictions directly limit the amount of building that can take place within a community. The policies of Petaluma, California, are the most widely known and provided the spearhead for this approach.[27] Other controls of this genre include the imposition of lengthy and complicated subdivision and permit approval processes, and the lack of expeditious treatment of permit applications.[28]

Official Maps[29] These are planning devices that complement official plans and the zoning map. They designate future streets, parks, and public infrastructure and provide a map of the community as it will look once fully developed. They provide a very useful means for guiding growth and can be combined with one or more of the land-use control techniques set out above. The maps do not usually control use, just the pattern of development and capital placement by public bodies.

Subdivision Controls[30] Subdivision controls provide communities with the wherewithal to regulate the subdivision and servicing of land. Local governments can prescribe servicing standards (sewage, water, utilities, curbs, storm sewers, etc.) as well as rules for laying out lots, allowing for drainage, flooding and snow removal, and for building on slopes, unstable or seismically active landscapes, or ecologically sensitive lands such as marshes, shorelines, or dunes. These tools provide local governments with very significant powers to limit the negative externalities arising from urban development. These limitations of the private property right are deemed constitutionally viable in the United States because they are seen as providing necessary protection for the general welfare of the entire community. The power to regulate property and urban development flows to local government directly from state governments, which are vested with so-called police powers under the U.S. Constitution. During the past decade, states have been active in exercising some of these police powers over urban land development directly, rather than delegating these powers to the local governments.

States have all of the land-use controlling powers of local government and then some, since they can control land use across local government boundaries. That the states have chosen to exercise these powers directly has been termed "the quiet revolution in land use controls."[31]

This country is in the midst of a revolution in the way we regulate the use of our land. It is a peaceful revolution, conducted entirely within the law. It is a quiet revolution, and its supporters include both conservatives and liberals. It is a disorganized revolution, with no central cadres of leaders, but it is a revolution nonetheless.

The *ancien regime* being overthrown is the feudal system under which the entire pattern of land development has been controlled by thousands of individual local governments, each seeking to maximize its tax base and minimize its social problems, and caring less what happens to all others. The tools of the revolution are new laws taking a wide variety of forms but each sharing a common theme—the need to provide some degree of state or regional participation in the major decisions that affect the use of our increasingly limited supply of land . . . [32]

In Chapter 8, we spent a good deal of time looking at this trend toward direct state involvement in land-use and environmental planning. We also saw that in Canada, despite a very different set of legal and constitutional property institutions, there was a parellel trend toward direct provincial control over land-use decisions and provincial review of local decisions.

Table 11–1 sets out, as of April 1975, the various types of land-use management programs in effect in the 50 states. Notice that state involvement is significantly broader than the environmental protection area shown earlier in Table 8–1. The table illustrates that the states are involved across a number of land-use activities and in a number of capacities, from acting as a coordinating agency for the environmental impact states mandated by the National Environmental Protection Act (NEPA) (see Table 8–1 for details) to the development of statewide land-use and land management programs (e.g., Hawaii and Vermont).

The states have stepped directly into the land management area in response to the repeated failure or inability of local government to do so. Local government is either too small or too narrowly based to take effective action on negative externalities that fall outside its boundaries—including, frequently, some that it generates, such as downstream water pollution from untreated or partially treated effluent. States have acted to protect endangered wetlands, farmlands, shorelands, and ecologically sensitive areas. Of more direct concern here are state attempts to minimize negative externalities arising from urban and regional development. Control of power plant siting is an excellent case in point, as 28 states, as of 1975, exercised such controls. Similarly, 31 states control surface mining.

Other statewide attempts to control such externalities include the following.[33]

Air Pollution States have an important role under the Clean Air Act of 1970. Through their power to regulate land use and transporta-

Table 11-1 Status of State Activity Related to Land-Use Management, April 1975

			Enabling Legislation		
State	**Municipalities**	**Counties**	**Regional Agency Advisory Only**	**Regional Agency Review Authority**	**Procedures for Coordination of Functional Programs**
Alabama	Yes	Yes	Yes	No	No
Alaska	Yes	Yes	NA	NA	Yes
Arizona	Yes	Yes	Yes	No	Yes
Arkansas	Yes	Yes	Yes	No	No
California	Yes	Yes	Yes	Yes	Yes
Colorado	Yes	Yes	No	Yes	No
Connecticut	Yes	NA	Yes	No	Yes
Delaware	Yes	No	Yes	No	Yes
Florida	Yes	Yes	No	Yes	Yes
Georgia	Yes	Yes	Yes	No	Yes
Hawaii	No	Yes	NA	NA	Yes
Idaho	Yes	Yes	Yes	No	No
Illinois	Yes	Yes	Yes	No	No
Indiana	Yes	Yes	Yes	No	Yes
Iowa	Yes	Yes	Yes	No	No
Kansas	Yes	Yes	Yes	No	No
Kentucky	Yes	Yes	Yes	No	No
Louisiana	Yes	Yes	Yes	No	No
Maine	Yes	Yes	Yes	No	Yes
Maryland	Yes	Yes	Yes	No	Yes
Massachusetts	Yes	Yes	Yes^c	No	No
Michigan	Yes	Yes	Yes	No	No
Minnesota	Yes	Yes	Yes^d	No	No
Mississippi	Yes	Yes	Yes	No	No
Missouri	Yes	Yes	Yes	No	No
Montana	Yes	Yes	Yes	No	No
Nebraska	Yes	Yes	Yes	No	No
Nevada	Yes	Yes	Yes	No	Yes
New Hampshire	Yes	Yes	Yes	No	No
New Jersey	Yes	No	Yes	No	No
New Mexico	Yes	Yes	Yes	No	Yes
New York	Yes	Yes	Yes	Yes	Yes
North Carolina	Yes	Yes	Yes	No	No
North Dakota	Yes	Yes	Yes	No	No
Ohio	Yes	Yes	Yes	No	No
Oklahoma	Yes	No	Yes	No	No
Oregon	Yes	Yes	Yes	No	No
Pennsylvania	Yes	Yes	Yes	No	No
Rhode Island	Yes	NA	No	No	Yes
South Carolina	Yes	Yes	Yes	No	No
South Dakota	Yes	Yes	Yes	No	No
Tennessee	Yes	Yes	Yes	No	Yes
Texas	Yes	No	Yes	No	Yes
Utah	Yes	Yes	Yes	No	Yes
Vermont	Yes	NA	Yes	No	Yes
Virginia	Yes	Yes	Yes	No	No
Washington	Yes	Yes	Yes	No	No
West Virginia	Yes	No	Yes	No	Yes
Wisconsin	Yes	No	Yes	No	Yes
Wyoming	Yes	Yes	No	Yes	Yes

^aCoastal Zone Management
No state has an approved Coastal Zone Management Program at present.
^bState Land Use Program Code:
1. No activity at state level
2. Study (executive or legislative) or state legislative consideration in progress.
3. State land (use program legislation enacted.
    Authorization for:
    (a) inventorying existing land resources, data and information collection
    (b) policy study or promulgation by agency or commission
    (c) identification of land areas or uses of more than local concern
    (d) regulation or management of land areas and uses identified
    (d) direct state implementation or state review of local government implementation
^cMassachusetts
Areawide Council for Martha's Vineyard has authority to administer controls

Functional Programs

Land Use-Value Tax Assessment Law	Surface Mining	Flood-plain Regulations	Power Plant Siting	Wetlands Management	Critical Areas	Coastal Zone Mgmt. Program Participation[a]	State Land Use Program (see Code)[b]
No	Yes	No	Yes	No	No	Yes	1
Yes	Yes	No	Yes	No	No	Yes	2
No	No	Yes	Yes	No	No	NA	2
Yes	Yes	Yes	Yes	No	No	NA	2
Yes	Yes	Yes	Yes	No	No	Yes	2
Yes	Yes	Yes	Yes	No	Yes	NA	3a-c
Yes	No	Yes	Yes	Yes	No	Yes	2
Yes	No	No	No	Yes	No	Yes	2
Yes	No	No	Yes	No	Yes	Yes	3a-e
No	Yes	No	No	Yes	No	Yes	2
Yes	No	Yes	No	No	No	Yes	3a-e
No	Yes	No	No	No	No	NA	2
Yes	Yes	No	No	No	No	Yes	2
Yes	Yes	Yes	No	No	No	No	2
Yes	No	Yes	No	No	No	NA	2
No	Yes	No	No	No	No	NA	2
Yes	Yes	No	Yes	No	No	NA	2
Yes	No	No	No	Yes	No	Yes	2
Yes	Yes	Yes	Yes	Yes	Yes	Yes	2
Yes	Yes	Yes	Yes	Yes	Yes	Yes	3a-c
Yes	No	No	Yes	Yes	No	Yes	2
Yes	Yes	Yes	No	No	No	Yes	2
Yes	No	No	Yes	Yes	Yes	Yes	2
No	No	No	No	No	No	Yes	2
No	No	No	Yes	Yes	No	NA	2
Yes	Yes	Yes	Yes	No	No	NA	2
Yes	No	Yes	Yes	No	No	NA	2
Yes[e]	No	No	Yes	No	Yes	NA	3a-c
Yes	No	No	Yes	Yes	No	Yes	2
Yes	No	Yes	No	Yes	No	Yes	2
Yes	Yes	No	Yes	No	No	NA	2
Yes	Yes	No	Yes	Yes	No	Yes	2
No	Yes	Yes	No	Yes	Yes	Yes	3a-c
Yes	Yes	No	No	No	No	NA	2
Yes	Yes	No	Yes	No	No	Yes	2
No	Yes	Yes	No	No	No	NA	2
Yes	Yes	No	Yes	No	Yes	Yes	3a-c
No	Yes	No	No	No	No	Yes	2
Yes	No	No	Yes[f]	Yes	No	Yes	2
No	Yes	No	No	No	No	Yes	2
Yes	Yes	No	No	No	No	NA	2
No	Yes	No	Yes[g]	No	No	NA	2
Yes	No	No	No	Yes	No	Yes	2
Yes	No	No	No	No	Yes	NA	2
Yes	No	Yes	Yes	Yes	No	NA	3a-e
Yes	Yes	No	No	Yes	No	Yes	2
Yes	Yes	Yes	Yes	Yes	No	Yes	2
No	Yes	Yes	No	No	Yes	NA	2
Yes	Yes	Yes	Yes	No	No	Yes	2
Yes	Yes	No	Yes	No	No	NA	3a-d

[d]Minnesota
Twin Cities Metropolitan Council has regulatory authority
[e]Nevada
Must be ratified in a referendum to take effect
[f]Rhode Island
Within the coastal zone a development permit is required from the Coastal Council
[g]Tennessee
Power plant siting is conducted by TVA only

Source: U.S. Department of Interior, Elaine Hess, ed. *Land Use Controls in the United Staes: A Handbook of the Legal Rights of Citizens* (New York, NY: The Dial Press for the National Resource Defense Council, Inc. 1977.

tion, states can exercise significant control over both stationary and mobile sources of air pollution.

Water Pollution   Under the Federal Water Pollution Control Act Amendments, the states are given a rather central role in ensuring that the water quality within the state is protected. States do this not only through direct involvement in supplying water, but also by sharing in the funding of sewage treatment facilities and enforcing state water-quality statutes.

Solid-Waste Pollution   Under the terms of the federal Solid Waste Disposal Act, states are provided with federal funds for developing statewide solid waste disposal plans. Again, states are envisioned as playing a key role in the implementation of solid waste management programs and in overseeing that such plans are adhered to by local governments and by developers in unincorporated parts of the various states.

Noise Pollution   While federal activities here are restricted to standards for airports and through general impacts via environmental impact statements, some states, such as Minnesota,[34] have moved to control this externality. This has traditionally been a local concern via nuisance ordinances.

States have also begun to involve themselves directly in two critical areas: statewide land-use planning and statewide transportation planning and management. As of 1975, six states had statewide land-use planning, all seeking to minimize the costs of continued urban expansion and to channel growth and protect endangered landscapes, environments, and resources. The costs may not be minimized, however, if the excess demand for urban space is channeled into congestion in existing improvements. Examples are illegal basement units and overcrowding. The regulations typically exempt existing land use.

During the 1970s virtually all state highway departments were broadened into state transportation departments, thus becoming concerned with modes other than roads and vehicles. In this regard, the A-95 budget review process of the Office of Management and Budgets (OMB) and the provisions of the 1956 National Defense Interstate Highway Act helped to coordinate land use and transportation and to rationalize transportation plans with land-use plans, and more recently with environmental protection and the control of negative externalities.

States have created regional agencies such as the Metropolitan Transportation Commission in the San Francisco Bay Area or the two-state Port Authority of New York–New Jersey. These regional agencies allow states to focus their policy activities in specfiic localized regions where air, water, and environmental externalities are found, yet enable them to deal with these external effects at a broader geo-graphical and political level than can local governments. Such regionalization is bound to create its own externalities if and when the functional geographical region spills over into another state or other states, as in the case of the New York metropolitan region and the Washington, D.C., metropolitan region. Such spillovers beyond state boundaries require federal intervention.

Federal Involvement in Land-Use Issues

Federal involvement derives from the negative effects of land-use ac-tivities, which endanger populations across wide regions of the country or are of sufficient national importance, even though highly localized (such as a unique environment like the Grand Canyon), to require fed-eral intervention. Direct federal intervention is difficult, land use be-ing a state concern under the U.S. Constitution. However, the federal government has exercised great control indirectly through its ability to make grants, levy taxes, grant subsidies, and in interstate issues control directly.[35] Such direct and indirect measures have a large, often domi-nant land-use element, since polluting activities must locate some-where and utilize land in the process. The federal government has enormous impacts on land use through its transportation investments, most notably through highway construction, and more recently the granting of capital and operating subsidies to urban mass transit and to intercity railroads.[36]

Finally, federal tax policies on artificial depreciation allowances and on the deductibility of the costs of holding potentially developable land have affected the urban development process and the negative and positive externalities that have flowed from that process. Clearly, the federal government must rationalize its tax policies to provide con-sistency with other measures such as environmental protection legisla-tion, to provide protection against, and discouragement of, the nega-tive effects of urban growth and land use. The U.S. government has already taken such measures vis-à-vis the preservation of valued his-toric buildings. Similar measures to reduce the incentive to use land for new depreciable structures would provide a complement to this preservation policy and to the other environmental protection meas-ures enacted by the U.S. government since the late 1960s.[37]

MARKET IMPERFECTIONS AND GOVERNMENT POLICIES TO CORRECT THEM

In government intervention to overcome market imperfections and improper pricing of land resources, there are two areas of difference between Canada and the United States, namely, in the nature of con-trols and in the perception of the problem. The issues to be discussed will differ for each country, as the perceived problems differ. For example, there is much talk in the United States about the need for government ownership to protect prime farmlands, rare and beautiful natural environments, and historic structures. In Canada, ownership is much less an issue, first because governments own much more of Canada than they do of the United States and second because governments can exercise much greater control over land in Canada without having to resort to direct ownership. There is a great deal of public policy in the United States directed toward environmental issues. Much recent U.S. legislation is aimed at protecting coastlines, unique environments such as wild and scenic rivers, and farmland. With the exception of farmland in British Columbia and Ontario, we will not see such concerns mirrored in Canada.

A possible explanation for many of the differences in defining issues between U.S. and Canadian cases stems from the relative population sizes of the two countries and from the patterns of land ownership. Tables 11–2 and 11–3 set out data on the tenure patterns of land in Canada and the United States. Private ownership accounts for over 58 percent of the 916.8 million hectares (3.539 million square miles) in the United States; whereas private ownership accounts for only 8 percent of Canada's 916.7 million hectares (3.540 million square miles). It should be recalled that Canada has 24 million people, whereas the United States has 230 million residents. It is clear from these aggregate figures that with much greater densities there are likely to be more land-use conflicts in the United States than in Canada.

Turning now to substantive issues, we shall be looking at Canadian approaches to the following land policy issues that Canadians have

Table 11–2 Land Tenure in United States—Ownership of Land, by Class, 1959–1978 (in million of acres, except percent)

Year	Total[a]	Private land[b]	Indian lands[c]	PUBLIC LAND			
				Total	Federal[d]	State[d]	County and Municipal
1959	2271	1332	53	886	765	103	18
1969	2264	1317	50	897	763	114	20
1974	2264	1316	51	897	761	116	20
1978	2264	1315	52	897	742	135	20
Percent distribution	100.0	58.1	2.3	39.6	32.7	6.0	.9

[a]Changes in total land area are due to variable methods and materials used in periodic remeasurements, and to the construction of artificial reservoirs.
[b]Land owned by individuals, partnerships, and corporations.
[c]Managed in trust by Bureau of Indian affairs.
[d]Changes in federal and state land holdings mainly represent federal land grants to the State of Alaska. Part of the change indicated after 1974 may have occurred prior to 1974.

Source: U.S. Statistical Abstract, 1981 (Washington D.C.: U.S. Bureau of the Census), Table No. 381, p. 224.

deemed important: monopoly and oligopoly control of urban land markets; speculation; and protection of unique resources, most notably farmland and historic or architecturally unique buildings.

Monopoly/Oligopoly Control of Urban Markets in Canada

Concern about this issue might seem somewhat ironic to non-Canadians in view of the size of the country and its land reserves. One would logically ask how anyone can exercise market control given such huge supplies of land? However, land markets are highly localized, particularly urban land submarkets for such land uses as housing, industry, and retail trade. The totality of land in Canada is irrelevant when considering control over urban land resources in each of Canada's 24 major urban regions. Concern for such monopoly/oligopoly control therefore becomes an empirical issue, it being conceptually easy to imagine large landowners virtually cornering the market in urban land.

Concern for artificial shortages and oligopolistic manipulation of prices of urban and urban fringe land escalated dramatically as prices escalated during the period 1972 to 1975. We will leave the empirical findings for the next section, but we will illustrate here the high level of concern on the part of the Canadian public and its elected representatives. Table 11–4 presents data on lot prices for houses financed under the National Housing Act (NHA) in Canada from 1966 to 1975. These have been further broken down within the table by region of the country. The markets are highly regional, with western markets growing more rapidly in general and experiencing higher house and lot price appreciation. This table reveals an enormous increase in residential lot prices during the 1972–1975 period (similar increases were recorded for house prices too). Some culprit had to be found, and attention was immediately directed toward the urban land market and its widely criticized oligopolistic structure and alleged manipulative practices.[38] Let us examine these criticisms at face value and explore some of the measures taken in Canada to halt the manipulative practices and restore competition and price stability to urban land markets.

Probably the most widely heralded and publicized programs to control monopoly and oligopoly price manipulations are the public land banking and public lot servicing activities undertaken by several local and provincial governments in Canada. Both Red Deer, Alberta, and Saskatoon, Saskatchewan, have had municipal land banking operations since the end of World War II.[39] Stated objectives include the following.

1. Improved planning and orderly community growth

2. Reduced cost of serviced land

3. Public participation in land price appreciation

Table 11–3 Land Tenure in Canada

Total Area Classified by Tenure, 1978 (km²)

Item	Province or Territory						
	Nfld.	PEI	NS	NB	Que.	Ont.	Man.
Federal Crown lands other than national parks, Indian reserves and forest experiment stations	440	16	181	1489	1178[a]	1158	259
National parks	2339	21	1331	433	790[b]	1922	2978
Indian reserves	—	8	114	168	779[c]	6703	2145
Federal forest experiment stations	—	—	—	91	28	103	—
Privately owned land or land in process of alienation from the Crown	17,992	4927	37,754	39,754	119,420	119,023	138,079
Provincial or territorial area other than provincial parks and provincial forests[d]	382,638	442	2652	28,495	674,819	891,261	481,951
Provincial parks	805	32	126	215	130,000	48,412	10,650
Provincial forests	303	211	13,732	2792	613,667	—	14,025
Total Area	404,517	5657	55,490	73,437	1,540,680	1,068,582	650,087

Item	Province or Territory					
	Sask.	Alta.	BC	YT	NWT	Canada
Federal Crown lands other than national parks, Indian reserves and forest experiment stations	5452	2844[e]	904	513,191	3,340,848	3,867,960
National parks	3875	54,084	4690	22,015	35,690	130,168
Indian reserves	6322	6566	3390	5	135	26,335
Federal forest experiment stations	—	59	—	—	—	281
Privately owned land or land in process of alienation from the Crown	246,939	183,521	55,040	170	73	962,292
Provincial or territorial area other than provincial parks and provincial forests[d]	35,481	63,313[f]	539,280	943	2937	3,104,212
Provincial parks	4944	7700	41,629	—	—	244,513
Provincial forests	348,887	343,098[g]	303,663	—	—	1,640,378
Total Area	651,900	661,185	948,596	536,324	3,379,683	9,976,138

[a]Includes Gatineau Park (35.1 km²) and Quebec Battlefields Park (0.93 km²), both under federal jurisdiction but not national parks. Excludes harbors of Gaspe, Chicoutimi, Quibec and ï'lsle Trois Rivières, Montreal and Sorel (under federal-provincial negotiation) and CNR properties.

[b]Includes Forillon and Mauricie parks.

[c]Includes reserves existing before 1851—Maria, Lorette, Bécancour, Odanak, Caughnawaga, and Saint-Régis. Excludes lands transferred provisionally under the James Bay and Northern Quebec Agreement (November 1975) and North-Eastern Quebec Agreement (January 1978).

[d]Includes freshwater area.

[e]Excludes Department of National Defence agreement areas (Primrose Lake, Camp Wainwright) and areas leased for agricultural experiment stations (Manyberries, Stavely).

[f]Includes lands held by the Department of National Defense under agreement with Alberta (Camp Wainwright) and areas leased for agricultural experiment stations (Manyberries, Stavely).

[g]Includes the area held by the Department of National Defense under agreement with Alberta (Primrose Lake Air Weapons Range).

Source: Canada Yearbook, 1980/81 (Ottawa: Minister of Supply and Services), Table 1.7, p. 27.

Table 11–4   Percent Changes in Average Cost Per Foot Frontage of Fully Paid, Fully Serviced Lots for New Housing Financed Under the NHA: Selected Averages of Urban Areas

	Percent Change 1966–1969		Percent Change 1969–1972		Percent Change 1972–1975	
	Nominal	Real	Nominal	Real	Nominal	Real
Ottawa to West Coast	42.4	26.3	29.4	16.1	102.9	53.4
Montreal to East Coast	25.2	11.1	21.8	9.3	31.4	− 0.6
Atlantic Provinces	17.5	4.3	51.2	35.7	47.0	11.2
Quebec	32.8	17.8	− 7.7	−17.1	15.9	−12.3
Ontario	42.8	26.7	35.5	21.6	95.2	47.6
Manitoba & Saskatchewan	21.5	7.8	9.2	− 2.0	98.2	49.9
Albert & British Columbia	56.8	39.1	26.1	13.2	129.4	73.5
All 25 Urban Areas	38.2	22.7	27.5	14.5	85.7	40.5

Source: Down to Earth, Volume II (Toronto, Ontario: Federal/Provincial Task Force Supply and Price of Serviced Residential Land), 1978, p. 7.

Each land bank operates via the market. Raw land is purchased and then improved through servicing. The lots are sold in the open market. The municipal land banking operations represent significant portions of the developed-lot market in their area.[40] Both land banking operations operate without subsidies and exist on the profits derived from their land development revenues. The success of these publicly operated land development programs has attracted attention outside Canada[41] and has provided the impetus for continued demands that such land banking activities be expanded in Canada.[42]

Closely related to land banking are public lot servicing programs undertaken during the 1972–1975 boom in land prices to put large numbers of lots on the market and thereby reduce lot prices. The province of Ontario was particularly energetic in its lot servicing program during this period. Its Home Ownership Made Easy (HOME) program was designed to acquire large tracts of land, provide site services, and market the lots at subsidized rates to first-time home purchasers. The allocation of some $500 million by the Canada Mortgage and Housing Corporation, over a five-year period beginning in 1973, to provinces for land assembly and servicing programs was clearly intended to provide HOME and analogous programs in other provinces with a boost.[43] This combination of federal and provincial financing of subdivision and lot servicing was intended to break the short-run supply shortage during the 1972–1975 period and provide serviced lots on the market at "reasonable" prices.[44] These programs are not without their problems. For instance, there are administrative costs. Also, in subdivisions under the HOME program where the public sector retained lot title, the property right was restricted. This was partially solved by conveying title, but at prices which bestowed all the windfall benefits of the subsidized land ownership on the first buyers.

Another policy directed toward restricting oligopoly control focused on changes in federal and provincial tax regulations relating to carrying costs of raw land. Begun by the province of Ontario and later implemented by Revenue Canada, from 1974 to 1979 developers could not deduct from taxable income interest charges for holding land inventories. The intent was to force developers to put additional land supplies on the market and discourage holding land off the market.[45] Such legislation was not only aimed at large-scale landowners but also at real estate speculators, who, it was alleged, also helped to manipulate and drive up land prices. Thus, we next turn to look at the problem of speculation.

Speculation in Urban Land Markets

Monopoly and oligopoly control was perhaps only overshadowed by speculation in popularity as a source of rising land prices. In fact, much of the public saw them as essentially the same issue. According to this view, land speculators bought and hoarded land with little or no intention of improving it, to take advantage of the rapid increases in land values that were being recorded in most urban areas in Canada. The above-mentioned removal of interest charges as deductible expenses for holding raw land was a federal and provincial effort to stem speculation as well as to coax large-scale developers to put more land on the market. Perhaps the most dramatic effort to influence speculation was the Ontario Land Speculation Tax imposed in the spring of 1974.[46] This tax was to be levied on all gains realized from transactions, with a number of important exceptions such as principal residences, vacation homes, and resource properties.[47] Land banking and public ownership of land were also frequently put forward as means for controlling speculation, the general notion being that any gains accruing from such speculative actions would be realized by the public and not by narrow private interests.

Protection of Unique Land and Building Resources

When it comes to protection of unique land and building resources, we see different patterns emerge in Canada and the United States. U.S. approaches need to be consistent with constitutional protection of property rights, while Canadian policy interventions do not operate under such constraints, only under the pressures of politics and social values and change.

One example is the British Columbia Land Commission Act to preserve agricultural land, as discussed in Chapter 8.[48] Another is the Ontario Land Speculation Tax, which made certain exemptions from the tax for farmland. Land that had been, and continued to be, farmed was exempt from the speculation tax; other tax exemptions are afforded farmland in every province—it is taxed for property tax purposes at use value instead of current market value. Such use-value taxation provides a significant incentive to keep the lands in farm use in Canada, since once they are removed from farm use back taxes on the difference between farm use value and market value are due.[49]

Other options that provincial governments have pursued in protecting unique resources have included the following.

1. The placing of large blocks of provincially owned land in provincial parks or in specially designated ecological reserves to protect them over time against future development.[50]

2. Designating historic buildings for protection from demolition or reuse that destroys their unique architectural qualities. Such designation is often made without any compensation to building owners.[51]

3. Regionwide planning of development and open space to protect open and recreational spaces for future public land, again often without compensation.[52]

4. Tight control of waterfront lots and shoreline and the common-law right of access to beaches all serve to ensure public enjoyment of such unique land resources.[53] Thus, despite less need to put aside unique resources in Canada because of the relatively greater abundance of such resources vis-à-vis the United States, it is interesting to observe the degree to which provincial and federal governments have acted to protect such resources for future Canadian generations.

Speculation in Urban Land Markets in ihe United States

Perhaps because there are many more urban areas in the United States than in Canada, or perhaps because there are more developers, or perhaps because Americans perceive their system to be highly competitive, monopoly or oligopoly control of urban land markets does not appear to be of general concern. Speculation is another matter, and the United States has a long history of land speculation.[54] More recently, Florida and Arizona land speculators have achieved some prominence. Much of the blatant abuses have been controlled by the U.S. government by prosecuting land fraud perpetrated across state boundaries. "Speculators" who deceive the public about land as an "investment" are not the focus here; we are concerned with urban land speculators who purchase land with little intent of improving it. Direct action in the United States has been as limited as it has been in Canada, a notable exception being the state of Vermont.

In 1973, as part of a comprehensive state land-use bill (passed as Act 250 of the Vermont state legislature), a capital gains tax on land was implemented, where the tax rate is a function of the number of years held and the size of the capital gain. The tax schedule appears as Table 11–5 below. As with the Ontario legislation, a number of exemptions have been included in the tax structure, generally smaller parcels and principal residences.[55] Paralleling the Ontario experience, the tax has been less successful than anticipated as a revenue-generating de-

Table 11–5 Vermont Land Gains Tax Rate

	Increase in Value (%)		
Years Land Held by Transferor	0–99	100–199	200 or more
		Rate of tax on gain	
Less than one year	30	45	60
One year, but less than two	25	37.5	50
Two years, but less than three	20	30	40
Three years, but less than four	15	22.5	30
Four years, but less than five	10	15	20
Five years, but less than six	5	7.5	10

Source: Robert G. Healy and John S. Rosenberg, *Land Use and States,* 2nd ed. (Baltimore: Johns Hopkins University Press), 1979, p. 70.

vice, and its actual effect on speculation and slowing the pace of development remains an open question.[56]

In sum, activity in the United States has been limited in controlling speculation and oligopoly in urban land markets. Based on the Canadian experience, we can envision this varying over time with the rise and fall of house and land prices and with the ebb and flow of public concern and political pressure.[57]

Protection of Unique Land and Building Resources

Desire to protect these resources has led to a range of innovative land-use control techniques. Among the resources that have come under protective legislation and policies are prime agricultural lands, historic and architecturally important buildings, open space and scenic vistas, coastal zones, and wild scenic rivers.

Prime Agricultural Lands Zoning land for agricultural purposes in the United States has been deemed to be unconstitutional without compensation.[58] Other approaches have to be sought. Four ideas have come forward.

Agricultural Easements or Preservation Districts The basic idea is to establish agricultural districts where farmland is thought worth preserving and involves purchasing open-space or preservation rights (usually easements, but also restrictive covenants levied by the present owner in favor of the community or the state). The farmer receives a cash payment in return for keeping the land in farm use or open space in perpetuity, or for some mutually agreeable period of time, after which the agreement is renewed.[59] The cost is significantly lower than purchasing the land directly, while simultaneously farmers receive compensation.

Use of Eminent Domain to Purchase Prime Farmlands The state, city, or country can resort to direct acquisition either through negotiated purchase or through compulsory acquisition. The cost is high for this option and includes the loss of tax revenue. Ownership by the public does provide greater control, which may or may not be necessary over and above the purchase of open-space or preservation rights.

Tax and Assessment Relief   Virtually every state provides tax relief for farmland, by taxing farmland at agricultural-use value instead of current market value, which usually includes a speculative and urban use component.[60] Sometimes, as in New Jersey and California,[61] taxes are owed if the land is later sold for another use.

Transferable Development Rights (TDRs)   The foregoing approaches are all based on traditional real property transactions or tax and assessment procedures. The TDR concept, however, is a significant departure from past practice and has received more attention because of its innovative nature or perhaps because it appeared at last to be a cure for the problem of protecting unique resources and buildings in the absence of public funds to purchase them on the open market. The TDR concept is necessitated by the inability of governments to take direct protective action without compensating current owners.[62]

Essentially, the TDR idea is to separate development or potential development rights from ownership and current use of land and buildings and to allow property owners to transfer their development rights from properties that the community desires to protect to other locations.[63] Such a scheme allows society to protect both the resource and the property development rights of the current owner. A frequently cited example would allow a southern New Jersey farmer to transfer development rights from the farm, thereby keeping it in farm use and protecting its food-growing capacity, to sites in Newark. The Newark landowner would purchase these extra-density rights from the farmer, who would thereby be compensated. Needless to say, the TDR notion gets extremely complicated as it gets closer to implementation and realization.[64]

Historic and Landmark Preservation   The problem here is analogous to that of farmland: The market underprices the value of the resource to society, yet society is powerless to preserve the land and building without compensating the current owner. In light of the similarities to the farmland preservation problem, most of the strategies and policies discussed in that regard have been applied to preserve valued buildings. Preservation has also been significantly aided by recent federal income tax changes that give extremely favorable treatment to developers who redevelop, and thereby preserve, buildings listed on the National Register of Historic Buildings.[65] This is a significant departure from traditional federal tax policy which, it is argued, promoted demolition and new construction and outward suburban expansion previously.[66]

Open Space and Scenic Vistas   Conservation (or open-space or scenic) easements have been particularly highly touted.[67] Direct purchase for parks and open space is also an extremely common form of preservation, limited to the availability of taxpayer willingness to allocate funds for such purchases.

Recently, a number of communities have sought to zone open space directly.[68] The courts have been loath to allow such measures in the absence of compensation for the loss of development potential.[69] Some notable exceptions, however, have been recorded, such as the Adirondack Park Agency in New York State, and some of the statewide land-use measures in Vermont and Maine.[70]

Coastal Zones   In contrast to the previous preservation problems and solutions, where the federal government has taken a limited role, federal involvement in both coastal zone management and wild and scenic river preservation is paramount, and has provided the essential leadership in both areas.[71]

In Chapter 8 it was noted that one of the most signficant forces redefining property rights in the United States was the growing role of the federal government in its environmental protection activities. The Coastal Zone Management Act of 1972 came about because "The increasing and competing demands upon the lands and waters of our coastal zone . . . have resulted in the loss of living marine resources, wildlife, nutrient-rich areas, permanent and adverse changes to ecological systems . . . ."[72] These socially valuable resources were being underpriced in the marketplace and government action was required. The Coastal Zone Management Act provided states in the coastal zone (30 of them) with federal funding. Table 11–1 (p. 314) showed that as of April 1975, 29 states had taken such action to plan for and protect coastal zone resources.

State programs vary from the highly innovative and protective California Coastal Zone Conservation Act of 1972 to the regional Bay Conservation and Development Commission (BCDC) for San Francisco Bay, a state-chartered agency that began life in the late 1960s to protect the shrinking San Francisco Bay from future encroachment by fill and development.

Scenic and Wild Rivers   Here, again, we find federal action at the forefront with the passage, in 1968, of the Wild and Scenic Rivers Act.[73] States have followed suit with their own designation of wild and scenic rivers within state boundaries, as more than half of the states currently have such legislation in force.

Summing up, we can make some rather general observations about government intervention to overcome market imperfections in land markets. First, unlike interventions that seek to minimize negative externalities, actions to overcome weaknesses in market operation have almost no local government base. The reason is not hard to identify: These problems are generally broader in geographic scope than a single municipality and require regional action at the minimum but more usually state land-use control action, or federal fiscal and tax action.

Second, while states have almost exclusive authority in regulating land use, the federal government has taken an enormous role in working to protect underpriced land and building resources. Moreover, additional federal intervention, through taxes and subsidies, is highly likely to extend federal involvement into the areas of monopolistic and oligopolistic control of urban land markets as occurred in Canada when the federal government acted to remove the deductibility of interest on holding costs on land as legitimate business expenses. Finally, the direct spending power of the federal government, with its ability to buy land to create parks and land reserves and with its enormous land holdings—still roughly one third of the entire land mass of the United States, including Alaska—cannot be overlooked.

THE EMPIRICAL EVIDENCE: LAND MARKET INTERVENTIONS

In the preceding sections we looked at a variety of land-use control measures, and related tax measures, that were intended to overcome a number of problems inherent in markets: the failure to account properly for negative externalities; positive externalities; and market imperfections, such as monopoly and oligopoly and discriminatory practices. In this final section of the chapter, we will look at evidence on the existence or severity of the problems and on the effectiveness of the various land-use policies.

Having established an empirical foundation for controlling negative externalities (or failing to do so), we move on to examine recent findings on the direct and indirect costs of land-use and urban development controls.

Controlling Negative Externalities: The Evidence to Date

Many land-use control devices are predicated on the assumption (usually implicit) that there are significant negative externalities in urban land markets. Zoning, the prototypical such control, has attracted a great deal of attention.[74] The work has largely been motivated by a desire to measure the cost of negative externalities to adjacent properties and to society.

Four studies, plus a much documented nonzoning example (the city of Houston, Texas), cast serious doubt on the existence of significant negative externalities from adjacent lower-status land uses (e.g., apartments and commercial uses adjacent to single-family housing). The earliest work was by Crecine, Davis, and Jackson in 1967, using data for the City of Pittsburgh.[75] They found that identical uses in different parts of the city sometimes appeared to have negative external effects and sometimes positive ones. On balance, it was impossible to assert a significant external effect from lower-order land uses. The authors were the first to qualify their results and methods, which led to the study, six years later, by Rueter, who, using more elaborate data and methods, confirmed the Crecine, Davis, and Jackson results.[76]

More recently, in 1977, Maser, Riker, and Rosett, using Rochester, New York, as their laboratory, studied two questions: the existence of significant negative externalities and the effectiveness of zoning in controlling them.[77] They found that there were no significant external effects and, moreover, that zoning appeared to have little, if any, effect on prices in any event. Goldberg and Horwood, and Goldberg and Mark, using data for Vancouver, B.C., found that rezoning an area from single-family to medium-density residential had no measurable negative effect on surrounding remaining single-family homes.[78] This may depend on how large the area affected must be. Immediately adjacent properties may rise in prices because of a speculative premium on rezoning, analogous to farmland. However, properties further away may experience the costs of congestion and view deterioration. Part of the effect may depend on the quality of the multiple units.

Finally, there is the much documented case of Houston, Texas, a city without traditional zoning. Much has been written about Houston, and the evidence leads one to conclude that it looks and functions much like any other American city of its vintage, with the automobile and expressways as important shapers of urban form.[79] The example of Houston lends further circumstantial evidence to the case against the importance of negative externalities.

There is only one recent study that provides empirical support for the existence of negative external forces in urban land markets. The 1974 work by Stull for the Boston metropolitan area suggests that negative externalities may be a factor, contrary to the findings in Pittsburgh, of Crecine, Davis, and Jackson and of Rueter.[80] However, Stull himself warns against placing too much weight on his study. Moreover, he concludes that zoning may be the wrong device to control negative externalities, given its frequent amendment by boards of variance and given its exclusionary and income distribution effects.

Figure 11–3 sets out the case on which zoning is based, and for which Stull found some support. There are land uses in the central part of the urban region (between the CBD and D_a) that are incompatible with the other land uses in the region (for example, let us assume central activities include office and retail activities, whereas the remaining uses are all residential in character). Because of this incompatibility, the outlying land uses suffer the negative external effects of the

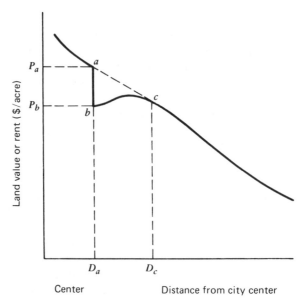

Figure 11–3. Effect of externalities on land values and rents.

central land uses and, accordingly, their prices or rents are depressed below what they would have been in the absence of the negative externality. Accordingly, as we move out past distance D_a, the land use changes, and normally (i.e., in the absence of the externality) land values should remain at the level P_a. However, they drop to the level P_b and do not regain their "normal" levels until they are far enough away from the incompatible uses to no longer suffer their negative effects (say, at point c). The dotted line on the figure denotes what land values or rents would have been if there were no external effects depressing them.

Zoning is predicated on the assumption that these negative externalities exist and are important determinants of land values and rents. Zoning could, in theory, protect the adversely affected land uses and thereby raise values to their "normal" level (i.e., the dotted line in Figure 11–3). Stull says that there is reason to believe that negative externalities do lower land values and rents. Rueter and others, however, say that this is not the case and that land values decline more or less smoothly along the long-run equilibrium path denoted by the dotted line. In this case, there is no need for zoning. Finally, there is additional evidence from Ohls, Wiesberg, and White that zoning in practice does not serve to maximize aggregate land values, further casting doubt on the correctness of the assumption on which zoning is predicated.[81]

Next, we move on to examine the empirical findings on the effects of zoning on the urban land markets. Two sorts of evidence are available. The first examines the effects of zoning on land values and rents, and therefore addresses questions of allocational efficiency. Second, we will look at the distributional effects of zoning, that is, the effects on the distribution of wealth and income among the various members of the population. The two effects are related, but are worth separating for analytical neatness.

First, in terms of the effectiveness of zoning in raising land values, the evidence forces us to draw the opposite conclusion. The work by Ohls et al., Maser et al., and Tunnicliffe (for the city of Vancouver) all point to the mixture of effects zoning can have, both raising and lowering land values and rents, in no readily predictable fashion.

On the second issue, the evidence is piling up that zoning's greatest impact appears to be on distribution, not on the efficient allocation of land. The principal result of zoning has been to raise the price of land for housing and to exclude effectively lower-income families from certain communities and submarkets, thereby raising the value of housing (wealth) in those communities. A redistribution occurs from lower-income groups to middle- and upper-income groups. The evidence is mounting that zoning has become socially costly with significant negative distributional consequences. The interested reader is directed to Bergman,[82] Scott,[83] Mills and Oates,[84] and Babcock and Bosselman.[85]

The empirical evidence on the costs of zoning is strong and consistent. Analytically, we can see why the effects of exclusionary zoning do act to raise land (and housing) prices in such a straightforward manner. Figure 11–4 shows what happens in supply-and-demand terms when municipalities exclude lower-cost housing. The supply of land for lower-cost housing shrinks, and with constant demand, price must inevitably rise. Allowed uses (usually high-technology research and development industries, or executive office parks and large-lot single-family homes) are usually overzoned, lowering their price. Large lots for more expensive houses become underpriced (compared to their equilibrium without exclusionary zoning) because of overzoning, and land for lower-cost housing becomes overpriced (again, compared with nonzoning), because of underzoning. The distributional inequities in this situation are clear and return us to Modesto in 1885, where we started our discussion.

Zoning appears to be largely unwarranted and ineffective on efficiency grounds. On distributional grounds, however, it appears to be all too effective and highly regressive. This result holds whether the exclusion is done on racial or environmental grounds. Excluded uses pay more for land than otherwise, while protected uses in essence realize subsidies through excess supplies of land for their use. One caveat should be stated: In the case of environmental protection of scarce resources, the resulting higher price is economically efficient since it reflects more closely true social costs rather than narrowly defined eco-

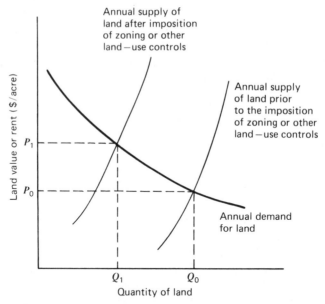

Figure 11–4. Demand and supply, with and without land-use controls.

nomic costs. Thus, higher prices need be neither inefficient nor indications of inefficiency, if the higher prices reflect the "true" social value of the resource whose price rises as a result of environmental controls and protection. However, the higher price shold reflect marginal private and social costs.

Regulating Monopoly/Oligopoly in Urban Land Markets

The possibility of monopoly and oligopoly control and of manipulation of urban land markets represents an important market imperfection. It is an empirical question basically. A major source of evidence is the Canadian Federal/Provincial Task Force on the Supply and Price of Serviced Residential Land. That task force was constituted in the face of enormous price increases in land and housing in Canada from 1972 to 1975. It delved into the ownership characteristics of vacant land ripe for development and surrounding the major cities in Canada. Its findings were clear and unequivocal: There does not appear to be any Canadian metropolitan area where land is held in sufficient quantity by a sufficiently small number of firms to allow these firms to manipulate the price of land.[86] Table 11–6 sets out ownership figures showing nominal ownership and then ownership combining separate firms if they had two or more directors in common.[87] The rule of thumb for market power (i.e., the power to manipulate prices) is that the top four firms control two-thirds of a market, the top ten firms control three-quarters; or the top 25 firms control 90 percent or more.

Table 11–6 Ownership Concentration: Nominal and Effective
Ownership Statistics

Metropolitan Area	% Owned by Top 4 Owners		% Owned by Top 10 Owners		% Owned by Top 25 Owners	
	Nominal	Effective	Nominal	Effective	Nominal	Effective
Calgary	30.4	46.1	51.5	62.2	70.3	72.2
Charlottetown	11.8	11.8	23.6	24.0	46.8	47.8
Edmonton	30.0	NA	50.0	NA	76.2	NA
Halifax	73.9	73.9	85.6	86.8	96.4	96.4
Hamilton	21.0	21.0	32.7	32.7	47.3	47.3
London	30.7	32.5	47.3	49.8	69.2	71.0
Montreal	13.6	NA	24.1	NA	39.0	NA
Ottawa	63.2	64.4	79.6	80.8	90.7	90.9
Regina	58.3	58.3	83.5	86.3	NA	NA
Saskatoon	84.5	98.1	99.2	99.8	NA	NA
Toronto	17.5	22.7	27.7	37.1	40.2	48.7
Vancouver	27.0	30.3	37.3	43.1	50.7	56.1
Winnipeg	48.7	49.5	64.8	66.4	74.2	75.5

Source: Federal/Provincial Task Force on the Supply and Price of Serviced Residential Land,
Down to Earth, Vol. 2 p. 73.

Only in Halifax, Ottawa, Regina, and Saskatoon are any of these criteria met; in these cities one or more government agencies were included in the top four landowners, hardly a case for private manipulation.[88]

There remain some problems with the data. First, the concentration ratio formula takes no account of the distribution of ownership. Second, the data are on stocks. Concentration ratios are usually constructed on flows, such as auto production. If there are passive owners or nondevelopers, developers may yet control a large component of the flow into production. Conversely, the data exclude all built-up areas and previously developed land, thus considerably understating the total stock supply. This is potentially a very significant oversight because homeownership is so prevalent, and thus the widespread stock of land under currently owned housing needs to be considered before one can speak about monopoly control of urban land markets.

We can see from the data in Table 11–7 that government ownership and land banking are not necessarily short-run solutions to rapidly rising housing and land prices. Those urban areas with significant public ownership experienced rates of price appreciation virtually identical to those for the average of the 25 urban areas studied by the task force. This is not at all inconsistent with our theoretical analysis in Part II, where we saw that in the short run land and housing supplies are relatively inelastic (the so-called stock-flow model of house and land price determination). Prices rise in the short run in the face of rising demand, since supply responses are relatively limited.

The task force also presented data that would lead one to question the effectiveness of land servicing policies such as that discussed for

Table 11–7 An Illustration of the Irrelevance of Public Versus Private Ownership for Short-run Housing Price Fluctuations

Urban Areas with High Government Ownership	Percentage Change, 1972–1975		
	NHA Lot	MLS Dwelling	NHA Dwelling
Regina	80.7	99.1	75.1
Saskatoon	59.2	101.5	71.7
Winnipeg	154.9	71.5	81.6
Ottawa	115.3	52.9	64.0
Halifax	15.9	44.9	26.7
Saint John	84.3	68.7	17.8
Average	85.1	73.0	56.2
Average of 25 areas	86.8	62.3	57.4
Difference	− 1.7%	+ 10.7%	− 1.2%

Source: Federal Provincial Task Force, *Down to Earth, Vol. 2* (Toronto, Ont.), 1978, p. 183.

Ontario. Toronto consistently ranked near the top of the 25 cities studies in terms of house and lot price appreciation, despite government efforts to service land in the urban region.[89]

The justification for government ownership and servicing programs is not strongly supported by available evidence; there does not appear to be monopoly or oligopoly power at work in Canadian urban land markets. Those ownership and servicing programs designed to increase the flow of lots and keep prices low are doomed to fail in the short run, and have not been successful. Equivalent United States data could not be found, but given the greater degree of competition in urban land markets in the United States, the Canadian findings should be relevant in the United States.[90]

Controlling Speculation in Urban Land Markets

Two sources of evidence can be brought into the analysis: theoretical and empirical. The theoretical evidence on speculation in organized markets is enormous and largely focused on financial and commodity futures markets.[91] The general finding is that speculators can be beneficial to adjustment processes in these markets by correctly anticipating changes and therefore easing the transition through guessing correctly in advance of (or in expectation of) the actual change.[92]

Recent work on speculation in urban land markets has reached mixed conclusions about the efficiency of such activities. Capozza notes that speculation can lead to higher prices, but that these higher prices might in fact be warranted due to the underpricing of scarce urban land resources.[93] Markusen and Scheffman conclude that the actual impact depends on a number of assumptions about landholding behavior.[94] Smith points out that there is little reason to expect that land markets will be substantially different from other markets, and there is therefore every reason to expect speculators to work as agents of stabilization rather than perpetuators of instability.[95]

Aside from the work in financial and commodity futures markets, there is a relative paucity of work done for land markets *per se*.[96] Data gathered by the previously cited Federal/Provincial Task Force on the Supply and Price of Serviced Residential Land lead one to conclude that speculation is risky. Figure 11–5 presents data from the task force for land prices within the Montreal urban region over a 26-year period. Two things are noteworthy: first, the incredible volatility of prices; second, that even in the same urban land market prices do not

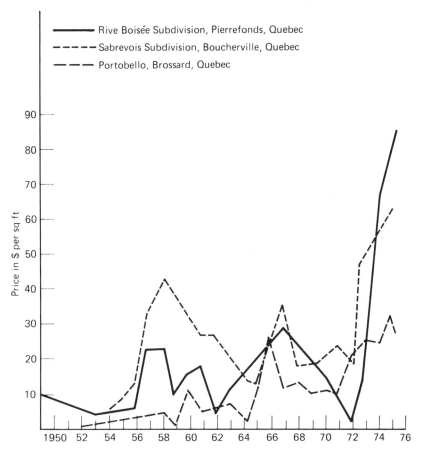

Figure 11–5. Land-price movements 1950–1976 in various Montreal suburbs. [*Source*: David Greenspan, ed., *Down to Earth, Volume II* (Toronto, Ontario: Federal-Provincial Task Force on the Supply and Price of Serviced Residential Land), 1978, p. 53.]

move together. Speculators can indeed lose, since prices can fall as well as rise.[97]

The empirical evidence on speculation in urban land markets leads us to conclude that speculators do not necessarily drive up prices.[98] This is consistent with many of the theoretical findings as well.

In sum, speculative activity does not appear harmful as purported, and can in fact serve useful stabilizing functions in urban land markets. The effectiveness of the Vermont and Ontario speculation taxes is questionable and requires additional research and a longer time horizon.[99]

Protecting Unique Land and Building Resources

Where our other analyses began with the question, "Does the stated problem exist in fact?" the present question rests on value judgments about the relative abundance or scarcity of a given resource, as well as on questions of the uniqueness of the "endangered" resource.

One aspect of protection legislation and policy has been investigated vigorously: the costs associated with growth and its control. The results are as varied as the studies and the clients commissioning the studies.[100] No clear answer has emerged, leaving the question of costs of growth and growth control wide open.

There has been a significant amount of work as well on assessing the costs of the continued pollution of air and water.[101] These studies have consistently demonstrated that there are significant and measurable costs not accounted for in the normal operations of the marketplace. There does, therefore, appear to be a strong empirical basis for imposing many of the air and water quality policies in urban areas.

The economic case for farmland, open space, scenic and recreation areas, and historic and architecturally interesting places is more difficult to substantiate since the benefits lost through continuation of present practices are difficult to estimate. Circumstantial evidence abounds. Older structures are continually being demolished to make way for parking lots or new buildings. Good farmland continues to be paved and developed.[102] Rivers continue to be dammed, and fertile valleys flooded. Development and pollution still threaten rich coastal areas.[103] Population increases still, and the supply of scenic areas, prime farmland, beautiful and productive coastal ecosystems, and older and architecturally interesting buildings decreases.

On the assumption that legislators are not capricious, evil, or power-hungry and react to real public pressures before enacting legislation, we can further assume that the growth in environmental protection legislation and policy stems from heightened general concern for the loss of high-quality natural and built environments.[104] Thus, the general public in Canada and the United States is becoming more aware of declines in environmental quality and is shifting its values toward environmental protection and against continued development.[105]

There are problems in assessing the impacts of the bevy of recent federal, state, and local protection and preservation legislation. The most frequently mentioned effects are those on price: environmental protection raises prices. It essentially does this through a mechanism similar to that displayed in Figure 11–4. By restricting development and directing it away from easily developed farmland and coastal areas, and by encouraging development in less sensitive areas and redevelopment and reuse of older but more expensively redeveloped buildings, environmental protection and preservation policies have served to restrict supply. Both of these effects are part and parcel of environmental preservation policies, since the tacit assumption is that market prices are too low. By raising prices, we more nearly reflect social costs and also slow down use and development.[106] We must pay for environmental quality, which is what economic theory tells us must be the case if a previously underpriced resource is priced at its social and opportunity cost.[107]

SUMMARY

Having reviewed the conceptual and empirical literature on the need for and effectiveness of land-use controls, the following generalizations appear consistent with current knowledge

1. *Controls on negative externalities* are poorly supported by the evidence. First, there appear to be few negative external effects among urban land uses. Second, the controls that have been imposed, largely zoning and its recent variants, seem to have little or no effect at improving the allocation of scarce urban land resources, as is called for by zoning proponents. One indirect effect, however, is the distributional effect, wherein zoning appears to have raised housing and land prices, to the detriment of lower-income households.

2. *Monopoly or oligopoly and speculative distortions* in urban land markets are similarly based on assumptions rather than empirical "fact." Detailed studies of 25 urban areas in Canada failed to provide evidence of oligopoly control of those land markets. Similarly, the purported effects of price manipulation and destabilization of urban land markets by speculators is not based on empirical findings, but rather on value-based assumptions. Attempts to control monopoly or oligopoly and speculative practices have not been successful to date.

3. *Protection of high-quality and/or unique natural and built environments* does appear to be based on sound thinking. Empirical evidence is difficult to compile, however, since there is so much room for judgment in the definition of environmental quality.

Footnotes

1. For additional historical detail, see: Richard F. Babcock, "Zoning," in Frank S. So, Israel Stallman, Frank Beal and David S. Arnold, *The Practice of Local Government Planning* (Washington, D.C.: International City Managers Association), 1979, pp. 416–443; Michael A. Goldberg and Peter J. Horwood, *Zoning: Its Costs and Relevance for the 1980's* (Vancouver, B.C.: The Fraser Institute), 1980; and Brian Porter, "The Land Use Contract," unpublished M.A. thesis (Vancouver, B.C.: School of Community and Regional Planning, University of British Columbia), 1973.

2. Quoted in Goldberg and Horwood, *op. cit.*, p. 11.

3. Goldberg and Horwood, *op. cit.*, p. 12.

4. For examples and an introduction to the voluminous literature, see: Fred Bosselman and David Callies, *The Quiet Revolution in Land Use Controls* (Washington, D.C.: Council on Environmental Quality), 1971; Donald C. Hagman, *Public Planning and Control of Urban and Land Development* (St. Paul, Minn.: West Publishing Company), 1973; Bill Shaw, *Environmental Law* (St. Paul, Minn.: West Publishing Company), 1976; Eva Hanks, A. Dan Tarlock, and John L. Hanks, *Environmental Law and Policy: Cases and Materials,* abridged edition (St. Paul, Minn.: West Publishing Company), 1975; and Jerome G. Rose, *Legal Foundations of Land Use Planning* (New Brunswick, New Jersey: Center for Urban Policy Research, Rutgers—The State University), 1979. See also: Gordon C. Bjork, *Life, Liberty and Property: The Economics and Politics of Land-use Planning and Environmental Controls* (Lexington Mass.: Lexington Books), 1982; Edith Netter, *Land-use Laws: Issues for the Eighties* (Washington, D.C.: Planners Press, American Planning Association), 1981.

5. See Porter, *op. cit.*

6. In certain municipalities in British Columbia and Ontario these development fees or impost charges could amount to $3000 per unit.

7. There is a long history of attempts to "recapture" the so-called unearned increment in land values that accrues to landowners as a result of urban growth and/or public policies such as provision of parks, streets, or sewers. The most well-known of these is the *Final Report by the Expert Committee on Compensation and Betterment* (London, England: His Majesty's Stationery Office), 1942, known as the Uthwatt Report after its chairman, Mr. Justice Uthwatt. The report espoused the idea that the increment belonged to the public, which idea was embodied in the 1947 Town and Country Planning Act in the United Kingdom. This act turned out to be unworkable concerning betterment and compensation, as did its 1968 successor. The idea of capturing the incremental value is very much alive and was among the most vigorously discussed items at the U.N. Conference on Human Settlements in Vancouver, B.C., in 1976 (called Habitat '76). Land-use contracts and development charges appear to be the most efficient way to extract the increment, however, as they are levied at the time of development in the bilateral bargaining situation between two legal entities: a developer and a municipality.

8. The notion of bilateral monopoly bargaining is an old one and traces its ancestry back to F. Y. Edgeworth and the Edgeworth boxes that depict this bilateral bargaining situation.

9. See Roderick M. Mackenzie, *The Development Approval Process* (Vancouver, B.C.: Executive Programmes, Faculty of Commerce and Business Administration, University of British Columbia), 1980.

10. The present system does raise a question about the equity of those already in residence in a community placing barriers to entry by new households ("closing the barn door," in common parlance). However, forcing new residents to pay the marginal costs that they impose on the community does make economic sense and is not inconsistent with equity objectives when one considers that high servicing standards and development charges do keep taxes low and public infrastructure at a high level of quality. For a more detailed argument along these lines see Michael A. Goldberg, "Municipal Arrogance or Economic Rationality: The Case of High Servicing Standards," *Canadian Public Policy* 6(1:1980):78–88.

11. Toronto, Calgary, and Winnipeg all make use of similar devices. So does the Boston Redevelopment Authority in its recent efforts to encourage innovative multiple use development.

12. For details of the Ontario system see: George A. Nader, *Cities of Canada*, Volumes I and II (Toronto: Macmillan of Canada), 1976; Gerald M. Adler, *Land Planning by Administrative Regulation: The Policies of the Ontario Municipal Board* (Toronto, Ontario: University of Toronto Press), 1971; Ontario Ministry of Municipal Affairs and Housing, *Land-Use Planning for Noise Control in Residential Communities* (Toronto: Ontario Ministry of Municipal Affairs and Housing), 1981; and John D. Bossons, *Reforming Planning in Ontario—Strengthening the Municipal Role* (Toronto: Ontario Economic Council), 1978.

13. Province of Ontario, *Planning Act* (Toronto: Queen's Printer for Ontario), 1983.

14. Porter, *op. cit.*, notes that 46 states and 1500 municipalities had adopted zoning and the Standard Zoning Enabling Act.

15. For details, see Robert W. Burchell, *Planned Unit Development: New Communities American Style* (New Brunswick, New Jersey: Center for Urban Policy Research, Rutgers University), 1972.

16. See Edwin S. Mills and Wallace E. Oates, eds., *Fiscal Zoning and Land Use Controls* (Lexington, Mass.: D.C. Heath), 1975; and Paul N. Courant, "On the Effect of Fiscal Zoning on Land and Housing Values," *Journal of Urban Economics* 3(1:1976):88–94.

17. The literature here is vast and growing. A good summary and bibliography appears in Randall W. Scott, "Exclusion and Land Use: A Comment and Research Bibliography," in Randall W. Scott, ed., *Management and Control of Growth, Volume* I (Washington, D.C.: ULI—The Urban Land Institute), 1975, pp. 445–464. An excellent statement of the issues is to be found in R. F. Babcock and F. P. Bosselman, *Exclusionary Zoning: Land Use Regulation and Housing in the 1970's* (New York: Praeger Publishers), 1973; and E. M. Bergman, *Eliminating Exclusionary Zoning: Reconciling Workplace and Residence in Suburban Areas* (Cambridge, Mass.: Ballinger Books), 1974. In addition, see: Penn Constance, *Everything In It's Place: Social Order and Land-use in America* (Princeton, New Jersey: Princeton University Press) 1977; and Robert Schafer, *Exclusionary Land-Use Controls: Conceptual and Empirical Problems in Measuring the Invisible Wall* (Cambridge, Mass.: Harvard University, Department of City and Regional Planning), 1975.

18. See Babcock and Bosselman, *op. cit.*, for details. Also see Hagman, *op. cit.*

19. For details and examples, see: Kate Thompson, *Innovative Techniques for Controlling Local Land Use* (Cambridge, Mass.: Graduate School of Design, Harvard University), 1975; Melvin R. Levin, Jerome G. Rose, and Joseph S. Slavet, *New Approaches to State Land-Use Policies* (Lexington, Mass.: D.C. Heath), 1974; Peter M. Wolf, *Land in America: Its Value, Use, and Control* (New York: Pantheon Books), 1981; and Lane Kendig, Susan Connor, Cranston Byrd, and Judy Hayman, *Performance Zoning* (Washington, D.C.: Planners' Press), 1981.

20. Levin *et al.*, *op. cit.* pp. 23–26.

21. New York City has an incentive scheme that combines performance criteria with development incentives. See Thompson, *op. cit.*, pp. 85–86.

22. See Thompson, *op. cit.*, pp. 29–44, and Scott *et al.*, *Management and Control of Growth, Volume II*, Chapter 12, pp. 355–487.

23. See Scott *et al.*, *op cit.*, Chapter 8, pp. 1–119.

24. See Scott *et al.*, *op cit.*, Chapter 12, pp. 355–487.

25. A complete discussion of the legal implications of growth controls appears in Fred Bosselman, David Callies, and John Banta, *The Taking Issue* (Washington, D.C.: Council on Environmental Quality), 1973. Also see Daniel R. Mandelker, *Environmental and Land Controls Legislation* (Indianapolis, Ind.: Bobbs-Merrill Company), 1976; Arden Herman Rathkopf, *The Law of Zoning and Planning: Analysis of the Law of Zoning, Comprehensive Citation of Cases, Excerpts from Court Decisions, Essential Forms* (New York: C. Boardman Co.), 1980; Norman J. Williams, *American Land Planning Law: Cases and Materials* (New Brunswick, New Jersey: Center for Urban Policy Research, Rutger's University), 1978; Robert H. Frielich and Eric Struhler, *The Land-Use Awakening: Zoning Law in the Seventies* (Chicago, Ill.: American Bar Association, Section of Urban, State and Local Government Law), 1981; and Robert V. Zener, *Guide to Environmental Law* (New York: Practising Law Institute) 1981.

26. Scott *et al.*, *op. cit.*, Chapters 8, 9, and 12, especially pp. 483–488.

27. Scott *et al.*, *op. cit.*, Chapter 9, pp. 127–210.

28. Scott *et al.*, *op. cit.*, presents an enormous range of growth controlling techniques that have been employed by governments with some success.

29. See Levin *et al.*, *op. cit.*, pp. 15–17, for details on official maps, with special reference to New Jersey.

30. For a good overview of the subject, see William Lamont, Jr., "Subdivision Regulation and Land Conversion," in Frank S. So, Israel Stollman, Frank Beal, and David S. Arnold, *The Practice of Local Government Planning* (Washington, D.C.: International City Managers Association), 1979, pp. 389–415.

31. Bosselman and Callies, *The Quiet Revolution in Land Use Controls, op. cit.*

32. *Ibid.* p. 1.

33. For a rather complete listing of various environmental controls, see Elaine Moss, ed., *Land Use Controls in the United States: A Handbook on the Legal Rights of Citizens* (New York: The Dial Press for the National Resources Defense Council, Inc.), 1977; J. Gordon Arbuckle, *Environmental Law Handbook* (Washington, D.C.: Government Institute Inc.), 1979; Robert V. Zener, *Guide to Environmental Law, op. cit.;* and Julie H. Saelig, Micheal A. Goldberg, and Peter Horwood,

Land-Use Legislation in the U.S.: A Survey and Synthesis (Ottawa: Economic Council of Canada), 1980.

34. Moss, *op. cit.*, p. 266.

35. *Ibid.;* plus references cited in footnote 4 of this chapter.

36. Moss, *op. cit.*, Chapter 10, pp. 168–223. Also see Peter deLeon and John Enns, "The Impact of Highways upon Metropolitan Dispersion: St. Louis," Research Memorandum P-5061 (Santa Monica, California: The RAND Corporation), 1973.

37. A strong case is made for the critical role that U.S. tax policy has had on urban development in George A. Peterson, "Federal Tax Policy and the Shaping of the Urban Environment," (New York: National Bureau of Economic Research), 1977, mimeographed.

38. The Federal/Provincial Task Force on the Supply and Price of Serviced Residential Land was established under the chairmanship of Toronto lawyer David Greenspan in late 1976 with a mandate to find out about the cause(s) of the land price spiral. See its final report, *Down to Earth, Volumes I and II* (Toronto: Federal/Provincial Task Force on the Supply and Price of Serviced Residential Land), 1978.

39. For details of some of the land banking activities in Canadian cities, see Stanley W. Hamilton, *Public Land Banking: Real or Illusory Benefits?* (Toronto: Urban Development Institute), 1974.

40. *Ibid.*

41. Neal Roberts, ed., *The Government Land Developers* (Lexington, Mass.: D. C. Heath), 1976.

42. For instance, in 1973 the National Housing Act was amended to enable municipalities to undertake land banking and servicing activities to speed the flow of serviced lots to the market.

43. See *Down to Earth, Volume II, op. cit.,* pp. 165–166, and more generally, Chapter 14, pp. 165–184.

44. Much has been written about what constitutes "reasonable" housing prices. A cynical view is that reasonable entails providing housing at less than cost. See Michael A. Goldberg, "Housing and Land Prices in Canada and the U.S.," in Lawrence B. Smith and Michael Walker, eds., *Public Property: The Habitat Debate Continued,* (Vancouver, B.C.: The Fraser Institute), 1976, pp. 207–254.

45. For additional detail, see *Down to Earth, Volume II, op. cit.,* Chapter 13, pp. 158–164.

46. See Lawrence B. Smith, "The Ontario Land Speculation Tax: An Analysis of an Unearned Increment Land Tax," *Land Economics* 52(1:1976):1–12.

47. *Ibid.,* p. 2.

48. For details, see David Baxter, *The British Columbia Land Commission Act—A Review,* Research Report #8 (Vancouver, B.C.: Urban Land Economics Program, Faculty of Commerce and Business Administration, University of British Columbia), 1974.

49. Smith, *op. cit.,* and *Down to Earth, op. cit.,* Chapter 13.

50. For example, from Table 11–3 we see that provincial parks (244,513) and provincial forests (1,640,378) contain about 19 percent of Canada's 9,976,138 square kilometers.

51. For example, until recently the *British Columbia Municipal Act* and the *Vancouver Charter* allowed buildings to be designated as landmarks severely restricting their use without compensation. This was changed in 1977 when land-use contracts were deleted from the *Municipal Act.* The point to note here is that cities can be given the right (or have it taken away) to drastically limit property rights through designation as landmarks and that compensation is only required if provincial legislation requires it. Compensation can also be expressly prohibited, as it was in the B.C. Land Commission Act. Again, there are not constitutional guarantees as in the United States, only political sensitivities on the part of provincial and federal governments.

52. The Greater Vancouver Regional District in the Vancouver metropolitan area has responsibility for broad zoning classes such as industrial, nonindustrial, agricultural, and open-space. Local governments cannot change their zoning if it conflicts with the regional zoning and the regional plan without first getting the regional plan and zoning amended. Regional governments in Ontario exercise more limited powers over land use but do influence infrastructure timing and placement and thus ultimately do have considerable land-use powers.

53. British Columbia and Prince Edward Island have taken some of the strongest actions on this front, especially with regard to foreign ownership. See John Spencer, *The Alien Landowner in Canada,* Research Report #1 (Vancouver, B.C.: Urban Land Economics Programme, Faculty of Commerce and Business Administration, University of British Columbia), 1974.

54. Peter Barnes, ed. *The People's Land: A Reader on Land Reform in the United States* (Emmaus, Pa.: Rodale Press Book Division), 1975, pp. 8–11. Also Robert G. Healy and John S. Rosenberg, *Land Use and States* Second Edition, (Baltimore: Johns Hopkins University Press), 1979.

55. Healy and Rosenberg, *op. cit.,* pp. 69–71.

56. *Ibid.,* p. 71. Also see Richard P. Fishman, "Public Land Banking: Examination of a Management Technique," in Randall W. Scott ed., *Management and Control of Growth, Volume III (Washington, D.C.: ULI—The Urban Land Institute), 1975, pp. 61–85.*

57. A debate has arisen in literature about the affordability of housing spurred on by the rapid rise in housing prices in the United States during the late 1970s. See John Weicher, "The Affordability of New Homes," *Journal of the American Real Estate and Urban Economics Association* 5(2:1977):209–226, and subsequent comments by Bernard J. Frieden and Arthur P. Solomon, "The Controversy Over Homeonwership Affordability," *AREUEA Journal* 5(3:1977):355–359, and Weicher's response in the same issue on pages 360–365. Table 11–8, below, comes from Weicher's initial article but has been updated to include 1979 data, as his data ended in 1976. For the evidence on the relationship between land-use controls and housing prices, see *Journal of the American Real Estate and Urban Economics Association* 9(4:1981), especially the papers by K. T. Rosen and L. F. Katz, "Growth Management and Land Use Controls: The San Francisco Bay Area Experience," pp. 321–344; F. E. Cae and J. Gale, "The Impact on Housing Costs of the California Coastal Zone Conseravtion Act," pp. 345–366; and J.

C. Nicholas, "Housing Costs and Prices Under Regional Regulation," pp. 384–396.

Table 11–8   New Home Prices and the New Price Index, 1963–1979

Year	Median New Home Price		1963 New Home Price Adjusted by the New Home Price Index		1974 New Home Price Adjusted by Index	
	Dollars	% Increase	Dollars	% Increase	Dollars	% Increase
1963	18,000	—	18,000	—	22,600	—
1964	18,900	5.0	18,200	1.0	22,700	0.4
1965	20,000	5.8	18,600	2.3	23,300	2.6
1966	21,400	7.0	19,300	3.6	24,200	3.8
1967	22,700	6.1	19,900	3.5	25,000	3.3
1968	24,700	8.8	21,000	5.1	26,200	4.8
1969	25,600	3.6	22,700	8.1	28,300	8.0
1970	23,400	−8.6	23,400	3.3	29,100	2.8
1971	25,200	7.7	24,600	4.9	30,700	5.5
1972	27,600	9.5	26,100	6.3	32,700	6.5
1973	32,500	17.8	28,800	10.5	35,600	8.9
1974	35,900	10.5	31,500	9.2	38,900	9.3
1975	39,300	9.5	34,700	10.2	42,800	10.0
1976	44,200	12.5	38,100	9.8	46,400	8.4
1977	48,800	10.4	—	—	52,100	12.3
1978	55,600	14.1	—	—	59,500	14.2
1979	62,900	12.9	—	—	67,700	13.8
1980	64,500	—	—	—	—	—
1980	68,900	—	—	—	—	—

Sources: U.S. Bureau of the Census, New One-Family Homes Sold and For Sale, Series C.-25; and U.S. Bureau of the Census, Price Index of New One-Family Houses Sold, Series C-27. Both are published by the U.S. Department of Commerce, the former monthly and the latter quarterly.

John Weicher, "The Affordability of New Homes," Journal of the American Real Estate and Urban Economics Association, 5 (2:1977):209–226 (table on p. 216).

Table 11–8 demonstrates rather dramatically the price changes that were taking place in the U.S. new housing market and provides evidence that there will be similar concerns voiced in the U.S. to those in Canada and a similar need to find one or more culprits for these escalating price increases in new housing. In this regard, the Canadian experience of the period 1972 to 1975 should provide useful analogies and lessons for U.S. researchers and policymakers.

58.   For some of the issues involved in agricultural and openspace zoning and land-use controls, see Bosselman, Callies and Banta, op. cit., p. 157, and Scott et al., op. cit., Volume III, pp. 52–60 and 114–126.

59.   Levin et al., op. cit., Chapter 3, pp. 31–42.

60.   Ibid., Chapter 4, pp. 43–54.

61.   Ibid., pp. 50–54.

62.   Development rights are in the public domain, a fundamental building block of the Alberta Planning Act and of comprehensive development districts in British Columbia, both of which would be of questionable legality in the United States.

63. The TDR concept has received a great deal of attention and has had much written about it. Among its leading advocates and clearest statements are the following, all of which have been reproduced in Scott *et al.*, Management and Control of Growth, Volume III, *op. cit.*, pp. 92–134: John J. Costonis, "Development Rights Transfer: Description and Perspectives for a Critique," pp. 92–107; John J. Costonis, "Space Adrift: A Synopsis," pp. 107–113); B. Budd Chavooshian, George H. Nieswand, and Thomas Norman, "Growth Management Programme: A New Planning Approach," pp. 114–126; and, finally, Frank Schnidman, "Transfer of Development Rights: Questions and Bibliography," pp. 127–134.

64. Both Costonis and Schnidman, *op. cit.*, raise relevant questions about the TDR notion. A thorough analysis is provided by Franklin J. James and Dennis E. Gale, *Zoning for Sale: A Critical Analysis of Transferable Development Rights Programs* (Washington, D.C.: The Urban Institute), 1977. Useful also are: Laura Lee Richard, *Implications of the Transfer of Development Potential in Vancouver* (Vancouver B.C.: Daon Development Corporation), 1981; and Dwight H. Merriam, *Making TDR Work* (New Haven, Conn.: Meram), 1978.

65. The Urban Land Institute monthly publication *Urban Land* has devoted considerable attention to the issue of historic preservation and the economics of rehabilitation. See, for example, the December 1977 issue, which dealt with the implications of the 1976 Tax Reform Act in the United States on the economics of rehabilitation and renovation. The December, 1979 issue dealt with tax incentives again, this time using developments in Little Rock, Arkansas, and Washington, D.C., as examples. That same issue also presented a detailed plan for historic preservation in Danville, Virginia.

66. See deLeon and Enns, *op. cit.*, and Peterson, *op. cit.* They provide evidence on federal transportation and tax policies, respectively, which demonstrate the centrifugal forces generated by these policies.

67. For details, see Healy and Rosenberg, *op. cit.*, pp. 198–199, and Levin, *et al.*, *op. cit.*, pp. 88–89.

68. See Bosselman, Callies, and Banta, *op. cit.*, pp. 147–175, and Levin *et al.*, *op. cit.* pp. 24–28 and 108–110.

69. Bosselman, Callies, and Banta, *op. cit.*

70. See Healy and Rosenberg, *op. cit.*, Chapters 3, 6, and 7.

71. See Healy and Rosenberg, *op. cit.*, Chapters 4 and 5, and Moss, *op. cit.*, Chapter 6.

72. Moss, *op. cit.*, p. 98.

73. Moss, *op. cit.*, Chapters 8 and 12.

74. See Goldberg and Horwood, *op. cit.*, for a review and analysis of much of the recent literature.

75. John P. Crecine, Otto A. Davis, and John E. Jackson, "Urban Property Markets: Some Empirical Results and their Implications for Municipal Zoning," *The Journal of Law and Economics* 10(1967):79–99.

76. Frederick H. Reuter, "Externalities in Urban Property Markets: An Empirical Test of the Zoning Ordinance of Pittsburgh," *The Journal of Law and Economics* 16(2:1973):313–350.

77. Steven Maser, William H. Riker, and Richard N. Rosett, "The Effects of Zoning and Externalities on the Price of Land: An Empirical Analysis of Monroe County, New York," *The Journal of Law and Economics* 20(1:1977):111–132.

78. Goldberg and Horwood, *op. cit.*, and Jonathan Mark and Michael A. Goldberg, "Land Use Controls: The Case of Zoning in Vancouver," *Journal of the American Real Estate and Urban Economics Association*, 9(4:1981):418–435.

79. The most complete study of Houston is that by Bernard Seigen, *Land Use Without Zoning* (Lexington, Mass: D. C. Heath), 1972. Also see Roscoe H. Jones, Appendix to Chapter 4 of Goldberg and Horwood, *Zoning: Its Costs and Relevance for the 1980's*, entitled "Houston City Planning and Zoning," pp. 45–58. Mr. Jones has been Houston's Director of Planning since 1964 and is in a unique position to comment on its land-use planning system. A recent analysis further supports the economic efficiency of the Houston approach. See Richard B. Peiser, "Land Development Regulation: A Case Study of Dallas and Houston Texas," *Journal of the American Real Estate and Urban Economics Association*, 9(4:1981):397–417.

80. William J. Stull, "Community Environment, Zoning, and the Market Value of Single Family Homes," *The Journal of Law and Economics* 18(2:1975):535–557. Also see Donald Jud, "The Effects of Zoning on Single-Family Residential Property Values: Charlotte, North Carolina," *Land Economics*, 56(2:1980):142–154.

81. James C. Ohls, Richard C. Weisberg, and Michelle J. White, "The Effect of Zoning on Land Value," *Journal of Urban Economics* 1(4:1974):428–44. Also see empirical evidence on the ambiguity of rezoning effects from George Peterson, "The Influence of Zoning Regulations on Land and Housing Prices," Working Paper 1207-24 (Washington, D.C.: The Urban Institute), 1974.

82. Bergman, *op. cit.*

83. Scott *et al.*, Volume I, Chapters 6 and 7, *op. cit.*

84. Mills and Oates, *op. cit.*

85. Babcock and Bosselman, *Exclusionary Zoning, op. cit.*

86. Federal/Provincial Task Force, *Down To Earth, Volume II, op. cit.*, Chapter 7, pp. 60–76.

87. *Ibid.*, Chapter 7, pp. 60–76.

88. *Ibid.*, p. 73.

89. *Ibid.*, Appendix Tables A1–A9, pp. 191–199.

90. Leo Grebler, *Large-Scale Housing and Real Estate Firms* (New York: Praeger Publishers), 1976: and John Herzog, *The Dynamics of Large Scale Housebuilding* (Berkeley, Cal.: Center for Real Estate and Urban Economics, University of California), 1963.

91. See, for examples, Jack Hirshleifer, "Speculation and Equilibrium: Information, Risk and Markets," *Quarterly Journal of Economics* 89(4:1975):519–542; Nicholas Kaldor, *Essays on Speculation and Economic Stability* (London, England: Duckworth), 1961, especially pp. 17–58; Martin S. Feldstein, "Uncertainty and Forward Exchange Speculation," *Review of Economics and Statistics* 50(2:1968):182–192; Jonathan Kesselman, "The Role of Speculation in Forward-Rate Determination: The Canadian Flexible Dollar, 1953–1960," *Ca-*

nadian Journal of Economics 4(3:1971):279–298; Tetteh Kofi, "A Framework for Comparing the Efficiency of Futures Markets," *American Journal of Agricultural Economics* 55(4:PartI:1973):584–594; and Holbrook Working, "New Concepts Concerning Futures Markets and Prices," *American Economic Review* 52(3:1962):431–459.

92. This case is made more strongly by Milton Friedman, "The Case for Flexible Exchange Rates," *Essays in Positive Economics* (Chicago: Aldine Publishers), 1954, pp. 157–203.

93. Dennis R. Capozza, "The Efficiency of Speculation in Urban Land," *Environment and Planning A* 8(1976):411–422. A dissenting argument is presented by George Gau in a number of papers where he establishes the relative efficiency of urban land markets and their ability to capitalize anticipated and speculative behaviors into prices and therefore normalize gains in the longer run. See George W. Gau, "Tests of Efficiency of Real Estate Investment Markets," paper presented to the American Finance Association Meetings, December 1982, (Vancouver B.C.: Faculty of Commerce, University of British Columbia), mimeographed.

94. James R. Markusen and David T. Scheffman, *Speculation and Monopoly in Urban Development: Analytical Foundations with Evidence for Toronto* (Toronto: Ontario Economic Council), 1977.

95. Lawrence B. Smith, "The Ontario Land Speculation Tax," *op. cit.*

96. In addition to Markusen and Scheffman, *op. cit.*, and Smith, *op. cit.*, relatively few studies could be identified with any empirical base. Among these is Richard U. Ratcliff and Stanley W. Hamilton, *Suburban Land Development* (Vancouver, B.C.: Union of B.C. Municipalities), 1972; and, of course, the Federal/Provincial Task Force materials cited throughout this chapter. A recent study of speculation and turnover rates in houses, as opposed to land, confirms these land speculation studies, further impairing the credibility of the speculation-manipulation view of urban land and housing markets. See A. Skaburskis, "Multiple Transactions and Housing Prices: A Study of Speculation Activity in Vancouver and Burnaby, 1979–1981," mimeographed (Ottawa, Ontario: Canada Mortagage and Housing Corporation), 1982.

97. Striking evidence for Vancouver, which has had a tumultuous history of booms and busts. See A. P. Morley, *Vancouver: From Milltown to Metropolis*, Revised Edition (Vancouver, B.C.: Mitchell Press), 1974.

98. The most persistent purveyor of this particular conspiracy view of urban development is James Lorimer, *The Developers* (Toronto: James Lorimer), 1978; and also his *City Magazine*.

99. Smith, *op. cit.*, and Healy and Rosenberg, *op. cit.*, pp. 69–71.

100. The cost-of-growth argument has spawned a large literature. See Scott *et al.*, *op. cit.*, Volume II, Chapter 13, pp. 489–596. The pieces collected here by Scott and his colleagues gives a good representative picture of the issues and the type of evidence being mounted on both sides of the issue.

101. *Environmental Quality*, the annual review of the Council on Environmental Quality, presents evidence each year. Specific technical studies include Jonathan H. Mark, "A Preference Approach to Measuring the Impact of David Harrison and Daniel Rubinfeld, "Hedonic Housing Prices and the Demand for Clean Air," *Journal of Environmental Economics and Management* 5(1:1978)81–102.

102. For figures on losses, see Healy and Rosenberg, *op. cit.*, pp. 18–20.

103. See Frank P. Grad, George W. Rathjens, and Albert J. Rosenthal, *Environmental Control: Priorities, Policies and the Law* (New York: Columbia University Press), 1971, pp. 11–22.

104. For insights into the politics of environmental land-use issues, see: Charles M. Lamb, *Land Use Politics and Law in the 1970's* (Washington, D.C.: Program of Policy Studies in Science and Technology, The George Washington University), 1975; Terry S. Peters, *The Politics and Administration of Land Use Control* (Lexington, Mass.: D. C. Heath), 1974; and Nelson Rosenbaum, *Land Use and the Legislatures: The Politics of State Innovation* (Washington, D.C.: The Urban Institute), 1976. Also see James Hite, *Room and Situation: The Political Economy of Land-use Policy* (Chicago Il.: Nelson-Hall), 1979: David E. Erwin, *Land-Use Control: Evaluating Economic and Political Effect* (Cambridge, Mass.: Ballinger Publishing Company), 1977; Guy Bienveniste, *Regulating and Planning: The Case of Environmental Politics* (San Francisco: Boyd and Fraser Publishing Company), 1981; and George Lefoe, *Urban Land Policy for the 1980's: The Message for State and Local Government* (Lexington Mass.: Lexington Books), 1983.

105. The movement to nonmetropolitan areas discussed in Chapter 1 and again in Chapter 13 bear witness to such changing values.

106. A fascinating analysis of the price increases of the recent past is provided by Maurice D. Levi and Martin Kupferman, *Slowth* (New York: Ronald Press), 1980.

107. Barry Commoner popularized the absence of free lunches in man-environmental relations and has continued to hit at the theme in a number of his books. See his *The Closing Circle* (New York: Alfred Knopf), 1971; and, more recently, *The Poverty of Power* (New York: Bantam Books), 1976. Also see Lester R. Brown, *Building a Sustainable Society* (New York: W. W. Norton), 1981. Of course, an adjunct to these critiques of growth and environment degradation must try to incorporate costs of these environmental protection measures, not just through higher prices but also in terms of their administrative and procedural costs, some of which may not be reflected or capitalized into higher prices. In short, some sort of benefit-cost calculation must be made. For an interesting attempt at such a calculation, see J. D. Belloit and H. C. Smith, "The Coastal Construction Control Line: A Cost-Benefit Analysis," *Journal of the American Real Estate and Urban Economics Association* 9(4:1981) :367–383.

12

HOUSING

ISSUES IN THE HOUSING MARKET

Introduction

Housing constitutes the most important source of consumer wealth in Western nations. It represents about half of the total physical and financial wealth in the United Kingdom, Canada, and the United States.[1] In terms of total measured consumer expenditures, an indication of flows rather than stocks, housing represents over one-third of the total in Canada[2] (the flow estimates are likely to be understated because measured expenditures exclude imputations for the rent on owner-occupied dwellings).

Apart from absorbing such a large component of personal consumption expenditures, housing occupies a central role in personal wealth and asset accumulation decisions. Favorable tax treatment is accorded housing investments as opposed to other vechicles. For instance, taxes are not levied on the imputed rent of owner-occupiers. Moreover, tax deductions are allowed for mortgage interest and property taxes against other income in the United States and most Western nations, Canada being an exception.

This chapter seeks to examine the efficiency and equity of the housing market. The approach taken starts from an economic perspective, though the social and racial aspects of housing are also discussed. In this economic context, however, no value judgments are made on existing allocations of housing. For example, some argue that housing is a right and not a commodity to be purchased in a market. Presumably, this implies that housing above some threshold or subsistence level could be subject to market forces, with the subsistence level provided by a grant. The problem is the determination of this minimum requirement. Another argument is that people spending more than a given proportion of their income on housing are allocating too much. This is also a normative statement, and requires inferences on the appropriate allocation of a household's budget.

Housing: Trends and Issues

Some of the many issues that have surrounded housing markets and housing policy in both Canada and the United States are discussed in general below, although the list considered is by no means exhaustive. These issues are: affordability, demographics, tenure choice (rent versus own), investment and inflationary hedges, taxes, and the supply side. To these could be added mortgages, but this issue is more fully examined in Chapter 6.

Affordability To deal with the issue of affordability, it has been proposed that direct shelter subsidies be paid to low-income groups. This constrains households to purchase only housing, and is socially less efficient than a direct income transfer. Housing may be regarded by some as meriting subsidy, but the increased demand by those receiving the subsidy may lead only to higher prices.

During the period 1971–1975, when prices rose particularly rapidly, the Canadian MLS average price increased from $24,581 to $45,878, or 86.6 percent. Median family income rose 60.2 per cent, from $10,368 to $16,613, and per capita income rose by 74.8 percent, from $3435 to $6005.[3] Considering the decade as a whole, the price of new houses as measured by the Canada Mortgage and Housing Corporation (CMHC) increased by 186.6 percent for 1971–1981, the Canadian MLS average price increased by 191.3 percent, the CMHC rent index by 54.8 percent, while household incomes increased by 226 percent and per capita income by 228 percent.

The above suggests that, for Canada, affordability did not become a problem during the 1970s. Rather, incomes increased by more than house prices and, as a result, the average person could more easily afford to purchase a house. The above does not provide information on the distribution of house prices and household incomes. If all house prices increased by the same percentage, while only a relatively few persons received large income increases, then affordability could have deteriorated. However, the age of the marginal buyer, according to new home sales insured under the National Housing Act, declined from 33.1 years in 1970 to 31.7 years in 1981. Thus, as income and wealth usually increase with age, it would appear that housing became more affordable during this period.

The above information is not part of a statistical model. The conclusion that housing was not necessarily less affordable in the 1970s can be altered by the following observations.

1. Although the average age of new home buyers declined in the 1970s, demographic shifts associated with the "baby boom" imply that the average age of the

population was declining also. The relevant consideration is the average age of home buyers relative to the population as a whole.

2.   Interest rates for mortgages were in nominal terms less than the rate of general inflation and the rate of house price appreciation during the early 1970s. By the late 1970s and 1980s, interest rates exceeded the rate of inflation, and substantially exceeded the rate of house price appreciation. In the United States, the tax deductibility of mortgage interest reduces the differential, but even here the relative differential between after-tax interest rates and inflation has narrowed.

Hence, while there is some evidence that affordability has not become a serious problem in the housing market, a complete analysis requires examination of age, sex, and family composition and the relationship between house carrying charges and after-tax family income.

For the United States, data on the relation between the cost of homeownership and net family incomes have been constructed.[4] The index of net effective costs, the sum of mortgage interest, property taxes, utilities, insurance, maintenance and repairs, less expected capital gains and tax savings for a constant quality 1974 house, was 100 in 1963 and had declined to below 80 in 1977. However, subsequent to that years, the index increased. If capital gains and tax savings are excluded from the calculation distributed across the population, the cost of homewonership increased even more substantially throughout the 1970s. Hence, the costs of homeownership have increased in the late 1970s and early 1980s.

Demographics   There are certain demographic movements which accounted for a large upward shift in the demand for housing units during the 1970s, but which are unlikely to be repeated. On the contrary, demographic projections suggest a declining demand for housing. This assumes that the other factors affecting demand, such as the inflationary environment and tax incentives, will remain constant.

The two demographic factors inducing demand for housing during the 1970s and 1980s were the "baby boom" and the increase in the divorce rate. The high birth rates of the period subsequent to World War II and up to the late 1960s has implied a continuing high rate of family formation for younger households.

In the early 1970s, the "baby boom" cohort exerted pressure on rental housing markets. By the late 1970s, this group was purchasing housing, thereby contributing to increases in demand for homeownership. The liberalized divorce laws in both Canada and the United States in the late 1960s also have increased the number of households, while reducing average household size. Between the 1960 and 1980 U.S. censuses, total annual population growth averaged 1.2 percent, but the number of households increased by 2.1 percent per year.

The decline in the birth rate did not commence until the 1960s in both the United States and Canada. This implies that the cohort aged 18 to 34 will remain large until the early 1990s, providing continued support for growth in housing demand. While projections for the future are of necessity uncertain, there is a likelihood that demand will decline in the 1990s, with a smaller cohort of young households. Immigration, both legal and illegal, remains unknown.

Population growth, and the consequent increases in household formation and housing demand, has not been even across the United States and Canada. In Chapter 1, evidence was presented of a reduction in the percentage of population in urban and suburban areas, and an increase in the rural share of total population. This occurred in the 1970s in both Canada and the United States, with the trend slightly more pronounced in the former. Population growth has also been dispersed regionally. In Canada, growth more rapid than average has occurred in the West, particularly in Alberta and British Columbia. Also, the Atlantic provinces have experienced above average population growth. Even a zero population growth rate nationally may be associated with regional dispersion in housing demand.

In the United States, Chapter 1 also indicated that population growth has been greatest in the South and West, the Sun Belt states, with the population growing slowly or even negatively in the Frost Belt states of the North and East. While a trend for the future cannot necessarily be extrapolated forward based on the recent past, there is reason to believe that some of the trends underlying the migration of the 1970s will continue in the future. Notable among these are:

1. *Aging population.* A larger percentage of the population is elderly and retired. For these groups and others, such as the independently wealthy and those from offshore seeking a haven, the advantages of leisure activities and sun are dominant.

2. *Employment opportunities.* In the United States, many states such as California, Texas and Florida are gateways to legal and illegal immigration. This immediately creates a demand for housing and reduces wages.

Hence, demographic factors associated with an aging population and a leveling off of the divorce rate will likely engender a decline in housing demand in the 1990s and subsequently. A feature of this may well be how to use efficiently the large amount of urban and possibly suburban land which has previously been assigned to single-family housing.

Tenure Choice A third general issue is that of tenure choice, or that between owning and renting. The general trend has been for a larger proportion of households becoming homeowners, even during the price escalation of the 1970s. In 1971, from the Census of Canada, the proportion of households owning a home was 60 percent, and this increased to 63 percent in the 1981 Census.

In the United States, census data reveal that in 1940 less than 45 percent of households were homeowners, but this had increased to 61 percent in 1971 and 63 percent in 1981. In fact, the group of renters, already a minority, now includes many people for whom tenure switching is expensive. These include:

1. *Transient workers.* These are people exposed to frequent moves or unstable employment, or those in search of work, notably the young.

2. *Low-income households.* This group lacks not only homeownership but also other goods.

Certain government policies contribute to households becoming tenants for longer than might otherwise be the case. Rent controls or stabilization result in the tenant paying a lower rent than that which clears the market. This lower rent creates a property right for the tenants, who are induced to become renters when otherwise some of them would be owners. Second, those on welfare or public assistance receive a partial subsidy on housing costs for rental. Homeowners have their equity counted as assets, so there is an incentive not to own.

In the reverse direction are government policies directed at increasing the rate of homeownership. These include the payment of grants for first-time purchase, deductibility of mortgage interest and property taxes from some income, and exemption or deferral of capital gains. These characteristics subsidize an increase in the homeownership rate.

Rates of homeownership also vary with certain household characteristics. They are lower for blacks than whites in the United States, even adjusting for differentials in education and income. In Canada, they are lower in Quebec and among French-speaking Canadians than among English-speaking Canadians. This suggests that these homeownership programs represent a cross-subsidization across household groups.

In both Canada and the United States, almost two-thirds of households are homeowners. In Canada, this arises despite the fact that mortgage interest and property taxes are not deductible from wage and salary income. While the rule in the United States is to mortgage oneself to the hilt, in Canada the rule is the opposite, to reduce the mortgage. The reason is that the return on this investment is the interest rate, paid from after-tax income. This accounts for the fact that in Canada about half of all homeowners have clear title to their property, with no mortgage.[5]

Inflation Hedge and Investment Confounding the examination of housing is its use as a tax shelter as well as providing physical shelter.

In the short run, land and improvements may be viewed as in perfectly inelastic supply. Shifts in demand because of inflationary expectations are thus captured immediately in prices.

The tax treatment of land and housing capital gains is usually preferential relative to that on other investments. In Canada, capital gains on a principal residence are fully exempt from tax. Further, a person need not live in a principal residence, which can be rented out for up to four years. In the United States, a rollover provision defers capital gains taxes virtually indefinitely. If the proceeds of a house sale are used to purchase another within 18 months, the tax is deferred.

The above refers to the nominal rate of tax on a taxpaying unit reporting capital gains in full. In practice, the reporting of capital gains on housing is likely to be understated, further reducing the effective tax burden. The problems are as follows. First, capital gains are based on a self-reporting mechanism. There is no outside verification, such as through the submission of payments documented by employers for wage and salary income. Second, the amount of capital gains can only be checked if tax identification records such as social security numbers are recorded on all land title transactions, and land registry offices forward this information to income tax authorities. Of course, large numbers of transactions are already exempt from tax, so methods would be required to determine which were taxable. The above suggests that the effective tax rate on capital gains is lower than the system intends.

If mortagage interest and property taxes are tax-deductible, carrying charges are reduced. For a house standing empty and not being utilized, the cost is $(MI + PTAX) \times (1 - TAX) + MAIN$, where MI is the mortgage interest rate; $PTAX$, the property tax rate; TAX, the marginal rate of personal income taxation; and $MAIN$, the maintenance rate. The return, if exempt from tax, is APP, where APP is the rate of appreciation in house prices. If MI is 10 percent and $PTAX$ 1 percent, with TAX 40 percent, $(MI + PTAX) \times (1 - TAX)$ is 6.6 percent. If $MAIN$ is 2 percent, the house empty is a profitable investment as long as prices are increasing by more than 8.6 percent.

Some risk premium may also be involved in the calculations. However, since the cost estimates in the example are plausible for the 1970s, and in many areas average price increases were in double digits, housing was a profitable investment even without regard to the shelter services provided. The demand for housing is thus akin to that for gold and art, namely, as a hedge against inflation.

In the 1980s, there are indications that the environment that gave rise to these increases is changing. Marginal personal income tax rates have been reduced, and interest rates have increased relative to other prices. This increases the cost per unit of holding a house. With a reduction in inflation rates, the advantage of having a tax-free shelter is reduced. The return from housing as an investment is reduced, leading to a decline in demand.

Taxes   Tax laws have tended to favor the housing industry relative to other sectors of the economy. Individuals and households bid up the price of housing to capitalize the value of these tax savings. However, this capitalization need not necessarily be realized, given the likelihood that a tax policy can be changed and the imperfect short-run supply elasticity.

Nevertheless, the cost to the government of these policies has been substantial. In the ownership sector, capital gains are exempt from tax, as is the imputed income to the homeowner. This is the income which would be received were the unit rented. This is in addition to the deductibility of mortgage interest and property taxes. In the rental sector, there are provisions for accelerated depreciation rates in excess of actual depreciation rates, and the ability to deduct rental losses against other income.

Depreciation deductions on rental property are on a basis of historical cost of purchase. In an inflationary environment, the cost of replacing an existing rental property rises. With depreciation based on historical cost, the provision does not replace the structure. By reducing the period over which a structure can be expensed, some of this is offset. However, the more appropriate procedure is for indexing of depreciation provisions.

The tax treatment of housing also has implications in the Consumer Price Index and other measures of inflation. The construction of such measures neglects the treatment of taxes and capital appreciation. If mortgage interest is tax deductible, the effective interest rate is reduced. There are several problems with including a tax-adjusted measure of housing costs in the Consumer Price Index. First, tax rates differ, even among households with similar income. Second, housing is illiquid, and there are costs of transacting. Expected capital gains can be realized only on the consumption of large transaction costs.

Supply Side   A final issue in housing markets is the supply side. While certain natural factors contribute to short-run inelasticity of land and the supply of improvements, part of this may also be attributable to government policies on zoning, construction regulations, and land usage. In this area, the *Report of the President's Commission on Housing* for the United States in 1982 is most instructive.[6] The Commission has argued that regulation denies consumers a choice in the marketplace, affects the production of housing for low- and middle-income people, increases the cost of the production of housing, and restricts substitution of materials, land, and labor in production.

In the 1970s, the cost of production of a new house increased more rapidly than the Consumer Price Index. A study of cost components on a typical single-family house reveals substantial increases. The Consumer Price Index in the United States itself increased by 112 percent over the decade 1970 to 1980. However, the cost of land increased by 248 percent, that for on-site labor by 130 percent, materials by 154 percent, financing by 381 percent, and overhead by 115 percent.

The weighted average increase over all costs is 176 percent, substantially in excess of general price increases. The source of this cost increase is at least partly attributable to government regulations restricting land use.

On the other hand, there are benefits from government regulations in areas such as servicing standards. The costs of overcrowding on sewer and transport systems are borne by all residents as an externality. Each additional housing unit adds pressure on such capacity not normally included in private cost. The issue is whether the additional requirements exceed those covering the externalities.

On financing, the period of the late 1970s and early 1980s has witnessed increases in the real interest rate chargeable for carrying land and any other durable good. This increase has affected housing costs. In addition, the cost of financing is also dependent on time spent obtaining approvals and permits. If these procedures become more lengthy and complicated, the cost of financing increases.

On construction technology, there is controversy surrounding the housing industry. Productivity appears to have declined more sharply in the housing industry than in any other. This is under both the definitions of output per unit of input, or total factor productivity, and output per hour worked, or labor productivity. Building codes restrict the substitution of capital for labor, and inhibit the introduction of new materials technology. Further, occupational licensing and restrictions in the subcontracting sector make it difficult to increase the supply or productivity of electricians and plumbers. In part, the public may be served by protection against low-quality work. However, the lack of retesting of qualified tradespeople assures that the industry is unlikely to benefit from individual upgrading and skills acquisition.

These are some of the issues surrounding housing markets and policy. The list is not meant to be exhaustive but to provide a framework that will permit the complete analysis of housing markets.

The second section of the chapter is devoted to the demand side of the housing market. In early research, housing was regarded as a homogeneous commodity like other economic goods. However, it differs in key characteristics such as location and quality. Recent housing demand studies explicitly acknowledge the importance of these characteristics. By way of introduction, and to posit the most basic model, homogeneous housing is discussed first. In the next section the modern hedonic, or characteristic, approach to housing is taken, where housing is not assumed to be identical across units. Following this, tenure choice is discussed, and the section concludes with implications for determining price and income elasticities of housing demand.

HOMOGENEOUS HOUSING

In the most straightforward case, a household derives utility from the consumption of housing services, h, and other goods, g.[7] Assume further no preferences for different types of housing or neighborhood location. Households do not differ in size, tastes, or incomes. The consumer maximizes utility subject to the constraint on his budget. Let d be the distance from the CBD; $r(d)$, the rent per unit of housing services; p_g, the price of goods; $c(d)$, the cost of a unit of transport services; $t(d)$, the quantity of transport services used; and y, income. Housing expenditures $r(d)h(d)$ and transport expenditures $c(d)t(d)$ are dependent on distance.

At any given utility level, let the budget constraint be satisfied exactly as:

$$y = r(d)h(d) + p_g g + c(d)t(d) \tag{12.1}$$

Income is spent on house rental, other goods, and transport. Now let all the variables remain constant except transport costs for commuting to the CBD—these may increase, for example, following a rise in fuel prices. Consider the compensating change in housing rental. In equation (12.1), let the increase in commuting cost per unit be $c(d)$. Then the change in commuting cost in total is $c(d)t(d)$. This is balanced by a decrease in rents $r(d)$ so that total income is constant. So:

$$-\Delta r(d)h(d) = \Delta c(d)t(d) \tag{12.2}$$

or the incremental change in commuting costs, $\Delta c(d)t(d)$, must be balanced by a fall in housing expenditures, $-\Delta r(d)h(d)$. In this model, the only commuting occurs to the CBD, and the "flat featureless plain" assumption of Chapter 4 is maintained.

Suppose the household makes a fixed number of commuting trips to the CBD, so $t(d) = t$ where t is constant. Assume that the transport cost, c, is proportional to the distance traveled, so $c(d) = cd$ where c is a constant charge per unit distance, for example, a mile. Then the marginal transport charge in (12.2) is $c(d) = c$, a constant, and the incremental transport charge is:

$$c(d)t(d) = ct \tag{12.3}$$

a constant, and independent of distance d, implying that marginal housing expenditure $-\Delta r(d)h(d) = ct$ is also constant and independent of location.

The next issue is to determine the pattern of demands, $h(d)$, and the distribution of rents, $r(d)$, with incremental housing expenditure equal to incremental transport costs, except opposite in sign. One specification adopted by Muth is to assume that rents decline exponentially with distance.[8] The marginal rent, $\Delta r(d)$, must also decline exponentially. The form is:

$$r(d) = ae^{-bd} \qquad (12.4)$$

where a and b are parameters. In the constant tansport cost case, any decline in rent must be offset by an increase in housing demand so that total expenditure is maintained.

By this method, Muth is able to determine the allocation of housing and rents. With rents declining exponentially, marginal rents also decline exponentially, and housing consumption increases with distance from the CBD.[9] Hence, suburban houses are likely to be larger than urban ones, all else being equal.

An alternative method of solution for (12.2) and the constant case, (12.3), is to assume $h(d) = h$, a constant, or housing services consumed are identical at all locations.[10] Rearranging and combining (12.2) and (12.3) yields:

$$-\Delta r(d) = \frac{ct}{h} \qquad (12.5)$$

or $\Delta r(d) = -ct/h$, so rent is $r(d) = -ctd/h$, indicating a decline with distance from the CBD.

These housing models depend on certain assumptions, the more notable being:

Homogeneous housing. All housing services are identical except for differences in location. However, housing units differ in age and structural characteristics. The definition of aggregate housing demand or supply is therefore not as straightforward as simply adding together the number of units or square feet, but rather includes an implicit quality index.

Homogenous people. Again, households are assumed identical except for location. Differences in household size, age, number of children, and tastes are assumed away. More important differences that arise in the parameters determining income before and after tax are also ignored. This is particularly weakening to these models, since housing services receive favored tax treatment.[11]

Since personal characteristics determining taxes differ across households, the same housing unit can have a widely differing price or rent depending on the user. Also, with a progressive tax structure involving higher marginal tax rates on higher incomes, as a household moves to upper income brackets, the tax benefits on housing increase in the United States. This implies that households do not face a constant price for housing services. In standard consumer theory, it is assumed that the price of apples or eggs is exogenous, that is, out of personal control. The user cost of housing services, however, is endogenous to the household, since it depends in part on household income and investment behavior.

Tenure choice: The choice of whether to rent or buy involves several issues. The tax legislation provides for alternative treatment of renters and owners, with preference given the latter. Risk is also a consideration here, with ownership providing for greater security of tenure, but higher risk on mortgage interest (particularly on renewal), household repairs, property taxes, and the possibility of capital losses. Renting is less secure, but avoids most of the risk associated with ownership just noted.

Equilibrium in housing markets. Differing estimates of price and income elasticities in housing demand have been presented, implying potential disequilibrium, although the usual assumption is of equilibrium. This requires that prices move immediately to clear markets, in violation of the frequent observation of significant vacancies, sluggish price responses, and supply lags.

HETEROGENEOUS HOUSING

The response to differences in the quality of housing services has led to the development of an hedonic price index, reflecting the importance of widely varying housing characteristics.[12] Suppose all housing units can be described by a list of characteristics $z_1, \ldots, z_m$, where an individual characteristic, z_i, could represent type of construction, age, or material in a given room. Then, housing services, h, are represented by a function of these, or:

$$h = h(z_1, \ldots, z_m) \qquad (12.6)$$

If there is some homogeneous unit that is used superficially as an aggregate, for example, "square feet" at the individual housing unit level, let this be n.

Specifically, data are frequently published on the "number of housing starts" or the "total housing supply," and this is the simple sum of all units available. The z_i elements can be expressed per square foot or per housing unit as z_i/n. Then, under certain conditions:

$$h = nh\left(\frac{z_1}{n}, \ldots, \frac{z_m}{n}\right) = nq(z_1, \ldots, z_m) \qquad (12.7)$$

where q is a quality index of housing services per square foot.[13] Total housing expenditure is rh, and a similar relation for the rental price can be derived. Let,

$$e = rh = rnq \qquad (12.8)$$

or $e/n = rq$ where e/n is total expenditure per square foot and rq is the rental price times the quality index. Finally:

$$r = \frac{e}{nq} \qquad (12.9)$$

is a hedonic rent index per square foot, since it is dependent on q, which in turn depends on the characteristics $z_1, \ldots, z_n$. If $q = 1$ and quality does not matter, then the previous homogeneous housing model is valid.

An analogous form can be used, with p, the asset price of housing, similarly explained, dependent on z. The actual form in which the characteristics determine r is usually unknown, but can be estimated statistically by a computer. The procedure is of use for both property tax assessment and real estate appraisal purposes.

In practice, survey data cannot usually observe r and h separately. For example, a renter may be asked, "What is your monthly rent?" A response of $300 per month indicates e, the product of rental price and the quantity of services. A homeowner may be asked, "What is your house worth?" but he or she, by responding, say, "$50,000," is indicating the product of the asset price of housing services and a stock of such services. From (12.8), r, the rental price, is common to all in a competitive market, so:

$$\frac{e(z_1, \ldots, z_m)}{n} = rq(z_1, \ldots, z_m) \tag{12.10}$$

where e/n is the "price" as reported by owners or renters per square foot. The right side is a constant, r, times a quality index. The theory of hedonic, or quality-corrected, price indices can also be derived from consumer theory.[14] Many have attempted to estimate this relationship, and an example is illustrated in Tables 12–1 and 12–2.

Table 12–1 presents a number of housing characteristics in a study of housing in New Haven by A. Thomas King. The variables describe a house, with FULLIN taking a unit value if a house is fully insulated.[15] Included are measures of neighborhood quality, GEN Q, representing schools and security, and SERVICE for local public goods.

Table 12–2 reports asset prices for the characteristics, estimating (12.10) for homeowners rather than renters. The numbers indicate the increase in house price arising from each characteristic. Suppose we have the following description of a house.

no insulation	FULLIN = 0
no garage(s)	GARG1 = GARG2 = 0
2 bathrooms	2 + BATH = 1
other characteristics	LAVTRY = BLAUND = HARDWD
	=FIREPL = 75 + AMP = STEAM = 0
realtor evaluation—very good	VGOOD = 1
brick facing	FACBSS = 1, FACASB = 0
age ten years (one decade)	AGE = 1
size—1000 square feet	AGESQ = 1
average room size 100 square feet	SQFT = 1
no basement	SQFTSQ = 1
one story	SQFT/R = .1
lot size—2000 square feet	FINBMT = NOBMT = 0
	2 story = 0
	SIZLOT = 2
	SIZLT2 = 4
distance to New Haven in logarithms times lot size general quality and services (scaled to unity)	GEN Q = SERVICE = 1
no garbage collection or sewer connection	GARBGE = CSEWER = 0

Table 12–1 Definitions of Variables for Hedonic Price Equations

FULLIN	0–1 dummy, 1 if house has full insulation (S).
GARG2	
GARG2	0–1 dummy, if house has a one-car garage or a two-car garage.
2 + BATH	0–1 dummy, 1 if house has two or more baths.
LAVTRY	0–1 dummy, if house a partial bath.
BLAUND	0–1 dummy, 1 if house has a basement laundry area with drains and spigots.
HARDWD	0–1 dummy, if house has hardwood flooring (S).
FIREPL	Number of fireplaces in house.
75 + AMP	0–1 dummy, 1 if house has wiring to supply, more than 75 amperes.
STEAM	0–1 dummy, 1 if house has a steam heating system (S).
EXCLNT	0–1, 1 if realtor's evaluation of house quality was excellent, very good, or fair; relative to good (S).
VGOOD	
FAIR	
FACBSS	0–1 dummy, 1 if house has facing, respectively, of brick, stone, or stucco; or of asbestos shingles (R).
FACASB	
AGE	Age and age squared of home in decades (S).
AGESQ	
SQFT	
SQFTS	Floor space and floor space squared in house in thousands of square feet.
SQFTIR	Average room size in thousands of square feet.
SMROOM	Number of small, special-purpose rooms.
FINBMT	0–1 dummy, 1 if house had a finished basement or no basement.
NOBMT	
2STORY	0–1 dummy, 1 if house had more than one story (S).
SIZLOT	Lot size and lot size squared in thousands of square feet.
SIZLT2	
DISCBD	Natural logarithm of distance from house to New Haven Green multiplied by lot size.
GEN Q	A measure of the quality of the local elementary school and high school, danger of crime and fire, amount of heavy traffic on neighborhood streets, and severity of air pollution. This measure is constructed from the perceptions of the purchasers of houses in each neighborhood. A high-quality neighborhood will receive a negative score on this measure: consequently, a negative hedonic price is expected. The measure is scaled by the lot size of the house.
SERVCE	A measure of the quality of local street lighting, sweeping, and maintenance, and the quality of garbage collection service. Like GEN Q, this measure is constructed from the perceptions of purchasers, and again a high-quality neighborhood will receive a negative score. The measure is scaled by the lot size of the house.
GARBGE	0–1 dummy, 1 if house receives municipal garbage collection.
GSEWER	0–1 dummy, 1 if house has connection to city sewer.
PRICE	Sales price of house in thousands of 1967 dollars.

Note: An (S) or (R) following the variables definition indicates that values are scaled by the square feet, or the square root of the square feet, of living space.

It is possible to construct an estimate of the value of this house. The term "INTERCEPT" is common to all houses, so we have as the value, in thousands, $11.0299 + 2.4398 + .5411 + 1.5686 - 1.1324 + .0545 + 6.6966 - .8491; -28.6988/10 + .2305 \times 2 - .0005 \times 4 - .0662 \times 4 - .0662 \times 4 - .0678 - .0192$, or $17,586.32. The numbers are based on

Table 12–2 Hedonic Prices for Housing Bundle (thousands of dollars)

	All Towns*	New Haven*	Hamden	North Haven
INTERCEPT	11.0299	.8079	12.9907	15.2537
FULLIN	.6517	.6465	.9557	.6517
GARG1	.9693	.3736	1.0724	.9710
GARG2	2.9139	1.2129	3.0659	3.4264
2+BATH	1.0045	1.0026	.9081	1.5998
LAVTRY	1.0045	1.0026	.9081	1.5998
BLAUND	.5467	1.7545	−.1908	.5323
HARDWD	.8791	1.2939	.8791	.7210
FIREPL	.8488	.9662	1.1845	1.1183
75+AMP	.3868	.8676	1.1500	.8021
STEAM	.6080	.7886	.3396	.6080
GOOD	.5411	1.2916	.1337	.6380
EXCLNT	1.3412	1.1213	1.1233	1.7103
FAIR	−1.0926	.3951	.2036	−3.5326
FACBSS	1.5686	2.5228	.7144	1.4391
FACASB	−1.8922	−.8831	−1.5611	1.8992
AGE	−1.1324	−1.2323	−.1958	−.3541
AGESQ	.0545	.1033	−.0917	−.0250
SQFT	6.6966	7.7909	3.6654	1.0753
SQFTSQ	.8491	.1476	1.5856	2.0239r
SQFT/R	−28.6988	12.2736	−32.6113	−25.1213
SMROOM	.6047	−.0448	.6858	.7522
FINBMT	.6834	−.7349	1.2947	.9674
NOBMT	.2351	−1.5000	1.1513	−1.1198
2STORY	.1100	−1.3043	−.1830	.5729
SIZLOT	.2305	.7128	.3707	.0513
SIZLT2	−.0005	−.0028	−.0014	.0002
DISCBD	−.0662	−.1870	−.1523	−.0424
GEN Q	−.0678	−.2164	−.0678	−.0678
SRVCE	−.0192	−.0192	−.1041	−.0456
GARBGE	.3068	.3068	.3068	.3068
GSEWER	.4664	.4684	.4684	.4684
$\bar{R}^2$	.82	.86	.71	.75
Standard Error	4.10	4.06	3.88	3.98
Number of Observations	1802	300	407	217

multiplying the coefficient estimate by the relevant dependent variable value. The data were based on 1967 prices. Hence, it is possible from this procedure to estimate the prices of houses with different characteristics.

By describing a standard house and pricing the different characteristics, meaningful price comparisons can be made. For example, if after the same procedure the standard house, is priced at $17,000, the relative hedonic price of this house is 17,586.32/17,000, or 1.034. The priced house is of a quality 3.4 percent higher than standard.

The hedonic procedure also facilitates appraisal of houses. The characteristics are priced as evaluated by the market.

TENURE CHOICE

The usual determinants of demand for a commodity are prices, here rents and incomes. For owners, there arises an imputed rent, or user cost, from renting a house to oneself.

Let the renter have the rental price r_R per unit of housing quality, now standardized, and income y_R. If the price of other goods is p_g, a utility level dependent on prices and income, $v_R(r_R, p_g, y_R)$, can be constructed. If rents increase, the consumer is worse off, but if income increases, utility increases.

Now suppose the renter has the option of buying the unit in which he lives and is deciding whether to exercise it. This does not include any imputation for the benefit attributable to being a homeowner. The user cost or rental price of owning is r_O, and the income obtained from owning is y_O, with corresponding utility. The decision rule, then, is to purchase if the utility obtained from owning is greater than that from renting.

The decision rule is:

$$V_O > V_R \quad \text{own } I = 1$$
$$V_O > V_R \quad \text{rent } I = 0 \tag{12.11}$$

where I is some index of the degree of homeownership. How these prices and incomes are determined depends on taxes, risk preferences, incomes, household size, stage in the life cycle, tastes, and other factors.

Some indication of observed tenure choice is contained in Table 12–3. This indicates tenure choice for England and Wales, the United States, and Canada. In the United States and Canada, about three in every five households are owners, and this conclusion appears to hold within local regions as well.[16]

Figures 12–1a and 12–1b indicate the patterns of consumer demand for housing. The personal characteristics of a homeowner are indicated by x, exemplified by age, sex, marital status, and race. Several studies have concluded that these characteristics are important in the

Table 12–3 International Housing Comparisons, 1970–71

Century	Owners (percentage)	Renters (percentage)	Household Size (persons)	Rooms/ Dwelling	Persons/ Room
England/Wales	50.1	49.9	2.9	4.9	0.6
United States	62.9	37.1	3.1	5.1	0.6
Canada	60.0	40.0	3.5	5.4	0.6

Source: British Columbia Ministry of Lands, Parks and Housing, *International Housing Comparisons,* Victoria, 1982.

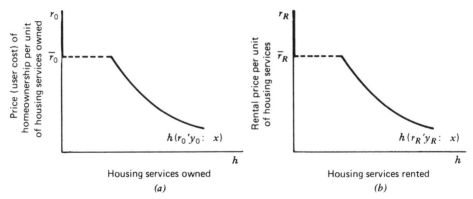

Figure 12–1. Housing tenure choices. (*a*) Ownership. (*b*) Rental.

United States. Housing demand, h, depends on the price of housing, r and y, which depends on ownership status.

A comparison of Boston and Baltimore 1970 census data reveals that a two-person husband–wife family with the head of household under 25 years of age, white, and with income under \$5000 has only a 6.3 (Boston) and 10.4 (Baltimore) percent probability of owning a home.[17] Blacks with the same characteristics fare even worse, at 2.1 and 3.5 percent, respectively.

Homeownership probabilities increase with age. Based on the same study, a household head in the 45–65 age group has a better than 90 percent chance of ownership. Homeownership also increased with family size, up to a point, and with income.

Other U.S. studies indicate that female household heads are less likely to be owners, and that ownership increases with distance from the CBD, confirming the strong negative correlation between homeownership and blacks.[18]

Figure 12–1a is the demand curve for an owner. As the price of ownership rises, the household reduces its demand for owner housing services, until at some ultimate price, $\bar{r}_O$, it finds renting more advantageous, and housing demand declines to zero. The demand curve then jumps to zero, and is discontinuous. Analogously, if rental becomes expensive and homeownership costs are held constant, people will ultimately shift from renting to owning.

In the United States, tax advantages accrue to homeownership, and income tax brackets are not adjusted for inflation. Hence, to avoid "bracket creep," individuals require methods of protecting or tax sheltering their income. The ability to offset inflation through homeownership provides an incentive to purchase homes when general prices are rising, and to switch tenure. This problem requires knowledge of the institutional structure, to derive r_O and r_R.

TAX POLICY AND EFFECTIVE PRICES FOR RENTING AND HOMEOWNERSHIP

A number of variables enter the calculation of the user cost or effective price of homeownership.[19] Several mortgages may be outstanding, with interest rate m_i and principal M_i, or payments $m_i M_i + \ldots + m_I M_I$, where the payments are for interest only. This can be rewritten as $MI = \bar{m}M$ where M is total mortgage debt and $\bar{m}$ is the weighted average interest rate payable.

The homeowner also has:

V market value of house

α rate of return on housing capital (opportunity cost of not investing funds elsewhere)

t effective property tax rate

q expenditures on depreciation, maintenance, insurance, and utilities, as a fraction of house value

ΔV capital gains or appreciation, in dollars

with a time period set at one year. Risk enters the calculation of capital gains. The owner forms expectations on these, and they may be positive or negative. Further, liquidity is curtailed by the transaction costs of changing location or of discharging mortgages. The homeowner makes a set of decisions on gross housing expenditures, some of which are recovered because housing is partly consumption, partly investment, and partly a tax shelter.

The tax shelter is that portion of housing expenditures which is exampt from tax and depends on actual legislation. First, most jurisdictions exempt net income, or the return on owner's equity, from taxation. This is:

$$NI = \alpha(V - M) + \Delta V \qquad (12.12)$$

or αV for those who hold clear title, or zero mortgage. In the United States the capital gains, ΔV, are nominally taxed, but can be deferred indefinitely. Other provisions arise in tax legislation, and are summarized in Table 12–4.[20] For the United States, the shelter term is:

$$S_{US} = NI + MI + tV - \Delta V \qquad (12.13)$$

assuming that capital gains on housing are eventually taxed. For a Canadian owner:

$$S_C = NI \qquad (12.14)$$

and in the U.K.:

$$S_{UK} = NI + MI + tV \qquad (12.15)$$

Table 12–4 Comparison of Alternative Treatment of Homeowner Housing Expenditures—Whether Part of Tax Shelter Term

Term	Canada	United States	United Kingdom
1. Gross imputed income on market value of house αV	Included[a]	Included in shelter	Included
2. Net imputed income on "equity" (less mortgage debt) $\alpha V - MI$	Included	Included	Included
3. Property taxes tV	Excluded	Included	Included
4. Operating expenses qV	Excluded	Excluded[b]	Excluded
5. Capital gains ΔV	Included	Excluded[c]	Included

Notes: [a]In Canada there is partial exclusion, since the equity portion is in the shelter.
[b]Some expenses are deductible, notably some taxes on materials.
[c]Capital gains can be deferred by a rollover provision, and persons over 55 have a one-time $100,000 exemption.

since capital gains on housing are tax-exempt in Canada and the United Kingdom.

The owner makes gross expenditures on housing for mortgage interest, MI, property taxes, tV, maintenance, qV, and the opportunity cost on his or her equity, NI, to cover the capital gains arising on housing, assuming these are positive. Then gross, pre-sheltered expenditures are:

$$GROSS = MI + tV + qV + NI \qquad (12.16)$$

and this represents an expenditure on housing services. Dividing by house value, V, the price of ownership is:

$$r_O = \frac{GROSS}{V} = m + t + q + n \qquad (12.17)$$

where $m = \bar{m}M/V$ is mortgage interest divided by house value, and $n = \alpha(V - M)/V$ is net equity income divided by house value.

If the homeowner had no taxable income, there would be no benefit from the shelter, and $GROSS/V$ would be an estimate of the user cost, or implicit rental, in percentage form. This is the sum of mortgage, tax, maintenance and opportunity costs.

The owner with any taxable income receives the benefit of a shelter. Let marginal and average tax rates on personal income be T.[21] so, the U.S. homeowner saves TS_{US}, and this is subtracted from gross expenditure. Gross expenditure net of shelter is:

$$
\begin{aligned}
NET &= GROSS - TS_{US} \\
&= MI + tV + qV + NI - T(NI + MI + tV - \Delta V) \qquad (12.18) \\
&= (1 - T)(MI + tV + NI) + qV + T\,\Delta V
\end{aligned}
$$

and dividing by V yields the rent paid by an owner to himself or herself as a percentage of market value. If p is the percentage increase of capital gains, this implies:

$$r_0(US) = (1 - T)(m + t + n) + q + Tp \qquad (12.19)$$

For example, consider an owner in the 40 percent marginal rate for federal and state income taxes, paying $800 a month interest on a mortgage of $80,000, with a house valued at $100,000. Suppose the following data obtain:

$$\begin{array}{ll} T = .4 & t = .01 \\ m = .096 & p = .10 \\ n = .13 & q = .05 \end{array}$$

So $m = \$9600/\$100,000$, or $.096$, and $T = .4$. His or her equity of $20,000 could be invested alternatively at 15 percent annually, yielding $.15 \times 20,000/100,000$, or $.03$. Capital gains on the house are expected at 10 percent, and so $n = .03 + .10 = .13$. The owner obtains all the capital gains despite having only 20 percent equity, an example of leverage. Property taxes and maintenance are, respectively, 1 and 5 percent. Thus, the expenditure without shelter (12.17) yields annual rent $u_0 = .096 + .01 + .05 + .13$, or $.286$.

The rent after shelter (12.19) is $.6 \times (.096 + .01 + .13) + .05 + .4 \times .10$, or $.232$. The ratio of rent after shelter to that before shelter is $.232/.286$, or 81 percent. This assumes that capital gains are taxed, but an indefinite deferral is possible. Taking this into account, the term Tp disappears from (12.19), further reducing the rent after shelter to $.192$, implying a reduction of almost one-third.

Two more observations are worth noting. First, for the same house, the higher the tax rate T of the household, the lower the sheltered rent. Hence, the individual does not face constant prices for housing services, nor are these prices exogenous. Second, capital gains occupy a central role. The assumption of 10 percent gains makes a substantial difference in rent calculations.

For Canada, the net expenditure is $NET = GROSS - TS_C$, and dividing by V:

$$r_0(c) = (1 - T)n + m + t + q \qquad (12.20)$$

or $.6 \times .13 + .096 + \cdot 01 + .05 = .234$, or 81.8 percent of the cost without shelter. In all cases, it is assumed that the alternative investment must compensate the owner for the capital gains earned in housing. This yields the rental price of housing for owners.

The income of owners, Y_0, is the sum of income after tax from other sources and net income from housing. So:

$$y_0 = (1 - T)y + NI \qquad (12.21)$$

assuming NI is untaxed and y is nonhousing income. For a renter, none of these considerations applies unless a subsidy program exists on rent or income.

The gap between tax-sheltered rent and the rent payable by a person with no taxable income leads to distortions in the housing market. The magnitude depends on the price and income elasticities of demand for housing, our subject for the following section.

PRICE AND INCOME ELASTICITIES OF HOUSING DEMAND

There has been extensive research on the income elasticity of demand for housing. If income changes by 1 percent, the objective is to determine the percentage response in demand. As a range, de Leeuw suggests that housing has an inelastic income demand for renters, with income elasticity ranging from 0.6 to 0.9, and from 0.7 to 1.7 for owners.[22] However, it is argued that when certain biases are eliminated, the income elasticity should be less than 1 and in the range of 0.7 to 0.9[23] for both groups.

As far as the price elasticity of demand is concerned, there is again a substantial range. A number of studies indicate that people are very price responsive in the housing market, with an estimate of -1.5 well grounded in empirical evidence. However, specification error and tax considerations combine to reduce this estimate to -0.75, indicating an inelastic demand.[24]

Some of the problems encountered in attempting to estimate these price and income responses are the following.

Use of aggregate data. Some researchers use average data, for example, as published in the United States decennial *Census of Housing*. There may be aggregation problems.

Lack of adjustment for taxes. Despite the role of taxes, many researchers have insufficient data to adjust for taxes.

The estimation of these price and income elasticities makes it possible to measure the losses caused by the tax distortions. The effect is indicated in Figure 12–2. Assume that each individual can purchase an unlimited quantity of housing at the prevailing rental price, r_O. Suppose this is indicated at the intersection of the compensated demand function, representing the effect of changes in income to leave a consumer no better off when prices change.

Clearly, price and income elasticity estimates are required here to derive the compensated demand. Let the rental price of housing fall to r_O (shelter) because of the tax benefits, resulting in increasing demand for housing ownership. The shaded triangle may be considered an excess burden in the sense that consumers are subsidized to purchase more housing than they otherwise would.

Since the triangle is an area, its unit of measurement is the product of r and h, in dollars. Based on a panel survey in the United States

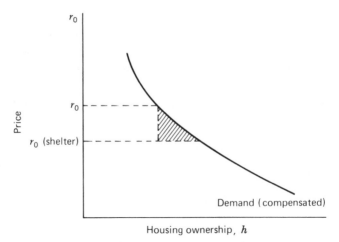

Figure 12–2. Subsidies to owner-occupied housing.

for 1970, an average excess burden of \$107 is estimated. The largest calculation arises for those in the \$16–\$20,000 income bracket that year, who have \$15,829 average disposable income, live in a house worth \$26,665 on average, and possess \$155 of excess burden.[25] The issue is whether or not this is large in comparison with other forms of taxation.

HOUSING SUPPLY: PRODUCTION

There are two sources of increased housing supply: new construction and renovation.[26] The typical method to specify the increases in supply comes from a production function aggregating land and improvements.

In terms of constructing data, suppose the market price of a newly constructed single-family home is known. The price of the house is equal to the price of land times land used, plus the price of improvements times the quantity improvements. Typically, the price of the lot to the builder is known, and to this should be added interest charges during construction, property taxes, and insurance. Suppose all builders have access to the same price information. In practice, builders may face a price distribution necessitating a search to secure the lowest price, and some builders may receive lower prices from dealing in large volume.

Once separate data on land and improvements are available, they may be combined in production function estimation. Some of the more important possibilities are indicated in Figure 12–3. Land is A, improvements N, with prices P_A and P_N. Figure 12–3a indicates the situation for a fixed-coefficients technology. This implies that land and improvements occur in fixed proportions and cannot be substituted. For example, each house requires a lot with a frontage of 50 feet. In

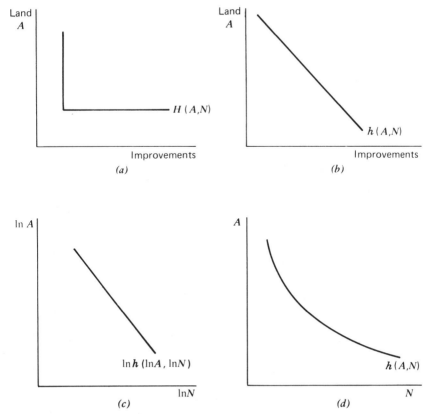

Figure 12–3. Specifications of housing production. (*a*) Fixed coefficients. (*b*) Perfect substitutes. (*c*) Cobb-Douglas. (*d*) General substitution.

Figure 12–3b, land and improvements are perfectly substitutable. Any change in the relative price of one reduces its demand to zero. The Cobb–Douglas function is linear in the logarithms of land and improvements (Figure 12–3c). Finally, a more general form exhibits some curvature, as shown in Figure 12–3d. The curvature depends on the rate of substitution between land and improvements. Knowing the price ratio of improvements to land as P_N/P_A, the elasticity of substitution is the percentage change in the land-improvements ratio when the price ratio changes. Percentage changes can be expressed as changes in the logarithm, so:

$$\sigma = \frac{\Delta 1n\ A/N}{\Delta 1n\ P_N/P_A} \tag{12.22}$$

where σ is the elasticity of substitution. Suppose lot prices increase, but construction costs remain constant. Then the denominator decreases. Builders will tend to economize on land and reduce A/N, so this decreases. If z is less than 1, the reduction in relative use of land is insufficient to compensate for the price increase, and it is relatively difficult to substitute. Most estimates of this elasticity confirm this finding, with the numbers ranging between 0.5 and 1.3, and averaging 0.9.

This difficulty in substitution suggests other issues on the supply side, including the following.

Technological change.   If there are methods to improve output with the same land and improvements—for example, by reducing wasted lumber or reducing construction time—supply increases.

Restrictions on usage.   A myriad of regulations applies to the construction industry. In the United States, the administration of building codes occurs at the local level, with communities free to choose their own standards. Regulations on site usage and coverage, together with the restrictions on types of materials, increase the cost of new construction. The benefit arises in the alleged improvement in safety and health standards, but typically these provisions do not apply to existing construction. In Canada there is a national building code, tending to standardize regulations.

Further, there is some question as to the policy implications of estimating a housing technology containing land and improvements. "Improvements" is an amorphous term encompassing labor, materials, and capital equipment separately. Adjustments for quality on the supply side are required as much as on the demand side. For wood-frame construction, #1 and #2 Douglas fir are of better quality than utility grade and SPF (spruce, pine, fir). It is therefore ideal to construct prices of all these lumber products for comparison purposes. This also applies to energy conservation in the appropriate use of insulation, double-glazed windows, and heating. Among houses passing inspection under building codes, there remains a distribution of quality. Embedded items such as storm drains or foundations cannot easily be observed by the buyer.

These considerations suggest that a broader examination of housing production is required, to include regulations and a wider selection of inputs. This is particularly necessary given government involvement on the supply side through programs of subsidizing mortgages for builders, placing subsidized land on the market, and programs requiring a prescribed minority employment content.

HOUSING SUPPLY: REGULATIONS

Building Codes

Building codes[27] and similar regulations reduce the choice of construction and housing. The exception is Houston, which has neither a building code nor zoning regulations, although restrictive covenants often serve in their place. The arguments in favor of building codes point out the benefit of regulation when consumers are ignorant of construction technology. Private markets for such quality control may fail because of difficulties in evaluating quality. Also, there are potential negative externalities on neighbors from low quality construction posing a fire or health hazard.

Opposing arguments center on costs of compliance. The requirement for frequent inspections increases the time period of construction. The use of materials with quality standards higher than otherwise demanded also increases costs. Several jurisdictions reserve some or all subtrade work, notably in electrical and plumbing services, to licensed or unionized workers. Local enforcement restricts the mobility of construction labor, particularly in the United States.

There has been some debate as to the degree of cost saving that deregulation would bring. Some researchers claim that the costs of the code are relatively small, increasing new construction costs by about 2 percent, but other estimates are as high af 15 percent.[28]

Oster and Quigley examine four modifications to the building code that would reduce materials demand and, hence, costs.

1. Using 2×3-inch instead of 2×4-inch studs on nonload-bearing partitions

2. Placing studs 24 inches apart instead of the present 16 inches

3. Using preassembled drain, waste, and ventilating systems

4. Using nonmetallic cable instead of metal conduit for wiring[29]

Applying estimates to a $50,000 house, the removal of the standard on studs would save $400, and the removal of other standards on wood stress would save an additional $1372. Eliminating prohibitions on preassembled water fixtures would save between $700 and $1000, and permission to use nonmetallic cable would save between $200 and $400. The historic trend toward acceptance of these innovations has been examined, and shown to be highly correlated with the eductional level of the chief municipal building official; the more education the greater the acceptance.

Clearly, further research is required on the costs and benefits of building codes and restrictions on new technology. It appears that many of the regulations have no practical benefit, for otherwise they would be applied. Rather, the regulation may serve as a tax on new construction and as a costly market imperfection.

Rent Controls

Rent controls have been applied in many jurisdictions. Consider the static illustration in Figure 12–4a. The variable of the vertical axis is rent expenditure, and both supply and demand curves are drawn to be extremely price-inelastic, in keeping with estimates. Note that since

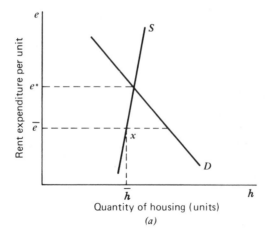

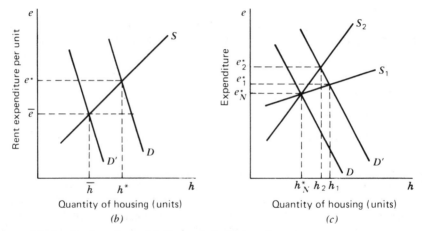

Figure 12–4. Rent controls. (a) No uncontrolled sector. (b) Rent controls, controlled sector. (c) Uncontrolled sector.

supply is perfectly inelastic, the rent control transfers some of the economic rent of landlords to the tenants.

For rent controls to be binding, the rent level, e, as a maximum must be below e^*, the rent level that clears supply and demand. The number of housing services in the market is h, and there is an excess demand, for rental units of x. People tend to search longer, the benefit being the ability to pay a lower rent in a rent-controlled unit.

The excess demanders in x and the landlords are the losers, but there is also an allocative inefficiency. With the lower rents of e, the opportunity cost of not using the units for rental purposes is lower and, ultimately, the number of units available declines as landlords do not reinvest in maintaining existing rental units. This shifts the supply curve to the left, further exacerbating the problem. New rental unit construction is also discouraged by rent controls. Therefore, long-term rent controls tend to reduce the number of rental units.

It is not clear either that average rents are reduced by the controls, paradoxical as that may appear. Suppose there is an uncontrolled sector. In typical legislation, there are exemptions for new construction and "amateur landlords" where either single rooms in a dwelling inhabited by the owner are rented or there are less than a prescribed number of units. Further, even if there is no officially uncontrolled sector, the presence of x may encourage illegal renting or the payment of "key money" or other similar inducements and black market practices.

The presence of the controlled sector is described in Figures 12–4b and 12–4c. The controlled sector contains excess demand, and ultimately the demand curve must shift downward through (e, h). In the uncontrolled sector, demand increases from D to D'. Two scenarios are indicated, depending on the elasticity of supply. Supply curve S is relatively elastic, assuming that a relatively large number of new units comes on stream with rent increases. The initial equilibrium was at (e^*_N, h^*_N) but now this changes to (e^*_1, h^*_1).

If there were no rental controls, then average rent expenditure per unit, assuming the markets remained separated, would be:

$$e_N = \frac{(e^*h^* + e^*_N h^*_N)}{(h^* + h^*_N)} \quad (12.23)$$

But after rent controls, average rent in the two cases is:

$$e_1 = \frac{(\bar{e}\bar{h} + e^*_1 h_1)}{(\bar{h} + h_1)} \quad (12.24)$$

and

$$e_2 = \frac{(\bar{e}\bar{h} + e^*_2 h_2)}{(\bar{h} + h_2)} \quad (12.25)$$

and it is possible for e_2 to exceed e_N, because of the crowding in the uncontrolled market. Furthermore, the hedonic rent faced by the tenants in the controlled sector is e/q, where q is a quality index along the lines already discussed. As controls continue and maintenance is reduced, q declines, implying e/q increases. The failure to account for negative quality change results in overstatement of the case for rent controls reducing rents.

Figure 12–5 summarizes the effects of rent controls. From an initial equilibrium of $D_0 = S_0$ (with price of P_0 and quantity of Q_0) we find a sudden increase in demand to D_1. Such short-run spurts in demand are consistent with observed fluctuations that can result from rapid increases in in-migrants or disposable income combined with de-

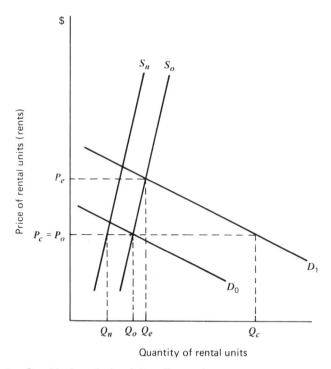

Figure 12–5. Graphical analysis of the effects of rent control.

clines in interest rates, and may even be government demand stimulating policies. As a result of this surge in demand, price should rise to P_e, the equilibrium price in the absence of controls. However, public authorities constrain price to its initial level P_0, also denoted here as P_c or the controlled-rent level.

Several points can be made about the effects of such controls. First, whereas at P_e (and Q_e) there is no excess demand, under rent controls excess demand exists and is equal to Q_c minus Q_0. The quantity supplied remains constant at Q_0 in the short run, while the demand on demand curve D_1 soars to Q_c at controlled price P_c. Thus, rent control converts a short-run increase in demand into considerable excess demand. Second, on the supply side, whereas without controls supply would normally rise to Q_e from Q_0, there is no supply response since price does not increase, exacerbating the rental shortage. Finally, to make matters worse, in the long run the supply curve shifts backward as landlords convert rental stock to condominium tenure and in extreme situations abandon their rental buildings completely, since they cannot earn an economic return with rent controls in place. Thus, effective supply falls from Q_0 at price P_c to Q_n, further worsening the excess demand and setting in motion additional cutbacks in supply and additional disincentives to rental housing investment.

Again, the supply to the controlled sector is ultimately reduced, further increasing rents in the long run. If the uncontrolled sector has a perfectly inelastic supply, the total amount available declines.

There are other regulations restricting the supply of housing. Land-use restrictions discussed in Chapters 5 and 11 also ultimately reduce the supply of housing. The myriad legal restrictions of zoning and environmental considerations detailed in Chapter 8 also reduce the supply. Productivity in construction could be enhanced by relaxing many of the present regulations.

Nevertheless, new construction represents only a small proportion, typically less than 5 percent, of the stock. The remaining potential supply is that from existing houses. Here, the regulations of the real estate brokerage industry may act to reduce availability of houses, or make the marketing of units less simple.

HOUSING POLICY

General Problems

The above discussions have spurred initiatives in the policy area of the housing market. *The Report of the President's Commission on Housing* examined the growing problem of affordability. The rapid inflation of the postwar era in the United States and Canada, together with demand for housing as a hedge, have created difficulty in home-ownership.[30]

The commission examined the problems faced by young people in purchasing a home, elderly "empty nesters", (who have children out of the home) in selling their house, and of newcomers to large cities in finding rental units. However, there is recognition of the general improvement in housing quality. For instance, in the United States, in the 1940 census over 40 percent of the housing units lacked plumbing facilities while by the 1980 census this had declined to about 4 percent.[31]

Low-income individuals and families in both the United States and Canada faced an increasing affordability problem during the 1970s, as the ratio of rental or user cost to income increased. On the supply side, the United States has established the Section 8 New Construction and Substantial Rehabilitation Program, providing a subsidy to rehabilitate or construct low-income housing, with rents accordingly reduced. In Canada, repair is subsidized by the Residential Rehabilitation Assistance Program (RRAP).

These programs are specific to the housing unit and not the low-income person. Two major problems arise. First, given relatively inelastic supply, the benefits of these programs may be capitalized in land prices. This increases user costs for the owners and the required subsidy, if rents are to be retained. Second, such policies may not account for changed tenant circumstances. If tenant income rises above the designated threshold, ejection may be difficult or impossible. The

United Kingdom, with its "council houses" owned by local governments and rented at low rents to tenants, has had this experience. The rent control experience in New York has created a secondary market for subletting.

The Commission proposes that any housing subsidies be directed to the person or family and not the dwelling. This permits tenants to choose location, is arguably simple to administer, and does not have the objections described above. In the United States, shelter allowances were provided on an experimental basis under the Experimental Housing Allowance Program (EHAP). The increased income of the recipients of shelter allowances can facilitate upgrading of properties without incurring the transaction costs of a move.

On directly owned public housing, the Commission propose decentralization, with local governments given more autonomy. In some cases, the direct involvement of the public sector implies similar costs to those in Section 8, essentially a private but subsidized program. In others, the government is an efficient housing producer.[32] This excludes the fact that, for the United States, in the directly operated case the revenues for public housing programs are derived from floating municipal bonds. The interest on municipal bonds is tax-free, and a tax expenditure, or subsidy, to issuer and holder is involved.

Housing for the Elderly and Handicapped

In North America, the elderly constitute a growing percentage of the population. In the United States, in the 1980 census 11.2 percent of the population was over 65 years old. This is projected to rise to 20 percent by the year 2030. One problem that arises with the elderly is their being house-rich and cash-poor. A large amount of equity, frequently clear title, is locked in the house. At the same time, cash flows of the elderly are relatively low.

One possible solution is the introduction of a reverse mortgage, where an investor takes a claim against a house in exchange for providing cash. This requires an investor with no short-term cash requirements, possibly a pension fund or life insurance company. Given variability in life expectancy, the contracts may be for a fixed duration. An alternative mechanism that provides cash flow is sale and leaseback. Here, an investor purchases the house, with resale to the individual owner. Given that in the United States persons over the age of 55 have a one-time exclusion of $125,000 from capital gains, this is an attractive option.

Zoning and municipal regulations frequently pose rigid restrictions on single-family house definitions. The regulations may prohibit rental of space in single-family homes or unrelated individuals sharing the same housing unit. Given high transaction costs, which may be higher than average for the elderly, individuals tend to stay in existing locations.[33] The cost of relaxing such regulations is increased density of population. The benefit is the sharing of overhead housing re-sources and a more efficient utilization of space. Alternatively, if trans-action costs were reduced, households could more efficiently choose smaller or communal housing, and would not be locked into existing accommodation.

Tenure Choice and Public Policy

Homeownership As noted earlier, approximately two of three house-holds in the United States are homeowners, despite demographic shifts in household composition with smaller family sizes and a greater proportion of households being single individuals and single parents. In the 1940 census, the homeownership rate was less than 50 percent in the United States. In terms of quality change, the average size of new conventional single-family homes increased about 20 percent be-tween 1964 and 1978, to an area of 1700 square feet. Subsequently, family size and energy cost considerations have caused a zero increase in house size.[34]

Apart from the user cost or price of homeownership, there are other prices associated with purchase. Financial markets are imperfect, partly because the credit risk characteristics of individuals are not com-pletely observable. Financial institutions do not have advance knowl-edge of a homeowner's ability to make payments on mortgages, remain as a stable household, or remain employed. Partly as an offset, down payment requirements as a percentage of total purchase price have in-creased. If capital markets were perfect, individuals or families would have the option of making no down payment. Another market imper-fection is the use of debt service ratios in computing PIT, or principal, interest, and tax payments as a proportion of cash income. These ra-tios typically range between 29 and 33 percent, and if debt service ra-tios are higher than indicated levels, the household cannot qualify for a mortgage. This requires the household to secure a mortgage debt with both a house and earnings or income-generating capacity.

Also affecting housing demand are demographic trends on house-hold and family formation, and the proportion of the population in the home-buying group aged 20 to 35. Finally, there is the rental price of homeownership, r_O. This rental price also includes the price of houses, which may capitalize various favorable tax treatments of owner-occupancy. During the 1960s and 1970s, deductibility of mort-gage interest and property taxes and sheltered treatment of capital gains implied a continuing subsidy to homeownership in the United States. Real income increases and "bracket creep" with high rates of inflation reinforced this trend.

In terms of policy, reduced rates of inflation or, even stronger, zero or negative inflation rates unravel the benefits to tax-sheltered housing. Further, marginal tax rates have been reduced in the United

States, also reducing the capital value of any tax shelter. The three-year program in the United States to reduce applicable federal tax rates by 25 percent has had the effect of raising the user cost of housing and reducing house prices.[35]

In Canada, the personal income tax was indexed to the Consumer Price Index commencing in 1974. Since the main shelter provision is the exemption of capital gains, reduced inflation rates also lessen the benefits from homeownership. The other main subsidy in Canada is the ability to use a house as a bank. Individuals have an incentive to discharge the mortgage as their first investment, since the interest is not deductible and the flow of housing services is not taxable.

In the United States, the policy initiative appears to be in the direction of reducing marginal tax rates. This is also true in Canada, where in 1981 the top combined federal and provincial rate was reduced to 50 percent. This policy has the effect of reducing the value of housing subsidies.

Rental About one-third of all households live in rental units, and of these about seven-eighths live in privately owned units. There has been extensive recommendation that rent control be removed. Rent controls have several effects, as outlined below.

1. They convey a property right on existing (and long-term) tenants, who tend to be immobile. They contribute to reducing mobility and migration from low-growth areas.

2. The property right may be sublet by leaseholders.

3. Landlords have no incentive to repair or maintain.

4. Landlords have increased costs in justifying pass-throughs of existing costs.

5. Under-the-table payments may result.

6. New construction is discouraged even if exempt, for there is a probability of controls being applied. Some potential tenants of new housing remain in subsidized, controlled units.

7. New entrants (young and mobile) face high rents.

On the supply side, there are various measures affecting rental housing. One is permitting deductibility by losses on rental property against other income. Another is permitting expensing rather than capitalization of interest incurred and taxes paid during construction. Both Canada and the United States have an investment tax credit: Up to 10 percent of an allowable investment can be deducted from tax otherwise payable. The investment tax credit typically applies to equipment and machinery and not to structures. The President's Commission on Housing recommends its extension in the United States to cover the rehabilitation of rental housing.[36]

SUMMARY

Throughout the preceding discussion we have touched on a number of factors that are relevant to housing market analysis. Demographic trends are important. As the large "baby boom" population of the 1950s and 1960s moves through the housing market, followed by a much smaller cohort, demand for housing will decline. Further, disequilibrium may arise in the housing market from a number of sources. For instance, in the United States mortgages provided by savings and loan institutions are an additional potential source of disequilibrium because of regulation. (We discussed these financial impediments in Chapter 6.)

Much has also been written on discrimination in housing markets. Particularly, as noted in the results reported, blacks have lower prospects for homeownership, even when income, age, education, and other factors are allowed for. Discrimination increases the price blacks must pay for housing. Further, competitive models of discrimination argue that those with a taste for not selling to minorities lose, since their effective market is smaller. This may not apply if neighbors also object to having blacks in the community. It is the case that factors such as income and education, if allowed for, reduce but do not eliminate the lower observed ownership rates for blacks. Interactive terms on race, sex of head of household, and marital status may further pinpoint the important characteristics affecting housing. For example, it is also known that women are less likely to be owners than men. Given the tax subsidy to ownership and against renters, if the problem arises from discrimination and not the preferences of blacks for renting, a large transfer of incomes is flowing from blacks to whites.

Another important aspect concerns housing and inflation. Housing is an important part of the Consumer Price Index, but this index has severe errors in measurement. Some of these are:

1. Individuals are assumed to renew their mortgages at current interest rates every six months in the United States, and every 60 months in Canada.

2. No allowance is made for capital gains in housing, either in increasing the income of the homeowner or in reducing his or her effective operating cost.

3. The user cost for owner-occupied housing in Consumer Price Index measurement includes interest and maintenance charges. However, the appropriate measure for the United States is interest charges net of tax, plus maintenance, less capital gains. It has been shown that the Consumer Price Index increased from 1.00 in 1968 to 2.369 (without adjustments, but to 2.014 with) by 1980.[37] In other words, the housing component alone causes the inflation index to be overstated by about 2 percent annually.

4. The distortion induced by inflation, fixed-rate and term mortgages, and the tax system is considerable. This distortion has made housing an attractive investment in inflationary times. A cautionary note is needed. If the user cost is the

sum of interest rates after taxes and maintenance, less capital gains, then if inflation declines or prices fall, housing becomes an unattractive investment. Certainly, the experience of the 1960s and 1970s suggests that housing is not a personal shelter but rather a tax shelter.

Footnotes

1. For the United Kingdom, see M. A. King, "An Econometric Model of Tenure Choice and Demand for Housing as a Joint Decision," *Journal of Public Economics* 14(1980):137–159. Extensive wealth time series for the United States are contained in P. Cagan and R. Lipsey, *The Financial Effects of Inflation* (New York: National Bureau of Economic Research), 1978.

2. For Canda, the 1974 estimate was 34.1 percent of total expenditures representing housing. This is a composite of owning and renting costs taken from the Survey of Consumer Finances, as represented in the *Consumer Price Index* (Ottawa: Statistics Canada), Catalogue 62-001.

3. The Canadian data are as summarized in M. Goldberg, *The Housing Problem: A Real Crisis?* (Vancouver, B. C.: University of British Columbia Press), 1983.

4. Douglas Diamond, "Taxes, Inflation, Speculation and the Cost of Homeownership," *Journal of the American Real Estate and Urban Economics Association,* Fall 1980.

5. *The Report of the President's Commission on Housing* (Washington, D.C.: Government Printing Office), 1982.

6. The data are from "The Housing Industry" of Merrill Lynch, January 1982, p. 28, cited in the Report of the President's Commission on Housing, p. 181.

7. The homogeneous housing model was pioneered by R. F. Muth, "The Spatial Structure of the Housing Market," *Papers and Proceedings of the Regional Science Association* 7(1961):207–220, and developed further in *Cities and Housing* (Chicago: University of Chicago Press), 1969. See also E. S. Mills, "An Aggregate Model of Resource Allocation in a Metropolitan Area," *American Economic Review Papers and Proceedings* 57(1967):200–209; and M. J. Beckmann, "On the Distribution of Urban Rent and Residential Density," *Journal of Economic Theory* 1 (1969):60–67.

8. Muth, *Cities and Housing, op. cit.,* Chapter 7, pp. 139–158.

9. Suppose that:

$$r(d) = ae^{-bd}$$

Then, marginal rents are:

$$\frac{\partial r}{\partial d} = abe^{-bd}$$

and marginal rents times housing services consumed are:

$$h(d)\frac{\partial r}{\partial d} = abh(d)e^{-bd}$$

If transport costs are constant at the margin at ct, as in the text, then:

$$abh(d)e^{-bd} = ct$$

Whereupon:

$$h(d) = \frac{cte^{bd}}{ab}$$

but c, t, a, and b are constants, and we can define $c^* = ct/ab$. So:

$$h(d) = c^*e^{bd}$$

and with $b > 0$, housing services consumed increase exponentially with distance from the CBD.

10. See Mills, *op. cit.*, and D. Pines, "The Exponential Density Function: A Comment," *Journal of Regional Science* 10(1970):107–110.

11. Some legislation provides for a rollover of capital gains, with capital gains not taxed if an individual purchases another property within a specified time period.

12. The number of papers in this area is extensive. These include E. F. Brigham, "The Determinants of Residential Land Values," *Land Economics 41* (1965):325–334; R. G. Ridker and J. A. Henning, "The Determinants of Residential Property Values with Special References to Air Polution," *Review of Economics and Statistics* 49(1967):246–257; J. F. Kain and J. M. Quigley, "Measuring the Value of Housing Quality," *Journal of the American Statistical Association* 65(1970):532–548; D. M. Grether and P. Mieszkowski, "Determinants of Real Estate Values," *Journal of Urban Economics* 1(1974):127–146; and A. T. King, "The Demand for Housing: Integrating the Roles of Journey-to-Work, Neighborhood Quality and Prices," in N. E. Terleckyj, ed., *Household Production and Consumption* (New York: National Bureau of Economic Research), 1976, pp. 451–484. The theoretical development is in S. Rosen, "Hedonic Prices and Implicit Markets," *Journal of Political Economy* 82(1974):34–56.

13. The basic requirement is that the function $h(z_1, \ldots, z_m)$ be linearly homogeneous, so that division of all elements by n and multiplication by n does not alter the value of the function.

14. Suppose the consumer is facing the problem of minimizing expenditure subject to utility being above a target level.

15. This exemplifies a problem with such binary values, for full insulation may have different meanings, depending on quality and thickness of material. An alternative possibility is to convert insulation measures to a common form, for example, an R-factor, if this is available.

16. For example, for the province of British Columbia, 63.3 percent of households are owners, and 36.7 percent are renters, based on the 1971 Census of Canada. Average household size, rooms per dwellings, and persons per room are, respectively, 3.2, 5.2, and 0.6.

17. See M. M. Li, "A Logit Model of Homeownership," *Econometrica* 45(1977):1081–1098. The theory operates by constructing odds of homeownership, being $f_i/(1-f_i)$ where f_i is the probability of ownership. Then the logarithm of the odds, or logit, is expressed as a linear relation of the characteristics, here:

$$\ln\frac{(f_i)}{(1-f_i)} = \beta_0 + \beta_1 x_1 + \beta_2 x_2 + \ldots + \beta_N x_N$$

where there are N characteristics, and the terms are the effects of the characteristics on the logit, to be estimated.

The family described in the test is the reference, or standard group, with all x values zero, and only a constant term. The constant was estimated at -2.699, so:

$$\ln\frac{(f_i)}{(1-f_i)} = -2.699$$

whereupon $f_i/(1-f_i) = 0.0672$, and $f_i = 0.0672 - 0.0672\ f_i$, or $f_i = 0.0672/1.0672$, or 6.3 percent as in the text.

18. See L. F. Lee and R. P. Trost, "Estimation of Some Limited Dependent Variable Models with Application to Housing Demand," *Journal of Econometrics* 8(1978) 357–382.

19. The pioneering work in this area is by D. Laidler, "Income Tax Incentives for Owner-Occupied Housing," in A. C. Harberger and M. J. Bailey, eds., *The Taxation of Income from Capital* (Washington, D.C.: Brookings Institution), 1969. See also H. Aaron, *Shelter and Subsidies* (Washington, D.C.: Brookings Institution), 1969; and H. S. Rosen, "Housing Decisions and the U.S. Income Tax: An Econometric Analysis," *Journal of Public Economics* 11(1979):1–24.

20. This assumes that capital gains are not sheltered, although favorable treatment is accorded. See Table 12–4 note c.

21. Although commonly used, this assumption may be implausible, given the large tax shelter effect of interest income and property taxes. These would be sufficiently large to change a marginal tax rate. Relaxing this would make the analysis more complicated.

22. See F. de Leeuw, "The Demand for Housing: A Review of Cross-Section Evidence," *Review of Economics and Statistics* 53(1971):1–10.

23. M. Polinsky, "The Demand for Housing: A Study in Specification and Grouping," *Econometrica* 45(1977):447–462.

24. For estimates, see M. Reid, *Housing and Income* (Chicago: University of Chicago Press), 1962; and G. Carliner, "Income Elasticity of Housing Demand," *Review of Economics and Statistics* 55(1973):528–532.

25. H. Rosen, *op. cit.*, Table 3.

26. The issues of housing supply are summarized in R. H. Edelstein, "The Production Function for Housing and its Implications for Future Urban Development," in M. A. Goldberg and G. Gau, eds., *North American Housing Markets into the 21st Century* (Cambridge, Mass.: Ballinger), 1983.

27. The regulations of the building code are examined in detail in S. M. Oster and J. M. Quigley, "Regulatory Barriers in the Diffusion of Innovation: Some Evidence from Building Codes," *Bell Journal of Economics* 8(1977):361–377.

28. The former conclusion is from Muth, *op. cit.*, with the larger estimate reported in R. J. Johnson, "Housing Technology and Housing Costs," in National Commission on Urban Problems, *Building the American City* (Washington, D.C.: Government Printing Office), 1968, pp. 53–64.

29. Oster and Quigley, *op. cit.*, pp. 367–368.

30. See A. Dougherty and R. Van Order, "Inflation, Housing Costs and the Consumer Price Index," *American Economic Review* 72(1982):154–164. The returns to owner-occupied housing deriving from inflation are estimated in P. Hendershott and S. Hu, "Inflation and Extraordinary Returns on Owner-Occupied Housing," *Journal of Macroeconomics* 3(1981):177–203.

31. President's Commission on Housing, *The Report of the President's Commission on Housing* (Washington, D.C.: Government Printing Office), 1982, p. 4.

32. The national average of the ratio of subsidy and grant in public-operated housing to Section 8 ranged from 93 to 100 percent. The source is J. Riley, *Integration of Public Housing with a Housing Voucher Program—An Overview* (Washington, D.C.: Department of Housing and Urban Development), 1981.

33. A large percentage of the elderly is infirm. The number of elderly impaired, as estimated by the 1979 Annual Housing Survey, exceeds 6 million in the United States. This increases the cost of searching and dealing with brokers, lawyers, and others involved in real estate transactions.

34. The data are as indicated in *The Report of the President's Commission on Housing* (hereafter, the *Report*), p. 71.

35. The individual tax burden has been somewhat counterbalanced by the increase in Social Security taxes. However, mortgage interest and property taxes are deductible only after deductibility of Social Security taxes.

36. *The Report,* p. 94.

37. See Dougherty and Van Order, *op. cit.*

13

URBAN COMMERCIAL AND INDUSTRIAL DEVELOPMENT AND CHANGE

INTRODUCTION

In Chapter 4 we introduced the concept of location when we looked at the locational behavior of firms and households as a prologue to the study of bid rents and the demand side of the urban land market. In this chapter we will extend the concept and combine it with current empirical knowledge about the locational behavior of firms. Of primary interest is the purported flight of jobs from both central cities and from older metropolitan areas.[1]

We begin by briefly reviewing the economics of firms in a spatial setting, and of their locational behavior. We then examine the empirical literature to try to ascertain exactly what is happening to the spatial economies of cities in Canada and the United States.[2] Lastly, we shall explore and evaluate some of the policies that have been put forward to deal with the economic decay of older cities and metropolitan areas. We shall then suggest some alternatives, based largely on the understanding of "the urban economic problem" provided by recent empirical work and by our conceptual analytical tools.

The Firm in a Spatial Setting: A Review

The locational requirements of economic activities including manufacturing, retail trade, and offices include the following:

1. Firms locate to maximize profits;

2. Urban areas traditionally provided such optimal locations because of the existence of *agglomeration economies*.[3]

384

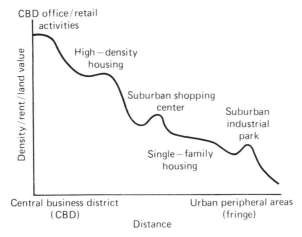

Figure 13–1. Typical declining density/rent and land-use gradient for an urban region.

3. Different firms in different industries have quite different site requirements for taking advantage of agglomeration economies.

4. As a result, firms can afford to pay different rents/prices for sites in different locations within the metropolitan area (bid rents).

5. The net outcome of this competitive bidding by users of land (firms and households) is the familiar downward-sloping density and land value gradient Figure 13–1. Note that while the curve slopes downward and to the right over its entirety, there are local peaks where activities tend to realize differential agglomeration economies within the urban area. Shopping centers, industrial parks, and suburban town centers would all be examples of this phenomenon.

Commercial Activities: The Locational Needs of Retail and Office Activities

Both retail and office activities are essentially people-serving activities. They therefore must be close to their respective client populations. Since these client populations differ somewhat, we should expect to see different locational needs for retail trade and for offices.

Retail trade needs people with spending power. The presence of large numbers of poor people, or a small number of very rich people, may not be sufficient. Retail trade locational requirements are nicely summarized in the following equations, taken from David Huff.[4] Let there be I locations. Then,

$$P_{ij}^t = \frac{\dfrac{S_j^t}{T_{ij}^{ht}}}{\displaystyle\sum_{j=1}^{J} \dfrac{S_j^t}{T_{ij}^{ht}}} \tag{13.1}$$

Where:

P_{ij}^t = the probability that someone living in location i will shop in location j for type t goods

S_j = a measure of retail activity in location j such as retail sales, square footage, or employment for type t goods

T_{ij}^t = the distance between locations and j, usually measured in time

h_t = a distance decay or inconvenience factor for type t goods such that the greater the inconvenience, the higher is h

Intuitively, equation (13.1) states that the probability that someone living in location i will shop in location j is directly proportional to the availability and scale of shopping in j and inversely proportional to the distance between i and j. Furthermore, it is inversely proportional to the existence of competing shopping opportunities represented by the denominator where all competing shopping opportunities are included.

This P_{ij}^t term is the first step in determining the suitability of a location, j, for shopping activities. Suitability is also dependent on income, population, and the proportion of income spent on retail goods. To take these factors into account, we set up equation (13.2).

$$SP_j^t = \sum_{i=1}^{I} P_{ij}^t \, (POP_i) \times (INCOME_i) \times (MPC_i^t) \qquad (13.2)$$

Where:

SP_j^t = the sales potential of location j for retail goods of type t

P_{ij}^t = the previously calculated probability for goods of type t

POP_i = the population in location i

$INCOME_i$ = disposable income in location i

MPC_i^t = marginal propensity to consume goods of type t out of disposable income of residents of i

Interpreting SP_j^t is quite straightforward. The sales potential (suitability for retail trade) of a location is affected by P_{ij}^t, POP_i, $INCOME_i$, and MPC_i^t all in a positive and proportional way. That is, the higher the probability of people traveling to j to shop for type t goods, the higher will be SP_j^t. Similarly, the higher is the income in each location, i, and the higher is the proportion of income spent by residents of i on goods of type t, the higher will be the sales potential of j for type t goods. Different types of goods will therefore be best merchandized at different locations, j. For example, for goods with low cost (value) such as bread and milk, we can anticipate a very high distance decay parameter, h, and therefore a very localized market. Good retail locations require both people, spending power, and a balance between competition—the denominator in (13.1)—and agglomeration economies—the numerator S_j in (13.1). Shopping centers in high-income suburbs will be successful by providing agglomeration economies while taking advantage of the high incomes of the surrounding residents. Similarly, central city shopping that caters to middle-income office workers can be successful because of the large number of such workers in close proximity to centrally located shopping.

Perhaps more than any other land-using urban activity, office activities locate with explicit concern for agglomeration economies, and show concern for two quite different office consumers. The first requires an office location that provides convenient access to the full range of support services that today's complex management tasks demand (e.g., financial, legal, and marketing services). Typical of this group would be administrative headquarters for manufacturing companies.

A second type of office user is much more market-oriented. Examples are such firms as accountants, advertising agencies, and business consultants. They need central locations in general, since that is where their corporate clientele can most often be found. Another type of market-oriented office activity is typified by doctors, real estate agencies, and small general-practice law firms. These office users are likely to be much more dependent on people as opposed to firms, and as a result will locate much more like retail establishments. Such office users will obviously not be tied to central locations, but are more likely to follow the population at large.

A third type of office user, one who is relatively indifferent about location, can be identified as well. Many consulting firms are free to locate in the urban core to service corporate clients, or in the suburbs to attract professional staff with short and convenient journeys to work. Other firms with significant travel requirements may prefer airport access over core access. Others may prefer peripheral locations where intercity automobile travel may be facilitated. The traditional trade-off between core and noncore locations in these instances is made with regard to considerations other than agglomeration economies or markets.

One characteristic does stand out as being a common thread in all location decisions by office users: Office activities are information processors, and such activities need to be understood with respect to their information flows and linkages. Access to labor markets, office rental rates and type of office, and access to support services are all secondary considerations that follow once the information flows and linkages are understood for a given office activity.[5]

Industrial Location in an Urban Setting

When dealing with the location of industrial activity, it is useful to distinguish between two types of locational issues.[6] The first deals with choosing an optimal region in which to carry out the industrial activity. This classic problem we will call the interregional industrial location problem. The second type of location issue relates to the selection of an appropriate site within the given region. These locational issues are clearly interrelated in practice; however, we can separate them conceptually at least to make their analysis more tractable.

Interregional industrial location problems are essentially *aspatial* (in Alonso's terms), since the amount of land and the precise location of the future industrial site are not of direct interest.[7] When trying to choose among competing potential locations in different regions, the factors of concern are energy and utility costs; transportation costs to markets; transportation costs of inputs; availability of labor, including the degree of unionization and skill levels among workers; tax rates; and, increasingly, environmental controls. Such factors can be seen to vary significantly from one region to the next. For example, the U.S. Northeast has very high energy costs but is an enormous and compact market for manufactured goods. If energy is an important input to an industrial process, then the Northeast will not be a favorable location. If, on the other hand, access to markets and the costs of transporting finished goods is important, then the Northeast has significant advantages.

The interregional industrial location problem revolves around the identification of the relative needs of each industry for such factors as energy, labor, access to markets, and public services. Having identified such locational factors, the interregional location problem is resolved by applying a selection criterion to the set of locational factors present in each of the regions under consideration. That region is chosen which possesses the best combination of factors to allow the locating establishment to maximize profits.[8]

Intraregional or intrametropolitan industrial problems differs dramatically from the interregional case, since the factors changing between regions are not likely to vary within a metropolitan region. Variations in attractiveness at the intrametropolitan level are site-dependent. The factors which impinge on the intrametropolitan location decision are size, shape, and slope of the site; soil conditions; zoning; proximity to deep-water, rail, or highway transportation; local government property taxes and regulations that affect industrial operations; availability of additional land for future expansion; and convenience of the site for the work force. These considerations are very specific and *microspatial* with their focus on detailed characteristics of the site.

One conceptual link that both types of industrial locations share is the previously mentioned notion of agglomeration economies. In both cases, locating firms seek economies to achieve lower costs, higher revenues, and greater operating efficiency.[9] Such economies help to explain the existence of specialized industrial enclaves within metropolitan areas (such as "Silicon Valley" south of San Francisco), as well as helping to explain the existence of specialized regions such as lumber and wood products in northwestern United States (southwestern Canada) and electronics and high technology in southern New England.

These rather general considerations provide the basics for understanding the locational trends that are emerging, or have been under way. Specific trends develop because, over time, technological change, tastes, and resource availability (including land, energy, and environmental amenities) change within and among regions. To understand these changing locational patterns, we must understand the changing locational needs of our employment activities (i.e., retail trade, offices, and industry), as well as the changing supply conditions within and among regions (e.g., the changing ability of individual regions and sites to satisfy these locational needs).

Emerging Locational Trends in Retail Trade, Office Activities and Industrial Plants

Retail Trade: Going After the Market   In (13.1) and (13.2), retail trade depended in part, on the levels of disposable income and population. Where people and spending power move, we can expect to find retail activity in pursuit of this spending power.

Retail customers are drawn primarily from places of residence and places of work. In both Canada and the United States residences have been decentralizing dramatically during much of this century. Urban populations have been moving outward over time, as population pressure, the desire to live in single-family housing, the advent of the automobile and highways, and central city crowding have all combined to push and pull population from the central city to the surrounding suburbs and even beyond.[10] Table 13–1 provides some quantitative measure of the magnitude of these outward shifts in both Canada and the United States for the period 1970 to 1975. Central cities in both Canada and the United States are growing very slowly in terms of population (0.9 percent in Canada's central cities versus 2.2 percent for those in the United States). While surrounding suburban areas have been growing quite rapidly in both countries (19.1 percent in Canada as opposed to 11.2 percent in U.S. suburban areas), although by the 1980s even this trend slowed down as the rural population began to grow relative to central city and suburban areas. Population growth is clearly centered outside the central cities of North America's urban regions, with significant variation from region to region.

Table 13–2 presents data on households for Canadian and U.S. central cities, surrounding areas, and metropolitan areas taken as a

Table 13–1 Household Change in U.S. and Canadian Metropolitan Areas

Percent Change Households	U.S. (1970–1975)			Canada (1971–1975)		
	Metro	Central City	Balance	Metro	Central City	Balance
more than −15%			1.2			
−14.9 to −10%		1.2				
−9.9 to −5%		3.1	1.9			3.4
−4.9 to 0%		10.8	1.5			
0 to 4.9%	5.0	18.1	2.3		9.4	6.9
5 to 9.9%	22.3	15.8	8.9	6.3	9.4	10.3
10 to 14.9%	26.2	13.1	33.4	15.6	31.3	6.9
15 to 19.9%	19.6	14.3	20.8	37.5	21.9	10.3
20 to 24.9%	8.8	5.0	12.0	21.9	12.5	6.9
25 to 29.9%	4.6	6.2	9.3	9.4	9.4	20.7
30 to 39.9%	8.8	8.1	10.0	9.4	6.3	10.3
40 to 49.9%	3.1	3.1	4.2			10.3
more than 50%	1.5	1.5	5.0			13.7
Mean	17.1	13.0	20.1	20.0	15.7	27.6
Standard deviation	11.1	13.5	14.9	6.7	7.9	20.3
N	257	257	254	32[a]	32	30

Notes: [a]Due to boundary changes since 1971, four metropolitan areas in Canada were removed from the data set due to a lack of comparable data and spatial units.

Sources: U.S. Bureau of Census, *County and City Data Book, 1977;* U.S. Census of Population and Housing: 1970, *Census Tracts, Final Reports,* P4C (1) Series, Table 4–1; "1976 Survey of Buying Power," *Sales and Marketing Management,* Volume 117, No. 2, July 26, 1976.
Statistics Canada, *Census of Canada: 1976,* Volume 3, Catalogue 93-802, Tables 7 and 8; *Census of Canada: 1971,* Volume 2, Part I: Catalogue 93–702, Tables 4, 5, and 6.

whole, for the same period. Central cities show considerable growth in numbers of households (13.0 percent for U.S. central cities, 15.7 percent for Canadian central cities). Surrounding areas show even more dramatic increases (20.1 percent for U.S. suburban areas; 27.6 percent for Canada's suburban areas). So, both population and households are growing much more rapidly in suburban areas in Canada and the United States. A parallel shift in retailing would be strengthened considerably if, in addition to the growing population, suburban areas were characterized as well by higher incomes, a subject to which we next turn our attention in Table 13–3.

This table compares central city incomes to those for the metropolitan area. In the United States, in 1970, central city household incomes averaged 91.1 percent (median) or 93.2 percent (mean) of metropolitan area household incomes. Central city incomes are thus considerably lower than the incomes in surrounding areas. In Canada, in 1971, the differences were not as pronounced, as central city household incomes were closer to metropolitan area averages (97.6 percent for median incomes and 98.0 percent for mean incomes of households).

Table 13–2 Population Change in U.S. and Canadian Metropolitan Areas

Percent Change in Population	U.S. (1970–1975) Metro	Central City	Balance	Canada (1971–1975) Metro	Central City	Balance
−19.9 to −15%		0.8				
−14.9 to −10%		4.2	1.2		8.3	
−9.9 to −5%	0.8	19.2	0.4	2.8	13.9	
−4.9 to 0%	14.6	27.6	3.4	8.3	25.0	5.9
0 to 4.9%	39.1	16.1	26.3	27.8	25.0	20.6
5 to 9.9%	18.8	13.4	26.3	36.1	16.7	5.9
10 to 14.9%	11.5	8.0	16.6	16.7	8.3	20.6
15 to 19.9%	6.1	6.1	10.4	5.6	2.8	14.7
20 to 24.9%	3.8	1.1	5.7	2.8		5.9
25 to 29.9%	3.8	3.4	2.7			8.8
30 to 39.9%	1.5		2.7			5.9
40 to 49.9%	0.4		2.3			
more than 50%			1.6			11.8
Mean	7.1	2.2	11.2	6.3	0.9	19.1
Standard deviation	8.3	9.5	11.4	5.4	7.1	19.4
N	257	257	254[a]	36	36	34[a]

Notes: [a]In the United States there are three cases were metropolitan areas are equivalent to the central cities, and in Canada there are two such instances.

Sources: U.S. Bureau of Census, County and City Data Book, 1977, U.S. Census of Population and Housing: 1970, Census Tracts, Final Reports, P4C(1) Series, Table 4–1; "1976 Survey of Buying Power," Sales and Marketing Management, Volume 117, No. 2, July 26, 1976.
Statistics Canada, Census of Canada: 1976, Volume 1, Catalogue 93-802, Tables 6 and 7.

Combining the income figures with the population figures, we should expect to see considerable decentralization of retailing to capture the market (population multiplied by income) that is growing more rapidly in noncentral locations. This growth is more marked in the United States than in Canada, where central cities have not experienced dramatic declines in income and where households are still increasing in numbers.

While people and incomes are dispersing, the outlook for central city retail trade need not be dismal if lost sales can be made up by increased daytime populations of working people and visitors to the central city. Unfortunately, data on central city employment outside of retail, wholesale, and manufacturing is scant. These data depict outward movement of jobs to match outward movements of people. However, it is obvious to even the casual observer that most downtown areas in central cities have been experiencing significant growth in the office sector. Little information exists systematically for office employment in metropolitan areas of Canada and the United States. The growth in highly concentrated central locations presents the only significant countertrend to dispersal. Due to lack of data, we cannot measure the strength of this concentrated office activity.

Table 13–3   Central City to Metropolitan Area Income Ratios

Ratio	U.S. (1970)		Canada (1971)	
	Median Household Income (percent)	Mean Household Income (percent)	Median Household Income (percent)	Mean Household Income (percent)
Under 59	1.4			
60–69	4.3	1.0		
70–79	19.5	8.1		
80–89	22.9	20.5	13.8	10.0
90–99	31.0	41.0	44.8	36.7
100–109	15.2	24.8	41.4	53.3
110–119	1.9	2.4		
120–129	1.4	1.8		
130–139	1.0	0.5		
140–149	0.5			
150–159	1.0			
Mean	91.1	93.2	97.6	98.0
Standard deviation	16.3	12.1	5.5	5.1
N	217[a]	217[a]	29[b]	30[b]

Notes: [a]Since 23 SMSAs in New England are excluded from analyses and there are 37 SMSAs formed since 1970, the N is 277 − 60 or 217.
[b]No data are available for one case.

Sources: U.S. Bureau of Census, Census of Population and Housing: 1970, *Census Tracts, Final Reports,* P4C(1) Series, Table P–4.
Statistics Canada, *Census of Canada: 1971; Population and Housing Characteristics by Census Tracts,* Catalogue 95-700 series.

One may conclude that there are strong centrifugal forces pulling retailing activity out of central areas into the suburban locations. However, the presence of a strong centrally located office sector mitigates against this dispersal.

Some recent innovations in commercial development also hold significant implications for the future spatial distribution of retailing activity. Since the 1960s, "mixed use developments" (MXDs) have become increasingly popular in both Canada and the United States.[11] These developments combine offices, shopping, and frequently housing in the same project. An important attraction is the fact that MXDs spread risk among several different urban land uses while providing an environment allowing different land uses to complement each other and enhance each other's marketability. MXDs exist in most large cities and in key suburban locations.

Office: Footloose and Fancy Free   Office activities have been exhibiting contradictory trends over the past several decades. They have been moving to the suburbs as office users began to search for lower-cost space and at the same time tried to avoid central area congestion.[12]

Decentralization has been spurred on by the suburbanization of population (labor supply) and by the existence of high-quality suburban office and shopping plazas. Arterial highways have enhanced the attractiveness of suburban centers as office locations. Conversely, centralization has been driven by agglomeration economies. Among these are the need for face-to-face communication; access to technical services such as marketing, finance, and insurance; access to clubs, restaurants, and other amenities; and the existence of a large number of other offices.

Recent innovations in computing and telecommunications make it possible to work at home or at neighborhood work centers, thus obviating the need to travel to work.[13] However, the growing depersonalization of society places a continuing premium on face-to-face interaction. Improvements in regional air service provide access to exurban locations. Rising energy costs and the prospect of better intercity rail service (especially in the U.S. Northeast and in California) provide stimuli for central cities. The movement of professionals into central cities to live provides an added impetus to keeping offices centrally located. However, residential locational preferences could change once these largely childless households have children.

Offices can be found in high-density structures downtown, and also in suburban locations. Office parks have sprung up around virtually every metropolitan core in both the United States and Canada. Shopping centers have been foci for recent office development. Airports have also attracted office activities, particularly those with travel needs. In short, office activities are virtually as ubiquitous as housing and shopping have become. Instead of the CBD as a focus, we now have many foci, providing enormous variety to service office needs, from headquarter activities in central areas, to regional offices in office parks in suburbia, to small neighborhood offices to service local populations.

Industrial Migration: Movement Within and Among Metropolitan Regions Perhaps more than any other land-use activity, manufacturing locational change conjures up visions of either pending disaster for the adversely affected area, or else ecstacy and almost limitless optimism for the recipient area.

Industrial activity is highly valued because of the ability of such activity to pay taxes and because of the minimal demands made on locational services, in marked contrast to housing. Industry provides needed tax bases for local governments. Movement of industry out of a jurisdiction spells a loss of tax revenue.

Manufacturing activity no longer prizes central city locations, preferring suburban and, increasingly, nonmetropolitan locations.[14] Using our previous terminology, there have been changes in both interregional industrial location patterns and intrametropolitan industrial location patterns. Among the driving forces of such changes are the following.

Changing Spatial Pattern of Labor Supply   Within metropolitan areas the movement of people into suburban areas has meant that the supply of skilled and semi-skilled labor can now be found outside the central city. Interregionally, the shift of people to Sun Belt states and to nonmetropolitan areas[15] of the United States has meant that supplies of appropriately skilled labor can now be found in a variety of regions. No similar trend is apparent yet in Canada, where metropolitan areas are holding jobs and people, though there is a shift toward the energy- and resource-rich western provinces.

Technological Change   Technological change in two areas has had enormous implications for industrial location. First, changes in manufacturing processes to capital-intensive, continuous-flow, high-volume production systems has necessitated movement to large sites where single-story continuous-flow processes can be housed. Storage of inputs and output also requires significant amounts of land. Taken together, these imply large sites, with room for expansion that cannot generally be found in central areas.

A second area of innovation that has greatly affected industrial location is transportation technology. Innovations such as unit trains and pipelines have enabled bulk raw materials to be shipped economically virtually anywhere in North America. Deep-water access is no longer a prerequisite even for heavy raw-materials users. Similarly, the growth of trucking and of the interstate highway system in the United States and the Trans-Canada Highway in Canada have made trucking competitive with rail even for hauls of several thousand miles. The advent of cargo planes and of wide-body jets (including wide-body cargo planes) has made air freight economical to previously inaccessible areas. Finally, the development of supertankers, bulk cargo ships, and, most importantly, of container ships (and trucks and railcars) has greatly increased the efficiency and lowered the cost of waterborne freight.

The net effect of all of these innovations in transportation has been to alter locational constraints. New constraints such as large-size sites with highway access have come to the fore. Industrial activities are able to move to locations with favorable labor supply conditions, or to regions with pleasant climates and environmental amenities.

Diseconomies at Old Locations   The two preceding factors served to free industrial activity from locational constraints and provided greater flexibility of locational choice. At the same time that industry was enabled to be *pulled* to new locations, a number of *push* factors acted to make extant central locations less attractive.

First, existing high-volume multi-story plants were no longer efficient, particularly in light of emerging continuous-flow production technologies. Second, central city locations are subject to serious disruption due to congestion, limited storage facilities, and the difficulties surrounding the movement of large quantities of inputs and outputs through crowded central city locations. Third, aging plant and equipment, inflexibility and high cost of maintaining old buildings, and growing costs of insurance against arson and theft and vandalism further added to the cost of central city manufacturing operations.

Miscellaneous Elements   Other forces conspired to move industry from its traditional locations in the Northeast and Midwest and from central city areas. Energy costs and availability were an inducement to move to the Sun Belt and to areas in the western United States and western Canada. In addition, new plants could be designed to be more energy-efficient than older ones.

Changing industrial technologies have also allowed firms to internalize many of the external economies that were formerly uniquely provided in central areas. Smaller-scale plants have allowed greater cost saving and locational flexibility. Finally, the shift in our industrial structure away from heavy industrial commodities to high-technology goods (and services) has further liberated manufacturing plants from old restraints.

One last implication of these changes in industrial structure is that newer, Space Age industries are virtually devoid of any locational requirements other than access to centers of learning and the ability to provide high-quality living and work environments for scientists, engineers, and technicians.

Summary

The above trends have worked in favor of noncentral areas within metropolitan regions, and in favor of nonmetropolitan regions within North America. As older plants are retired, they are often replaced with new plants in peripheral areas. Newer manufacturing techniques and products have tended to favor less central locations. The net result has been a decline in central city industrial activity and an increase in industrial activity in less central locations. For all of the reasons discussed above, costs associated with central locations have risen while costs associated with noncentral locations have tended to fall as shown in figure 13–2. Given that firms face relatively constant prices for their products, we see that noncentral locations have gained the advantage and provide higher profit potential than central locations.

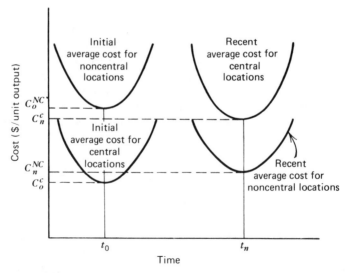

Figure 13–2. Long-run average costs of operating in central and noncentral locations.

RECENT CHANGES IN THE LOCATION OF ECONOMIC ACTIVITY WITHIN AND AMONG URBAN AREAS

The previous section raised a number of arguments about the likely trends in the location of economic activity (jobs) both within and among metropolitan areas. In this section we will look at some of the empirical findings that have been put forward to answer the following questions: "What is the nature of the flight of jobs from central cities?" "What is the nature of the flight of jobs from established and older metropolitan areas?"

The Flight of Jobs from Central Cities: Myth, Reality, and Unknowns

There are significant differences between the cities of the United States and those of Canada, and we divide our discussion by country to see how the locational dynamics of retail trade, offices and manufacturing industry have varied.

Retailing Data are available for the metropolitan areas of both Canada and the United States with respect to retail sales in metropolitan areas and in principal central city areas. Table 13–4 sets out these data. First, retail activity is significantly more concentrated in Canadian central cities than in the United States. This is so whether one looks at retail sales or at the number of retail establishments or at retail employment. Second, the trend toward decentralization appears to progress in Canada and the United States, since in both countries central city retail trade grew more slowly than did metropolitan retail trade,

Table 13–4 Retail Trade Data

	U.S.						Canada					
	Metro Area			Central City			Metro Area			Central City		
	Mean	S.D.	N	Mean	S.D.	N	Mean	S.D.	N	Mean	S.D.	N
Central city sales as % metro sales (1967/1966)				64.5	19.2	244				77.1	18.2	29
Central city sales as % metro sales (1972/1971)				60.9	21.1	252				75.9	18.5	38
% Change in retail sales (1967–1972/1966–1971)	56.2	18.9	253	45.2	25.9	244	50.4	20.4	29	42.0	22.6	38
Central city unincorporated establishments as % metro total (1972/1971)				51.2	19.2	252				69.8	19.3	38
Central city establishments as % metro total (1972/1971)				54.3	19.3	252				72.9	18.6	38
Sales/Establishment (1972/1971) in $000's	255.6	38.7	251	287.9	53.3	251	264.5	54.5	38	276.9	61.1	38
People employed in trade (retail and wholesale) in central city as % metro total (1970/1971)				50.5	19.8	252				67.6	22.0	39

Source: Michael A. Goldberg and John Mercer, *Canadian and American Cities* (forthcoming).

Table 13–5 Service Activities Within Metropolitan Areas

	U.S.						Canada					
	Metro Area			Central City			Metro Area			Central City		
	Mean	S.D.	N	Mean	S.D.	N	Mean	S.D.	N	Mean	S.D.	N
Central city sales as % metro sales (1967/1966)				68.6	18.6	243				80.3	15.5	38
Central city sales as % metro sales (1972/1971)				66.4	19.0	252				81.0	15.0	38
# establishments in central city as % metro total (1972/1971)				57.3	18.8	253				74.8	17.1	38
Sales/establishment (1972/1971) in $000's	60.8	25.8	253	72.6	39.4	252	81.1	21.1	38	90.0	25.8	38
% Change in sales (1967–1972/1966–1971)	99.5	35.6	252	92.3	39.2	244	105.8	40.9	29	101.2	41.7	39
Persons employed in finance, insurance, real estate, and public services in central city as % metro total (1970/1971)				72.1	26.0	209				69.6	21.1	39

Source: Michael A. Goldberg and John Mercer, *Canadian and American Cities*, (forthcoming).

though again the difference is less pronounced in Canada than in the United States.

This evidence suggests that retail activity is growing in the suburban rings of metropolitan areas. Central city retailing is growing less rapidly than suburban retailing. Given the continued decentralization of population, there is every reason to anticipate that retail activity will follow.[16]

Offices Earlier we observed that it is extremely difficult to get information directly on office activities in suburban and central city areas. We must approach the subject obliquely, drawing on extant information about service and other office-type jobs, as well as selectively using data for individual cities where office space and employment information is available.

First, it is interesting to observe that while central city sales of services declined in U.S. central cities between 1967 and 1972 (from 68.6 percent of metro total to 66.4 percent), in Canada's central cities analogous service activities increased their share of metro area service activity (from 80.3 percent to 81.0 percent) from 1966 to 1971. Second, these activities tend to be considerably more concentrated in Canada's central cities than they are in the central cities of the United States.

Turning to offices specifically, we see many of the same trends that we have seen in the changing pattern of retailing: relatively high concentrations in central cities but more rapid growth in outlying suburban rings. Table 13–6 provides information on the intraregional locations of corporate headquarters from Fortune's 500 largest U.S. corporations. It shows that between 1965 and 1969 these headquarters were moving from central city locations to suburban ones. Table 13–7 demonstrates that this decentralization trend holds not just for intraregional office locations, but for relocations among regions as well.

Central locations retain enormous numbers of office workers, as can be seen from Table 13–8, which presents estimates of the amount of central city office space in 1970 in selected SMSAs. Even given these decade-old figures, the picture could not have changed dramatically in view of the massive stock of central city office space. Despite rapid growth in suburban space, the central city retains its primacy.[17]

A more recent study (1976) by Quante entitled *The Exodus of Corporate Headquarters from New York City*[18] provides data on the Fortune 500 that confirm that the central city and previously central regions are losing headquarters offices. Unfortunately, these data do not refer to total office space and office employment, only to Fortune 500 firms. They do not give us any idea about regional headquarters and the localization of smaller national firms. Thus, they are suggestive of trends, but not hard empirical proof.

Table 13–6 The Intraregional Location of Corporate Industrial Headquarters in Selected SMSAs, 1965 and 1969

	Central City		Suburban Ring	
	1965	*1969*	*1965*	*1969*
New York	131	126	6	5
Los Angeles	7	13	7	8
Chicago	39	37	9	12
Philadelphia	11	10	5	4
Detroit	12	9	3	4
San Francisco	11	8	1	3
Boston	6	5	3	4
Pittsburgh	21	14	1	—
St. Louis	11	10	1	—
Washington	—	—	—	1
Cleveland	16	16	—	1
Newark	2	3	5	4
Minneapolis-St. Paul	9	10	1	1
Houston	2	2	—	—
Milwaukee	8	9	2	2
Paterson	—	—	3	7
Dallas	5	7	—	—
Cincinnati	4	4	—	—
Kansas City	2	2	—	—
Atlanta	1	3	—	—
Wilmington	3	3	—	—
Total SMSAs	301	291	47	56

Source: Regina Armstrong, *The Office Industry,* (Cambridge, Mass.: M.I.T. Press) 1972. p. 52.

Turning to the situation in Canada's central cities, Tables 13–11, 13–12, and 13–13 present data for office space in Montreal, Toronto, and Vancouver, respectively. The picture is clouded somewhat by the different dates during which the data were collected. The Montreal data (Table 13–11) show that from 1949 to 1962 there was considerable growth in offices and that the city core roughly held its own. However, the data for Toronto (Table 13–12) show that while the core did grow from 1962 to 1973, suburban areas grew even more rapidly. Finally, the data for Vancouver (Table 13–13), from the period 1971 to 1978, show that suburban locations grew at roughly twice the rate in terms of new office space as compared with the city of Vancouver and its central core (the Downtown Peninsula).

The strength of the office sector in central cities is in some measure a result of the strength of the office sector nationally: The white-collar work force has grown rapidly over the past several decades, creating a continentwide demand for office space. Tables 13–14 to 13–16 present data for the United States and Canada that illustrate the growth of office-type activities and provide the underpinning for the strength of offices in all regions and all sections of metropolitan areas.

Table 13–7   The Location of Headquarters for the Largest Industrial Corporations, 1958, 1963, 1965, 1969

	Corporate Headquarters				CAO & A Establishments[a]	
	1958	*1963*	*1965*	*1969*	*1963*	*% in Corp. Hdqrs.*
United States	500	500	500	500	17,569	2.8%
New York–N.E., N.J., SCA	151	163	151	148	2,246	7.3
New York SMSA	142	147	137	131	1,738	8.5
Newark SMSA	4	7	7	7	235	3.0
Paterson SMSA	3	6	3	7	131	4.6
Chicago–N.W., Ind. SCA	50	50	48	49	987	5.1
Chicago SMSA	50	50	48	49	965	5.2
Los Angeles SMSA	17	16	14	21	780	2.1
Philadelphia SMSA	17	16	16	14	431	3.7
Detroit SMSA	16	15	15	13	392	3.8
San Francisco SMSA	13	12	12	11	512	2.3
Boston SMSA	7	10	9	9	355	2.8
Pittsburgh SMSA	23	22	22	14	287	7.7
St. Louis SMSA	14	14	12	10	282	5.0
Washington SMSA	—	—	—	1	264	—
Cleveland SMSA	15	14	16	17	276	5.1
Minneapolis-St. Paul SMSA	7	10	10	11	264	3.8
Houston SMSA	1	3	2	2	242	1.2
Milwaukee SMSA	6	8	10	11	122	6.6
Dallas SMSA	6	6	5	7	306	2.0
Cincinnati SMSA	4	4	4	4	149	2.7
Kansas City SMSA	3	2	2	2	251	.8
Atlanta SMSA	—	—	1	3	252	—
Wilmington SMSA	4	3	3	3	45	6.7
Total SCAs and SMSAs	354	368	352	250	8,443	4.4

[a]Total central administrative offices and auxiliaries.

Source: Regina Armstrong, *The Office Industry* (Cambridge, Mass: M.I.T. Press), 1972, p. 37.

Office activities are characterized simultaneously by decentralization, both within and among regions, and centralization, in well-defined office pockets, the largest and strongest of which is the traditional central city core. Central cities continue to attract because of their agglomeration forces, and suburbs continue to grow because that is increasingly the focus of population and other activity in the metropolitan regions. This office space situation is summarized in Figure 13–3 for Vancouver, where there is great centralization in the core and great suburban office growth.

Industry   The so-called flight of industry from the central city has caused concern. In this section we want to examine the evidence concerning the "flight" and ascertain its magnitude and character, before getting on with possible curative policies and programmes.

Table 13–8 Total Office Employment in Selected SMSAs and Estimated Intraregional Distribution

	Office Employment, in Thousands (1960)				Estimated Gross Private and Public Office Space in Downtown (× 1 million sq. feet)	
	SMSA	Central City	Suburban Ring	Downtown	% of Office Employment in Downtown	1960	1970
New York SMSA	1334	1113	221	840	63%	179	247
Los Angeles SMSA	703	376	327	100	14	16	33
Chicago SMSA	688	488	200	275	40	47	63
Philadelphia SMSA	397	240	157	120	30	26	34
Detroit SMSA	316	183	133	80	25	16	23
San Francisco SMSA	306	175	131	100	33	16	26
Boston SMSA	297	142	155	120	40	24	34
Pittsburgh SMSA	188	79	108	70	37	15	22
St. Louis SMSA	188	110	78	35	19	4	8
Washington SMSA	288	199	89	180	63	36	54
Cleveland SMSA	183	126	57	50	27	8	11
Newark SMSA	178	85	93	50	28	12	14
Minneapolis-St. Paul SMSA	168	124	44	65	39	10	12
Houston SMSA	118	100	18	80	68	13	22
Milwaukee SMSA	120	90	30	60	50	12	14
Paterson SMSA	97	24	72	5	5	1	1
Dallas SMSA	124	93	31	80	65	16	22
Cincinnati SMSA	106	71	35	45	42	10	12
Kansas City SMSA	113	76	37	30	27	6	9
Atlanta SMSA	111	77	34	45	41	8	17
Wilmington SMSA	34	17	17	10	29	2	3
Total SMSAs	6055	3990	2065	2440	40	477	681

Source: Regina Armstrong, *The Office Industry* (Cambridge, Mass.: M.I.T. Press), p. 49.

Table 13–17 sets out information on manufacturing employment, establishments, and value for metropolitan areas and central cities in both Canada and the United States. The data confirm that central cities have been receiving a smaller proportion of manufacturing employment, as growth has been more rapid in the metropolitan area as a whole than in the central city. The situation appears more pronounced in Canada than in the United States, where industry grew at the rate of 1.7 percent from 1966 to 1971 for central city employment and 9.9 percent for the total of Canadian metropolitan areas. In the United States, the corresponding figures for the 1967–1972 period were 7.7 percent for central city manufacturing employment and 9.0 percent for the metropolitan areas.

One other point is worth observing. Once again, manufacturing jobs tend to be much more highly concentrated in Canada's central cities than in those of the United States. This view is confirmed in Table

Table 13–9 Distribution of Fortune 500 Headquarters by Region: 1956–74

Regions	Share of Headquarters 1956		Share of Headquarters 1974		Changes 1956–74		Share of Headquarters 1980		Changes 1974–1980	
	Number	Percent	Number	Percent	Number	Percent	Number	Percent	Number	Percent
Northeast	242	48.4	214	42.8	–28	–11.6	215	43.0	+1	+0.5
North Central	181	36.2	170	34.0	–11	– 6.2	158	31.6	–12	–7.1
South	40	8.0	63[a]	12.6	+23	+57.5	65	13.0	+ 2	+ 3.2
West	37	7.4	53[b]	10.6	+16	+43.3	62	12.4	+ 9	+17.0
Total	500	100.0	500	100.0	0	—	500	100.0	0	—

Note: All the losses and gains by region do not necessarily represent the interregional movement of headquarters. They might indicate, however, the preference of headquarter location for various reasons.

[a]Includes one form in Puerto Rico.

[b]Includes one firm in Hawaii.

Sources: Wolfgang Quante, *The Exodus of Corporate Headquarters* (New York: Praeger Publishers), 1976, p. 63. *Fortune Double 500 Directory* 1981.

Table 13–10   Number of Fortune 500 Companies in Ten Cities by City, Suburb and Region, 1956–1974

	Central City 1956	1974	Changes (%)	Suburbs 1956	1974	Changes (%)	Region 1956	1974	Changes (%)
New York	140	98	−30.0	16	46	+187.5	156	144	− 7.7
Chicago	47	33	−29.8	4	10	+150.0	51	43	−15.7
Pittsburgh	22	15	−31.8	2	—	—	24	15	−37.5
Detroit	18	6	−66.7	2	4	+100.0	20	10	−50.0
Cleveland	16	14	−12.5	—	2	—	16	16	0.0
Philadelphia	14	8	−42.9	8	6	− 25.0	22	14	−36.4
St. Louis	11	10	− 9.1	1	—	—	12	10	−16.7
Los Angeles	10	13	+30.0	5	6	+ 20.0	15	19	+26.6
San Francisco	8	7	−12.5	4	6	+ 50.0	12	13	+ 8.3
Boston	7	5	−28.6	2	4	+150.0	9	9	0.0
Total	293	209	−29.7	44	85	+ 93.2	337	293	−13.1

Source: Wolfgang Quante, *The Exodus of Corporate Headquarters* (New York: Praeger Publishers), 1976, p. 61.

Table 13–11   Floor Space ('000 sq. ft.) by Land Use and Sub-Area, Montreal's City Center, 1949 and 1962

	Core 1949	1962	Frame 1949	1962	Total CBD 1949	1962
Office	7,174.4	13,960.8	4,186.2	6,191.3	11,360.6	20,152.1
Retail	3,744.8	3,751.8	3,860.6	3,676.1	7,605.4	7,427.9
Manufacturing	838.7	324.2	4,397.1	3,995.3	5,235.8	4,319.5
Wholesale	161.9	144.7	4,417.9	3,949.3	4,579.8	4,094.0
Public and institutional	602.3	468.5	4,259.9	5,376.9	4,862.2	5,845.4
Residential	400.8	211.8	4,740.9	3,083.5	5,141.7	3,295.3
Other	1,790.2	3,588.1	2,338.2	2,507.4	4,128.4	6,095.5
Total	14,713.1	22,449.9	28,200.8	28,779.9	42,913.9	51,229.7
Floor space index	4.3	6.9	1.9	2.0	2.3	2.9

	Periphery 1949	1962	Total City Center 1949	1962
Office	497.7	861.3	11,858.3	21,013.4
Retail	2,703.5	2,307.8	10,308.9	9,735.7
Manufacturing	6,060.0	6,230.2	11,295.8	10,549.7
Wholesale	2,392.6	2,677.6	6,972.4	6,771.6
Public and institutional	4,745.5	6,128.8	9.607.7	11,974.2
Residential	16,783.4	16,490.0	21,925.1	19,785.5
Other	1,755.2	2,023.6	5,883.6	8,119.1
Total	34,937.9	36,719.3	77,851.8	87,949.0
Floor space index	1.5	1.7	1.9	2.2

Note: Floor space index (FSI) equals total floor space divided by buildable area (i.e., excluding streets).

Source: George A. Nader, *Cities of Canada,* Volume 1 (Toronto Ontario: Macmillan of Canada), 1976, p. 118.

Table 13–12   Office Space[a] by District, Metro Toronto: 1962–1973

	1962 Sq. Ft.	%	1973 Sq. Ft.	%
Downtown core	7,488,470	40.0	14,396,429	34.5
Rest of downtown	5,040,534	26.8	8,618,695	20.6
Midtown district	4,687,574	25.0	10,138,683	24.3
Suburban district	1,551,858	8.2	8,629,752	20.6
Total	18,768,436	100.0	41,783,559	100.0

[a]Excludes buildings of less than 20,000 square feet.

Source: George A. Nader, The Cities of Canada, Volume I (Toronto, Ontario: Macmillan of Canada), 1976, p. 124.

Table 13–13   Office Space Summary, Greater Vancouver, 1971 and 1981

	Rentable Area (thousand sq. ft)		Annual Growth (%) 1971–81	Rental Range ($/sq. ft.)	Vacancy Rate (%)	Under Construction (thousand sq. ft.)
	May 1971	May 1981				
Vancouver						
Downtown Peninsula[a]	8,917	15,997	6.0	7.00–16.00 NNN 11.00–21.00 G	1.8	1,543
Broadway	1,318	3,149	9.2	7.50–11.00 NNN	2.0	269
Kingsway	230	441	6.0	6.50–11.00 NNN	2.2	—
Main	184	243	2.8	—	0.0	—
Fraser	254	308	1.9	—	0.0	—
East Hastings	309	408	2.8	—	0.0	—
Other areas	685	1,881	10.6	6.50–10.00 NNN	0.2	14
	11,897	22,397	6.5		1.6	1,826
Suburbs						
Burnaby	322	2,217	20.8	7.00–11.00 NNN	0.6	235
New Westminster	781	1,203	4.4	5.50– 9.50 NNN	9.8	22
North Van. City	270	725	10.4	8.00–12.00 NNN	0.9	295
North Van. D.M.	120	218	6.2	6.00–10.00 NNN	2.2	11
West Vancouver	162	415	9.9	6.00–11.00 NNN	1.4	23
Richmond	129	1,136	24.3	6.00–10.00 NNN	1.3	362
	1,784	5,824	12.6		2.8	948
Total	13,681	28,221	7.5		1.9	2,774

[a]Includes government-owned space
NNN = Triple Net Lease
G = Gross Lease

Source: Real Estate Trends 1981 in Metropolitan Vancouver (Vancouver, B.C.: Real Estate Board of Greater Vancouver), 1982, p. 65.

13–18, which sets out employment and unemployment in U.S. and Canadian central cities as compared with metropolitan areawide figures.

The picture that emerges is consistent with one we obtained from looking at retail and service activities (offices): Peripheral locations are

Table 13–14 United States Work Force by Industry Characteristics, 1870–1981 (in millions)

	1870	1880	1890	1900	1910	1920	1930	1940	1950	1960	1970	1981[a]
Tertiary (trade, finance, service, transportation, government)	3.2	4.5	7.3	10.1	13.9	16.7	23.0	29.5	30.4	38.3	49.1	67.9
Secondary (manufacturing, construction)	2.6	3.9	5.5	7.2	10.7	12.9	14.1	14.5	18.1	21.3	24.1	27.9
Primary (agriculture, forestry, mining)	7.1	9.0	10.5	11.8	12.8	12.8	11.7	11.1	7.9	5.0	3.0	4.6
Total	12.9	17.4	23.3	29.1	37.4	42.4	48.8	55.1	56.4	64.6	76.2	100.4
Tertiary as percentage of total employment	24.8	25.9	31.3	34.7	37.2	39.4	47.1	53.5	53.9	59.3	59.9	67.6

Sources: Regina Armstrong, *The Office Industry*, p. 16.

[a]*US Statistical Abstract 1982/3*, p. 390, table 652. Note that 1981 figures are taken from a different source, and measure employment by industry.

Table 13–15 United State Labor Force by Major Occupation Groups, 1870–1981 (in millions)

	1870	1880	1890	1900	1910	1920	1930	1940	1950	1960	1970	1981[a]
White collar	1.2	1.9	3.2	5.1	8.0	10.5	14.3	16.1	21.6	28.7	35.8	52.9
Professional	.4	.6	.9	1.2	1.7	2.3	3.3	3.9	5.1	7.4		16.4
Managerial	.4	.6	.9	1.7	2.5	2.8	3.6	3.8	5.2	6.7		11.5
Clerical	.1	.2	.6	.9	2.0	3.4	4.3	5.0	7.2	9.7		18.6
Sales	.3	.5	.8	1.3	1.8	2.0	3.1	3.4	4.1	4.8		6.4
Blue collar (craftsmen, operatives, laborers)	3.7	5.4	8.0	10.4	14.2	17.0	19.3	20.6	24.3	25.6	28.4	31.2
Service (household and other)	1.2	1.5	2.1	2.6	3.6	3.3	4.8	6.1	6.2	8.3	9.8	13.4
Farm	6.8	8.6	9.9	10.9	11.5	11.4	10.3	9.0	6.9	5.4	2.2	2.7
Total	12.9	17.4	23.2	29.0	37.3	42.2	48.7	51.7	59.0	68.0	76.6	100.4
White collar as percentage of total	9.3	10.9	14.2	17.6	21.4	24.9	29.4	30.9	36.6	42.2	46.7	52.7

Sources: Regina Armstrong, The Office Industry, p. 16.

[a] US Statistical Abstract 1982/3, p. 386, table 648. Note that these figures are taken from a different source than the others, and represent the number of employed persons by occupation.

Table 13–16 Occupation and Structure of the Canadian Work Force (in percent)

1921	Canada	B.C.	Prairies	Ontario	Quebec	Atlantic
Primary	36.6	29.4	55.2	28.2	30.9	43.4
Manufacturing	20.8	19.3	7.1	26.4	26.9	17.4
Construction	5.8	8.0	3.2	6.7	6.5	5.4
Transportation	7.8	11.2	7.2	8.1	7.1	7.7
Trade	9.4	11.2	8.3	10.7	9.9	8.2
Services	19.2	20.8	19.3	19.9	17.9	16.9
Total	100.0	100.0	100.0	100.0	100.0	100.0

Note: The labor force is composed of noninstitutional population 10 years of age and over, who were employed or unemployed.

1951	Canada	B.C.	Prairies	Ontario	Quebec	Atlantic
Primary	19.8	13.7	37.3	13.1	17.2	27.1
Manufacturing	25.1	24.0	13.6	29.8	29.4	20.1
Construction	6.2	6.8	4.8	6.4	6.8	5.9
Transportation	9.5	11.9	8.8	9.4	9.3	10.9
Trade	10.1	11.9	10.1	10.7	9.3	9.3
Services	28.2	31.7	25.1	30.6	27.9	26.1
Total	100.0	100.0	100.0	100.0	100.0	100.0

Note: The labor force is composed of civilian noninstitutional population 14 years of age and over who, during the reference week, were employed or unemployed. That portion of the labor force enumerated as "clerical" is included here in the Services classification. That portion of the labor force enumerated as "laborers" is included here in the Manufacturing classification.

1971	Canada	B.C.	Prairies	Ontario	Quebec	Atlantic
Primary	8.3	7.3	19.5	5.4	5.2	8.4
Manufacturing	22.2	17.8	10.1	27.4	26.2	15.0
Construction	6.0	7.0	6.2	5.8	5.3	7.5
Transportation	8.8	10.5	9.7	7.5	8.7	10.4
Trade	16.9	19.2	17.2	16.4	15.9	19.8
Services	16.9	19.2	17.2	16.4	15.9	19.8
Total	100.0	100.0	100.0	100.0	100.0	100.0

Note: The labor force is composed of civilian noninstitutional population 14 years of age and over who, during the reference week, were employed or unemployed.

Source: Michael Ray, editor, *Canadian Urban Trends*, Vol. I., (Ottawa, Ontario: Minister of Supply and Services), 1976, pp. 64–65.

growing more rapidly, but there is still manufacturing activity in the central cities. One characteristic that does set manufacturing apart is the significant losses (albeit from large bases) of employment from central cities. Tables 13–19 and 13–20 illustrate that older industrial cities in the U.S. East and Midwest are losing jobs in manufacturing, though their surrounding SMSAs are not. Table 13–20 shows that, in a strict sense, manufacturing firms are not leaving central cities, but rather that central cities are experiencing higher "death rates" for their manufacturing establishments than are surrounding areas. A number of

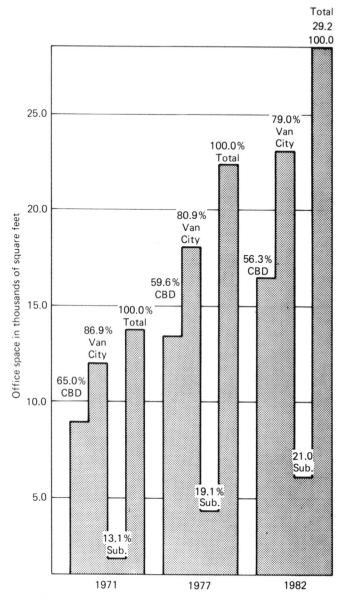

Figure 13–3. Office space: central city and suburban Vancouver, 1971, 1977, 1982. [*Source:* Real Estate Board of Greater Vancouver, *Real Estate Trends in Metropolitan Vancouver, 1973–1974 and 1982* (Vancouver, B.C.: Real Estate Board of Greater Vancouver), 1974 and 1982.]

Table 13–17 Manufacturing Data

| | United States | | | | | | Canada | | | | | |
| | Metro Area | | | Central City | | | Metro Area | | | Central City | | |
	Mean	S.D.	N	Mean	S.D.	N	Mean	S.D.	N	Mean	S.D.	N
Central city establishments as % of metro total (1972/1971)	—	—	—	55.2	19.6	243	—	—	—	71.9	21.2	27
Central city employees as % of metro total (1972/1971)	—	—	—	57.3	22.3	211	—	—	—	69.4	26.5	27
Employees per establishment (1972/1971)	71.9	39.5	250	76.3	48.3	212	73.1	40.9	28	64.3	36.6	38
Change in manufacturing employees in % (1967–72/1966–71)	9.0	29.1	194	7.7	20.4	212	9.9	30.1	17	1.7	27.3	33
Change in value added in % (1967–72/1966–71)	59.5	80.7	200	54.2	54.4	222	53.5	46.1	17	47.3	46.1	33
Central city payroll as % of metro total payroll (1972/1971)	—	—	—	57.5	23.2	211	—	—	—	69.0	27.0	27
Pesons employed in central city manufacturing as % of total metro persons employed in manufacturing (1970/1971)	—	—	—	45.4	20.3	252	—	—	—	66.2	22.7	39

Source: Michael A. Goldberg and John Mercer, *Canadian and American Cities* (forthcoming).

Table 13–18 Employment and Unemployment in Canadian and U.S. Central Cities

	United States			Canada		
	Central City			Central City		
	Mean	S.D.	N	Mean	S.D.	N
Labor force in central city as % of metro total (1970/1971)	48.8	19.5	252	67.7	21.2	39
Total persons employed in central city as % of total persons employed metro (1970/1971)	48.7	19.5	252	67.5	21.2	39
Total persons unemployed in central city as % of total persons unemployed metro (1970/1971)	51.6	19.5	252	70.1	20.8	39

Source: Michael A. Goldberg and John Mercer, *Canadian and American Cities* (forthcoming).

Table 13–19 Manufacturing Employment in Central Cities and Central Industrial Districts of Four Sample Metropolitan Areas, 1965–1968

	Manufacturing Employment			
	1965		1968	
	Number	Number as Fraction of SMSA Total	Number	Number as Fraction of SMSA Total
	Central Cities			
Cleveland	187,190	.627	168,544	.594
Minneapolis	58,262	.384	45,028	.315
St. Paul	44,073	.291	41,498	.299
Boston	92,601	.311	89,636	.289
Phoenix	41,063	.777	50,558	.753
	Central Industrial Districts			
Cleveland	44,319	.148	43,338	.153
Minneapolis	16,720	.110	13,491	.094
St. Paul	12,781	.084	8,799	.061
Boston	13,634	.046	7,724	.025
Phoenix	4,007	.076	904	.058

Source: Raymond Struyk and Franklin James, *Intrametropolitan Industrial Location: The Pattern and Process of Change* (Lexington, Mass.: D. C. Heath), 1975, p. 94.

earlier studies have confirmed that the "flight" from the central city is much more the result of differential birth and death rates for firms in central cities relative to those in surrounding suburban locations.[19] Older central areas are less suited to the needs of modern industry, as we have noted earlier. Thus, older central area firms experience higher death rates than peripherally located firms and also have lower birth rates as new firms choose to locate in more suitable peripheral areas.

Table 13–20 Components of Net Employment Change in Central Cities of the Metropolitan Area, 1968 Relative to 1965 (number of employees)

	Total Net Change	Net in-migration	Net Natural Increase	Net Change in Stationary Establishments
Boston				
Central city	− 2,965	−2,362	−10,735	10,132
Rest of SMSA	14,182	664	− 8,870	22,748
Cleveland				
Central city	−18,646	−4,441	−11,144	− 3,061
Rest of SMSA	4,636	4,606	4,240	4,383
Minneapolis-St. Paul				
Central city	−14,599	−2,764	− 6,200	− 5,635
Rest of SMSA	6,007	2,869	− 1,446	4,422
Phoenix				
Central city	9,495	− 86	374	9,216
Rest of SMSA	4,813	− 36	3,205	1,573

Source: Ray and Struyk and Franklin James, *Intrametropolitan Industrial Location: The Pattern and Process of Change* (Lexington, Mass.: D.C. Heath), 1975, p. 96.

To recapitulate, there does appear to be a decline in central city manufacturing activity. This decline varies greatly from one metropolitan area to the next, with older areas suffering more than newer ones. However, in many cases the decline is only relative and not absolute, with the central city shrinking relative to surrounding and more rapidly growing suburan areas. If present trends continue or accelerate and are not ameliorated by offsetting increases in office and retail activities, then central cities could face dire consequences. For the time being, it appears that, despite sluggish growth or even decline, the amount of manufacturing activity in central cities is still significant. This is true even in the United States. In Canada, the situation is quite different, and concern has stemmed not so much from the flight of manufacturing as from its continued high concentration and ensuing congestion, pollution, and diminished urban environmental quality.[20]

The Flight of Jobs from Metropolitan Areas

In chapter 1, evidence was presented that demonstrated a dramatic shift in population movements in the United States during the 1970s. Previously, metropolitan regions grew rapidly as residents of rural and small urban communities moved to cities and their surrounding suburban areas. Beginning in 1970 this trend, which had lasted for nearly half a century, began to change: Nonmetropolitan communities with 50,000 or fewer inhabitants began to experience growth instead of continued decline.[21] The trend continued through the decade, so that states with historically declining populations, such as Montana and Wyoming, have grown at rates well above the national average.

Manufacturing in particular has found nonmetropolitan settings conducive to production. However, while nonmetropolitan areas are growing relatively faster than metropolitan areas, metropolitan areas are not likely to become extinct, only less dominant than they are at present.

Changing Patterns of Employment within the United States

The following set of tables (13–21 through 13–25) depict shifts in employment within the United States, first from the perspective of metropolitan and nonmetropolitan areas, then by major regions of the United States. Over the period 1962 to 1978, employment in all major categories grew considerably more rapidly in nonmetropolitan areas than in metropolitan areas (Table 13–20). Metropolitan areas in the West and South were gaining employment at rates well above the rest of the United States, while the older metropolitan regions in the Northeast and North Central portions of the United States were growing less slowly (Table 13–22). However, as can be seen from Tables 13–21 through 13–24, metropolitan area employment levels are still substantial. Thus, while so-called Sun Belt areas in the South and West are experiencing growth in both their metropolitan and nonmetropolitan areas, and while nonmetropolitan areas are gaining employment more rapidly than metropolitan areas, it is still fair to conclude that metropolitan areas, even in the Northeast and North Central regions, remain important employment centers.[22]

Finally, turning to Table 13–25, we get some idea about the dynamics of this employment redistribution process. Nonmetropolitan areas were net recipients of some 19,300 workers during the 1970–73 period, the vast bulk of this in-migration from larger (and generally older) metropolitan areas, and were losing workers to smaller metropolitan areas (those with core counties of less than two million persons) and to the suburbs. These trends, first noted in the early 1970s, are continuing.

The larger view that emerges is that metropolitan areas are economically viable and gaining employment. However, the largest metropolitan areas (and usually the oldest) are not growing and are losing employment to smaller metropolitan areas, to nonmetropolitan areas, and to the suburbs.

These data lead one to conclude that nonmetropolitan area gains in employment have been impressive, particularly in light of their previous economic and population decline. In such a context it is clear that metropolitan regions of the United States are growing in the West and South and continue to be large employment centers, even in older declining regions such as the Northeast and North Central regions. In absolute terms, metropolitan area decline is a myth; in relative terms, it is apparent that nonmetropolitan areas have experienced a new surge of growth and economic prosperity that has very much reversed past trends. Nonmetropolitan America in the aggregate must still take a back seat to metropolitan America in terms of total employment and

Table 13–21 Comparisons of Nonfarm Wage and Salary Employment, United States, March 1962–78

Area and Industry Group	March 1962 N (thou.)	Distribution (%)	March 1967 N (thou.)	Distribution (%)	March 1970 N (thou.)	Distribution (%)	March 1974 N (thou.)	Distribution (%)	March 1978 N (thou.)	Distribution (%)
Total	54,192	100.0	64,701	100.0	70,369	100.0	77,509	100.0	83,323	100.0
Goods–Producing	19,759	36.5	22,893	35.4	23,545	33.5	24,424	31.5	24,192	29.0
Manufacturing	16,662	30.7	19,390	30.0	19,764	28.1	19,983	25.7	19,870	23.8
Construction	2,495	4.6	2,897	4.5	3,171	4.5	3,778	4.9	3,644	4.4
Mining	642	1.2	606	0.9	610	0.9	663	0.9	678	0.8
Service–Performing	30,572	56.4	37,606	58.1	42,377	60.2	48,425	62.5	54,437	65.3
Private sector	21,572	39.8	26,126	40.3	29,553	42.0	34,112	44.0	38,492	46.2
Trade	11,215	20.7	13,257	20.5	14,695	20.9	16,592	21.4	18,547	22.3
Services	7,603	14.0	9,735	15.0	11,264	16.0	13,373	17.3	15,420	18.5
FIRE[a]	2,754	5.1	3,134	4.8	3,594	5.1	4,147	5.3	4,525	5.4
Government	9,000	16.6	11,480	17.8	12,824	18.2	14,313	18.5	15,945	19.1
TCU[b]	3,861	7.1	4,202	6.5	4,447	6.3	4,660	6.0	4,694	5.7
Metro[c]	41,030	75.7	48,754	75.4	53,249	75.7	57,843	74.6	61,628	73.9
Goods–Producing	14,823	27.4	16,906	26.2	17,285	24.6	17,319	22.3	16,955	20.3
Manufacturing	12,715	23.5	14,541	22.5	14,654	20.8	14,320	18.4	14,141	16.9
Construction	1,899	3.5	2,160	3.4	2,422	3.5	2,776	3.6	2,592	3.1
Mining	209	0.4	205	0.3	209	0.3	223	0.3	222	0.3

Service–Performing	23,191	42.8	28,527	44.1	32,431	46.1	36,880	47.6	41,039	49.2

Service–Performing	23,191	42.8	28,527	44.1	32,431	46.1	36,880	47.6	41,039	49.2
Private sector	16,935	31.2	20,526	31.7	23,393	33.3	26,736	34.5	29,794	35.7
Trade	8,606	15.9	10,205	15.8	11,372	16.2	12,641	16.3	13,924	16.7
Services[a]	5,990	11.0	7,669	11.8	8,957	12.7	10,601	13.7	12,090	14.5
FIRE[a]	2,339	4.3	2,652	4.1	3,064	4.4	3,494	4.5	3,780	4.5
Government	6,256	11.6	8,001	12.4	9,038	12.8	10,114	13.1	11,245	13.5
TCU[b]	3,016	5.5	3,321	5.1	3,533	5.0	3,644	4.7	3,634	4.4
Nonmetro	13,162	24.3	15,947	24.6	17,120	24.3	19,666	25.4	21,695	26.1
Goods–Producing	4,936	9.1	5,987	9.2	6,260	8.9	7,105	9.2	7,237	8.7
Manufacturing	3,907	7.2	4,849	7.5	5,110	7.3	5,663	7.3	5,729	6.9
Construction	596	1.1	737	1.1	749	1.0	1,002	1.3	1,052	1.3
Mining	433	0.8	401	0.6	401	0.6	440	0.6	456	0.5
Service–Performing	7,381	13.6	9,079	14.0	9,946	14.1	11,545	14.9	13,398	16.1
Private sector	4,637	8.6	5,600	8.6	6,160	8.7	7,376	9.5	8,698	10.5
Trade	2,609	4.8	3,052	4.7	3,323	4.7	3,951	5.1	4,623	5.6
Services[a]	1,613	3.0	2,066	3.2	2,307	3.3	2,772	3.6	3,330	4.0
FIRE[a]	415	0.8	482	0.7	530	0.7	653	0.8	745	0.9
Government	2,744	5.0	3,479	5.4	3,786	5.4	4,169	5.4	4,700	5.6
TCU[b]	845	1.6	881	1.4	914	1.3	1,016	1.3	1,060	1.3

Notes: [a]Finance, insurance, and real estate

[b]Transportation, communication, and utilities

[c]Includes 225 (mostly larger) of the 278 SMSAs through December 31, 1977.

Source: of Claude C. Haren and Ronald W. Holling, "Industrial Development in Non-Metropolitan American: A Locational Perspective," in Richard E. Lonsdale and H. L. Seyler, *Non-Metropolitan Industrialization* (New York: John Wiley and Sons), 1979, p. 18.

Table 13-22 Changes in Nonfarm Wage and Salary Employment, United States, March 1962–78

	1962–1978		1962–1967		1967–1970		1970–1974		1974–1978	
	N (thou.)	(%)	N (thou.)	(%)	N (thou.)	(%)	N (thou.)	(%)	N (thou.)	(%)
Total	29,131	53.8	10,509	19.4	5,668	8.8	7,140	10.1	5,814	7.5
Goods–Producing	4,433	22.4	3,134	15.9	652	2.8	879	3.7	232	0.9
Manufacturing	3,248	19.5	2,768	16.7	374	1.9	219	1.1	113	-0.6
Construction	1,149	46.1	402	16.1	274	9.5	607	19.1	134	-3.5
Mining	36	5.6	-36	-5.6	4	0.7	53	8.7	15	2.3
Service–Performing	23,865	78.1	7,034	23.0	4,771	12.7	6,048	14.3	6,012	12.4
Private Sector	16,920	78.4	4,554	21.1	3,427	13.1	4,559	15.4	4,380	12.8
Trade	7,332	65.4	2,042	18.2	1,438	10.8	1,897	12.9	1,955	10.0
Services	7,817	102.8	2,132	28.0	1,529	15.7	2,109	18.7	2,047	15.3
FIRE[a]	1,771	64.3	380	13.8	460	14.7	583	15.4	378	9.1
Government	6,945	77.2	2,480	27.6	1,344	11.7	1,489	11.6	1,632	11.4
TCU[b]	833	21.6	341	8.8	245	5.8	213	4.8	34	0.7
Metro[c]	20,598	50.2	7,724	18.89	4,495	9.2	4,594	8.6	3,785	6.5
Goods–Producing	2,132	14.4	2,083	14.1	379	2.2	34	0.2	364	2.1
Manufacturing	1,426	11.2	1,826	14.4	113	0.8	-334	-2.3	179	-1.3
Construction	693	36.5	261	13.8	262	12.1	354	14.6	-184	-6.6
Mining	13	6.2	-4	-1.9	4	2.0	14	6.7	-1	-0.4

Service–Performing	17,848	77.0	5,336	23.0	3,904	13.7	4,449	13.7	4,159	11.3
Private sector	12,859	75.9	3,591	21.2	2,867	14.0	3,343	14.3	3,058	11.4
Trade	5,318	61.8	1,599	18.6	1,167	11.4	1,269	11.2	1,283	10.1
Services	6,100	101.8	1,679	28.0	1,288	16.8	1,644	18.4	1,489	14.0
FIRE[a]	1,441	61.6	313	13.4	412	15.5	430	14.0	286	8.2
Government	4,989	79.7	1,745	27.9	1,037	13.0	1,106	12.2	1,101	10.9
TCU[b]	618	20.5	305	10.1	212	6.4	111	3.1	-10	-0.3
Nonmetro	8,533	64.8	2,785	21.2	1,173	7.4	2,546	14.9	2,029	10.3
Goods–Producing	2,301	46.6	1,051	21.3	273	4.6	845	13.5	132	1.9
Manufacturing	1,822	46.6	942	24.1	261	5.4	553	10.8	66	1.2
Construction	456	76.5	141	23.7	12	1.6	253	33.8	50	5.0
Mining	23	5.3	-32	-7.4			39	9.7	16	3.6
Service–Performing	6,017	81.5	1,698	23.0	867	9.6	1,599	16.1	1,853	16.1
Private Sector	4,061	87.6	963	20.8	560	10.0	1,216	19.7	1,322	17.9
Trade	2,014	77.2	443	17.0	271	8.9	628	18.9	672	17.0
Services	1,717	106.4	453	28.1	241	16.7	465	20.2	558	20.1
FIRE[a]	330	79.5	67	16.2	48	10.0	123	23.2	92	14.1
Government	1,956	71.3	735	26.8	307	8.8	383	10.1	531	12.7
TCU[b]	215	25.4	36	4.3	33	3.7	102	11.2	44	4.3

Notes: [a]Finance, insurance, and real estate

[b]Transportation, communication, and utilities

[c]Includes 225 (mostly larger) of the 278 SMSAs through December 31, 1977.

Source: Claude C. Haven and Ronald W. Holling, "Industrial Development in Non-Metropolitan America; Locational Perspectives," in Richard E. Lonsdale and H. L. Seyler, *Non-Metropolitan Industrialization* (New York: John Wiley and Sons), 1979, p. 19.

Table 13–23 Comparisons of Nonfarm Wage and Salary Employment, United States and by Regions, March 1962–78

Area and Industry Group	Overall		Northeast		North Central		South		West	
	1978 (thou.)	1962 (thou.)	1978 (thou.)	1962 (thou.)	1978 (thou.)	1962 (thou.)	1978 (thou.)	1962 (thou.)	1978 (thou.)	1962 (thou.)
Total	83,323	54,192	19,197	15,430	22,695	15,557	25,991	14,676	15,440	8,529
Goods–Producing	24,192	19,759	5,599	6,111	7,249	6,052	7,668	5,006	3,656	2,590
Manufacturing	19,870	16,622	5,001	5,475	6,319	5,350	5,813	3,818	2,737	1,979
Construction	3,644	2,495	564	576	838	587	1,489	837	753	495
Mining	678	642	34	60	92	115	386	351	116	431
Service–Producing	54,437	30,572	12,514	8,246	14,209	8,399	16,818	8,619	10,896	5,308
Private sector	38,492	21,572	9,179	6,176	10,227	6,047	11,500	5,795	7,586	3,554
Trade	18,547	11,215	4,029	2,964	5,126	3,264	5,802	3,144	3,590	1,843
Services	15,420	7,603	3,921	2,288	3,993	2,059	4,394	1,965	3,112	1,291
FIRE[a]	4,525	2,754	1,229	924	1,108	724	1,304	686	844	420
Government	15,945	9,000	3,335	2,070	3,982	2,352	5,318	2,824	3,310	1,754
TCU[b]	4,694	3,861	1,084	1,073	1,237	1,106	1,485	1,051	888	631
Metro[c]	61,628	41,030	16,188	13,399	16,033	11,289	17,055	9,363	12,352	6,979
Goods–Producing	16,955	14,823	4,587	5,227	5,158	4,603	4,287	2,825	2,923	2,168
Manufacturing	14,141	12,715	4,122	4,700	4,574	4,169	3,150	2,121	2,295	1,725
Construction	2,592	1,899	458	502	568	413	986	579	570	405
Mining	222	209	7	25	16	21	141	125	58	38

Service-Performing	41,039	23,191	10,656	7,220	9,969	5,875	11,697	5,791	8,717	4,305
Private sector	29,794	16,935	7,927	5,518	7,418	4,415	8,204	4,011	6,245	2,991
Trade	13,924	8,606	3,433	2,625	3,579	2,309	4,010	2,145	2,902	1,527
Services	12,090	5,990	3,365	2,029	2,966	1,526	3,179	1,344	2,580	1,091
FIRE[a]	3,780	2,339	1,129	864	873	580	1,015	522	763	373
Government	11,245	6,256	2,729	1,702	2,551	1,460	3,493	1,780	2,472	1,314
TCU[b]	3,634	3,016	945	952	906	811	1,071	747	712	506
Nonmetro	21,695	13,162	3,009	2,031	6,662	4,268	8,936	5,313	3,088	1,550
Goods-Producing	7,237	4,936	1,012	884	2,091	1,449	3,401	2,181	733	422
Manufacturing	5,729	3,907	879	775	1,745	1,181	2,663	1,697	442	254
Construction	1,052	596	106	74	270	174	493	258	183	90
Mining	456	433	27	35	76	94	245	226	108	78
Service-Performing	13,398	7,381	1,858	1,026	4,240	2,524	5,121	2,828	2,179	1,003
Private sector	8,698	4,637	1,252	658	2,809	1,632	3,296	1,784	1,841	563
Trade	4,623	2,609	596	339	1,547	955	1,792	999	688	316
Services	3,330	1,613	556	259	1,027	533	1,215	621	532	200
FIRE[a]	745	415	100	60	235	144	289	164	121	47
Government	4,700	2,744	606	368	1,431	892	1,825	1,044	838	440
TCU[b]	1,060	845	139	121	331	295	414	304	176	125

Notes: [a]Finance, insurance, and real estate
[b]Transportation, communication, and utilities
[c]Includes 225 (mostly larger) of the 278 SMSAs through December 31, 1977.

Source: Claude C. Haven and Ronald W. Holling, "Industrial Development in Non-Metropolitan America: A Locational Perspective," in Richard E. Lonsdale and H. L. Seyler, Non-Metropolitan Industrialization (New York: John Wiley and Sons), 1979, p. 28.

Table 13–24 Comparisons of Changes in Nonfarm Wage and Salary Employment, United States and by Regions, March 1962–78

Area and Industrial Group	Overall N (thou.)	Overall (%)	Northeast N (thou.)	Northeast (%)	North Central N (thou.)	North Central (%)	South N (thou.)	South (%)	West N (thou.)	West (%)
Total	29,131	53.8	3,767	24.4	7,138	45.9	11,315	77.1	6,911	81.0
Goods–Producing	4,433	22.4	−512	−8.4	1,197	19.8	2,682	53.6	1,066	41.2
Manufacturing	3,248	19.5	−474	−8.7	969	18.1	1,995	52.3	758	38.3
Construction	1,149	46.1	−12	−2.1	251	42.8	652	77.9	258	52.1
Mining	36	5.6	−26	−43.3	−23	−20.0	35	10.0	50	43.1
Service–Performing	23,865	78.1	4,268	51.8	5,810	69.2	8,199	95.1	5,588	105.3
Private sector	16,920	78.4	3,003	48.6	4,180	69.1	5,705	98.4	4,032	113.4
Trade	7,332	65.4	1,065	35.9	1,862	57.0	2,658	84.5	1,747	94.8
Services	7,817	102.8	1,633	71.4	1,934	93.9	2,429	123.6	1,821	141.1
FIRE^a	1,771	64.3	305	33.0	384	53.0	618	90.1	464	110.5
Government	6,945	77.2	1,265	61.1	1,630	69.3	2,494	88.3	1,556	88.7
TCU^b	833	21.6	11	1.0	131	11.8	434	41.3	257	40.7
Metro^c	20,598	50.2	2,789	20.8	4,744	42.0	7,692	82.2	5,373	77.0
Goods–Producing	2,132	14.4	−640	−12.2	555	12.1	1,462	51.8	755	34.8
Manufacturing	1,426	11.2	−578	−12.3	405	9.7	1,029	48.5	570	33.0
Construction	693	36.5	−44	−8.8	155	37.5	417	70.0	165	40.7
Mining	13	6.2	−18	−72.0	−5	−23.8	16	12.8	20	52.6

Service–Performing	17,848	77.0	3,436	47.6	4,094	69.7	5,906	102.0	4,412	102.5
Private sector	12,859	75.9	2,409	43.7	3,003	68.0	4,193	104.5	3,254	108.8
Trade	5,318	61.8	808	30.8	1,270	55.0	1,865	86.9	1,375	90.0
Services	6,100	101.8	1,336	65.8	1,440	94.4	1,835	136.5	1,489	136.5
FIRE[a]	1,441	61.6	265	20.7	293	50.5	493	94.4	390	104.6
Government	4,989	79.7	1,027	60.3	1,091	74.7	1,713	96.2	1,158	88.1
TCU[b]	618	20.5	-7	-0.7	95	11.7	324	43.4	206	40.7
Nonmetro	8,533	64.8	978	48.2	2,394	56.1	3,623	68.2	1,538	99.2
Goods–Producing	2,301	46.6	126	14.5	642	44.3	1,220	55.9	311	73.7
Manufacturing	1,822	46.6	104	13.4	564	47.8	966	56.9	188	74.0
Construction	456	76.5	32	43.2	96	55.2	235	91.1	93	103.3
Mining	23	5.3	-8	22.9	-18	-19.1	19	8.4	30	38.5
Service–Performing	6,017	81.5	832	81.1	1,716	68.0	2,293	91.1	1,176	117.2
Private sector	4,061	87.6	594	80.3	1,177	72.1	1,512	84.0	778	138.2
Trade	2,014	77.2	257	75.8	592	62.0	793	79.4	372	117.7
Services	1,717	106.4	297	114.7	494	92.7	594	95.7	332	166.0
FIRE[a]	330	79.5	40	66.7	91	63.2	125	76.2	74	157.4
Government	1,956	71.3	238	64.7	539	60.4	781	74.8	398	90.5
TCU[b]	215	25.4	18	14.9	36	12.2	110	36.2	51	40.8

Notes: [a]Finance, insurance, and real estate
[b]Transportation, communication, and utilities
[c]Includes 225 (mostly larger) of the 278 SMSAs through December 31, 1977.

Source: Claude C. Haven and Ronald W. Holling, "Industrial Development in Non-Metropolitan America: Locational Perspectives," in Richard E. Lonsdale and H. L. Seyler, *Non-Metropolitan Industrialization* (New York: John Wiley and Sons), 1979, p. 29,

Table 13–25   Place-to-Place Net Migration of Work Force for Metropolitan and Nonmetropolitan Counties, 1960–63 and 1970–73 (in thousands)

| | Central Counties with Populations of: | | | | | | | |
| | 2 Million or More | | Less than 2 Million | | Suburban | | Non-Metropolitan | |
Type of County	1960–63	1970–73	1960–63	1970–73	1960–63	1970–73	1960–63	1970–73
Central with population of:								
2 million or more	NA	NA	− 13.4	141.5	65.1	75.8	− 24.6	53.5
less than 2 million	13.4	−141.5	NA	NA	−35.1	−14.7	−109.5	−30.9
Suburban	−65.1	− 75.8	35.1	14.7	NA	NA	− 25.4	− 3.3
Nonmetropolitan	24.6	− 53.5	109.5	30.9	25.4	3.3	NA	NA

Note: Positive numbers indicate net in-migration; negative numbers indicate net out-migration.

Source: "Brian J. Berry and Donald C. Dahmann, "Population Redistribution in the United States in the 1970's," *Population* and Development Review 3(4:1977):462.

economic activity. A somewhat different pattern appears in the Canadian context, making generalization of the U.S. experience questionable.

Changing Patterns of Employment in Canada

Are there analogous shifts evident in Canada? Is the extant or emerging Canadian pattern of employment different from what we just observed in the United States? Answering these questions is the focus of this section.[23]

Specifically, Tables 13–26 and 13–27 set out demographic and employment figures for provinces and Census Metropolitan Areas (CMAs), respectively. Looking first at the data for the provinces (Table 13–26), we can see that the traditional central areas of Ontario and Quebec are not keeping pace with the West (especially British Columbia and Alberta), and on some dimensions, such as in the growth of personal and per capita income, are even losing out to the Maritimes. If we look at data for CMAs, we see from Table 13–27 that CMAs in Saskatchewan, Alberta, and British Columbia are growing in employment at rates that are considerably faster than the national average and those for cities in Ontario and Quebec. The focus of economic activity appears to be shifting away from Ontario and Quebec, a trend that seems to be accelerating according to partial but more recent data.[24]

A review of population trends, particularly migration between the provinces from 1961 to 1976, reinforces this impression that a shift is under way from the central provinces of Ontario and Quebec to peripheral provinces both east and west. Table 13–28 presents the relevant data. Interestingly, the traditionally declining Atlantic provinces of eastern Canada have shown a strong resurgence of population

Table 13–26 The Variations of Growth: Provinces, 1971–76

Province	Demographic Growth			Employment Growth			Income Growth		
	Natural Increase	Net Migration	Total Growth	Change in Participation Rate	Change in Employment Rate	Number of Jobs	Gross Provincial Product	Personal Income	Personal Income/Capita
Newfoundland	8.9%	−1.9%	6.8%	6.2%	−6.5%	12.0%	32.7%	75.5%	64.3%
P.E.I.	2.3	3.6	5.9	4.4	−3.4	12.2	39.0	87.6	71.2
Nova Scotia	3.1	1.9	5.0	1.5	−0.4	10.6	34.3	59.2	51.6
New Brunswick	3.5	3.2	6.7	2.5	−2.1	12.4	39.4	66.0	55.5
Quebec	3.6	−0.2	3.4	8.5	2.8	22.9	29.4	52.6	47.5
Ontario	3.1	4.2	7.3	0.5	0.8	13.8	27.0	41.8	32.2
Manitoba	3.3	0.1	3.7	1.8	2.1	12.1	35.9	54.2	49.2
Saskatchewan	3.3	−3.8	− 0.5	7.5	2.4	14.7	53.9	81.1	82.2
Alberta	6.0	6.9	12.9	4.3	2.6	28.3	81.6	79.6	59.0
B.C. and Territories	3.8	9.3	13.1	1.4	0.3	20.6	74.8	58.8	39.6
Canada	4.3	2.3	6.6	3.4	1.2	17.8	35.9	52.6	43.2

Source: Larry S. Bourne and James W. Simmons, *Canadian Settlement Trends* (University of Toronto: Centre for Urban and Community Studies, Major Report #15), p. 48.

Table 13–27 Metropolitan Growth in Canada, 1961–1981

Rank (1976)	Census Metropolitan Area (CMA)	Population (in 000's)							% Change				1976 Employment Index 1961 = 100
		1961	(1966)	1966	(1971)	1971	1976	1981	1961-66	1966-71	1971-76	1976-81	
1	Toronto	1,825	(2,157)	2,290	(2,628)	2,602	2,803	2,999	18.2	14.8	7.6	7.0	157.4
2	Montreal	2,110	(2,436)	2,571	(2,731)	2,729	2,802	2,828	15.5	6.7	2.6	.9	137.8
3	Vancouver	790	(892)	933	(1,082)	1,082	1,166	1,268	12.9	16.0	7.6	8.8	171.6
4	Ottawa-Hull	430	(495)	529	(596)	620	693	718	15.1	13.9	11.8	3.6	175.0
5	Winnipeg	476	(509)	509	(540)	550	578	585	6.8	6.2	5.1	1.2	134.9
6	Edmonton	337	(401)	425	(491)	496	554	657	18.9	16.4	11.7	19.0	196.3
7	Quebec	358	(413)	437	(481)	501	542	576	15.6	10.1	8.1	6.3	140.9
8	Hamilton	395	(449)	457	(496)	503	529	542	13.6	9.0	5.2	2.5	138.4
9	Calgary	279	(331)	331	(403)	403	470	593	18.5	21.6	16.5	26.2	203.7
10	St. Cathrines-Niagara	217	(229)	285	(302)	286	302	304	5.9	6.2	5.6	.7	146.0
11	Kitchener-Waterloo	155	(192)	192	(227)	239	272	288	24.3	18.0	14.0	5.9	177.0
12	Kondon	181	(207)	254	(286)	253	270	284	14.4	12.9	6.8	5.2	137.1
13	Halifax	184	(198)	210	(223)	251	268	278	7.7	6.3	6.9	3.7	148.1
14	Windsor	193	(212)	238	(259)	249	248	246	9.5	8.5	-0.4	-0.8	166.0
15	Victoria	154	(175)	175	(196)	196	218	234	12.5	11.7	11.4	7.3	160.4
16	Sudbury	111	(117)	137	(155)	158	157	150	5.7	16.0	-0.4	-4.5	120.4
17	Regina	112	(131)	132	(141)	141	151	164	16.9	6.3	7.4	8.6	162.0
18	St. John's	91	(101)	118	(132)	132	143	155	11.0	12.1	8.7	8.4	166.1
19	Oshawa	80	(100)	106	(120)	120	135	154	30.8	13.0	12.3	14.1	152.4
20	Saskatoon	96	(116)	116	(126)	127	134	154	21.3	9.1	5.7	14.9	165.2
21	Chicoutimi-Jonquere	105	(109)	133	(134)	126	129	135	5.9	0.9	1.7	4.7	81.7
22	Thunder Bay	92	(96)	108	(112)	115	119	121	17.6	3.2	2.9	1.7	156.2
23	Saint John	96	(101)	104	(107)	107	113	114	5.2	2.4	5.8	.9	138.4
24	Sherbrooke	—	—	80	(85)	97	104	111	—	6.2	7.2	6.7	133.2

Sources: L. S. Bourne, "Emergent Realities of Urbanization in Canada: Some Parameters and Implications of Declining Growth" (University of Toronto: Centre for Urban and Community Studies), Research Paper No. 96, July 1978, p. 14.
Statistics Canada, *1981 Census of Canada*, Catologue Number 95-903 (Ottawa, Ontario: Statistics Canada), 1982.

Table 13–28   Provincial Growth Rates and Interprovincial Migration, 1961–76

Province	Average Annual Geometric Growth Rate			Net Interprovincial Migration		
	1966–71	*1971–76*	*1976–81ᵃ*	*1961–66*	*1966–71*	*1971–76*
Newfoundland	1.14	1.33	0.35	−15,213	− 19,344	− 1,856
Prince Edward Island	0.57	1.15	0.72	− 2,970	− 2,763	+ 3,754
Nova Scotia	0.86	0.98	0.45	−27,125	− 16,396	+11,307
New Brunswick	0.57	1.31	0.55	−25,679	− 19,596	+16,801
Quebec	0.84	0.68	0.64	−19,860	−122,735	−77,610
Ontario	2.05	1.42	0.86	+85,369	+150,712	−38,559
Manitoba	0.52	0.66	0.09	−23,470	− 40,690	−26,828
Saskatchewan	−0.62	−0.11	1.00	−42,094	− 81,398	−40,753
Alberta	2.16	2.46	4.00	− 1,984	+ 32,008	+58,571
British Columbia	3.12	2.46	2.15	+77,747	+114,966	+92,285
Canada	1.51	1.29	1.14			

Source: L. S. Bourne, "Emergent Realities of Urbanization in Canada: Some Parameters and Implications of Declining Growth" (University of Toronto: Centre for Urban and Community Studies), Research Paper No. 96, July 1978, p. 19.
ᵃCalculated from Statistics Canada, *1981 Census of Population,* Catalogue Number 92-901 (Ottawa, Ontario: Statistics Canada), 1982.

growth. Such growth augurs well for future employment growth, as population-serving activities (see Chapter 3) move to the region to cater to the growing population.

Available data do not point to the boom in nonmetropolitan population and employment that we witnessed in the United States. Tables 13–29 and 13–30 however do demonstrate that the movement of Canadians into metropolitan regions has slowed considerably. The three largest CMAs (Montreal, Toronto, and Vancouver) all grew at a slower rate than did the Canadian population during the period 1971 to 1976. The most rapid growth was recorded by metropolitan regions of the next echelon, such as Edmonton, Calgary, and Ottawa.

This leveling off of metropolitan concentration in Canada may be a preamble to future relative decline, as has happened in the United

Table 13–29   Degree of Metropolitan Population Concentration Canada, 1941–1976

	1941	*1951*	*1971*	*1976*	*1981ᵃ*
Population of three national metropolises (in 000's)	2,449	3,244	4,725	6,771	7,095
Total national population (in 000's)	11,507	14,009	18,238	22,993	24,343
% In three national metropolises	21.3	23.2	29.7	29.5	29.1
% In 23 metropolitan areas	40.2	44.9	55.4	55.5	55.9

ᵃCalculated from 1981 Canada population figures in Statistics Canada, *1981 Census of Canada.* Catalogue Number 95-903 (Ottawa, Ontario: Statistics Canada), 1982.

Source: L. S. Bourne, "Emergent Realities of Urbanization in Canada: Some Parameters and Implications of Declining Growth" (University or Toronto: Centre for Urban and Community Studies), Research Paper No. 96, July 1978, p. 16.

Table 13–30 Population Growth of Urban Centered Regions, by Level in the Urban Hierarchy, 1971–1976

	Number of Centers	*Population 1976 (in 000's)*	*Growth Rate 1971–76 (%)*
National metropolises	3	6,771	4.9
Major regional centers	8	4,829	8.4
Regional centers	14	3,453	3.7
Small regional centers	36	4,308	8.1
Local centers	64	3,633	5.1
Total	125	22,993	6.4

Source: L. S. Bourne, "Emergent Realities of Urbanization in Canada: Some Parameters and Implications of Declining Growth," Research Paper No. 96, July 1978, Centre for Urban and Community Studies, University of Toronto, p. 14.

States. We can conclude that the Canadian urban system is stable, though there does appear to be a shift of people and jobs toward peripheral provinces.

Summing Up the Myth and Reality of Metropolitan Decline

The evidence for the United States demonstrates that there has been a rather dramatic shift of population and employment into nonmetropolitan areas during the 1970s. This shift reversed a period of decline that confronted nonmetropolitan areas for most of this century, and has been most notable in the South and West and in the nonmetropolitan areas of these rapidly growing regions. Employment shifts have largely been concentrated in the manufacturing sector, though it is reasonable to expect that services will grow rapidly in the future to keep pace with population growth. [25] Despite the impressive gains in people and jobs in nonmetropolitan America, metropolitan America still holds over 70 percent of manufacturing jobs and nearly 70 percent of the nation's population.

For the beneficiaries of this change, community growing pains and the loss of those very amenities that attracted people in the first place are real possibilities. It is likely that growth policies will become popular in rapidly growing nonmetropolitan areas. Growth, as we learned during the 1970s, is no longer perceived as an unquestioned good. The "go-go" boosterism that has tended to typify many of the Sun Belt and nonmetropolitan areas is most likely going to be replaced by the kind of protectionism we have witnessed in suburban areas. [26]

In Canada, metropolitan areas have lost neither people nor jobs. Rather, they have stabilized their share of people and jobs. Whether or not this is a precursor to the relative decline of metropolitan areas observed in the United States remains an unknown. Canadians appear to perceive their cities in more favorable terms than do Americans, and thus Canadian cities and the surrounding suburbs are more likely to hold population and continue to grow at or above the national rates.[27]

Overall, therefore, it is safe to conclude that the "myth of metropolitan job flight" is just that, a myth. Metropolitan areas in the United States have held their own, even if we look at the largest and oldest areas that have suffered job loss. The jobs that remain still constitute a considerable employment pool. In Canada, we can make a stronger statement and assert that metropolitan areas remain the focus of economic activity and, though their rate of growth has diminshed, show no signs of losing jobs at this point.

POLICY INTERVENTIONS: FAILURE AND SUCCESSES

In the absence of any "problem" concerning metropolitan decline, we can focus our attention here on those attempts to alter recent experience vis-à-vis central city employment trends. We can typify Canadian concerns as focusing on job deflection and growth management to maintain the viability of central cities and avoid congestion, environmental decay, and loss of households.

In contrast, U.S. central cities have sought a range of growth-promotion policies to attract and retain employment. These policies include subsidies, advertising campaigns, and even direct grants. The net result of these policies was not as intended: Central cities in the United States on average continued to lose jobs, though we cannot know to what extent job loss was minimized by policy interventions.

The overall strategy to be followed might instead focus on altering the present actual or perceived profitability of doing business in central city locations in large metropolitan areas, given the failure of past approaches. Subsidized land and building costs and property taxes often are insufficient to compensate for higher costs due to labor unrest, crime, congestion, and a whole host of uncertainties related to doing business in declining central city areas. Policy should take into account the profitability of carrying on business at different locations, and then seek to influence the profitability through policy intitiatives. Lowering costs on nonessential inputs will do little to change locational patterns. A knowledge of locational economics is a necessary prerequisite to policy formulation and implementation.

One of the principal devices to encourage relocation or growth of firms has been the use of a variety of tax subsidies and incentives.[28] The evidence does not support the use of such subsidies and incentives[29], and such special treatment does not rate very highly on the locational criteria of surveyed firms.[30] It does not appear to address the needs of those firms that provide the bulk of new employment in urban regions—new and small firms.[31] Given the great expense of these inducements and given their ineffectiveness in actually influencing location decisions, there appears to be little justification for their continuation.

The reasons for the poor showing of tax subsidies and other inducements to firms are not difficult to trace. They are aimed exclusively at the cost side of the profit equation. They ignore revenue and productivity factors that could be strongly influenced by the provision of high-quality publicly provided services such as education and training programs.

Another class of locational incentives relates to the importance placed on land for expansion by industrial firms. The inability to expand in central city locations has been shown by Hamer and others to be a key impediment to central city industrial locations holding their own when compared with suburban or nonmetropolitan locations.[32] To overcome these problems, local governments, particularly in older central cities, have sought to assemble large parcels of land to encourage central city industrial development. Most new jobs come from small and volatile (and often new) firms that possess relatively modest land needs but require a host of services and amenities in their economic environment.[33]

Recent work has stressed the importance for firms in most industries of the existence of strong and growing markets,[34] of the availability of factors of production, particularly skilled and dependable supplies of labor,[35] of the adequacy of credit,[36] and of the existence of reasonably high-quality urban environments in the broadest sense (e.g., crime, pollution, crowding, noise, etc.)[37] These factors lie largely outside the purview of government action, particularly short- and medium-term local government action.

A number of innovative suggestions have been propounded recently, but they have not yet been implemented through legislation or other policy changes. Virtually all of the suggestions discussed below appeared in some form in the much-publicized (it was widely both damned and acclaimed) National Urban Policy Report of the President of the United States, unveiled in the summer of 1978.[38] The document dealt with an enormous range of urban policy issues. We will focus on those that related to urban economies and to job creation or retention, particularly for the ailing older urban economies in the Northeast and North Central states. We will also briefly examine some of the responses and policy alternatives spawned by the publication of the National Urban Policy Report.

A National Urban Policy for the United States

The 1978 President's National Urban Policy Report presented a sweeping set of proposals to assist urban areas. It documented at some length the plight of older cities and then developed a set of nine policy objectives to overcome these difficulties. These objectives proceeded along a broad front, from increased federal coordination via urban impact analysis of federal agency expenditures and policies, to greater community involvement. The main thrust of all the objectives was to put distressed cities back on their feet through providing investment and job creation incentives and improving the delivery of social, economic, and health services.[39]

Despite the defeat of the Carter Administration and the anti-intervention philosophy of the Reagan Administration, the report is still worth discussing as a take-off point.[40] Specific policy proposals can be grouped under the following four headings:

1. Capital incentives. Included here were proposals to establish a National Development Bank to attract capital investment into distressed areas. Tax incentives were put forward in the form of investment tax credits for new industrial investment in distressed urban areas. Estimated cost: $11 billion.

2. Labor incentives. Public works projects and employment tax credits are the focal points here. An estimated 60,000 jobs would be created at a cost of perhaps $500 million.

3. Direct aid. Several forms of direct aid are envisioned. Targeted aid to cities with unemployment rates above the national average is to replace some of the extant revenue sharing. In addition, small sums were to be made available to neighborhood groups for rehabilitation and revitalization.

4. Federal coordination. An Inter-Agency Coordinating Council at the Cabinet level was proposed to channel, among other things, federal facilities and procurement into distressed urban areas. The development of Urban Impact Statements for federal programs was also suggested as a means for helping to achieve coordination.

The response to these proposals was as varied as the proposals themselves. An entire issue of the *Journal of Regional Science* devoted a majority of its pages to five analyses of the *Report.*[41] The *Report* also stimulated a variety of comments and analyses from citizen action groups[42] and academics.[43] Several important critical themes emerged and are worth summarizing here.

1. The Wrong Model of Urban Development is Implicit in the Report. The *Report* proceeds from the implicit assumption that industry (e.g., manufacturing and related warehousing activity) is the basis for a sound and growing urban economy. Evidence is presented by both Birch[44] and Hirschhorn[45] that seriously questions this assumption and strongly suggests that service and higher-technology employment is really the road to the future, not merely a larger dose of the economic activities of the 1950s and 1960s.

2. The Wrong Firms are Being Targeted for Assistance. A number of people noted that new and young firms are the sources of employment gains, not merely expanding existing plants or attracting new branch plants.[46]

3. The Wrong Techniques are Being Employed. Given the preceding weaknesses of the *Report,* it is not at all surprising that critics focused on the proposed tech-

niques to provide assistance, namely tax incentives, capital subsidies, and other grants. Daniels and Kieschnick summarize these weaknesses when focusing on an alternative development financing system (alternative to the National Development Bank). However, their comments have general utility in the present context. It is more important to avoid certain past pitfalls at the outset than necessarily to focus on the details of more appropriate aid systems. The three items on their avoidance list are:

- the use of tax and financial incentives, both of which have been shown to exert little influence on the pattern of economic development;

- the use of development finance to try and overcome all of the cost and quality-of-life problems, leading ultimately to economic distress; and

- the financing of large corporations whose activities create few new jobs and whose decisions are not affected by either lowered cost or increased availability of capital.[47]

Similarly, the use of employment tax credits and public works spending are seen as having been largely ineffective in the past.[48]

4. The Wrong People are Being Helped. The investment and job creation programs that are the crux of the *Report* are not seen as reaching the neediest groups, the urban poor and unemployed. The various incentives are seen as assisting large and wealthy corporations, and skilled and middle- to upper-income workers.[49] Little trickle-down effect is seen likely to occur at the neighborhood level.

In view of the criticisms then, what policies are likely to be appropriate and effective? First, critics point out that knowing which programs to avoid based on current research is in itself an enormous step in the right direction. If an economic turnaround is to be achieved in depressed central city areas, it must be rooted in those small and young, volatile firms that point the way to future economic activities.[50] Such firms require significant capital to finance their uncertain beginnings and the provision of a financing system that gives such firms access to capital markets.[51]

Once we leave the development financing area, the suggestions begin to diverge. Some groups stress more funding of grass roots, neighborhood-based activity.[52] Others focus on income maintenance and the provision of needed public services.[53] Finally, it is suggested that a more fundamental approach be taken that looks at the institutional and cultural base of distressed areas.[54]

The important point to note in all of the above is that old approaches have finally been demonstrated to be ineffective and perhaps even harmful.[55] The effort and debate stimulated by the *Report* has had significant positive benefit. Ultimately, the process must move from debate and discussion to legislation and progarm evaluation.

A National Urban Policy for Canada

As we have stressed, it is absolutely essential that we develop an appreciation of the differences that exist among and between cities as well as an appreciation of generalities. We saw above that it was incorrect to say that metropolitan areas were in decline. Metropolitan areas of less than two million people in Sun Belt states have been thriving. We must therefore be extremely careful when attempting generalizations. This is particularly true when trying to generalize from the American experience to develop urban economic policy in the Candian context. The constitutional basis for federal action in cities is severely restricted in Canada, which helps to explain in large measure the relative absence of federal urban policies.

A national urban policy in Canada is largely impossible because of the allocation of powers under the Canadian constitution, the Canada Act. This act (originally of British Parliament) allocates powers to the federal parliament (in Section 91) and to the provincial legislatures (in Section 92). One of the powers allocated to provinces is over "municipal institutions" [Section 2(8)] and "property and civil rights" [Section 92(13)].[56] This allocation has been held to be the exclusive purview of provinces, largely precluding direct federal involvement and discouraging even indirect involvement.[57] The system has worked well, in general.[58]

However, during the 1960s, American perceptions of urban crises spawned two notable efforts in Canada to search for national urban policies. The first was the Task Force on Housing and Urban Development (the Hellyer Task Force, after its chairman, then Minister of Transport and Minister Responsible for Housing, Paul Hellyer). After touring the country to gather evidence about the nature and dimensions of the urban crisis, the task force published its findings in December 1968.[59] Paramount among these was the call for a Department of Urban Affairs at the federal level.

However, within two years, Harvey Lithwick of Carleton University was asked by Robert Andras, the Minister Responsible for Housing at the time, to prepare a report on the nature of the urban crisis in Canada and to suggest approaches to solving the crisis. The report appeared in 1970 under the title *Urban Canada: Problems and Prospects.*[60] Its primary conclusion and its implications are at great variance with analogous policies in the United States. Specifically, the report notes:

The assumption, then,is that controlling urban growth can expand choice in the future. This emerges from our findings that rapid urban growth exacerbates the scarcity of land in large urban areas, and thereby distorts the housing market, the transport system, and urban public economy—indeed the whole mix of urban problems. A policy that moderates these growth impacts—that strives for a more optimal growth process—eases these pressures in the largest metropolitan areas. This arrests the degenerative process which limits choice, and it permits the accumulation of public resources to deal with the backlog of extant problems. it also provides the opportunity to plan for new, more desirable urban alternatives.[61]

The Lithwick Report did in fact lead to some federal action. In June 1971 the Ministry of State for Urban Affairs was instituted with the express role of coordinating federal policy and fostering cooperation with provincial and municipal governments.[62] The role of MSUA was tightly defined and its powers carefully proscribed.

By the late 1970s however, it was becoming increasingly obvious that Canada's urban areas suffered from few of the actual and perceived ills of those in the United States. The federal role in housing and its impacts on urban environments was clearly established with procedures for carrying out the provisions of the National Housing Act via the Canada Mortgage and Housing Corporation (CMHC). Where federal policies do impinge on local areas, the decade of the 1970s had provided a format for federal/provincial/municipal discussion.

The Ministry of State for Urban Affairs was discontinued by decision of the federal Cabinet, and it ceased operations on March 31, 1979, its policy and planning activities largely reverting to CMHC where they have resided since. One may conclude that the demise of MSUA is indicative of the success that Canada's urban areas have had in dealing with urban development and the various dimensions of urban problems. The intergovernmental bargaining and coordinating devices that have evolved out of the Canadian system of federalism provide for many of the needs that were the genesis of MSUA.[63]

SUMMARY

In this chapter we explored two widely held and growing beliefs, that central cities are suffering severe commercial and industrial decline and major employment losses, and that the metropolitan areas are suffering an analogous decline brought on by the recent rapid growth of nonmetropolitan areas. These views were subjected to empirical analysis for both Canada and the United States.

In Canada, we found that both beliefs did not apply. To the extent that concern for cities and metropolitan areas exists, it is focused on questions of growth management and the maintenance of high-quality urban environments.

When turning to the case of U.S. cities, there is evidence to support the fears concerning job losses.[64] Two caveats need to be inserted. First, these losses do not represent a wholesale migration of central city activities. Rather, they appear to be the result of older and more slowly growing industries and economic activities in central cities. Surburban and nonmetropolitan areas are the recipients of new and growing firms in new and growing industries. Thus, over time, central cities are losing out.[65] Second, despite documented employment and population losses, central cities still contain large numbers of jobs and people. They are far from extinct, though they are in need of revitalization.[66]

When we look at the questions of metropolitan decline, a different picture emerges. There is little evidence to support the proposition that metropolitan areas are losing out in terms of people and jobs to nonmetropolitan areas. It does appear that older and larger metropolitan areas are suffering some declines, though metropolitan areas taken as a whole, particularly those in Sun Belt states, are continuing to grow.

Against this background, two very different policy approaches have emerged in Canada and the United States. Essentially, the status quo is being accepted in Canada and there are no grand initiatives either at the federal or the provincial level to promote urban growth. In fact, quite the reverse seems to be the case, with lingering fears that continuing rapid urban growth must be controlled and managed so as to avoid "big city" problems such as those perceived as plaguing big cities in the United States.

In the United States, where the need for policy initiatives is clearer, especially to help ailing older cities, we saw that a number of policy proposals have recently come to the fore. The federal basis for action is predicated on the proposition that industrial growth and the attraction of any and all types of firms is the route to success. Recent work demonstrates that new and young firms, usually smaller firms, in new and young industries are the real sources of future growth, yet the needs of these firms are little understood and little appreciated in present policy statements.

One final note: We have been stressing the need to understand the institutions and particulars of specific urban problems and policies[66] This chapter has once again pointed to the merit of such an approach. While generalization as a process of reasoning and problem solving is powerful, it must be tempered with an appreciation of specific local conditions.

Footnotes

1. An earlier attempt to force greater focus and clarity on urban problem solving and problem defining is Raymond Vernon, *The Myth and Reality of Our Urban Problems* (Cambridge, Mass.: Harvard Univesity Press), 1962.

2. The utility of this comparative perspective and some of the details of the differences that exist between U.S. and Canadian cities are spelled out in Michael A. Goldberg and John Mercer, "Canadian and U.S. Cities: Basic Differences, Possi-

ble Explanations, and Their Meaning for Public Policy," *Papers of the Regional Science Association* 45(1980): 159–183.

3. For an excellent discussion of the variety of agglomeration economies, see Hugh O. Nourse *Regional Economics* (New York: McGraw-Hill), 1968, pp. 85–92.

4. David L. Huff, *Determination of Intraurban Retail Trade Areas* (Los Angeles, Cal.: University of California, Real Estate Research Program), 1962. An interesting and equally usable variant of Huff's approach is to be found in T. R. Lakshmanan and W. G. Hansen, "A Retail Market Potential Model," *Journal of the American Institute of Planners* 31(2:1965):134–143.

5. Two studies that address these linkages explicitly and are forerunners of more recent work are: Michael J. Bannon, *Office Location in Ireland: The Role of Central Dublin* (Dublin, Ireland: An Foras Forbartha), 1973; and J. B. Goddard, *Office Linkages and Location: A Study of Communications and Spatial Patterns in Central London* (London, England: Pergamon Press), 1973.

6. For a more detailed discussion of this point, see Michael A. Goldberg, *Intrametropolitan Industrial Location and the Theory of Production* (Berkeley, Cal.: University of California, Center for Real Estate and Urban Economics), 1969.

7. William Alonso, "A Reformulation of Classical Location Theory and Its Relation to Rent Theory," *Papers of the Regional Science Association 19(1967):23–44.*

8. See Goldberg, *op. cit.*, and Alonso, *op cit.*, for elaborations of the central, but often overlooked, point.

9. See Nourse, *op. cit.*, on agglomeration economies. Also see Benjamin Chintz, *City and Suburb* (Englewood Cliffs, N.J.: Prentice-Hall), 1964, pp. 3–50; Harry W. Richardson, *Urban Economics* (New York: Holt, Rinehart and Winston), 1978, especially Chapter 3, pp. 41–54; and George A. Nader, *Cities of Canada,* Volume 1 (Toronto: Macmillan of Canada), 1975, pp. 10–12 and 102–103.

10. See a discussion of this recent growth of nonmetropolitan areas in the United States presented in Chapter 1 of this text. Also see Peter Morrison, "The Current Demographic Context of National Growth and Development," RAND Corporation Publications P-5514 (Santa Monica, Cal.: The RAND Corporation), 1975; Gene F. Summers, Sharon D. Evans, Frank Clemente, E. M. Beck, and Jon Minkoff, *Industrial Invasion of Nonmetropolitan America: A Quarter Century of Experience* (New York: Praeger Publishers), 1976; and, most recently, Richard E. Lonsdale and H. L. Seyler, eds., *Nonmetropolitan Industrialization* (New York: John Wiley and Sons), 1979.

11. ULI—The Urban Land Institute, *Mixed Use Development* (Washington, D.C.: ULI—The Urban Land Institute), 1973.

12. This trend was noted as early as 1957 by Donald L. Foley, *The Suburbanization of Office Activities in the San Francisco Bay Area* (Berkeley, Cal.: University of California, Real Estate Research Program), 1957. More recently, it has been documented by Regina B. Armstrong, *The Office Industry* (New York: The Regional Plan Association), 1972; and by Leland S. Burns and Wing Ning Pang, "Big Business in the Big City: Corporate Headquarters in the CBD, " *Urban Affairs Quarterly* 12(4:1977):533–544.

13. Richard C. Harkness, *The Impact of Changing Telecommunica-Technology* (Menlo Park, Cal. Stanford Research: Institute), 1975.

14. See Lonsdale and Seyler, *op. cit.*; Summers *et al.*, *op. cit.*,; Andrew S. Hamer, *Industrial Exodus from Central City* (Lexington, Mass.: D. C. Heath), 1973; and Donald N. Stone, *Industrial Location in Metropolitan Areas,* (New York: Praeger Publishers), 1974.

15. See footnote 10 above, and also David C. Perry and Alfred J. Watkins, eds., *The Rise of Sunbelt Cities* (Beverly Hills, Cal.: Sage Publications), 1977; and Leonard F. Wheat, *Urban Growth in the Nonmetropolitan South* (Lexington, Mass.: D. C. Heath), 1976. .

16. See supporting evidence from Avery M. Guest, "Nighttime and Daytime Populations of Large American Suburbs," *Ruban Affairs Quarterly* 12(1:1976):57–82; William J. Young, "Distance Decay Values and Shopping Center Size," *The Professional Geographer* 27(3:1975):304–309; and J. Dennis Lord, "Locational Shifts in Supermarket Patronage," *The Professional Geographer* 27(4:1975):310–313.

17. See Armstrong, *op. cit.*, and also Peter Cowan, Daniel Fine, John Ireland, Clive Jordan, Dilys Mercer, and Angela Sears, *The Office: A Facet of Urban Growth* (New York: American Elsevier Publishing Company, Inc.), 1969; P. W. Daniels, *Office Location: An Urban and Regional Study* (London, England: G. Bell and Sons Ltd.), 1975; and Ian C. Alexander, *The City Centre* (Perth, Australia: The University of Western Australia Press), 1974.

18. Wolfgang Quante, *The Exodus of Corporate Headquarters from New York City* (New York: Praeger Publishers), 1976.

19. See Vernon, *op. cit.*; Goldberg, *op. cit.*; and David L. Birch, *The Job Generation Process* (Cambridge, Mass.: MIT Program on Neighborhood and Regional Change), 1979.

20. Len Gertler and Ron Crowley, *Changing Canadian Cities: The Next 25 Years* (Toronto, Ontario: McClelland and Stewart), 1977, Chapters 5, 7, and 9.

21. Morrison, *op. cit+.*

22. Perry and Watkins, *op. cit.*, and Wheat (1976), *op. cit.*

23. We question the generality of these trends both in the United States and certainly across national boundaries, as we have clearly stated with respect to their relevance for Canada. Brian J. L. Berry, "The Counterurbanization Process: How General? in Niles M. Hansen, ed., *Human Settlement Systems: International Perspectives on Structure, Change and Public Policy* (Cambridge, Mass.: Ballinger Publishing Co.), 1978, pp. 25–49, also questions the generality of the phenomenon.

24. For details, see: *Canada's Business Climate* (Toronto, Ontario: Department of Economic Research, The Toronto Dominion Bank), issued quarterly; *Economic Review* (Ottawa, Ontario: Department of Finance), issued annually in April; *Canada Yearbook* (Ottawa, Ontario: Statistics Canada), annually; and Larry S. Bourne and James W. Simmons, *Canadian Settlement Trends: An Examination of the Spatial Pattern of Growth, 1971–76* (Toronto, Ontario: Centre for Urban and Community Studies, University of Toronto), 1979.

25. Lonsdale and Seyler, *op. cit.*

26. We already reviewed the growth control issue in Chapter 11. A convenient collection of articles and views is available in the four-volume compendium from

the Urban Land Institute. See Randall W. Scott, ed., *Management and Control of Growth* (Washington D.C.: ULI—The Urban Land Institute), 1975.

27. The summary of this survey of just over 11,000 households appears in Canada Mortgage and Housing Corporation, *Public Priorities in Urban Canada: A Survey of Community Concerns (Ottawa, Ontario: Canada Mortgage and Housing Corporation), 1979.*

28. For a detailed account of the major subsidy instruments, see John E. Moes, *Local Subsidies for Industry* (Chapel Hill, N.C.: The University of North Carolina Press), 1962.

29. See Belden H. Daniels and Michael Kieschnick, *Theory and Practice in the Design of Development Finance Innovations* (Washington, D.C.: U.S. Economic Development Administration), 1978, especially Chapter 1. Also see Birch, *op. cit.,* and R. W. Schmenner, *The Manufacturing Location Decision: Evidence from Cincinnati and New England* (Washington, D.C.: U.S. Economic Development Administration), 1978.

30. Two well-known and frequently consulted survey research studies rank such special treatment low in importance. See Eva Mueller and James N. Morgan, "Location Decisions of Manufacturers," *American Economic Review* 52(3:1962):204–217; and Melvin L. Greenhut and Marshall R. Colberg, *Factors in the Location of Florida Industry* (Tallahassee, Fla.: The Florida State University), 1962. More recently, an econometric study to forecast industrial location in the United States for 24 industries and 3097 counties in the 48 contiguous states did not even use a tax variable or any other proxy for government subsidy. See James C. Burrows, Charles E. Metcalf, and John B. Kaler, *Industrial Location in the United States* (Lexington, Mass.: D.C. Heath), 1971.

31. Birch, *op. cit.,* and Daniels and Kieschnick, *op. cit.*

32. See Hamer, *op. cit.,* for evidence from Boston; Schmenner, *op. cit.,* with evidence for Cincinnati; and Henrik Van de Linde, *Demand for Industrial Property and Metropolitan Location,* unpublished M.Sc. thesis, (Vancouver, B.C.: The University of British Columbia), 1973, presenting data for Vancouver.

33. Raymond, J. Struyk and Franklin J. James, *Intrametropolitan Industrial Location: The Pattern and Process of Change* (Lexington, Mass.: D.C. Heath), 1975; and Goldberg, 1969, *op. cit.*

34. Schmenner, *op. cit.,* and Wheat (1973), *op. cit.*

35. Hamer, *op. cit.,* Birch, *op. cit.,* and Stone, *op. cit.*

36. Daniels and Kieschnick, *op. cit.,* and Peter Bearse, "Toward a National Growth Policy—Critical Reviews: Influencing Capital Flows for Urban Economic Development: Incentives or Institution Building?" *Journal of Regional Science* 19(1:1979):79–91.

37. Birch, *op. cit.,* Lonsdale and Seyler, *op. cit.,* and Goldberg (1969), *op. cit.*

38. Office of the President of the United States, *The President's National Urban Policy Report* (Washington, D.C. : U.S. Department of Housing and Urban Development), 1978.

39. *Ibid.,* pp. 122–128.

40. William W. Goldsmith and Michael J. Derian, "Toward a National Urban Policy—Critical Reviews: Is There an Urban Policy?" *Journal of Regional Science* 19(1:1979):93–108, quoted on p. 95.

41. *Journal of Regional Science,* 19(1:1979):67–129.

42. For example, see The National Urban Policy Collective, "Carter's National Urban Policy: A Response," (San Francisco, Cal.: National Urban Policy Collective), mimeographed, 1978; and Marc Allan Weiss and Erica Schoenberger, "Carter's 'New' Urban Strategy: Peanuts" (San Francisco, Cal.: The National Urban Policy Collective), 1979.

43. Daniels and Kieschnick, *op. cit.,* and Belden H. Daniels and Michael Kieschnick, *Development Finance: A Primer for Policymakers,* Parts I–III (Washington, D.C.: The National Rural Center), 1978; and Birch (1979), *op. cit.*

44. Birch, *op. cit.*

45. Larry Hischhorn, "Toward a National Urban Policy—Critical Reviews: The Urban Crisis: A Post-Industrial Perspective," *Journal of Regional Science* 19(1:1979):109–118.

46. Daniels and Kieschnick, *op. cit.,* Birch, *op. cit..,* and Bearse, *op. cit.*

47. Daniels and Kieschnick, *op. cit.,* Part III, p. 1.

48. National Urban Policy Collective, *op. cit.,* and Robert P. Inman, "Toward A National Urban Policy—Critical Reviews: Federal Policy and the Urban Poor," *Journal of Regional Science* 19(1:1979):119–129.

49. National Urban Policy Collective, *op. cit.,* Inman, *op. cit.,* and Goldsmith and Derian, *op. cit.*

50. Daniels and Kieschnick, *op. cit.,* and Birch, *op. cit.*

51. Daniels and Kieschnick, *op. cit.,* Birch, *op. cit.,* and Bearse, *op. cit.*

52. National Urban Policy Collective, *op. cit.,* and Weiss and Schoenberger, *op. cit.*

53. Inman, *op. cit.*

54. Bearse, *op. cit.*

55. National Urban Policy Collective, *op. cit.,* p. 2.

56. Elmer A. Driedger, ed., *The British North America Acts, 1867–1975* (Ottawa, Ontario: Supply and Services Canada), 1976.

57. Peter H. Russell, *Leading Constitutional Cases* (Toronto, Ontario: MacMillan of Canada), 1978.

58. The virtues of the present federal-provincial-municipal sharing of powers and responsibilities are set out in Michael A. Goldberg, "The BNA Act, NHA, CMHC, MSUA, etc.: 'Nymophobia' and the On-Going Search for an Appropriate Canadian Housing and Urban Development Policy," in Michael Walker, ed., *Canadian Confederation at the Crossroads: The Search for a Federal-Provincial Balance* (Vancouver, B.C.: The Fraser Institute), 1978, pp. 320–361.

59. Paul Hellyer, *Report of the Task Force on Housing and Urban Development* (Ottawa, Ontario: Queen's Printer), 1969.

60. N. H. Lithwick, *Urban Canada: Problems and Prospects* (Ottawa, Ontario: Central Mortgage and Housing Corporation), 1970.

61. Lithwick, *op. cit.,* p. 228. Gertler and Crowley, *op. cit.,* p. 420, make a similar point.

62. See *Hansard,* "A Speech by Ron Basford," House of Commons, March 13, 1972, pp. 766–770.

63. George Sternlieb and James W. Hughes, eds., *Post-Industrial America: Metropolitan Decline and Inter-Regional Job Shifts* (New Brunswick, N.J.: Center for Urban Policy Research, Rutgers—The State University), 1975.

64. John R. Mollenkopf, cited in Hirschhorn, *op. cit.*, p. 117.

65. See, for example, James H. Boykin, *Industrial Potential of the Central City* (Washington, D.C.: ULI—The Urban Land Institute), 1973.

66. The need for institutional context cannot be stressed enough. The U.S. experience cannot easily be generalized, even to Canada, where it should be of relevance, if anywhere. As an example of the need to get behind surface similarities, see the study of the decline of the central city in Britain by Colin Jones, ed., *Urban Deprivation and The Inner City* (London, England: Croom Helm), 1979. Ian Alexander's study for Australia, *op. cit.*, provides yet another point of comparison of apparent similarities.

14

ISSUES IN LOCAL PUBLIC FINANCE

INTRODUCTION

The earlier chapter on the local public sector detailed the principal revenues and expenditures incurred. Primacy on the revenue side goes to the real property tax, accounting for almost two-thirds of the total of locally raised revenues. This revenue source has been under broad political attack.

The property tax revolt has been extensive across the United States. In the state of California, the passage of Proposition 13 has limited property tax payments to 1 percent of market value, implying a substantial reduction in both the taxes to property owners and revenues to governments.[1]

Further, the future increase in property tax payments also has been limited. In Massachusetts, an issue is the relatively large proportion of total assessable property owned by tax-exempt institutions such as religious organizations, governments at the federal, state, and local levels, and educational institutions. For a given level of local public goods, this requires relatively high effective property tax rates on land and improvements not exempt. Hence, the passage of Proposition 2½, limiting property tax liabilities to 2½ percent of market value, marks a substantial reduction in property tax liabilities for that state.

There are several implications of drastic property tax reductions and limitations. First, given the lack of access of local government to money creation, expenditures must be reduced. This leads to questions about the stability of local government institutions, and whether new residents are willing to pay higher prices for property with access to fewer services. Second, the theory of property tax capitalization is required to determine whether tax reductions increase market values. If so, paradoxically, the tax cut could ultimately increase local government revenue through increasing the value of real property in a jurisdiction with lower taxes, yielding a local government analog of the Laffer curve.[2]

The general equilibrium consequences of the property tax are discussed next. Not only does the property tax affect allocation of resources to the real estate sector, but also to other activities as well. If property taxes, housing costs, or labor are high, immigration is reduced. Higher labor costs and capital costs for property reduce output. The property tax thus has effects on employment and capital markets well beyond the bounds of local real estate markets alone.

In the next section, a detailed discussion of the progressive or regressive aspect of the property tax is carried out. If the property tax is regressive, there are distributional considerations to examine as well. Next we examine the relationship between property taxes, the delivery of local public services, and land prices. Higher property taxes do not necessarily imply lower land prices. The result depends on the degree to which services are affected and the degree to which taxes are capitalized into (or discounted from) property values. A further issue is whether the property tax is an excise or profits tax. If it is an excise tax levied on a commodity, the relatively inelastic demand for land causes this tax to be shifted to consumers, or homeowners in the case of residential property. This may account for homeowner resentment of the property tax as manifested in Proposition 13. An alternative theory is that the property tax is a tax on profits, and thus falls on business owners rather than tenants. Of course, this still involves taxes falling on owner-occupiers as producers and consumers of housing services.

These are some of the more salient issues that surround the problem of financing the local public sector. The chapter ends with some conclusions about the appropriateness of the tax and with some implications for public policy vis-à-vis financing local government.

PROPERTY TAX CRISIS

Introduction

The major confrontation over property taxes in the late 1970s in the United States surrounds the passage of Proposition 13 in California on June 7, 1978. It is worth examining this proposition in detail. There are three main provisions.

1. *Limit on property tax rate.* The maximum proportional rate of property taxation is 1 percent of the full cash value of the property. The only exception concerns taxes used to pay the interest and redemption charges on any indebtedness approved by the voters prior to the passage of Proposition 13.

2. *Restricted definition of full cash value.* For purposes of the legislation, full cash value is defined as the county assessor's evaluation of real property as shown on the 1975–76 tax bill. Subsequent to 1975, the full cash value is the market value at which the property changes hands.

3. *Limited increase in full cash value.* Increases in the full cash value are limited to an annual rate of 2 percent, with the exception of properties changing hands.

Since the previous average property tax rate in California had been 2.6 percent, the initiative reduces tax rates by more than one-half. In addition to the above, state and local governments are prohibited from levying any further taxes on property. There are some obvious implications of the above provisions. Specifically, differential tax rates apply to similar property, since new purchasers are typically being heavily taxed at a full cash value based on their actual purchase price, while existing homeowners are taxed on much lower property values reflecting the lags in assessment procedures.

Returning to the discussion of Chapter 7, recall the argument that property taxes may be capitalized in the price of houses. The issue here is whether residents of a given jurisdiction benefit from a property tax revolt in increased house prices, and if so, by how much. The key assumption in all models is that service levels are equated across communities. If this is not the case, whether through imperfect information by homeowners or disequilibrium in specific local submarkets, the model must be amended to take account of capitalization of benefits and services.

Table 14–1 indicates pre- and post-Proposition 13 house prices in the San Francisco metropolitan area.[3] The indication is that prices did increase, most notably in the most expensive areas. However, these are

Table 14–1 House Prices in San Francisco Metropolitan Area Pre- and Post-Proposition 13

Municipality	January–June 1978 (Thousands of $)	January–June 1979 (Thousands of $)	Change Post/Pre (%)	Change Pre/1976 Base (%)
Alameda	79.0	85.0	7.6	56.5
Albany	64.0	74.0	15.6	41.8
Berkeley	80.0	94.0	17.5	45.4
Fremont	69.5	85.0	22.3	58.6
Hayward	60.0	70.0	16.7	39.5
Livermore	67.0	78.0	16.4	50.0
Newark	65.0	77.0	18.5	48.8
Oakland	50.0	56.0	2.0	—
Pleasanton	78.0	87.0	11.5	46.3
San Leandro	62.0	76.0	22.6	39.5
Union City	62.0	67.0	8.1	53.6
Antioch	52.0	58.0	11.5	34.2
Clayton	87.0	108.0	24.1	37.5
Concord	64.0	68.0	6.2	35.4
El Cerrito	73.0	87.0	19.2	42.3
Hercules	75.0	78.0	4.0	61.7
Martinez	62.0	67.0	8.1	46.3
Moraga	121.0	135.0	11.6	57.5

Table 14–1 *(Continued)*

Municipality	January–June 1978 (Thousands of $)	January–June 1979 (Thousands of $)	Change Post/Pre (%)	Change Pre/1976 Base (%)
Pinole	63.0	69.0	9.5	36.3
Pittsburg	52.0	55.0	5.8	40.0
Pleasant Hill	88.0	109.0	23.9	39.3
Richmond	42.0	49.0	16.7	38.7
San Pablo	44.0	51.0	15.9	33.3
Walnut Creek	88.0	94.0	6.8	33.8
Corte Madera	80.0	132.0	51.7	29.7
Fairfax	89.0	105.0	20.7	44.8
Larkspur	109.0	149.0	36.7	18.8
Mill Valley	116.0	143.0	23.3	37.5
Novato	95.0	122.0	24.4	47.4
San Anselmo	90.0	131.0	33.7	15.0
San Rafael	98.0	114.0	21.3	36.0
Sausalito	135.0	181.0	34.1	47.8
Tiburon	179.0	259.0	44.7	77.1
Napa	64.0	71.0	10.9	43.2
St. Helena	66.0	82.0	24.2	38.7
Yountville	63.0	83.0	31.7	34.0
Atherton	236.0	337.0	42.8	38.2
Belmont	103.0	128.0	24.3	27.6
Burlingame	121.0	138.0	14.1	46.9
Daly City	69.0	76.0	10.1	34.6
Half Moon Bay	91.0	129.0	41.7	—
Hillsborough	243.0	337.0	38.7	29.1
Menlo Park	103.0	123.0	19.4	42.1
Millbrae	110.0	116.0	5.4	35.0
Pacifica	70.0	78.0	11.4	36.0
Portola Valley	187.0	246.0	31.6	53.0
Redwood City	92.0	106.0	15.2	30.2
San Bruno	81.0	84.0	3.7	45.6
San Carlos	94.0	113.0	20.2	39.7
San Mateo	101.0	105.0	4.0	42.8
South San Francisco	76.0	82.0	7.9	50.0
Woodwide	226.0	269.0	19.0	86.1
Cotati	61.0	83.0	36.1	—
Healdsburg	63.0	70.0	11.1	—
Petaluma	65.0	78.0	20.1	—
Rohnert Park	59.0	70.0	18.6	—
Santa Rose	60.0	75.0	25.0	—
Sebastopol	73.0	77.0	5.5	—
Sonoma	64.0	82.0	28.1	—
Benicia	59.0	73.0	23.7	—
Fairfield	47.0	50.0	6.4	—
Suisun City	53.0	51.0	−3.8	—
Vacaville	55.0	61.0	10.9	—
Vallejo	50.0	52.0	4.0	—

Source: K. T. Rosen, "The Impact of Proposition 13 on House Prices in Northern California: A Test of the Interjurisdictional Capitalization Hypothesis," *Journal of Political Economy* 90 (1982): 197–8, Table 2.

average prices, and there may be changes in the composition and quality of houses sold. Atherton and Hillsborough, already the most expensive areas prior to Proposition 13, recorded respective increases of 42.8 percent and 38.7 percent. In other areas, the percentage increases were smaller, and it should be noted that the initiative was passed during a period when large house price increases were already occurring.

Tax Effects

Assuming perfect mobility and equal benefits in communities 1 and 2, the model states that, all else being equal, house prices should differ in percentage terms by the difference in tax rates. If community 1 has an effective tax rate of 1 percent and community 2 has a corresponding rate of 1.25 percent, house prices in community 2 should be 25 percent lower. The percentage difference in prices is the difference in prices in logarithms, so:

$$\ln \left(\frac{P_1}{P_2}\right) = t_2 - t_1 \tag{14.1}$$

Suppose property taxes are cut with no reduction in service. For the short run, as occurred in California, state general revenues may be used to fund the shortfall, in which case the homeowner is virtually a free rider. House prices then increase by the capitalized value of the tax saving, or:

$$\Delta P_i = \sum_{n=1}^{\infty} (1 + r)^{-n} T_{ni} \tag{14.2}$$

where T_{ni} is the tax liablility in future years n in community i, with $T_{ni} = t_{ni} P_{ni}$, or the product of the tax rate and the market value of the house. Note that there is some feedback effect, for the reduction in property tax rates may increase house prices, thereby increasing liabilities. The limit in changes in full cash value prohibited this from occurring in California.

House prices obviously change for many reasons in addition to the capitalization factor given on the right side of (14.2). One must therefore determine the weight (or capitalization coefficient) in an expression such as

$$\sum_{n=1}^{\infty} (1 + r)^{-n} T_{ni}$$

to estimate property tax effects on house prices to use the model appropriately. Rosen indicates that $1 in annual tax saving increases house prices by $7. He concludes that the results are consistent with full capitalization at an interest rate of 12 to 15 percent, the inverse of the capitalization factor.[4]

Several points should be noted, apart from the usual issues of whether perfect mobility or equal community service levels and quality actually exist. First, the observation of substantial house price increases in some areas implies that some houses face tax liability increases if they change hands. This provides an economic rent to an immobile owner and reduces the number of housing transactions, for the tax rate changes on purchase. A benefit arises to an owner that does not accrue to the market generally. An interesting testable hypothesis is whether long-term rental contracts or delayed interim and closing contracts to preserve the tax benefits have emerged in post-Proposition 13 California. This is because on sale, market value becomes the assessment base. If a house is not sold, the assessment remains at the existing level. Second, there may be a reduction in service, another testable hypothesis. This has a further effect in reducing house prices as these capitalizations take place. Third, given that property taxes are deductible in computing state and federal income tax liabilities, the effect on house prices must be attenuated somewhat. In fact, it implies that the state and federal governments receive an increase in net taxes. Such governments are beneficiaries of the reduction in local taxes. Depending on marginal tax rates, higher levels of government may receive as much as half the tax savings.

In terms of the context in which the property tax crisis has developed, an increasing share of the total state and local tax burden was assumed by residential property during the 1970s. Single-family houses accounted for 44.3 percent of all property tax revenue in the state in the 1978–79 fiscal year, in comparison with 36.2 percent in 1964–65. Further, assessment occurs in California every three years, and in 1978–79 the rising house prices of the period had not been completely reflected in assessments.

The problems with a large increase in house prices, perhaps created by people seeking an inflationary hedge, is that some people may not be generating the income flows to pay large tax increases.[5] People obtain large capital gains that can be realized only on sale of a house, but increased assessments call for increased taxes immediately. If capital markets were perfect, the homeowner could borrow against his or her housing equity to finance the additional tax liability. Typically, financial institutions also require collateral that involves cash flow, such as earnings, prior to the advancement of a mortgage.

To examine this in detail, consider a homeowner facing a market mortgage rate of r, and a single mortgage. Suppose that title owners or those with some equity could invest this holding at the same rate r. Maintenance expenditures are q in percentage terms, property taxes are t, and expected capital gains on housing in percentage terms are p^e, all in percentage rates. For an owner with a zero marginal rate of personal state and federal income tax, and for all households in Canada,

$$u = r + q + t - p \qquad (14.3)$$

is the user cost of one unit of housing services. If mortgage interest is tax-deductible and the homeowner is not in a zero marginal tax bracket, the formula is altered.

If all capital is substitutable, then the user cost of housing should be proportional to the user cost of any other capital. View the homeowner as an investor. If he or she were not owning housing, the net equity would be invested in an alternative form of capital, with rental price u_a. So:

$$u = \lambda u_a \tag{14.4}$$

where λ is a constant, reflecting the substitution between housing and other capital. If $\lambda = 1$, housing is perfectly substitutable with, or identical to, other capital.

As in the case of the United States during the mid-1970s, let there be no adjustments in interest rates or maintenance. This implies:

$$\begin{aligned} -\lambda \Delta p_a &= -\Delta u \\ &= -\Delta(t - p) \end{aligned} \tag{14.5}$$

or $\Delta = \Delta p - \lambda p_a$. The change in tax rate depends on house prices and general inflation. If house capital gains are untaxed, so that housing is an attractive inflationary hedge, then the required tax rate increase is even larger.

Expenditure and Service Effects

For Proposition 13, the estimate was that the property tax bill for Californians would be reduced by $7 billion, or 57 percent.[6] The property tax yields about 40 percent of gross local revenues. However, given that the state possessed a surplus, the transfer of resources prevented a major reduction in local services.

Whether there is a long-run reduction in services depends on institutional arrangements facing the local public sector. Welfare expenditures, the largest component of which provides assistance to single parents with dependent children, is administered by local governments and partially funded by them in the United States. Eligibility for receiving benefits is tied to criteria established by state and federal governments.

An attempt to reduce school expenditures faces similar difficulties, apart from rigidities in areas such as teacher contracts and job security. Legislation and judicial rulings on education finance and the provision of services may make reductions difficult. In the area of police and fire services, local governments must maintain these facilities at given levels or risk losing emergency state assistance.

The potential effect of Proposition 13 on local revenues is substantial. However, the effect is mitigated by the transfer of funds from the state to local governments, as indicated in Table 14–2. The property tax load was reduced to less than half, from $12.448 billion to $5.404 billion, but the overall reduction in revenue amounted to only 4 percent. This effect may ultimately become larger if the state reduces its transfers to local government. In California's case, the state transferred its immediate surplus to the municipalities.

Table 14–2 Reduction in the Average Level of Local Public Service Caused by Proposition 13 ($ millions)

Changes in local revenues caused by Proposition 13		
1977–78 property tax collection	$11,452	
1978–79 officially estimated property tax collections	5,404	
Net Change		−$6,048
Adjustments		
State relief	4,100	
Additional property tax revenue due to higher assessments	405	
Total		4,505
Projected increase in other revenues, 1977–78 to 1978–79		1,716
Net change in revenues		173
Changes in revenue necessary to maintain 1977–78 service levels		
1.08 × 1978–78 expenditure	2,288	
Less wage share (55%)	1,258	1,030
Revenue deficiency	857	
Percent revenue deficiency	2.8%	

Source: G. Kaufman and K. Rosen, eds., *The Property Tax Revolt: The Case of Proposition 13* (Cambridge, Mass.: Ballinger), 1981, p. 46.

Tax Reductions and the Market of Real Estate

It has been argued earlier that because tax reductions are geared toward existing owners, not only in Proposition 13 but in similar initiatives, there is an effect to reduce turnover and transactions. This is dampened slightly because the user cost of homeownership is also reduced relative to renting, since property taxes are reduced for all owners and there is an incentive to purchase.

The annual allowed increase of 2 percent in assessment implies that even if a property changes hands and is immediately revalued, the subsequent assessment may lag behind fair market value as long as house prices are increasing at more than 2 percent annually. This occurs if assessments are not made on an annual basis. Further, jurisdictions with low turnover rates will have a tax base relatively lower than those with higher turnover rates, again provided house prices increase at more than 2 percent annually.

As an example of the effect of such a policy on the municipal revenue base, let α be the turnover rate. Then, in the first year after a tax reduction, all houses are reassessed to A_L, an earlier assessment. To simplify, suppose the houses are identical, as in a tract or subdivision. The market price is $A > A_L$, and let the effective property tax rate be t_e. Were market value assessments in force, tax revenue would be:

$$T = t_e A(1 + \pi) \tag{14.6}$$

where T is the collection on any one house and π is the rate of house inflation. As an alternative to the identical-house assumption, the collection T can be assumed to apply to the average house.

Subsequent to the revaluation, houses are reduced to A_L in assessment. At the end of the first year, with α of the houses trading and with t the new reduced rate, average tax liabilities are:

$$T = t(1 + \pi_a)[\alpha A + (1 - \alpha)A_L] \qquad (14.7)$$

in comparison with $t_e A(1 + \pi)$ under market value assessments, with π the rate of inflation in house prices and π_a the allowed rate of increase. Consider the following example.

$$
\begin{array}{llll}
\alpha = .1 & \pi_a = 0.02 & t = .01 & A_L = \$50,000 \\
t_e = .026 & \pi = 0.10 & & A = \$80,000
\end{array}
$$

where the t_e estimate of .026 corresponds exactly to that prevailing in California prior to the passage of Proposition 13, and t is the reduced rate of taxation. So $T = .026 \times \$80,000 \times 1.1 = \$2288$, the total tax bill had there been market value assessments.

Now $\alpha A_L + (1 - \alpha)A$ is $0.1 \times \$80,000 + 0.9 \times \$50,000 = \$53,000$. With $t(1 + \pi_a)$ being .0101, the liability is \$535.30, a substantial reduction from the previous \$2288. If the turnover rate declines, the tax liability is further depressed. In fact, the marginal change in tax liability with respect to the turnover rate is $t(1 + \pi_a)(A - A_L)$, which means that reduced turnover reduces taxes.

The distribution of turnover is also relevant. An area where the same houses tend to turn over repeatedly, for example, in rental properties, will have lower tax revenue, all else being equal, than one where turnover is distributed more uniformly. The reason is that as inflation progresses, houses with the same owner have a valuation well behind market value.

The issues and implications for the housing market may be summarized as follows.

1. Mobility and efficiency in housing are reduced by skewing the benefits of tax reductions toward long-term residents.

2. Service and tax reductions may be disproportionate.

3. The offset from the increase in the federal and state governments reduces the tax saving (in the United States only).

The Effect on Financial Markets

Another effect occurs in financial markets. In the case of the United States, municipal authorities issue debt securities, frequently under federal-tax-exempt status. The implicit or explicit collateral for these securities is the tax revenue collected and the property base which underlies it. If the tax revenue is reduced substantially, the implied risk of holding municipal bonds may be viewed by financial markets as greater. In such an instance, potential bondholders will require a premium, and interest rates on these bonds will increase and municipal finances worsen further.

Two other considerations arise. First, the usual tax-exempt status implies that the market interest rate is below that of securities carrying no tax-free position. If the market rate of interest is r, and the rate of return on municipal bonds is r_e, where r_e is less than r, then:

$$r_e = (1 - t)r \tag{14.8}$$

where t is a threshold marginal tax rate. Investors whose personal marginal tax rate is greater than t will hold municipal bonds, all else being equal. Those with a rate less than t hold the alternative bonds.

Second, the reduction in property taxes has the effect of raising the marginal tax rate for homeowners, since the property tax deduction is reduced for those who itemize. This occurs in U.S. jurisdictions, but in Canada, where property taxes are not deductible, there is no effect. If the threshold marginal tax rate rises, the required return on municipal bonds falls.

In short, there are two effects from property tax reductions in the financial market. The first may be termed the revenue risk effect, where investors require a higher return as compensation for the reduced municipal tax capacity. The second is a marginal tax rate effect, where a lower return is required as tax rates for investors increase on the marginal dollar, which holds for resident bondholders only.

Municipal bonds are legally classified by the sources of revenues from which interest and principal payments are made.[7] An important category is that of general obligation bonds, which depend on the above-mentioned capability of municipalities to levy and collect taxes. This is the "full faith and credit" provision.

A test of the theory has been applied to California bonds.[8] Suppose that people did not expect the passage of Proposition 13. Let the return on bond i be $r_i(NO)$ if Proposition 13 had not been passed. The actual post-passage return is r_i, leaving a residual:

$$e_i = r_i - r_i(NO) \tag{14.9}$$

And if the e_i values are negative, it shows that Proposition 13 had an effect. Empirical estimates on e_i suggest that the passage had no effect on general obligation bonds. However, bonds tied to tax collections were affected by the passage. The latter would be bonds whose repayment of principal and interest depend on specific revenue sources.

THE PROPERTY TAX: INCIDENCE

We now turn to some more fundamental aspects of property taxation. Consider the property tax as falling on structures and land. If the supply of structures is perfectly elastic and the supply of land perfectly in-

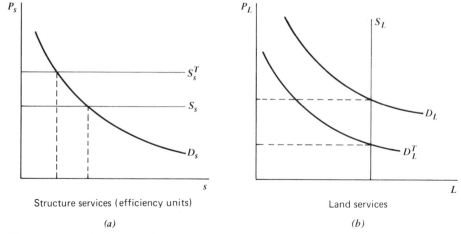

Figure 14–1. Incidence of the property tax. (*a*) Structures. (*b*) Land.

elastic, the incidence, the tax, or who bears it, is, respectively, on tenants for structures and owners for land. This is detailed in Figures 14–1a and 14–1b. In the former, the tax causes the rental price of the structure services (housing in the case of residential property) to increase. The user cost increases from S_s to S_s^T, and demand falls. The incidence of the tax thus falls on demanders, or tenants. In Figure 14–1b, for land, the supply is perfectly inelastic. Hence, the property tax falls on the landowners.

Under these assumptions, the incidence is straightforward, and in the case of land, this argument underlies the single-tax movement. However, both elasticity assumptions are open to question. There are cases where the supply of structures is not perfectly elastic, and may be upward sloping. As a city develops with a given land supply, adding structures must involve increased density, or more structures per unit of land. If housing technology involves higher marginal cost per unit with added density, then marginal costs increase. As an example, construction costs might increase with the height of a structure.[9]

If constant marginal costs obtain in construction, then the supply is perfectly elastic. In the case of land, there may be a fixed acreage of land, with its usage and allocation restricted by zoning. However, zoning variances, relaxation of building and servicing standards, and illegal building activity may all increase the supply. Further, the property tax itself can alter the allocation of land between residential and nonresidential uses.

To examine the effect of the property tax, consider the following model.[10] The household derives utility, as in the core model of Chapter 4, from housing services and other goods. Housing services are produced, as in the supply section of Chapter 12, by land and improvements as:

$$H = H(L,S) \qquad (14.10)$$

with L denoting land and S representing structures, as in Figure 14–1, with H as housing. If this production function exhibits constant returns to scale, a proportional increase in land and structures increases housing services in the same proportion. If this proportional factor is the amount of land, then:

$$H = LH\left(1, \frac{S}{L}\right) \qquad (14.11)$$

$$= Lh(s)$$

where $s = S/L$ is the improvement to land ratio, otherwise known as structural density.

Suppose a household lives distance d away from the CBD, and per unit commuting costs are $c(d)$. So, total commuting costs are $c(d)d$. The rental price of housing services is $r(d)$ and the effective property tax rate is t_e, using the notation of previous chapters. The rental price inclusive of tax is then $(1 + t_e)r(d)$, and total housing expenditure is $(1 + t_e)r(d)h(d)$, where housing also depends on distance $h(d)$. As one specification, $h(d) = h$. The budget constraint is:

$$y = p_g g + (1 + t_e)r(d)h + c(d)d \qquad (14.12)$$

where y is total expenditure on all goods, with $p_g g$ being expenditure on goods. The consumer maximizes utility subject to (14.12).

Consider now the problem facing the producer of housing, according to $h(s)$, the production function. Let the cost per unit of housing structural density be $P(s)$. As an example, the cost of building a high-rise apartment building, with a relatively high ratio of improvements to land, or s, may differ from that for a low-rise duplex.

The builder attempts to minimize the cost of producing housing services.[11] The condition occurs where the marginal cost of building horizontally is equal to that for building vertically.

EFFECT OF THE PROPERTY TAX ON PUBLIC SERVICES

There is considerable discussion of the effect of the shifting of the property tax. On the tax revenue side, one view is that the tax is shifted forward to consumers through higher house prices. There may be an effect not only on the prices of land and housing, but also on factors of production such as labor and capital.[12] The effect is argued to reduce the amount of housing construction and the demand for the factors that produce housing.

There is also some disagreement on the services side. An improvement in benefits can be capitalized in higher land and housing prices. People receiving an improvement in police or fire protection will be willing to bid up the prices of land and structures in that jurisdiction.

The higher quality of public goods may elicit a reduction in the wage rate. People may be willing to accept lower wages as a trade-off for the improved amenities.

One structure examining the effect of property taxes on the level of public services is discussed in Polinsky and Rubinfeld.[13] They examine three types of land: a central business district, a surrounding residential ring, and an outer rural area. A private consumption good is produced in the CBD from land, labor, and capital, and sold locally and nationally. Housing services are produced at each site in the residential area from land and capital. Capital and labor are perfectly mobile and each city is small. Each individual works in the CBD and allocates his budget among the private consumption good, housing services, property taxes, and journeys to work. Local public goods are also consumed, the level of which depends on the individual's location.

When the property tax rate is increased and public services are held fixed, the wage rate and prices of housing and capital increase while the prices of housing and land net property taxes fall. If u_H is the cost of housing services prior to taxes, and t_e is the tax rate, the cost after taxes is $u_H(1 + t_e)$. Any investor in housing services receives a reduced return after taxes. The city decreases in area and per capita housing consumption falls.

When public services are increased and the tax rate is held constant, the price of land rises and the wage rate falls. The price of housing services and the price of business land, both net of property taxes, increase.

Some of the other characteristics of the property tax depend on whether it is an excise or profits tax.[14] It is argued that such taxation does not necessarily increase the price of housing services. Owners have higher costs of operation, but the price of rental housing is not increased.[15]

Suppose two types of goods are produced within a municipality— industrial or export goods and home goods. The latter are exemplified by activity in residential real estate, trade, and services. The following example is constructed. Suppose there are three towns—A, B, and C. The taxes are as follows.

City	Units of Residential Capital	Tax Rate (%)
A	1,000	2
B	10,000	3
C	1,000	4

The simple and weighted average of the tax rate are 3 percent. Suppose that before the imposition of property taxes the return on capital is 10 percent. This implies that, assuming there is no increase in benefits and services, residents of high-tax communities decrease demand for residential capital and some households shift residential capital to low-tax areas. The after-tax return on capital falls by the amount of the tax, from 10 percent to 7 percent. The overall tax rate may fall as people shift to the lower-tax jurisdiction.

Further, community C must provide a before-tax return of at least 11 percent to compensate for the tax, since the rate there is 11 percent. The cost of capital increases by a percentage point, and the price of capital services increases by 10 percent (or 1 in 10). Moreover, community A, which has a tax rate of 2 percent, will see a relative decline of 10 percent in capital service prices, it being 9 percent there versus 10 percent in the market. The above assumes that services are maintained at the same level in all three jurisdictions. The tax may be borne also by industries in the given jurisdiction.

An above-average rate of tax in a community, as in C, increases the cost of capital, thereby shifting it to low-tax areas. If high-tax areas produce capital-intensive goods and elasticities of substitution are high, the average return on industrial capital will fall.

In general, Mieszkowski observes:

. . . the system of property taxes imposed by local governments decreases the overall return to capital by the average rate of tax in the nation as a whole, and changes the supply price of capital to different cities according to the relationship of the specific rates relative to the mean rate of property tax. Cities with a relatively high tax rate will pay more for the services of capital, low tax rates resulting in a lower cost of capital.

Changes in the cost of capital lead to a reallocation of residential and industrial activities which in turn influences site values and the returns to other imperfectly mobile factors of production . . . changes in wage rates will be small in magnitude as labor is partially mobile and labor can be substituted for capital. Changes in land values are likely to be substantial but because of the low share of land rents in total costs are quite unlikely to increase sufficiently to offset the tax. Commodity prices will rise and I venture to guess that at least 75% of the burden of the tax differential falls on consumers, when capital is perfectly shiftable. In cities where the level of new construction is negligible tax increases will lead to a downward re-evaluation of the existing capital stock.[16]

There are several problems with the Mieszkowski view.

1. It is generally assumed that benefits are equal across jurisdictions or that these are pure taxes. This is not usually the case with property taxes, for individuals are expecting a benefit offset by their willingness to pay property taxes.

2. A partial tax on some capital, which is the property tax, will not usually reduce the return to capital in general. It depends on the share of real estate in total capital, and the substitutability between real estate and other capital.

3. Mobility of factors of production depends on substitutability between real estate and these factors.

As regards housing and the property tax, two points are worth noting.[17] First, taxes on owner-occupied residential structures will be borne by owners, not as capitalists but as consumers of housing services, unless the price elasticity of demand for housing is high and factors engaged in production of owner-occupied housing are relatively immobile. If the price elasticity of demand for housing is -1, the burden of taxation is shared between suppliers of factors to the industry and homeowners.

For renters, there may be incidence between consumers, landlords, and the construction industry. The argument is that the short-run elasticity of supply for rental units is close to zero, so there is no shifting of the tax.

Calculation of Property Tax Capitalization

The calculation of property tax capitalization follows that for any other capital asset. In this case, the capital asset is the reduction in property values arising from the tax. The capital value depends on the real interest rate, or discount rate, to be used, and the expected life of the given tax changes. The calculations are sensitive to the choice of both the discount rate and the expected life.

Suppose the property produces an annual rental value of A_i. If the discount rate is R in percent, and N is the expected duration of house life, then:

$$P = \sum_{i=1}^{N} \frac{A_i}{(1 + R)^i} \tag{14.15}$$

$$= \sum_{i=1}^{N} \frac{(A - \tau P)}{(1 + R)^i}$$

where the annual rent is the same every year, P is the value of the property, and τ is the property tax rate. Solving for P:

$$P = \left[A \left(\sum_{i=1}^{N} \frac{1}{(1 + R)^i} \right) \right] \left[1 + \tau \left(\sum_{i=1}^{N} \frac{1}{(1 + R)^i} \right) \right]$$

$$= \frac{Ax}{(1 + \tau x)}$$

where x is the multiplier factor, $x = \sum_{i=1}^{N} \frac{1}{(1 + R)^i}$ the present value of \$1 per period at an interest rate R and period N. This x can be obtained from mathematical annuity tables. For $N = 40$ and $R = 0.02$, the capitalization value of $x = 27.355$.

As an example, suppose the tax rate is $\tau = 0.008$, or 8/10 of 1 percent. If P is \$64,095, the capitalization formula yields \$2856. A one mill increase, from 0.008 to 0.009, would cause the price of the property to change to \$62,692. With 100 percent capitalization, then, the change in value of the property is \$64,095 $-$ \$62,692, or \$1403.[18] Further, in logarithms $\ln P = \ln A + \ln x - \tau x$. In usual studies of capitalization, the coefficient of the tax variable τ in a regression is the measure of capitalization. More generally, let b be the degree of capitalization. Then $\ln P = \ln A + \ln x - b\tau x$, and if $b = 1$, there is 100 percent capitalization. In turn, the price equation is:

$$P = \frac{Ax}{(1 + b\tau x)} \tag{14.16}$$

to allow for capitalization. If $b = 0$, there is no capitalization, and if $b < 1$, there is incomplete capitalization.

The effect of taxes on prices can be obtained by the correlation between τ and $\ln P$. The effect of a change in taxes is bx on prices, so if this effect is $\partial \ln P/\partial \tau = B$, then the capitalization is B/x. Of course, the capitalization estimates depends on the selection of the multiplier factor x.

Local Expenditures

It is also possible to estimate the effect of local expenditures on prices. The procedure is exactly identical to that for taxes. The formula for the effect on prices is:

$$P = \frac{Ax(1 + cEx)}{(1 + b\tau x)} \tag{14.17}$$

where E is a measure of expenditures and c is the degree of expenditure capitalization. Expenditures can be in dollars total or per household. Taking the logarithms of the above, $\ln P = \ln A + \ln x + cEx - b\tau x$. If E is included as a variable to explain prices, its coefficient is cEx. If $c = 0$, there is no capitalization, and if $c = 1$, there is full capitalization. Hence, expenditures can be examined by procedures analogous to those for taxes.

Empirical Results—Tax Capitalization

Estimates of property tax capitalization are typically performed in a regression equation of the hedonic type. A hedonic equation assumes that a property has certain characteristics, in given proportions. Each of these characteristics, such as bedrooms and bathrooms in a house, or proximity to amenities in land, has a price. This follows the procedure developed in Chapter 12.

The capitalization estimate is derived by including the effective property tax rate in such a hedonic equation. The issue of whether the effective or actual property tax rate should be used has generated controversy. Within a jurisdiction, some properties may be overassessed in the sense that the assessment for tax purposes exceeds the market value. People can vote with their feet by locating in subareas that are underassessed.

The original formulation of the Tiebout model for empirical testing is by Oates.[19] In the Oates estimation, effective property taxes were used. An alternative form is to use total annual property taxes, rather than the tax rate. Oates examined 53 residential municipalities in New Jersey. The estimated equation is:

$$\ln V = d_O + \sum_{i=1}^{N} X_i + \alpha_t \tau \qquad (14.18)$$

where the X_i are variables and τ is the effective tax rate. In the model, V is the median house value in the municipality, with school expenditures, distance from midtown Manhattan, median number of rooms, percent of houses built since 1950, median family income, and percent of families with income less than \$3000 included in X. The results indicated that α_t, the coefficient of tax capitalization, is negative. Several issues arise, including whether the variables in the model appropriately measure site and structural characteristics. With the addition of municipal spending, Oates finds that property taxes are fully capitalized in reductions in price.

Several subsequent papers followed, but the relevant issues are as follows.

1. The adjustment period to complete capitalization may be substantial. Studies indicating incomplete capitalization may obtain only in the short run.

2. The property tax rate may be correlated with site or structural characteristics. If some of these are excluded from the capitalization formula, the coefficient is biased.

3. The property tax is deductible in computing taxable income in the United States. The effect of the tax thus varies across individuals, and there are distributional implications.

4. Market value may be obtained by possibly incorrect subjective assessment.

5. The property tax bill rather than the tax may be the more appropriate variable.

The issue of capitalization has ramifications for other types of local public sector activities. Zoning regulations restrict the highest and best use to which land can be put. Environmental and land-use controls also impose restrictions. Both of these impacts can be examined analogously to those for property taxes, however, the same types of problems apply.

In terms of empirical results there has been a diversity of estimates. Generally, full capitalization is indicated. However, Wales and Wiens, in examining Surrey, British Columbia, found that there was no capitalization of property taxes.[20] They introduce two possible explanations for their results. First, buyers may not have complete information or may expect that tax changes are temporary rather than permanent. Second, buyers do not offer to pay more for the prospect of lower tax payments because they distrust their own judgment.

There is another issue associated with voting with one's feet. If property taxes are made specific to local public goods, the type of preferences indicated may arise only in cases where local public goods have essentially private characteristics. In such a case, the theory degenerates.

SUMMARY

The property tax remains a large source of local government revenue. There remain pressures because the tax falls on a specific form of local capital, namely, land and its improvements. Competition among jurisdictions can lead to distortions in local markets in terms of employment and public goods levels.

There remain other issues with the property tax, including whether or not it is regressive. This implies that a larger proportion of income is paid in property taxes by low-income groups. The appropriate measure of income here is permanent income, abstracting from any short-run, transitory fluctuation in measured income.

The benefit, or expenditure, side is also important. The quality of local public goods, including maintenance of streets, garbage collection, and sewers, appears higher in Canada than in the United States. This may arise because Canada does not have the same problems with security and crime as the United States, and this may affect the allocation of expenditures on local public goods.

Footnotes

1. The proposition is also known as the Jarvis–Gann initiative. For details, see Frank Levy, "On Understanding Proposition 13," *Public Interest* 56(Summer 1979):66–89.

2. The argument here is that as tax rates increase, so does total revenue; but, ultimately, as tax rates continue to increase, revenue declines.

3. The table and model reported are from K. T. Rosen, "The Impact of Proposition 13 on House Prices in Northern California: A Test of the Interjurisdictional Capitalization Hypothesis," *Journal of Political Economy* 90(1982):191–200.

4. Rosen, *op. cit.*, p. 199. The implicit assumption is that the house price feedback is minimal.

5. See W. H. Oakland, "Proposition 13, Genesis and Consequences," in G. Kaufman and K. Rosen, eds., *The Property Tax Revolt: The Case of Proposition 13* (Cambridge, Mass.: Ballinger), 1981, pp. 31–65.

6. Oakland, *op. cit.*, p. 45. This section on expenditures relies on the discussion there.

7. See A. R. Thomas, "Fiscal Limitations and Municipal Debt," in Kaufman and Rosen, *op. cit.*, pp. 105–116; and R. Forbes, A. Frankle, and P. Fischer, "The Effects of Proposition 13 on Tax-supported Municipal Bonds in California," in Kaufman and Rosen, *op. cit.*, pp. 117–163.

8. Forbes, Frankle, and Fischer, *op. cit.*, p. 122 *et seq.*

9. The discussion and model here are based on R. J. Arnott and J. G. MacKinnon, "The Effects of the Property Tax: A General Equilibrium Simulation," *Journal of Urban Economics* 4(1977):380–407. The construction technology assumption is in R. E. Grierson, "The Economics of Property Taxes: The Elasticity of Supply of Structures," *Journal of Urban Economics* 1(1974):367–381.

10. Arnott and MacKinnon, *op. cit.*, p. 392, construct the model on which the following is derived.

11. The minimization problem for the builder is:

$$\text{minimize} \quad P(S)S$$
$$\text{subject to} \quad LH(S) \leq \bar{H}$$

where $\bar{H}$ is some critical level of housing services. The builder minimizes expenditure on housing $P(S)S$, subject to the technology $LH(S) < \bar{H}$. Now let p be the price of housing. The difference between $\bar{H}$ and $LH(S)$ may represent wastage of housing services, since produced output is not equal to the critical level. So the value of this loss is $p(\bar{H} - LH(S))$, and the builder minimizes, by choosing S:

$$E = P(S)S + p(\bar{H} - LH(S))$$

By setting the change in E equal to zero:

$$\frac{\partial E}{\partial S} = 0 = \left(\frac{\partial P}{\partial S}\right)S + P(S) - \frac{pL\partial H}{\partial S}$$

So $pL\partial H/\partial S = (\partial P/\partial S)S + P(S)$, and this is the equation of the text. Now total revenue from housing must be equal to total expenditures on factors of production, so:

$$ph = rL + Ps$$
$$= rL + PLS$$

and $ph/L = r + PS$. Further $ph/LS = r/S + P$. Since $pL\partial H/\partial S = (2P/\partial S)S + P(S)$, dividing one by the other:

$$\frac{1}{L^2 S} \frac{h}{\partial H/\partial S} = \frac{r/s + P}{(\partial P/\partial S)S + P(S)}$$

Alternative specifications involve $\partial H/\partial S$ or $P(S)$ being constant.

12. The view that the property tax is shifted to housing is in D. Netzer, *The Economics of the Property Tax* (Washington, D.C.: Brookings Institution), 1966. The effect on labor and capital markets is in P. Mieszkowski, "The Property Tax: An Excise Tax or a Profits Tax?" *Journal of Public Economics* 1(1972):73–96.

13. A. M. Polinsky and D. L. Rubinfeld, "The Long-Run Effects of a Residential Property Tax and Local Public Services," *Journal of Urban Economics* 5(1978):241–262.

14. Mieszkowski, *op. cit.,* pp. 73–96.

15. *Ibid.,* p. 76.

16. *Ibid.,* pp. 79–80.

17. See D. Netzer, "The Incidence of the Property Tax Revisited," *National Tax Journal* 26(1973):515–535. Netzer also argues that residential housing is subject to above average rates of effective property taxation, but this is prior to deductibility of these taxes for computing federal income tax liability in the United States, and prior to any offset for benefits received.

18. The example estimates are obtained for the city of Edmonton, Canada, in A. M. Chaudry, *Capitalization of Local Property Taxes and Public Services with Applications to Efficiency and Equity Issues,* Ph.D. dissertation, University of Alberta, 1983.

19. See Tiebout, *op. cit.,* and W. Oates, "The Effects of Property Taxes and Local Public Spending on Property Values: An Empirical Study of Tax Capitalization and the Tiebout Hypothesis," *Journal of Political Economy* 77(1969):957–971.

20. T. J. Wales and E. G. Wiens, "Capitalization of Residential Property Taxes: An Empirical Study", *Review of Economics and Statistics* 56:329–333 (1974).

15

GOVERNING URBAN AREAS: SOME ECONOMIC, ORGANIZATIONAL AND POLITICAL ISSUES

INTRODUCTION

Local governments are key actors in land-use and subdivision activities, which are fundamental to urban land market operations, as we discussed in Chapter 11. Local governments also play central roles in urban economic development through their interest in attracting new jobs and in financing themselves, as we saw in Chapters 13 and 14. Finally, local governments exert enormous influence over urban housing markets through their ability to regulate land use and urban development, a topic touched on in Chapters 11 and 12.

A number of difficulties arise, however, as local governments seek to guide and finance their development. Spillover effects provide an example where pollution from one community along a river imposes costs on downstream communities. Local governments also face problems in financing the services demanded of them by residents, and they must concern themselves with organizational structures to raise funds, provide programs, and deal with neighboring local governments and with senior governments. Accordingly, in this chapter we will look at the various functions of local government, and then examine old and emerging difficulties, and their suggested solutions.

The Various Roles of Local Government

We have already explored three areas where local government has important roles: land use and management; housing; and urban economic development. We have seen that the ability to control land use and urban development had significant impacts on and implications for housing location, type, availability, and cost. Local governments also occasionally become involved in provision of housing directly, for example, the cities of Toronto and of New York.[1] Local governments involve themselves in economic development through redevelopment grants and tax and service subsidies.

They are also established to provide a range of services that are generally deemed best provided by government as opposed to private interests, largely "public goods" in economic parlance.[2]

Local government expenditure patterns provide interesting insights into local functions. From Table 15–1 in 1980–81, local governments accounted for a total of US$245.1 billion in expenditure, 42 percent less than the US$422.3 billion spent by the federal government and 53 percent more than the US$160.5 billion spent by state governments. Within the category of local government expenditures, education accounted for 43 percent of the total, followed by police and fire protection (9.1 percent), public welfare (11.1 percent), health and hospitals (7.4 percent), and highways (5.7 percent).

In Canada's local governments a similar picture emerges, with differences at the margin (Table 15–2). First, local government expenditures totaled C$21.8 billion in 1978, compared with federal expenditures (including transfers to provinces and local governments) of C$49.0 billion and provincial government expenditures (including transfers to local and federal governments) of C$45.3 billion. Since some of the local government expenditures are based on federal transfer payments, the total size of government is somewhat less. In the Canadian case, provincial and federal expenditures are similar in size.[3] This reflects the significantly stronger position of provinces vis-à-vis the federal government in Canada, as contrasted with the role of states and the U.S. federal government.[4]

Looking more closely at the categories of expenditures, education comprises 41.8 percent of total local government expenditure, followed by transportation and communications, including roads, transit and parking (12.3 percent), sanitation and water (8.7 percent), protection (fire and police) (8.1 percent), and recreation and culture (5.7 percent). Allowing for differences in accounting definitions, we see that there are few major differences between local spending in Canada and the United States.

In summarizing the changing role of local governments in Canada from the provision of essential local services (so-called hard services such as engineering and public works) to broader considerations falling under the rubric "quality of life," Plunkett and Betts observe:

These new concerns involve the conditions and circumstances that affect the quality of life. In very recent years individuals and groups in a number of cities have found that some of the matters which specifically affect the quality of city living include social dislocation caused by urban development, the need to preserve neighbourhoods with a particular lifestyle, the allocation of the resources to urban transportation facilities between urban transit systems and expressways, the provision and location of public housing, effective land use control, land prices, to name but a few.[5]

Another measure of the importance of local government is their sheer numbers. Tables 15–3 and 15–4 present data for the United States and Canada, respectively, setting out the numbers of local governments.

First, there is a very large number of local governments in the United States, with 82,688 of them being recorded in 1982, an increase of 2826 from the previous Census of Governments in 1977. Second, the data are not strictly comparable between Canada and the United States. The data for the latter include counties and special-purpose districts, both of which are largely absent from the Canadian data. There are 35,831 municipal and township governments in the United States and 4071 unitary municipalities in Canada. These municipal governments are roughly comparable and proportional to the respective urban populations of the two countries.[6]

The presence of such large numbers of special-purpose districts and counties in the United States (together comprising another 31,774 governments at the local level) does pose difficulties in making comparisons since there are no consistent data on special-purpose and school districts in Canada. A 1967 study in Ontario did reveal the data presented in Table 15–5 concerning special purpose bodies in that province. The 3220 special-purpose bodies enumerated in the study compared with 964 municipalities in the province in 1968. If this ratio holds over time and in other provinces, then we would anticipate that there would be a total of nearly 13,600 additional special-purpose bodies in Canada at the local level, compared with 45,000 such bodies in the United States. However, it is not possible to make very strong inferences because of the definitional differences that underly the classification of such local government bodies as special-purpose bodies in the two countries. All we can say with certainty is that there are a very large number of such local government bodies in both Canada and the United States.

The growing role of local governments is evidenced by the growth in their expenditures, by their diversity, and by the growth in the numbers of such governments. There are numerous problems faced by local governments, however, and these require our attention here. Some of these difficulties derive from the nature of public goods (e.g., the free-rider problem), while some derive from the scale and spatial arrangement of local governments within metropolitan areas (e.g.,

Table 15–1 Governmental Direct General Expenditure, by Function and Level of Government: 1980–81

Function	Amount (millions of dollars)					Per Capita		
	All Governments	Federal Government	State and Local Governments			Total	Federal Government	State and Local governments
			Total	State	Local			
Total	827,877	422,301	405,576	160,474	245,102	3,654.33	1,864.08	1,790.25
Selected federal programs:								
National defense and international relations	174,564	174,564	—	—	—	770.54	770.54	—
Postal service	20,466	20,466	—	—	—	90.34	90.34	—
Space research and technology	5,523	5,523	—	—	—	24.38	24.38	—
Education services:								
Education	158,012	12,228	145,784	39,664	106,121	697.48	53.98	643.51
Local schools	100,534	—	100,534	1,040	99,494	443.77	—	443.77
Institutions of higher education	38,114	—	38,114	31,488	6,626	168.24	—	168.24
Other	19,364	12,228	7,136	7,135	—	85.47	53.98	31.50
Libraries	2,045	180	1,865	140	1,725	9.03	.79	8.23
Social services and income maintenance:								
Public welfare	74,643	22,395	52,248	38,580	13,667	329.48	98.85	230.63
Categorical cash assistance	21,516	8,683	12,833	7,579	5,254	94.97	38.33	56.65
Other cash assistance	1,517	—	1,517	799	718	6.70	—	6.70
Other public welfare	51,610	13,712	37,898	30,202	7,696	227.81	60.53	167.28
Hospitals	32,132	5,802	26,330	12,697	13,633	141.83	25.61	116.22
Health	15,246	5,475	9,771	5,331	4,440	67.30	24.17	43.13
Social insurance administration	5,075	2,799	2,276	2,269	7	22.40	12.36	10.05
Veterans' services	13,833	13,776	57	57	—	61.06	60.81	.25

Transportation:								
Highways	34,909	306	34,603	20,688	13,915	154.09	1.35	152.74
Air Transportation	6,994	4,251	2,743	316	2,427	30.87	18.76	12.11
Water transport and terminals	4,675	3,167	1,508	509	999	20.64	13.98	6.66
Parking facilities	377	—	377	—	377	1.67	—	1.67
Public safety:								
Police protection	16,851	1,904	14,947	2,270	12,677	74.38	8.40	65.98
Fire protection	6,336	—	6,336	—	6,336	27.97	—	27.97
Correction	7,806	413	7,393	4,817	2,576	34.46	1.82	32.63
Protective inspection and regulation	2,557	—	2,557	1,724	833	11.29	—	11.29
Environment and housing:								
Natural resources	43,599	37,424	6,175	4,725	1,451	192.45	165.19	27.26
Sewerage	11,121	—	11,121	345	10,776	49.09	—	49.09
Housing and urban renewal	13,894	6,808	7,086	402	6,684	61.33	30.05	31.28
Parks and recreation	8,536	1,472	7,064	1,329	5,735	37.68	6.50	31.18
Sanitation other than sewerage	3,777	—	3,777	—	3,777	16.67	—	16.67
Governmental administration:								
Financial administration	10,944	3,714	7,230	3,272	3,958	48.31	16.39	31.91
General control	11,514	1,973	9,541	3,291	6,250	50.82	8.71	42.11
General public buildings (state–local)	3,230	—	3,230	803	2,426	14.26	—	14.26
Interest on general debt	97,641	80,510	17,131	7,844	9,288	431.00	355.38	75.62
Other and unallocable	41,577	17,151	24,426	9,404	15,022	183.53	75.71	107.82

Source: U.S. Bureau of the Census, *Governmental Finances in 1980–81,* ASI 2466-2.

Table 15–2 General Expenditures of Local Canadian Governments, Fiscal Year Ended December 31, 1978 (thousands of Canadian dollars)

Function	Nfld	PEI	NS	NB	Que	Ont	Man	Sask	Alta	BC	YT	NWT	Canada
General government	9270	1080	23,228	10,477	356,682	336,750	49,365	37,349	85,846	104,188	1349	2838	1,018,422
Executive and legislative	915	146	2192	1241	17,012	23,226	1713	1563	5711	5735	87	215	61,756
Administrative	6682	836	18,399	8301	208,533	303,495	42,225	29,399	69,663	83,261	1103	2458	774,355
Other	1673	98	2637	935	131,137	10,029	4427	5387	10,472	15,192	159	165	182,311
Protection of persons and property	3450	2175	39,900	32,783	502,508	695,490	67,993	52,382	163,883	197,235	1064	1239	1,760,502
Police services	449	1561	18,630	15,165	336,796	398,862	33,614	29,857	85,920	92,985	—	9	1,013,848
Courts of law & correctional service	—	—	5152	—	15,006	391	82	1153	349	5119	157	366	27,775
Fire-fighting services	2516	585	14,125	14,981	125,244	229,636	25,395	17,891	61,567	79,133	731	608	572,412
Emergency measures	—	5	138	1478	—	20,067	3482	1034	2385	2720	1	114	31,424
Regulatory	234	18	1037	758	—	38,177	3852	1645	6419	13,827	124	110	66,201
Other	251	6	818	401	25,862	8357	1568	802	7243	3451	51	32	48,842
Transportation & communications	1008	2705	55,818	48,339	645,434	987,589	112,744	150,493	453,835	206,212	3539	3678	2,691,394
Common services	1182	98	3897	6355	6700	30,387	4095	7368	31,897	21,661	125	382	114,147
Road	9640	2607	48,672	41,229	514,661	947,139	107,358	142,817	421,608	181,445	3341	2984	2,433,503
Administration	277	51	1796	682	48,480	45,347	4984	2135	4294	5053	60	70	113,229
Engineering	—	—	2161	646	—	28,324	1196	3730	3564	6777	—	58	46,456
Roads and streets	4915	1628	36,459	29,981	273,099	637,503	76,283	122,127	324,733	140,413	2778	2185	1,662,104
Snow and ice removal	1470	403	2962	5771	122,361	100,858	8085	4104	17,349	4036	168	299	267,866

Bridges, subways, tunnels	20	—	83	67	10,529	41,417	5205	1990	40,807	2352	—	50	102,520
Street lighting	2437	391	3924	2940	38,318	34,414	7024	5564	15,418	12,863	162	264	123,719
Traffic services	116	86	985	761	16,204	33,896	3165	2081	12,055	7500	166	52	77,067
Parking	191	48	119	363	5670	23,187	717	929	2940	1792	5	8	35,969
Other	214	—	183	18	—	2193	699	157	448	659	2	—	4573
Public transit	—	—	—	612	119,042	554	—	83	—	1231	—	28	121,550
Other	186	—	3249	143	5031	9509	1291	225	330	1875	73	282	22,194
Environment	22,465	3692	49,592	43,466	545,161	662,474	52,453	60,140	215,974	219,800	8818	7552	1,891,587
Water purification and supply	9984	1850	25,610	24,474	212,751	239,053	24,545	26,626	97,246	82,723	3894	5221	753,977
Sewage collection and disposal	7798	1455	16,364	14,645	243,271	265,719	13,053	24,239	87,324	102,607	4493	1229	782,197
Garbage & waste collection disposal	4627	387	7467	4082	78,628	150,348	14,640	9027	29,853	33,451	426	836	333,772
Other	56	—	151	265	10,511	7354	215	248	1551	1019	5	266	21,641
Health	6	10	40,084	45	5562	406,987	63,580	130,949	319,817	21,500	69	149	988,758
Preventive services	6	10	797	45	5562	122,511	1960	3776	1623	16,792	69	55	153,206
Medical care	—	—	30	—	—	—	1863	553	—	3055	—	—	5501
Hospital care	—	—	39,220	—	—	283,463	59,558	126,549	317,205	1578	—	57	827,630
Other	—	—	37	—	—	1013	199	71	989	75	—	37	2421
Social welfare	—	—	46,436	—	22,252	463,935	11,394	5949	33,501	29,176	—	—	612,643
Administration	—	—	3616	—	22,252	17,187	2356	273	2599	167	—	—	48,450
Assistance	—	—	21,374	—	—	208,785	8869	3651	22,159	27,311	—	—	292,149
Services	—	—	18,555	—	—	235,685	167	1984	8599	971	—	—	265,961
Other	—	—	2891	—	—	2278	2	41	144	727	—	—	6083

465

Table 15–2 (Continued)

Function	Nfld	PEI	NS	NB	Que	Ont	Man	Sask	Alta	BC	YT	NWT	Canada
Housing—general assistance	9966	1199	9014	9571	71,889	82,556	14,156	7681	30,842	61,287	2362	1071	301,594
Environmental planning and zoning	—	63	1986	920	21,286	40,747	2465	1641	6839	15,476	8	31	91,462
Community development	9876	1104	6119	8651	35,857	36,356	11,573	5650	12,130	44,457	2133	1029	174,935
Other	90	32	909	—	14,776	5453	118	390	11,873	1354	221	11	35,197
Natural resources	—	—	159	140	—	64,214	2746	1387	22,325	3024	28	11	94,026
Agriculture, trade & industry, & tourism	115	263	652	1195	13,619	17,570	1240	1371	7809	1868	33	22	45,747
Agriculture	—	—	—	—	—	—	—	—	—	—	—	—	
Trade and industry	100	—	466	375	10,352	15,292	846	490	6530	1391	—	—	35,842
Regional development commissions	100	—	419	364	10,348	14,359	347	490	6157	1080	—	—	33,664
Industrial parks and commissions	—	—	47	11	4	933	499	—	393	311	—	—	2178
Tourism	15	263	186	820	3257	2278	394	881	1279	477	33	22	9905

Recreation and culture	13,532	2201	17,588	19,785	293,857	467,553	46,597	35,656	168,497	176,464	1610	1546	1,244,886
Recreational facilities	12,571	1971	11,235	15,322	226,106	326,990	38,387	23,186	144,421	141,817	1581	1339	944,926
Cultural facilities	961	114	6146	4137	44,485	125,396	7841	12,111	19,389	33,259	29	191	254,059
Other	—	116	207	326	23,266	15,167	369	359	4687	1388	—	16	45,901
Education—primary and secondary	10,222	41,009	332,672	—	2,720,637	3,340,134	378,442	396,003	806,995	1,089,181		6494	9,121,789
Fiscal services	22,369	2842	40,019	17,458	763,671	595,082	79,654	41,142	209,127	264,415	1593	1331	2,035,994
Debt changes	20,078	2554	30,556	16,616	558,727	355,484	50,394	23,482	124,221	215,335	664	1284	1,399,395
Interest on short-term borrowing	709	140	2542	1927	70,401	14,317	1138	1551	4509	6671	10	180	104,095
Interest on long-term borrowing	19,077	2387	26,047	14,483	478,302	337,167	46,401	17,834	116,349	206,597	653	1049	1,266,346
Other	292	27	1967	206	10,024	4000	2855	4097	3363	2067	1	55	28,954
Transfers to reserves and allowances	517	288	7967	90	12,031	85,475	6554	12,454	49,599	46,993	640	47	222,655
Transfers to own enterprises	1774	—	1496	752	192,913	154,123	19,997	5206	35,307	2087	289	—	413,944
Other services	565	50	536	17	7673	453	1598	289	621	516	2	21	12,342
Total general expenditure	112,968	57,226	655,698	183,276	5,949,335	8,120,787	879,253	920,791	2,519,072	2,374,866	20,467	25,944	21,819,683

Source: Canada Yearbook, 1980/81 (Ottawa: Ministry of Supply and Services), 1981, Table 22.24, p. 843.

467

Table 15-3 Number of Local Governments, by Type—States: 1977 and 1982

[Limited to governments actually in existence. Excludes, therefore, a few counties and numerous townships and "incorporated places" existing as areas for which statistics can be presented as to population and other subjects, but lacking any separate organized county, township, or municipal government]

| | 1977 | | | 1982 | | | | | | | | |
| | | | | Local Government units | | | | | Special Districts | | | |
State	All Governmental units[a]	School districts	Special districts	All Governmental units[a]	Counties	Municipalities	Townships	School Districts	Total[a]	Natural resources	Fire protection	Housing and community development
U.S.	79,862	15,174	25,962	82,688	3,041	19,083	16,748	15,032	28,733	6,276	4,567	3,308
Ala	949	127	336	1,019	67	434	—	127	390	67	2	157
Alaska	150	—	106	157	8	142	—	—	6	—	—	6
Ariz	420	230	106	459	14	76	—	231	137	89	—	—
Ark	1,346	380	424	1,430	75	472	—	376	506	227	29	135
Calif	3,806	1,109	2,227	4,112	57	428	—	1,115	2,511	530	382	88
Colo	1,459	185	950	1,568	62	267	—	207	1,031	174	201	56
Conn	434	16	236	481	—	33	149	16	282	1	49	91
Del	210	25	127	219	3	56	—	19	140	135	—	3
D.C.	2	—	1	2	—	1	—	—	1	—	—	—
Fla	911	95	361	972	66	391	—	95	419	132	56	94
Ga	1,263	188	387	1,271	158	534	—	188	390	30	—	210
Hawaii	19	—	15	19	3	1	—	—	14	14	—	—
Idaho	972	117	612	1,018	44	198	—	117	658	175	101	12
Ill	6,620	1,063	2,745	6,464	102	1,280	1,434	1,050	2,597	905	767	98
Ind	2,854	307	885	2,873	91	565	1,008	306	902	116	—	52
Iowa	1,852	464	334	1,874	99	955	—	457	362	220	62	5
Kans	3,725	327	1,219	3,819	105	627	1,380	326	1,380	263	—	103
Ky	1,183	181	478	1,253	119	426	—	180	527	76	21	103
La	458	66	30	469	62	301	—	66	39	19	—	—
Maine	779	86	178	808	16	22	475	98	196	13	—	31

Md	426	—	252	443	23	152	—	—	267	196	—	2
Mass	766	75	328	799	12	39	312	81	354	14	13	219
Mich	2,633	606	168	2,646	83	532	1,245	601	184	85	—	—
Minn	3,437	440	263	3,530	87	855	1,795	436	356	111	—	163
Miss	835	166	304	860	292	—	169	316	235	—	59	—
Mo	2,937	574	1,007	3,128	114	929	324	559	1,201	152	116	142
Mont	958	465	311	1,045	54	126	—	412	452	119	98	20
Nebr	3,485	1,195	1,192	3,336	93	535	469	1,080	1,158	111	426	136
Nev	182	17	132	186	16	17	—	17	135	31	18	16
N.H	506	159	103	507	10	13	221	149	113	8	15	19
N.J	1,517	549	380	1,597	21	323	244	553	455	15	148	78
N. Mex	313	88	100	320	33	96	—	89	101	71	—	6
N.Y	3,309	740	964	3,301	57	615	932	773	923	1	841	—
N.C	874	—	302	910	100	484	—	325	325	147	278	113
N. Dak	2,707	346	587	1,798	53	365	1,360	325	694	85	—	37
Ohio	3,285	631	312	3,353	88	941	1,318	627	378	99	22	53
Okla	1,675	625	406	2,262	77	582	—	653	949	114	6	137
Oreg	1,447	375	797	1,460	36	241	—	354	828	193	249	24
Pa	5,246	581	2,035	5,317	66	1,019	1,549	618	2,064	6	1	91
R.I	120	3	78	125	—	8	31	3	82	4	38	27
S.C	585	93	182	652	46	265	—	92	248	46	61	46
S. Dak	1,727	194	148	1,768	64	312	996	195	200	105	16	40
Tenn	905	14	471	914	94	335	—	13	471	128	—	104
Tex	3,883	1,138	1,425	4,192	254	1,121	—	1,125	1,691	388	18	398
Utah	492	40	207	506	29	224	237	40	212	72	4	9
Vt	647	272	67	668	14	57	—	85	14	18	8	—
Va	389	—	65	408	95	229	—	—	83	42	412	—
Wash	1,666	302	1,060	1,735	39	265	—	300	1,130	163	—	42
W. Va	595	55	258	637	55	231	—	55	295	15	—	38
Wis	2,518	410	190	2,596	72	580	1,269	409	265	155	44	101
Wyo	385	55	217	401	23	91	—	56	230	114	—	—

— Represents zero.

[a]Includes other types of governments not shown separately.

[b]Includes "town" governments in the 6 New England States and in Minnesota, New York, and Wisconsin.

Source: 1982 Statistical Abstract of the U.S., Table 489, p. 294.

Table 15–4 Number of Muncipalities Classified by Type and Size Group, by Province, as at Jan. 1, 1977 and 1978

Year, Type, and Size Group	Nfld	PEI	NS	NB	Que	Ont	Man	Sask	Alta	BC	YT	NWT	Canada
1977													
Type													
Regional municipalities	—	—	—	—	75	39	—	—	—	28	—	—	142
Metropolitan and regional municipalities[a]	—	—	—	—	3	12	—	—	—	—	—	—	15
Counties and regional districts	—	—	—	—	72	27	—	—	—	28	—	—	127
Unitary municipalities	129	36	65	112	1496	784	185	783	327	140	3	7	4067
Cities[b]	2	1	3	6	66	45	5	11	10	33	2	1	185
Towns	127[c]	8	38	21	193	144	35	135	102	10	1	4	818
Villages	—	27	—	85	241	120	40	344	167	59	—	2	1085
Rural municipalities[d]	—	—	24	—	996	475	105	293	48	38	—	—	1979
Quasi-municipalities[e]	171	—	—	—	—	13	17	7	22	269	4	10	513
Total	300	36	65	112	1571	836	202	790	349	437	7	17	4722
Population Size Group (1976 Census)													
Unitary municipalities													
Over 10,000	—	—	1	—	4	17	1	2	2	3	—	—	30
50,000–99,999	1	—	2	2	17	14	—	—	—	9	—	—	45
10,000–49,999	5	1	17	5	71	76	3	6	14	26	1	—	226
Under 10,000	123	35	45	105	1404	677	181	775	311	102	2	7	3766
Total	129	36	65	112	1496	784	185	783	327	140	3	7	4067
1978													
Type													
Regional municipalities	—	—	—	—	75	39	—	—	—	28	—	—	142
Metropolitan and regional municipalities[a]	—	—	—	—	3	12	—	—	—	—	—	—	15
Counties and regional districts	—	—	—	—	72	27	—	—	—	28	—	—	127

	Nfld.	PEI	NS	NB	Que.	Ont.	Man.	Sask.	Alta.	B.C.	YT	NWT	Total
Unitary municipalities	133	37	65	112	1502	785	185	791	330	140	3	7	4090
Cities[b]	2	1	3	6	66	45	5	11	10	33	2	1	185
Towns	131	8	38	21	192	144	35	135	104	11	1	4	824
Villages	—	28	—	85	240	120	40	346	168	58	—	2	1087
Rural municipalities[d]	—	—	24	—	1004	476	105	299	48	38	—	—	1994
Quasi-municipalities[e]	174	—	—	—	—	13	17	—	21	26	4	10	508
Total	307	37	65	112	1577	837	202	791	351	437	7	17	4740
Population Size Group (1976 Census)													
Unitary municipalities													
Over 100,000	—	—	1	—	4	17	1	2	2	3	—	—	30
50,000–99,999	1	—	2	2	17	14	—	—	—	9	—	—	45
10,000–49,999	5	1	17	5	71	76	3	6	14	26	1	—	225
Under 10,000	127	36	45	105	1410	678	181	783	314	102	2	7	3790
Total	133	37	65	112	1502	785	185	791	330	140	3	7	4090

[a] Includes urban communities in Quebec, and metropolitan Toronto, regional municipalities and the district municipality in Ontario.

[b] Includes the five boroughs of metropolitan Toronto.

[c] Includes 11 rural districts.

[d] Includes, municipalities in Nova Scotia; parishes, townships, united townships and municipalities in Quebec; townships in Ontario; rural municipalities in Manitoba and Saskatchewan, municipal districts and counties in Alberta; and districts in British Columbia.

[e] Includes local government communities, local improvement districts, and the metropolitan area in Newfoundland; improvement districts in Ontario and Alberta; local government districts in Manitoba; local improvement districts in Saskatchewan; British Columbia and Yukon; and hamlets in Northwest Territories.

Abbreviations: Nfld. Newfoundland   Man. Manitoba
PEI. Prince Edward Island   Sask. Saskatchewan
NS Nova Scotia   Alta. Alberta
NB New Brunswick   B.C. British Columbia
Que. Quebec   YT Yukon Territories
Ont. Ontario   NWT Northwest Territories

Source: Canada Yearbook 1980/81 (Ottawa: Ministry of Supply & Services), 1981, Table 3.7

Table 15–5 Special-Purpose Bodies in Ontario

Utility commissions	360
Planning boards	225
Community center boards	250
Parks commissions	150
Public library boards	220
Health boards	270
Police boards	93
Police villages	158
	——
	1726
Public school boards	777
Separate school boards	482
Secondary school boards	235
	——
	1494
Total	3220

Source: Higgins, *Urban Canada* (Toronto: Macmillan of Canada), 1977, p. 105, taken from Bureau of Municipal Research, *Regional Government—The Key to Genuine Local Autonomy* (Toronto), May 1968, page 10.

mismatches between the spatial distribution of service needs and the ability to raise tax revenues).

Problems Facing Local Governments in Providing Services in Metropolitan Areas

We can divide the several problems into those relating to the demand for local government services and those relating to supply.[7] Demand-related problems would inlcude:

1. Spillover effects and free-riders.

2. Growing expectations and wants on the part of the public.

3. Migration within urban regions.

4. Imbalances between revenues and service demands.

Supply-related problems include:

1. Inefficient scale of local government services.

2. Fragmentation and balkanization.

3. Competition among local governments.

4. Spatial imbalances between demand and supply.

Let us look at the demand-related issues firsʳ. A common theme is their spatial character and the mobility of demand, while supply is often fixed in location, as with public parks, schools or museums. The nature of these spatially fixed public goods allows people from outside the service area of the local government to take advantage of the service without bearing the cost.[8] The classic instance of this spatially mobile demand is the so-called free-rider problem.

Free-riders and Spillovers   These were introduced in Chapter 7, where our focus was on urban public finance. These ideas are relevant because they provide insights into problems faced by spatially defined and separated local governmental units in providing services to spatially mobile residents. In the case of free-riders, we have the phenomenon of residents of one local jurisdiction taking advantage of public goods provided by another local government. They are therefore free-riders in that they do pay neither through taxes nor user charges. Spillovers involve the imposition of costs by the residents of one jurisdiction on other jurisdictions and their residents. Users or cost imposers need not bear the cost of their actions due to the spatial nature of local government services and demands for these services.

Growing Expectations   An interesting outgrowth of the much-vaunted Proposition 13 property tax revolt in California is that the most recent effort to extend government taxing and spending limits in that state have gone down to significant defeat, as we discussed at length in Chapter 14.[9] California taxpayers have realized that their desire for low taxes was inconsistent with their desire for high levels of service such as education, recreation, and libraries and other cultural activities. This California experience highlights the problem that local governments face. The public has increasingly become used to such services but has only recently begun to realize the costs involved in the provision of such services. Often, local government has to satisfy local taxpayer demands and desires while not being able to raise taxes readily to pay for such services. Actual and perceived waste in government has made this situation more acute.

Migration Within Metropolitan Areas   The great mobility of metropolitan area residents has also caused significant problems for local governments. First, as noted in Chapter 3 and again in Chapter 13, central city populations are not growing. Higher-income residents are being replaced by lower-income residents (in the United States). The net effect has been that costly capital in the form of schools, roads, and other public infrastructure is being used in the U.S. central city at lower rates than initially designed. Fewer taxpayers are around to pay for these social investments. The fixity of social overhead capital and its long gestation period and longer life poses difficulties in the face of a highly mobile metropolitan population. While this has not yet been a major problem in Canada, as it has been in the United States, the potential is there in light of the above.[10] A second problem raised by mobility is that service demands can increase significantly (the obverse of the previous problem), causing local governments to spend on schools, libraries, streets and parks.[11] This phenomenon of "voting with your feet" has been much studied and discussed in the literature, and most agree on the basic fact that mobile populations do put strains on recipient jurisdictions.[12]

Imbalances Between Revenues and Service Demand Expenditures   The net effect of the above is periodic fiscal crisis, where revenues and expenditures cannot keep pace with each other at the local government level. This may not be a problem of demand excesses alone, but may also be a function of the ways in which services have been provided at the local level. It may be that supply is not being provided efficiently, a problem which occupies our attention next.

Scale of Local Government Services   A frequently made claim by urban reformers is that local governments, being small in scale, cannot provide services at minimal cost with maximal efficiency.[13] A number of conceptual problems stand in the way of determining optimal scale for various governmental units and services. First, different services have different optimal scales and it is difficult to have a local governmental unit of a fixed size providing optimal scale services for each service. Alternatively, if we assume a fixed bundle of services and then try to determine optimal local government scale, we run into the completely analogous problem of optimality for some services in the bundle at given sizes of local government, but suboptimal scales for other services in the bundle. Higher costs in and of themselves may be misleading, for example, since many of the higher costs associated with larger-size cities could be attributable to higher quality and broader coverage of services.[14]

The search for the optimum-size urban place is fraught with great conceptual and empirical difficulty.[15] Deriving optimal scales for the diversity of publicly provided urban services remains an elusive, and perhaps impossible, goal. Even were we able to develop optimal-size units, there still remains the difficult equity issue, which is ignored in discussions of efficiency of delivery systems: the need for political input and public involvement in the allocative processes of local government. It has not yet been possible to make the case for larger-scale regional governmental units even on the relatively narrow grounds of economic efficiency. Proponents of efficiency are seemingly undeterred by a growing body of evidence that questions their basic assertion: that local governments are inefficient as presently constituted.

Fragmentation and Balkanization of Local Governments   The existence of numerous local governments is closely tied to the previous argument about scale economies. The existence of so many local governments within metropolitan areas is counterproductive as each balkanized local entity stands to serve its own residents and their narrow interests. We saw this phenomenon in exclusionary and fiscal zoning in Chapter 11 where the pursuit of local interests could lead to higher land and housing prices for the society as a whole, with significant distributional and equity consequences.[16] There is a trade-off, therefore, between the rights of individuals and those of society.

Table 15–6 presents indices of municipal fragmentation for metropolitan areas in Canada and the United States. The table demonstrates that there is significantly more fragmentation in U.S. metropolitan areas. This still begs the question in absolute terms as to whether there are too many municipal governments in U.S. metropolitan areas. The existence of more municipal governments in the United States could signify the greater diversity of preferences of United States urban area residents for different municipal service bundles. The observed difference between metropolitan areas in Canada and the United States could thus be reasonably interpreted as illustrating that there is relatively greater diversity (or, conversely, more homogeneity

Table 15–6 Distribution of Scores on the Index of Municipal Fragmentation[a]

Score	*Cumulative Percent of Metropolitan Areas with Scores Within the Specified Class*	
	U.S.A. (1972)	*Canada (1971)*
0.000 to 0.014	10.0	26.5
0.015 to 0.025	20.0	50.0
0.026 to 0.039	30.0	73.5
0.040 to 0.054	40.0	82.4
0.055 to 0.064	50.0	88.2
0.065 to 0.079	60.0	91.2
0.080 to 0.102	70.0	100.0
0.103 to 0.121	80.0	100.0
0.122 to 0.163	90.0	100.0
0.164 to 0.434	100.0	100.0
	(*n* = 264)[b]	(*n* = 34)
Mean	0.082[c]	0.031[c]
Standard Deviation	0.068	0.033

[a]The index of municipal fragmentation is the ratio of the number of municipalities in a metropolitan area to the per-thousand population resident in municipally governed areas. The higher the score, the more fragmented is an area.
[b]There were 264 SMSAs in the United States in 1972.
[c]Significant at .001 level.
Source: Calculated by authors from U.S. Bureau of the Census, *1972 Census of Governments,* Vol. 1, Governmental Organization, Table 19, Local Governments and Public School Systems in Individual SMSAs: 1972; D. M. Ray *et al., Canadian Urban Trends* (Toronto: Copp Clark), 1976, Volume 1, National Perspective: Table A1.3.

in Canada) of preferences. The Tiebout hypothesis is consistent with the above interpretation wherein U.S. urban residents "vote with their feet" and seek out those municipalities that provide the bundle of services and costs (taxes) that are consistent with personal preferences. In such a setting, more diverse units could legitimately be interpreted as representing more diverse underlying service preferences of U.S. metropolitan area residents compared with residents of Canada's metropolitan regions. While the evidence in support of the hypothesis is not conclusive, it is still a useful construct to understand some of the issues surrounding local services and taxes in urban regions.[17]

Competition Among Local Governments   It is further claimed that the existence of numerous competing local governments unnecessarily duplicates services and wastes taxpayers' dollars. One could first of all invoke the Tiebout argument again, that the existence of numerous competing local governments provides consumers of local public services with maximum choice of residential and work locations. The existence of such competition forces local governments to be efficient for fear of losing residents to neighboring local governments with more favorable services and lower taxes.[18] Despite the lack of rigorous support for this argument, there is no evidence that the claim is unfounded and baseless.[19]

There is evidence though that competition among local governments for tax base is inefficient and wasteful. First, there is the work on fiscal zoning, which has shown that there are real losses associated with such practices.[20] Fiscal zoning can restrict land supply and increase prices of residential land and simultaneously lower prices of industrial/commercial land through overzoning of these preferred tax-base land uses. The distributional impact is double-barreled: higher house prices especially affecting lower income groups and subsidies for businesses.[21]

The efficacy of this competition for tax base can also be questioned on the basis of work we discussed in Chapter 13 on locational incentives. Effectively, these locational incentives add costs to local governments that need not be incurred.[22] The result is higher costs of local government without offsetting benefits.

Spatial Imbalances Between Demand and Supply for Local Services   Demands on local governments exceed their ability to supply services out of their own revenue sources. Local governments in the United States and Canada are dependent on transfers from federal and state and provincial governments. In the United States, in 1980–81, local government units received US$22.4 billion from the federal government and US$89.0 billion from the states, together comprising 38.7 percent of all local government revenue. Table 15–8 indicates the local government expenditures for Canada.

Table 15–7 Governmental Revenue by Source and Level of Government: 1980–81

	Amount (millions of dollars)					Per Capita		
			State and Local Governments					State and Local governments
Sources	All Governments	Federal Government	Total	State	Local	Total	Federal Government	
Total revenue	1,075,387	660,759	506,728	310,828	287,834	4,746.86	2,916.65	2,236.75
Total general revenue	820,814	489,509	423,404	258,159	257,179	3,623.15	2,160.74	1,868.94
Intergovernmental revenue	—	1,804	90,294	70,786	111,443	—	7.96	398.57
From federal government	—	—	90,294	67,868	22,427	—	—	398.57
Public welfare	—	—	29,176	28,892	285	—	—	128.79
Education	—	—	15,831	14,100	1,731	—	—	69.88
General revenue sharing	—	—	5,649	1,118	4,531	—	—	24.93
Highways	—	—	9,508	9,369	140	—	—	41.97
Housing and urban renewal	—	—	4,867	286	4,581	—	—	21.48
Health and hospitals	—	—	2,809	2,601	208	—	—	12.40
Other and combined	—	—	22,453	11,502	10,951	—	—	99.11
From state governments	—	1,804	—	—	89,017	—	7.96	—
Education	—	—	—	—	57,251	—	—	—
Public welfare	—	1,804	—	—	9,901	—	7.96	—
Highways	—	—	—	—	4,477	—	—	—
Health and hospitals	—	—	—	—	2,356	—	—	—
Other and combined	—	—	—	—	15,031	—	—	—
From local governments	—	—	—	2,918	—	—	—	—
Revenue from own sources	1,075,387	658,954	416,433	240,042	176,391	4,746.86	2,908.69	1,838.17
General revenue from own sources	820,814	487,705	333,109	187,373	145,736	3,623.15	2,152.78	1,470.38
Taxes	650,228	405,714	244,514	149,738	94,776	2,870.17	1,790.86	1,079.31
Property	74,969	—	74,969	2,949	72,020	330.92	—	330.92
Individual income	331,977	285,551	46,426	40,895	5,531	1,465.38	1,260.45	204.93
Corporation income	75,280	61,137	14,143	14,143	—	332.30	269.86	62.43

Table 15–7 (Continued)

| | Amount (millions of dollars) | | | | | Per Capita | | |
| Sources | All Governments | Federal Government | State and Local Governments | | | Total | Federal Government | State and Local governments |
			Total	State	Local			
Sales and gross receipts	134,532	48,561	85,971	72,751	13,220	593.84	214.35	379.49
Customs duties	8,161	8,161	—	—	—	36.02	36.02	—
General sales and gross receipts	55,641	—	55,641	46,412	9,229	245.61	—	245.61
Selective sales and gross receipts	70,730	40,400	30,330	26,339	3,991	312.21	178.33	133.88
Motor fuel	14,537	4,678	9,859	9,734	125	64.17	20.65	43.52
Alcoholic beverages	8,487	5,667	2,820	2,613	206	37.46	25.01	12.45
Tobacco products	6,631	2,584	4,047	3,893	154	29.27	11.41	17.86
Public utilities	9,038	2,326	6,712	4,296	2,417	39.90	10.27	29.63
Other	32,038	25,145	6,893	5,803	1,089	141.42	110.99	30.42
Motor vehicle and operators licenses	6,108	—	6,108	5,695	413	26.96	—	26.96
Death and gift tax	9,016	6,787	2,229	2,229	—	39.80	29.96	9.84
All other	18,345	3,678	14,667	11,075	3,592	80.98	16.24	64.74
Charges and miscellaneous general revenue	170,586	81,991	88,595	37,636	50,960	752.98	361.92	391.07
Current charges	90,534	40,296	50,238	18,775	31,463	399.62	177.87	221.75
National defense and international relations	6,138	6,138	—	—	—	27.09	27.09	—
Postal service	18,373	18,373	—	—	—	81.10	81.10	—

Education	15,326	—	15,326	10,517	4,808	67.65	—	67.65
School lunch sales	2,105	—	2,105	7	2,098	9.29	—	9.29
Institutions of higher education	11,803	—	11,803	10,312	1,491	52.10	—	52.10
Other	1,418	—	1,418	199	1,220	6.26	—	6.26
Hospitals	14,829	69	14,760	4,085	10,675	65.46	.30	65.15
Sewerage	4,500	—	4,500	3	4,496	19.86	—	19.86
Sanitation other than sewerage	1,202	—	1,202	—	1,202	5.31	—	5.31
Parks and recreation	1,395	25	1,370	326	1,043	6.16	.11	6.05
Natural resources	10,942	10,111	831	567	263	48.30	44.63	3.67
Housing and urban renewal	2,322	976	1,346	109	1,237	10.25	4.31	5.94
Air transportation	2,120	92	2,098	206	1,892	9.36	.10	9.26
Water transport and terminals	1,364	460	904	267	637	6.02	2.03	3.99
Parking facilities	369	—	369	—	369	1.63	—	1.63
Other	11,655	4,122	7,533	2,693	4,839	51.44	18.19	33.25
Miscellaneous general revenue	80,053	41,695	38,358	18,861	19,497	353.36	184.05	169.31
Special assessments	1,353	—	1,353	35	1,319	5.97	—	5.97
Sale of property	1,014	437	577	79	498	4.47	1.93	2.55
Interest earnings	36,234	15,776	20,458	9,756	10,702	159.94	69.64	90.30
Other	41,451	25,482	15,969	8,991	6,979	182.97	112.48	70.49
Utility revenue	26,617	—	26,617	1,823	24,794	117.49	—	117.49
Liquor stores revenue	3,278	—	3,278	2,805	474	14.47	—	14.47
Insurance trust revenue	224,678	171,249	53,429	48,041	5,388	991.75	755.91	235.84

Note: Because of rounding, detail may not add to totals. Local government amounts are estimates subject to sampling variation.

Source: U.S. Bureau of the Census, *Government Finances in 1980–81* (Washington, D.C.: Government Printing Office), 1982, p. 17.

Table 15—8 Gross General Revenue and Expenditure of Provincial and Territorial Governments, years ended Mar. 31, 1976 and 1977 (thousand dollars)

Year, source or function	Nfld.	PEI	NS	NB	Que.	Ont.	Man.	Sask.	Alta.	BC	YT	NWT	Canada
1977													
Gross general revenue by source													
Income tax													
Individuals	107,815	17,242	172,551	146,494	3,279,519	2,200,175	291,314	277,097	439,265	725,316	—	—	7,656,788
Corporations	26,662	3,548	49,700	30,813	465,001	785,478	111,858	91,501	384,487	231,907	—	—	2,180,955
General sales tax	139,963	19,733	137,259	113,400	1,341,111	1,787,261	182,074	171,990	—	673,139	—	—	4,565,929
Motive fuel tax	37,665	8,405	57,890	49,582	428,450	587,091	72,619	59,983	91,356	178,517	2,835	2,644	1,577,037
Health insurance premiums	—	—	—	—	—	798,656	—	—	76,958	129,473	833	—	1,005,920
Social insurance levies	10,409	1,946	16,785	18,251	341,336	481,160	26,248	41,254	81,313	165,781	1,940	—	1,186,422
Other provincial taxes	20,095	12,778	22,877	57,990	1,348,537	537,417	64,750	52,071	57,822	188,912	3,768	3,187	2,370,202
Natural resource revenue	14,540	490	4,741	12,713	68,187	110,585	28,462	298,953	2,213,777	268,568	211	193	3,021,419
Privileges, licenses and permits	24,872	2,723	25,777	19,192	260,593	365,794	34,616	23,551	62,212	72,266	1,527	1,246	894,369
Liquor profits	18,971	5,586	53,371	34,674	164,983	299,859	56,456	59,304	110,149	159,597	2,411	5,020	970,382
Nontax revenue from own sources	85,177	19,452	110,466	65,412	985,722	1,103,390	152,968	211,221	526,221	539,432	6,365	13,332	3,819,159
General purpose transfers from other levels of government	255,543	60,548	309,193	237,106	1,245,139	508,537	217,026	36,922	105,748	127,960	20,861	124,335	3,248,919
Specific purpose transfers from other levels of government	192,192	59,295	248,141	345,027	1,211,246	2,150,213	319,413	302,923	509,371	639,943	33,271	58,930	5,969,967
Total	933,903	211,747	1,208,749	1,030,654	11,139,824	11,715,617	1,557,805	1,626,772	4,658,680	4,100,812	74,021	208,886	38,467,469

Gross general expenditure by function													
General government	38,176	12,865	52,046	44,572	536,041	648,212	96,494	115,228	333,736	323,575	10,494	76,841	2,288,279
Protection of persons and property	29,567	5,072	39,185	32,625	435,594	500,451	66,757	63,893	136,032	130,528	3,871	5,591	1,449,167
Transportation and communications	107,696	20,307	110,007	123,880	887,986	872,212	86,334	147,575	261,116	346,904	15,433	2,896	2,982,345
Health	196,132	38,730	303,496	232,125	2,741,388	3,439,234	431,116	347,535	936,224	1,043,970	9,595	19,551	9,739,094
Social welfare	107,247	21,232	115,357	146,620	1,872,374	1,841,378	260,929	225,921	358,417	614,413	7,421	9,676	5,580,985
Education	264,293	57,566	305,815	301,650	3,122,601	2,918,936	311,117	321,062	783,577	683,515	12,160	36,714	9,119,004
Natural resources	34,997	2,946	20,121	30,250	165,770	167,566	33,790	63,033	377,427	123,162	750	3,064	1,022,875
Agriculture, trade and industry, and tourism	32,705	17,830	44,622	50,200	270,614	164,499	69,141	116,313	143,187	94,626	1,159	7,538	1,012,435
Housing	651	—	8,008	6,115	98,490	155,013	92	22	25,217	169,682	210	—	463,499
Debt charges	122,589	13,363	99,440	70,628	580,895	1,030,299	132,825	80,706	153,511	89,729	913	1,137	2,376,037
General purpose transfers to other levels of government	8,661	2,085	47,394	36,540	361,709	454,338	17,513	12,295	57,338	68,903	—	—	1,066,775
All other expenditures	130,595	20,047	91,580	41,573	397,847	548,965	110,335	81,699	150,448	250,607	7,318	42,473	1,873,488
Total	1,073,308	212,041	1,237,071	1,116,778	11,471,309	12,741,103	1,616,442	1,575,282	3,716,229	3,939,613	69,324	205,482	38,973,983

Source: Canada Yearbook 1980–81, Table 22.22, p. 837.

In Canada, provinces transferred C\$9.6 billion of the C\$20.2 billion of local government revenues in 1978, or 47.3 percent of such revenues, while there were effectively no transfers from the federal government, compared with over US\$22.4 billion of federal transfers to local governments in the United States in 1980–81. The direct federal impact on local government spending is minimal in Canada, whereas federal support represents 7.8 percent of local government total revenues in the United States.

Local governments cannot cover current operating demands out of current revenues. The alternative open to local governments is debt financing, though most states and provinces forbid their local governments from running operating deficits. Debt is permissible for capital expenditures, though there is the problem of distinguishing between current and capital expenditures. Road repair and maintenance is an example.

Some rather striking differences are apparent in debt structures between Canada and the United States. First the ratio of state to local indebtedness in 1981 in the United States is 1:1.69 (Table 15–9), whereas the corresponding ratio between provincial and local government debt in Canada for 1977 is 1:0.50. Thus, local governments in Canada bear much less of the burden of debt vis-à-vis the provinces than do local governments in the United States vis-à-vis the states.[23] Moreover, these figures exclude liabilities guaranteed by the provinces which amounted to C\$21.2 billion in 1976.[24] Local governments get relatively greater support from provinces in Canada than they do from states in the United States.[25]

Summarizing Problems of Local Governments

The expansion of local government services beyond providing hard services has put strains on local government resources. It has also lifted local government out of its traditionally apolitical role as a mere provider of technical and infrastructure services and placed it more squarely in the political arena.[26] The classic trade-off between efficiency ("clean government") and representativeness ("political") arises.

One criticism is that the supply side of the local government service market is inefficient. An alternative view focuses on the demand side for locally provided services, which notes that demand is spatially mobile while supply is relatively fixed. Over time, inter- and intrametropolitan mobility can lead to imbalances between the demand for services and the ability to provide services.

Numerous solutions have been put forward. The more prominent solutions can be grouped along two complementary lines: demand-satisfying schemes that seek to increase local government resources to enable them to meet increasing levels of demand; supply-improvement schemes aimed at increased efficiency and cost-effectiveness in the provision of locally based public services.

Table 15–9   State and Local Governments: Indebtedness and Debt Transactions, 1970–1977[a]

Item	Debt Outstanding						Long-Term		
	Total	Per Capita (dol.)	Local Schools	Utilities	All Other	Short-Term	Net Long-Term	Debt Issued	Debt Retired
1970: Total	143.6	704	31.5	19.6	80.3	12.2	121.7	12.8	7.0
State	42.0	206	3.0	(NA)	35.9	3.1	34.5	3.9	1.9
Local	101.6	498	28.6	19.6	44.4	9.1	87.3	8.9	5.1
1975: Total	219.9	1,032	40.5	30.0	129.6	19.8	183.4	21.1	10.9
State	72.1	338	3.9	(NA)	63.7	4.6	58.4	8.4	2.9
Local	147.7	693	36.6	30.0	65.9	15.2	125.0	12.7	8.0
1976: Total	240.5	1,121	41.1	20.8	49.9	18.8	195.7	31.7	11.3
State	84.8	395	4.0	(NA)	74.8	6.0	62.9	13.9	3.0
Local	155.7	725	37.0	30.8	75.1	12.8	132.8	17.8	8.4
1977: Total	259.7	1,200	38.0	40.2	168.5	12.8	214.9	34.4	13.6
State	90.2	417	4.0	3.3	79.9	3.0	67.6	12.4	4.0
Local	169.5	783	33.9	36.8	88.7	9.8	147.3	22.0	9.5
1978: Total	280.4	1,286	33.0	42.4	193.6	11.4	225.2	40.0	16.7
State	102.6	472	4.1	3.7	91.9	2.9	72.1	17.0	5.9
Local	177.9	814	28.9	38.7	101.7	8.5	153.1	23.0	10.8
1979: Total	304.1	1,382	31.8	49.6	210.9	11.8	248.5	42.1	27.1
State	111.7	509	4.0	4.3	101.1	2.3	81.2	16.9	8.0
Local	192.4	873	27.8	45.3	109.8	9.5	167.3	25.2	19.1
1980: Total	335.6	1,482	32.3	55.2	235.0	13.1	262.9	42.3	17.4
State	122.0	540	3.8	4.6	111.5	2.1	79.8	16.4	5.7
Local	213.6	942	28.5	50.6	123.5	11.0	183.1	25.9	11.7
1981: Total	363.8		40.1	60.1	127.0	15.7	273.7	43.8	18.9
State	134.8		3.6	4.9	104.5	2.3	81.5	18.2	6.2
Local	229.0		36.5	55.2	122.5	13.4	192.2	25.6	12.7

[a]In billions of dollars, except per capita. Local government amounts are estimates subject to sampling variation.

Source: U.S. Statistical Abstract, 1979, Table 490, p. 297. U.S. Bureau of the Census, *Governmental Finances in 1980–81,* (Washington, D.C.: Government Printing Office), Table 17, p. 54, ASI-81 2466-2.4.

OVERCOMING THE DIFFICULTIES: ORGANIZATIONAL AND FISCAL REFORMS

Previously, we have described the nature and functions of local government. We also explored some of the difficulties of providing local services in a spatial setting. We will not be discussing the financial crunch in older Eastern United States cities but concentrating instead on more general questions of balancing revenues and expenditures in the urban spatial public economy.[27]

Expanding the Resources Available to Local Governments

Three general approaches have been put forth to expand local government revenue bases. Within each approach a number of specific variations have been proposed. The approaches are revenue sharing among different levels of government; property tax reforms; and user charges for local government services.

Revenue Sharing   Two broad types of revenue sharing are already in effect: general, or unconditional, revenue sharing where local governments are free to spend additional revenues; and specific, or conditional, revenue sharing where the donor government specifies the use of the funds. Local governments prefer unconditional transfers. Senior levels of government prefer conditional grants of various kinds to ensure performance and the meeting of senior-level government objectives.

Looking at specific program categories, we find that transfers, usually in the form of conditional grants, are even more important. For example, 47.6 percent of U.S. local government direct educational expenditures were financed by state intergovernmental transfers, including funds from the federal government.[28] In Canada, provincial governments accounted for roughly 70 percent of local government educational expenditures.[29]

Another form of revenue sharing that is implied by such legal decisions as *Serrano* v. *Priest* is intrametropolitan revenue sharing where local governments contribute, according to their revenue capacity, to the provision of a public service such as education, on a regional basis.[30] Such a form of revenue sharing raises questions about regionalization of function and regionalization of the tax base. The general idea is that governmental units that can raise revenues more easily should redistribute to units that have relatively greater difficulty in raising revenues.

Property Tax Reforms and Modifications   In Chapter 14 we discussed the pros and cons of the property tax. Foremost is the regressivity of the tax, wherein low- and middle-income groups are taxed disproportionately relative to upper-income groups. Other shortcomings of the property tax as the major source of local government revenue are problems in administration and assessment, and the fact that revenues are spatially fixed, while costs are not necessarily imposed by fixed property within the taxing jurisdiction but can be imposed from outside by free-riders, spillover, and spatially varying demands.

There is a large literature that questions the regressivity of the property tax.[31] The evidence on the property tax itself is that it is regressive (i.e., the poor pay disproportionately).[32] When placed in a larger context, there is room to question the regressivity if we include the service benefits provided by local governments compared with the tax.[33] Some of the regressivity results from assessment procedures wherein property is not reassessed frequently and, as a result, declining lower-income neighborhoods are overassessed and growing middle- and upper-income neighborhoods are underassessed.[34]

The need for frequent reassessment (particularly in changing urban areas) has spawned an enormous amount of interest in mass appraisal and assessment.[35] It has led to centralization of assessment at the state and provincial level in the belief that assessment and property appraisal involves economies of scale, particularly in technical expertise.[36] The political decision is vital in real property taxation, but should focus on the setting of tax rates and not on tax assessments. The ideal reform model in property tax assessment and administration has assessment done over states or provinces by assessors who rely increasingly on advances in the hedonic price index work of economists,[37] while the local governments are left to make the hard political decisions which revolve around setting property tax rates.[38] Each jurisdiction retains the setting of rates and thus leaves open the possibility that poor areas are taxed higher because of their limited tax base, while rich areas may be taxed at lower rates.

Growing areas experience growing tax bases and declining areas declining tax bases, our third issue relating to property tax reform. Two arguments are put forward in this regard. First, in the longer run, growing areas experience higher prices than declining areas. Initially, low property taxes are capitalized into prices as consumers seek to save on taxes and therefore bid up property values in low-tax areas. These related phenomena serve to equalize tax burdens somewhat.[39] This depends on the degree of property tax capitalization. The evidence is mixed, however, and we cannot state with much confidence that the tax capitalization mechanism is working at all, let alone that it is working in such a way as to equalize tax burdens.[40]

To overcome the difficulties of spatially mobile demand and relative fixity of tax revenues, it is argued that the property tax base should be regionalized. By having a regional property-taxing authority within entire metropolitan areas, it is thought that problems of growth and decline, rich and poor areas, and mobility generally can be overcome.[41] Such proposals are met with enthusiasm by poorer jurisdictions (the prototypical declining central city in the United States) and with horror and scorn by surrounding suburban jurisdictions. Little success has been achieved, except where metropolitan governments have been created out of local jurisdictions and where certain functions (such as sewage and drainage) have been regionalized.[42]

Despite the difficulties associated with the property tax, it has a number of very desirable characteristics: It is relatively stable and predictable, although real estate markets do experience turbulence at times; it is difficult to escape, since the property is immovable; finally, it is a well-defined tax that, if levied within the context of a modern assessment authority, does provide horizontal equity.[43] Alternatives such as locally administered income taxes are more expensive and too easy to avoid paying.[44] Similarly, reliance on sales and excise taxes is likely to be at least as regressive as the present property tax is supposed to be.[45]

Thus, we are left with the following reforms of the property tax system. First, reduce horizontal (and some vertical) inequality through more frequent assessments conducted over larger jurisdictions, such as states and provinces, using uniform assessment procedures. This can be combined with regionalization of tax bases, which is practical if done by function instead of across the board. Finally, much of the regressivity of the tax can be removed by lump-sum payments by state and provincial governments to local property owners. Such payments lower the tax for relatively inexpensive housing, while lowering taxes for more expensive properties only marginally.[46]

It seems that the virtues of the property tax to local governments (stability, inescapability, and ease of administration) outweigh the current social costs. The property tax appears destined to continue as a major source of local government revenues.

User Charges   To the extent that the property tax is for services to real property it represents a kind of generalized user charge.[47] There are many public services which are not services to real property specifically (such as education), and there are also services to real property which are only imperfectly reflected in the property tax (e.g., water and garbage service, where they are included in property taxes but where level of use and level of tax are unrelated).

Because of the inefficiencies built into a general tax covering a range of services, local governments are finding it more efficient to tax users directly. Moving water service out from beneath the general umbrella of the property tax and putting it on a user charge basis is an example of the potential gains in efficiency that result from appropriate marginal pricing.

User charges are firmly grounded in the *benefits principle* of taxation where the person (or property) that benefits from a public action or service pays for the benefit. As Maxwell and Aronson note,

Nevertheless, state and local governments do provide many services—higher education, recreation and parking facilities, and so on—that yield direct and measurable benefits to individuals for which collection of user charges would bring a desirable linkage between individual payment and benefit; they would not result in significant shrinkage of collective benefits; and they would provide needed revenues.[48]

The usual rationale given for including education under general property tax levies is the existence of significant externalities that benefit the community at large. Another stated virtue of general property tax levies is that any public good financed under such levies benefits all, independent of income, and thus possesses an important equity or redistributive component. Maxwell and Aronson state,

Development of nontax revenues seems to have promise. In the past, considerations of equity and of redistribution have led public enterprises to price their services far below cost, and have persuaded local governments to levy user charges for noncommercial activities that do not reflect particular benefits. The probability is that, in these respects, the pursuit of equity has been misdirected; the inefficiencies of applying an equity test at the state and local level have been forgotten. Subsidization in kind has, moreover, serious built-in defects, and these are exaggerated when action is confined to a small geographic area. It would seem, therefore, that if public service enterprises followed a more rational system of pricing, they could provide local governments with additional revenue.[49]

From Tables 15–10 and 15–11, user charges constitute large components of local government revenues in both the United States and Canada. They represent an efficient means of raising revenues at the local government level. However, there may be limits on their continued growth on equity grounds and, in the United States, because of the deductibility of property taxes from federal income taxes, which does not apply to user charges.[50]

Cutting Costs and Increasing Efficiency of Services by Local Governments

Means to improve efficiency and expand revenue are two complementary approaches and are being pursued simultaneously.[51] We explore four approaches to cost cutting and greater efficiency: regionalizing functions to take advantage of economies of scale; stemming the growth of local government fragmentation; creating new local government boundaries that more closely correspond to service areas; reducing services provided with no marginal charges and putting them on a pay-as-you-go basis. The most widely heralded approach deals with regionalization of local government.

Regionalizing Local Government Function   This approach has long been a favorite with urban reformers who view politics as a barrier to the provision of services.[52] If provision of services in an efficient manner is the sole goal of local government, and politics obstructs the pursuit of this goal, then regionalizing local government has an efficiency gain. Regionalizing functions overcomes the diseconomies of small-scale local government services, leading to further improvements in efficiency. However, from the previous evidence, it was not possible to conclude that there are large economies of scale in the provision of public services at the regional, instead of the local, level.[53]

Turning to the notion that regionalization takes service delivery out of the political realm and into the professional, one finds general agreement on this point. However, do we want to leave service delivery exclusively to professional and technical people, or do we desire to maintain political input and public surveillance? Three quite different forms of regionalization provide different solutions to these problems.

The prototype metropolitan government is Toronto's Metro. Metro began its operations on January 1, 1954. Out of 13 municipal governments was created the Metro Council with 25 members (12 from the city of Toronto and one each from the surrounding municipalities, plus the chairman). Initially Metro Council was responsible for relatively few services, including capital borrowing, major roads, and property assessment. The lower tier of 13 municipal governments was left with the responsibility of providing for police and fire protection, libraries, licensing, and local planning. The vast bulk of local government services therefore was left to be shared with Metro Council and the member municipalities. Thus, Metro supplied water and sewage treatment services at wholesale rates to the municipalities, which in turn sold water to local customers and collected sewage.[54]

The Metro Toronto government was viewed as an experiment subject to periodic review. In 1957 the 13 local police departments were merged into a Metro Police function. Pollution control was also added as a Metro responsibility in that year. Finally, 1957 also saw the first in a series of reviews of Metro performance. The initial metropolitan amalgamation proposed in the Cumming Report of 1953 was turned down, but Metro did eventually grow out of this report. The 1958 Cumming review suggested no changes despite the appearance of significant difficulties tied to the imbalance of power in Metro Council, where Toronto possessed 12 votes yet represented a smaller share of Metro population and jobs.

In 1963 the city of Toronto made its second request to the Ontario Municipal Board (the Cumming Report of 1953 being the first request) for amalgamation with the 12 neighboring municipalities. The provincial government sidestepped the issue by establishing a Royal Commission under Carl Goldenberg (who had just reviewed municipal organization in New Brunswick) to review the Metro situation. Two

Table 15–10 Local Government User Charges, by Major Categories of Governmental Service 1953, 1963, 1968, and 1973 to 1980

Government Service	1953	1963	1968	1973	1974	1975	1976	1977	1978	1979	1980
Millions of Dollars											
Nonhighway transportation	128	335	490	956	1,067	1,245	1,362	1,524	1,726	1,912	2,208
Air	42	216	331	682	798	920	1,002	1,109	1,253	1,385	1,636
Water	87	119	159	274	269	325	360	415	473	527	572
Hospitals	230	815	1,411	3,405	3,879	4,248	5,051	5,722	6,506	7,921	9,236
Housing	225	446	514	689	688	757	842	916	975	1,124	1,208
Sewerage and other sanitation	154	633	678	1,951	2,229	2,542	2,906	3,150	3,587	4,204	4,870
Natural resources, parks, and recreation	91	238	243	443	479	522	596	756	838	1,014	1,137
Education	357	1,240	1,829	2,714	2,908	3,301	4,079	3,492	3,734	4,109	4,490
Highways	96										
Other	343	932	1,729	2,128	2,419	2,286	2,566	2,669	3,499	4,013	4,345
Total	1,625	4,639	6,894	12,285	14,736	16,146	18,764	19,753	22,591	26,209	29,702
User charges as percentage of general revenue from own revenue	12.8	16.3	16.9	17.4							
Percentage of Expenditure											
Nonhighway transportation	55.7	59.7	73.4	59.5	69.8	73.5	80.9	92.5	91.3	80.0	74.9
Air	NA	65.5	73.9	58.0	74.1	79.0	82.7	97.4	91.3	84.0	76.4
Water	NA	51.5	72.3	63.4	59.4	61.3	76.3	21.7	91.3	71.1	70.8
Hospitals	27.1	41.5	46.3	59.3	60.5	57.4	63.1	66.7	29.2	73.2	73.8
Housing	35.8	36.1	31.9	23.8	22.3	24.8	29.2	28.3	27.6	24.9	21.1
Sewerage and other sanitation	17.0	28.9	25.0	36.7	37.2	37.8	35.3	35.5	37.5	36.6	37.8
Natural resources, parks, and recreation	16.6	16.2	12.6	13.8	13.0	12.1	12.2	15.9	16.0	17.3	17.1
Education	4.6	6.5	6.1	5.3	5.2	5.1	5.7	4.6	4.6	4.7	4.6
Highways	4.3										

Source: J. Maxwell and R. Aronson, *Financial State and Local Governments*, 1977 Third Edition (Washington, D.C.: The Brookings Institution), p. 273. 1974–1980 from U.S. Bureau of the Census, *Governmental Finances* (Washington, D.C.: Government Printing Office), 1974, 1975, 1976, 1977, 1978, 1979, 1980.

Table 15–11 Revenue Sources of Local Governments in Canada 1969–1978

Revenue Source	1969		1970		1971		1972		1973		1974		1975		1976		1977		1978	
Taxes																				
Taxes on corporations	263	3.8	297	3.8	315	3.7	335	3.5	351	3.4	378	3.3	508	3.6	586	3.4	706	3.8	748	3.7
Real and personal property taxes																				
Municipal	1338	19.1	1486	18.9	1570	17.8	1791	18.7	2000	19.6	2218	19.4	—	—	—	—	—	—	—	—
School	1681	24.0	1766	22.5	1802	20.4	1855	19.3	1782	17.4	1884	16.5	—	—	—	—	—	—	—	—
Subtotal	3019	43.1	3249	41.3	3371	38.1	3645	38.0	3728	37.0	4103	35.9	4989	35.4	5901	34.6	6510	35.4	7422	36.8
Other taxes	37	.5	58	.7	41	.5	30	.3	41	.4	38	.3	29	.2	79	.5	73	.4	78	.4
Total tax revenue	3316	47.3	3602	45.8	3726	42.1	4010	41.8	4173	40.8	4517	39.5	5527	39.2	6567	38.5	7288	39.6	7875	39.0
Privileges, licenses, etc.	73	1.0	74	.9	57	.6	63	.6	68	.7	71	.6	92	.6	88	.5	105	.6	113	.6
Sales of goods and services																				
Water	184	2.6	202	2.6	304	3.4	334	3.5	354	3.5	372	3.3	436	3.1	523	3.1	568	3.1	616	3.1
General	148	2.1	171	2.2	251	2.8	306	3.2	316	3.1	350	3.1	491	3.5	630	3.7	718	3.9	776	3.8
Subtotal	331	4.7	374	4.8	555	6.3	639	6.7	667	6.5	722	6.3	927	6.6	1153	6.7	1286	7.0	1392	6.9
Return on investments	62	.9	70	.9	64	.7	78	.8	80	.8	68	.6	—		—		—		—	
Other own-source revenue	175	2.5	182	2.3	212	2.4	207	2.2	213	2.1	210	1.8	463	3.3	702	4.1	583	3.2	624	3.1
Total own-source revenue	3955	56.5	4298	54.7	4615	52.2	4995	52.1	5203	50.9	5590	48.9	7009	49.7	8854	51.9	9639	52.3	10423	51.6

Grants in lieu of taxes																				
Federal government	41	.6	44	.6	45	.5	50	.5	51	.5	56	.5	81	.6	105	.6	114	.6	123	.6
Provincial government	17	.2	19	.2	21	.2	30	.3	46	.4	48	.4	60	.4	60	.4	67	.4	77	.4
Federal and provincial enterprises	35	.5	36	.4	41	.5	45	.5	53	.5	59	.5	84	.6	120	.7	132	.7	142	.7
Other	—	—	—	—	16	.2	20	.2	39	.4	41	.4	58	.4	59	.3	65	.4	76	.4
Subtotal	92	1.3	98	1.2	121	1.4	144	1.5	189	1.8	203	1.8	283	2.0	344	2.0	377	2.0	419	2.1
General-purpose transfers (provincial)	290	4.1	307	3.9	361	4.1	429	4.5	565	5.5	668	5.9	943	6.7	1048	6.1	1172	6.4	1266	6.3
Special-purpose transfers																				
Federal	37	.5	31	.4	87	1.0	95	1.0	80	.8	125	1.1	101	.7	257	1.5	174	.9	209	1.0
Provincial	2633	37.6	3127	34.8	3656	41.3	3926	40.9	4186	40.9	4841	42.4	5771	40.9	6896	40.4	7427	40.3	8285	41.0
Subtotal	2669	38.1	3158	40.2	3744	42.3	4021	41.9	4267	41.7	4965	43.5	5872	41.6	7153	41.9	7646	41.5	8494	42.1
Total revenue	7006	100.0	7862	100.0	8842	100.0	9589	100.0	10223	100.0	11426	100.0	14107	100.0	17055	100.0	18413	100.0	20184	100.0

Source: Plunkett and Betts, *The Management of Canadian Urban Government* (Kingston, Ontario: Queen's University Press), 1978, p. 84; and *Canada Yearbook, 1978/79* (Ottawa, Ontario: Minister of Supply and Services), Table 20.23, pp. 833–834, for 1975 data; *Canada Yearbook 1980–81*, Table 20.23, pp. 838–839.

years later, in 1965, he suggested that the 13 governments be amalgamated into four governments, with the mayors of the four municipalities sitting on the Metro Council chaired again by a provincial government appointee. In 1967 the provincial government did reorganize Metro. Six municipalities were created (not four, as suggested by Goldenberg), called boroughs. Welfare was added as a Metro function and the Metro School Board was empowered to equalize school facilities and costs in the area.

The final review of the Metro experience is embodied in the Robarts Commission Report of 1977. Its principal contribution was to acknowledge the effectively running Metro. The Commission noted that the six mayors, four members of the city of Toronto executive committee (elected councillors), and the appointed chairman could not deal with the details of day-to-day management very efficiently. The Commission also noted that the Metro Council members were not in a good position to supply needed political leadership, since they all held elected office in their respective boroughs and, thus, did not have a true metropolotan mandate but rather a more narrow borough mandate.

Over the past 27 years Metro Toronto has evolved considerably. As a result of this evolution it has managed to provide regionwide services efficiently, and yet its federal structure gives heed to local concerns. It seems to provide a workable compromise between technical efficiency and political responsiveness. While its specific structure and operations may be difficult to duplicate elsewhere, its evolutionary approach should be transferable across regions and indeed across national boundaries, as Metro served as the model for two of the first metropolitan governments in the United States—in Miami, Florida, and Nashville, Tennessee.

The federal two-tier structure embodied in Metro has spawned innovations in both British Columbia and Quebec.[55] It has also led to the development of regional governments in other parts of Ontario, as Table 15–12 illustrates. In short, it is an innovation that has had far-reaching impact and which, as a result, is deserving of our attention.

The Dade County (Florida) experiment provides an interesting example of the problems of creating metropolitan governments in the United States. It is also worth discussing briefly because it followed on the heels of Metro and has served as an American prototype.

Metropolitan Dade County was created in 1957 by a vote of 44,404 to 42,620 (26 percent voter turnout). The Dade County approach leaves intact the preexisting 26 municipalities. Metropolitan area responsibilities are now under the aegis of the county, including transportation (expressways, transit, and traffic); fire and police; health and hospitals and welfare programs; housing and urban renewal; servicing standards; overall zoning and planning; pollution control; flood and beach erosion control; drainage; and public utility regulation.[56]

Table 15–12 Regional Governments in Ontario

Name	Date of Operation	Area (sq. miles)	Population (1972)	Units Before Reform	Units After Reform
Ottawa-Carleton	January 1969	1100	467,700	16	16 (11 by 1974)
Niagara (St. Catherines)	January 1970	720	345,200	26	12
York	January 1971	645	173,700	14	9
Muskoka	January 1971	1688	31,100	25	6
Waterloo (Kitchener)	January 1973	519	258,900	15	7
Sudbury	January 1973	1088	167,800	15	7
Peel (Mississauga)	January 1974	484	302,700	10	3
Halton-(Burlington)	January 1974	405	202,300	7	4
Durham (Oshawa)	January 1974	875	220,200	21	8
Hamilton-Wentworth	January 1974	432	398,200	11	6
Haldimand-Norfolk	April 1974	1117	83,900	28	6

Source: D. J. Higgins, *Urban Canada: Its Government and Politics* (Toronto, Ontario: Macmillan of Canada, 1977.

County government was also reorganized with the elimination of many elected offices and the creation of the county manager. The Metropolitan Dade County experiment has achieved some notable success in providing regional services, (such as transportation planning), though it still faces periodic political attacks. It does stand as a model for metropolitan government in the United States, where heavy reliance is placed on county governments (unlike Canada) and where city–county infighting frequently arises.[57]

Before leaving the subject of metropolitan and regional government, a brief look at the British Columbia system of regional districts is in order. This system is unique and provides a useful prototype for many states and provinces with large areas of unincorporated territory and also areas of significant concentration of population.

At the time of the creation of the regional districts in British Columbia, it was estimated that less than 3000 square miles of territory lay within organized municipalities, leaving slightly more than 363,000 square miles in unorganized territories, directly managed by the provincial Department of Municipal Affairs.[58] A system of 28 regional districts was established, virtually spanning the province, with the exception of the northwesternmost corner. Begun in 1965, by 1968 boundaries had been established for all 28 regional districts. They ranged in size from roughly 800 square miles to 80,000 square miles, and have from 40,000 to 1.1 million inhabitants.[59] In the rural and remote areas of the province, the regional districts represent the major form of local government. The precise functions of each regional district appear in the Letters Patent that establish each district. All are responsible for hospital financing and regional planning, while the more urban regional districts have taken on a form similar to Metro Toronto. For example, the Greater Vancouver Regional District (the most populous) has responsibility for regional land-use planning; hospitals and their financing; senior citizen housing; regional parks; water and sewage facilities for the region; managing municipal debt; regional transportation planning; and air pollution control.

In rural and remote areas, the regional districts function as a unitary government regulating development, while in urban areas they function in a two-tier federal fashion similar to Toronto's Metro.[60] Regional districts are run by an elected board from member muncipalities and from unincorporated areas. The general consensus appears to be that the idea has been adaptable to, and has achieved the objectives of, the development process and the efficient provision of local public services,[61] although the 1983 reelection of the Social Credit government is likely to spell major changes in regional district functions.

Reducing the Numbers of Local Governments: Amalgamation and Annexation   If there are economies of scale (and the evidence is spotty), then efficiency can be achieved through the reduction in the number of governmental units at the local level and an incease in their size. Two approaches exist: amalgamating existing units and annexing neighboring units by the primary, or core, city.

Amalgamation has been the more difficult of the two approaches in the United States, while it has been the preferred approach in Canada, with the exception of the province of Alberta where both Edmonton and Calgary have grown as a result of annexation.[62] The most dramatic, and perhaps the best documented, recent amalgamation was the creation of the present Winnipeg out of 12 existing municipal governments and a two-tier regional government.[63] The City of Winnipeg Act of July 1, 1971, became effective on January 1, 1972, and created a unitary city of 520,000 people with an elected city council of 50 and a directly elected mayor. A major innovation in the Winnipeg experiment (called Unicity) is the creation of 12 community committees, each comprised of from 3 to 6 wards (out of the 50 wards in the city). These community committees include both the elected ward councillor plus appointed local citizens.[64]

While there is some reason to be sceptical about the effectiveness of the advisory community committees, there is little question that the Unicity amalgamation has provided for the rationalization of municipal services and the end of competition among municipalities for tax base, staff, and services. The contribution of the Unicity experiment is that it sought to deal directly with the problems of government responsiveness and efficiency. As with British Columbia's regional districts, Toronto's Metro, and regional governments in Ontario, Unicity should be viewed as an ongoing experiment rather than a finished product. While similar amalgamations took place in four locations in British Columbia during the early 1970s, they can be contrasted directly with Unicity since they lacked the notion of community participation and were designed for efficiency only.[65]

Annexation has been particularly popular in rapidly growing areas of the United States where fringe growth has motivated cities to annex surrounding lands.[66] Annexation usually meets less political resistance than amalgamation because annexed territories tend to be sparsely inhabited and because there is usually less conflict than with amalgamation.[67] Indeed, most annexation has been in the South, Southwest, and West, all of which have been experiencing rapid growth.[68]

Some striking examples about the results of annexation exist. Oklahoma City after World War II comprised about 50 square miles of territory. Today it encompasses over 650 square miles. It was the largest city in area in the United States until Jacksonville, Florida, and its surrounding county merged in 1967 to to create a city of 740 square miles.

Whether through amalgamation or annexation, previously fragmented governmental structures (either incorporated or unincorporated) are consolidated under one municipal government. Such consolidation of territory under one municipal government overcomes some of the weaknesses inherent in the federal form, such as Metro Toronto, in that all powers are concentrated in the consolidated municipality.

Creating Alternative Jurisdictional Boundaries There are instances where neither regionalization of existing functions nor consolidation of existing units can be effective. Such instances arise where the function to be provided does not correspond to political boundaries of any sort, but rather is dictated by broader considerations such as water or air sheds or unique ecological environments.

In general, these functions are carried out through the creation of special-purpose districts that transcend existing political boundaries. Special-purpose districts have been the one areas of consistent growth at the local government level, growing in number from 14,405 in 1957 to 28,733 in 1982. School districts diminished in number from 50,446 to 15,032 over that period, and the number of municipalities and townships remained essentially unchanged (these figures are all for the United States).[69]

One of the most innovative and important special-purpose districts transcended not only municipal and county boundaries but also state borders. The Port Authority of New York and New Jersey was created by a bi-state compact to provide for functions which include not only the region's airports (three major airports plus one for general aviation), its bus terminals, and its deep-water shipping facilities, but commuter railroads, bridges and tunnels, heliports, truck terminals, and the famed World Trade Center, the largest office complex in the world, with nearly 9 million square feet of leasable space (roughly 200 acres of building).[70]

Special-purpose districts abound in the provision of sewage, drainage, and water. They have gained popularity in providing regional transportation, starting with San Francisco's Bay Area Rapid Transit District (BART), being followed more recently by Washington, D.C.'s METRO, and Atlanta's Metropolitan Area Rapid Transit Authority (MARTA), and Boston's Massachusetts Bay Transit Authority (MBTA), and so on. The San Francisco Bay Conservation and Development Commission (BCDC) started in the mid-1960s as a prototype regional conservation agency that provided leadership for the burgeoning environmental concern during the 1970s. If successful, the implications of special-purpose districts for existing levels of government are significant as they hold the promise of easing environmental strains, reducing pollution and congestion, and generally improving the management of public resources inside metropolitan areas in both the United States and Canada. There are some problem areas, including the establishment of districts to obtain the tax-free status on municipal bonds for coporate placements, distorting the market for both bonds and industrial sites in the process.

User Charges   Another means of reducing costs is the imposition of user charges. By putting local public services on a pay-as-you-go basis, cost savings can be realized as overconsumption and waste can be discouraged. The movement from publicly provided goods to a system of user charges contains equity and distributional issues noted earlier, which must be traded off against economic efficiency criteria.[71]

Administrative Devices   One last set of approaches to cutting costs and duplication in local government derives from administrative procedures propounded by the U.S. federal government. At the urging of the Office of Management and Budget (OMB), the A-95 procedures noted in Chapter 11 were put in place to deal with duplication in local government efforts in gaining federal support. These procedures require metropolitan area coordination (the so-called clearinghouse function) of federal grant applications and expenditures. The A-95 Bureau of the Budget Circular extended an earlier Circular A-80 in bringing federal pressure to bear to coordinate planning on a regionwide basis. Similar provisions for areawide planning and coordination in the use of federal funds appears in the National Interstate Highway Act of 1956 and its 1962 amendments and the HUD "701" planning program.[72] Recent federal environmental legislation has tended to place additional demands on areawide planning.[73] The result of these federal initiatives has been the formation of councils of government (COGs) or metropolitan government organizations (MGOs) to serve this clearinghouse and coordination function. Among the more active and well-documented MGOs are San Diego's Comprehensive Planning Organization (CPO), the San Francisco Bay Area's Association of Bay Area Governments (ABAG), and Seattle's Puget Sound Council of Governments (PSCOG). These regional agencies and their analogs elsewhere in the United States have served to coordinate and thereby rationalize local government plans and grants, though at some cost in terms of local representation since MGOs are functionally creatures of federal making.

Summary

We have explored a range of devices intended to increase the efficiency of local governments. We first examined various organizational approaches such as the creation of regional or metroplitan governments. Next, we looked at annexation and amalgamation. Finally, we explored special-purpose districts which transcend traditional boundaries and are organized along functional rather than historical political lines. These organizational approaches combined with the imposition of user charges and rationalized procedures for obtaining and spending federal grants (in the United States but not in Canada, where federal monies do not flow directly to local government), are all aimed at increasing efficiency and lowering the unit costs of local government services.

SUMMARY

We have looked at local government as a provider of services that form the background against which urban markets function. That local government services can have direct and important impacts on urban land values has been clearly demonstrated.[74]

Local governments in both Canada and the United States have consistently expanded their initial roles as providers of so-called hard services (e.g., engineering and public works, planning and financial administration) and have increasingly sought to provide broader ranges or amenities. We reviewed the various sources of funds available to local governments in the United States and Canada and found some regularities (reliance on property taxes and intergovernmental transfers) and some differences (relatively greater role played by provinces vis-á-vis states). There are other problems that are directly related to revenues but tied to the spatial heterogeneity of urban areas and the existence of many local governments which, of necessity, are fixed in location. Demand is highly mobile, as the tax base itself can be. Thus, local governments are faced with imbalances in revenues and expenditures.

Revenue-oriented reforms provide one means for overcoming these problem areas. Cost-cutting and efficiency schemes constituted another major thrust. A range of solutions exist, all of which embody, in one form or another, basic trade-offs between economic efficiency and responsiveness in government.

All governments must successfully confront a number of fundamental trade-offs. First, every government must come to terms with protecting the rights of individuals and the rights of the entire society. Laws are passed that infringe on individual rights for the good of the society. Next, governments must cope with a schizophrenic requirement to provide both followership (e.g., responsiveness to popular demands) and leadership, often making decisions against the popular will in the short run (such as tax or interest rate increases) in the longer-run interests of the society. Of central importance in the present context of local government is the trade-off between efficiency and responsiveness to public demands. Engineering efficiency in road alignments needs to be traded off against the disruption of nieghborhoods and political upheaval. In the case of regionalizing or amalgamating local government functions and units, the central political concern is always the loss of the political power or voice of the absorbed territories, or the absence of input to the more efficient regional function. (Unicity Winnipeg has attempted to deal with this issue head-on, with as yet limited success.)

Footnotes

1. The experience in Canadian cities is best documented in Michael Dennis and Susan Fish, *Programs in Search of a Policy (Toronto, Ontario: Haggert), 1972; and George A. Nader, Canadian Cities, Volumes 1 and 2,* (Toronto, Ontario: Macmillan of Canada), 1975 and 1976. In the United States, New York City stands out. See David Dreyfuss and Joan Hendrickson, *A Guide to Government Activites in New York City's Housing Markets* (Santa Monica, Cal. The RAND Corporation), RM-5673-NYC, 1968. See also Jewel Bellush and Murray Hausknecht, eds., *Urban Renewal* (Garden City, N.Y.: Anchor Books), 1969.

2. Public goods are those goods and services which generate benefits that are generally available to the public and not easily captured (and therefore sold) by private intersts. In essence, these are goods with very large external positive effects. Because public external benefits (soical benefits) are greater than private benefits accruing from such goods, they are generally provided by the public sector. Parks and recreation facilities would be a good example, as would urban open space and scenic vistas. See Richard F. Muth, *(Urban Economic Problems* (New York: Harper and Row), 1975, pp. 372–374, for additional detail.

3. Canada Department of Finance, *Economic Review* (Ottawa, Ontario: Minister of Supply and Services), annually.

4. Much has been written on comparative federalism. See Ivo Duchacek, *Comparative Federalism* (New York: Holt, Rinehart and Winston), 1970. Also see A. Breton and A. D. Scott, *The Economic Constitution of Federal States* (Toronto, Ontario: University of Toronto Press), 1979.

5. T. J. Plunkett and G. M. Betts, *The Management of Canadian Urban Government* (Kingston, Ontario: The Institute of Local Government, Queen's University), 1978, pp. 29–30.

6. More specifically, in the United States in 1980 there were a total of 167,000,000 urban residents out of a total population of 226,500,000, or 73.7 percent. In Canada in 1981 the comparable figures are 16,411,000 out of a total population of 24,189,000 or 76.1 percent. Canadian data are from *Canada Yearbook, 1980/81* (Ottawa, Canada: Ministry of Supply and Services), 1981, while U.S. data are from *the Statistical Abstract of the U.S.* (Washington, D.C.: U.S. Government Printing Office, 1982.

7. We could also view fragmentation as a demand problem, given the spatial dispersion of urban area residents and the general desire to overcome spatial separation with minimal effort. We have chosen here, somewhat arbitrarily, to view fragmentation as a supply side phenomenon by concentrating on the fragmentation of local governments (suppliers of locally demanded services).

8. New England town beaches, which require town parking stickers, local library cards for residents, and minimal community and recreation center fees for residents, are all attempts to deal with the free-rider problem.

9. Proposition 9 was an attempt to limit and cut California state income taxes and would have resulted in service cuts similar to those that ensued in the wake of Proposition 13. For an analysis of Proposition 13, see Frank Levey, "On Understanding Proposition 13," *Public Interest*, 56 (Summer 1979):66–89.

10. That central cities in Canada have faired well in holding families and middle-income groups has been documented recently by Michael A. Goldberg and John Mercer, "Canadian and U.S. Cities: Basic Differences, Possible Explanations, and Their Meaning for Public Policy," *Papers and Proceedings of the Regional Science Association*, 1980 45:159–183.

11. Again, this is much more a U.S. problem than a Canadian one. Canadian cities have been able to deal with many of the costs of growth by passing them along to developers. See Michael A. Goldberg, "Municipal Arrogance or Economic Rationality: The Case of High Servicing Standards, *Canadian Public Policy*, 6(1:1980):78–88.

12. The ability of local area residents to move about metropolitan areas in search of preferred combinations of taxes and services has been loosely dubbed "voting with one's feet" and is traceable to Charles M. Tiebout, "A Pure Theory of Local Expenditures," *Journal of Political Economy*, 64(4:1956):416–424. This model of local expenditures has stimulated an enormous amount of interest and empirical work. For a review and criticism of the literature, see M. Edel and E. Sclar, "Taxes, Spending and Property Values: Supply Adjustment in a Tiebout-Oates Model," *Journal of Political Economy*, 82(6:1974:941–954.

13. The question of optimal scale of urban services is tied to questions of optimum city size. The optimum scale of service question is addressed by R. Kirwan, "The Contribution of Public Expenditure and Finance to the Problems of Inner

London" (London: England: Centre for Environmental Studies), 1972, which questions the existence of scale economies; and by R. W. Bahl, *Metropolitan City Expenditures: A Comparative Analysis*, (Lexington, Kentucky: Kentucky University Press), 1969, which shows diseconomies of scale. On the optimum-city-size question, see William Alonso, "The Economics of Urban Size," *Papers and Proceedings of the Regional Science Association* 26(1971:67–83; and also Harry W. Richardson, *The Economics of Urban Size*, (Farnsborough, England: Saxon House), 1973.

14. The book by Bahl, *op. cit.*, is a prime example of this problem of dealing with mix and quality of services.

15. See Alonso, *op. cit.*, and Richardson, *op. cit.*, for some of the conceptual and empirical issues facing the quest for optimal-size cities. Also, see Irving Hoch, "Income and City Size," *Urban Studies* 9(3:1972): 299–328.

16. See Chapter 11 in this volume. Also see Edwin S. Mills, "Economic Analysis of Land-Use Controls," and Daniel L. Rubinfeld, "Judicial Approaches to Local Public-Sector Equity: An Economic Analysis," Chapters 15 and 16, respectively, in Peter Mieszkowski and Mahlon Straszheim, eds., *Current Issues in Urban Economics* (Baltimore: Johns Hopkins University Press), 1979, pp. 511–576.

17. Again we are back to the Tiebout Hypothesis and "voting with one's feet." See Tiebout, *op. cit.*, and Edel and Sclar, *op. cit.*

18. Another spin-off from the Tiebout hypothesis is the phenomenon of tax capitalization where it is postulated that urban area residents capitalize tax differentials (savings) into their bids for residential units. Thus, it is hypothesized, low-tax jurisdictions should have higher housing prices reflecting the capitalized value of the stream of tax savings. Once again, sound economic reasoning has not been substantiated empirically. As was the case with scale economies and diseconomies, the case for tax capitalization is hard to document unequivocally. See, for examples of the existence of tax capitalization, the following papers: J. P. Moody, "Measuring Tax and Benefit Capitalization from a Local Rapid Transit Investment in the San Francisco Bay Area," unpublished Ph.D. dissertation (Berkeley, Cal.: University of California), 1973; and D. N. Hyman and E. C. Pasour, "Real Property Taxes, Local Public Services, and Residential Property Values in North Carolina," *Southern Economic Journal* 29(3:1973):601–611. Only partial capitalization of property tax differences has been shown by W. E. Oates, "The Effects of Property Taxes and Local Spending on Property Values: An Empirical Study of Tax Capitalization and the Tiebout Hypothesis," *Journal of Political Economy* 77(5:1969):957–971.

19. Reformers who decry local government inefficiency and argue for improvements are discussed in Robert L. Lineberry and Edmund P. Fowler, "Reformism and Public Policies in American Cities," *American Political Science Review* 61(3:1967):701–716.

20. For a discussion of fiscal zoning, see Chapter 11 in this book. Also see J. C. Ohls, R. C. Weisberg, and M. J. White, "The Effects of Zoning and Land Value," *Journal of Urban Economics* 1(4:1974):428–444.

21. This double-barreled effect is raised by Ohls, Weisberg and White, *op. cit.*, and by Ohls, R. C. Weisberg, and M. J. White, "Welfare Effects in Alternative Models of Zoning, *Journal of Urban Economics* 3(1:1976):95–96, which is a reply to Paul N. Courant, "On the Effect of Fiscal Zoning on Land and Housing Values," *Journal of Urban Economics* 3(1:1976):88–94.

22. This point was discussed at some length in Chapter 23 in this text. The interested reader should see the references in that chapter, and particularly John Moes, *Local Subsidies for Industry* (Chapel Hill, N.C.: University of North Carolina Press), 1962.

23. This point comes out in a number of ways in Elliot J. Feldman and Neil Nevitte, eds., *The Future of North America: Canada, the United States, and Quebec Nationalism* (Cambridge, Mass.: Center for International Affairs, Harvard University), 1979.

24. Liabilities guaranteed by the provincial and territorial governments, such guarantees being over and above the direct debt borne by these governments, amounted to C$10.4 billion in 1975, C$12.6 billion in 1976, C$25.8 billion in 1977, and C$29.8 billion in 1978. See *Canada Yearbook* (Ottawa, Ontario: Minister of Supply and Services), various years, for details.

25. This appears to be especially the case for such vital local government expenditures as education, where local governments needed to raise only C$2.3 billion out of C$8.5 billion in 1975–76.
This povincial funding of a central service such as education might go part of the way in explaining the relative absence in Canada of the need for such decisions as *Serrano* v. *Priest,* which sought to redistribute property tax revenues across local government boundaries so that poorer taxing jursidictions could finance adequate schools. The provincial legislatures appear to have avoided such need by redistributing needed funds themselves.

26. The mixture of technical and political elements in today's local government reflects the reality of differing technical opinions and differing political views regarding these technical opinions, as the Spadina Freeway revolt attests in Toronto and the absence of the Embarcadero Freeway does in San Francisco, where public (political) values won out over technical engineering values. The conduct of local government today closely reflects public views on how to allocate scarce resources and scarce technical expertise. This appears to be another phase in the eternal movement of the proverbial pendulum, which moved from machine (e.g., political) government to reform (e.g., technical and efficient) government in the post-World War II era.
A balance is presently in the process of being established. For more detail on this perennial problem (technical versus political bases for local government), see any of the following texts and studies. For the United States, see: Robert L. Lineberry and Ira Sharkansky, *Urban Politics and Public Policy,* (New York: Harper and Row), 1974, especially Chapters 1 through 5; and Jay S. Goodman, *The Dynamics of Urban Government and Politics* (New York: Macmillan), 1980, especially Chapters 4, 8, 9, and 10. For Canada, see: C. R. Tindal and S. N. Tindal, *Local Government in Canada* (Toronto, Ontario: McGraw-Hill Ryerson), 1979, especially Chapters 2, 8, and 9; and Donald J. Higgins, *Urban Canada: Its Government and Politics* (Toronto, Ontario: MacMillan of Canada), 1977, especially Chapters 5, 6, 7, and 8.

27. Several points should be made concerning the fiscal plight of cities. First, it is not generally observable in Canada, and we should be careful to extend U.S. work to Canada in this context. Second, it is not even generally true of U.S. local governments, which recorded a US$3 billion surplus in 1975–76 in the aggregate. For some interesting insights into the nature of the urban fiscal dilemma, see William H. Oakland, "Central Cities: Fiscal Plight and Prospects for Reform," in Peter Mieszkowski and Mahlon Straszheim, eds., *Current Issues in Urban Econom-*

ics (Baltimore: Johns Hopkins University Press), 1979, pp. 322–358. Also see Michael A. Goldberg and John Mercer, "The Fiscal Condition of American and Canadian Cities" (Vancouver, B.C.: U. B. C., Faculty of Commerce), mimeographed, 1983.

28. U.S. Bureau of the Census, *Local Government Finances, 1975–76, (Washington, D.C.: U.S. Government Printing Office), 1977, p. 6.*

29. See footnote 25 for details.

30. The *Serrano* v. *Priest* decision was noted earlier, in footnote 26. For details of the attempt by courts to redistribute resources among taxing jurisdictions, see Lineberry and Sharkansky,*op. cit.*, pp. 232–234.

31. See George E. Peterson, ed., *Property Tax Reform* (Washington, D.C.: The Urban Institute), 1973, especially the papers by Peterson, Aaron, and Gaffney (e.g., Chapters 1, 4 and 5).

32. Lots of support can be found for the generally regressive nature of the property tax. In Peterson, *op. cit.*, papers by Netzer and by Shannon (Chapters 2 and 3) argue strongly that the tax is regressive.

33. See Aaron, in Peterson *op. cit.*, and also Henry Aaron, *Who Pays the Property Tax? (Washington, D.C.: The Brookings Institution), 1975,* who argues that when considering permanent income and benefits, the tax is best considered neutral and much of the regressivity can be traced to poor property tax assessment and administration.

34. See Aaron, *op. cit.*, and also Richard R. Almy, "Rationalizing the Assessment Process," in Peterson, *op. cit.*, Chapter 10, pp. 175–188. Also see, Daniel M. Holland and Oliver Oldman, *Estimating the Impact of 100% of Market Value Property Tax Assessments of Boston Real Estate* (Boston, Mass.: The Boston Uran Observatory), 1974, Chapter 2.

35. See John B. Rackham and Theodore R. Smith, eds., *Automated Mass Appraisal of Real Property* (Chicago: International Association of Assessing Officers), 1974: and *Proceedings of Colloquium on Computer Assisted Mass Appraisal Potential for Commercial and Industrial Real Property* (Cambridge, Mass.: Lincoln Institute of Land Policy), 1977.

36. Both British Columbia and California have actively experimented with such techniques and are presently implementing them.

37. See, for example, Erik Stenehjem, "A Scientific Approach to the Mass Appraisal of Residential Property," in Rackham and Smith, *op. cit.*, Chapter 2, pp. 22–43.

38. Most Canadian provinces follow the model of British Columbia, with a provincial assessment authority carrying out assessment valuations of all real property within the province against which property tax rates can be set. Many states have state boards of equalization or their equivalent which carry out analogous functions. (See James A. Maxwell and J. Richard Aronson, *Financing State and Local Government, Third Edition,* (Washington, D.C.: The Brookings Institution), 1977, pp. 66–71.

39. See footnote 18 for more on the tax capitalization argument.

40. Remember that similar indeterminacy confronted us when we looked at questions of scale economies and diseconomies and the search for optimum-size cities.

41. For the need for such regionalization, see Higgins, *op. cit.*, pp. 125–126, and Lineberry and Sharkansky, *op. cit.*, p. 129.

42. Unicity Winnipeg provides an example of the merging of local governments to achieve some sort of balance between revenue and expenditures spatially. In the United States, special-purpose districts that rely on property taxes for servicing areas have achieved similar balancing. The Metropolitan District Commission (parks and recreation) and the Massachusetts Bay Transportation Authority in the Boston area are examples of such regional agencies which are supported in large measure through property taxes and local user charges.

43. The Royal Commission of Inquiry into Real Property Taxation and Assessment in British Columbia recommended just such virtues for keeping the property tax in its present form, but with uniform assessment and administration procedures. These recommendations were put into law in the revisions to the B.C. Assessment Act in 1976, and represent a very fine example of good theory and sound practice in action and complementing each other.

44. Maxwell and Aronson, *op. cit.*, pp. 167–173.

45. See Joseph A. Pechman and Benjamin A. Okner, *Who Bears the Tax Burden?* (Washington, D.C.: The Brookings Institution), 1974.

46. In British Columbia, for example, all homeowners receive a basic "homeowner grant" from the provincial government at the time they pay their property taxes. The basic grant is C$380. Those over 65 years of age are eligible to receive another C$300 or a total of C$680 in 1983.

47. It also follows that to the extent that if the property tax is a use tax and higher-income households occupy larger units and require higher-quality and more costly site services (such as police and fire protection and water and sewer), then the property tax need not be regressive given that Peterson, *op. cit.*, finds the tax neutral if permanent as opposed to current income is taken as the appropriate income measure. In such a circumstance house price, permanent income, and services to property and property taxes could be proportional and not regressive.

48. Maxwell and Aronson, *op. cit.*, p. 185.

49. *Ibid.*, p. 188.

50. This point is made by Charles Goetz, "The Revenue Potential of User-Related Charges in State and Local Governments," in Richard A. Musgrave, ed., *Broad-Based Taxes: New Options and Sources*, (Baltimore: Johns Hopkins University Press), 1973, p. 114. The following, quoted by Maxwell and Aronson, *op. cit.*, p. 185, sums up Goetz's argument:

> unless technological developments or changes in social attitudes are postulated, it is not clear why state and local governments would be expected to place an increased emphasis on user charges. In most cases, moreover, federal tax deductibility suggests advantages for the more traditional forms of taxation.

51. For example, in British Columbia the Greater Vancouver Regional District, a form of local government, achieves efficiency through regional provision of sewer, water, and other revenue-producing services.

52. For a review of the arguments in favor of regional or metropolitan government, see Tindal and Tindal, *op. cit.*, Chapter 4; C. R. Tindal, *Structural Changes in Local Government: Government for Urban Regions* (Toronto, Ontario: The Institute of Public Administration of Canada), 1977; Lineberry and Sharkansky, *op. cit.*, pp. 128–134; and Goodman, *op. cit.*, Chapter 7. Goodman has a detailed discussion of various models of reform for metropolitan government as well as numerous examples.

53. See footnote 13 for references. Also see the following works: Werner Z. Hirsch, "The Supply of Urban Public Services," in H. S. Perloff and L. Wingo, eds., *Issues in Urban Economics* (Baltimore: Johns Hopkins University Press), 1968, pp. 477–525; J. T. Hughes, "Economic Aspects of Local Government Reform," *Scottish Journal of Political Economy*, 14(1:1967):118–137; and D. O. Popp and F. D. Sebold, "Quasi-Returns to Scale in the Provision of Public Services," *Public Finance* 27(1:1972:46–60.

54. For details on the Canadian experience, see Tindal and Tindal, *op. cit.*, Chapter 4; Higgins, *op. cit.*, Chapter 4; and George A. Nader, *Cities of Canada, Volume I* (Toronto, Ontario: Macmillan of Canada), 1975, Chapter 8.

55. For details, see George A. Nader, *Cities of Canada, Volume II* (Toronto: Macmillan of Canada), 1976, pp. 160–162 for Montreal, and pp. 415–417 for Vancouver. For the British Columbia approach as a whole, see Higgins, *op. cit.*, pp. 153–155, and Tindal and Tindal, *op. cit.*, pp. 57–58. For Quebec, see Tindal and Tindal, *op. cit.*, pp. 58–60, and Tindal, *Structural Changes in Local Government*, pp. 24–26.

56. See Goodman, *op. cit.*, pp. 191–192, for details on the Dade County amalgamation. Also see Edward Sofen, *The Miami Metropolitan Experiment, Second Edition*, (New York: Anchor Books), 1966.

57. For details on country governments, see Goodman, *op. cit.*, pp. 143–146; and Charles R. Adrian, *State and Local Government*, (New York: McGraw-Hill Book Co.), 1976, pp. 172–180. See Adrian, pp. 213–216, for background on city-county difficulties.

58. Tindal and Tindal, *op. cit.*, p. 57.

59. Higgins, *op. cit.*, pp. 153–154.

60. *Ibid.*, p. 154.

61. The minor changes being suggested on representation and election of directors support this conclusion, since there does not appear to be any move afoot to abolish the regional districts, merely a desire to make marginal changes and fine-tune them to the changing environment of the 1980s.

62. Higgins, *op. cit.*, p. 152.

63. Ibid, pp. 147–151, for background and detail on Unicity. For a more thorough analysis, see Tindal, *Structural Changes in Local Government*, Chapter 4, "Manitoba: The Winnipeg Experience," pp. 27–38.

64. Higgins, *op. cit.*, p. 151.

65. The cities that underwent consolidation during the early 1970s in British Columbia include Prince George, Nanaimo, Kamloops, and Kelowna.

66. Consolidations either through amalgamation or annexation have been accompanied by bitter controversy in many U.S. urban areas. For details of such consolidations, see Goodman, *op. cit.*, pp. 193–197.

67. Goodman, *op. cit.*, p. 193. Also, Adrian, *op. cit.*, pp. 212–213.

68. Goodman, *op. cit.*, p. 193.

69. These data come from Maxwell and Aronson,*op. cit.*, p. 78, updated using date from Table 15–3.

70. For more information on the Port Authority of New York and New Jersey, see recent annual reports from the Port Authority. The success of the venture can be gleaned from its present scale of assets and operations. For instance, in 1979 the Port Authority had assets of US$3.6 billion and net assets of US$1.3 billion. Its gross operating revenues were US$588 million and its net income stood at US$52 million. For an earlier but reasonably comprehensive history of the Port Authority and the Port of New York, see John I. Griffin, *The Port of New York* (New York: ARCO Publishing Company), 1959, especially Chapter 6. While the Port Authority stands as the most dramatic example of special-purpose districts, we can see a whole range of special-purpose functions in urban transit, water, and sewer districts and the like across a broad spectrum of functions and scales of operation.

71. Maxwell and Aronson, *op. cit.*, pp. 181–188; and Wayland D. Gardner, *Government Finance: National, State, and Local* (Englewood Cliffs, N.J.: Prentice-Hall), 1978, pp. 397–401.

72. For some of the details involved in the various federally mandated review processes such as the A-80, A-95 and HUD 701 programs, see Donald G. Hagman, *Public Planning and Control of Urban and Land Development: Cases and Materials* (St. Paul, Minn.: West Publishing Company), 1973, Chapter 3, especially pp. 62–76.

73. See Hagman,*op. cit.*, especially Chapter 20, pp. 970–1047; Bill Shaw, *Environmental Law: People, Pollution, and Land Use* (St. Paul Minn.: West Publishing Company), 1976; and Eva H. Hanks, A. Dan Tarlock, and John L. Hanks, *Environmental Law and Policy: Cases and Materials, Abridged Edition* (St. Paul, Minn. West Publishing Company), 1975.

74. Two particularly well-documented examples are James T. Little, High O. Nourse, R. B. Read, and Charles L. Leven, *The Contemporary Neighborhood Succession Process* (St. Louis, Miss. Institute for Urban and Regional Studies, Washington University), 1975; and C. Lowell Harris, ed., *Government Spending and Land Values* (Madison, Wis.: University of Wisconsin Press), 1973.

16

URBAN
TRANSPORTATION

INTRODUCTION:TRANSPORTATION AND LAND-USE INTERACTIONS

As we saw in Chapter 4, transportation costs were a key element in the determination of bid rent functions for land. We also saw that changes in transportation costs had significant consequences for land values. The interactions between the transportation system and the urban land market are of central concern to the urban land economist. Up to this point, however, we have focused on land and land-using activities and not on transportation per se. Accordingly, in the present chapter we address major urban transportation issues in both Canada and the United States and then explore their consequences for urban land markets.

Transportation and Urban Land Market Interactions

Transportation has been an important shaper of urban land uses and land values. It has also been directly and significantly affected by those very land-use and urban development patterns that it has shaped. The transportation and urban land market interaction is therefore a pivotal one, and one that has attracted attention from both urban land economists and transportation analysts.

As early as 1826, Johann von Thünen observed the linkages between land use and transportation access and costs.[1] This early work provided the foundation for the bid rent analysis of Chapter 4 in which transportation costs were seen to play a central role in bid rent and land value determination.[2]

The essence of the linkage between the urban transportation and urban land-use systems is the complementarity between transportation costs and site rents (or land values). This complementarity has formed

506

the backbone of much of the urban land economics literature during this century, wherein access has been seen as a prime element in location (or "situs" in Ratcliff's terminology), and location in turn is the key determinant of land value and land use.[3] More recently, the complementarity has received attention from urban transportation planners and analysts who have come to realize the centrality of land-use and development patterns in the spatial patterns and levels of demand for the urban transportation system.[4]

This extensive body of research into transportation and land market interactions is of particular importance to the urban land market analyst as it provides a vital bridge between the focus of this chapter, urban transportation systems, and the workings of the urban land market. Moreover, the urban land economist has increasingly been relied on to assist the transportation economist in assessing the impacts of transportation systems. Accordingly, the urban transportation problems and their proposed and implemented solutions must be of special concern to the analyst of urban land market behavior.[5]

Urban Transportation Problems

Initially these problems were rather narrowly defined. In fact, they were all loosely fitted into "the urban transportation problem," which was viewed as a peak capacity issue largely related to roads for handling private automobiles. Among the strongest adherents of this view of "the problem" were Meyer, Kain, and Wohl, who in 1965 observed:

... the primary focus is on the problem of moving passengers into and out of cities during the peak or rush hours, occurring mornings and afternoons of weekdays. It is these movements that tax the capacity of existing urban transport facilities and create the congestion and delays that most people associate with what has come to be known, for better or worse, as "the urban transportation problem." Intracity freight movements and passenger trips at other times of the day or week can and do create important problems but these are almost always of second-order importance.[6]

The demand for urban transportation exceeds available supply at these peak hours. As a result, the costs borne by individuals at peak hours are almost always less than the costs borne by society in the course of using urban transportation facilities. This is as true for public transit as it is for automobiles. For example, at rush hour, individuals impose costs on each other and on society as a whole, not the least of which is the need for massive excess capacity over most of the week to handle peak hour travel. Figure 16–1 summarizes this by depicting both social and private costs. Where demand intersects private costs, costs are lower and usage is higher (excess demand) than where the same demand curve intersects public (or social) costs. The allocational

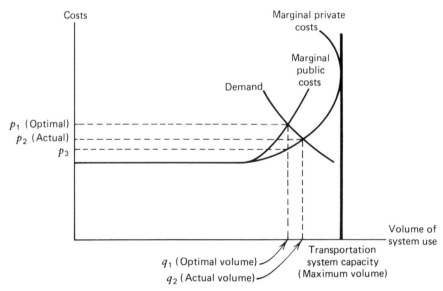

Figure 16–1. Demand and supply in urban transportation systems.

inefficiency in such a situation should be obvious: Too much use is made of underpriced transportation resources.

Two obvious, and polar opposite, strategies immediately come to mind to solve such a problem: Increase supply so that social and private costs intersect demand in the horizontal portion of the marginal cost curve; and decrease demand to achieve a similar result, albeit at a lower level of travel.

During the 1970s the earlier view of "the problem" was expanded considerably as we began to realize that the urban transportation problem was really a series of complex and interrelated problems. Alan Altshuler distinguishes among objective *condition,* which describe the state of the urban transporation system; *problems,* which are perceived conditions that are unsatisfactory; and *values* which both define conditions as problems and also define the efficacy of solutions intended to remedy problems.[7]

Altshuler's framework for looking at urban transportation problems is particularly helpful in understanding how the list of transportation problems has broadened during the 1970s, as perceptions and values changed along with conditions such as the Arab oil embargo and its jarring effect on energy consumption and awareness. Following this framework, we can list, in rough chronological order, the current slate of transportation problems.[8]

1. Congestion (the original transportation problem).

2. Decline of mass transit usage and rising costs (largely a U.S. phenomenon, as Canadian transit usage has been quite healthy over the 1970s and 1980s).

3. Disruption of neighborhoods through expressway construction.

4. Safety (the more than 50,000 auto deaths a year, plus billions of dollars of damage).

5. Air pollution and, more recently, noise pollution from motor vehicles.

6. Energy consumption principally from private automobile use.

7. Equity issues resulting from the access needs of nonautomobile users (the poor, the elderly, the handicapped) and from the subsidy of roads and automobiles by society (a similar issue exists in subsidizing transit by automobile owners and users).

8. Increasing fiscal demands of mass transit (again largely a U.S. issue).

9. The sharply reduced ability of recession-struck federal and state/provincial governments to deal with this growing list of urban transportation problems.

The transportation problem in urban areas is therefore not one problem but many. Its treatment must be necessarily diverse, encompassing economics, engineering, planning, and political considerations.

AN OVERVIEW OF URBAN TRANSPORTATION IN CANADA AND THE UNITED STATES

There are significant differences in urban travel and transportation between Canada and the United States. This is indicated in the following three tables. Table 16–1 compares the journey to work in 10 Canadian urban areas with that in 41 U.S. urban areas. The dominance of automobile travel in the United States is quite dramatic, with nearly 4 out of every 5 journey-to-work trips being made by automobile, whereas less than 2 out of every 3 such trips in Canada are made by automobile. The correspondingly greater use of public transit in Canada, as compared with its use in the United States, is entirely consistent with the differences in automobile use.[9] Table 16–2 sets out information on automobiles in operation in the two countries. U.S. figures per capita are consistently 50 percent greater than those in Canada. Finally, Table 16–3 presents data on public transit systems in Canada and the United States during the 1970s and once again our inferences from Table 16–1 are supported: Public transit usage has grown considerably in Canada, while it has been relatively stable or declining in the United States.

While rush hour demand might be a problem in both Canada and the United States, the sources differ. Given the massive use of automobiles in the United States, solutions that take advantage of the enormous stock of automobiles and roadways will come to the fore. In Canada, with its relatively greater reliance on public transit (and walking), transit and land-use alternatives hold promise.

Table 16–1 Mode of Transportation for Journey to Work in Metropolitan Areas

Mode	United States				Canada				
	1975	*1976*	*1975 & 1976*	*1977*	*1976*	*1977*	*1978*	*1979*	*1980*
	(n = 21)	(n = 20)	(n = 41)		(n = 10)	(n = 10)			
Driving alone	64	59	62	72	45	48	52	52	53
Riding as passenger	7	6	7	7	7	6	7	7	7
Shares driving	6	6	6	7	NA	NA	12	12	12
Total Auto	82	76	79	82	64	65	73	74	74
Public transit	12	18	15	7	26	25	15	15	15
Walking	5	5	5	4	8	8	10	10	10
Other	1	1	1	2	2	2	2	2	1
	100%	100%	100%	100%	100%	100%	100%	100%	100%

Sources: U.S. Bureau of the Census, *Current Population Reports*, Series P-23, No. 68, "Selected Characteristics of Travel to Work in 21 Metropolitan Areas, 1975", and Series P-23, No. 72, "Selected CHaracteristics of Travel to Work in 20 Metropolitan Areas, 1976" (Washington, D.C.: 1978). *Current Population Reports*, Series P-23, "Special Studies: Selected Characteristics of Travel to Work in 20 Metropolitan Areas" (AS1-S1 2546-2). Statistics Canada, Education, Science and Culture Division, "Travel to Work Survey, November 1976," Catalogue 81-001 (November 1977); and "Travel to Work Survey, November, 1977," Catalogue 87-001 (September 1978). Statistics Canada, *Travel to Work*, Catalogue 87-503 (1976–80).

Table 16–2 Automobiles in Operation

	United States		Canada	
Year	Thousands	Per Capita	Thousands	Per Capita
1953	—	—	2,044	0.14
1954	38,828	0.24		
1960	57,103	0.32	3,255	0.18
1975	95,241	0.45	7,074	0.31

Source: Ward's 1976 Automotive Yearbook; Automotive Industries Statistical Issue, March 1962; Statistics Canada, Household Facilities and Equipment, Catalogue 64-202) (Ottawa, Ontario: Statistics Canada), 1977.

Table 16–3 Public Transit Data for U.S. and Canadian Transit Systems

Item	United States					Canada			
	1970	1972	1977	1979	1980	1971	1976	1979[a]	1980[a]
Revenue passengers (millions)	5932	5253	5723	6370	6358	856	1076	1205	1315
Revenue miles (millions)	1883	1756	2021	2045	2095	222	300	381 (km)	409 (km)
Deficits (millions $)[b]	184	400	1836	NA	NA	3.8	235.3	390	502
Deficits (including taxes) (millions $)[b]	288	513	2025	3008	NA	23.8	235.3	390	502
Service area population (millions)	NA	NA	NA	NA	NA	8.2	9.4	13	14
Number of systems	1079	1045	1009	1027	1044	17	17	66	73

[a]Compare figures of previous years with caution as different sources are cited.
[b]Dollar figures are in U.s. and Canadian dollars, respectively.

Source: U.S.: Statistical Abstract of the U.S., 1979, Table 1115, p. 654 (1970–1977); Ibid., 1981, Table 1101, p. 630 (1979); Ibid., 1982, Table 1080, p. 623.
John Sewell, "Public Transit in Canada: A Primer," City Magazine 3(4: 1978): 40–55 (1971, 1976).
Canadian Urban Transit Association, 1981 Transit Fact Book and Membership Directory, p. 99.

URBAN TRANSPORTATION PLANNING

Because of the close ties between urban transportation and urban land use, the transportation planning process is increasingly envisioned as an integrated "transport/land use" planning process. Most recent transportation planning theory and practice stress this complementarity, a complementarity we noted previously from the perspective of the urban land market analyst.[10]

For planning to be effective, there is a necessity to *understand* how an urban area "works" in terms of land use, traffic and transport *before attempting to devise solutions*. The preparation of alternative land-use and transport plans must be based therefore on a sound understanding of the way that the urban area functions, how it might evolve over time, if left to develop alone, or most importantly, how it might react to different policies.[11]

This process is nicely represented in Figure 16–2 which provides a schematic overview of the urban transportation planning process. This figure also depicts the sort of framework implicit in Alan Altshuler's approach to defining and solving urban transportation problems discussed previously. We begin the process with a set of goals and objectives (closely related to and derived from the values in the Altshuler analysis), and then analyze existing transportation system conditions in light of these goals and objectives. From this point on, the process continues in two parallel streams: one dealing with transportation policy options and their analysis, one dealing with land-use policy options and their analysis. It is clear from the direction of the arrows in Figure 16–2 that transportation and land use both impact on the transportation planning model, which in turn impacts on the land-use and transportation systems.

The output of the transportation planning model (whether it be quantitative and computer-based, or qualitative and based on verbal, graphical, and geographic mapping) is an evaluation of the various transportation policy options considered in the analysis. Given this evaluation, the transportation planning process concludes by selecting the preferred alternative, or combinations of alternatives, and by actually implementing this solution in the urban setting under consideration. Selecting and implementing policies are highly political activities which are firmly rooted in our goals and objectives and political values, thus returning the process to where it started: societal values.

With the growth of inflation and the economic instability of the late 1970s and early 1980s, the idealized transportation planning process depicted above became less usable. The process in Figure 16–2 is essentially a medium- to long-term planning exercise and was not well suited to the volatility and shrinking government planning and capital budgets of the late 1970s. Commenting on the emergence of a different kind of transportation planning during this period, Douglas Lee notes:

The "old" process in this somewhat overdrawn dichotomy can be described long range, comprehensive, top-down, end state, closed option planning, based on the engineer-architectonic approach that requires a detailed, fixed end product from which everything else is subsequently determined, the whole predicated on the belief that it is possible to forecast future events. The alternative, or the emerging 'new' process, is characterized as short range, incremental, politically open, and multi-optioned in the sense of narrowing but not eliminating choice. Methodologies and techniques for the emerging paradigm have not been settled upon, but the intent of sketch planning and quick response analytic procedures is in the direction.[12]

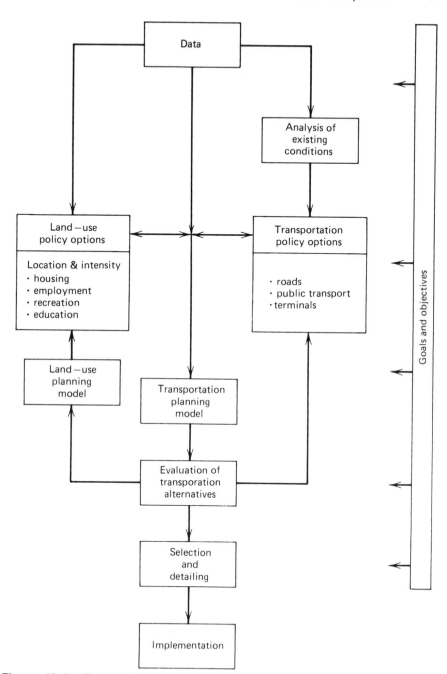

Figure 16–2. Transportation planning process. (*Source:* Roads and Transportation Association of Canada, *Urban Transportation Planning Guide* (Toronto, Ontario: University of Toronto Press), 1977, p. 8.)

In practice, of course, this dichotomy is not nearly so neatly drawn. Even in the heyday of the large-scale transportation studies, smaller-scale incremental efforts were being used to augment large plans or to implement portions of them. Similarly, despite the greatly increased interest in more modest approaches to transportation planning during the late 1970s and early 1980s, long-range and large-scale activities were continuing, particularly with respect to mass transit planning.[13] Lee's characterization above is, however, helpful in providing insights into the changing nature of the process. As the process has changed, so have the kinds of policies that the process is being employed to analyze. The scale of solutions has diminished along with their costs and timeframe, and increased emphasis is being placed on operational innovations to parallel capital investments, such as para-transit and transportation systems management techniques, all of which we discuss next.

URBAN TRANSPORTATION POLICIES AND ALTERNATIVES

For convenience, we can divide policies and proposals into supply and demand orientations. Effective policies and programs, however, will be liberally sprinkled with policies which treat both supply and demand in an integrated manner.[14]

On the demand side, conceptually, there are two alternatives: the first is to move backward along a demand curve; the second is to lower the demand curve. By raising the costs of peak-hour travel for all modes, people will be induced to move their trips, if possible, to less crowded travel periods. "Flex-time," wherein federal employees in Ottawa were able to alter their working hours, provides the basis for such a switching of hours; so does the policy of staggered working hours in, for example, New York's World Trade Center (to avoid congestion delays in the elevator system). Lowering the demand curve for a given mode of travel can be achieved by making other competing modes more attractive (in essence, this has happened already, as cheaper, more attractive automobile travel has reduced the demand for transit in the United States).

A number of techniques have been proposed and implemented that raise the price of travel during peak hours in the hope of reducing peak-hour demand (i. e., moving back along the demand curve in Figure 16–1). Among the more celebrated schemes is Singapore's Auto Restricted Zone, which requires cars entering the downtown zone to have either three or more passengers or else a permit purchased either by the day or for longer periods of time (taxis and public transit are exempt).[15] The scheme has achieved only limited success to date, in part because the permit costs have not increased very rapidly whereas automobile ownership and incomes in Singapore have risen dramatically during the past decade.

The more general question of peak pricing of transportation resources has received a great deal of study by economists, and there is surprising agreement: Current underpricing leads to overuse of roads (and transit) at peak hours, and a peak pricing scheme, which varies by travel mode and city, is called for.[16] Other examples such as preferential tolls for car pools on the San Francisco Bay Bridge and access to exclusive bus lanes for car pools on the Santa Monica Freeway further illustrate the attempts to impose peak pricing on motorists.[17]

Transit systems are among the easiest places to impose peak-hour pricing. The Washington Metro system uses peak-hour prices. Providing senior citizens with free travel at off-peak hours, as is done in New York City, is another means of shifting demand away from the peak hours of use.

A final area where much can be done to raise the costs of travel and improve both technical and economic efficiency is that of parking. Currently, federal tax laws in both Canada and the United States permit business to claim as deductible expenses the parking fees paid on behalf of employees, while not taxing such benefits in the hands of the employees. Some studies show that as much as 20 percent of the users of such parking can be shifted away from automobiles if parking were priced at full cost.[18]

When we consider lowering the demand curve for given modes, we find a number of approaches. Suggestions include improving transit through purchasing additional and more efficient vehicles (be they buses, minibuses, railcars, or subway cars). The more efficient mobilization of existing facilities in all modes, known as Transportation System Management (TSM) seeks to improve service through the use of the most modern operating procedures, which effectively expands supply.[19] To the extent that greater gains can be made in the transit field through scheduling and maintenance improvements, transit can, in theory at least, be made more competitive with automobiles, shifting demand away from cars and correspondingly reducing street congestion.

Among the most innovative schemes to shift demand away from the individual driver and car are the so-called para-transit options. Para-transit spans an enormous range of urban transportation policies and programs (most of them quite mundane), which for the first time have been brought together systematically to provide alternatives to the single automobile and its driver.[20] For example, minibuses and jitneys can cover more diverse routes than can the traditional large buses. Another para-transit idea centers on the removal of local taxi monopolies, throwing the taxi business into a much more competitive state and also encouraging the use of limousines (somewhat between taxis and jitneys in the above scheme). The development of other demand-responsive systems include dial-a-bus systems, which combine minibuses/jitneys with taxicab responsiveness.[21] Car pools are another popular approach to reducing single-car and driver use of scarce road capacity.[22] Finally, flex-time systems, providing the freedom to choose both working hours and working days, hold great promise in easing peak-hour congestion, particularly in cities where there is one dominant firm or industry (such as state, provincial, and national capitals).[23] All such para-transit concepts seek to reduce road congestion through spreading demand across more modes or hours and to build on well-known and proven transportation modes (such as taxis).

The final means for reducing peak-hour congestion is based on more efficient land use. Such innovative land uses as mixed use and planned unit developments hold potential to cluster land-using activities, which may reduce the demand for travel. Land use and transportation are inextricably linked, as we keep stressing here, and thus thinking of them as complements and coordinating land use and urban transportation planning can lead to major benefits for any transportation system.[24]

Managing and altering the composition of demand is not without its potential costs, however. Foremost among them are the distributional costs involved in raising the prices of travel for urban area residents. If the costs fall on higher-income groups, then distributional equity need not be sacrificed. However, to the extent that peak prices (particularly for public transit systems) are being borne by middle- and lower-income groups, while senior executives still get free and highly subsidized parking, distributional equity is not being served. The equity/efficiency trade-off is central here as the social costs of inequitable policies could be as high as the gains in economic and operating efficiency.[25]

Turning our attention now to supply-expanding options, we find an enormous array of approaches. Urban transportation has been an area where technology can display its wares.[26] The most dramatic supply-expanding schemes to date have involved the automobile, though mass transit is the most recent focus for technological innovation.[27]

One estimate of the cost of highways in the United States since the 1956 passage of the National Defense Interstate Highway Act runs as high as $300 billion through the early 1970s.[28] However, this includes the vast majority of the interstate highway network that lies outside of urban areas. A more recent estimate puts the cost of urban expressways built under the program at $70 billion for 8800 miles of urban highways (out of a contemplated total of 42,500).[29] By any measure, the sums are enormous and understate considerably the costs of urban expressway development in the United States, since the estimates include neither the costs of state and local improvements to connecting roads, nor the social costs for urban neighborhoods and their residents.[30] There is one other important cost that is grossly understated by the capital costs of the expressway system, and that is its maintenance. Recent studies estimate that perhaps as much as $10 billion needs to be spent on bridges alone to repair corrosion and wear.[31] The heyday of urban expressway building is clearly over. Remaining bottlenecks will be dealt with, though even here it is not clear that citizen resistance to further expressway development will not win the day. Battles loom in New York City, over the construction of the much delayed Westway project, and on the Pacific Coast, where residents of Seattle are vigorously opposing the completion of Interstate 90, a major connector, through an old and stable Seattle neighborhood, and the proposed construction of another bridge across Lake Washington. Rather, we can expect improvements in the road system to result from better management and utilization.[32] Better management, development of alternatives to individual automobiles, and the selective construction of particularly critical highway links appear to be the future course of urban highway development and planning.

Among the most highly recommended transit options is the development of adequate bus service. Buses are relatively inexpensive, and bus routes highly malleable. The bus transit option usually includes the purchase of more efficient buses, including larger buses to cut unit labor costs, more energy-efficient buses to cut energy costs, and more durable buses to trim maintenance costs and reduce losses due to vandalism. The allocation of exclusive bus lanes on urban freeways and major arteries can dramatically upgrade bus service (with existing fleets) to make it more convenient and competitive with automobile travel.[33] Combining bus with automobile use through the development of peripheral parking lots for park-and-ride commuting has also been widely tried, and with considerable success. New technology has also surfaced with the use of articulated buses and a limited return to electrified trolley buses, both of which improve efficiency and reduce energy consumption of scarce fossil fuels. Buses that "kneel" or have movable platforms to aid the handicapped have also been developed. Lastly, recent technical improvements in engines, brakes, and door-opening systems are less dramatic but equally important.

The next step up from buses involves light-rail vehicles (LRVs), also referred to as light-rail transit (LRT). In an earlier day this innovation was called the streetcar or trolley and, ironically, during the 1950s in particular, enormous energy was devoted to ripping up streetcar tracks and eliminating streetcar rights-of-way to improve traffic flow. Long popular in Europe, LRT systems can be constructed at grade in either exclusive or nonexclusive rights-of-way or else combined with subways, as has been done very successfully in Boston for nearly a century and in Edmonton during the past decade. LRTs have the advantage of being less costly than heavy-rail, full-scale subway systems and, though less flexible than buses, they can be combined into trains of several cars in length and thus carry many more passengers. Construction costs are also considerably less than for heavy-rail systems, since LRTs most often run at grade, obviating the need for costly tunneling and underground stations. The Edmonton, Alberta, LRT system is a frequently cited model, having opened in 1978 for the Commonwealth Games and costing roughly $80 million (Canadian) for its 7.7 kilometers. It has been extended another 2 kilometers to the northeast to link with a large-scale residential-commercial development planned for the northern portion of the city, and more ambitious plans are afoot to extend the system under the city (its present underground portion totals roughly 3 kilometers) for another 3 or 4 kilometers and then run at grade on existing railroad tracks (as does the majority of the present system) for another 15 to 20 kilometers to service the southern portion of the city.

The success of the Edmonton system in a city of just over 600,000 people led to the construction of a system in Calgary, Alberta, of approximately the same size and physical form. Active consideration is being given to LRT systems in a number of U.S. urban areas, and San Diego, California, recently completed an LRT system from the old Sante Fe Railroad Station in the center of the city to San Ysidro, California, on the U.S.—Mexico border some 25 miles south.[34]

The utility of sticking with known technologies and with known and reliable operating characteristics is nowhere better illustrated than by the experience of the BART system in the San Francisco Bay Area, which will introduce us to the third transit option: heavy-rail rapid transit. The initial $792 million bond issue passed by residents of three Bay Area counties in 1962 signaled the beginning of the 75-mile BART system. Costs subsequently escalated, and when the system finally opened to trans-bay service in the fall of 1974 (five years late), the total price was estimated at over $1.6 billion. Aside from cost overruns and lengthy delays, BART has also been plagued by operating problems, equipment failures, and fires in the trans-bay tunnel. Hailed initially as the first modern subway in the United States, its reliance on Space Age technology proved a setback, and recent heavy-rail systems in Atlanta and Washington, D.C., had to overcome BART's bad image to be sold to area residents.[35] Successful systems in Montreal and Toronto, using rather conventional "but reliable and usable" technology, did provide examples of postwar heavy-rail systems that worked well, thus helping to overcome some of the adverse BART publicity. The major drawback of rail rapid transit is its enormous expense (the Washington system has been called the largest public works project in the United States, and could cost as much as $8 billion when over 100 miles are completed). Another important shortcoming is the almost total lack of flexibility. Its main advantage is its enormous peak hauling capacity: 35,000 to 40,000 passengers per hour, compared with 3000 to 6000 passengers per hour for buses, and with speeds twice the 10 miles per hour recorded by buses on average in urban areas.[36] In comparison, freeways can carry from 1400 to 1800 cars per hour at rush hour per lane, at speeds of 40 to 50 miles per hour.[37]

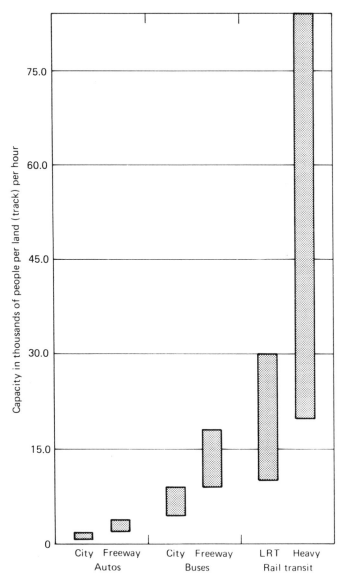

Figure 16–3. Capacity ranges for various modes of urban transportation. *Sources* G. Smerk, *Urban Mass Transportation* (Bloomington, Indiana: Indiana University Press), 1974, p. 99; J. Black, *Urban Transport Planning* (London: Croom Helm), 1981, p. 48.

In addition to subway systems, heavy-rail options also exist for carrying commuters. Such well-known commuter railroads as the Long Island Railroad and the New York Central Railroad, serving New York City and its suburbs, and the Reading and Pennsylvania Railroads in Philadelphia have long served this function. In 1967 the government of Ontario initiated its GO system bringing commuters along Lake Ontario from the eastern and western suburbs. In 1974, GO service was extended northwest, and at the present time consists of well over 100 miles in rail line and feeder bus service.[38]

Heavy-rail systems are well suited to dense urban areas with large passenger volumes. More dispersed urban areas are less likely to find such expensive systems viable. This is essentially the point made by Meyer, Kain, and Wohl and other heavy-rail critics when they recommend strongly against rail rapid transit in favor of an integrated multimodal transit system.[39]

The arguments against heavy-rail rapid transit systems are sufficiently weighty that their utility is greatly restricted. Light-rail systems, though less restricted, are more expensive and less flexible than are buses and cars. The para-transit options, in all their diversity, provide both long- and short-run options at reasonable costs.[40] The cost is largely in behavioral terms: Commuters must rely increasingly on group travel in car pools, minibuses, LRTs, or other modes.

In addition to these major options, a number of other approaches have been tried. In Vancouver, B. C., after a 20-year lapse, ferry service was reintroduced across Vancouver harbor. Present plans call for expanding the service and encouraging development in and around its two terminals. San Francisco Bay Area commuters have also enjoyed improved ferry service from Marin County, supplementing the overcrowded Golden Gate Bridge. Not all cities have the option of using ferries, but in many places ferries can provide a viable, economical, pleasant, and flexible alternative to bridges and their approaches.[41]

Finally, the U.S. Department of Transportation has been experimenting with "people-movers" for a number of years. Essentially, small versions of subway cars, people-movers have been used in a number of U.S. airports (Dallas–Fort Worth most notably) among terminal buildings and parking lots.[42]

All of the options have been tried, either singly or in combination, in various areas of the United States. In Canada, much heavier and sustained emphasis on transit options characterizes planning and policy making. The differences reflect, in part, the differences in current urban travel behavior that we observed earlier. In part they also reflect the much larger federal presence in urban transportation planning and funding in the United States and differences in urban form between Canada and American cities.[43]

Preferred Urban Transportation Alternatives

The era of large-scale transportation plans over long-run futures is gone, at least for the present.[44] Instead, transportation planning for urban areas is becoming more open-ended, as noted above. Transportation planning must satisfy energy and citizen constraints as well as technical ones. Such a planning process differs dramatically from the one that was practiced into the early 1970s. The earlier process was linear and goal-oriented; it was very much an engineering paradigm.

In the emerging process and planning environment there is likely to be a mix of urban transportation options. We can expect to see urban transportation planners pursue several parallel courses. Vancouver, B. C., has already moved toward some form of light-rail system while also expanding ferry service, parking capacity, and bus service. Even such auto-dominated cities as Los Angeles and Houston are pursuing multiple strategies including transit, road, para-transit, and TSM approaches. The costs of traditional road and heavy-rail systems is too great; so is the likely cost perceived by residents in having to give up their present travel behaviors.[45] Accordingly, transportation policies that wean urban travelers from their automobiles while providing flexible alternatives are the way of the future.

There is one other need that must be fulfilled: Various levels of government will have to coordinate their separate efforts. It will not be very effective in the future if, for instance, the U.S. federal government continues to allow free parking as a deductible business expense while encouraging transit and para-transit options through its Department of Transportation.[46] Similarly, mortgage and tax policies encouraging land-extensive suburban development are not entirely consistent with efforts to contain urban growth. Both transportation and land-use planning and policies must be coordinated to ensure that they are not working against each other.

TRANSPORTATION AND URBAN LAND MARKETS AGAIN

We come full circle now to look at some of the urban land market impacts of transportation improvements, thus completing the path on which we set out at the beginning of the chapter. Impacts to be reviewed are of three types: land use, land value, and urban form impacts. Given the high degree of interaction among these three impacts, it is not always possible to isolate effects on one type of impact. However, the classification does allow us to separate transportation impacts on urban land markets into more digestible pieces for study.

Land Use Impacts

Initial concerns here were focused on highway impacts, particularly on the development of suburban areas. Of primary interest were such land-use changes as those arising from the development of metropolitan a rearing by-pass roads like Route 128 in the Boston area and the Washington Beltway system surrounding the U.S. capital region.[47] These roads significantly affected employment locations and led to the suburban movement of industrial and office activities to take advantage of the accessibility created by these highways. Analogous studies examined the impacts on smaller communities that were bypassed by interstate highways in the United States. Again we find that these highway investments attracted economic activities to them very often at the direct expense of the bypassed community.[48]

Public transportation investments have also had significant impacts on land use, particularly on land near mass transit stations. Studies in Berkeley, California, suburban Philadelphia, and Washington, D.C., all point to the increase in density and the shift to higher-order uses that result from transit investments.[49]

Land Value Impacts

Transportation improvements have two opposite effects on land and property values. First, through increasing the accessibility of sites within their service area, transportation improvements increase land and property values via the bid rent mechanism discussed in Chapter 4. Second, because of the noise, air, and visual pollution that frequent ly result from a transportation investment, such investments have depressing effects on land and buildings in close proximity to the investment. As such, the affected properties capitalize (discount) the negative externalities resulting from noise, air, and visual pollution. Empirical studies point out both kinds of land value impacts, whether the transportation improvement consists of roads or highways or mass transit.

Negative effects on land values can be seen from the literature on highway corridors where adjoining properties suffer significant declines in value.[50] One recent study done in the state of Washington suggests, however, that these negative effects deriving from externaliti es can be more than compensated for by the positive effects of increased access provided by the highway.[51]

Several rail transit studies confirm the negative impacts on land values in proximity to rail rapid transit lines. Most studies demonstrat e a rather continuous decline of these negative impacts with distance from the line.[52] However, negative impacts from noise, air, and visual pollution of transportation investments seem to be swamped by the positive externalities provided by improved access. The evidence overwhelmingly suggests that property values do indeed capitalize transportation costs savings realized through increased accessibility, just the way our bid rent models suggest that they should. This is the case both for highways and for transit investments. The limited access highway significantly affects the land values of the hinterland which it serves, whether one considers residential, commercial, retail, or industrial uses.[53] At interchanges, nonresidential land values are particularly advantaged and realize very significant increases with the advent of highway improvements.[54]

Rapid transit investments have similar affects. Studies of service areas show that the opening of suburban rail rapid transit lines significantly increases property values.[55] Perhaps the most dramatic consequences of rapid transit investments are those surrounding station areas where property appreciation is greatest. However, these positive price effects usually diminish rapidly with distance from the station area, with noticeable impacts being minimal beyond 1500 feet (e.g., 5 to 7 minutes' walking time for most people).[56]

Urban Form Impacts

Impacts of transportation on urban form have been noted from the earliest studies of urban growth dating back to the Chicago School sociologists Park and Burgess.[57] Subsequently, the urban growth patterns of Hoyt and of Harris and Ullman also were implicitly built on a foundation of then existing transportation systems.[58] More recent empirical work has focused on the impacts of highways, especially on urban growth patterns, and particularly on the growth (or decline) of central areas. A well-known study by deLeon and Enns in St. Louis demonstrated the suburbanizing effects of the freeway system in that urban region, and its negative consequences for the core area.[59] Stern generalizes the St. Louis findings and also questions the environmental impacts of highway development in pointing out the suburbanizing power of highway development.[60]

More recently, policymakers have focused on the urban form consequences of transportation investments. This recent concern grows out of a wish to use transportation investments, particularly transit improvements, to rejuvenate the core area of large metropolitan regions, especially those older and declining regions outside the United States Sun Belt. Whereas highways clearly had a strong decentralizing effect, it is less clear that transit investments can lead to a recentralizing and rebirth of older central areas.[61] What is interesting in this new policy perspective, however, is the explicit appreciation of the role of transportation investment in shaping urban form and development patterns, a clear (if somewhat belated) appreciation of the inextricable links between the urban transportation system and the urban land market with which it interacts so closely.

SUMMARY

In this chapter, we returned to study the interactions between urban transportation and urban land use and land values that we last considered in the derivation of bid rent functions. We began by reviewing some of the fundamental issues in these interactions and we traced briefly the extensive literature on transportation and land market links. Our essential finding in this review was the complementarity of transportation and land use and land value, a complementarity forecast in our bid rent analyses.

With this as background, we proceeded to explore the dimensions of the urban transportation problem. From its earliest statement in the

1960s as a road congestion problem, the problem has grown in complexity to the point where it is now a complex of interrelated problems ranging from congestion to air pollution to energy conservation.

We next moved on to look at some of the important dimensions of the urban transportation systems in Canada and the United States. Significant differences were apparent, with the United States being much more dependent on private automobiles and the highways to support them. In Canada, much greater reliance has been placed on the use of public mass transit. These differences are obvious from the contrasting ways Canadians and Americans get to work and in the relatively greater ownership of automobiles in the United States.

As the transportation problem has broadened so has the planning process to plan transportation investments. In our review of that process we saw that it has become considerably broader over time, reflecting the broader demands being placed on it. It has also become more open-ended, inviting greater public input and greater diversity of policy outputs.

Against a backdrop of a more flexible planning process we then reviewed some of the more frequently suggested transportation policies. These included means to regulate demand to bring it into conformity with available supply, as well as means to increase effective supply through more efficient management of existing transportation facilities and through the expansion of transportation investment and the development of new transportation technologies. An essential ingredient here was also seen to be proper coordination of transportation with land-use decisions. Such coordination has the possibility of significantly decreasing demand for transportation through the placement of land-using activities in proper spatial juxtaposition so as to reduce travel demands.

Finally, we explored some of the empirical evidence linking the transportation and land-use systems. We saw that transportation had major impacts on both land use and land value. It also was clear from our review that transportation investments have a significant ability to influence urban form and development patterns, and that policymakers are trying to utilize transportation investments to help rejuvenate declining central areas.

Footnotes

1. Johann von Thünen, *The Isolated State*, (Hamburg, Germany), 1826.

2. See William Alonso, *Location and Land Use* (Cambridge, Mass.: Harvard University Press), 1964, for details of the bid rent derivation and its relation to transportation costs and access.

3. See the classic study by Richard U. Ratcliff, *Urban Land Economics* (New York: McGraw-Hill Book Co.), 1949. Also see the historically important work by Rob-

ert Murray Haig, *Major Economic Factors in Metropolitan Growth and Arrangement* (New York: Regional Plan Association of New York and Its Environs), 1927.

4. Among the recent urban transportation planning studies that explicitly acknowledge the centrality of the transportation/land-use linkage are: Roads and Transport Association of Canada, *Urban Transportation Planning Guide* (Toronto, Ontario: University of Toronto Press), 1977; John Black, *Urban Transportation Planning*, (London, England: Croom-Helm), 1981; and Rodney E. Engelen, *Coordination of Transportation System Management and Land Use Management* (Washington, D.C.: Transportation Research Board, National Cooperative Highway Research Program Synthesis of Highway Practice No.93), 1982.

5. An excellent survey of the transportation and urban land market literature, which focuses on the two-way interaction of these systems, can be found in Roger E. Alcaly, "Transportation and Urban Land Values: A Review of the Theoretical Literature," *Land Economics* 52(1:1976):42–53.

6. John Meyer, John Kain, and Martin Wohl, *The Urban Transportation Problem*, (Cambridge, Mass.: Harvard University Press), 1965, p. 5. The recently updated and extended version of Meyer, Kain, and Wohl is also an excellent source of detail on the urban transportation problem. See John R. Meyer and Jose A. Gomez-Ibañez, *Autos, Traffic, and Cities* (Cambridge, Mass: Twentieth Century Fund Report, Harvard University Press), 1981. Another recent and challenging view of urban transportation is Alan Altschuler, *Urban Transportation Planning* (Cambridge, Mass: MIT Press), 1979. It should also be noted that since the writing of this book, urban goods movement has become an important and much researched area. See, for example, *Transportation Research Record 496*, "Urban Goods Movement," 1974.

7. Altshuler, *op. cit.*, p. 2.

8. *Ibid.*, pp. 3–7.

9. Also consistent with greater automobile use in the United States is the greater work-trip length average of 7.6 miles, compared with 6.0 miles in Canada. Michael A. Goldberg and John Mercer, "Canadian and U.S. Cities: Basic Differences, Possible Explanations, and Their Meaning for Public Policy," *Papers and Proceedings of the Regional Science Association* 45(1979):159–183.

10. In addition to the citations above in footnote #4, see D. N. M. Starkie, *Transportation Planning, Policy and Analysis* (Oxford, England: Pergamon Press), 1976; and Michael J. Bruton, *Introduction to Transportation Planning*, 2nd edition (London, England: Hutchinson), 1975.

11. Black, *op. cit.*, p. 42.

12. Douglas B. Lee, Jr., "Improving Communication Among Researchers, Professionals, and Policy Makers in Land Use and Transportation Planning," (Washington, D.C.: U.S. Department of Transportation), 1977, p. 6. Also see the proceedings of a conference sponsored by the U.S. Department of Transportation, appearing in: Transportation Research Board, *Urban Transportation Planning in the 1980s*, Special Report #196, (Washington, D.C.: Transportation Research Board), 1982.

13. For transit, see Robert L. Knight and Lisa L. Trygg, *Land Use Impacts of Recent Major Rapid Transit Improvements* (Washington, D.C.: U.S. Department of Transportation), 1977. For highways, see National Technical Information Service

(NTIS), *Highway and Freeway Planning: Social and Economic Affects, 1964–July 1981* (Springfield, Va.: National Technical Information Service), 1981.

14. A number of examples of competing policies come to mind. The BART system in the San Francisco Bay Area was frequently built in freeway median dividers and in conjunction with freeway expansion projects. Similarly, federal policy attempts to stimulate transit use and discourage automobile use is not consistent with federal tax policies that allow firms to deduct parking costs for employees while not taxing such fringe benefits as income. See Don H. Pickrell, "Free Parking and Urban Transportation Policy" (Cambridge, Mass.: Department of City and Regional Planning, Harvard University), mimeographed, April, 1980.

15. The Singapore experience is unique and its consistency with sound economic arguments has attracted considerable attention and support from urban transportation economists. See, for example, Herbert Mohring, "The Benefits of Reserved Bus Lanes, Mass Transit Subsidies, and Marginal Cost Pricing in Alleviating Traffic Congestion," in Peter Mieszkowski and Mahlon R. Straszheim, eds., *Current Issues in Urban Economics* (Baltimore: Johns Hopkins University Press), 1979, p. 166.

16. For a good review and statement of the economic principles involved in urban transportation planning, see Mahlon R. Straszheim, "Assessing the Social Costs of Urban Transportation Technologies," in Mieszkowski and Straszheim, *op. cit.*, pp. 196–232; and Michael Beesley, *Urban Transport: Studies in Economic Policy* (London, England: Butterworth), 1973.

17. The Santa Monica case is particularly well documented in Peter Gordon, "The New Disincentives" (Los Angeles, Calif.: Department of Economics, University of Southern California), mimeographed, 1976.

18. Pickrell, *op. cit.*

19. Transportation Research Board, Special Report #172, "Transportation System Management" (Washington, D.C.: Transportation Research Board), 1977.

20. The following publications of the Transportation Research Board provide details of recent para-transit discussions: *Special Report #164,* "Paratransit," 1976; *Transportation Research Record #650,* "Paratransit Services," 1977; *Special Report #186,* "Paratransit," 1979; and *Transportation Research Record #724,* "Current Paratransit and Ride-Sharing Activities," 1979.

21. Once again, the following Transportation Research Board publications provide insights into recent demand-responsive transportation planning ideas: *Special Report #184,* "Urban Transport Service Innovations," 1979; and *Special Report #154,* "Demand-Responsive Transportation Systems and Services", 1975.

22. See Pickrell, *op. cit.*, for some evidence on the potential of car pooling vis-à-vis parking. Also see para-transit references in footnote #20 above.

23. For some recent evidence on the potential utility of flexible working hours, see Wilfred Owen, *Transportation for Cities: The Role of Federal Policy* (Washington, D.C.: Brookings Institution), 1976, pp. 40–41.

24. The necessity of carefully coordinating transportation and land-use planning has been frequently noted over the past 20 years in the urban transportation planning field. Seldom, however, until recently have land-use and transportation problems become so serious and complex, and has much more than lip service been paid to the concept. For details on the nature of the argument for such integrated transportation and land-use planning, see Owen, *op. cit.,* Chapter 5; Alan M. Voorhees, Walter G. Hansen, and A. Keith Gilbert, "Urban Transportation," in Frank S. So, Israel Stollman, Frank Beal, and David S. Arnold, eds., *The Practice of Local Government Planning* (Washington, D.C.: The International City Management Association), 1979, Chapter 8, pp. 214–245; and from the point of view of the land-use planner, F. Stuart Chapin, Jr., and Edward Kaiser, *Urban Land Use Planning,* third edition (Urbana, Ill.: University of Illinois Press), 1979. More general readings on transportation planning and some of its attendant conflicts are to be found in John W. Dickey, *Metropolitan Transportation Planning* (New York: McGraw-Hill), 1975; David R. Miller, ed., *Urban Transportation Policy: New Perspectives* (Lexington, Mass.: D. C. Heath), 1972; K. H. Schaeffer and Elliot Sclar, *Access for All: Transportation and Urban Growth* (Harmondsworth, England: Penguin Books), 1975; Melvin R. Levin and Norman A. Abend, *Bureaucrats in Collision: Case Studies in Area Transportation Planning* (Cambridge, Mass.: MIT Press), 1971; and Alan Lupo, Frank Colcord, and Edmund P. Fowler, *Rites of Way: The Politics of Transportation in Boston and the U.S. City* (Boston, Mass.: Little, Brown and Company), 1971. Recent studies of the interaction between transportation and land use can be found in *Transportation Research Record #820,* "Land Use and Economic Development," 1981; and *Transportation Research Record #861,* "Transportation and Land Use Impacts on Major Activity Centers," 1982.

25. The equity and transportation pricing is dealt with at some length and detail in Straszheim, *op. cit.,* pp. 223–227. Also see Mark Frankera, *Urban Transportation Economics* (Toronto, Ontario: Butterworths), 1979, especially Chapter 4.

26. For a frequently noted discussion of the issue, see Lewis Mumford, *The Culture of Cities* (New York: Harcourt Brace Jovanovich), 1970.

27. The Advanced Light Rapid Transit (ALRT) system currently under construction in Vancouver, British Columbia, is typical of the high technology being used in new transit systems. The system is completely automated, uses a new power system (a linear induction motor) and steerable wheel carriages that reduce noise and wear and tear, and is built around a new lightweight car.

28. Wilfred Owen, *The Accessible City* (Washington, D.C.: The Brookings Institution), 1972.

29. Owen, *Transportation for Cities,* p. 15.

30. For discussions of some of these social costs, see Lupo, Colcord, and Fowler, *op. cit.*; Schaeffer and Sclar, *op. cit.* + r Lewis Mumford, *The Highway and the City* (New York: Harcourt Brace Jovanovich), 1963; and D. Nowlan and A. Nowlan, *The Bad Trip: The Untold Story of the Spadina Expressway* (Toronto, Ontario: Harvest), 1972.

31. Transportation Research Board, *National Cooperative Highway Research Program Synthesis of Highway Practice, #58,* "Consequences of Deferred Maintenance," 1979.

32. Recent emphasis by candidates in virtually all elections on government restraint at all levels of government augurs well for heightened economy and poorly for new construction programs.

33. The Shirley Highway experiment in Virginia is perhaps the best known and documented exclusive bus lane program. See Dickey, *op. cit.,* p. 371. Also see Trans-

portation Research Board, *National Cooperative Highway Research Program Report #155,* "Bus Use of Highways: Planning and Design Guidelines," 1975.

34. The newly constructed and highly successful San Diego Trolley is one of the more innovative additions to mass transit in the United States because of its extreme simplicity and economy. It stands in marked contrast to the BART system 500 miles to the north in the San Francisco Bay Area. See Paul Van Slambrouck, "San Diego's Do-It-Yourself Trolley," *Mass Transit,* June 1981, p. 64.

35. BART stories are numerous and the number of studies of the system is large indeed. Perhaps the most thorough study of BART's operations was performed by A. Alan Post, Legislative Analyst for the California Legislature during the early 1970's. Post's analysis pointed up numerous examples of equipment failures and poor design and received a great deal of notoriety at the time of its publication. See A. Alan Post, *An Analysis of the Bay Area Rapid Transit District,* (Sacramento, Caifornia: Legislative Analysts Office), 1973. For a very different approach to rapid transit see Paul Van Slambrouck, "San Diego's Do-It-Yourself Trolley", *Mass Transit,* June 1981, p. 64.

36. George A. Nader, *Cities of Canada, Volume I* (Toronto, Ontario: Macmillan of Canada), 1975, p. 359.

37. Meyer, Kain, and Wohl, *op. cit.,* pp. 69–70.

38. Nader, *op. cit.,* p. 359.

39. The detailed analysis of the various conditions under which different transportation systems yield minimal costs if found in Meyer, Kain, and Wohl, *op. cit.,* pp. 290–306.

40. While technical problems are on the way to being solved, getting people and institutions to accept the sorts of changes implied by para-transit is another story. People will not easily give up the independence and comfort represented by the private automobile. Nor will the creation of new institutions that coordinate various modes of travel necessarily be without problems. See, for example, Transportation Research Board, *National Cooperative Highway Research Program Report #205,* "Implementing Packages of Congestion-Reducing Techniques: Strategies for Dealing with Institutional Problems of Cooperative Programs," 1979.

41. Seabus (as the ferry system is called) was constructed at an estimated cost of $80 million for the two twin-hulled passenger ferries and the two terminals, including all other planning and engineering studies. In contrast, a proposed bridge and approaches with the same capacity as Seabus (assuming the primary use of individually driven automobiles) would have cost nearly $1 billion. Thus, for less than the cost of one year's debt service (at 10 percent interest), Vancouverites have a flexible and economical cross-harbor facility.

42. For details of some of the alternative personal rapid transit possibilities, see Brian Richards, *Moving in Cities* (London, England: Macmillan), 1976, pp. 71–83.

43. For details of some of the more important differences, see John Mercer and Michael A. Goldberg, "Value Differences and their Meaning for Urban Development in Canada and the United States," in Gilbert A. Stelter and Alan F. Artibise, ed., *Comparative Urban History,* (Vancouver, B.C.: The University of British Columbia Press), forthcoming.

44. Two papers on urban transportation planning set out in detail how the process has changed from the 1960s, when large-scale capital projects were the rule. See Douglas B. Lee, Jr., *op. cit.,* and Michael A. Goldberg, "Modelers, Muddlers and Multitudes: Establishing a Balanced Transportation Planning Process," *Transportation Research Record* #677, 1978, pp. 23–28.

45. Owen, *Transportation for Cities,* pp. 5–7, sets out some of the many advantages perceived by automobile users. So do Meyer, Kain, and Wohl, *op. cit.,* pp. 248–259. It is these advantages which must be overcome or neutralized if automobile usage is to be successfully slowed.

46. Pickrell, *op. cit.,* and Donald C. Shoup and Don H. Pickrell, *Free Parking as Transportation Problem,* Discussion Paper 130 (Los Angeles, Cal.: School of Architecture, University of California at Los Angeles), 1979.

47. For Boston's Route 128, see: A. J. Bone and Martin Wohl, *Economic Impact Study: Massachusetts' Route 128* (Cambridge, Mass.: M.I.T. Transportation Engineering Division), 1958; and Don Levitan, "Massachusetts Route 128: A Nonemulative Enigma," Transportation Research Record #583, 1976, pp. 45–54. For Washington, D.C., see: Bureau of Population and Economic Research, *The Socio-Economic Impact of the Capital Beltway on Northern Virginia,* (Charlottesville, Va.: Bureau of Population and Economic Research, University of Virginia), 1968. Finally, for a review of beltway impacts on eight cities, see: Payne-Maxie Consultants, *The Land Use and Urban Development Impacts of Beltways: Case Studies* (Washington, D.C.: U.S. Department of Transportation and U.S. Department of Housing and Urban Development), 1980.

48. For sample studies see: George E. Bardwell and Paul R. Merry, "Measuring the Economic Impact of Limited-Access Highways on Communities, Land Use, and Land Values," *Highway Research Board Bulletin* 268, pp. 17–27 1960; and Iowa Highway Department, *Economic Effects of Interstate 80: Ginnell, Iowa* (Des Moines, Iowa: Iowa Department of Highways), 1972.

49. See Knight and Trygg, *op. cit.,* for general overview and review. For San Francisco Bay Area impacts, see John Blayney and Associates and David M. Dornbusch and Co., *Station Area Land Use,* BART Impact Program WP-38-5-77 (Berkeley, Cal.: Metropolitan Transportation Commission). For the impacts of Philadelphia's suburban Lindenwold Line, see David E. Boyce, *Methods for the Assessment of the Impact of an Urban Transportation Improvement,* Studies of the Philadelphia-Lindenwold Rapid Transit Line, Discussion Paper No. 7 (Philadelphia, Pa.: Transportation Program, University of Pennsylvania), 1971.

50. Hayes B. Gamble and Owen Sauerlander, *The Influence of Highway Environmental Effects on Residential Property Values,* Research Publication No. 78 (University Park, Pa.: Institute for Research on Land and Water Resources, Pennsylvania State University), 1974; and John C. Langley, Jr., *Highways and Property Values: The Washington Beltway Revisited* (Knoxville, Tenn.: Department of Marketing and Transportation, College of Business Administration, University of Tennessee), 1981.

51. Raymond B. Palmquist, "Impact of Highway Improvements on Property Values in Washington State," *Transportation Research Record* 887, pp. 22–29, 1982.

52. L. C. L. Poon, "Railway Externalities and Residential Property Prices," *Land Economics,* 54(2:1978): pp. 218–227; and Caj. O. Falcke, *BART's Effects on Property*

Prices and Rents, BART Impact Program WP-52-5-78 (Berkeley, Cal.: Metropolitan Transportation Commission), 1978.

53. For positive effects of highways, see Palmquist, *op. cit.;* and Herbert Hohring and Mitchell Harwitz, *Highway Benefits* (Evanston, Ill.: Northwestern University Press), 1962.

54. For interchange effects of highways, see: Snehamay Khasnabis and Willard F. Babcock, "Impact of a Beltway on a Medium-Sized Urban Area in North Carolina: A Case Study," *Transportation Research Record* 583, pp. 219–227, 1976; and Gale A. Long, *A Corridor Land Use Study: The Impact of an Interstate Highway on Land Values, Private Investment and Land Use in Southwestern Wyoming* (Laramie, Wyo.: College of Commerce and Industry, University of Wyoming), 1970.

55. For impacts of transit on service areas, see: Boyce, *op. cit.,* for Philadelphia; and Falcke, *op. cit.,* and Blayney/Dornbusch, *op. cit.,* for San Francisco.

56. See Falcke, *op. cit.,* for station area impacts. Also see: Colin Gannon and Michael J. Dear, *The Impacts of a Rail Rapid Transit System on Commercial Office Development: The Case of the Philadelphia-Lindenwold High Speedline* (Philadelphia, Pa.: Transportation Studies Center, University of Pennsylvania), 1977; and Donald N. Dewees, "The Effect of a Subway on Residential Property Values in Toronto," *Journal of Urban Economics* 3(4:1976):357–369.

57. Robert Park and Ernest Burgess, *The City* (Chicago, Ill.: University of Chicago Press), 1925, developed a descriptive model of urban growth based on a pedestrian and streetcar access system.

58. Two essentially automobile-based models of the city are provided by Homer Hoyt, *The Structure and Growth of Residential Neighborhoods in American Cities* (Washington, D.C.: U.S. Federal Housing Administration), 1939; and Chauncey D. Harris and Edward L. Ullman, "The Nature of Cities," *Annals of the Americas,* Academy of Political and Social Science, Vol. 242, pp. 7–17.

59. Peter deLeon and John Enns, *The Impact of Highways Upon Metropolitan Dispersion: St. Louis* (Santa Monica, Cal.: The RAND Corporation), RAND Report P-5061, 1973.

60. Martin O. Stern, "The Use of Urban Roads and Their Effect on the Spatial Structure of Cities," in Paul B. Downing, ed., *Local Service Pricing Policies and Their Effect on Urban Spatial Structure* (Vancouver, B.C.: The University of British Columbia Press), 1974.

61. See a detailed analysis of the potential role of transportation in urban redevelopment and shaping in Michael D. Meyer, Ralph Gakenheimer, Paul Haven, Brendon Hemily, and Eric Ziering, *Urban Development and Revitalization: The Role of Federal and State Transportation Agencies* (Cambridge, Mass.: Center for Transportation Studies, M.I.T.), 1979. For a specific application of the concept, see Tomoki Noguchi, "Shaping a Suburban Activity Center Through Transit and Pedestrian Incentives: Bellevue CBD Planning Experience," *Transportation Research Record* 861, pp. 1–6, 1982. At a more conceptual level, see Leo H. Klaassen, Jan A. Bourdez, and Jacques Volmuller, *Transport and Reurbanisation* (Aldershot, England: Gower), 1981.

17

SOME POSSIBLE
URBAN FUTURES

SUMMING UP: WHAT HAVE WE LEARNED?

To the various tools of urban macroeconomics and microeconomics we
have added institutional settings. We then broadened our discussion to
include a range of substantive issues such as the regulation of urban
development; the periodic fluctuations in housing markets; urban economic decline and change; fragmentation of and financing local governments; and the perceived need for metropolitan governments. In
the last chapter, we examined issues of urban access and
transportation.

We now want to move on to speculate on the nature of cities and
urban regions in the future. This chapter will present some of the
emerging forces and factors that will likely shape our cities in the years
to come, ingredients we feel are worth including in recipes for the
course of future urban events.

DIFFICULTIES IN THE FUTURE DEVELOPMENT OF URBAN AREAS

In the course of our discussion we encountered several areas that constitute potential pitfalls or bottlenecks to the continued development of
urban areas. These include the following

1. Financing urban development (both public and private).

2. Land for urban development.

3. Costs (both hard and soft, and public and private) of urban development.

4. The provision of access within and among urban areas.

We deal with these issues in sequence. There are other factors closely related to these issues that also might put limits on urban development (the periodic shortage of materials such as gravel and reinforcing steel is one very specific example of a bottleneck that can be very disruptive to the urban development process). In general, we can observe that anything that interferes with the urban development process in any one stage holds significant implications for all the phases of urban development, the phases being highly interconnected.

Financing Urban Development

We can divide this topic into two parts: private sector financing and public sector financing.

The fiscal crisis of cities is much talked about and the focus of significant controversy in the United States. The prototypical example is New York, whose financial woes have filled volumes.[1] Older cities in the U.S. Midwest and Northeast have received considerable attention as their tax bases have declined and their expenditure demands remained constant or increased.[2] These widely publicized problems of financing central cities are part of the larger question of financing local governments that we discussed earlier in Chapters 14 and 15. We can organize these fiscal difficulties of local governments into three categories

1. Spatial mismatch between revenues and expenditures.

2. Spatial array of local governments and fragmentation of function.

3. Growing diversity of local government services and emerging intergovernmental relations.

We noted that items 1 and 2 in particular were of significantly greater concern in the United States than they were in Canada. Given our discussions, it is easy to understand the U.S. emphasis on the fiscal viability of central cities and local governments, and the relative lack of such concerns in the Canadian context.[3]

We are dealing with a problem that is largely centered in the United States and in its older central cities, and we should not minimize the potential importance the U.S. experience has for Canada.[4] In Canada, with a federal structure similar to that of the United States (though with a parliamentary form of government), the problems of local governments in other federal states such as the United States should not be dismissed out of hand, since some of the financial difficulty arises from the nature of the federal system itself.[5]

For the problem being faced by older U.S. cities, and potentially by all U.S. local governments, we find the following comments by William Oakland most germane:

Local governments, consciously or not, engage in the redistribution of income. Because most local government services are rendered without regard to the tax contribution of the recipient, those who pay little in taxes (i.e., the poor) are subsidized by those who pay a lot (i.e., the rich). For a number of reasons, the nation's older central cities house a disproportionate share of their area's poor. Hence, income redistribution is greater in the central cities than in the suburbs, creating incentives for the well-to-do and business firms to relocate to the suburbs. Equally important, it is in the interest of suburban localities to attract and retain individuals who yield "fiscal surpluses" and repel those who create "fiscal losses." The process, then, may be self-reinforcing and cumulative in its effect. "Rich" governments grow richer and "poor" localities grow poorer.[6]

Some comparisons by Oakland are indicated in Table 17–1.

The outlook for these older cities is therefore fraught with considerable uncertainty over their ability to finance the services vital to their residents.[7] The picture does not appear nearly so grim when we look at financing growth and urban development. This is because the rapidly growing areas of the United States, in the Sun Belt of the South and West, have received more than their share of federal funds in particular, as Table 17–2 clearly shows. (This table comes from Richard Morris's *Bum Rap on America's Cities,* which seeks to document the shortfall in federal support for older cities.) Redevelopment, in contrast to new development, is likely to be hampered by fiscal stress and the inability of older central city governments to provide both the hard and soft services necessary to promote and facilitate urban redevelopment within their boundaries.[8]

We have found that central cities, particularly older ones in the U.S. Northeast and Midwest, are experiencing fiscal difficulties.[9] These fiscal difficulties present barriers to redevelopment, though the existence of enormous capital already in place does mitigate against these difficulties.[10] The main problem facing local governments is that they have been given a larger role in redistributing income, entirely inconsistent with their revenue-raising ability.[11] Looking at the public finance elements of future urban development, we can conclude that problems lie ahead, but so do solutions such as relieving local governments of their redistributional role and increasing the efficiency of locally provided services.[12]

First, let us return to the subject matter of Chapter 6, where we considered private capital markets and some of the problems they have faced in providing adequate funding to the urban development sector, most usually to housing.[13] In Canada the private market generally has functioned well, despite recurrent fears to the contrary. For example, among the recommendations of the 1969 Hellyer Report was the creation in Canada of thrift institutions similar to mutual savings banks and savings and loan associations operating in the United States. The idea

Table 17–1 Property Tax Base and Own Source Revenues for Central Cities and Suburbs in Select Metropolitan Areas

City	Market Value of Taxable Property per Capita[a] 1971				Market Value of Taxable Property per Capita[a] 1961				Local Revenues per Capita[b] 1970			
	CC (1)	OCC (2)	SMSA (3)	(3) ÷ (1) (4)	CC (5)	OCC (6)	SMSA (7)	(7) ÷ (5) (8)	CC (9)	OCC (10)	SMSA (11)	(11) ÷ (9)
New York	10,459	16,157	12,271	1.17	6,801	7,128	6,891	1.01	493	402	462	.94
Chicago	11,150	13,189	12,205	1.09	8,046	8,247	8,133	1.01	281	303	292	1.04
Philadelphia	5,363	9,019	7,540	1.40	3,255	3,666	3,477	1.07	321	232	268	.83
Baltimore	5,889	11,701	9,160	1.55	4,022	5,683	4,801	1.19	286	240	260	.91
Cleveland	11,893	14,389	13,482	1.13	9,226	9,867	9,573	1.04	376	299	327	.87
St. Louis	9,173	10,548	10,186	1.11	5,920	6,701	6,422	1.08	375	210	253	.67
Pittsburgh	6,182	6,674	6,572	1.06	5,021	4,534	4,656	.92	315	205	229	.73
Buffalo	7,856	7,247	7,456	.95	7,024	5,338	6,025	.86	289	293	292	1.01
Cincinnati	10,732	11,043	10,941	1.02	7,700	6,783	7,153	.92	475	177	274	.58
Newark	4,634	12,378	10,787	2.32	3,953	5,773	5,336	1.35	421	331	350	.83
Washington, D.C.	12,371	13,666	13,323	1.08	7,048	7,361	7,246	1.03	594	296	375	.63
Milwaukee	9,527	13,168	11,308	1.19	5,304	6,556	5,699	1.07	371	239	306	.82
Boston	8,058	8,928	8,763	1.09	5,483	5,274	5,321	.97	443	299	333	.77
Kansas City	11,555	12,682	12,226	1.06	7,949	6,674	7,229	.91	347	213	285	.82
Atlanta	14,547	12,259	13,078	.90	8,117	3,849	5,978	.74	318	196	240	.75
Rochester	9,955	9,002	9,322	.93	—	—	—	—	359	293	309	.86
Providence	8,665	9,218	9,089	1.05	—	—	—	—	236	181	192	.81
Akron	11,838	13,898	13,063	1.10	—	—	—	—	298	200	240	.81
Louisville	9,695	9,064	9,341	.96	5,752	6,414	6,058	1.05	302	186	240	.78
New Orleans	8,842	11,391	9,945	1.12	5,176	3,406	4,630	.89	288	162	199	.87

[a]Compiled from information in U.S. Bureau of Census, Taxable Property Values, 1972 and 1962.
[b]U.S. Advisory Commission on Intergovernmental Relations, City Financial Emergencies, (Washington, D.C., 1973).

Source: William H. Oakland, "Central Cities: Fiscal Plight and Prospects for Reform," in Peter Mieskowski and Mahlon R. Straszheim, ed. *Current Issues in Urban Economics* (Baltimore: John Hopkins University Press), 1979, p. 327.

Table 17–2 Federal Taxes and Federal Spending in the Northeast and Sun Belt Compared, 1975

Northeast

State	*Federal Taxes (in millions)*	*Federal Spending (in millions)*	*Surplus (+)/ Deficit (−) (in millions)*
Maine	$ 760	$ 1,277	+ 517
Massachusetts	7,622	8,474	+ 852
Vermont	319	641	+ 322
Connecticut	5,946	5,137	− 809
New Hampshire	714	1,145	+ 431
Rhode Island	1,204	1,243	+ 39
New York	39,007	24,269	−14,738
New Jersey	11,083	8,395	− 2,688
Pennsylvania	17,697	14,462	− 3,235
Ohio	17,194	10,822	− 6,372
Indiana	6,860	5,412	− 1,448
Illinois	21,774	13,462	− 8,312
Michigan	14,778	9,095	− 5,683
Minnesota	6,150	4,497	− 1,653
Wisconsin	5,422	4,443	− 979
Total	$156,530	$112,774	−43,756

Sun Belt

State	*Federal Taxes (in millions)*	*Federal Spending (in millions)*	*Surplus (+)/ Deficit (−) (in millions)*
Virginia	$ 5,035	$ 8,906	+ 3,871
North Carolina	1,875	6,100	+ 4,225
Tennessee	3,511	5,425	+ 1,914
South Carolina	1,875	3,485	+ 1,610
Georgia	4,784	6,786	+ 2,002
Florida	7,787	11,512	+ 3,725
Alabama	2,684	4,816	+ 2,132
Mississippi	1,167	3,740	+ 2,573
Louisiana	3,287	4,596	+ 1,309
Texas	16,048	15,806	− 242
Arkansas	1,241	2,544	+ 1,303
Oklahoma	3,361	3,871	+ 510
Arizona	1,789	3,646	+ 1,857
New Mexico	708	2,264	+ 1,556
California	28,510	35,838	+ 7,328
Total	$83,662	$119,335	+35,673

Source: Richard S. Morris, *Bum Rap on America's Cities* (Englewood Cliffs, N.J.: Prentice-Hall), 1978, p. 112.

was that such new institutions, with primary interests in residential mortgage lending, would help to overcome the periodic shortages that plague mortgage markets during periods of tight money.[14] Several years later, under the editorship of J. V. Poapst, a three-volume report sponsored by the Central Mortgage and Housing Corporation argued for the creation of several new institutions to improve the efficiency of the primary mortgage market and to create a viable secondary market in residential mortgages.[15]

The implication of these studies was clear: Canadian mortgage markets were not functioning effectively and needed to be overhauled on a number of fronts to increase the flow of mortgage funds. In retrospect, these fears were ill-founded. For example, between 1968 and 1980 total mortgage loans outstanding in Canada rose more than fivefold, from C$25.2 billion to C$125.6 billion,[16] despite the absence of government-mandated new financial institutions.[17] The earlier demands for reform were founded on U.S. mortgage market institutions and predicated on the assumption that capital markets in the two countries were so similar that mortgage market institutions could be readily transferred from the United States to Canada. However, the underlying structure of the Canadian mortgage market and the government policies that impinged on it were different from those in the United States, largely obviating the need for such institutions as organized secondary mortgage markets and government-backed mortgage securities. The absence of deposit rate ceilings and usury laws and the shortening of the standard mortgage to a five-year renegotiable term allowed Canadian mortgage markets to attract these additional funds.

In the United States, mortgage markets have been under somewhat different pressures, and have responded differently. The existence of deposit rate ceilings, state usury laws, long-term mortgage lending, and a host of federally sponsored mortgage market agencies and institutions all combine to create a different constellation of mortgage market stumbling blocks.[18] Among the most widely documented is disintermediation and the resulting liquidity crunch faced by U.S. mortgage lenders during periods of tight money. While vastly more complex and varied than their Canadian counterparts, these U.S. mortgage market institutions have, nevertheless, achieved considerable success. Mortgage loans outstanding in the United States rose almost fivefold between 1965 and 1980, from US$333 billion to US$1452 billion.[19] While not as buoyant a performance as in Canada (where there was nearly a sevenfold increase between 1965 and 1980), the U.S. response was impressive, dampened undoubtedly by the very weak performance of the U.S. housing industry during the early and late 1970s, in contrast to record activity in Canada during the same period. Moreover, recent legislation in the United States has sought to make mortgages even more attractive as financial instruments by encouraging shorter terms with variable conditions and interest rates, and by encouraging new deposit instruments to attract savings to the mortgage sector.[20] U.S. capital markets have been able to meet the demands for mortgage funds, despite institutional rigidities and imperfections.[21]

In summary, there do not appear to be major bottlenecks in financial markets. Caveats would include the general level of economic activity both nationally and within the local real estate market. We also assume implicitly that inflation will be kept within reasonable bounds; otherwise it may be difficult to forecast future capital market and real estate investment behavior, as the period of the early 1980s has shown us.

Land for Urban Development

It must come as something of a shock, for Europeans in particular, to read in the 1970 Lithwick report, *Urban Canada: Problems and Prospects,* that one of the more critical problems facing Canada's cities during the 1970s and 1980s was the availability of land, this in a country with 3.9 million square miles of land area and a 1971 population of only 21.6 million persons.[22] In the United States similar fears have been expressed, usually in relation to growth controls and the housing affordability debate.[23] How is it possible for such vast countries with relatively low population densities to worry about land availability when countries like Holland and Denmark actually face much more severe land supply situations? The answer lies in part with past land-use practices in urban areas in both Canada and the United States. Another contributing factor is life-style expectations.

Beginning with the Canadian situation, we find the decade-old concern expressed by Lithwick being reaffirmed more recently by the Federal/Provincial Task Force on the Supply and Price of Serviced Residential Land.[24] Specifically, the Task Force observed that rising lot (and house) prices were the results of short-run increases in the demand for residential land and housing. In the longer run, supply restrictions rather than demand bouyancy were likely to be the cause of rising lot and house prices. The Task Force concludes:

To permanently reduce the price of land in the face of strong demand, it will be necessary for planners and municipalities to permanently increase the rate at which lots are produced. We are concerned, however, that various planning concepts such as contiguous or sequential development policies, greenbelts and higher servicing standards—all of which may be warranted—will lead to a more restrictive subdivision approvals process and higher house prices.[25]

Gertler and Crowley also focus on land-use and development policies.

Land—its use, cost, ownership and development—is a concern that has run through our book. The overview of land as a public policy issue in Canada leads to one over-riding conclusion: the land in the urban fringe of places with 10,000 and more people is the most critical 85,000 square miles in Canada.[26]

However, counter to the Task Force findings, they go on to recommend the following.

A land use policy would not only preserve good farm land, but by defining urban development constraints and potentials should—if the authorities demonstrate that they mean business—gradually restrain land price.[27]

Gertler and Crowley are advocating greater control of the urban land resource, which, as our own analyses and that of the Task Force suggest, may lead to higher, not lower, prices for urban land. Growing environmental and aesthetic concerns, combined with fiscal pressures, can lead to supply limitations so that effective supply is indeed restricted and residential land prices rise.

Given the greater involvement in environmental protection by all levels of government, especially the U.S. federal government, and the trends toward growth controls, the foregoing observations from the Canadian viewpoint appear equally relevant in the United States.

Levin, in *The Urban Prospect,* observes that there is no shortage of land in the United States (only 3 percent of the U.S. land mass has been built on to date).[28] There is more to usability than mere quantity, however.

As any real estate developer can testify, it is not enough for land to be open; it must be "ripe," or capable of being developed and marketed at reasonable cost. This means that land must be well located with respect to transportation, employment, and private and public facilities and services, and properly zoned or susceptible to requisite zoning alterations. Viewed from this perspective, prime land—well-located, properly zoned, reasonably priced and in "good" neighborhoods—is extremely limited; hence its high cost.[29]

Availability of land is not enough. It must be combined with capital, suitable location, and appropriate government approvals to be usable. Thus, the desire to protect land from future development or from certain kinds of development (e.g., exclusionary and fiscal zoning) can affect the supply of developable land.

Healy and Rosenberg make a similar observation about the total available land in the United States being irrelevant, since battles over use arise on individual parcels.[30] Everyone is delighted to have certain types of development ("dirty" industry, low-income and higher-density housing) go elsewhere, leading to a shortage in the aggregate if many jurisdictions adopt exclusionary policies.[31]

Since housing is the largest user of urban land, it has borne the brunt of many policies restricting land use. Thus, it is often difficult to separate land availability from housing costs. When housing and housing land studies are added to a more general concern about developable land, a rather formidable literature begins to take shape.[32]

Summing up, there is no shortage of land available for urban development in either Canada or the United States. However, when we consider developable land, we are faced with another one of our trade-off situations where continued development of vacant land can lead to environmental degradation. Environmental protection and land-use controls have a cost. Whether the costs are worth the benefits depends on who bears the costs or enjoys the benefits.

Servicing costs and access are important determinants of the effective urban land supply, as distinct from total vacant or reusable land. Both are related to government action, but both have characteristics quite separate from local government attitudes toward growth. We now consider servicing and construction costs and the provision of access.

Cost of Urban Development

The first cost of interest here relates to servicing land and bringing it into the status of "developable" land. The second set of costs relates to the construction of the building or improvement itself. Table 17–3 sets out a range of construction cost data for the United States for the period 1965 to 1981. Single-family residential construction costs rose by 140.7 percent between 1970 and 1981, while sewer construction costs (a key hard service) rose by 177.7 percent during those 11 years. Meanwhile, house prices rose by 184.6 percent over the same period. The rise in construction costs shown in Table 17–3 cannot be accounted for by labor costs (which averaged just over 101 percent between 1970 and 1980) and must be accounted for in part by higher materials and financing and soft costs (e.g., architectural, engineering design, planning and approval costs). Table 17–4 provides insights into materials costs, which rose considerably more rapidly than did wages over the 1970–1980 period, rising by 136.8 percent for all materials (note that the table uses a 1967 base instead of the 1977 base of Table 17–3). Construction costs and the materials used in construction were under considerable inflationary pressure during the 1970s in the United States, which, when combined with our previous comments on land availability, lead us to conclude that there appear to be some potential bottlenecks in the construction industry (consumer prices over the period rose by 112.2 percent).[33]

Turning to the Canadian situation, we find similar forces at work. According to Table 17–5, between 1971 and 1982 prices of residential building materials rose by 143.7 percent while wage rates rose by 181.4 percent (the reverse of the U.S. situation, where labor costs rose less steeply than materials costs). The composite residential building cost index rose by 185.9 percent over the period, noticeably faster than the 140.7 percent rise recorded in the United States.

The Federal/Provincial Task Force on the Supply and Price of Serviced Residential Land developed information on lot servicing costs (e.g., the cost of bringing raw land into the effective land supply).[34] These data appear below. Figure 17–1 shows that for most of the urban areas in the Task Force sample (13 of them across Canada),

Table 17–3 Price, Wage Scale, and Cost Indexes for Construction: 1965 to 1981

Item	1965	1970	1973	1974	1975	1976	1978	1979	1980	1981
Price index for new one-family houses sold[a]	44.4	55.3	67.5	73.8	81.7	88.7	114.5	130.8	145.2	157.4
Union hourly wage scales, building trades[b]	59.3	84.1	105.0	113.2	122.9	130.9	146.5	156.6	169.1	(NA)
Construction cost indexes										
Dept. of Commerce composite[c]	43.6	56.8	69.6	81.8	89.3	92.4	113.0	128.7	143.3	152.5
Federal Highway Admin. Highways[d]	41.7	58.0	70.8	96.3	96.7	93.4	119.4	142.6	163.0	156.7
Environmental Protection Agency										
Sewers	39.9	51.2	68.2	78.8	88.5	94.1	109.5	123.2	133.6	142.2
Sewage treatment plant	40.2	51.6	65.6	78.0	89.8	94.3	109.5	120.4	131.3	142.5
Federal Energy Regulatory Commission Pipelinle	48	54	64	76	93	98	112	121	133	145
American Appraisal Co. Building construction[e]	41	57	76	80	86	94	109	118	125	132
Turner Construction Co. Building construction[f]	45	62	78	91	95	97	106	118	131	144
E. H. Boeckh, building cost index[g]										
Small residential structures	41.8	56.5	73.5	79.4	84.7	91.7	109.0	119.0	128.9	136.0
Apartments, hotels, and office buildings	41.9	57.5	71.3	77.9	85.6	92.4	106.5	114.7	125.1	137.4
Commercial and factory buildings	40.7	55.6	69.8	77.3	85.3	92.6	107.5	117.1	127.7	140.1
Engineering News-Record[h]										
Building construction	40.6	54.1	73.7	78.0	84.6	92.3	108.4	117.8	125.9	135.8
General construction	37.7	53.8	73.5	78.4	85.8	93.1	107.7	116.5	125.6	137.1
Handy-Whitman public utility[i]										
Building	41	53	69	84	93	95	109	122	135	142
Electric light and power[j]	41	52	63	75	88	94	106	116	127	139

[a]Includes value of site.

[b]1972 = 100. Based on minimum wage rates agreed upon through collective bargaining: excludes overtime. As of first work day in July: includes Honolulu, Hawaii, beginning in 1976. Source: U.S. Bureau of Labor Statistics. *Union Wages and Hours: Building Trades annual.*

[c]Covers both building and nonbuilding construction, excluding maintenance and repair Represents a weighted average of various indexes used for different types of construction.

[d]Based on average contract unit bid prices for composite mile (involving specific average amounts of excavation paving, reinforcing steel, structural steel, and structural concrete).

[e]Average for 30 cities of 4 types of buildings: wood frame, back-wood frame, brick-steel frame, and reinforced concrete. Covers materials and labor costs in structural portion of building, but excludes those for plumbing, heating, lighting, sprinklers, and elevators. Reflects employee-benefit costs, and allows for contractors' overhead and profit.

[f]Eastern cities. Based on firm's cost experience with respect to labor rates, materials prices, competitive conditions, efficiency of plant and management and productivity. Reflects payment of sales taxes and employee-benefit costs. Wage rates used for both common and skilled labor. Reflects payment of sales taxes and social security payroll taxes.

gAverage of 20 cities for types shown. Weights based on surveys of building costs.
hBuilding construction index computed on basis of hypothetical unit of construction requiring 6 bbl of Portland cement, 1088 M bd ft of 2″ × 4″ lumber, 2500 lb of structural steel, and 68.38 hours of skilled labor. General construction index based on same malterials components combined with 200 hours of common labor.
iBased on data covering public utility construction costs for 95 items in six geographic regions. Covers skilled and common labor; does not reflect tax payments nor employee-benefit costs.
jAs derived by U.S. Bureau of the Census. Covers steam production plants only; excludes hydraulic plants.
Note: 1977 = 100, except as indicated. Excludes Alaska and Hawaii, except as noted. Indexes of certain of these sources are published on bases different from those shown here.

Table 17-4 Construction Materials—Producer Price Indexes: 1970 to 1981

Commodity	1970	1972	1973	1974	1975	1976	1977	1978	1979	1980	1981
All materials	112.5	126.6	138.5	160.9	174.0	187.7	204.9	228.3	251.4	266.4	283.0
Softwood lumber:											
Douglas fir	108.7	161.1	209.6	213.7	212.0	250.7	291.4	339.7	383.9	353.0	311.8
Southern pine	114.7	151.5	187.9	184.5	175.3	217.4	262.5	304.6	324.2	297.4	291.6
Hardwood lumber	114.6	126.2	169.0	198.5	160.3	176.0	200.3	235.8	260.0	252.0	255.2
Millwork	116.0	128.4	144.2	157.1	160.4	176.9	193.7	235.4	254.3	260.4	273.4
Plywood	108.4	130.7	155.2	161.1	161.2	187.0	212.2	235.6	250.5	246.5	245.7
Building paper and board	101.0	106.4	112.8	123.5	127.1	138.8	157.0	187.4	182.4	206.2	231.7
Prepared paint	112.4	118.0	122.2	145.7	166.9	174.4	182.4	192.3	204.4	235.3	249.8
Finished steel products:											
Structural shapes	115.3	134.6	140.7	179.0	216.3	227.1	241.2	272.0	300.4	329.9	368.1
Reinforcing bars	110.3	114.7	124.1	201.5	199.2	182.5	185.8	208.4	261.1	274.8	275.5
Black pipe, carbon	113.3	132.5	137.8	178.7	204.6	219.1	247.9	279.8	301.8	323.6	380.4
Wire nails, 8d common	114.8	133.5	140.4	207.1	241.4	243.6	261.3	273.5	298.5	331.9	356.9
Nonferrous metal products	124.7	116.9	135.0	187.1	171.6	181.6	195.4	207.8	261.7	305.0	285.8
Building wire	123.2	92.9	108.2	169.7	125.8	118.4	126.7	125.5	167.7	209.4	163.7
Plumbing fixtures	111.2	119.7	125.8	149.1	162.3	174.1	186.6	199.1	217.1	246.7	267.5
Heating equipment	110.6	118.2	120.4	135.0	150.7	158.0	165.5	174.4	187.1	206.5	224.2
Metal doors, sash, trim	113.0	120.5	124.5	147.3	162.5	171.3	188.7	207.6	229.6	255.2	278.8
Concrete ingredients	112.6	126.9	131.2	148.7	172.3	186.7	199.0	217.7	244.0	274.0	296.3
Concrete products	112.2	125.6	131.7	151.7	170.5	180.1	191.8	214.0	244.1	273.9	291.2
Structural clay products	109.9	117.3	123.3	135.2	151.2	163.5	179.8	197.2	217.9	231.5	249.8
Gypsum products	99.7	114.7	120.9	137.6	144.0	154.4	183.5	229.1	252.3	256.3	256.2
Asphalt roofing	107.7	131.2	135.5	196.0	225.9	238.3	253.0	292.0	325.3	396.8	407.5
Insulation materials	123.2	136.9	137.4	156.5	196.2	212.6	235.9	250.7	256.3	287.9	(NA)

Note: 1967 = 100. Covers materials incorporated as integral part of a building or normally installed during construction and not readily removable. Excludes consumer durables such as kitchen ranges, refrigerators, etc.

Source: Statistical Abstract of the United States, 1982/83 (Washington, D.C.: U.S. Government Printing Office), 1983, Table No. 1331, page 742.

Table 17-5 Indexes of Construction Costs, Canada 1971–1982 (1971 = 100)

| | Building Materials | | Composite Indexes | | | |
Period	Residential	Nonresidential	Residential Construction Labor Costs	Residential Building Material and Wage Rates	Nonresidential Building Material and Wage Rates	Implicit Index of Residential Construction
1971	100.0	100.0	100.0	100.0	100.0	100.0
1973	124.0	113.1	121.8	123.2	117.5	123.8
1974	135.2	137.3	133.8	134.7	136.1	147.9
1975	139.7	147.0	151.6	144.0	150.4	167.8
1976	153.6	156.6	172.8	160.5	165.7	187.7
1977	165.2	165.6	193.9	175.5	179.7	208.2
1978	184.1	179.4	206.2	192.0	193.2	227.9
1979	207.0	208.7	219.5	211.4	214.6	255.5
1980	215.1	230.2	236.3	222.7	234.0	281.0
1981	236.4	253.2	258.5	244.3	256.6	277.6
1982	243.7	275.4	281.4	257.2	279.3	285.9

Source: Canadian Housing Statistics, 1981 (Ottawa: Canada Mortgage and Housing Corporation), Table 92, p. 77. *Canadian Housing Statistics, 1982*, (Ottawa: Canada Mortgage and Housing Corporaiton), Table 89, p. 75.

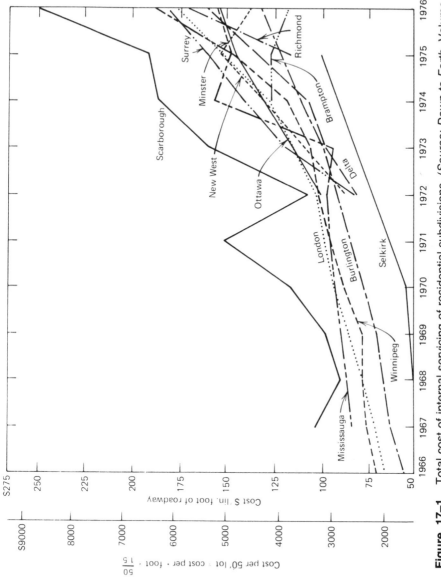

Figure 17–1. Total cost of internal servicing of residential subdivisions. (*Source: Down to Earth*, Volume Two, Figure 8.1, p. 86.)

servicing costs for residential subdivisions accelerated beginning in 1972, reflecting the general inflation in the country at the time (the Consumer Price Index rose by just over 40 percent during 1972–76, compared with a mere 15 percent rise in the previous four years). So, as in the United States, construction costs displayed a unique vulnerability to inflation.

To conclude, construction costs have risen dramatically during the 1970s, although the pattern was somewhat different in the United States and Canada, with materials costs leading the way in the former and labor cost at the forefront in the latter. Despite periodic shortages in such varied inputs as reinforcing rods, gravel (for concrete), and lumber and plywood, there seems to have been no crippling bottleneck in either country. There is little reason to believe that the construction industry will not suffer from higher-than-average inflation as it is the classic increasing-cost industry and exhibits strongly pro-cyclical behavior.[35] Increasing costs and periodic materials shortages (and occasional shortages of skilled labor as well) should continue to typify urban development in the future.[36]

Of equal importance are the intangible costs of urban development related to environmental quality. Some of these costs are being internalized and are showing up as added costs for land and for development.[37] These internalized environmental costs have taken many forms, from growing citizen awareness and involvement to the passage of stringent environmental and urban development restrictions. Higher costs of housing and development reflect the willingness of North Americans to pay for higher-quality urban environments. So does the increased movement in the United States of people to nonmetropolitan urban areas. Whether such costs will continue to be borne by the public in the United States and Canada remains to be seen,[38] though it is extremely unlikely that there will be any retrenchment to pre-1960s thinking. What is more likely is explicit recognition that the trade-off exists.[39]

We have considered a number of potential pitfalls that lie in the path of continued urban development. The development process itself might be self-limiting, since the process creates space, and unless there is some means for overcoming space and the spatial separation of people and activities in urban areas, severe limits to further urban expansion could be faced.[40]

The old saw about the importance of location in urban land economics is very much to the point here.[41] The importance of access in determining land use and value has been well established. Of equal importance is the role that land use plays in the determination of the demand for different modes of urban travel. Access provides the means whereby land can be brought into use, while land use provides the demand for access.

The provision of access in urban areas is likely to be as constrained as local finances for developers and governments. Dramatic large-scale public investments are not in the future of urban transportation systems at the present time. Instead, we are much more likely to see urban transportation systems that look remarkably like the ones of today, though with marginal improvements. It is highly probable that urban access will improve considerably by the turn of the century, but those improvements will be very much along the lines of improvements already in the works, and not at all discontinuous, as urban futurists would have us believe.[42] Patterns are already beginning to emerge based on rather modest changes in our urban transportation system, such as renewed interest in central areas and their redevelopment in the face of rising energy and automobile prices, growing congestion, and increasing travel time costs.[43]

FUTURE CONCERNS AND CLOSING OBSERVATIONS

Land availability, credit, costs of urban development, and access all hold important keys to the future of urban areas. In this final section we want to raise some questions about future development patterns, future problems facing urban areas and their residents, and some of the proposals that have been put forward about how our cities are likely to develop.

Potential Problems

We can easily envision a number of areas where bottlenecks and shortages could stem the urban development process. Above we discussed land and capital, but we could also conceive of situations where shortages of labor (especially skilled tradespeople) could be a severe limiting factor. Materials shortages have occurred in the past. Further, energy is an enormous unknown and a potential stumbling block not only to future urban development, but also to the smooth functioning of areas already developed. While in its relative infancy as an area of study, energy and its relationship to urban growth has already attracted considerable interest.[44] The potential impacts of energy shortages, policies, and innovations are very much at the core of urban development and urban functioning.[45]

Aside from these input questions, other difficulties loom. Central cities in urban areas have had trouble keeping up with economic developments nationally. The supply of jobs has not kept pace, and has frequently contracted. Old and often shrinking housing stocks in central cities also threaten to diminish their ability to attract and keep residents. Low vacancy rates, demolitions, growth of rent controls, and environmental and land-use restrictions combine to make the outlook for housing construction a gloomy one in central cities. Suburban supplies have been restricted by land-use and environmental protection policies. Questions about the affordability of housing have cropped up with growing frequency and stridency.[46]

Urban areas face continuing threats from their own success and growth. Loss of open space, various types of pollution, and congestion are all in part the results of urban growth. Failure to protect environmental quality and provide for open space and other urban amenities can act as a self-regulating mechanism to slow or stall future urban growth.

Changing Preferences and the Urban Future

We observed that there was a marked slowdown in the growth of metropolitan areas in the United States. Nonmetropolitan growth appears to augur changes in life-style preferences, the usual explanation being that people want to avoid the negative externalities of big cities yet remain in an urban setting, thus the compromise of nonmetropolitan urban regions. If the desire for such a life-style is broadly based, then we can expect a continuation and strengthening of the trend, with the obvious consequence that larger urban regions will decline.

Within urban areas, continued suburbanization and the simultaneous movement back into central city areas (where, until recently, lower-priced housing stock existed) provide two diametrically opposed models of behavior, one with favorable consequences for central cities, one unfavorable. Understanding the dynamics of these forces remains a very high priority in urban research.[47]

Housing preferences and demographic behavior are also closely linked. Past trends toward smaller families, nonfamily households, delayed marriage, lower fertility, and higher divorce all combined to shape recent urban growth in both Canada and the United States.[48] Depending on household formation behavior, households will opt for smaller housing (which could also be more central and in duplex, row, or apartment units) or larger units (which could be centrally located, but more likely would be suburban or exurban).

Travel behavior and the trade-off between work and leisure are closely related. Desire for a shorter commuting distance to work could lead to either central city preferences or to nonmetropolitan locations where access is also easy. Growing demand for leisure could signal more suburban and nonmetropolitan growth as people want to be close to recreational amenities. It also might imply smaller, more central housing and second homes.

Given the diversity of possible futures, it is not hard to understand the diversity of alternative urban prospects. Accordingly, a look at some of these often imaginative forecasts and predictions can provide us with another dimension of the urban experience that awaits us.

Urban Change: The Futurists

Probably no other aspect of human societies has evoked as much utopian and futurist thinking as cities. Early thinking was confined to the creation of utopian towns largely in response to the oppressive conditions of British cities of the Industrial Revolution. Industrialist Robert Owen's factory communities of the early 19th century are the models of early utopias.[49] Later in the century, utopian farming communities began to spring up in the midwestern United States. By the end of the century, Patrick Geddes and Ebenezer Howard were arguing passionately for planning and open spaces, and "the city beautiful" movement was born.[50] Central Park in New York, Golden Gate Park in San Francisco, Lincoln Park in Chicago, and Stanley Park in Vancouver were products of this school of thought and of this era.

It remained for the 20th century, however, to usher in the high-technology and "science fiction" views of urban futures. Early films led the way, followed by the wave of Art Deco architecture and streamlining during the 1920s and 1930s. Fantastic cities were imagined, with people being whisked about by aerial and underground trains, ramps and driverless vehicles, all of this activity taking place in a fantastic landscape of enormous Art Deco skyscrapers.[51]

More recently, we can identify two rather different streams of urban futures thought. The first is a direct descendant of the technologically based fantasies of the 1920s and 1930s. The second is more in keeping with contemporary social science thought, being relatively sober and firmly rooted in research methodologies and empirically measurable trends and patterns.

Paolo Soleri and Kenzo Tange are the best-known proponents of the first stream. In both cases, megastructures are envisioned that provide a complete (and man-made) environment. Soleri's Arcology is under construction at the present time. The original Arcology was visualized as a home for 1 million people, while the prototype rising in the Arizona desert will hold perhaps 30,000 inhabitants.[52]

Tange and Soleri stress building technology. Another strong technological stream in present-day thinking about cities of the future lies in access systems. Even more fanciful solutions have been put forward involving automated highways systems of moving sidewalks, and automated buses and trains.[53]

Closely related to evolving transportation technologies are ideas about planned communities and land uses. The fully planned community, or so-called *new town*, is the best example, and its combination of dense mixed land uses with clusters of pedestrian-oriented activities can be combined easily with the most innovative transportation technologies.[54]

The second stream of urban futures thinking constructs the future out of the present and observable trends in travel, housing, demography, employment, and economic growth. Limited by current empirically measured realities, this school foresees marginal changes in cities.[55]

The Urban Future: A Synthesis

Looking over the past century of urban change in North America leads us to side with the more conservative views of the urban future. Doubtless this comes in part from our social science training as economists. It is also based on observation. The serious "innovations" in transportation and land use that loom ahead are firmly rooted in the past. Light rapid transit and light-rail vehicles used to be trolley cars. Mixed land uses existed before zoning. Condominium town houses, "zero-lot line zoning" (no side or back yards), and planned unit developments have all existed in one form or another for a century or more, as have subways (fixed-guideway heavy-rail rapid transit), moving sidewalks and escalators, and large building complexes (Rockefeller Center incorporates almost all of the Space Age innovations, and it is 50 years old).

There is little cause to believe that our society will embrace the creation of urban environments that bear no relation to past urban environments.[56] New towns, especially in Britain, have not worked, except as they have become older.[57] Almost certainly such grand and expensive designs as those of Soleri and Tange are impractical from economic, energy, and purely social perspectives.

In short, the city of the future is likely to look very much like the city of the present and the past. Such changes as will occur are much more likely to be at the margin than at the core of urban change. Our parents and grandparents might be awed by some of the technology of the next century, but they would have little trouble finding their way about future cities, since most of them have already been built in the form of the city of today.

A Final Word

Forecasting on any front is extraordinarily hazardous, but the hazards become extreme when trying to forecast the nature of cities and city living well into the next century. Such forecasts must deal with some very crucial unknowns. Human behavior (household and family formation, residential location and work location preferences, and travel behavior) leads the list of unpredictables, followed closely by materials availability (particularly energy), labor (especially skilled trades), and capital (both private and public).

Economics in general, and urban land economics in particular, provides key ingredients for the urban policy process. We have explored a number of forces that are likely to shape cities into the next century, with obvious relevance for the conduct of urban land markets. Urban land markets are shapers of that very same urban future. Urban land economists must continually take such prospective views of the environment within which urban land markets function. The immobility of land and buildings and their relative permanence demand long-run views. The present exercise in urban futures is indicative of the kinds of considerations that must be made. Since all activities in urban areas must locate somewhere, knowing what kinds of activities are likely to exist in the future, and being cognizant of their locational possibilities, holds great relevance for urban land markets, which in turn affect the constellation of activities and locational possibilities, and so on. This knot cannot be unraveled (never, in all probability). We can gain some understanding, however, of the various strands that come together to form it, as we have tried to do in other areas where urban land markets are both determinants and determined. This book is intended to be a start toward such an understanding.

Footnotes

1. For details, see: Roger E. Alcaly and David Mermelstein, *The Fiscal Crisis of American Cities* (New York: Vintage Books), 1976, especially Part III; Marian Lief Palley and Howard A. Palley, *Urban America and Public Policies* (Lexington, Mass.: D. C. Heath & Co.), 1977, Chapter 11; and Richard S. Morris, *Bum Rap on America's Cities: The Real Causes of Urban Decay* (Englewood Cliffs, N.J.: Prentice-Hall), 1978.

2. Roy Bahl, Bernard Jump, Jr., and Larry Schroeder, "The Outlook for City Fiscal Performance in Declining Regions," in Roy Bahl, *The Fiscal Outlook for Cities: Implications of a National Urban Policy* (Syracuse, N.Y.: Syracuse University Press), 1978, pp. 147.

3. In this regard, it is most telling that two influential volumes that looked into the prospects for Canada's cities over the coming decades did not stress urban fiscal crises in the Canadian context. Much greater stress was placed on the ability to provide jobs and the need for coordinated planning of urban development. See N. H. Lithwick, *Urban Canada: Problems and Prospects* (Ottawa, Ontario: Central Mortgage and Housing Corporation), 1970; and Len Gertler and Ron Crowley, *Changing Canadian Cities: The Next 25 Years* (Toronto, Ontario: McClelland and Stewart), 1977.

4. The reader is referred back to Chapter 15, where we presented data on transfers of funds from provincial and federal government sources to local governments. In studying the readings concerning local government in Canada, one is once again struck by the relative absence of discussion of fiscal crisis facing such governments.

5. Several authors have raised concerns about the continued financial viability of Canada's local governments. See, for example: *Report of the Tri-Level Task Force on Public Finance* (Toronto, Ontario: Tri-Level Task Force on Public Finance), 1976; and David Nowlan, "Towards Urban Home Rule in Canada," *Ekistics* 262(September 1977):144–149. More general questions relating to the function of local governments in federal systems and the difficulties associated with being

a "junior" government in the U.S. federal system (though with some considerable relevance in Canada) are raised in Michael Dear and Gordon L. Clark, "Dimensions of Local State Autonomy" (Cambridge, Mass.: Department of City and Regional Planning Harvard University), mimeographed, 1980.

6. William H. Oakland, "Central Cities: Fiscal Plight and Prospects for Reform," in Peter Mieszkowski and Mahlon R. Straszheim, eds., *Current Issues in Urban Economics* (Baltimore: Johns Hopkins University Press), 1979, pp. 322–358.

7. Bahl *et al.*, *op. cit.*, made similar points. Also see Robert P. Inman, "The Fiscal Performance of Local Governments: An Interpretative Review," in Mieszkowski and Straszheim, *op. cit.*, pp. 270–321.

8. Morris, *op. cit.*, presents a range of very interesting evidence concerning the direct and indirect ways in which an enormous array of U.S. policies adversely affect older cities in the U.S. Northeast and Midwest and appear to promote urban development in rural Southern and Western states and regions. Also see Jerome Rothenberg, *Economic Evaluation of Urban Renewal* (Washington, D.C.: Brookings Institution), 1966.

9. Central cities have, on average, lower property tax bases per capita than the SMSA within which they are located, yet at the same time local revenues per capita were greater than the SMSA figure, thus demonstrating that central cities were stretching their tax base considerably more than the rest of their respective SMSAs.

10. This point is made by George Peterson, who also notes that considerable capital is likely needed to upgrade the infrastructure in older cities, though these capital needs are unlikely to be as great as building from scratch. See George E. Peterson, "Capital Spending and Capital Obsolescence: The Outlook for Cities," in Roy Bahl, *op. cit.*, pp. 49–74.

11. This point is made very strongly by Oakland, *op. cit.*, and Inman, *op. cit.*, and also occupies a central place in the argument by Dear and Clark about the nature of local governments in the United States.

12. Once again, support for this point can be found in Oakland, *op. cit.*, and Bahl *et al.*, *op. cit.* Also see materials in Chapter 15 dealing with suggestions for trimming local government costs and increasing local government efficiency.

13. To see how important mortgages are to North America's capital markets, see Chapter 6, Tables 6–5 and 6–6, for details on the magnitude of mortgage debt compared with other financial instruments.

14. Task Force on Housing and Urban Development, *Report* (Ottawa, Ontario: Queen's Printer), 1969.

15. J. V. Poapst, *Developing the Residential Mortgage Market, Volumes I, II and III* (Ottawa, Ontario: Central Mortgage and Housing Corporation), 1975. Also see J. Hatch, *The Canadian Mortgage Market* (Toronto, Ontario: Treasury Board), 1975.

16. Central Mortgage and Housing Corporation, *Canadian Housing Statistics, 1978* (Ottawa, Ontario: Central Mortgage and Housing Corporation), 1979, Table 82, p. 72.

17. Real Estate Investment Trusts (REITs) and Mortgage Investment Companies (MICs) did appear along the lines suggested by Poapst and his associates. However, the more important reasons why mortgage funds were not in short supply

during the boom in housing demand during the 1972–1975 period can probably be traced not to new institutions, but rather to changes in the mortgage document such as the five-year renewal provision and the floating rate for NHA mortgages, which combined with 1967 changes in the Bank Act to make mortgage lending more attractive to banks, in the first instance, and to financial institutions more generally. For more detail see Chapter 6.

18. The existence of deposit rate ceilings (Regulation Q and the Interest Rate Adjustment Act) and state usury laws created a very different institutional environment in the United States, necessitating different solutions to periodic shortages of mortgage funds, such as the development of a secondary mortgage market based on Ginnie Mae, Fannie Mae, and Freddie Mac instruments (see Chapter 6 for details). In contrast, the secondary mortgage market in Canada has been relatively small and unorganized and the periodic liquidity crises faced by U.S. mortgage lenders has not been a characteristic of the Canadian market. See J. R. Ostas, "The Effects of Usury Ceilings in the Mortgage Market", *Journal of Finance*, June 1976; and R. Lindsay, *The Economics of Interest Rate Ceilings* (New York: New York City Institute of Finance), Bulletins Nos. 68–69, December 1970.

19. *U.S. Statistical Abstract, 1981* (Washington, D.C.: U.S. Government Printing Office), 1981, p. 518.

20. See The Financial Reform Act of 1979 as the major thrust in the direction of more flexible mortgage lending. For reviews of the issues and suggested reforms, see Patrick H. Hendershott and Kevin E. Villani, "Housing Finance in America in the Year 2001," in M. A. Goldberg and G. W. Gau, eds., *North American Housing Markets into the 21st Century* (Cambridge, Mass: Ballinger Publishing Company), 1983, pp. 181–202.

21. Lawrence D. Jones, "The Future of Community Production Systems in the United States," in *The Construction Industry: New Adaptations to a Changing Environment* (Washington, D.C.: ULI—The Urban Land Institute), 1977, p. 124.

22. N. H. Lithwick, *op. cit.*, pp. 156–158 and pp. 222–236.

23. Much of the four-volume series from the Urban Land Institute is devoted to similar themes about the effects of land-use and environmental controls on costs. In particular, see Frank Schnidman, Jane A. Silverman, and Rufus C. Young, Jr., eds., *Management and Control of Growth, Volume IV* (Washington, D.C.: ULI—The Urban Land Institute), 1978, especially Chapter 29, pp. 311–326.

24. Federal/Provincial Task on the Supply and Price of Serviced Residential Land, *Down To Earth, Volume II*, (Toronto, Ontario: Federal/Provincial Task Force on the Supply and Price of Serviced Residential Land), 1977.

25. *Ibid.*, p. 186.

26. Gertler and Crowley, *op. cit.*, p. 144.

27. *Ibid.*, p. 448.

28. Melvin R. Levin, *The Urban Prospect* (North Scituate, Mass.: Duxbury Press), 1977, p. 67.

29. *Ibid.*, p. 68.

30. Robert G. Healy and John S. Rosenberg, *Land Use and the States*, second edition, (Baltimore: Johns Hopkins University Press), 1979, p. 34. For some of the costs associated with such growth controls, see David E. Dowall, *The Suburban Squeeze:*

An Examination of Suburban Land Conversion in the San Francisco Bay Area (Berkeley, Calif.: Institute of Urban and Regional Development, University of California), 1981.

31. This is the classic problem faced by individual decision units in free markets, typified perhaps by the periodic swings in agricultural markets. The general class of problems are called "fallacies of composition," and governments as well as individuals are prone to them.

32. See Schnidman *et al.*, *op. cit.*, especially the Bibliography, pp. 325–326; Bernard J. Frieden, "The Environmental Attack on Home Building," in Arthur P. Solomon, ed., *The Prospective City* (Cambridge, Mass.: MIT Press), 1980, pp. 288–308; and Healy and Rosenberg, *op. cit.*, Chapters 2 and 7. Also see: Edwin Mills, "Economic Analysis of Urban Land-Use Controls," in Mieszkowski and Straszheim, *op. cit.*, pp. 511–541; and David Dowall and John Landis, "Land-Use Controls and Housing Costs: An Examination of San Francisco Bay Area Communities" (Berkeley, Calif.: Center for Real Estate and Urban Economics, University of California), 1981.

33. The data came from the *U.S. Statistical Abstract, 1981*. More specifically, the construction data came from pp. 775–777, while the Consumer Price Index data came from pp. 483–485. The increasing cost nature of the construction industry has been well established in the past. See, for example, Leo Grebler, *Large-Scale Housing and Real Estate Firms: Analysis of a New Business Enterprise* (New York: Praeger Books), 1974. for Canada, see L. Auer, *Construction Instability in Canada* (Ottawa, Ontario: Economic Council of Canada), 1970.

34. Federal/Provincial Task Force, *op. cit.*, Chapter 8.

35. The highly cyclical nature of the construction industry is another much discussed and documented characteristic. See Economic Council of Canada, *Toward More Stable Growth in Construction* (Ottawa, Ontario: Information Canada), 1974. See also J. H. Chung, *Cyclical Instability in Residential Construction in Canada* (Ottawa, Ontario: Economic Council of Canada), 1976.

36. *Project Breakthrough*, sponsored by the U.S. Department of Housing and Urban Development, and the ongoing research at Canada's National Research Council on building are two visible means by which governments attempt to improve efficiency and lower building costs, though with limited success.

37. Federal Provincial Task Force, *op. cit.*, and Schnidman *et al.*, *op. cit.*

38. Government willingness to ease environmental restrictions on automobiles to aid the ailing U.S. automobile industry is an example of the trade-off in action, and also perhaps an indication of the future outcome when economic and environmental issues meet in the crunch.

39. The whole issue of environmental, livability, and economic trade-offs is the focal point of the book by Maurice Levi and Martin Kupferman, *Slowth* (New York: Ronald Press), 1980, and provides interesting examples and documentation of the trade-off.

40. Access and overcoming spatial separation was fundamental to early work in urban land economics, as we saw in Chapters 4 and 5. See, for example, Robert Murray Haig, "Toward an Understanding of the Metropolis," *Quarterly Journal of Economics* (February–May 1926):179–208, 402–434; and Richard U. Ratcliff, *Urban Land Economics* (New York: McGraw-Hill), 1949, especially Chapter 13, pp. 368–405.

41. Real estate analysts and developers like to repeat the three most important facets of a property: "Location, location, location."

42. Among the more fanciful thinkers, one finds: R. Buckminster Fuller, *Utopia or Oblivion* (New York: Bantam Books), 1969; Paolo Soleri, *Arcology and the Future of Man* (Montgomery, Ala: Montgomery Museum of Fine Arts), 1975, and *The Sketchbooks of Paolo Soleri* (Cambridge, Mass.: MIT Press), 1971; Udo Kultermann, ed., *Kenzo Tange, Architecture and Urban Design* (New York: Praeger Publishers), 1970; and Kenzo Tange, "Images of the Future Urban Environment," in Gwen Bell and Jaqueline Tyrwhitt, eds., (Harmondsworth, England: Penguin Books), 1972. For a collection of futurist designs, see Justus Dahinden, ed., *Urban Structures for the Future* (London, England: Pall Mall Press), 1972.

43. See Franklin J. James, "The Revitalization of Older Urban Housing and Neighborhoods," in Arthur P. Solomon, ed., *The Prospective City* (Cambridge, Mass.: MIT Press), 1980, pp. 130–160. Also see Shirley B. Laska and Daphne Spain, eds., *Back to the City: Issues in Neighborhood Renovation* (New York: Pergamon Press), 1980.

44. See Sale L. Keyes, "The Influence of Energy on Future Patterns of Urban Development," in Solomon, *op. cit.,* pp. 309–325.

45. Among the many difficulties in forecasting the impact of energy availability on urban form is the multiplicity of outcomes that one could envision for each energy scenario. For example, will energy shortages lead to more compact cities or to more decentralized ones? Will shortages favor older renovated areas and cities or is the energy efficiency of building anew more attractive? The absence of definitive findings about the relative efficiencies (in energy terms) of building or rebuilding, highlights the difficulty involved in forecasting energy impacts. This task is made considerably more difficult by the newness of energy-saving technologies and by the renovation/rehabilitation experience making any short-run findings of dubious value in the longer run as new approaches evolve. A key element in assessing energy impacts on urban form is the effect of energy on urban transportation and the resulting impact on urban form. For a very good review of the literature on urban form and transportation, see Caj O. Falcke, *Methodologies for Assessing the Impacts of Major Transportation Facilities on Land Use and Land Prices* (Cambridge, Mass.: Transportation Systems Center, U.S. Department of Transportation), 1982.

46. Frieden, *op. cit.,* has raised numerous questions about affordability and environmental protection. On a larger front, questions about affordability more generally have been raised by John C. Weicher, "New Home Affordability, Equity, and Housing Market Behavior," *American Real Estate and Urban Economics Association Journal* 6(4):1979):395–416.

47. For some insights into the complexity of the problem and recent evidence, see G. Sternlieb and J. W. Hughes, eds., *Post-Industrial America: Metropolitan Decline and Interregional Job Shifts* (New Brunswick, N.J.: Center for Urban Policy Research, Rutgers University), 1975. Also see Charles L. Leven, *The Maturing Metropolis* (Lexington, Mass.: D. C. Heath), 1978; and G. Stemlieb and J. Hughes, "Back to the Central City," *Traffic Quarterly* 33(4):1979):617–636.

48. Recent demographic trends and some of their manifold implications have been discussed by the following people: William Alonso, "The Population Factor and Urban Structure," in Solomon, *op. cit.,* pp. 32–51; Melvin R. Levin, *The Urban Prospect, op. cit.,* Chapter 2, pp. 21–64; and Heather Hamilton-Wright, *Canadian*

Housing Policy and The Future Demand for Housing: A Demographic Analysis and a Look into the Future, unpublished M.Sc. thesis (Vancouver, B.C.: Faculty of Commerce and Business Administration, University of British Columbia), 1977.

49. For background on these and other utopian thoughts, see: Lewis Mumford, *The Story of Utopias* (New York: Peter Smith), 1941; George Kateb, *Utopia and Its Enemies* (New York: Schocken Publishers), 1972; Robert Fishman, *Urban Utopias of the Twentieth Century* (New York: Basic Books), 1977; and George Lockwood, *The New Harmony Movement* (New York: Dover Books), 1971.

50. Ebenezer Howard, *Garden Cities of Tomorrow* (London, England: Swan and Sonnenschein), 1902. For an application of the garden city idea to community development, see C. B. Purdom, *The Letchworth Achievement* (London, England: J. M. Dent), 1963, Letchworth and Welwyn Garden City being among the first towns to employ Howard's ideas on any scale. An updated emphasis on open space and landscaping can be found in Ian McHarg, *Design with Nature* (New York: Natural History Press), 1969.

51. Perhaps the classic example of futurism and fantasy as it was often combined during the 1920s and 1930s is Fritz Lang's 1926 film *Metropolis.* The general futurist spirit of the period comes across very strongly in its architecture and architectural writings. For details, see C. Robinson and R. H. Bletter, *Skyscraper Style* (New York: Oxford University Press), 1975.

52. See Solari, *Arcology and the Future of Man.*

53. A range of technological innovations that are either extant or on the horizon and which possess interesting future implications for urban growth and structure can be found in the following collections of essays, drawings, and ideas: Gideon Golanyi, ed., *Innovations for Future Cities* (New York: Praeger Publishers), 1976, especially the papers by Richard C. Harkness ("Innovations in Telecommunications and Their Impact on Urban Life," Chapter 2, pp. 21–53) and by Orville G. Lee ("Potential Solar Energy Conservation Systems and Production Devices for The Community of the Future," Chapter 10, pp. 222–245); Richards, *Moving in Cities;* and Peter Wolf, *The Future of the City: New Directions in Urban Planning* (New York: Whitney Library of Design), 1974.

54. See, for example, Frederick J. Osborn and Arnold Whittick, *The New Towns: The Answer to Megalopolis,* New Revised Edition, (Cambridge, Mass.: MIT Press), 1969, and also Frank Schaffer, *The New Town Story* (London, England: MacGibbon and McKee), 1970.

55. The relatively more conservative futurism of the social sciences is well illustrated by the following works: Ely Chinoy, ed., *The Urban Future* (New York: Lieber-Atherton), 1973; John N. Jackson, *The Urban Future* (London, England: George Allen and Unwin), 1972; Sara Mills Mazie, *Population, Distribution, and Policy: The Commission on Population Growth and the American Future, Research Reports* (Washington, D.C.: U.S. Government Printing Office), 1973; Arthur P. Solomon, *The Prospective City;* and Andrew Blowers, Chris Hamnett, and Philip Sarre, eds., *The Future of Cities* (London, England: Hutchinson Educational Ltd.), 1974.

56. The conservatism and resistance to change that typify human societies have considerable survival value. Recent work in anthropology and the emerging field of sociobiology present considerable evidence on the subject which should be considered when designing future urban change. See, for example, Edward O.

Wilson, *On Human Nature* (Cambridge, Mass.: Harvard University Press), 1978; and Roy A. Rappaport, "Sanctity and Adaptation," *Io* 7(1970):46–51.

57. Some of the glamour has recently worn off new towns as evidence has mounted regarding their costs and association difficulties. See, for example, Albert J. Robinson, *Economics and New Towns* (New York: Praeger Publishers), 1975; and New Communities Administration, *New Communities: Problems and Potentials* (Washington, D.C.: New Communities Administration, U.S. Department of Housing and Urban Development), 1976.

INDEX

F
N